ORIGINAL TREATISES ON THE
ARTS OF PAINTING

ORIGINAL TREATISES ON THE
ARTS OF PAINTING

By

MRS. MARY P. MERRIFIELD

WITH A NEW INTRODUCTION AND GLOSSARY BY

S. M. ALEXANDER

Conservation Center
Institute of Fine Arts
New York University

In Two Volumes
VOLUME I

DOVER PUBLICATIONS, INC.
NEW YORK

Published in Canada by General Publishing Com-
pany, Ltd., 30 Lesmill Road, Don Mills, Toronto,
Ontario.
Published in the United Kingdom by Constable
and Company, Ltd., 10 Orange Street, London
WC 2.

This Dover edition, first published in 1967, is an
unabridged and unaltered republication of the
work originally published by John Murray, London,
in 1849. A new Introduction and Glossary of Technical Terms have been prepared specially for the
present edition by S. M. Alexander.

Library of Congress Catalog Card Number: 64-18860

Manufactured in the United States of America
Dover Publications, Inc.
180 Varick Street
New York, N.Y. 10014

INTRODUCTION TO THE DOVER EDITION

It is a tribute to Mrs Merrifield's scholarship that her *Original Treatises* merits republication in its original form. Not only are the treatises of interest *per se*, and the translations still adequate, but the author's presentation of her material is a monument of diligent and thoughtful enquiry which continues to take its place with the best of such work today.

Since its appearance in 1849, the *Original Treatises* has been the only publication and English translation of most of the compilations and manuals it contains; it has become one of the standard reference texts in the technology of painting from the Middle Ages to the seventeenth century. Unfortunately, the book has been virtually unobtainable for a considerable time, and current interest in historical materials and methods of production of art objects, manifest among historians in many fields, serves to emphasize the urgent need for a new edition of the volumes.

Mrs Merrifield's work was undertaken during a period of keen interest in the methods of painting of previous centuries, when it was hoped that a close study of ancient texts on the techniques and materials of the Old Masters would contribute to a revival of ancient achievements. A British Royal Commission initiated research in the field and employed Mrs Merrifield as a participant in the work; her books *The Art of Fresco Painting as Practised by the Old Italian and Spanish Masters* (1846) and the *Original Treatises* (1849) were a direct outcome of this

activity. Mrs Merrifield seems to have been well equipped
for the task of collecting, translating and explaining early
texts on painting techniques. We assume from her later
publications—*Practical Directions for Portrait Painting
in Watercolours* (1851) and *Handbook of Light and Shade
with Especial Reference to Model Drawing* (1855)—that she
had some skill as an artist and therefore an understanding of the purpose and character of the treatises she was
presenting. Although she states that her two sons
prepared the translation of the recipes[1] from Latin,
French, Spanish and Italian texts of different periods,
Mrs Merrifield herself must have been proficient in these
languages in order to supervise the work; her familiarity
with Italian is demonstrated by the publication in 1844 of
her translation of Cennino Cennini's *Treatise on Painting.*[2]
Her capacity for painstaking and thorough research is
exemplified in the lengthy introduction to the *Original
Treatises*, in which she traces the history of each significant
material referred to in the recipes, through literary sources
and surviving examples, recording a vast amount of
relevant and highly interesting information, interspersed
with anecdote and comment. From her introductory pages
we get little idea of the author as an individual, the wife
of a lawyer and mother of at least three children, with the
opportunity in her early forties to spend a period of several
years on the preparation of her great book.[3] The personality
behind the work is more clearly defined in her *Dress as a
Fine Art, with Suggestions on Children's Dress*, published in
Boston in 1854, in which she reveals herself as a forceful
character with an agreeable sense of humour, and very
much the Victorian gentlewoman.

Mrs Merrifield states in the preface to the *Original*

[1] In the prefaces to *The Art of Fresco Painting* and the *Original
Treatises.*

[2] *A Treatise on Painting, Written by Cennino Cennini . . . ,*
London, E. Lumley, 1844.

[3] A short account of Mrs Merrifield's life and work appears in
A. C. Sewter's introduction to the 1952 edition of *The Art of Fresco
Painting*, London, A. Tiranti (Scopas Handbooks).

Treatises that the research for the work was primarily directed towards establishing the historical techniques of painting, Italian oil painting in particular, as recorded in the early recipes relevant to the subject. However, her selection of texts gives us information of a far wider scope, as the author decided to include treatises outside the area of Italian painting, as well as those predating the appearance of the oil medium in Italy, in order to show the techniques of the period. Thus the treatises of Petrus de S. Audemar and Alcherius, and the greater part of Jean Le Begue's compilation, relate almost entirely to the illumination of manuscripts; Eraclius has a great deal on painting on glass; the Bologna Manuscript has sections on dyeing leather and the fabrication of artificial gems; and the later texts, included for their information on oil painting, also contribute a great deal to our knowledge of ancient practice in other media. The complete title of the book, therefore, *Original Treatises, Dating from the XIIth to XVIIIth Centuries on the Arts of Painting, in Oil, Miniature, Mosaic, and on Glass; of Gilding, Dyeing, and the Preparation of Colours and Artificial Gems*, is fully justified.

The treatises cover a more extensive period of time than was indicated by the information available in 1849. Eraclius, Books I and II, are now thought to be tenth-century[4] and represent one of the few surviving technical manuscripts of that period. Several recipes which Mrs Merrifield traces to the twelfth-century *Mappae Clavicula* may be redated with the bulk of the *Clavicula* text to the eighth or ninth century[5] and probably much earlier, as the

[4] A. Giry, *Notice sur un Traité du Moyen Age, entitulé De Coloribus et Artibus Romanorum*, Bibl. de l'Ecole des Hautes Etudes, Fasc. 35, Paris, 1878; J. C. Richards, "A New Manuscript of Heraclius," *Speculum* XV, 1940, 255–271.

[5] H. Leclercq, *Dictionnaire d'Archéologie Chrétienne et de Liturgie*, vol. X, part ii, 1932, col. 1719–1728.

R. P. Johnson, "Notes on Some Manuscripts of the Mappae Clavicula," *Speculum* X, 1935, 72–81.

———, "Some Continental Manuscripts of the Mappae Clavicula," *Speculum* XII, 1937, 84–91.

Mappae Clavicula itself is a compilation from earlier sources. Similarly, many of the formulae of Jean Le Begue's manuscript are known to be from sources considerably earlier than the fifteenth century. In the history of technical literature generally, however, the manuscripts included in the *Original Treatises* are comparatively late, and fit mainly into a transitional period between the few surviving works predating the thirteenth century, and the more plentiful examples of the sixteenth century and later. It is of considerable assistance to the student of medieval technical literature that Mrs Merrifield published each treatise in full, both in its original language and in English translation, "in order to satisfy the reader that nothing important has been omitted."[6]

The advantage of the manuals dating from the twelfth century and later is the relative ease with which we can understand most of them today. There are very few individual recipes in Mrs Merrifield's collection which we are entitled to view with amused scepticism or to dismiss as unpractical. Several of the ingredients may seem unusual to the modern reader, and the claims made by each author with respect to the efficacy of his recommended procedure may have little consistency with the truth; nevertheless, the validity of the recipes should not be underestimated, at least until practical tests have been made. Apparent confusion on the part of the medieval craftsman, as, for example, in *Experimenta de Coloribus* 30, may be the result of generations of scribes recording each other's misreadings or omissions. The greatest problem facing the modern reader is likely to be the interpretation of technical terms. Over the centuries, most pigments and many other substances have acquired a confusing variety of names, some of which can no longer be identified with accuracy. This edition, therefore, adds a glossary which attempts to collect in one place the data concerning difficult or foreign names and phrases gained from a study of the individual recipes, and the

---

[6] *Original Treatises*, Preface, vi.

information in Mrs Merrifield's introduction and footnotes to the text.

With this edition of the *Original Treatises*, a classic is restored to the medieval art-technical literature available to the reader of English, and Mrs Merrifield's position is assured in the affections of modern students in the field.

Conservation Center   S. M. ALEXANDER
Institute of Fine Arts
New York University
30 June 1966

GLOSSARY OF TECHNICAL TERMS

This glossary includes terms from Mrs Merrifield's Introduction and footnotes, as well as from the text. The spelling in the text is retained. The interpretation of terms is confined to their use in the treatises included in this book; similar terms in use today frequently have different interpretations.

A word is not included in this glossary if there is only one mention of it with a footnote by Mrs Merrifield on the same page—unless the word happens to be of general interest.

A word is not included if it is mentioned in Mrs Merrifield's Introduction but has no reference to the texts in her *Original Treatises*—unless the word is not explained by her, or unless it is of general interest.

Terms from the "Table of Synonymes" (pp. 18–39) not translated by Mrs Merrifield are included here if they represent actual identifiable materials.

Cross references are indicated by the abbreviation *"q.v.,"* since many of the words are synonyms.

Where other researchers may wish to verify the interpretations given here by reference to the recipes, the number of the page in question, or of a typical page, has been supplied along with the definition. Well-known terms, and words extracted from Mrs Merrifield's Introduction which do not refer directly to the treatises she includes, do not have page references.

ABBOZZO. Preliminary sketch of a painting before the colours were applied.

ADAMANT. Fictitious stone of extreme hardness.

AFRONITRE. Perhaps synonymous with saltpetre (*see* Nitre).

AGATINO. Colour made by mixing white lead and red ochre (p. 650).

ALBA CRETA. White earths or chalk, used as a ground (*q.v.*, no. 1) or as a bulk material in pigments made from plant juices and dyes. *Syn.:* Argilla, Creta alba, Gersa, Gypsum, Plastrum (p. 19).

ALBUM HISPANIE. White lead (*q.v.*).

ALBUM PLUMBUM. White lead (*q.v.*).

ALBUS. General term for white pigments. *Cf.* p. 18, note 1; *cf.* Candidus.

ALEMBIC. Early distilling apparatus.

ALOES. Condensed juice from leaves of *Aloe spicata* used as a colouring agent in varnish. The names Hepatic Aloes, Socotrine Aloes and Caballine Aloes indicate juices of different colours from different species.

ALUM. A variety of astringent substances was classed under the name of alum. Sulphates of iron and aluminium, or a mixture of the two, were commonly understood by the term.

ALUME DI PIUMA. Alun de plume (*q.v.*).

ALUMEN. 1. Alum (*q.v.*).

2. White pigment requiring a medium of egg-white (p. 232). Mrs Merrifield suggests that this was the alum scagliuolo used in the preparation of grounds for paintings and for gesso d'oro (*q.v.*), which is not precisely identified.

ALUMEN GLACIAE. Alun de glace (*q.v.*).

ALUMINE ZUCCARINO. Alum ground and heated with rose water, sugar and white of egg, and allowed to harden by cooling. Used as a carrier for lake pigments (p. 62) and as a thickening agent in one of the preparations of verdigris (p. 66).

ALUM OF JAMENI. Alum (*q.v.*).

ALUN DE GLACE. Crystallised alum. *Syn.:* Alumen glaciae.

ALUN DE PLUME. Feather or plume alum, a naturally occurring crystalline ferric potassium sulphate. *Syn.:* Alume di piuma.

AMASSETTE. Early type of palette knife, made of horn, wood or ivory.

AMBER. Translucent fossil resin of the *Pinites succinifer* and other conifers, used as an ingredient in varnish. *Syn.:* Carabé, Glassa.

ANGUILLARIA, ANGULARIA. White pigment prepared from chalk and powdered glass (p. 250).

A PUTRIDO. Technique of painting with decomposed white (p. 282) or yolk (p. 610) of egg as the medium for the pigment.

AQUA DI RAGGIA. *See* Turpentine.

AQUA FORTIS. Nitric acid.

AQUA TARTARI. Water of tartar (*q.v.*).

ARGENTUM. Silver (*q.v.*).

ARGILLA. Alba creta (*q.v.*).

ARMENIAN BOLE. *See* Bole.

ARSICON, ARZICON. Orpiment (*q.v.*).

ARXICA, ARZICA. 1. Yellow lake prepared from the plant weld (*q.v.*) (p. 482).
2. Yellow earth used as a pigment (p. 19). *Syn.:* Terra crocea.

A SECCO. Method of painting on a dry lime-plaster wall with pigments applied in an aqueous medium.

A SFREGAZZO. Method of applying a thin glazing with oil, whereby the finger was dipped into the colour and passed once over the area where a soft shadow was required.

ASPHALTUM. Brownish-black native organic substance; bitumen. Mixed with a drying agent for use as a pigment (p. 748); dissolved in oil or turpentine (*q.v.*) for use as a glaze.

ASSAFOETIDA. Gum resin, mainly from the root of *Ferula fetida*, and probably from other species, used to increase the permanence of a dye (p. 434) and as an insecticide.

ASSISIAM AURI. Gold size (*q.v.*).

ATRAMENTUM. 1. Artificial black pigments including lamp black (*q.v.*) and charcoal black, made from the soot of a variety of carbonised materials (p. 248).
2. Writing ink, incaustum (*q.v.*) (p. 242).
3. Soot of burnt wood, perhaps beech, which when mixed with salt, served as a substitute for gold in the gilding of metal surfaces (p. 220, 222). *See* Bistre.
4. Black dye for leather, made by boiling oil and scales of iron (scoria of iron, *q.v.*) (p. 138, 562). Usually called atramentum sutorium (shoemaker's black).

AURARE. Deaurare (*q.v.*).

AUREOLA. Auripetrum (*q.v.*).

AURIPETRUM. Lacquer, made of gall or saffron or similar materials, applied over base metals such as tin, to represent gilding (p. 158, 240). *Syn.:* Aureola.

AURIPIGMENTUM. Orpiment (*q.v.*). Substitutes such as gall on white earth or chalk base are mentioned (p. 19).

AURUM. Gold, prepared as powder for ink and paint, or laid on as gold leaf.

A VELATURA. Method of glazing large painted surfaces by rubbing on the glaze with the fingers or with the flat of the hand.

AZURE, AZZURRIUM. General term for blue colours. *Syn.:* Lasur, Lazurium.

GERMAN. Azurite (*q.v.*).

INDIAN. Ultramarine (*q.v.*).

LOMBARDY. Azurite (*q.v.*).

PERSIAN. Ultramarine (*q.v.*).

SPANISH. Azurite, or prepared from azurite (*q.v.*).

TEUTONIC. Azurite (*q.v.*).

AZURE D'ACRE. Ultramarine (*q.v.*).

AZURITE. Native blue carbonate of copper, used as a pigment. *Syn.:* German azure, Lombardy azure, Spanish azure, Teutonic azure, Azzurro della Magne, Biadetto, Cendre bleue, Cendrée, Ceneri azzuri, Hungarian blue, Mountain blue, Spanish blue.

AZZURRO DELLA MAGNE, AZZURRUM DE ALEMANNIA. Azurite (*q.v.*).

BAGADEL, BAGADON, BAGUEDEL. Indigo (*q.v.*).

BENZOIN. Balsamic resin from the *Styrax benzoin* tree, dissolved in spirit of turpentine or spirit of wine as an ingredient for varnish.

BERETTINUS. Lombard term for elbidus (*q.v*).

BIACA, BIACCA, BIACHA. White lead (*q.v.*).

BIADETTO. 1. Azurite (*q.v.*).

2. Artificial blue pigment made from copper.

3. Artificial blue pigment made from verdigris (*q.v.*), sal ammoniac (*q.v.*) and tartar.

BIRSUS. Dark red colour made by mixing black and red (p. 21). *Syn.:* Fulvus, Ravus.

BISETUM. Small pieces of rag saturated with plant juices of various shades, which were extracted for use when required, by boiling in an appropriate solution. *Syn.:* Pezzette.

BISTRE. Yellowish-brown soot from charred beech and pine, here used as an ingredient for "gilding" metal. *See* Atramentum 3. *Syn.:* Caligo, Fuligo.

BLACHA. White lead (*q.v.*).

BLANC. French coin of very small value.

BLANCHET. White lead (*q.v.*).

BLAUCCUS. General name for blue colours (p. 20).

BLONDUS. Name applied to different mixtures of blue and white, red and white, green, white and yellow, etc. (p. 21).

BLOODSTONE. *See* Haematite.

BOCALE. Liquid measure, approximately one litre, varying according to locality.

BOLE. Clay material, usually reddish in colour, applied as a ground for gold leaf. The best was thought to come from Armenia. *Syn.:* Armenian bole, Bularminium.

BONE BLACK. Black pigment prepared from the charred bones of various animals.

BRACHA. White lead (*q.v.*).

BRASILEUM, BRASILIUM, BREXILIUM, BREXILLIUM, etc. Brazil wood (*q.v.*).

BRAZIL WOOD. Wood of several kinds of *Caesalpinia* yielding a red dye. Dye extracted by boiling the finely chipped wood, the final colour depending on the acidity or alkalinity of the solution. Used as a pigment or as underpainting for gold leaf (p. 154). *Syn.:* Brasileum, Brexilium, Lignum Braxillii, Verxillium, Verzino.

BRUNO DI SPAGNA. Red ochre (*q.v.*).

BRUNUS. Red ochre (*q.v.*).

BRUSLÉ. Sil atticum (*q.v.*).

BULARMINIUM. Bole (*q.v.*).

BUON FRESCO. Painting on newly applied wet plaster with pigments mixed with water; the colours penetrate the plaster and remain fixed on drying.

BURNT ORPIMENT. Realgar (*q.v.*).

BURNT ROCHE ALUM. White powder left after heating alum to remove water of crystallisation, used to prepare lake pigments from plant dyes (p. 658, 678).

BURNT TERRE VERTE. Brown pigment made by heating terre verte (*q.v.*).

BURNT UMBER. Brown pigment made by heating raw umber (*q.v.*).

BURNT VITRIOL, BURNT ROMAN VITRIOL. Artificial red pigment made by heating iron sulphate.

CALCANTHUM, CHALCANTHUM. Copper sulphate, blue vitriol.

CALIGO. Bistre (*q.v.*).

CALX. 1. Product of calcination (*i.e.*, strong heating).
2. Lime (p. 24).

CALX OF GOLD. Powdered gold (p. 532, 334).

CALX OF IRON. Iron oxide (p. 534).

CALX OF TIN. Tin oxide (p. 86, 402).

CALX VIVA. Quicklime, calcium oxide.

CAMILLINA, CAMILLINUS. Colour made by mixing vermilion (*q.v.*), azure and ceruse (*q.v.*); vermilion and ceruse; azure and ceruse, etc. (p. 480, 486).

CAMPEACHY WOOD. Logwood (*q.v.*).

CANDIDUS. Shining white, as opposed to albus, which is matt white (p. 24). *Cf.* Albus.

CANDIDUS CALX. Lime white (p. 20).

CAPRIFOLIUM. Honeysuckle. The ripe berries, after pounding, were boiled in wine; the addition of iron rust gave a bright green ink and dye (p. 158). *Syn.:* Galetrice, Gaterice.

CARABÉ. Amber (*q.v.*).

CARBO. Charcoal black (p. 25).

CARMINE, CARMINIUM. 1. Lake (*q.v.*) from cochineal (*q.v.*) (p. 698).
2. Cinnabar (*q.v.*) (p. 238).
3. White and ochre mixed (p. 252).

CARNATURA, CARNATION. Colour used to represent flesh tint (p. 22, 770).

CEDRA, CEDRE. Excedre (*q.v.*).

CELESTE. Mixture of white lead, smalti and indigo (p. 650).

CENDRE BLEUE. Azurite (*q.v.*) or artificial copper blue.

CENDRÉE. Azurite (*q.v.*) or artificial copper blue.

CENDRE VERTE. Native green ore of copper.

CENERI AZZURI. Azurite (*q.v.*) or artificial copper blue.

CERATE. Unctuous preparation.

CEROSIUS. Green pigment.

CERULÉE. Frit (*q.v.*).

CERUSA, CERUSE. White lead (*q.v.*).

CERVISIA. Beer, used as a medium for pigments (p. 232).

CHIAROSCURO. The disposition of light and shade in a picture.

CHOPINE. Liquid measure, about half a litre.

CHRISARE. *See* Deaurare.

CHRYSOCOLLA. Native green carbonate of copper, malachite (*q.v.*), used as a pigment (p. 248).

CILACETUS. Sillacetus (*q.v.*).

CINERIS PENCHOLINI. Brass burnt and reduced to powder (p. 532).

CINNABAR. Vermilion (*q.v.*).

CINOBRIUM. Vermilion (*q.v.*).

CINOPIS. Red ochre (*q.v.*).

CINOPLE. Red ochre (*q.v.*).

CITRINUS. Colour obtained by mixing yellow with red (p. 22).

CLARE. Solution of gum in water, used as a medium for pigments (p. 294); *cf.* glair, well-beaten egg-white and water, used for the same purpose.

COCCICUS, COCCUS. Kermes (*q.v.*).

COCHINEAL. Natural scarlet or crimson dyestuff obtained from the egg-bearing bodies of the female *Coccus cacti*, introduced into Europe from Mexico in the sixteenth century. *Syn.:* Carmine, Cremisi, Cremisino, Grana.

COLLA. Gum water, size.

COLOPHONY. Rosin (*q.v.*).

COMMON GREEN. Verdigris (*q.v.*).

CONCHILE. Oster (*q.v.*).

COPEROSA. Zinc sulphate.

COPPERAS. Ferrous sulphate, green vitriol, used in dyeing and tanning, and as an ingredient in iron-gall ink. *See also* Shoemaker's black.

CORISCOS. *See* Saffron.

CORROSIVE SUBLIMATE. Mercuric sulphide.

CREMISI, CREMISINO. 1. Cochineal (*q.v.*).
2. Dragon's blood (*q.v.*) with the addition of a substantial amount of alkali.

CRETA ALBA. Alba creta (*q.v.*).

CRETA CIRINA. Terre verte (*q.v.*).

CRETA VIRIDIS. Terre verte (*q.v.*).

CRISICULA. Chrysocolla (*q.v.*).

CROCEA TERRA. Yellow earth (*q.v.*).

CROCEUS. General name for yellow colours.

CROCUS. Saffron (*q.v.*).

CROCUS MARTIS. Saffron of Mars (*q.v.*).

CUBIT. Measurement of length, 45.72 cm.

CUCURBIT. Flask for distillation, forming part of an alembic.

CUM(M)IN. *Cuminum cyminum*, a plant cultivated for its aromatic fruits, used as a spice in the Middle Ages.

CYNOBRE. Vermilion (*q.v.*).

DEAURARE. Latin infinitive, meaning "to gild." *Syn.:* Aurare, Chrisare.

DENARIUS. Coin, mentioned in the recipes as a weight, just over a gram.

DISTEMPER (verb). To add a binding medium to pigments, synonymous with "to temper."

DRAGON'S BLOOD. Dark red resin obtained from the outer surface of the fruit of the *Calamus draco*. Formerly used as a pigment in miniature painting, or as a colouring agent for varnishes. *Syn.:* Sanguis draconis.

DUTCH VERMILION. Artificial vermilion.

EDERA. *See* Gum edere.

ELBIDUS, ELBUS. Latin term for grey colour mixed from black and white (p. 650) with or without the addition of other pigments (p. 654). *Syn.:* Berettinus, Grisus, Neveda, Veneda.

ENDICO BAGATELLO. Indigo (*q.v.*).

ENGLISH RED. Red ochre (*q.v.*).

ESSENTIAL OIL. Volatile oil, such as turpentine.

ESTERLIN. Goldsmith's weight, eighteen and a half grains.

EUPHORBIA. Large genus of plants whose milky juice was used in the preparation of certain substitutes for expensive pigments.

EXCEDRE. Shadow colour for flesh made by mixing red and black (p. 26). *Syn.:* Cedra, Cedre, Exedra.

EXEDRA. Excedre (*q.v.*).

FEL. Gall (*q.v.*).

FENIX. Phenix (*q.v.*).

FENUGREEK. Asiatic herb *Trigonella foenumgraecum*. Oil from the seeds was used in dyeing skins (p. 546).

FERULA. Galbanum (*q.v.*)

FIG TREE MILK. Juice extracted from the young shoots of the tree in spring, or obtained from the young leaves by soaking them in water and alcohol until decomposed. Used as a medium for pigments (p. 96), or as an ingredient in mordant for gold (p. 462).

FLANDERS BLACK. Black pigment made from vine twigs.

FLAVUS. Massicot (*q.v.*).

FLOUR PASTE. Sometimes used instead of size (*q.v.*) for covering canvas before priming (p. 772).

FLOWER OF NITRE. Efflorescence of nitre (*q.v.*) used in the composition of frit (*q.v.*) (p. 804).

FLOWER OF WOAD, FROTH OF WOAD. Scum floating on dyers' vats when woad was boiled after fermentation, used as a colouring agent in the preparation of some blue pigments (p. 390, 414).

FOGLIECTO. Liquid measure, approximately a quarter of a litre.

FOLIUM. Vegetable colour used in painting and dyeing, prepared from the juice of *Croton tinctorium*. The hue could be changed from red, through purple, to blue by the addition of alkali (p. 132). *Syn.:* Morella, Turnsole, Worina.

FRANKINCENSE. Yellowish aromatic gum resin from the genus *Boswellia*. Used as an ingredient in varnish and in the purification of ultramarine (*q.v.*). *Syn.:* Incense, Olibanum.

FRIT. Blue pigment made by melting siliceous material with copper and other metallic salts, and grinding the mass to a very fine powder. *Syn.:* Cerulée, Smaltino, Turchino.

FULIGO. Bistre (*q.v.*).

FULVUS. Birsus (*q.v.*).

FUMUS. Lamp black (*q.v.*).

FUSCUS. Lamp black (*q.v.*).

GADUS. Madder (*q.v.*).

GALBANUM. Gum resin from *Ferula galbanifera* used in the preparation of varnish. *Syn.:* Ferula.

GALETRICE. Caprifolium (*q.v.*).

GALL. Secretion of liver from several fish or animals, used as a yellow pigment (p. 198) and as a substitute for gold (p. 160, 308). *Syn.:* Fel.

GALL NUTS, GALLS. Vegetable excrescences, especially on oak trees, produced by an insect. Tannin, extracted from the galls, was used in making ink, as a mordant in dyeing, and for tanning leather.

GAMBOGE. Yellow gum resin from the bark of the *Garcinia hanburii* tree, used as a pigment and as a colouring agent for varnishes. *Syn.:* Gutiambar.

GARANCIA. Gallic name for madder (*q.v.*).

GATERICE. English term for caprifolium (*q.v.*).

GAUDE. French term for woad (*q.v.*).

GENESTRA. Myrrh (*q.v.*).

GERMAN AZURE. *See* Azure.

GERMAN GIALLOLINO. Massicot (*q.v.*).

GERSA. Alba creta (*q.v.*).

GESSO. Aqueous white priming used in the preparation of panels or other supports for painting and gilding. Usually consisted of gypsum (*q.v.*) mixed with glue or size (*q.v.*).

GESSO D'ORO. Very fine and smooth gesso (*q.v.*), called "honey of the plasterers," used as a ground for gilding.

GESSO MARCIO. Type of fine gesso (*q.v.*).

GESSO SOTTILE. Gesso (*q.v.*) prepared from plaster of Paris soaked for several weeks in excess water to prevent setting. Used as a final coat for grounds in panel painting and as a mordant for gold leaf on parchment.

GIALDOLINO, GIALLOLINO. 1. Massicot (*q.v.*).

    2. Massicot mixed with giallo di vetro (*q.v.*).

    3. Native yellow earth used as a pigment.

GIALDOLINO DI FIANDRE. Massicot (*q.v.*).

GIALDOLINO DI FORNACE. Massicot (*q.v.*).

GIALLO DI VETRO. Pigment made by heating tin and lead together.

GIALLO SANTO. Yellow lake made from a variety of flowers.

GIALORINO. Natural and artificial massicot (*q.v.*).

GIPSUS. Gypsum (*q.v.*).

GLADIUS. 1. Vegetable green from leaves of *Gladiolus communis*.

    2. Green colour made by mixing orpiment and indigo (p. 28).

GLASSA. 1. Amber (*q.v.*) (p. 162).

    2. Crystallised alum (p. 240).

GLASSE AROMATIQUE. May mean amber (*q.v.*) or sandarac (*q.v.*) (p. 312).

GLAUCUS. Here synonymous with white lead (p. 18, 29), possibly through confusion with *leucos* (*q.v.*).

GLAZING. The last thin coat of transparent colour which softens and gives brilliancy to the pigments.

GOLD SIZE. Ground, usually consisting of bole in a liquid medium, with or without the addition of chalk and pigments, applied under gold which was to be burnished (p. 94, 282). *Syn.:* Assisiam auri.

GOMMA DI GINEPRO. Sandarac (*q.v.*).

GRANA. Kermes (*q.v.*); cochineal (*q.v.*).

GRANETUM, GRANETUS. Colour made by mixing green and white (p. 28).

GRANZA. Madder (*q.v.*).

GREEK GREEN. Verdigris (*q.v.*).

GREEK PITCH. Rosin (*q.v.*).

GREEN CHALK. Terre verte (*q.v.*).

GRENUSPECT. Plant yielding yellow juice which was added to verdigris and wine medium to give green colour (p. 158).

GRISUS. Gallic name for elbidus (*q.v.*).

GROSSINUM. French weight, the *gros*, weighing 3.82 grams at Paris.

GROUND. Used by Mrs Merrifield to mean:

1. The layer of a painting applied to the support to provide a suitable surface for the application of pigment or gold.

2. The background of a picture.

GUADO. Italian term for woad (*q.v.*).

GUM AMMONIAC. Aromatic gum resin from the *Dorema ammoniacum*, used as an ingredient in mordants for gold (p. 156, 622).

GUM ANDRIANUM. Mrs Merrifield suggests this is synonymous with amber (?) or native bitumen (?).

GUM ARABIC. Gum obtained from various species of *Acacia*. The gum is completely soluble in water and was used as a medium for pigments (p. 58), as an adhesive (p. 156), and as an ingredient in gold mordants (p. 156).

GUM EDERE. Gum of certain species of ivy. The dye extracted from the stem turned red on exposure to the air, and was prepared as a pigment by boiling to concentrate the colour. Also used in dyeing and as an ink (p. 190).

GUM LAC. Red pigment prepared from natural red organic dyestuff obtained from the secretion of larvae of *Coccus lacca*. The dye is similar to cochineal in composition, but duller in colour (p. 50, 62). *Syn.:* Indian gum lac, Indian lac lake, Lac.

GUM TRAGACANTH. Gum obtained from several species of *Astragalus*, chiefly used as a binder for pastels and chalks, and as a medium for pigments.

GUTIAMBAR. Gamboge (*q.v.*).

GYPSUM. Native calcium sulphate, used to prepare gesso (*q.v.*) and as a carrier for vegetable pigments (p. 184). Stated to be synonymous with alba creta (*q.v.*).

HAEMATITE. 1. Ferric oxide, highly polished and shaped to form a burnisher (p. 220). *Syn.:* Bloodstone.

2. Red earth used as a pigment (p. 806).

HARTSHORN GLUE. Ammoniacal liquor obtained by the distillation of horn shavings.

HEPATIC ALOES. *See* Aloes.

HERBA MORELLA. The plant *Solanum nigrum* ground with chalk to give a green colour (p. 29).

HERBA ROCCIA. Weld (*q.v.*).

HERBA SANDIX. Madder (*q.v.*).

HERBA VACCINIUM. 1. Plant giving red juice which was mixed with milk to give a violet colour.

2. Plant yielding yellow juice.

HOLCHUS. Membrana (*q.v.*).

HONEY OF ROSES. Mixture of infusion of roses, white sugar and honey, used as an ingredient in mordants for gilding (p. 468).

HUILE DE SAPIN. Pine resin used as an ingredient in varnish (p. 840).

HUNGARIAN BLUE. Azurite (*q.v.*).

INCAUSTUM. Latin term for "ink," including black pigment mixed with gum for writing, and iron-gall ink (p. 30, 150). *Syn.:* Atramentum.

INCENSE. *See* Frankincense.

INDIAN AZURE. *See* Azure.

INDIAN GUM LAC. *See* Gum lac.

INDIAN LAC LAKE. *See* Gum lac.

INDICUS. Indigo (*q.v.*).

INDIGO. 1. Blue vegetable dye from the leaves of plants of the genus *Indigofera*. *Syn.:* Bagadel, Bagadon, Baguedel, Endico Bagatello, Indicus.

2. Blue dye from woad, *Isatis tinctoria* (p. 806).

INTONACO. Final layer of lime plaster on the ground of a fresco painting.

ISINGLASS. Pure form of gelatine prepared from the air bladders of certain fish, especially the sturgeon. Used as an ingredient in some types of media and as an adhesive for gold (p. 192).

IVORY BLACK. Carbon black made by burning ivory chips.

KERMES. Red dyestuff prepared from the egg-bearing bodies of the kermes insect *Coccus ilicis*. Used as a dye and a pigment. *Syn.:* Coccus, Grana, Rubea de grana, Sanguineus, Vermiculus.

LAC. Gum lac (*q.v.*).

LACCA DI CIMATURA, LACHA. Red pigment made by boiling small pieces of cloth dyed with kermes in lye, then precipitating the colour with alum.

LAKE. Transparent dye precipitated on to a translucent base (p. 50, 144).

LAMP BLACK. Pigment made from soot obtained by burning oil or fat and collecting the material on a metallic or other cold surface. *Syn.:* Fumus, Fuscus, Sanctonicus.

LAPIS LAZULI. *See* Ultramarine.

LAPIS NIGER. Terra nigra (*q.v.*).

LASUR, LAZURIUM. Azure (*q.v.*).

LESSIVE FONDISSE. Perhaps a lye solution.

LEUCOS. White lead (*q.v.*).

LEY, LYE. Alkaline solution made from mixing wood ashes in water.

LIGNUM BRAXILLII. Brazil wood (*q.v.*).

LINSEED OIL. Drying oil expressed from the seeds of the flax plant *Linum usitatissimum*, purified for use.

LIQUID VARNISH. Thick varnish composed of oil and resin—usually linseed oil (*q.v.*) and sandarac (*q.v.*)—rubbed while warm on panel paintings.

LITHARGE. Orange-yellow monoxide of lead used as a dryer in paints and varnishes. It is produced as an intermediate step in the preparation of red lead from white lead. Not used as a pigment. *Syn.:* Terraghetta.

LOADSTONE. Magnetite, magnetic iron ore.

LOGWOOD. Heartwood of *Haematoxylon campechianum* from which a purple dye is produced. *Syn.:* Campeachy wood.

LOMBARDY AZURE. *See* Azure.

LOT. Weight, 14.2 grams approximately.

LUMINA, LUMINE. Mixture of pink flesh-tint (membrana, *q.v.*) with lead white, malachite and vermilion, perhaps used as highlight for flesh (p. 314).

LUSTRO DI RASA. Turpentine dissolved with rosin, used as a medium for pigments in painting on glass (p. 696).

LUTUM SAPIENTIAE. Philosopher's lute (*q.v.*).

MADDER. Natural red dyestuff prepared from the roots of the shrub *Rubia tinctorium*. Used as a lake, dye and pigment. *Syn.:* Gadus, Garancia, Granza, Herba sandix, Rubea radix, Sandis, Sandix, Warancia.

MAESTRA. Mordant, used in dyeing.

MALACHITE. Native green carbonate of copper, used as a pigment. *Syn.:* Chrysocolla, Crisicula, Verde azzuro.

MARCHESITE. Iron pyrite, iron disulphide.

MARZACHOTTO. Mixture of sand, soda and potash used as the base material in the production of coloured glass.

MASSICOT. In these recipes it is yellow oxide of lead, an intermediate step in the production of red lead from white lead. *Syn.:* Flavus, German giallolino, Gialdolino, Gialdolino di Fiandre, Gialdolino di Fornace, Gialorino.

MASTIC. Resin from the *Pistachia lentiscus*. Had several uses, mainly as an ingredient in varnish and in media (p. 306).

MEDIUM. Liquid such as water, oil, or a solution of gum, in which a pigment is suspended for painting. *Syn.:* Vehicle.

MELINE EARTH. White earth from Melos used as a pigment (p. 244).

MELLANA. Sinopis de Mellana (*q.v.*).

MEMBRANA, MEMBRAYNE. Pink colour for flesh tints, mixed from red, white and green (p. 144). *Syn.:* Holchus, Olchus.

MENECH, MENESCH. 1. Blue juice used as a colour (p. 31).
2. Medium red tone, perhaps synonymous with madder (p. 31).
3. Dark green colour, the juice of the elder (p. 31). *Cf.* Succus sambuci.

METADELLE. Liquid measure, approximately half a litre.

MILK OF LIME. Solution of calcium hydroxide in water, made by dissolving slaked lime in water. Used for mixing the sand and lime of the plaster coats for fresco painting (p. 788).

MINEVER. White fur from the ermine.

MINIUM. 1. Red lead (*q.v.*).
2. Perhaps sometimes synonymous with vermilion (*q.v.*) (p. 68).

MIRCA. Myrrh (*q.v.*).

MOMMIA. Mummy (*q.v.*).

MORDANT. 1. In dyeing, a mordant is a substance which produces a fast colour on a fibre by combining with the dye-stuff and the fibre to form an insoluble compound or lake.
2. In gilding, a mordant is an adhesive for the metal or a ground over which the gold leaf was laid and against which it could be burnished (p. 94, 152).

MORELLA. Folium (*q.v.*).

MORELLO. Violet colour made by mixing blue with various other pigments.

MORELLO DI FERRO. Red pigment from an ore of iron.

MORELLO DI SALE. Unidentified. Perhaps a reddish clay left over from the purification of rock salt.

MOTTÉE DE SIL. Native red or yellow ochre (*q.v.*) used as a pigment (p. 804).

MOUNTAIN BLUE. Azurite (*q.v.*).

MUMMY. Brown bituminous pigment said to be warmer in tone than asphaltum. Used as a pigment, varnish and dryer. *Syn.:* Mommia.

MYRRH. Reddish-brown gum resin from the tree genus *Balsamodendron* boiled with aloes to coat varnished tin in imitation of gold (p. 162). *Syn.:* Genestra, Mirca.

NAPHTHA. Liquid obtained by the distillation of petroleum, used as a solvent for mastic (*q.v.*) in the preparation of varnish (p. 670) and as a thinner for varnish (p. 628).

NATRON. Impure mixture of a variety of saline substances found in the natural state, especially in arid regions. Probably native sodium sesquicarbonate.

NEVEDA. Elbidus (*q.v.*).

NIELLO. Technique in fine metalwork, whereby an engraved design on a gold or silver ground is filled with a black composition of copper, lead, silver and sulphur fused together by heat. *Syn.:* Nigellum.

NIGELLUM. Niello (*q.v.*).

NIGER. General name for black (p. 32).

NIGRI PRUNI CORTEX SECUNDUS. Inner bark of black plum, boiled to give a yellow dye which was mixed with vitriol (*q.v.*) and gum arabic (*q.v.*) to make ink (p. 162).

NITRE. A variety of white substances was classed under the name of nitre, not necessarily corresponding to the modern nitre, which is potassium nitrate. *Syn.:* Afronitre, Sal nitrinum, Saltpetre.

OCHRE. Variety of natural earths coloured in the brown, red, yellow range by iron oxide and iron hydroxide. *Syn.:* Ogra.

OCRA DE RU. Dark-coloured ochre (p. 786).

OGLIO COTTA. Nut or linseed oil boiled with litharge.

OGRA. Ochre (*q.v.*).

OIL OF CHAMOMILE. Oil extracted from the camomile flowers by soaking in olive oil in direct sunlight. Used to dilute pigments.

OIL OF COPAIBA. Resin from the trunk of a species of *Copaifera*, used as an ingredient in varnish.

OIL OF SPIKE. Oil distilled from *Lavandula spica*, used as a diluent for varnish. Its properties are similar to those of turpentine (*q.v.*).

OIL OF TARTAR. Concentrated solution of potassium carbonate, used in one of the preparations of "azure" (p. 398) and of lake (p. 712).

OLCHUS. Membrana (*q.v.*).

OLIBANUM. Frankincense (*q.v.*).

OLIO DI ABEZZO. Resin from the *Pinus picea*. Used as an ingredient in varnish (p. 670), or was mixed with the oil in which brushes had been cleaned, and painted on the back of oil paintings on canvas to re-attach flaking grounds (p. 740).

OR DE COULEUR. Mordant for gold made of oil and yellow ochre (*q.v.*) or bole (*q.v.*) (p. 836).

ORICELLO. Lichen *Roccella* or archil used for dyeing a purple colour (p. 582) or as underpainting for gold (p. 474).

ORPIMENT. 1. Naturally occurring yellow sulphide of arsenic, formerly used as a pigment. *Syn.:* Arsicon, Arzicon, Auripigmentum.

2. Gall adsorbed on to white chalk, used as a substitute for orpiment (p. 19, 198).

OSTER. Purple dye mentioned by Vitruvius, obtained from several types of shellfish. *Syn.:* Conchile.

PAGLIONAZO. Pavonazzo (*q.v.*).

PALLIDUS. Off-white.

PANICELLA. Weld (*q.v.*).

PARAMENTUM. Saline efflorescence found on old walls.

PARATONIUM. White mineral used as a pigment.

PARIS CARMINE. Parisian red (*q.v.*).

PARISIAN RED. Brazil wood (*q.v.*) boiled in lye and mixed with alum (*q.v.*). *Syn.:* Paris carmine.

PASTA DI VESICHA. Sap green (*q.v.*) kept in pigs' bladders (p. 664, 808). *Syn.:* Verde di vesicha.

PASTA VERDE. Sap green (*q.v.*).

PAVONAZZO. Purple colour.

1. Mixture of white lead, azure and red lake (p. 610). *Syn.:* Paglionazo.

2. Purple dye from *Roccella tinctoria* (p. 583). *Cf.* Oricello.

PECE GRECA. Rosin (*q.v.*).

PENCIL. This term, as used by Mrs Merrifield, usually refers to the modern word "paintbrush."

PERSIAN AZURE. *See* Azure.

PERSICUS, PERSUS. Dark blue colour.

PETITTO. Liquid measure.

PEZZETTE. Bisetum (*q.v.*).

PHENIX. Scarlet dye or pigment. *Syn.:* Fenix.

PHILOSOPHER'S LUTE. Cement for sealing vessels; composed of white of egg beaten to a froth, mixed with iron filings and applied in three or four coats. *Syn.:* Lutum Sapientiae.

PIETRA FOCARA, FOCAIA. Flint?

PIGNOLATO. Cloth of linen or hemp.

PINCELIER. Vessel containing oil in which oil-painting brushes were cleaned or placed to prevent hardening.

PLASTRUM. Gypsum (*q.v.*).

PLUMBAGO. Graphite, used for drawing (p. 780).

PLUMBUS ALBUS. White lead (*q.v.*).

PONTELLO. Pontil or punty, working rod for holding glass objects during the process of manufacture.

POSC(E), POSCH, POSECH. Shadow colour for pink flesh, made of ochre, green and membrayne (*q.v.*) (p. 33).

POTTER'S EARTH. Clay used for priming canvas (p. 772).

POUNCE (verb). To perforate for the purpose of using as a stencil in ornamentation.

PRASINUS. 1. Prasin: red pigment, burnt ochre (p. 33, 298).
2. Prasminum, prasis. (a) General term for green. (b) Dark green colour of indeterminate nature (p. 33).

PRUNI NIGRI SECUNDUS CORTEX. Nigri pruni cortex secundus (*q.v.*).

PUMICEUS, PUNICEUS. Reddish colour made by adding red to yellow (p. 34).

PURPLE OF CASSIUS. Richly coloured pigment produced by the action of a solution of tin and iron salts on a solution of gold (p. 388).

PURPUREUS. General name for purple colours.

PURPURINUS. 1. Red colours of various types.
2. Composition of quicksilver, tin or brass, and sulphur heated to produce a yellow metallic powder which, with a medium of gum or egg-white, was used as a substitute for gold (p. 54, 64).

QUICKSILVER. Mercury.

RADIX RUBEA. *See* Rubea radix.

RAVUS. Birsus (*q.v.*).

REALGAR. Artificial or naturally occurring red sulphide of arsenic formerly used as a pigment, and as a preservative for glair (*cf.* clare) (p. 676). *Syn.:* Burnt orpiment, Red orpiment, Red sulphur, Sandaraca, Sandaraque.

RED LEAD. Red oxide of lead made by heating white lead. *Syn.:* Minium, Stupium.

RED OCHRE. Native red clay containing oxide of iron. *Syn.:* Brunus, Bruno di Spagna, Cinopis, Cinople, English red, Rubea terra, Rubigo, Sinople, Spanish red, Synople, Terra rossa, Terra rossa d'Inghilterra, Terra rossa di Spagna, Terra rubea; Vermilion (*q.v.*).

RED ORPIMENT. Realgar (*q.v.*).

RED SULPHUR. Realgar (*q.v.*).

ROCAILLE. White glass or flux to which different minerals were added in the manufacture of coloured glass for painting (p. 792).

ROCHE ALUM. Pure form of alum prepared from alunite.

ROMAN VITRIOL. Copper sulphate, blue vitriol.

ROSA, ROSE. Pink colours of various hues. *Syn.:* Rosette.

ROSACEUM. Pink colour made by adsorbing brazil-wood dye on to white chalk.

ROSETTE. Rosa (*q.v.*).

ROSIN. Resinous constituent of the oleo-resin exuded by various species of pine, i.e., the residue left after the extraction of turpentine from the crude exudation. *Syn.:* Colophony, Greek pitch, Pece greca, Spanish pitch.

ROTHOMAGENSIAN GREEN. Verdigris (*q.v.*).

ROTOLO. Weight of about 907 grams, but varying greatly with locality.

ROUGET. Brazil wood boiled with lime water and alum (p. 808).

RUBEA DE GRANA. Kermes (*q.v.*).

RUBEA RADIX. Madder (*q.v.*).

RUBEA TERRA. Red ochre (*q.v.*).

RUBEUS. General name for red colours.

RUBIGO. Red ochre (*q.v.*).

SAFFRON. Yellow dye obtained by soaking the dried stigmas of *Crocus sativus* in water or white of egg. The best sort, from Sicily, was called coriscos (p. 132). *Syn.:* Crocus.

SAFFRON OF MARS. Native yellow earth used as a pigment. *Syn.:* Crocus Martis.

SAFIREUS. Lapis lazuli. *See* Ultramarine.

SAGIUM. Weight of approximately 1.6 grams.

SAL ALKALI. Potassium carbonate.

SAL AMMONIAC. Ammonium chloride used in the manufacture of purpurinus (*q.v.*) and as a mordant for gold leaf (p. 54).

SAL GEM. Rock salt, sodium chloride.

SAL NITRINUM. Nitre (*q.v.*).

SALT GREEN. Type of verdigris. Green pigment made by sprinkling salt over pieces of copper and subjecting them to the fumes of vinegar or urine in a sealed vessel (p. 116).

TRAVERTINE. Calcium carbonate used as the bulk material in the preparation of lakes. *Syn.:* Tavertinus.

TRIPOLI POWDER. Decomposed siliceous limestone, called rotten stone, used as a polishing powder.

TUCHIA, TUCIA, TUZIA. Impure zinc oxide found adhering to the walls of furnaces for roasting zinc ores.

TURCHINO. 1. Frit (*q.v.*) (p. 804).
2. Mixture of white and blue pigments (p. 651).

TURNSOLE. Folium (*q.v.*).

TURPENTINE. In the recipes, turpentine is the crude resinous liquid from pine trees, used as an ingredient in varnish and in the refining of lapis lazuli. Today, turpentine is the volatile distillate of the above resinous sap. *Syn.:* Terebinthina.

ULTRAMARINE. 1. Blue pigment made from the mineral lapis lazuli by a complicated process of separating it from its associated rock. It was the most expensive pigment of the Middle Ages. *Syn.:* Azure d'acre, Indian azure, Persian azure.
2. Substitute for ultramarine was made from calcined silver, nitric acid and sal ammoniac sealed together in a leaden vessel (p. 808).

ULTRAMARINE SOAP. Mrs Merrifield suggests that this was the Roman soap or alkaline material used in the washing of azure (p. 512).

UMBER. Native brown earth, a hydrate of iron oxide with manganese oxide and clay, varying in colour between yellow- and purple-brown. Used as a pigment (p. 770). *Syn.:* Terra d'ombra.

USTICIUM. Of a colour produced by burning (p. 39).

VACCINIUM. Purple colour prepared from herba vaccinium (*q.v.*, no. 1).

VEHICLE. Medium (*q.v.*).

VENEDA. Elbidus (*q.v.*).

VENETIAN LAKE. Red lake, of which cochineal appears to have been the main ingredient.

VENICE TURPENTINE. Resinous liquid from *Pinus larix*, used in the preparation of varnish.

VERBLEA. Perhaps synonymous with Verde azzuro (*q.v.*, no. 1).

VERCANDE. Vernide (*q.v.*).

VERD DE TERRE, VERDE TERRA. Terre verte (*q.v.*).

SALTPETRE. Nitre (*q.v.*).

SANCTONICUS. Lamp black (*q.v.*).

SANDALICA. Sandalwood (*q.v.*).

SANDALWOOD. Wood of the *Pterocarpus santalinus*, yielding a red dye used for colouring varnishes. *Syn.:* Sandalica.

SANDARAC. Yellowish resinous body obtained from the stems of the conifer *Callitris quadrivalvis*, used in the preparation of varnish. *Syn.:* Gomma di ginepro, Vernix.

SANDARACA. 1. Red lead, minium (p. 140).
2. Massicot (p. 314).
3. Realgar (p. 246, *n.* 3).
Syn.: Sandaracum, Sandaraque.

SANDARACUM, SANDARAQUE. Sandaraca (*q.v.*, nos. 1, 2 and 3).

SANDIS, SANDIX. Madder (*q.v.*).

SANGUINE. General term for red and purple lakes.

SANGUINEUS. Kermes (*q.v.*).

SANGUIS DRACONIS. Dragon's blood (*q.v.*).

SAP GREEN. Colour made from crushed buckthorn berries boiled in alum (p. 662, 808). *Syn.:* Pasta di vesicha, Pasta verde, Succo verde.

SAPPHIRE. Lapis lazuli. *See* Ultramarine.

SBIADATO. Pale yellow colour made by mixing yellow ochre with white (p. 650).

SCAMMONY. Resin obtained from the dried roots of *Convolvulus scammonia* by soaking in alcohol.

SCORIA OF IRON, SCALES OF IRON. Iron oxides from the forging of iron.

SCRINIUM. Container for rolls or books, frequently round, sometimes rectangular.

SCUDELLA. Liquid measure.

SEPIA. Dark brown pigment obtained from ink sacs of various species of cuttlefish. The ink sac is dried immediately after extraction, to prevent putrefaction, is then powdered, dissolved in caustic alkali and precipitated from the solution by neutralising with acid.

SEXTARIUS. Dry and liquid measure, 0.55 litre.

SHOEMAKER'S BLACK. Ferrous sulphate, used as a black dye for leather (p. 138). *See* Atramentum 4. *Syn.:* Atramentum sutorium, Copperas.

SIL ATTICUM. Purple pigment made by quenching heated yellow ochre in vinegar. A substitute was made from plant juices (p. 250). *Syn.:* Bruslé.

SILLACETUS. Yellow lake made from the colour extracted from *Viola lutea* adsorbed on to chalk. *Syn.:* Cilacetus.

SILVER. The metal was used in powdered form as ink or paint, and was a supposed source of blue colour made by subjecting the metal to vinegar fumes (p. 46, 48, 136). *Syn.:* Argentum.

SINDONE. Fine linen.

SINOBRIUM. Vermilion (*q.v.*).

SINOPIA. 1. Red ochre. (*q.v.*).
2. Sinopis de Mellana (*q.v.*).

SINOPIS. Sinopia (*q.v.*).

SINOPIS DE MELLANA. Red lake made from gum of ivy, sometimes boiled with madder (p. 144). *Syn.:* Mellana.

SINOPLE. Red ochre (*q.v.*).

SIZE. 1. Solution of glue or gelatine in water, used for filling pores in supports or to render supports suitable for receiving coatings (p. 772).
2. Gold size (*q.v.*).

SMALT. A frit made by strongly heating a cobalt ore with other ingredients, probably introduced during the later Middle Ages. *Cf.* Frit. *Syn.:* Zaffre.

SMALTI. Coloured glass or enamel used in painting glass.

SMALTINO. Frit (*q.v.*).

SPANISH AZURE. *See* Azure.

SPANISH BLUE. Azurite (*q.v.*).

SPANISH GREEN. Verdigris (*q.v.*).

SPANISH PITCH. Rosin (*q.v.*).

SPANISH RED. Red ochre (*q.v.*).

SPANISH WHITE. White lead (*q.v.*).

STANNUM. Tin, recommended as a substitute for silver or— with the addition of suitable colouring—for gold.

STECCA. Scraper.

STIL DE GRAIN. Transparent yellow lake made by mixing the juice of certain flowers with white earth (p. 808).

STIPATUM. Plant from whose root "gelantina" was extracted for use as a medium for pigments.

STONE YELLOW. Perhaps native yellow ochre.

STUCCO. Fine plaster used for walls or for relief decorations on walls; made of powdered white marble, fine sand, gypsum and water.

STUPIUM. Red lead (*q.v.*).

SUCCO VERDE. Sap green (*q.v.*).

SUCCUS SAMBUCI. Dark green juice from elder (p. 36). *Cf.* Menech 3.

SULPHUR VIVUM. Impure sulphur.

SUMACH. Dried and powdered leaves of sumach, *Rhus coriaria*, used in dyeing

SYNOPLE. Red ochre (*q.v.*).

TALC. A hydrous magnesium silicate, calle compact form. The term was formerly and to foliated gypsum. Used to cover pa them from dust (p. 774, 784).

TAVERTINUS. Travertine (*q.v.*).

TEMPER. Distemper (*q.v.*).

TEMPERA. Medium for pigments.

TEREBINTHINA. Turpentine (*q.v.*).

TERRA CROCEA. 1. Yellow ochre (*q.v.*).
2. Arxica 2 (*q.v.*).

TERRA DA BOCCALI. China clay.
1. When mixed with earth colours and lin used for priming in oil paintings (p. 730).
2. Sometimes mixed with lamp black and charcoal for drawing.
Syn.: Terra di cava, Terretta.

TERRA DI CAVA. Terra da boccali (*q.v.*).

TERRA DI SIENA. Variety of yellow ochre, r ent than the usual kind.

TERRA D'OMBRA. Umber (*q.v.*).

TERRAGHETTA. Litharge (*q.v.*).

TERRA GIALLA. Yellow earth (*q.v.*).

TERRA NERA DI CAMPANA. Black colour m crust which forms on moulds for casting bell

TERRA NEREA. Native black unctuous eart pigment.

TERRA NIGRA. Black chalk or graphite. *Syn.:*

TERRA ROSSA, TERRA RUBEA. Red ochre

TERRA ROSSA D'INGHILTERRA. Red ochre

TERRA ROSSA DI SPAGNA. Red ochre (*q.v.*).

TERRA VIRIDIS. Terre verte (*q.v.*).

TERRETTA. Terra da boccali (*q.v.*).

TERRE VERTE. Native green earth coloured b manganese. Used as a pigment. *Syn.:* Creta ci viridis, Green chalk, Terra viridis, Theodotian Verd de terre, Verde terra, Viride terrenum, Vi

TEUTONIC AZURE. *See* Azure.

THEODOTIAN, THERDOTE. Terre verte (*q.v.*).

TRAGACANTH. Gum tragacanth (*q.v.*).

VERDE AZZURO. 1. Malachite (*q.v.*).

    2. Green colour made from blue and saffron (p. 422).

VERDE DI VESICHA. Pasta di vesicha (*q.v.*).

VERDE ETERNO. Purified verdigris (*q.v.*).

VERDE PORRO. Whitish-green colour; Mrs Merrifield suggests that it might be synonymous with prasinus (*q.v.*).

VERDERAME. Variety of verdigris (*q.v.*).

VERDET. Type of verdigris (*q.v.*).

VERDETTO. 1. Native green pigment from Germany.

    2. Yellow-green colour, the juice of certain flowers precipitated on to a white earth.

VERDIGRIS. Hydrated copper acetate, a green substance prepared by suspending pieces of copper over strong vinegar. One of the earliest artificial pigments, no longer in use. Used as a dye (p. 84), as a pigment, as an ink (p. 126, 194), and mixed with varnish for glazing (p. 812). *Syn.:* Common green, Greek green, Rothomagensian green, Spanish green.

VERGAUT. Grey-green colour made by mixing "azure" or indigo with orpiment or yellow ochre.

VERJUICE. Acid liquor from sour apples, grapes and other sour fruit.

VERMICULUS. 1. Kermes (*q.v.*) (p. 38).

    2. Vermilion (*q.v.*) (p. 139, 141).

VERMILION. 1. Mercuric sulphide (p. 138). Red pigment artificially produced in the Middle Ages, the natural ore of mercury being used in classical antiquity. *Syn.:* Cinnabar, Cinobrium, Cynobre, Minium, Sinobrium, Vermiculus.

    2. Red ochre (*q.v.*). [Perhaps in error.]

VERNICE COMMUNE. Varnish made of turpentine, oil of turpentine and resin melted together. *Syn.:* Vernice grossa.

VERNICE GROSSA. Vernice commune (*q.v.*).

VERNIDE. Undetermined substance used in dyeing (p. 314). *Syn.:* Vercande.

VERNIX. Sandarac (*q.v.*).

VERXILLIUM, VERZILIUM, VERZINO. Brazil wood (*q.v.*).

VERZINO COLUMBINO. Possibly brazil wood (*q.v.*) from Ceylon, thought to be the best quality (p. 554).

VIOLA. Pigment prepared from blue flowers, pounded to press out the juice, which is adsorbed on to chalk.

VIOLACEUS, VIOLETUS. Colour obtained by mixing red and blue (p. 37).

VIRIDE TERRENUM, VIRIDIS TERRE. Terre verte (*q.v.*).

VIRIDIS. General term for green colours.

VITRIOL. Native or artificial sulphates of metals.

WARANCIA. Madder (*q.v.*).

WATER OF TARTAR. Solution of potash. *Syn.:* Aqua tartari.

WELD. The plant *Reseda luteola*, from which a yellow dye is obtained, especially from the seeds and the upper portions of the plant. *Syn.:* Herba roccia, Panicella.

WHITE COPPERAS. Zinc sulphate used as a dryer in oil painting.

WHITE EARTH OF THE FELLMONGERS. Lime.

WHITE LEAD. Basic lead carbonate, a white pigment made by exposing lead metal to the fumes of strong vinegar in a sealed vessel. *Syn.:* Album Hispanie, Album plumbum, Biacca, Biacha, Blacha, Blanchet, Bracha, Ceruse, Leucos, Plumbus albus, Spanish white.

WOAD. The plant *Isatis tinctoria*, whose leaves yield a blue dye, similar in composition to indigo (*q.v.*). *Syn.:* Gaude, Guado.

WORINA. Folium (*q.v.*).

YELLOW EARTH. A native earth, not synonymous with yellow ochre, used as a pigment (p. 810) and as an ingredient in the priming for canvas (p. 772). *Syn.:* Crocea terra, Terra gialla.

YELLOW OCHRE. Natural yellow earth containing iron oxides and clay minerals, used as a pigment. *Syn.:* Mottée de sil, Terra crocea.

ZAFFIRRO, ZAFIRRO. 1. Blue-coloured precious stone. 2. Blue mineral.

ZAFFRE, ZAFFERA. Smalt (*q.v.*).

ORIGINAL TREATISES ON THE
ARTS OF PAINTING

ORIGINAL TREATISES,

DATING FROM THE XIIth TO XVIIIth CENTURIES

ON THE

ARTS OF PAINTING,

IN

OIL, MINIATURE, MOSAIC, AND ON GLASS; OF GILDING, DYEING, AND THE
PREPARATION OF COLOURS AND ARTIFICIAL GEMS;

PRECEDED BY A GENERAL INTRODUCTION; WITH TRANSLATIONS, PREFACES, AND NOTES.

BY

MRS. MERRIFIELD,

HONORARY MEMBER OF THE ACADEMY OF FINE ARTS AT BOLOGNA, TRANSLATOR OF
THE TREATISE ON PAINTING OF CENNINO CENNINI, AND AUTHORESS OF
'THE ART OF FRESCO-PAINTING.'

IN TWO VOLUMES.—VOL. I.

LONDON:
JOHN MURRAY, ALBEMARLE STREET.

1849.

TO

THE RIGHT HONOURABLE

SIR ROBERT PEEL, BART.,

THESE TREATISES,

COLLECTED UNDER HIS AUSPICES,

ARE GRATEFULLY AND RESPECTFULLY DEDICATED BY

THE EDITOR.

PREFACE.

In the autumn of 1845 I was honoured by Her Majesty's Government with a commission to proceed to the North of Italy, for the purpose of collecting MSS. relative to the technical part of painting, with a view principally of ascertaining the processes and methods of oil-painting adopted by the Italians. I was also instructed generally to endeavour to procure traditional and practical information on this subject from other sources.

I succeeded in obtaining copies of the MSS. contained in the following volumes. On my return to this country, Sir Robert Peel was pleased to entrust me with the publication of the MSS., and to intimate that a part of the expenses of publication would be defrayed by Government.

I need not say how highly I was gratified by this distinction, for an occupation more congenial to my inclinations could scarcely have been suggested; and I accepted the offer without, perhaps, properly considering the magnitude of the undertaking, and my own incapacity.

The following work, in which I have endeavoured to supply by diligence what I have wanted in ability, is the result of my labours.

In preparing the MSS. for publication, I have adopted, as nearly as possible, a chronological arrangement, considering it was best adapted to show the progress of the art, and the technical methods in use from the twelfth or thirteenth to the eighteenth centuries.

The early MSS., although they do not treat of oil-painting, properly so called, are useful in showing the state of the art of painting at the period when they were written, and the importance attached to the preparation and purification of colours. In an antiquarian and historical point of view these MSS. are also highly interesting. Some of the most valuable facts to be collected from them are mentioned in the preliminary observations prefixed to each treatise. With a view of rendering the MSS. more generally useful, I have prefixed to them a brief sketch of the history and technical processes of the different kinds of painting and other arts, which are alluded to in the MSS.

Among the various recipes, many of which may be traced to a very early period, it will not occasion surprise that some should be found which partake of the barbarism of the times when they were written. Absurd, and perhaps useless, as a few of these may be considered, except as forming part of the History of Art, it has been thought advisable to publish the whole of the MSS. in order to satisfy the reader that nothing important has been omitted. The orthography of the originals has been always scrupulously followed; and no emendations have been permitted, except in one or two instances which are mentioned in the notes.

Much information relative to oil-painting was communicated to me orally by several eminent Italian artists during my tour. This information, which I endeavoured to preserve by committing the substance of their communications immediately to writing, is now published in the original form, with such explanatory notes as appeared necessary to make them intelligible.

It also occurred to me that the statements made in these memoranda would require other confirmation than the oral testimony of living persons, who, although possessing much valuable knowledge acquired by their practice and researches, and much information derived from tradition and the study of works on art, are yet unknown to the reader, and their statements are frequently contradictory. It, therefore, appeared to me, that it would be important to examine and compare the statements of the Italian professors with the treatises contained in these volumes, and with many of the best English and foreign works connected with the fine arts, in order to ascertain how far the statements and practice of these artists were supported in their view of the practice of the old masters; inasmuch as, in these points where they did coincide, it might fairly be concluded that the practice of the old masters was correctly stated by these modern professors. I have accordingly made this examination by comparing these statements with the most esteemed works on this subject. The more important points connected with this examination I communicated to Sir Robert Peel in October, 1846. They are now more fully stated, with additions and corrections, in the following work. I have referred to the authorities from which I have framed my opinions, and from which the reader will be enabled to judge of the correctness of my conclusions.

In arranging this brief account of the methods and materials adopted in oil-painting in Italy, it is to be observed, that it has not been my intention to give a complete history of all the processes employed in this art, and of the practice of the different schools, but merely to give such a general outline as will render the oral and documentary evidence and information contained in these volumes and now scattered through so many pages, available to the reader. The only variations from the original memoranda which I have permitted myself to make consist in some necessary verbal corrections, and in some omissions of statements and opinions, which, on inquiry, could not be satisfactorily substantiated. I have also considered it unnecessary to mention the names of the professors who favoured me with the communications, although I was careful to ascertain that they were considered by competent judges eminent in their profession.

Although no exertion has been wanting on my part to make the work as useful as possible by a dispassionate and unprejudiced inquiry into the former processes of oil-painting, it may yet be feared that many errors have crept in, or been overlooked, and that many links in the chain of evidence as well as in the technical processes are still wanting. As I have been particular in stating my authorities, the former may be corrected by reference to the works indicated, the latter will be supplied by Mr. Eastlake's promised volume on the Technical Processes of the Italian Painters.

I cannot dismiss the subject of oil-painting without acknowledging the great assistance I have derived from Mr. Eastlake's recent and very valuable work, 'Materials for a History of Oil-Painting;' and I take this opportunity of expressing my sincere thanks to him for the important assistance and encouragement he has so kindly and readily afforded me during the progress of the work.

To the Earl of Ellesmere I beg also to offer my very grateful acknowledgments for the loan of many valuable books, without which it would have been impossible for me to have completed the work.

To Sir Thomas Phillipps I am also indebted for a copy of an interesting work of the middle ages, entitled 'Mappæ Clavicula,' which I have found very useful.

To my highly-esteemed friend, Mr. Seymour, of Dorset Gardens, Brighton, my acknowledgments are also especially due for loans of books, and valuable references to others, which his extensive reading qualified him to give. To Mr. Charles Carpenter, of the Brighton Bench of Magistrates, I am indebted for similar assistance

I beg also to thank Mr. Robert Hendrie, junior, whose recent edition of Theophilus has been of great assistance to me; Mr. Borrer, of Henfield, Sussex; and Mr. Albert Way, Secretary of the Archæological Institute, for their ready attention to my applications.

Mr. Hermann Schweitzer, of Brighton, the eminent analytical chemist, has also afforded me much valuable professional assistance, which I feel great pleasure in acknowledging.

By means of the introductions with which I was
favoured by Sir Henry Ellis and Sig. Panizzi, of the
British Museum ; by M. Champollion-Figeac, of the
Bibliothèque Royale, at Paris ; and the Cav. Gazzera,
of the Library of the University at Turin, I obtained
access to the public libraries of many of the principal
cities of the North of Italy, and to some private
libraries : especially those of the King of Sardinia ; the
Marquis Trivulzio, and Conte Pompeo Litta, of Milan,
author of the ' History of the Noble Families of Italy ;'
Conte Francesco de' Lazara, of Padua, the nephew and
heir of the Cav. Lazara, whose valuable collection of
MSS. and works on art is so frequently mentioned by
Lanzi ; of Sig. Giuseppe Riva, of the Monte Berici,
near Vicenza, author of several works of antiquarian
interest; of the Canon Ramelli, of Rovigo ; of Sig. M.
A. Gualandi, of Bologna, editor of an interesting series
of original documents and letters of painters ; of Professor Longhena and Sig. Vallardi, of Milan : to all of
whom I beg to express my obligations for the facilities
afforded me.*

---

* My acknowledgments and thanks are also due to many eminent in
literature, science, and art on the Continent. I regret to omit the names
of any of them, and among others named in these volumes, I feel gratified
in expressing my obligations to M. le Comte Charles de l'Escalopier, and M.
Delaroche, of Paris ; the Cav. Promis, of the Private Library of the King of
Sardinia, and Conte Galiteris, of Turin ; Conte Giberto Borromeo, and the
Cav. Rossi, of the Brera Library, Dr. Zardetti, of the Cabinet of Medals,
Drs. Capelli and Vallardi, of Milan ; Conte Lochis, President of the Ac-
cademia Carrara, Conte Pietro Moroni, Sig. Salvioni of the Public Library,
and Sig. Arrigoni, of Bergamo ; Conte Luigi Lechi, of Brescia ; Conte
Orti Manara, and Conte Jacomo Mosconi (known to the literary world as
the translator of some of the works of Sir Walter Scott), of Verona ; the
Ab. Furlanetto, the Ab. Barbaran of the Library of the Seminario, the Ab.
Roncetti of the University Library, and Prof. Poli of the University of

In preparing the following treatises for publication, I have been greatly assisted by my sons, Charles and Frederic, who translated the whole of the MSS.

In conclusion I would observe, that the work has been begun and finished under the pressure of great domestic anxiety and ill health, which sometimes rendered it scarcely possible to give that attention which so arduous a task required. Under these circumstances I have to request the indulgence of the reader for any oversights and mis-translations which may be found in the work. These errors will, however, be less important, inasmuch as the translations are accompanied by the original text, and any mistakes in the former may be corrected by reference to the latter. The fatigue of comparing the translations with works in MS. so numerous and so long, can only be appreciated by those who have been engaged in similar undertakings.

The labour, however, has been far from irksome: on the contrary, it has been pursued from beginning to end with intense interest; and from the consolation and stimulus I have derived from the pursuit, in many a

Padua; the Baron Galvagna, President of the Academy of Fine Arts at Venice; Sig. Gio. O'Kelly Edwards, son of Sig. Pietro Edwards, who restored the public pictures at Venice; Mr. Rawdon Brown, the Ab. Cadorin, the biographer of Titian ; the Ab. Valentinelli, of the Marciana Library ; Dr. Vincenzo Lazari, editor of a recent edition of the ' Travels of Marco Polo;' Sig. Cigogna, author of the valuable work entitled ' Iscrizioni Venetiane ;' Signori Felice Schiavone, Tagliapietra, and Quarena, of Venice; Dr. Devit, of the Public Library of Rovigo; the Ab. Antonelli, of the Ducal Library, and Sig. N. Cittadella, of Ferrara; Sig. Vegetti, of the Library of the University of Bologna ; Sig. Gaetano Giordini, Inspector of the Pinacoteca, and Sig. Masini, Secretary of the Academy of Fine Arts at Bologna; the Cav. Pezzana, of the Ducal Library, and Sig. Scaramuscia, of Parma; Sig. Bombardini, and Sig. Giambatista Baseggio, President of the Athenæum, of Bassano.

weary hour, I take leave of it with the regret which one always feels on parting with an old and agreeable companion.

M. P. M.

Brighton, 6th Nov., 1848.

CONTENTS OF VOL. I.

INTRODUCTION—

CHAPTER I.

Page

ON THE STATE OF SOCIETY AND OF THE ARTS DURING THE
MIDDLE AGES xvii

CHAPTER II.

MINIATURE PAINTING xxvi

CHAPTER III.

MOSAICS xxxviii

Tarsia Work lvii

CHAPTER IV.

GLASS—

§ 1. Early History of Glass Painting in Italy . . lix

§ 2. Windows lxxvi

§ 3. Various Methods of Painting on Glass . . lxxxi

§ 4. Other Uses to which Glass was applied . . lxxxvii

Note.—On Jewish Glass xcii

CHAPTER V.

On Gilding and other Arts—   Page
  § 1. On Gilding xcv
  § 2. On Auripetrum and Porporino xcviii
  § 3. On the Use of Wax in Painting . . . c
  § 4. On Painting Statues cii
  § 5. On the Implements used in Painting . . . cvii
  § 6. On Leather, Dyed and Gilt cix
  § 7. On Niello cxii
  § 8. On Dyeing cxiii

CHAPTER VI.

Painting in Oil—
Introduction cxvi
  § 1. Opinions of Eminent Italian Artists as to the Practice
     of the Old Masters cxvii
  § 2. Colours used in Painting cxlviii
  § 3. On Oils and Varnishes—
    On Grinding and Diluting the Colours . . ccxxx
    On the Purification of Oils ccxxxii
    On Dryers and Drying Oils ccxxxvi
    On Essential Oils ccxlv
    On Resins ccxlviii
    On Varnishes cclxi
    On Varnish in Painting cclxxv
    On Varnishing Pictures cclxxx
  § 4. On the Preparation of the Grounds . . . cclxxxi
    Methods of Painting ccxciii
      Note.—On MS. of Fra Fortunato of Rovigo . cccxi

MANUSCRIPTS OF JEHAN LE BEGUE—   Page

Preliminary Observations **1**

TABULA DE VOCABULIS SINONIMIS ET EQUIVOCIS COLORUM   .   **18**

(*Table of Synonymes and Words of uncertain signification.*)

Alia Tabula Imperfecta et sine Inicio **39**

(*Another Table, imperfect and without a beginning.*)

Experimenta de Coloribus **47**

(*Experiments on Colours.*)

MANUSCRIPTS OF S. AUDEMAR—

Preliminary Observations **112**

Liber Magistri Petri de Sancto Audemaro de Coloribus Faciendis **117**

(*The Book of Master Peter, of S. Audemar, on making Colours.*)

MANUSCRIPTS OF ERACLIUS—

Preliminary Observations **166**

De Coloribus et Artibus Romanorum—

(*On the Colours and Arts of the Romans*)—

     LIB. I. **183**

     LIB. II. **199**

     LIB. III. **205**

MANUSCRIPTS OF ARCHERIUS—

De Coloribus Diversis Modis Tractatur   .   .   .   **259**

(*A Treatise on preparing many kinds of Colours.*)

De Diversis Coloribus **281**

(*On Colours of different kinds.*)

Additional Recipes by Jehan le Begue   .   .   .   **291**

ERRATA.

Page 4, line 12 from bottom, *for* Again at Milan, *read* at Genoa.

16,	20	top, *for* Jacobo, *read* Jacobus.
„	10	bottom, dele " the."
68,	12 & 18	top ⎫
82,	5	bottom, ⎬ *for* in Janua, *read* at Genoa.
224,	17	bottom, *for* mixed however with oil and a little varnish, *read* a little varnish being mixed with the oil.

INTRODUCTION.

CHAPTER I.

ON THE STATE OF SOCIETY AND OF THE ARTS DURING THE MIDDLE AGES.

HISTORY gives but a melancholy view of the state of society in Europe towards the close of the dark ages. The domestic habits and accommodations of the people were rude in the extreme. The nobles were devoted to the pursuit of arms, and when not actually engaged in war their time was occupied in hunting and hawking, of which they were passionately fond. Nor did they disdain, in the intervals of these employments, to become highway-robbers, and to possess themselves by force of the money and baggage of the travellers whom chance threw in their way.[1]

Men so employed could have but little relish for the elegancies and comforts of domestic life. Their castles were merely a retreat from the pursuit of their enemies, and were more suited to secure the defence and safety of their possessions than to display their wealth and magnificence. The walls of these edifices were lofty and substantial, the openings for the admission of light few and narrow, the apertures unclosed with glass; the interior walls, which were bare, had no decorations but arms and the trophies of the chase. The intellectual condition of the nobles was scarcely more advanced

---

[1] See Hallam's Middle Ages, vol. iii. p. 368.

than their domestic arrangements ; the accomplishment
of reading was possessed by few, that of writing was
still more rare.   Neither Frederic Barbarossa, John,
King of Bavaria, nor Philip the Hardy of France,
could read ; nor could Theodoric or Charlemagne
write.[1]   Of the barons whose names are affixed to
Magna Charta very few could write.

The domestic accommodations were in accordance
with the edifices.   A passage quoted by Mr. Hallam,[2]
from a work written about the year 1300, shows the state
of manners in Italy during the age of Frederic Barbarossa.[3]   " In those days," the author observes, " the
manners of the Italians were rude.   A man and his
wife eat off the same plate.   There were no wooden-
handled knives nor more than one or two drinking-cups
in a house.   Candles of wax or tallow were unknown ;
a servant held a torch during supper.   The clothes of
men were of leather unlined ; scarcely any gold or
silver was seen on their dress."

Such a state of society, it may be readily supposed,
afforded small scope for the development of the arts.
They were not, however, totally lost.   The cloister,
while it afforded a shelter and retreat from the more
active pursuits of life, afforded also to the monks leisure
and opportunity for cherishing the arts, the technical
processes of which were preserved in their convents.
The magnificent cathedrals which were erected during the
eleventh, twelfth, and thirteenth centuries,[4] not only in

1 Hallam, Middle Ages, vol. iii. p. 329.   2 Ibid., p. 409.

3 Frederic Barbarossa was born A.D. 1121, ascended the throne A.D. 1152,
and died A.D. 1190.

4 In the eleventh and twelfth centuries the Basilica of St. Mark's at Venice,
and the Cathedrals of Pisa and Siena, were erected ; and in the thirteenth the
Basilica of S. Francesco di Assisi, the Duomo of Florence, that of Orvieto,
and the churches of S. Antonio at Padua, Sta. Maria Novella at Florence,
S. Croce, SS. Giovanni and Paulo, and the Frari at Venice, and the Campo
Santo of Pisa.   In other parts of Europe, the Cathedrals of Cologne, of
Beauvais, Chartres, Rheims, Amiens, Brussels, York, Salisbury, West-
minster, Burgos, Toledo, &c., were built.   See, on this subject, Marchese,
Memorie dei più insigni Pittori, &c. Domenicani, vol. i. p. 17.

Italy, but in the more northern parts of Europe, gave an additional impulse to the study of painting. It was the delight of the monks to adorn these edifices with painted windows of the most brilliant colours, to cover the interior with pictures representing Scripture stories, which were to serve for the catechism and instruction of the common people,[1] and to embellish the choral books with the most elaborate miniatures.

It is impossible to study the history of the arts of the middle ages without considering the immense influence exercised over society by monastic institutions. It is unnecessary to inquire here whether this influence was the cause or the effect of the darkness which hung over Europe at this period; it is sufficient to state that it extended over all classes of society, for the monks, who were the legislators[2] and physicians[3] of that period, and who possessed almost exclusively all the learning of the age, were almost the only persons skilled in the arts of sculpture, painting, and architecture. Marchese observes, with reference to the services rendered to the arts by the monks in Italy,[4] that "after having taught their ferocious conquerors the duty of forgiveness, struggled against the pride of the powerful, and preached the Gospel in the midst of the barbarous feudal laws, they prepared themselves to build bridges, to embank rivers, to construct magnificent cathedrals and abbeys, many of which remain to record the variety of their genius and the benefits they conferred on mankind. In vain would the patronage of Charlemagne, of Theodo-

---

[1] An inscription formerly over the principal door of the Church of S. Nixier de Troyes states that a certain curé had caused three windows to be painted " for the catechism and instruction of the people."—L'Anglois, Essai sur la Peinture sur Verre, p. 16.

[2] Mosheim's Eccles. Hist., vol. ii. pp. 26 and 377 n.

[3] See Introduction to Mr. Eastlake's ' Materials for a History of Oil Painting.'

[4] Memorie de' Pittori, &c., p. 13.

linda,[1] of Theodoric, and of some of the popes have
sufficed to save the arts from total ruin, if the monks
had not, with so much affection, protected and practised
them during so many centuries.   They preserved to us
the traditions transmitted to them by the Byzantines,
and bequeathed them to future ages, stamping them
with that expression and melancholy which transpires
in them in spite of the inelegance of the forms; and
they ennobled by their profession the arts which their
barbarous conquerors despised."

The proof that Europe is indebted to the religious
communities for the preservation of the arts during the
dark ages, rests on the fact that the most ancient
examples of Christian art consist of the remains of
mural pictures in churches, of illuminations in sacred
books, and of vessels for the use of the church and the
altar, and on the absence of all similar decorations on
buildings and utensils devoted to secular uses during
the same period, to which may be added that many of
the early treatises on painting were the work of ecclesiastics as well as the paintings themselves.   A similar
remark may be made with regard to architecture, many
of the earliest professors of which were monks.

Painting was essentially a religious occupation.   The
early professors of the art believed that they had an
especial mission to make known the works and miracles
of God to the common people, who were unacquainted
with letters, "agli uomini grossi che non sanno lettere."[2]
Actuated by this sentiment, it is not surprising that so
many of the Italian painters should have been members
of monastic establishments.   It has been observed that
the different religious orders selected some particular
branch of the art, which they practised with great suc-

---

1 Theodolinda caused to be painted on the walls of the palace of Monza
the principal events in the history of the Lombards.   See Rio, de la Poésie
Chrétienne, p. 20, n.

2 See the Statutes of the Sienese Painters—Carteggio Inedito, &c., vol. ii.

cess in the convents of their respective orders. Thus the Gesuati and Umiliati attached themselves to painting on glass and architecture, the Olivetani to Tarsia work, the Benedictines and Camaldolites to painting generally, and the monks of Monte Casino to miniature painting, while the Dominicans appear to have practised all the various branches of the fine arts (with the exception of mosaics) and to have produced artists who excelled in each.

The various remains of the artistic skill of the monks of the middle ages which have escaped the ravages of time sufficiently attest their mechanical dexterity in these arts, and the excellence of the traditionary practices of which they were for some time the sole depositaries.

Great, however, as the technical skill of the monks undoubtedly was at this period, their paintings were distinguished neither for accuracy of drawing nor for elegance or variety of design. Until the time of Cimabue and Giotto the Byzantine type was adhered to with little variation in Italy, or at least in the northern and southern parts; but in Rome a somewhat different style prevailed, which has been called the Italian. The mural pictures and mosaics throughout Lombardy presented everywhere the same lengthened [1] and attenuated figures, standing on the tips of their toes (for the painters of those days did not possess the art of representing the feet in perspective), with ample and flowing draperies, narrow and ill-shaped extremities, solemn and severe aspects, and large, open, and staring black eyes; the outlines of the figures were hard and black, cutting sharply the gold back-ground, and the expression of the features inspired awe and terror. The same type prevailed in the districts of Southern Italy.

---

[1] The figures of the Byzantine school were sometimes thirteen heads in height.

The good taste of Cimabue introduced in the thirteenth century a better style of art, which was much improved by his gifted pupil Giotto ; and such was the influence of their example that the Byzantine style was banished from Tuscany, and wherever the works and influence of these artists extended.

The improvement in the civil condition of the people followed, if it did not keep pace with the advancement of the arts. In the twelfth century there were many influences which had been for some time silently producing a change in the manners of the people. Among these may be enumerated the Crusades, which, by making the turbulent and warlike nobles of Europe acquainted with the arts and luxuries of the more refined and polished Saracens, awakened in them a taste for dress and the elegant enjoyments of life; the commercial enterprise of a few cities,[1] which, in spite of wars and tumults, succeeded in establishing an uninterrupted intercourse with Constantinople and Palestine, and introducing the merchandise of Asia and Africa into the interior of Europe;[2] the settlements in Sicily, in the kingdom of Naples, and in Spain, of the Saracens, who, less distracted with wars than the Europeans, had leisure to attend to the erection of palaces and to the cultivation of the arts; and the establishment of the silk and woollen manufactories,[3] and the consequent increase in the comforts and conveniences of life. To these may be added the occasional cessation of war, which enabled the laity to devote themselves to the study of the arts. During this period the kind

---

[1] Venice, Amalfi, Pisa, Genoa. See Hallam, Mid. Ages, vol. iii. pp. 367, 388, 389, 390.

[2] Saggio sull' Antico Commercio, sull' Arti, e sulla Marina de' Veneziani, da Jacopo Filiasi, pp. 27 n., 153.

[3] A silk manufactory was established at Palermo in 1148, and in the same century at Genoa. There were woollen manufactories in England in the twelfth century.—Hallam, Midd. Ages, vol. iii. pp. 367, 393.

of painting most practised in Italy was mosaic, but in the western part of Europe painting on glass appears to have been exercised in preference to all others.

In the thirteenth century the manners of the people were still rude and uncultivated, but towards the latter end of this century a sensible refinement took place, especially in Italy. In Venice there were at this period laws in which were mentioned the tariffs regulating the manufactories of gauzes, purple cloth, and cloth of gold;[1] this is sufficient evidence of the establishment of manufactories of these articles and of the increased taste for dress. At this period the commerce of Marseilles with the Levant was in its greatest prosperity. Montpellier and Arles were also engaged in the same pursuit, and at the end of this century or the beginning of the fourteenth the first Venetian vessels arrived at Antwerp laden with spices, drugs, and silk stuffs; to these were added perfumes, cotton, and colours.[2]

The amelioration of the manners and habits of the people was decidedly favourable to the development of the arts in Italy, and the influx of Greek artists, after the taking of Constantinople by the Latins in 1204, gave them an additional impulse, and contributed to their revival in different parts of the country. From the ancient mosaic on the Duomo of Spoleto, dated 1207,[3] works of art, bearing the names of the artists and the date, are of frequent occurrence in the annals of art. Guido da Siena painted the large Madonna in S. Domenico at Siena in 1221; and the works of Giunto da Pisa were executed during the early part of this century.

These artists were succeeded by Cimabue, to whose influence is ascribed the revival of painting in Florence.

---

[1] See Filiasi, Saggio, &c., p. 153.
[2] Guicciardini, Belgii Descript., Amsterdam, 1613, quoted by Depping.
[3] Kugler, Handbook of Painting in Italy, p. 28.

In the middle of this century arose the Florentine school of mosaic painters under Andrea Tafi, who was taught the art by the Greeks; and the family of Cosmati, also painters in mosaic, flourished at Rome about the same period.

In France and England other branches of the art were cultivated with success, especially painting on glass; and a taste for mural paintings appears to have arisen in England.

The arts had also made some progress in Spain during this century, for the corporation of the painters and sculptors of Barcelona dates from the same period.[1] The incorporation of similar societies in Italy appears to have taken place at a later period.[2]

During this century the kings of England found leisure to attend to the decoration of the interior of their palaces. It is ascertained from records preserved at Winchester, that there was a " painted chamber" in this the favourite city of the kings of England, as early as the year 1216;[3] and it appears also from another document that this apartment was decorated with historical pictures.[4] In other documents, paintings, the subjects of which are mentioned, were ordered to be executed in the Hall at Winchester, in the Painted Chamber and Palace at Westminster, in the Castle of Nottingham, and other Royal residences.[5]

---

[1] A.D. 1291. Capmany, Memorias, &c., tome iii., cited by Depping, vol. i. p. 264.

[2] The statutes of the Sienese painters are dated 1355; those of the goldsmiths, 1361; of the Florentine painters in 1339. Those of Padua were probably some years earlier. The Florentine painters were included in the same company as the physicians and apothecaries. See Gaye, Carteggio Inedito, vols. i. and ii. p. i.

[3] Rol. Claus. 4 Hen. III., mem. 16, cited in the Archæological Journal for 1845, p. 69.

[4] See Mr. Eastlake's ' Materials,' p. 556.

[5] Rol. Liberat. 17 Hen. III. mem. 6, and other documents quoted in the Archæological Journal for 1845, pp. 70–77; and in Mr. Eastlake's ' Materials for a History of Painting in Oil,' vol. i. pp. 552–561.

The analysis of early mural pictures, and the directions of Le Begue, Theophilus, and the author of the Bolognese MS., place it beyond a doubt that the greater part of these paintings were executed in tempera. Many of those which are called fresco paintings, were merely commenced in fresco and finished in distemper.[1] The art of fresco-painting, properly so called, did not arise until some time after the period of which I am now speaking. The paintings on the walls of the Chapel of S. Jacopo di Pistoia were ascertained by Professor Branchi to have been executed upon a ground composed of sulphate of lime (plaster of Paris, the *gesso* of the Italians), carbonate of lime, and a yellowish colouring matter tempered with glue. It has also been ascertained that many of the beautiful mural paintings by Bernardino Luini, in the Chapel of the Monastero Maggiore at Milan, were not painted in buon-fresco, but on white stucco, in the ancient manner.[2]

It appears, from MSS. of this period, that it was sometimes the custom in England to whitewash the exterior of castles, and sometimes to paint them of three colours.[3]

" This castel is paynted without with thre maner colours :
    Rede brennand colour is above toward the fair tours,
    Meyne colour is y-middes of ynde and of blewe,
    Grene colour be the ground that never changes hewe."

In the thirteenth and fourteenth centuries the houses of the English, of the middle and lower classes, consisted in general of a ground-floor only, divided into two apartments, namely, a hall, into which the principal door opened, and which was the room for cooking, eating, and receiving visitors ; and a chamber adjoining the hall, and opening out of it, which was the private apartment of the females of the family and the bed-

---

[1] See the First and Second Reports of the Commissioners of Fine Arts.
[2] Milano e il suo Territorio, vol. ii. p. 254.
[3] See Archæological Journal, Part IV., Jan. 1845, p. 304.

room at night. The greater part of the houses in London were built after this plan.[1] The habitations of the more wealthy classes differed from those of the middle ranks only in having an upper floor, called a *soler*, or *solar*, on which was an apartment called a " saloon." The access to this was by a flight of stairs on the outside of the house.[2] The soler is mentioned in the Le Begue MS., p. 88, probably with reference to an English house, since the term occurs in the recipes given by Theodore of Flanders to Alcherius. A different style of architecture prevailed on the Continent, for it is related that when Henry III. visited S. Louis at Paris, he greatly admired the houses of that city, consisting for the most part of many stories.[3] In houses of this description there was but little room for decoration; and they appear to have been but scantily provided with furniture. Even at a much later period, neither looking-glasses nor chairs are mentioned in the catalogue of the furniture of Contarini, the rich Venetian trader, who resided at St. Botolph's, in London, in 1481;[4] or in that of a nobleman in 1572. The Bolognese MS., however, mentions glass mirrors, in a manner which proves that they were not uncommon in Italy at the time that MS. was written.

In the fifteenth century the taste for decoration extended, as might be supposed, to the castles of the nobility, and the apartments were decorated with historical paintings from the Old and New Testament.

> " Ther men myzth se, ho that wolde,
> Arcangeles of rede golde,
> ffytly mad of o molde,
> Lowynge ful lyzth ;

---

1 See notice of the ' Chronicle of the Mayors and Sheriffs of London from 1188 to 1274,' in the Arch. Journ. for Sept. 1847, p. 282.

2 Illustrations of the Domestic Architecture of the Middle Ages, by Mr. Wright, Arch. Journ., Sept. 1844.

3 Arch. Jour., Sept. 1847, p. 282.

4 Hallam's Middle Ages, vol. iii. p. 428.

> With the Pocalyps of Jon,
> The Powles Pystoles everychon,
> The paraboles of Salamon,
>   Paynted ful ryzth.
> And the foure gospellores,
> Sytting on pyllores,
> Hend, herkeneth and heres,
>   Gyf hyt be zoure wyll.
> Austyn and Gregory,
> Jerome and Ambrose,
> Thus the foure doctores
>   Lystened than tylle.
> Ther was purtred in ston,
> The fylesoferes everychon,
> The story of Absolon,
>   That lykyd full ylle."[1]

It will be observed that in all the early MSS. published in this volume clocks are not mentioned, but the hours of the day were reckoned from sun-rise, and shorter periods by the time occupied in repeating Ave Marias, Paternosters, and Misereres. From this we may collect that, although the apartments of castles and palaces might reckon among their articles of domestic convenience—

> " An orrelegge (horloge) one hyzth
>   To rynge the ours at nyzth,"

they were unknown in convents, and among the middle classes, at least until the later half of the fifteenth century.

---

[1] From a manuscript of the fifteenth century, in the Public Library at Cambridge, quoted in the Arch. Jour., Sept. 1844.

CHAPTER II.

MINIATURE PAINTING.

HAVING thus taken a cursory view of the state of society and of the arts during the middle ages, it may not be uninteresting to treat more particularly of those arts, the technical processes of which are described in the following MSS., in order to render the various practical directions more available to the student, and more interesting to the general reader.

It has been observed [1] that the rise and progress of painting is better shown by miniatures than by large pictures, because the altar-pieces and frescoes were frequently repetitions of smaller works painted in choral books, and the parchment on which they are executed being better preserved than pictures on walls, and less injured by retouching, represented more exactly the types and traditions of the early schools. Besides the miniatures painted in books, it was also the custom to affix to every picture a predella or gradino, [2] on which the different events of the life of the Saint represented in the picture were portrayed in miniature; the frames were also ornamented with small figures, so that the study of miniature-painting was necessary to all painters. We turn, therefore, with increased interest to the early history of miniature-painting, which, after the revival of the art, [3] must be sought chiefly in the archives of the

---

[1] Marchese, Memorie, &c., vol. i. lib. i. cap. xi. p. 175.

[2] The step on the top of the altar was so called.

[3] The school of miniature painters was very important during the eighth and ninth centuries. Kugler mentions some interesting illuminations executed in manuscripts of this period. (See Handbook of Painting in Italy, p. 20.)

convents of the Benedictine, Camaldolese, and Dominican monks, and in those of the Canons Regular. It is
impossible to imagine any employment more congenial
to the peaceful and contemplative lives of the monks, in
the intervals of their religious duties, than the pleasing
and almost luxurious occupation of illustrating the
sacred books with stories from Scripture, and of ornament-
ing with elaborate miniatures the works of Virgil and a
few of the other classic authors. It is not surprising,
therefore, that this kind of painting should have found
so many followers in the cloisters.

The art of miniature painting was divided into two
branches: the professors of the first were styled
" Miniatori," or miniature painters, or illuminators of
books; and those of the second, " Miniatori caligrafi,"
or "pulchri scriptores." To the first class belonged the
task of painting the Scripture stories, the borders, and
the arabesques, and of laying on the gold and ornaments
of the MSS.

The second wrote the whole of the work, and those
initial letters generally drawn with blue or red, full of
flourishes and fanciful ornaments, in which the patience
of the writer is frequently more to be admired than his
genius. The wood-cut[1] in the next page shows a writer
of the fifteenth century engaged in this occupation and
surrounded with his various implements. With the
miniatori may be classed the authors and collectors of
many of the MSS. now published, and others of a similar
nature. To the second class belongs Alberto Porzello,
who is mentioned in the Le Begue MS. to have been
" perfect in all kinds of writing, and to have kept a
school at Milan, where he taught the art to young men
and boys." But the two branches were frequently prac-

---

[1] Copied from the work of M. Aimé Champollion-Figeac, entitled
' Louis et Charles, Ducs d'Orléans, leur Influence sur les Arts, la Littéra-
ture, et l'Esprit de leur Siècle, d'après les Documents Originaux et les
Peintres des Manuscrits,' Paris, 1844.

A WRITER OF THE FIFTEENTH CENTURY.
From a Manuscript in the Bibliothèque Royale at Paris.

tised by the same person, whence the term "writing" was also extended to painting, and the word was not confined to miniature painting only, but was applied to painting on glass, which was also called "writing on glass." As to the origin of the word "miniature," it received its name from the practice of writing the rubrics and initial letters with minium or red lead. The French term "illuminer" is supposed to be derived from the custom of illuminating or heightening the lights with gold. The term occurs in the Lucca MS., in the chapter "De Lazuri."

Previous to the invention of printing the art of calligraphy was of great importance. It was the custom and the pride of the large religious establishments to have the books used in the celebration of Divine Service exquisitely written, and adorned with miniatures. The recent researches into the archives of the different Italian cities have brought to light the minutes of expenses of some of these books, which prove the

time occupied in painting them, and the large sums
paid to the artists for executing them, or for the purchase of the materials; for the monks did not receive
payment for the works intended for their own convents.
The choral books of the convent of S. Marco, at
Florence, were written and painted by Fra Benedetto
del Mugello (the elder brother of Frate Angelico[1]),
with the assistance of the monks. The cost of these
books was 1500 ducats, and the time occupied in completing them was five years.[2]

The choral books belonging to the cathedral of
Ferrara are thirty in number; twenty-two of which
are 26 inches long by 18 in breadth, and the remaining
eight smaller. They were begun in the year 1477,
and completed in 1535.[3] The most interesting of
these books, for the beauty of the characters, as well as
for the miniatures, were executed by Jacopo Filippo
d'Argenta, Frate Evangelista da Reggio, a Franciscan,
Andrea delle Veze, Giovanni Vendramin of Padua,
and Martino di Giorgio da Modena. The parchment
on which these books are written is in excellent preservation. It is worthy of remark that great part of
the parchment or vellum for these books was brought
from Germany, or, at least, was manufactured by
Germans. There is an entry in the records of the
cathedral, for the year 1477, of a sum of money paid
to M. Alberto da Lamagna for 265 skins of vellum;
of another sum, paid in 1501, for 60 skins, to Piero
Iberno, also a German; and to Creste, another German, for 50 skins, furnished by them on account of
these books.

The magnificent choral books, thirteen in number,
which formerly belonged to the Certosa of Pavia, are

---

[1] Called also Beato Angelico.

[2] Marchese, Memorie, &c., vol. i. p. 189.

[3] Documenti risguardanti i Libri Corali del Duomo di Ferrara, communicated by the Ab. Antonelli, of the Public Library at Ferrara, to Sig. Gualandi, by whom they were published in his Memorie, &c., ser. vi. p. 153.

now in the library of Brera, at Milan. They are of very large size, probably three feet by two, and many of the illuminations are very beautiful.

As a work of art, the choral books of the Monastery degli Angeli in Florence are perhaps more remarkable than those of Ferrara. They are twenty in number, and were all written by one writer, and embellished by one miniature painter. The former, Don Jacopo, was a Camaldolese monk, of the same religious house at Florence; and, according to Vasari,[1] was not only a most excellent person, but the best writer of initial letters that ever lived, not only in Tuscany, but in Europe; and he adds, that these choral books are perhaps, as regards the writing, the finest and largest in Italy; Don Jacopo also wrote other books at Rome and at Venice. The miniatures in the above-mentioned choral books, which are all by the hand of Don Silvestro, are not less excellent than the writing; and so great was the esteem in which these two monks, D. Jacopo and D. Silvestro, were held in their convent, that the right hand of each was preserved in a casket with the utmost veneration. Vasari adds that he, who had seen these books so many times, was astonished at the skill in design and ability with which they were executed, at a period when the art of design was all but lost; for these monks flourished about the year 1350.

The choral books of the Cathedral of Siena have been preserved with the greatest care. They were all attributed by Vasari to Piero di Perugia,[2] but they are known to have been painted by several artists, among whom may be mentioned Liberale di Verona and Ansino di Pietro, whose names are inscribed on their paintings.[3] There were also fourteen magnificent choral books in the convent of Sta. Maria del Sasso,

---

[1] Life of Don Lorenzo.

[2] Life of Agnolo Gaddi.   [3] Marchese, Memorie, &c., vol. i. p. 197.

near Bibbiena, which were executed by Fra Pietro di
Tramoggiano, and which were valued at upwards of
1500 scudi.   Many of the miniatures were cut out
and carried away, others were sent to Sta. Maria
Novella, at Florence; but the books are now lost, and
the convent does not at the present time possess a
single miniature.[1]

The sister arts of calligraphy and miniature painting
flourished simultaneously in Italy and in the countries
north of the Alps.   The celebrated monastery of St.
Gall possessed a school of painters, who were distinguished even in the ninth century.   In the tenth
century, Tutilo, a member of this community, was
equally famous as a painter, poet, musician, sculptor,
and statuary.   But the best miniature painter of the
tenth century was Godemann, who was chaplain of the
Bishop of Winchester from A.D. 963 to 984, and afterwards Abbot of Thornley.   His benedictional, ornamented with thirty beautiful miniatures, is in the
possession of the Duke of Devonshire.   In the eleventh
century schools of painting were formed at Hildesheim
and Paderborn; and the art was exercised by ecclesiastics of the highest rank.[2]   The reputation of the
French miniature painters had reached Italy in the
time of Dante, who alludes to the practice of the art
        " Ch' alluminare è chiamato in Parigi,"
while recording the merit of Oderigi da Gubbio and
Franco Bolognese.   Many artists who followed this
branch of the profession are enumerated by Alcherius in
the work of Le Begue.   Some of these were natives of
Italy, others of France, and others of Flanders.   The
Italian miniature painters are numerous.   Among the

---

[1] Compendio Storico Critico sopra le due Immagine di Maria S. S. nella
Chiesa di Sta. Maria del Sasso, presso Bibbiena, dato in luce dal P. Vincenzo Fineschi, Firenze, 1792, cap. x. p. 72; cited by Marchese, vol. i.
p. 209.

[2] See Rio, de la Poèsie Chrétienne, p. 32–34.

most celebrated miniatori of the fifteenth century was
Francesco dai Libri, a native of Verona, called the Old,
to distinguish him from his son Girolamo. He obtained
the appellation "dai Libri" from his employment,
which consisted in illuminating MSS.; and, as he lived
before the discovery of the art of printing, he found
constant occupation, because those persons who paid
the expense of the writing, which was very great, were
also desirous of seeing their books ornamented with
miniatures. Francesco lived to a great age, and died
contented and happy, because, says Vasari, "in addition to the peace of mind which he derived from his
own virtues, he left a son who was a better painter than
himself." This son was Girolamo dai Libri, whose
merits as a miniature painter fully equalled the sanguine
expectations of his father. Vasari is warm in his
praises. He says, "Girolamo painted flowers with such
skill, truth, and beauty, that they appeared like nature
itself; and he imitated small cameos and other engraved
stones and jewels in such a manner that it was impossible to make them more like, or more minute; and
among the figures which he made on cameos and factitious stones, may be seen some which are not larger
than a small ant, yet all their limbs and muscles are
seen distinctly." Girolamo illuminated many books
for religious societies, and especially for the rich monastery of the Canons Regular of S. Salvatore, at Can-
diani, where he went to work in person, which he would
not do at any other place; whilst at this monastery he
taught the first principles of the art to Don Giulio
Clovio, who was afterwards reputed to be the best
miniature painter of his time.[1] Lanzi calls him the prince
of miniature painters. Great part of his works were
painted for sovereigns and princes, in whose libraries
they may be seen, executed with such surprising truth

---

[1] Vasari, Vita di Fra Giocondo ed Altri, vol. iii.

and liveliness, that they appear rather to be reflections in a camera obscura than works of art. Some idea of the labour of executing these minute pictures may be formed from the fact, that one work alone, which he illustrated for Cardinal Farnese, with twenty-six subjects, occupied him during nine years. His works are very scarce, but some may be found in the libraries of private individuals. The Sloane Library contains a MS. illuminated by Don Giulio Clovio.

Among the miniature painters of the order of St. Dominic was P. Alessandro della Spina, who flourished during the fourteenth century. Padre Alessandro deserves the gratitude of posterity, and of all miniature painters especially; for to him we are indebted for making known the invention and use of spectacles. Indeed P. Marchese attributes the *invention* [1] of spectacles to Padre Alessandro, but the memorial of him in the Chronicle of St. Katherine, at Pisa, proves that he had seen spectacles made by one who would not communicate the secret, before he made them himself, and that with a cheerful and willing heart he communicated all he knew. The notice in the Chronicle runs thus:—

" Fra Alexander de Spina vir modestus et bonus, quæ vidit oculis facta scivit et facere. Ocularia ab alio primo facta comunicare nolente, ipse fecit, et omnibus comunicavit corde hilari et volente. Cantare, scribere, miniare, et omnia scivit quæ manus mechanicæ valent." [2]

Another monk and miniature painter of the same order, Fra Benedetto, usually called " Bettuccio," deserves remembrance for his brave defence of Giro-

---

[1] " Spectacles had been known at Haarlem since the beginning of the 14th century, and a monument in the church of Sta. Maria Maggiore, at Florence, alludes to Salvino degli Armati, who died in 1317, as their inventor (inventore degli occhiali). Some accurate notices of the use of spectacles by old men appear to have been made in 1299 and 1305." Humboldt's Kosmos, vol. ii. p. 497.—Is it possible that Padre Marchese can have overlooked the monument alluded to by the accurate and scientific Humboldt?   [2] Memorie de' Pittori, &c. Domenicani, vol. i. p. 177.

lamo Savonarola, when the latter was torn from the shelter of his convent of S. Marco, at Florence, to meet a cruel and painful death. Fra Pacifico Burlamacchi, in his Life of Savonarola, relates that " Fra Benedetto armed himself from head to foot, and joined the party of the Piagnoni,[1] to defend a life so dear to him ; but Savonarola seeing him, desired him to lay down his arms, adding that the professors of religion should use spiritual weapons only. When Benedetto saw them carrying away his beloved master to prison, he entreated to be allowed to follow him. Then Savonarola, turning round to him, said, ' Brother Benedetto, I command you by your vow of obedience not to follow me, because Brother Domenico and I must die for the love of Christ.' At this instant he was torn from the sight of his sons, who all wept for him. And it was then the ninth hour of the night." [2]

Fra Eustachio, another Dominican monk, was, perhaps, one of the greatest miniature painters that Italy has produced.[3] His merits, passed over by historians, and especially by Vasari, whom gratitude should have prompted to remember him, are recorded by his own order. Padre Timoteo Bottonio,[4] a contemporary of Fra Eustachio, relates that when Vasari was writing the first edition of his Lives of the Painters, he used to come frequently to converse with this old man, who related to him many interesting facts concerning the early and illustrious artists. A Psalter, exquisitely painted by him, still exists in the Convent of S. Marco, at Florence. He has been styled the Porta of miniature painting.

The French miniature painters were undoubtedly numerous, but a Vasari is still wanting to record their merits. The beautiful choral book, painted by Daniel d'Aubonne, in 1621, must not be forgotten. This volume

---

[1] The partisans of Savonarola.
[2] See Marchese, Memorie, &c., vol. i. p. 199.   [3] Ibid., p. 202-207.
[4] Annale MSS., vol. ii. p. 303, ann. 1555.

is preserved in the public library at Rouen; it is of very large size, and the writing and illuminations are exquisitely beautiful. Daniel was thirty years in completing it.

Missals and livres d'heures of great beauty are so common in all rich libraries, that it is unnecessary to particularise any in the present work.

As a private collection, perhaps there is no single volume of greater beauty or value than that belonging to Mr. Rogers the poet, whose elegant and correct taste is well known. The volume, formed at great expense, consists of miniatures from different works and different countries; and it is scarcely possible to see more exquisite specimens of the art.

The manner in which these works were executed may be collected from the following Treatises: it is sufficient to observe that the colours were prepared with the greatest care, and that the vehicle was egg, gum, or glue. D'Agincourt, however, mentions some miniatures, the colours of which were insoluble in water; and Dr. Dibdin,[1] in describing the illuminations of a MS. of the Codex Justinianus of the fourteenth century, states that on close examination the colours appear to have been mixed up with a glossy material not unlike oil. These instances appear to have been exceptions to the general character of miniatures, the surface of which usually does not shine. It will be observed that the shades in miniatures were not generally painted with transparent colours, but that white was mixed with them.

The parchment or paper on which these MSS. were written was usually left white; but a purple colour was sometimes communicated to it, by tinging it with a decoction of oricello.[2] When the tint was dry, the letters were written on it with gold or silver. Several MSS. of this kind are preserved in the Bibliothèque Royale at Paris.

---

[1] Northern Tour, p. 603.   [2] See Bol. MS., p. 474.

CHAPTER III.

MOSAICS AND TARSIA WORK.

In enumerating the arts of the middle ages, we must not omit to mention the beautiful art of working in mosaic, the most durable of all the methods of painting now in existence. Domenico Ghirlandaio used to say that it was the only painting for eternity.[1] Vasari also has a similar remark; he says, with regard to the durability of all works composed of colours, there are none which resist the action of the winds and waters like mosaics.[2]

The art of working in mosaic was known to the ancients. It was practised by the Byzantine Greeks, and appears never to have been entirely lost in Italy. Specimens of this art may still be seen at Rome and at Ravenna, which date from the fourth and fifth centuries.

There were various kinds of mosaics.[3] Those intended for the decoration of vaulted ceilings and other elevated parts of buildings, consisted of cubes of coloured glass, the older specimens being generally inlaid either on a white ground, as in the Romano-Christian school,[4] or on a gold ground, as in the early Christian mosaics of the Byzantine school. The mosaics in the church of SS. Cosmo and Damiano in the Forum at Rome were the work of Roman artists, while the old mosaics

---

[1] Vasari, Life of Domenico Ghirlandaio.

[2] Life of Gherardo.

[3] For an account of the different kinds of mosaic, and of the process employed at Rome, see Transactions of the Society of Arts, Part I., New Series, 1847.

[4] Rio, de la Poésie Chrétienne, p. 41.

in the Apsis [1] of the Basilica of S. Ambrogio, at Milan,
which are said to be not later than the ninth century;
those in S. Lorenzo, also in Milan; those in the Duomo
of Torcello, reputed to be of the tenth century; and
some of the ancient mosaics in the church of S. Marco,
at Venice, which are of the eleventh century, are represented to be the work of Byzantine artists. Some of
the mosaics in the last-mentioned edifice are stated to
have been actually brought from the East.

It appears that there were in Italy two principal
schools of mosaic painting, established as early as the
eleventh century. One of these was formed by the
Greek artists employed on the church of S. Mark, at
Venice, from which the Florentine school afterwards
sprung; the other subsisted in Rome, from an early
period until the thirteenth century.[2]   Both schools have
been praised by different authors as superior to all
others; Vasari gives the preference to that of Venice,
while Lanzi considers that the Roman artists excelled
the Venetians.   The Venetian school undoubtedly
originated in the decoration of the church of S. Mark,
which afforded for several centuries constant occupation
to the musaicisti. This church, observes Lanzi, was and
is an incomparable museum, in which, commencing
from the eleventh century, may be traced, in the mosaics
begun by the Greeks and continued by the Italians, the
gradual progress of design of every period until the
present day.

The earliest artists were undoubtedly Greeks, and
the work appears to have been continued by Greek
artists and their disciples until about 1250.   From that
time until 1350, Zanetti states [3] that he was unable to
find any records of the progress of the work; but at the

---

[1] The *Apsis* was also called the *Tribune*.   It was the semicircular recess
at the east end of the church.   [2] Lanzi, vol. i. p. 6 n.

[3] Notizie de' Musaici della Chiesa Ducale di S. Marco—Zanetti, della
Pittura Veneziana, p. 561.

last date the doge Andrea Dandolo caused the chapel
of the Baptistery to be covered with mosaics. The
fourteenth and fifteenth centuries produced many artists,
the best of whom was Michele Zamboni, who was the
first to abandon the ancient manner, and to improve
his design, by studying the works of the best painters
of his time. Many of the ancient mosaics having
perished, they were replaced by Zamboni, according to
the old design. The sixteenth century was the golden
age of mosaic painting at Venice. Among the great
names of the period may be enumerated Vincente
Bianchini, more remarkable for his talents than his integrity, and his brother Domenico, called Il Rosso or
Rosetto; Alberto Zio, the priest; Marco Luciano
Rizzo; the celebrated Francesco Zuccato, the friend of
Titian, who received his first instructions in painting
from the father of Zuccato; Valerio Zuccato, the brother
of Francesco; and Giovanni Visentin.

The distinctions enjoyed by the brothers Zuccati
excited the envy of the other artists, and when the
former had completed the pictures from the Apocalypse,
the quarrels among the rival painters ran so high, that
they reached the ears of the Procuratore Cassiere. A
process was instituted to discover the truth. The Zuccati were accused, among other things, of having added
to the effect of their mosaics by painting on certain
parts, and of having joined the squares badly; Valerio
especially was accused of not knowing his business.
Among the most violent of the accusers was Bartolommeo Bozzo, a former pupil of the Zuccati, who pointed
out some small campanili, and also some clouds in the
mosaic of the Apocalypse, which were executed with the
pencil, and not with coloured glass and stones, as they
ought to have been, according to the rules of the Procuratori. The Bianchini supported the accusation of
Bozzo, and an accidental circumstance gave additional
weight to the charge against the Zuccati. A mistake

having been discovered by the latter in the word *saxibus*, which formed part of the inscription, they had corrected the error by affixing to it a small piece of painted paper; and when the mosaic was washed to ascertain whether it had been painted or not, the piece of paper was separated, and the Procuratore believed accordingly that some deception had been used. He therefore caused several persons employed in the church to inquire into the affair, and finally he summoned a council of the greatest painters of that time, among whom were Titian, Paolo Veronese, Tintoretto, and Andrea Schiavone, who decided that it could not be denied " that the pencil had been used in some parts, but that when these touches had been removed with a sponge and sand, the mosaics were not injured by it, but were even considered to be improved." Every one praised the design, and the skill of the artists, and Titian, especially, defended his friends the Zuccati with great warmth, saying that the cartoons ought to be examined, to see whether the campanili which had been painted were in them as well as in the mosaics ; thinking that the degree of blame attached to these masters depended upon this circumstance. It is doubtful who made the cartoons; Valerio asserted that they were made by " Messer Tiziano," and that they did not contain the campanili, and said that if it were necessary he would produce them with the outlines pricked, as they were. Titian, however, did not acknowledge that these cartoons were his work, although he owned having made others for the Zuccati. The trial concluded by the Zuccati being adjudged to execute again, at their own expense, the parts on which the pencil had been employed; but this decree was never executed, and the painted parts, particularly the small campanili, remain to this day.[1]

The dispute concerning the execution of this mosaic

---

[1] Zanetti, p. 576.

by the Zuccati led to the examination of the other pictures, which had been the work of their rivals; and it was finally concluded unanimously, that the two Bianchini and Bozzo were the best workers in mosaic, but that Francesco Zuccato excelled them all in the knowledge of the art, and next to him in skill was Vincente Bianchini.

The designs for the mosaics executed about this period were by the most celebrated painters, Titian, Tintoretto, Salviati, Sansovino, Domenico Tintoretto, Maffeo Verona, and others; and many of the musaicisti were so little acquainted with the principles of art, that the painters who made the designs were obliged to colour as well as draw them, and they were then servilely copied by the musaicisti. The Procuratori being satisfied by the representations of the professors of the bad consequences likely to ensue from the ignorance of the musaicisti, new regulations were made, the number of masters employed in St. Mark's was reduced, and every one was required, before his election, to give a proof of his skill. In order to determine the respective merits of the rival artists, a design representing S. Jerome was made, and Francesco Zuccato, the two Bianchini, and Bozzo were required to copy it in mosaic. Sansovino, Titian, and Paolo Veronese were the judges, and it was agreed unanimously that Zuccato's picture was the best, Gian Antonio Bianchini's was next, then that of Bozzo, and Domenico Bianchini's was the last, although it was considered the most faithful copy of the design.

Among the later Venetian artists may be enumerated Gio. Antonio Marini, Lorenzo Ceccato, Luigi Gaetano, Jacopo Pasterini, and Francesco Turessio; these worked from the designs of Palma Giovane, of Maffeo Verona, of Leandro Bassano, Aliense, Padovanino, and others. The artists of the seventeenth century were less celebrated, and their works in mosaic executed in the style of that period were employed as decorations on new walls only ; according to Zanetti,[1] it was decreed in the year 1610, that no ancient mosaic should be removed, although the work might be Greek, and the style bad ; but that where the danger of ruin was imminent, the design should be copied, and the picture restored exactly as it was at first.   By this means a complete series of monuments, unique in their kind, not only in Italy, but in all the world, has been preserved to posterity.

In the middle of the thirteenth century the fame of the Greek artists, who were still employed on the mosaic decorations of St. Mark's, was spread far and wide ; it reached to Florence, where Andrea Tafi then practised the art of painting.   Andrea, ambitious of transmitting his name to posterity, and having greater confidence in the durability of the materials than in his own talents, prudently determined to adopt the art of mosaic painting ; but as the technical part of this art was unknown in the north of Italy, he found it necessary to go to Venice.   While residing in this city, he gained the good will of a Greek painter named Apollonio so entirely, that he was persuaded not only to teach him the art, but to accompany him to Florence, where, in the middle of the thirteenth century, he executed, in conjunction with Andrea Tafi, some mosaics in the Tribune of the old church of S. Giovanni.[2]   Vasari[3] says that this work was entirely in the Greek manner, that the design was rude and without skill, but that the mechanical part was well executed, the pieces extremely well joined, and the surface even.[4]   He adds, that the latter part of the work is much better, or to speak more correctly, not so bad as the portions first completed. After this, Andrea executed in mosaic, without the assistance of Apollonio, a figure of Christ 14 feet high,

[1] Della Pittura Veneziana, p. 570 n.

[2] Now the Basilica of S. Giovanni Battista—the Battistero.

[3] Vita di Andrea Tafi.   [4] See also Morrona, Pisa Illustrata, vol. i. p. 254.

a work which, Vasari says, spread his fame throughout Italy. "Andrea was really," observes this author, "very happy in living at a time when works of so little merit were so much esteemed." It may be added, that he was fortunate in forming so correct an estimate of his own powers, as to prefer being the head of a new school of painting in the north of Italy, to remaining in the obscurity to which his want of skill in design appeared to consign him. Andrea died in 1294, and his merits were recorded in an epitaph preserved by Vasari—

> " Qui giace Andrea, ch' opre leggiadre, e belle
>   Fece in tutta Toscana, ed ora è ito
>   A far vago lo Regno delle stelle."

Contemporary with Andrea was Jacopo da Turrita,[1] or, as he was called in Siena, Maestro Mino,[2] a Franciscan friar, to whose merits Lanzi says that Vasari did not do justice. Perhaps the latter judged from the specimens of the works of Jacopo at Florence, which were by no means equal to those conducted by him in Sta. Maria Maggiore at Rome. Some writers have believed that Fra Mino and Tafi both worked in mosaic in the Tribune of the Duomo of Pisa, but Prof. Ciampi has shown that this mosaic was not begun until 1301, at which time Fra Mino and Tafi were no longer living. The mosaic at Pisa, the subject of which was a Maestà, was commenced by one Maestro Francesco,[3] assisted by his son Vittorio, Lapo of Florence, Michele, Duccio, Tura, Turetto, Dato, Tano, and others. Francesco either died or abandoned the work the same year, and was succeeded as Capo Maestro by Cimabue,[4] under whom worked Bardo, Ganaccio, Upechino, and Turetto. The S. Giovanni, on the left hand of the Saviour in the

---

1 Vasari, Vita di Andrea Tafi. Baldinucci, Vite.
2 Morrona, Pisa Illust., vol. i. p. 247.
3 Ciampi, Notizie, &c., p. 144, and Docum. xxv.   4 Ibid., Doc. xxvi.

same design, is said to be the work of Cimabue, who
however left it incomplete; and it was, together with
the figure of the Saviour, finished by Vicino, the pupil
of Gaddo Gaddi, in 1321. As this is the only work in
mosaic ascribed to Cimabue, it has been supposed by
some persons that he merely executed the design.
The repeated payments, however, to him, on account
of this work,[1] in the books of the Duomo, seem to
warrant the belief that he actually worked on the
mosaic. Giotto also exercised his talents in mosaic
painting, and the celebrated mosaic called the " Nave
di Giotto," which was executed for the ancient basilica
of St. Peter at Rome, attests his eminence in this
branch of the art.[2] This work, observes D'Agincourt,
" by its ingenious and picturesque composition, as well
as by a more correct design, fixes the epoch of the
revival of this kind of painting." Kugler says[3] that
the mosaic has so frequently changed its place, and thus
undergone so many restorations, that the composition
only can now be considered as belonging to Giotto.

Gaddo Gaddi was the father of Taddeo Gaddi,[4] and
the grandfather of Agnolo, the master of Cennino
Cennini.[5] He was the friend of Cimabue and of
Andrea Tafi; from the example of the former he
learned to improve his style of design, and from the
latter he acquired the art of working in mosaic. As
he united the mechanical skill of Andrea to a better
taste in design, it will readily be supposed that his
works were in much request. He executed, in the
semicircle over the principal door in Sta. Maria del
Fiore in Florence, the mosaic representing the Corona-
tion of the Virgin, which, on the authority of Vasari,

[1] Ciampi, Notizie, &c., Doc. xxvi.; Morrona, Pisa Illust., vol. i. p.
249 n.; and see Kugler, Handbook of Painting in Italy, p. 32.
[2] Vasari, Int., cap. xxix.
[3] Handbook of Painting, Italian School, p. 51.
[4] Vasari, Vite di Gaddo, Taddeo, e Agnolo Gaddi.
[5] Cennino Cennini, Trattato.

was considered by all masters, foreign as well as native, as the finest work of the kind which had ever been seen in Italy. He afterwards worked at Rome and at Pisa, and died in 1312.

The secret of working in mosaic was inherited by Agnolo, the son of Taddeo,[1] who in 1346 repaired some of the mosaics executed by Andrea Tafi in the roof of S. Giovanni at Florence. He fixed the cubes of glass so firmly into the ground, with a stucco composed of mastic[2] and wax melted together, that neither the roof nor the vaulting had received any injury from water from the period of its completion until the time of Vasari. From Agnolo Gaddi the secrets of the art were transmitted to Cennino Cennini, who, in his Treatise on Painting, left them as an heir-loom to posterity. That Cennini actually treated on mosaics in his work, is related by Vasari;[3] but as this subject is not mentioned in the MS. published by Tambroni, it was considered that Vasari was mistaken, and that he had spoken of the MS. without having read it. Subsequent researches,[4] however, have proved that he was right. Besides the MS. in the Laurenziana, the Riccardiana Library (at Florence) contains a more perfect copy made in the sixteenth century, probably soon after the year 1500, which contains many things omitted in the Vatican MS., among which may be mentioned the arts of working in glass and in mosaic.

It is gratifying to learn that a second edition of this highly interesting work will probably be published at Florence, which will contain the new passages in the MS. of the Riccardiana, and which will be collated with both the Florentine MSS. It has been con-jectured from the last words of the MS. of Cennini in

---

[1] Vasari, Vita di Agnolo Gaddi ; Bald., Vita di Agnolo Gaddi.

[2] Bald., Vita di Agnolo Gaddi. Vasari says " mastrice," which signifies cement or glue.

[3] Vita di Agnolo Gaddi.   [4] Antologia—Firenze, 1821.

the Vatican, "Finito libro referamus gratia Christi
1437 a dì 31 di luglio.   Ex stincarum f.,"[1] that
Cennini was an inmate of the debtors' prison at
Florence called "Le Stinche," and our sympathies
were excited on behalf of the patient and religious old
man, who at an age approaching to eighty could so
abstract his mind from the adversity into which he had
fallen, as to compose his Treatise on Painting during
his confinement in a prison, and to allow no expressions
of regret or discontent to escape from his pen.   The
researches, however, of Signor Benci of Florence
prove that the name of Cennini does not occur in the
books belonging to the prison of the Stinche in the
year 1437, or in some of the later years of the fourteenth century.   The addition of the above mentioned
words has been accounted for[2] by the fact that it was
the custom to employ the prisoners for debt in copying
MSS.; and it was conjectured that these words, so
expressive of the distaste we may suppose a person
indifferent to the art to have felt on the completion of,
to him, so irksome a task, were added by the unfor-
tunate prisoner who copied the MS. afterwards placed
in the Vatican.   If then the date 1437 be that of the
copy, the original MS. must be older, and perhaps may
be actually a work of the fourteenth century.

Many, if not all, of the early Florentine painters
practised this branch of the art.[3]   It is said[4] that
Alesso Baldovinetto spared no pains to discover the
best method of working in mosaic, and that he would
never have succeeded in this pursuit, if he had not

---

[1] These words are wanting in the Riccardiana MS.   See Antologia—
Firenze, 1821.

[2] Edinburgh Review, 1847, p. 193.

[3] Prof. Ciampi (Notizie, &c., p. 92) says the *Musaicisti* called themselves
painters, and he quotes the inscription on the mosaic by Torriti (or Turrita)
in the church of S. Giovanni Laterani at Rome :—" Jacobus Torriti pictor
hoc opus mosaycen fecit."

[4] Vasari, Vita di Alesso Baldovinetto.

accidentally met with a German who was travelling through Florence on his way to Rome. Alesso gave this man a lodging, and learned from him the whole process, so that he was enabled to set to work with confidence, and to execute some figures in mosaic in the church of S. Giovanni. This work so increased his reputation that he was employed in cleaning the whole roof of the edifice, which had been covered with mosaics by Andrea Tafi, and was then in want of repair. He completed this work also to the satisfaction of his employers. Alesso lived to be eighty years old, and then feeling the infirmities of age stealing over him, he sought a retreat for his declining years in the Hospital of S. Paul. It is related that in order to ensure for himself a better reception, he took with him to his apartments in the hospital a large chest which was thought to contain money, and in this belief the officers of the hospital treated him with the greatest respect and attention. But their disappointment may be imagined when, on opening the chest, after the decease of the aged artist, they found nothing but drawings on paper, and a small book which taught the art of making the mosaics (pietre del musaico), the stucco, and the method of working. At the present time we should have considered this little book a greater treasure than the money which was so much desired. The remarks of Vasari on this occurrence are highly honourable to the venerable old man; he says, "It was no wonder that they did not find money, for Alesso was so bountiful, that everything he possessed was as much at the service of his friends as if it had been their own."

Alesso taught the art of working in mosaic to Domenico Ghirlandaio, who executed, in conjunction with Gherardo, some mosaics in the Duomo of Florence.[1]

The only artists of the early Roman school whose

---

[1] Vasari, Vite di Alesso Baldovinetto e Domenico Ghirlandaio.

names have descended to posterity are the family of
Cosmati.[1] Adeodati di Cosmo Cosmati worked in
Sta. Maria Maggiore in 1290, two years after the
arrival of Giotto in Rome, and probably about the time
that he was employed upon the "Navicella." Jacopo
and Giovanni Cosmati also worked in mosaic about
1299 in Rome, and in the Duomo of Orvieto. It is
said that these artists were all superior to the Greeks
employed in S. Mark's at Venice. It is certain, however, that much encouragement was given at Rome to
artists from other parts of Italy, and especially to many
Florentines. This city was in fact the general ren-
dezvous of all who were distinguished for more than
ordinary skill in the arts, as the place where they might
not only improve themselves in their profession by the
contemplation and study of works of art, but where
their talents might meet with encouragement and
reward. The art of working in mosaic was brought to
perfection in this city. It became in time the rival of
painting, not only by the artful combination of various
coloured stones cemented together, but by means of a
composition, by which it was possible to produce every
colour, to emulate every half tint, to represent every
gradation, every touch, as perfectly as with the pencil.[2]
As the building of S. Mark's at Venice called forth all
the talent of the artists of that period, so the construction and decoration of S. Peter's at Rome occasioned
employment to Roman artists. Natural causes con-
curred in promoting the cultivation of mosaic painting
at Rome, for the humidity of S. Peter's was found
inimical to paintings in oil, and it was considered
advisable, even in the time of Urban VIII.,[3] to substitute mosaics in the place of paintings in oil.

The Roman school in mosaics produced Muziani,

[1] Lanzi, vol. i. p. 6 n. ; Ciampi, Notizie, &c., p. 46.
[2] Lanzi, vol. ii. p. 230.   [3] Ibid.

Paolo Rossetti, Marcello Provenzale, Gio. Batt. Calandra, a native of Vercelli, by whose discoveries the mechanical part of the art was greatly improved, and the family of Fabio, who copied in mosaic some of the works of Guercino, Domenichino, and Carlo Maratta.

The earliest document known which gives an account of any of the processes of mosaic painting, is the Lucca MS.; but this merely contains some recipes for colouring the glass of which the work was composed. These recipes are repeated in the Mappæ Clavicula. The Bolognese MS. contains directions for making coloured glass, and "Materia Musica;" and the subject is alluded to by Theophilus. The recipes for coloured glass in the MS. of Eraclius may also relate to mosaics. Neither of these authorities, however, describe the stucco in which the mosaic was embedded, nor do they speak of any cement for fastening the pieces of glass together. The omission has, however, been supplied by Vasari,[1] who has mentioned the materials employed for this purpose.

According to this author the stucco, which would remain in a state fit for working for a period of from two to four days according to the weather, was composed of lime, pounded brick, gum tragacanth, and white of egg, and it was kept moist by laying wet cloths upon it. In the Life of Agnolo Gaddi, Vasari mentions that the mosaics of Andrea Tafi in S. Giovanni in Florence, having been injured by the penetration of damp, were repaired by Agnolo, who employed stucco made of mastrice (or mastic according to Baldinucci) and wax, and this composition effectually answered the purpose of excluding the damp. From the same account it also appears that the squares were deeply embedded in the stucco and firmly cemented together. The repairing of these mosaics also gave the artists employed on the work an opportunity of observing that

---

[1] Intr., cap. xxix.

the design had been marked out on the stucco with red outlines, and that it had been entirely worked on the stucco. Prof. Branchi of Pisa thus describes the ground in which the before-mentioned mosaics in the Tribune of the Duomo of that city were embedded:—" The cement or bed of the beautiful mosaic of the Tribune of the Duomo of Pisa consists of two thick strata one upon the other. The lower stratum, which is white, tasteless, of a texture apparently homogeneous, soluble in acids, with liberation of carbonic acid, consisted undoubtedly of a mixture of slaked lime and marble dust. Having tested the weight of 2 denari (grammi 2·358) with acetic acid, there remained only silica and yellow oxide of iron, weighing $1\frac{3}{4}$ gr. (grammi 0·085). The superior stratum in which the parallelopipeds of coloured glass were embedded, consisted of a yellowish mixture some-what hard, which acquired on lighted charcoal a colour that was first grey and then blackish. The same acetic acid, to the action of which I exposed an equal quantity of this layer as of the lower, dissolved the lime with slight ebullition, and left $12\frac{1}{2}$ gr. (grammi 0·613) of a substance of a dark-yellow colour, which I found was composed of linseed oil dried, and a small portion of turpentine, and of other resinous matter. The cement of the mosaics of the cloisters of the Basilica of S. Paolo without the walls at Rome was composed of slaked lime and brickdust more or less finely pulverized. It was of a flesh colour, unalterable by fire or by exposure to the sea wind, and of a taste slightly saline. By means of an analysis, sufficiently accurate for the pur-pose, I found in the same quantity, namely 2 denari, that its constituents were nearly as follows :—

	Denari.	Grains.	Grammi.
Carbonate of lime	1	$3\frac{1}{2}$	(1·350
Pulverized bricks deprived by acetic acid of their cal-careous parts	0	$11\frac{2}{3}$	(0·572
Muriate of soda, earthy muriates, and a little calca-reous sulphate	0	$8\frac{5}{6}$	(0·433

By these results I have learned, that the grounds of the mosaics were not always prepared in the same manner. Chambers [1] informs us, that "the composition adapted to retain the different pieces of glass, consisted of lime, and powder of fine bricks, with gum tragacanth and white of egg. From the Encyclopédie we learn, that anciently the cement of the mosaics was composed of white of egg and water, three parts of pulverized bricks, and one part of slaked lime, but that the materials generally employed, and which were preferable to the preceding, were slaked lime, pulverized marble, and linseed oil. As this last composition does not differ essentially from that which formed the superior layer of the Pisan mosaics, it is evident that it was known to the most eminent workers in mosaic of the thirteenth century."

With regard to the oil and turpentine or other resin of which Prof. Branchi found traces in the upper stratum of the ground, I may add that notices have been found by Prof. Ciampi, in the records of the Duomo of Pisa for the year 1303, of payments for oil and turpentine which belong to the mosaics of the Duomo.[2]

---

[1] Dict., Art. Mosaics, in which he mentions those of Pisa. [Note by Branchi.] Chambers probably learned this from Vasari (Intr., cap. xxix.), who adds travertine to the other ingredients.

[2] "Docum 26 . . . . . Johannes Orlandi coram me Ugolino notario recepit a D. Burgundio operario pro pretio librarum 76 olei linseminis ab eo, et operato. . . . . ad operam Magiestatis* que fit in Majori Ecclesia, lib. iii. Sol. xviiii. . . . . Johannes Orlandi sua sponte dixit se habuisse a d. Operario libras duas den. pis. pro pretio libre viginti novem trementine operate ad operam Magiestatis." Da lib. di am. dell' an. 1301 st. pis. dell' opera del Duomo di Pisa.

"Libras quinquaginta quatuor et solidos decem et octo den. pisanorum minutorum pro pretio centinarum quatuor olei linseminis ad operam Ma-

---

* By a "Majesty" or "Maestà," is meant a representation of the Virgin or Saviour enthroned. See Mr. Eastlake's 'Materials,' &c., p. 170, n. In the present case the maestà consists of the gigantic figure of the Saviour seated on a throne, and holding in his hand a book, on which are inscribed the words " Ego sum Lux Mundi." On one side is the Virgin, and on the other St. John; these figures also are gigantic, and the effect is said to be most grand and sublime. Morrona, Pisa Illust., vol. i. p. 247, 249, n. Murray's Guide to North Italy.

It will be observed that wax does not occur in these
documents, neither does it appear that it was found by
Prof. Branchi in his analysis of the ground.   From this
it may be inferred, that it was not used generally, but
was employed by Agnolo Gaddi merely as a hydrofuge.
Prof. Branchi analysed also some of the glass or
enamel of which the coloured cubes were composed, for
the purpose of ascertaining the metals with which they
were coloured.   On this subject he has the following
observations:—

"The art of composing the glass and enamels of
various colours, by uniting them with glass liquefied by
metallic oxides, is at the present time more extensively
and perfectly conducted than it was among the ancients.
Some chemists assert that the use of the oxide of cobalt
in colouring glass blue was known to the ancient Egyptians,[1] but this opinion, as far as I am aware, has never
been confirmed by experience.   In the observations of
the Cav. Rossi, on the vase preserved at Genoa under
the name of the 'Sacro Catino,'[2] &c. (Torino, 1807),
inserted in the fifth number of the Giornale della
Società d'Incoraggiamento delle Scienze e dell' Arte

---

giestatis, et aliarum figurarum que fiunt in Majori Ecclesia, ad rationem
denariorum xxviii. pro qualibet libra. . . . . . Upechinus pictor pro libris
quadraginta tribus vernicis emptis ab eo ad operum Magiestatis." See also
Morrona, Pisa Illustr., vol. i. pp. 249, 250, 256.

[1] M. de Brongniart (Traité des Arts Céramiques, p. 563) says, that
having analysed some of the Egyptian blue glass, he found it to contain
silica, alkali, cobalt, and a small quantity of lime. He also says that the
Egyptian figurines are coloured blue with copper, and not with cobalt.

[2] This was a vessel for a long time supposed to have been formed of a
single emerald. There is little doubt, however, that it is composed of glass.
As a work of art its value will scarcely be diminished on this account; since
it affords evidence of the perfection to which the art of making and colouring glass was brought at a very early period ; for this vessel formed part of
the spoils won at the taking of Cæsarea in 1101. The author of the Handbook for North Italy observes (p. 106), "The extraordinary perfection of
the material, as well as the workmanship, must always cause it to be considered as a very remarkable monument, and of remote antiquity. The colour
is beautiful, the transparency perfect, but a few air-bubbles sufficiently dis-
close the substance of which it is made."

stabilita in Milano,' the following passage occurs :—
' Sig. Millin infers from the blue glass, that cobalt was
known to the ancients ; but this was unnecessary, says
the author, because the oxide of copper, which naturally
takes a blue colour, was sufficient for this purpose.' I
have not been able to analyse the blue glass of the two
works in mosaic above mentioned, because too small
a quantity was sent me, and because my own private
occupations did not permit me to devote as much time
to these experiments as was necessary. I observed,
however, that in the Roman mosaic and in the fragments of the Pisan [1] seen by refracted light, the charac-
teristics pointed out by Bergman which distinguish
glass coloured with cobalt were entirely wanting. I
observed also that the last-mentioned glass preserved,
as it should do, its own colour after being pulverized and
fused by the combined action of fire and of a small
quantity of carbonate of soda ;[2] whilst that from Rome
passed to an amethystine colour, which the Pisan glass
also acquired, although in a less degree, having been
both pulverized, mixed with carbonate of soda, and
exposed to the same degree of heat. Having treated
in the same manner the other enamels of various
colours and more or less opaque of the mosaic of Pisa,
I saw that the red passed to a blue colour; that the
purple was changed to an amethystine colour, and that
the black became a transparent yellow glass, on the
surface of which was an alkaline stratum of a bluish

---

[1] The blue glass of the mosaic of S. Paolo is transparent ; that of the
mosaic of Pisa is opaque, and of much greater thickness. [Note by Branchi.]

[2] Sig. Clovet remarks on this subject, " The blue obtained from an oxide
of cobalt is the most permanent of all colours ; it is equally fine at a low or
at a great heat."—Annales du Chimie, Paris, tome xxxiv. p. 222. And in
tome ii. p. 434, of the Dictionnaire Portatile des Arts et des Métiers, Paris,
1776, is found the following passage :—" The most permanent colours are,
the blue from cobalt, which resists without changing the greatest heat of the
fire ; then the purple from gold, certain reds prepared from iron, &c."—
[Note by Branchi.]

green. Having repeated these last experiments, I obtained from the dark green, light green, and purple enamels, results differing from the preceding in the gradation of colour only. From the red I afterwards obtained a transparent glass of yellowish green colour; from the black, a violet or amethystine glass. These alterations and anomalies, some of which throw light on the nature of the blue glass of the ancients, are to be ascribed to the greater or less degree of oxidation of the metallic colouring matters."

It will be interesting to the practical artist to compare the recipes for the mosaic glass and enamels in the Bolognese MS. with these results of Prof. Branchi's researches. In the Pisan mosaics, the red colour appears to have been produced from copper, while in the MS. it is produced from gold as well as from copper. Another variation also occurs in the blue, which in the old Pisan and Roman mosaics was produced from copper, while in the Bolognese MS. it was coloured with " azzurri ultramarini." The green of the Pisan mosaic was produced by copper, that of the Bolognese MS. by " crocus martis " and salgem.

The gilding of the mosaics of which the backgrounds of the figures were composed was next examined by Professor Branchi. On this subject he observes:— " The gilding of the cubes of common glass and enamel of these mosaics is very beautiful; the leaf of gold is itself defended by a vitreous varnish, which, although not distinguishable on account of its thinness in the Pisan mosaic, except by having a shining surface, different from that of gold, and by the resistance it offers to iron tools, to the action of mercury, and nitro-muriatic acid, is also of such a thickness in the Roman mosaic that even the sight of it alone is sufficient to remove all doubt.

" Chambers,[1] in speaking of the method of gilding

---

[1] Dict., Art. Mosaics. This also is from Vasari.

glass for mosaics, does not mention this varnish.
' The pieces,' he says, 'to be gilded, are moistened
with gum-water, and the leaves of gold are applied;
they are then placed at the entrance of the furnace
until they are hot. By this means the metal remains
fixed to the glass so firmly that it cannot be detached.'
In order to varnish the gilded glass and enamels, it is
very probable that glass or crystal, easily fusible, was
reduced to an impalpable powder; that this powder
was distempered with water, or with a solution of gum,
or of borate of soda or other liquid; that this mixture
was spread over the gilded surface, and that finally the
pieces of glass thus prepared were exposed to a degree
of heat sufficient to fuse this fine powder, which, when
fused, would form the desired varnish.[1]

"The gilding by fire on crystal[2] and porcelain is
much superior in beauty to that of our mosaics. The
latter, however, besides resisting the above-mentioned
reagents, appears, as it were, after the lapse of six centuries, without the slightest alteration, and in the same
state in which it left the hand of the artist. This observation, confirmed by so many others, proves that the
old masters had the stability of their works much at
heart, and that they wished to preserve them, not only
for their own sons and grandsons, but also for posterity."
The method alluded to by Professor Branchi of mixing

---

[1] Leon Battista Alberti recommends fixing the gold to the glass with calcined lead (calcina di piombo), which he says becomes more liquid than any
kind of glass. Arch., book 6, cap. x.

[2] Kunckel, in the additions to the Arte Vetraria of Neri, treats at length
of gilding with greater or less permanence on glass. For gilding which
was to be fixed by fire, he recommends that the leaves of gold should be
applied with the solution of borate of soda, or the borax of commerce, or
with gum and a small quantity of this salt dissolved in a proportionate quantity of water. By bathing that part of the crystal which is to be gilded with
a solution of nitro-muriate of gold, mixed with a sufficient quantity of sulphuric acid, and exposing it afterwards to a sufficient degree of heat, a fine
and permanent gilding is produced, according to the assertion of Struve and
Exsaquet, Giornale di Torino, tom. ii. part i. [Note by Branchi.]

pulverized glass with gum-water, and spreading it over
the gold leaf, and afterwards fusing the glass, appears
to have been the method followed by Theophilus: while
the process described by Count Caylus of placing the
design in gold between two plates of glass, and fixing
the surfaces together by fire, was the method which
Eraclius says was practised by the Romans, and which
he describes in Lib. I. cap. v.[1]

TARSIA WORK.

Another art, allied to mosaic painting, was practised
in Italy, and was called "Mosaic of wood," "Tarsia"
or "Tarsie" work, or "Tarsiatura." This consisted in
representing houses and perspective views of buildings
by inlaying pieces of wood of various colours and
shades into panels of walnut wood.

Vasari[2] says, that at first this kind of work was
executed in white and black only; but Fra Giovanni
Veronese, who practised it extensively, much improved
the art by staining the wood with various colours by
means of waters and tints boiled with penetrating oil, in
order to produce both light and shadow, with wood of
various colours, making the lights with the whitest
pieces of the spindle tree. In order to produce the
shades, it was the practice of some artists to singe the
wood by the fire; while others used oil of sulphur and
a solution of corrosive sublimate and arsenic.

St. Audemar (No. 165) mentions that saffron was
used to stain box-wood yellow; but he does not say to
what use the wood was put when stained.

The subjects most proper for Tarsia work are perspective representations of buildings full of windows
and angular lines, to which force and relief are given
by means of lights and shades. Vasari speaks rather
slightingly of this art, and says that it was practised

---

[1] See pages 187, 188. [2] Int., cap. xxxi.

chiefly by those persons who possessed more patience than skill in design ; that although he had seen some good representations of figures, fruits, and animals, yet the work soon became dark, and was always in danger of perishing from the worms and by fire.

Tarsia work was frequently employed in decorating the choirs of churches, as well as the backs of the seats and the wainscotings. It was also used in the panels of doors. The art was cultivated to the greatest extent in the Venetian territories, where three Olivetani monks were particularly distinguished for their skill. The most celebrated of these was Fra Giovanni da Verona, who was called to Rome by Pope Julius II. to decorate the doors and seats of the Vatican with Tarsia work, the designs of which were made by Raffaelle. Fra Damiano da Bergamo, a Dominican monk, attained equal celebrity in this art. So great was his skill that Charles V. refused to believe that the Tarsia work executed by him in the Arca of S. Domenico, at Bologna, really consisted of pieces of wood inlaid, but he thought it must have been the work of the pencil.[1] Nor would he be convinced of the fact until part of the stucco was removed and a piece of the wood taken out; in remembrance of this circumstance the work was left in that state, and has never been repaired.

The inlaid work in wood of various kinds called " Tunbridge ware" is a kind of mosaic, but it cannot be compared with the Italian Tarsia work in the delicate gradations of colour, or the intricacy of the subject represented.

---

[1] Marchese, Vite de' Pittori, &c. Domenicani, vol. ii. p. 257.

CHAPTER IV.

GLASS.

§ 1. Early History of Painting on Glass in Italy.

WHILE the history of painting on glass has been studied in France and Germany, where it has been illustrated by the works of Le Vieil, Langlois, Thibaud, Lasteyrie, and of Fathers Martin and Cahier, its rise and progress in Italy has been but little investigated. A sufficient reason for this may perhaps be found in the superiority of the glass painters of France and Germany [1] over those of Italy in all the mechanical parts of the art, as well as in the fact that all the improvements introduced into this branch of painting may be traced to the northern nations, who in their turn are represented to have received their first instruction from the East. [2] It might be supposed from the celebrity of the glass works at Murano, that the Venetians would have excelled in this art, but this has not been the case; the art of painting on glass was but little practised by them, [3] and the glass manufactured at Murano was found too opaque for this purpose. [4] Still the art was occasionally practised in Italy, sometimes by native artists, who employed their skill either on Venetian glass, or on glass manufactured for the purpose by German or French artists, and some-

---

[1] See Vasari, Int., cap. xxxii.

[2] In 687 many Greek workmen went to France, for the purpose of working in glass. Filiasi, Saggio sull' Antico Commercio, &c., p. 148, n.

[3] The windows of churches in the Venetian territories are usually filled with small circular panes of colourless glass, about 6 inches in diameter.

[4] Vasari, Introduction, cap. xxxii.

times the painted glass was executed entirely by foreign artists invited into Italy for this purpose. The designs, however, were frequently made by the Italians, who excelled the Germans in design and composition. The names of but few painters on glass have descended to posterity, and this is partly explained by the rule which prevailed among the Flemish artists at least, of not affixing their names to their works, or of marking them with their monograms only. [1] The notices of the Italian painters on glass are few and scanty, and have never yet been published collectively. It may, therefore, not be uninteresting to give a short account of some of the most distinguished painters in this branch of the profession.

History has not preserved the name of the artist who executed those glass windows, considered to be the earliest of the kind in Italy, which were painted or stained by order of Pope Leo III. at Rome, A.D. 795 ; [2] neither is it recorded whether they were by a Greek or an Italian artist. That they were the work of the latter is probable, from the existence of recipes for coloured glass in the Lucca MS., published by Muratori, which was apparently written by an Italian.

From this time until 1303 [3] no certain notices of painting on glass in Italy are found. The archives of the House of Savoy show that at this period a sum of money was paid to one Johanneto (Giannetto) for painting certain windows in the Castle at Chambery. [4]

In the fourteenth and fifteenth centuries the art was

---

[1] See Le Vieil, de la Peinture sur Verre, p. 33. Albert Dürer is an exception to this rule ; he is said not only to have written his name on his works, but to have added sometimes his portrait also.

[2] Mur., Rer. Ital., tom. iii. part i. p. 196, 197.

[3] At Altare, a village in the midst of the central range of the Ligurian Alps, glass-works are said to have existed from time immemorial. They are reported to have been founded by some fugitive Gauls.—Murray's Handbook for North Italy.

[4] Lettera dal Vernazza al P. Guglielmo della Valle. Giornale di Pisa, 1794.

much cultivated in Tuscany, especially by the Gesuati, who worked in the Cathedrals of Florence, Arezzo, and elsewhere. The names of a few only of these artists have survived. The necrology of the Dominicans, in the convent of Sta. Maria Novella in Florence, has preserved the name of Fra Giacomo di Andrea, a Dominican and painter on glass, who flourished during this century.[1]

Fra Domenico Pollini, a native of Cagliari in Sardinia, lived at Pisa during the first half of the fourteenth century. The Chronicle of the Convent of Sta. Catherine of Pisa thus records his merits: " Frater Dominicus Sardus de Pollinis Kallaritanis fuit valde gratiosus et probus, soavissime conversationis. Cantabat bene, scribebat pulcre, et fenestras vitreas operabatur optime."[2]

The same Chronicle also eulogizes more copiously Fra Michele Pina of Pisa, who is said to have been a perfect master in painting on glass, and who painted the large window in the church of the Dominicans at Pistoia now destroyed, and one in the refectory of the convent of Sta. Katherine. He died in 1340. A lay Dominican named Andrea painted the window of the choir in the same church of Sta. Katherine, as appears by his name being at the foot of it.[3]

The large window in the choir of the church of S. Francesco at Pisa was painted in 1340, but the name of the artist has not been preserved. This window was repaired in 1585 by P. Johanne Antonio Nerucci.[4]

Another window in the same church was painted in 1390 by Jacopo Castelli, of Siena, as is proved by an inscription on the glass.[5] It appears from these notices and from the records of the Duomo that a school of

---

[1] Marchese, Vite de' Pittori, &c., Domenicani, vol. i. p. 391.

[2] Ib., p. 390.

[3] Valtancoli, Annali Pisani, vol. i. p. 428.   See Marchese, vol. ii. p. 438.

[4] Ciampi, Notizie, &c., p. 116, n.   Morrona, Pisa Illust., vol. iii. p. 56.

[5] Pisa Illust., vol. iii. p. 60.

painters on glass subsisted in Pisa from the early part of the fourteenth century until 1685, if not later. Lunardo, M. Simone di Domenico of Florence, and Bartolomeo da Scarperia, painted, between 1460 and 1464, the glass for the large windows which sheltered, on the sides exposed to the north and to the marine winds, the walls of the Campo Santo. The remains of the iron employed in fixing the windows may still be seen opposite the pictures of Buffalmacco and Orgagna.[1]

About the same time flourished at Venice one Maestro Marco, who painted certain windows in the church of S. Francesco at Treviso, "which were well executed; for a certain German friar painted [the originals of] all those works formerly in the convent (of the Frate Minori) at Venice, and Maestro Marco copied and sent them to Treviso." This Marco is stated to have been living in 1335.[2]

In the fifteenth century the notices of painters on glass in Italy are more numerous; among those who flourished in the first half of this century may be named Angioletto da Gubbio, who painted some windows in the cathedrals of Orvieto and Siena, and the large window in the chapel of S. Ludovico in the Basilica of Assisi. The original designs for this window, executed in distemper, are preserved in the collection of Conte Francesco Ranghiasi Brancaleone in Gubbio.[3]

In the beginning of this century flourished a Dominican friar named Ambruogio di Bindo, an excellent painter on glass, whose name appears in the archives of the Duomo of Siena from 1404 to 1411.[4]

[1] Ciampi, Notizie, &c., p. 116, n.

[2] Zanetti, Nuova Raccolta delle Monete e Zecche d' Italia, vol. iv. p. 151, cited by Lanzi, vol. i. p. 151, and by Mr. Eastlake, ' Materials,' &c., p. 90, 91.

[3] Memorie Storiche di Ottaviano Nelli. Da Luigi Bonfatti. Gubbio, 1843.

[4] Marchese, Vite de' Pittori Domenicani, vol. ii. p. 440.

Fra Bartolommeo di Pietro di Vanni Accomandati of Perugia painted a beautiful window in the church of S. Domenico at Perugia,[1] which is said to exceed in the dimensions, in the composition, and in the beauty of the colouring, every other painted window in Italy, with the exception of those by Gulielmo de Marcillat in Arezzo. On the lowest compartments of this window there is an inscription purporting that the window was painted by Fra Bartolommeo in 1411. It has been doubted whether the inscription actually belonged to the window below which it is placed, but the fact appears to be satisfactorily proved by Marchese.[2] A contract for making a glass window in the sacristy of the church of the Dominicans proves that Bartolommeo was living in 1415. The dates of his birth and death are unknown, but he was resident in his convent in 1370, and was elected superior of it in 1413.

It is much to be regretted that the annals of the convent should have been discontinued (excepting a few brief notices) for nearly a century, so that there are no means of ascertaining how Fra Bartolommeo acquired his skill in glass-painting, or where he procured the glass. Even twenty-five years after Bartolommeo completed his celebrated work, the glass made in Italy was not considered good enough for the windows of the Duomo of Florence; for we read that Lorenzo Ghiberti, who delighted greatly in this kind of work, and who had undertaken to paint some of the windows in this cathedral, having considered how large a quantity of glass of the finest workmanship would be required for so great a work, and having heard of a native of Tuscany named Francesco Dominici Livi di Gambasso, who was then living in the city of Lubeck, and who was considered the most eminent master of this art then living, determined to recall him with his whole

---

[1] Marchese, Vite de' Pittori Domenicani, vol. i. p. 393.
[2] Ibid., vol. i. p. 391-402.

family to his own country, for the benefit of which he might exercise his profession.

This design was executed; Livi came to Florence in 1436, and made the glass, which was all painted by Ghiberti, with the exception of one window, which was painted by Donatello. Baldinucci proves the truth of these facts by an entry in the 'Libro di Deliberazione de' Signori Operai,' b. 1436, A.C. 8,[1] which he quotes in his Life of Ghiberti, and thus disproves the assertion of Vasari, that the glass used for this purpose was Venetian.

In reading the history of Italian art there is nothing that strikes the mind more forcibly than that versatility and universality of genius for which so many of the medieval and cinque-cento artists were distinguished, and by which they were enabled to attain so high a degree of eminence in *all* the fine arts. At the present time, in which division of labour is the order of the day, the exercise of one branch of the arts is considered a sufficient employment for the mental powers of an artist during his whole life. When we remember the long period of pupilage through which the Italian artists were accustomed to pass, it is not surprising that there should have been artists who have succeeded in all kinds of painting, as I have mentioned with regard to the painters in mosaic and on glass, who frequently excelled also in oil and fresco painting; but it does appear astonishing that the greatest architect should have been, as was frequently the case, not only the greatest painter of his time, but the greatest sculptor also. Vasari accounts for this fact by saying that " design and invention are the father and mother of all the arts, and not of one only." There is no doubt that he was right, and that the great Italian masters owed

---

[1] The same document is published in the Carteggio Inedito, vol. ii. p. 441.

their celebrity to their mental endowments, and not merely to their practical skill. It is said [1] on the authority of Lorenzo Ghiberti that Giotto, painter, architect, and poet, sculptured some of the subjects in marble on his own beautiful campanile at Florence. At a later period the great Raphael changed his manner of painting after having examined the paintings of Michael Angelo, the greatest architect and the greatest sculptor of his age. Francia was a goldsmith before he was a painter. The genius of Benvenuto Cellini was as conspicuous in the jewelled ornaments he made for the pope as in his Perseus. The names of painters who have possessed high mathematical attainments are numerous. But the most remarkable man among the moderns was undoubtedly Lionardo da Vinci, who was at once a painter, poet, musician, mathematician, and natural philosopher, and, as some say, architect and statuary also, whose sagacity anticipated Bacon in declaring that experiment should precede theory—who had described the camera obscura before it was made known by Porta—who wrote on the descent or attraction of heavy bodies to the earth forty years before Copernicus—whose discoveries in hydraulics preceded by a century those of Castelli—and whose observations "on flame and air" were made nearly three centuries before the modern theory of combustion was promulgated. [2] Did Lionardo, when he registered these discoveries in characters that could only be read by reflection in a glass, think, like Bacon, that mankind

---

[1] Vasari, Vita di Giotto. Lorenzo Ghiberti left a MS., in which he gives a short account of ancient and modern painters. The most interesting parts of this Essay have been published by Cicognara in his Storia di Scultura.

[2] See Amoretti, Memorie Storiche di Lionardo da Vinci, p. 135-142, citing Venturi, Essai sur les Ouvrages Mathématiques de Léonard da Vinci, 1797. See also Humboldt's Kosmos, vol. ii. p. 322, 380, 389, and Hallam's Hist. of Literature, vol. i. p. 303, and note.

were not at that period sufficiently enlightened to profit by his researches into the arcana of nature?

Second to Lionardo only in fame, but his equal in talent, was Leon Batista Alberti. His genius was universal: he was a skilful architect, an accomplished painter, sculptor, poet, and musician, a mathematician and inventor of optical instruments, an author of treatises on painting, sculpture, and architecture, and a moral and dramatic writer.

Lorenzo Ghiberti was another of these distinguished men. He began his career as a goldsmith, but being more partial to the arts of design and sculpture, he sometimes practised painting, and sometimes cast small bronze figures, which he finished with infinite grace. In his maturer years he seems to have occasionally worked at all these arts. He painted an apartment for Pandolfo Malatesta at Rimini soon after the year 1400. In 1439 he made for Pope Eugenius a golden mitre which weighed fifteen pounds; the weight of the pearls with which it was decorated was five pounds and a half, and which, with the other jewels, were estimated at 30,000 golden ducats. It is said that six of these pearls were as large as filberts, and Vasari remarks that, to judge from the design, nothing could be imagined more beautiful than the arrangement of the jewels and the variety of the figures and other ornaments. But the capo d'opera of Ghiberti was the bronze doors of the Baptistery at Florence, one of the finest works of the middle ages, and which alone was sufficient to immortalise the name of Ghiberti. His predilection for painting on glass has been already mentioned. Besides the windows in the Duomo of Florence, he painted others at Arezzo; but in spite of his precautions to secure the best kind of glass, it is related that the buildings were too much obscured by these windows, and this was undoubtedly Vasari's reason for saying they were made of Venetian glass. Lorenzo taught the art of painting on glass to Parri Spinello, who introduced it into Arezzo.[1]

At Milan during this century the art was practised less successfully. It appears from an entry in the records of the Duomo, dated November 10, 1449,[2] that a dispute having arisen between Stefano da Pandino, the painter, and the authorities on account of some window which he had painted, his work was adjudged to be so badly executed that the artist was obliged to repaint great part of it at his own expense.

In the Venetian territories painting on glass was occasionally practised at this period. In 1473 the window of the choir in the south transept of the church of SS. Giovanni and Paolo at Venice, and another at Murano, were painted by Mocetto from the designs of Vivarini.[3]

But the most distinguished painter on glass of the fifteenth century in Italy was Beato Giacomo da Ulmo, a native of Ulm, in Germany. He was born in 1406, and acquired the art of painting on glass in this city. At the age of twenty-five he travelled to Rome, where he spent his time and money in visiting the sacred edifices of that city; but finding himself at last pennyless, he became a soldier in the service of Alphonso of Arragon, king of Naples, and fought in the great battle in which the Genoese were victorious, and Alphonso lost both his throne and his life. Giacomo having served four years in the army, became disgusted with the profession, and engaged himself as servant to a citizen of Capua. In 1440 or 1441 he determined to return to his native land and embrace

[1] Vasari, Vita di Lorenzo Ghiberti.

[2] Memorie de' Pittori, Scultori, e Architetti Milanesi, Opera MS. dell' Abate Ant?. Albuzzi, vol. i. This MS. is now in the possession of Co. Gaetano Melzi, to whom I am indebted for the loan of it.

[3] See Lanzi, vol. i. p. 152, and Murray's Hand-book for North Italy, p. 354.

once more his aged father. With this view he arrived at Bologna, where, praying before the altar of S. Domenico, he felt himself inspired to renounce his earthly home, and think only of the heavenly. In the thirty-fourth year of his age he entered his noviciate in this monastery, where he lived for fifty years a life so holy that he obtained the honours of canonization. His death took place in 1491.

With the religious habit Fra Giacomo resumed his early occupation of painting on glass. It appears from public archives preserved in Bologna, that he painted windows in the convent of S. Domenico in 1464 and 1465; in the library from 1467 until 1472; and the last time his name was mentioned was in 1480, when he was in his seventy-third year. Some painted glass in a window of the first dormitory in this convent has been attributed to him; but it is considered by Bianconi [1] and by Marchese to be much more ancient—indeed to be the most ancient specimen of painted glass in Bologna.

But the principal works of Fra Giacomo were in the church of S. Petronio in Bologna.[2] It is much to be regretted that it cannot now be ascertained what glass was painted by him, for the windows in this church were the work of several artists, among the best of whom was Frate Ambrogino da Soncino, who had been pupil of Fra Giacomo for thirty years. Besides the glass in S. Petronio, Fra Giacomo is said to have

---

[1] Guida di Bologna.

[2] The colours in the old glass in S. Petronio are extremely vivid—ruby red, emerald green, ultramarine blue, and opaque black. The two former are transparent, but the blue is semi-opaque, resembling in effect thin plates of ultramarine, rather than blue glass. I could imagine the colour was produced by stirring the ultramarine in powder into glass, as described by Suger when speaking of the blue glass for the abbey of S. Denys. In one of the windows is another kind of blue, more transparent, but the colour is neither so deep nor so pure.—This resembles the blue seen in the old Venetian coloured glass windows.

painted several other windows in Bologna, which still remain.

It appears from an entry in the records of the convent that Fra Giacomo was assisted in the designs by a certain Michele. Bianconi states[1] that the designs for some of the windows in S. Petronio were by the great Michael Angelo Buonarroti. On considering the dates, it will be seen that these designs by Michael Angelo could not have been for the windows painted by Fra Giacomo, because it does not appear that the latter painted after 1480, when Michael Angelo had only attained his sixth year. The reputation of Beato Giacomo was as great in France as in Italy. He was there called "Jacques l'Allemand." Le Vieil (p. 34) says, "The miracles that were wrought at his tomb caused him to be placed among the saints of his order, and the company or guild of the master glass-makers, painters on glass at Paris, celebrate his fête as their second patron on the second Sunday in October."

The discovery of the art of staining glass a transparent yellow with silver has been by some authors ascribed to Van Eyck, but it is attributed with greater reason to Fra Giacomo da Ulmo. The discovery is said to have originated in an accident. Le Vieil (p. 108) gives the following account of it:—Fra Giacomo being one day occupied in placing his glass in the furnace in order to fix the colours, let fall a silver button from one of his sleeves without perceiving it. The button sank into the lime, which is always placed in the furnace under the glass. The furnace being closed, the enamels melted. The button, or at least a part of it, was fused, and it imparted a yellow stain to the glass which lay above it, and this yellow stain was found to have penetrated into the substance of the glass.

---

[1] Guida di Bologna.

Fra Ambrogino da Soncino, the pupil of Giacomo, was also an excellent painter on glass, and his works may be seen in many churches at Bologna. He died in 1517. He wrote the life of his master, Giacomo, from which the biographical facts relative to the latter have been extracted.[1]

Frate Anastasio, also a lay brother of the convent of S. Domenico at Bologna, was another pupil of Fra Giacomo. He died in 1529, having instructed in his art a pupil who left, in a book of Memoranda concerning the Arca of S. Domenico, begun in the year 1521, the following affectionate and pathetic memorial of his master :—" After him (one Fra Petronio, who held the office of Archisti, or guardian of the Arca, until 1521) came my beloved and dear master and predecessor Frate Anastasio, a lay brother, a devout man, a man of God, and of our father S. Domenico. Cheerful, of middling stature, the beauty of his mind was reflected in that of his body ; in him I frequently seemed to behold a cherub ; one of his hands was worth my whole body ; he had great genius, was most skilful in painting on glass, a disciple and imitator of the blessed Giacomo, and during the space of eight years he most faithfully, most fervently, and most devotedly served with the greatest charity and integrity of life, his and our good father S. Domenico, and by him he was richly rewarded." [2]

That affectionate and lasting attachment which so frequently subsisted between the master and the pupils, and which is a beautiful trait in the character of the Italian painters, could only have arisen under their system of working together for a long period of years. The lengthened term of the apprenticeship, frequently extending to twelve years, and the consequent inter-

---

[1] Marchese, vol. i. p. 409, 410.
[2] Ibid., p. 411.

change of benefits given and received by master and pupil, frequently gave rise to a friendship as sincere as it was affectionate, and which terminated only with the death of one of the parties. Thus Taddeo Gaddi, the godson and favourite pupil of Giotto, was the disciple of the latter for twenty-four years; Cennini was for twelve years the pupil of Agnolo, the son of Taddeo. Many other instances are noticed in these pages; many also are recorded by Vasari.

In the 'History of the Duomo of Orvieto'[1] it is stated that in 1444 a certain Fra Mariano di Viterbo, a Dominican, offered himself to paint the windows of the cathedral, and proposed to paint one as a specimen. He did so, but his painting was not approved of, and D. Gasparro di Volterra, a priest, was then invited to paint a specimen. This also was disapproved of, and ultimately the celebrated Benedictine monk D. Francesco di Barone Brunacci was selected, who executed the work to the satisfaction of all parties. Marchese[2] conjectures that he was a pupil of Fra Bartolommeo di Pietro.

In the Necrology of the convent of S. Domenico at Siena, under the year 1515 is mentioned the name of Frater Raphael Peregrini; he is said to have been skilful in painting on glass.[3]

The names of two other professors of this art, Fra Cristophano and Fra Bernardo, have been preserved in the archives of the Duomo of Arezzo. The contract is dated March, 1477, and the colours were to be " *cotti al fuoco, e non messi a olio.*" [4]

A similar stipulation is contained in the contract, dated August, 1513 (preserved in the same archives), relative to the windows to be painted in the cathedral

---

[1] Storia del Duomo di Orvieto, Document lxviii. p. 71.
[2] Vol. i. p. 413.   [3] Id. ibid.
[4] Carteggio Inedito d' Artisti, vol. ii. p. 446.

by Domenicho Pietro Vannis de Pechoris[1] and Stagio Fabiani Stagii;[2] and in another contract, dated April 25, 1515,[3] it was stipulated that Domenicho should execute certain paintings *on good Venetian or German glass.* The price paid for the last windows was at the rate of fourteen "lire piccole" the square braccio.[4] The execution, however, of these works was not such as to satisfy the good people of Arezzo, and one M. Lodovico Bellichini, a physician, and intimate friend of Guglielmo de Marcillat, persuaded the latter, who was then resident at Cortona, to visit Arezzo, where Stagio had the liberality to invite him to reside in his house.[5]

The greatest of all the artists who practised painting on glass in Italy was Guglielmo de Marcillat, whose name is generally translated William of Marseilles. Dr. Gaye, the editor of the 'Carteggio Inedito,' has, however, discovered his real name and designation in a document preserved in the archives belonging to the Bishop of Arezzo. He is there[6] described as "Messer Guillelmo de Piero, Franceze, Priore di S. Tibaldo, di Sto. Michele, diocesi di Verduno" (Verdun, in France), and he subscribes his name thus: "Io Guillelmo de Piero de Marcillat." From this Marchese (vol. ii. p. 212) thinks that *Marcillat* was his family-name, and *Piero* that of his father. He was born in 1475, and acquired the art of painting on glass in France. In order to escape the consequence of being concerned, with some of his friends, in the death of an enemy, he sought refuge in a Dominican convent,

---

[1] Carteggio Inedito d' Artisti, vol. ii. p. 446. See also Vasari, Life of Don Bartolommeo, Abate di S. Clementi.

[2] Carteggio Inedito, vol. ii. p. 446. Vasari, in the Life of Lazzaro, calls this artist Fabiano Sassoli.

[3] Carteggio Inedito, vol. ii. p. 449.   [4] A braccio is about 23 inches.

[5] Vasari, Vita di Guglielmo de Marcillat, and see Marchese, vol. ii. p. 211, &c.

[6] Carteggio Inedito, &c., vol. ii. p. 449.

where he assumed the habit of the order and continued
to practise his art.

About this time Pope Julius the Second commissioned Bramante to introduce many windows of glass
into the palace.   In reply to the inquiries made by the
latter for the most excellent among those who practised
this art, he was informed that these things were done
in a wonderful manner in France, and he was shown a
specimen by the French ambassador at the Court of
Rome, who had for the window of his study a piece
of white glass, on which was painted a figure with an
infinite number of colours fixed on the glass by the
action of fire.   Bramante caused an invitation to be
sent to these French artists, offering them good emolu-
ment.   Claudio, a brother monk, and excellent painter
on glass, and intimate friend of Guglielmo, persuaded
the latter to accept the offer, and the two artists set out
together for Rome, where they were employed by the
Pope to paint several windows of the palace, which are
now no longer in existence; two only remain of those
painted in Sta. Maria del Popolo.   About this time
his friend Claudio died, leaving him heir to his designs,
and the implements used in the art; and Guglielmo
henceforward worked by himself.   From Rome he
went to Cortona, where he painted the front of the
house of Cardinal Passerini, and several windows.
Leaving Cortona he went to Siena, where he painted
a window in Sta. Lucia, in the chapel of the Alber-
gotti, in the bishopric of Arezzo; "which," says Vasari, "may truly be said to be living figures, and not
coloured or transparent glass."   Some parts of these
still remain, and the parts deficient are filled up with
white glass.   He also painted three windows in the
Duomo di Arezzo, as appears by the following contract,[1] dated 31 Oct., 1519 :—

_____

[1] Carteggio Inedito, vol. ii. p. 449.

"I signori operai al Vescovado ano alogato a fare tre finestre di vetro in Vescovado a Maestro Guglielmo di Pietro, franceze, maestro a far finestre di vetro, coiè una finestra sopra la cappella di San Francesco, una finestra sopra la cappella di San Matio, una finestra sopra la cappella di San Niccolò, per prezzo di lire 15 per ciascheduno braccio, *cotti a fuoco, non a olio*, e debale avere finite per tutto Gugno prossimo 1520."

For each of these windows he received 180 ducats, as appears by a record dated 31st Dec., 1520.

He also painted a window in the church of the Dominicans, for which he would receive no recompense, "because," he said, "he was much indebted to that society," alluding to the shelter and protection the Dominicans had formerly afforded him.

Besides other windows, he painted several frescoes which are still in good preservation ; the design and composition of these works are good, but the colouring is rather feeble.[1]

He lost his life from his too great application to fresco painting, which he followed summer and winter; the exhalations from the lime occasioned an illness which carried him off in a few days, in the year 1537, at the age of 62.[2]

Many practical details relative to painting on glass are given in the Life of Guglielmo by Vasari, who united to his other attainments a knowledge of this art. Vasari attributes to Guglielmo de Marcillat the honour of having carried the art of painting on glass to perfection in Tuscany. He particularly eulogizes the skill of Guglielmo in the arrangement of the colours, whereby the most forcible colours were employed for the figures in the foreground, while the darker colours were reserved for the more distant objects. He praises also his invention and composition, and the great skill

---

[1] Marchese, vol. ii. p. 223.
[2] Vasari, Vita de Guglielmo de Marcillat.

with which he arranged the joinings of the lead and iron, which he disposed in such a manner in the joints of the figures, and the folds of the draperies, that they were scarcely visible, and even imparted to the figures a grace which could not be exceeded by the pencil. Vasari mentions more than once the great dexterity of Guglielmo in applying different colours to the same piece of glass by grinding away the coloured surfaces, so as to leave the white glass, to which another colour was afterwards given ; and he informs us that the Gesuati of Florence, by whom this art was much cultivated, having obtained possession of a window painted by Guglielmo, took it to pieces in order to ascertain how it was put together, and removed and experimented on many of the pieces of glass, which they replaced by new ones.

Guglielmo left the materials belonging to the art to Pastorino da Siena, his assistant, who had worked for him many years.[1] Pastorino painted in 1549 the beautiful round or rose window (occhio) in the Duomo of Siena, and others in St. Peter's at Rome. He usually worked from the designs of Pierino del Vaga.

Maso Porro, of Cortona, who was more skilful in joining and in burning the glass than in painting, and Battista Borro, of Arezzo, were also pupils of Guglielmo de Marcillat. The latter taught the art to Benedetto Spadari and Giorgio Vasari, the biographer of the painters.

To these artists may be added Gondrate, who in 1574 painted a window in the Duomo of Parma, from a design by Lattanzio Gambara.

The first glass furnace was introduced into Rimini in 1551 by Geminiano da Modena, whose sons became excellent painters on glass.[2]

---

[1] Vasari, Life of Guglielmo ; Bald., Vite, Dec. iv. Part i. del Sec. iv.
[2] Vedriani, Pittori Modenesi, p. 86.

§ 2. On Windows.

We have been so long accustomed to see glass windows in our houses, that few, perhaps, except antiquaries
and archæologists, have ever inquired whether they were
possessed by our ancestors. It may not, therefore,
be deemed uninteresting to relate briefly a few facts
relative to this subject, gleaned from history and
archæology.

There is reason to believe [1] that glass windows were
employed occasionally in ecclesiastical buildings during
the early centuries of the Christian era; but the practice was by no means universal, and the most ancient
glass windows mentioned to have been constructed in
Italy were those ordered by Pope Leo the Third in
the eighth century [2] at Rome. The windows of some
sacred edifices were closed with valves, or shutters of
stone, like those of the Duomo of Torcello [3] erected in
1008. Others were filled with slabs of a transparent
kind of talc or alabaster. [4] The only example now
known to exist of this kind of window is in the church
of St. Miniato at Florence, built in the commencement
of the eleventh century, under the Emperor Henry
and his wife Cunegonda. The windows, five in number, are in the apsis, and are each filled with a single
slab, formed of a kind of transparent alabaster, or
marble, called by the Italians "fengite." [5] The effect
of these windows is singular. When illuminated by
the morning sun, they appear shining with a cloudy
roseate light. [6]

---

[1] See Theoph., E. Ed., p. 185.

[2] Coloured glass is mentioned in the Lucca MS., which is said to be of
this century.

[3] The windows are now glazed, but this is thought to be a later addition.

[4] Vasari, Int., cap. xxxii.   [5] Fantozzi, Guida di Firenze, p. 770.

[6] Murray's Guide to North Italy, p. 583.

Bede relates that glass was brought to England, A.D. 674, by certain ecclesiastics for the purpose of decorating the churches then erecting in this country; but although makers of glass were brought to England at the same time, the progress of the art in this country must have been inconsiderable, since Matthew Paris relates that, in the reign of Henry the Third, a few churches only had glass windows. In 1135, glazed frames, called "verrinæ," were made for the windows in the chapel and hall of Winchester, and in some of the chambers.[1] The earliest painted glass in York Cathedral was painted about 1200. This slowness of progress must, however, have been the effect of want of encouragement rather than of want of ability, for in 1153 the Queen of England sent a present of a painting on glass to the Comte de Dreux, and his third wife, the Comtesse of Braine, in Normandy.[2] The beauty of the early English painted glass is evident from the windows of Lincoln Cathedral: some of these, which are remarkable for the brilliancy of the colours, were executed in 1220.

In France the art must have been extensively cultivated. A great many churches were erected during the eleventh century, and Le Vieil considers that the art of painting on glass, properly so called, arose in France about this period. In the twelfth century Suger adorned the Abbey of St. Denys with painted windows, and his example was followed in most of the churches newly erected.

The use of glass windows in private houses was

---

[1] Archæological Journal for 1845, p. 54.

[2] Le Vieil (de la Peinture sur Verre, p. 24), quoting the Chartularium of the Abbey, and the Index Cœnobiorum Ordinis Præmonstratensis. According to Lavoisne, Matilda of Boulogne, wife of Stephen, died in 1152, consequently there was no Queen of England in 1153. The window, however, might have been ordered to be painted some years previously, and perhaps was not completed and fixed in its destined place until 1153.

extremely limited during the middle ages. In France it was not employed until the fourteenth century.[1] At the close of this century, however, and the beginning of the next,[2] several windows were painted for the hotel of the Duke of Orleans in the Rue de la Poterne lez Saints Pol, at Paris. It may be interesting to know that the price paid for this painted glass varied from four to eight Parisian sous the foot. In the document which contains an account of these windows, there is also a charge for "taking down, washing, and replacing several panes of glass, painted and recoloured, in the chamber of Louis Monseigneur de Bourbon." This makes it probable that the glass had been fixed in the windows for some time, since it had become necessary to wash and recolour it. It also suggests the idea that these paintings were not executed with enamel or vitrified colours, which would not have required recolouring, but probably with pigments mixed with egg or oil.

It appears from recent archæological researches that many of the royal residences in England had glazed windows in the thirteenth century. In the twentieth year of the reign of Henry the Third (1235-6), the windows of the chapel and hall of Winchester, and some of the chambers, were glazed.[3] The accounts of Rockingham Castle for the year 1279 also contain an entry of payment "for glazing the windows, 5s."[4] It is probable that the dwellings of the nobility were furnished with glass windows in the fourteenth century,

---

[1] Hallam's Midd. Ages, vol. iii. p. 425.

[2] Between 1399 and 1429. See 'Louis et Charles, Ducs d'Orléans, leur Influence sur les Arts, la Littérature, et l'Esprit de leur Siècle, d'après les Documents Originaux et les Peintures des Manuscrits. Par Aimé Champollion-Figeac (de la Bibliothèque Royale). Paris, 1844.' This extremely interesting publication is very scarce, the work having been suppressed.

[3] Archæological Journal for 1845, p. 54, 74.

[4] Ibid., Jan. 1845, p. 370.

since they are mentioned in a description of the interior of a castle in a MS. of the fifteenth century [1] (in
the public library at Cambridge), containing the metrical romance of Sir Degrevant:—

> " Square windows of glas
> The richest that ever was,
> Tho moynells (mullions) was off bras,
> Made with menne handes."

Glass, however, was not in common use in England
until the reign of Henry the Eighth;[2] but it appears
to have been employed for windows in Vienna during
the fifteenth century. Æneas Sylvius mentions that
the houses in that city had glass windows and iron
doors.[3]

During the middle ages, glass windows, instead of
being affixed to the buildings, were frequently fastened
into wooden frames; they were considered as moveable
furniture, and were removed with the other effects of
families when they travelled. Upon the arrival of the
family at the mansion, the glazed frames, or verrinæ,
were placed in the windows, where they remained
during the residence of the family, and on their depar-
ture they were taken out and laid by carefully.[4] A
passage in Vasari's Life of Guglielmo de Marcillat
proves that this custom of using moveable windows prevailed in France and Italy until the beginning of the
sixteenth century. Vasari says that at this period Pope
Julius the Second commissioned Bramante of Urbino
to make many glazed windows in the palace; and while
the latter was making inquiries for persons skilled in
this art, he was shown a specimen of one belonging to
the French ambassador at the Papal court. This,
which he had used for the window of his study, con-

---

[1] Arch. Journ., Sept. 1844.
[2] Hallam's Midd. Ages, vol. iii. p. 425.   [3] Ibid.
[4] Northumberland Household Book, Preface, p. 16, quoted in Hallam's
Midd. Ages, vol. iii. p. 425.

sisted of a piece of white glass fixed in a frame (telaro), on which was painted a figure with an infinite variety of colours burnt in by the action of fire.

It must not, however, be inferred, because the glasses were moveable, that the windows of houses were destitute of any protection from the weather. The Bolognese MS.[1] describes no less than three contrivances for excluding the air, softening the light, and concealing the inmates of the houses from the gaze of passengers in the streets. The three methods described in this MS. were probably for the windows of the nobility, for it is unlikely that private individuals would incur the expense of painting these substitutes for glass in the manner described. The first substitute was thin parchment stretched on a frame, and afterwards painted and varnished; the second consisted also of parchment, painted as before, but instead of varnish, a coat of linseed oil was applied to make it transparent; the third consisted of linen, stretched on a frame, and then painted. When dry, a coat of white of egg and gum water was applied, and it was then varnished. It is not at all improbable that some of the early transparent paintings executed in Germany, France, and England, may have been intended, and used occasionally, instead of glass for windows.

In France, paper was much employed as a substitute for glass in domestic architecture even at a late period. Le Vieil[2] devotes a chapter of his work to this subject. He says that at the close of the seventeenth century, the persons whose business it was to fix the paper in the windows were called "chassissiers," and the glazier who repaired or cleaned the glazed windows on the inside of the apartments of the palace and its dependences left to the chassissier the care of renewing the double windows of paper. From this it seems

---

[1] Nos. 214, 215, 216.   [2] De la Peinture sur Verre, p. 235.

probable that glass windows were limited to the habitations of the higher ranks, and that these windows were
further defended with other windows, the frames of
which were filled with paper.   In Le Vieil's time these
paper windows were found only in the studios of
painters and engravers, who found them useful in
diminishing the noise from the street.   The light which
passed through them was more equal, and less fatiguing
to the sight.   He adds there was no place of study or
religious community, the windows of which were not
defended by double casements filled with paper: these
had also the additional recommendation of affording an
obstacle to the indiscretion and curiosity of those
within, as well as without.   At Lyons they were used
constantly in the time of Le Vieil in the silk manufactories, where they were found to yield a more
uniform light than glass.   In France, the paper, after
being fixed in the windows, was made transparent by
the application of poppy oil, or mutton suet, instead of
which some persons whose olfactory nerves were more
susceptible, employed wax.   Paper windows being constantly exposed to the rain, the sun, and the wind,
required to be renewed annually, and were consequently found more expensive than glass ; this perhaps
was a principal cause of their falling into disuse.

These paper windows may still be seen in many
villages in the north of Italy.

§ 3. Various Methods of Painting on Glass.

The origin of painting on glass, properly so called, is
involved in obscurity.   Le Vieil, as has been before
observed, attributes it to the French in the eleventh
century.   It appears certain, however, that it was
known and practised at Constantinople in the preceding
century.   Perhaps the earliest historical notice yet
recorded of painting on glass, is the portrait of Con-

stantine VII., which the Arab historian, Ibn Hayyan, states was presented by the ambassadors of that Prince in 949 to Abdurrahman at Cordova. Ibn Hayyan relates that the ambassadors of Constantine, son of Leo, Lord of Constantinah the Great (Constantinople), presented to the Moorish prince a letter, of which he gives the following description:—

" It was written on sky-blue paper, and the characters were of gold. Within the letter was an enclosure, the ground of which was sky-blue like the first, but the characters were of silver: it was likewise written in Greek, and contained a list of the presents which the Lord of Constantinah sent to the Khalif; on the letter was a seal of gold of the weight of four mithkals, on one side of which was a likeness of the Messiah, and on the other those of King Constantine and his son. The letter was enclosed in a bag of silver cloth, over which was a case of gold, with *a portrait of King Constantine admirably executed on stained glass.* All this was enclosed in a case covered with cloth of silk and gold tissue. On the first line of the *Inwan* or introduction was written, 'Constantine and Romanin (Romanus), believers in the Messiah, kings of the Greeks;' and in the next, 'To the great and exalted in dignity and power, as he most deserves, the noble in descent, Abdurrahman the khalif, who rules over the Arabs of Andalus; may God preserve his life!'" [1]

In the absence of all information relative to the manner in which this portrait was painted, conjectures must be useless; it is sufficient for the present purpose to

---

[1] The description of Ibn Hayyan is quoted by the Arab historian, Al Makkari, in his History of the Mohammedan Dynasties in Spain. The work has been translated, with critical Notes, by Pascual de Gayangos, late Professor of Arabic in the Athenæum of Madrid. Printed for the Oriental Translation Fund, 2 vols. 4to. 1840-43. See Blackwood's Mag., vol. 54, p. 442, where the account of the visit of the ambassadors to Abdurrahman is given at length.

establish the fact that a portrait was actually painted on
glass at Constantinople and sent to Spain as early as the
year 949.

It is generally considered that the earliest glazed
windows were filled with stained glass,[1] for it is said to
require more skill to make colourless glass than to tinge it
with some of the ordinary colours. The pieces of stained
glass of which the early windows were composed were
small, and they were arranged in a kind of mosaic
pattern. The next improvement consisted in forming
pieces of stained glass into figures, the outlines and
strong shades of which were afterwards formed with
black,[2] and fixed by the heat of the furnace. This
kind of semi-painting afterwards gave place to painting
on glass, properly so called. This was executed in
various ways. The colours were sometimes diluted with
white of egg,[3] and sometimes mixed with oil, and then
varnished.[4] But as it was found that in both kinds of
painting, the colours were affected by the weather, a
new plan was adopted of employing vitrified colours or
enamels, which were applied to the glass with gum
water, and then fixed by burning them into the glass in
the furnace. This method of painting is described by
Eraclius and Theophilus. The invention is generally
ascribed to the Flemings or Germans. It is quite
certain that Italy was supplied with these coloured
glasses or "smalti"[5] by some transalpine nation; the
Marciana MS. states that they were brought from
Germany.[6]

---

[1] See Theoph., E. Ed., lib. ii. cap. xxix.

[2] The black used for this purpose is described by Eraclius, Lib. ii. No.
20, Lib. iii. Nos. 8 and 49; the MS. of the Marciana, No. 325; Bulengerus de Pictura, &c.

[3] See Marciana MS., p. 615.

[4] Ibid. See also the Paduan MS., p. 693.

[5] The smalti of the modern Italians consist of pieces of glass, about $\frac{1}{2}$ an
inch thick, and 6 or 8 inches in diameter.

[6] See the Marciana MS., p. 617.

The method of painting on glass practised by Guglielmo de Marcillat and his pupils has been described by Vasari. The following is a condensed account of it.

To produce a good picture on glass, three things were considered necessary, namely, a luminous transparency in the glass selected, good composition, and brilliant colouring without confusion. Transparency was to be secured by selecting the clearest glass, and in this respect the French, English, and Flemish glass was preferable to the Venetian; for the former was very clear, whilst the latter was dark; "and," observes Vasari, "when clear glass is shaded, the light is not totally lost, but appears through the shadows; but Venetian glass, being naturally dark, and being made still darker by the shadows, loses its transparency. Many persons delight in loading the colours artificially applied upon the surface, which being exposed to the sun and air, appear more beautiful than the natural colours; it is better, however, that the glass should be light rather than dark, that it may not be rendered opaque by the thickness of the colour."

To paint on glass it is necessary to be provided with a cartoon, on which are drawn the outlines of the figure, and of the folds of the drapery, which will serve as a guide in joining the glass. The various pieces of red, yellow, blue, and white glass are then arranged in their places as required; and in order to reduce each piece to the form and size indicated by the cartoon, the pieces are laid upon the cartoon and the outline marked with a pencil full of white lead, and a number is affixed to each piece in order to find its place more readily when uniting the various fragments. These numbers are obliterated when the painting is finished. This being done, the pieces of glass must be cut according to the form and size required; for this purpose, the point of an emerald must be drawn along the part to be cut, and the division must be completed by passing a pointed piece of hot iron over the outline (which is to be first moistened with saliva), being careful not to go too near to it. The superfluous glass is then to be removed with the emerald,[1] and the pieces of glass reduced to the exact size and shape, by filing them with an iron tool called "grisatoio" or "topo," until they fit together accurately. The cartoon being laid on a table, and the pieces of glass thus fitted and laid upon it, the shades of the drapery must be painted with scales of iron ground, and another sort of red rust found in iron mines, or the hard red hæmatite ground, and with this the flesh is shaded, using more or less red or black as required.[2]   But in painting flesh, the glass should be previously covered with a coat of this red, and the drapery should be painted with the black, in the same manner tempering the colour with gum, and painting and shading it by degrees until it resembles the cartoon. The painting being completed, in order to produce the high lights, a short and thin pencil of bristles, with which the colour is removed from the lights, is necessary. The high lights in the beards, hair, draperies, casements, and landscapes are to be produced by marking them out with the handle of the brush. There are, however, many difficulties in exercising this art, and he who delights in it may lay various colours on the glass; for if it be required to paint on a red ground a leaf or other small object, which, after being in the furnace, should become of another colour, the surface of the painted glass may be ground away within the outlines of the leaf with the

---

[1] It is evident, from the Bolognese MS., p. 495, that the diamond was used for cutting glass long previous to the time of Vasari. It appears, however, not to have been used for this purpose in France until the time of Francis I. (if the story related by Le Vieil be true), and this will account for the emerald being used by Guglielmo de Marcillat and his pupils.

[2] In addition to the hæmatite, Guglielmo de Marcillat is said to have used for the flesh, scales of copper (scaglia di rame).

iron point, which removes the surface of the glass; for
by so doing, the glass remains white, and that red
colour (composed of several mixtures), which, when
fused by heat becomes yellow, is applied to it.[1] And
this may be done with all the colours, but yellow
is better when applied over white than over other
colours; but when blue is laid on it, it becomes green
by the application of heat, because yellow and blue
mixed, make green. This yellow colour[2] can be used
only on the back of the painting, because by fusing, it
would spoil and unite with that colour, which being
heated remains red on the surface, but which being
rasped away with an iron, leaves the yellow visible.
The pieces of glass being painted, they should be placed
in a muffle or coffin, on a layer of sifted ashes mixed
with burnt lime, then another layer of glass, and another
of ashes, until all the glass is disposed of; the whole is
then to be placed in the furnace, and heated gradually
by a slow fire, until the colours are fused and become
fixed to the glass. This burning in of the colours requires the greatest caution, for if the heat be too great
it will cause the glass to crack, and if insufficient it
will not fix the colours. Neither should the glass be
withdrawn, until by repeated trials it is ascertained that
the iron coffin and the ashes are red hot, and that the
colours are fused.

The windows of the Duomo of Milan were once filled
with painted glass of the greatest brilliancy ; much still
remains, but a great quantity was destroyed by the
French, who it is said, on some occasion of rejoicing,

---

[1] From this description it is apparent that the colours were "flashed"
on the colourless glass. This is said to have been the case with the red
glass which was found among the ruins of old St. Paul's in London. See
Boyle's Philosophical Essays, vol. i. p. 458.

[2] In the Life of Guglielmo de Marcillat, this is said to be calcined silver.

placed cannon in the piazza immediately under the windows, which were shattered by the discharge.[1]

The restoration of the painted glass has however been undertaken by the Austrian Government, and several of the windows, including those very large ones in the apsis, have again been filled with glass painted in the vicinity of Milan.

The original windows were painted in the ancient manner, in a kind of mosaic of coloured glass; the result was a picture of the utmost brilliancy. The modern glass is painted with coloured " smalti " mixed with some flux which accelerates the fusion and fixes them firmly to the plate of glass before it melts.[2]

§ 4. Of the various Uses to which Glass was applied.

Another important application of glass was in the composition of factitious gems, which appear to have been made, not for the purpose of personal decoration, but for adorning covers of sacred books, reliquaries,[3] and pictures of the Virgin and saints. It is not, therefore, surprising that so many recipes of this kind should occur in MSS. belonging to convents. Bibles and psalters were frequently bound in ivory covers, beautifully carved, and inlaid with artificial gems, the surfaces of which are always smooth, from their having been formed in moulds, and not cut. Sometimes the covers of books were of silver, or silver-gilt; sometimes they were solid, and carved in relief; sometimes they consisted of a sort of filigree-work in silver, over crimson velvet; and sometimes they were covered with velvet,

---

[1] Murray's Guide for North Italy.

[2] Dizionario delle Invenzione e Scoperte nelle Arti, nelle Scienze, &c., Milano, 1830. Art. Pittura.

[3] A reliquary of brass gilt, set with false stones, was exhibited by Mr. Way at the meeting of the Archæological Institute at Winchester, in 1845. It was of the 11th century, and was of French workmanship.

and strengthened and ornamented with silver or gold studs.

The application of factitious gems to pictures was common. They are expressly mentioned by Cennini, who describes the method of attaching them to the pictures; and they may be frequently seen on paintings executed in Italy during the middle ages. The most remarkable picture decorated with these gems is one by Carlo Crivelli, in the gallery of Brera, at Milan. The picture is highly interesting, not only on this account, but because several portions of it are in relief. It is not less remarkable for the extreme brilliancy of the colours, which are as bright as if just painted. The picture is divided into three compartments. The centre contains the Virgin and Child; on the right hand are St. Peter and St. Dominic; and on the left St. Peter Martyr and St. Geminiano. The surface of each compartment is slightly convex, rising about one inch or one inch and a half in the centre of each compartment; it is quite perfect, without a flaw of any kind. The figures are placed on a gold ground. St. Peter has on his head the papal crown, the gilded ornaments of which are in high relief; and it is set with precious stones, or rather imitations of such. The keys are in his hand, and these are actually modelled, the stem-part of the keys being quite round, and merely attached by a small part of the surface to the picture; the other key lies on this, so that here the relief must be at least one inch and a half. The keys are gilded. The mantle of the Virgin is fastened with a gold or gilt ornament, in which a sapphire is set. The drapery of St. Geminiano is painted to represent crimson velvet, on which is a collar of gold, set with real or factitious pearls, some of which having dropped off, show small holes made in the panel to receive them.

The picture by the same artist, placed next to this in

the same gallery, is, in some respects, a contrast to it.
The colours are as brilliant as those in the former
picture, and the ground also is of gold; but the glories,
instead of being in relief, are indented, and the jewels,
with which the mitre is decorated, are painted, instead
of being actually affixed to the picture.   The artist has
given as much transparency and brilliancy to these as
if they were actually inlaid, like those in the picture
above mentioned.   The period of the birth of Crivelli
is unknown, but he was living in 1476.

Sacramental cups, both of metal and of glass, were
also frequently set with gems, real or factitious; hence
the directions given in old MSS. for cements for gems.
It is certain that glass was in use in Italy for drinking-
vessels in the first half of the fifteenth century.   Glass
drinking-vessels are frequently mentioned by Cennini,
who calls them by the name by which they are still
known in Italy—*bicchieri*.   Representations of them,
of the same shape as those now in use, may be seen
in early Italian pictures of the Last Supper, and
particularly in the Cenacolo of Lionardo da Vinci.
Glass vessels were frequently embossed, or enamelled,
with the armorial bearings of their owners, sometimes parcel gilt, sometimes set with jewels, and
occasionally they bore designs of high pretension.[1]
The museum of antiquities of the middle ages in the
Louvre, and in the Hôtel de Cluny, at Paris, afford
many interesting specimens of glass of the middle ages,
enriched with enamels and jewels.   The drinking-
vessels and flasks, executed at Murano, were particularly esteemed.   Many beautiful specimens of the latter
are in the possession of the Marquess Trivulzio, at
Milan.

It is generally considered that the art of colouring
glass was introduced from the East into Venice.   The

---

[1] Arch. Journ., Sept., 1845, p. 264.

time of its introduction is uncertain, but it is known
that as early as the commencement of the twelfth
century the manufacture of what is called *crystal*, and
the art of colouring glass, were carried on at Venice.[1]
The mirrors and other works executed in glass in this
city were, during the middle ages, the finest works of
the kind; and the flasks and other small articles were
much sought after, not only in Europe, but also in
Asia, and even in the deserts of Africa.[2]   Murano
was, during four or five centuries, the seat of this
manufacture, which the Venetians knew how to vary
according to the taste of the times, and for which they
found a ready market in the countries of the East.
As long ago as 1275 there was a law mentioned in the
Chronicle of Dandolo, which prohibited the exportation,
not only of sand and the other substances used in the
fabrication of glass from Venice, but also of the fragments of broken glass, which other nations might melt
and fashion into new forms.   It seems that there were
formerly large masses of glass, which were employed
in the factories.[3]   Filiasi supposes that they were
brought from Greece, where the composition of glass
had attained a certain degree of perfection.   By an
ancient Venetian law masters of vessels were permitted
to import these masses of glass as ballast.   Sabellino
speaks with admiration of the works executed at the
commencement of the fourteenth century in the glass-
works at Murano.

It is much to be regretted that no work should be
known to exist in which the art of making glass, as
practised at Murano, is accurately described.   All inquiries for such a work are, however, rendered useless
by the fact that the workmen at Murano have always

---

[1] Depping, Histoire du Commerce, &c., vol. i. p. 191.
[2] Ibid., vol. ii. p. 322, n.
[3] Are these the masses of glass mentioned by Eraclius, p. 208, 210 ?

been sworn to preserve secrecy with respect to all technical processes.[1]

Much information, however, relative to this subject, will be found scattered through the pages of Neri's ' Arte Vetraria,' and the Commentary on this work by Dr. Merret, an Englishman. Cardanus mentions a Venetian MS. on the manufacture of glass, which fell into his hands. This would undoubtedly be a great acquisition if it could be discovered. It was said to have been written by a Venetian named Panteo.

Besides the uses already enumerated, glass was employed in making beads for paternosters, a manufacture which is still carried on to a great extent at Murano. But the favourite material of which the beads or rosaries used in the middle ages were composed, appears to have been amber.[2] The scarcity and high price of genuine amber placing it beyond the reach of the people generally, various attempts were made to imitate it; hence the numerous recipes in old MSS. for " making amber for paternosters;" and hence also the adoption of the term " amber " as a synonyme for beads, in which sense it is frequently used in the Bolognese MS.,[3] where we find directions for colouring the composition red, green, or blue, at pleasure. This fact is a sufficient proof of the estimation in which amber was held during the middle ages. Genuine amber was so highly prized that a statue of the Virgin made of this material, and a set of altar furniture in

---

[1] Gallipado Tallier (author of the ' Nuovo Plico d' ogni sorte di Tinture,' published at Bologna without a date) observes (p. 152), that " The red colour called ' rubino,' which, as every one knows, is made at Murano, is composed of ' oro di zecchino,' but few are acquainted with the process of combining the calcined gold with the liquid crystal." He adds, " The method of calcination is, however, known to me, but it is not lawful for me to discover it."

[2] Secreti di Don Alessio Piemontese, Part ii., p. 35. MS. of the Marciana, p. 609.

[3] Nos. 249—254.

amber, studded with jewels,[1] were considered among the
treasures of the Santa Casa at Loreto.   At the meeting of the English Archæological Society in 1845, a
necklace of rough amber was exhibited, which was
found round the neck of a skeleton near Ely, and which
was supposed to be of the Romano-British period.[2]

Another art practised during the middle ages was
the manufacture of artificial pearls from the bones of
the heads of fish, from mother-of-pearl, and other substances; many recipes for these occur in MSS.,[3] as
well as for making large pearls out of small ones.
Beckmann treats these inventions with contempt, and
thinks it impossible to give to any pulverized calcareous
matter the hardness and lustre of real pearls.   The
varnish of caseum, mixed with the milk of the fig-tree,
described in the Bolognese MS., No. 245, is certainly
curious, and perhaps may hereafter receive a trial.

NOTE ON JEWISH GLASS.

I⊤ would appear, on the authority of the third book of Eraclius (p. 245),
that lead-glass (see Eraclius, p. 217) was called Jewish glass. I have
mentioned in the note to this passage,* that a ruby-coloured glass was formerly sold at Birmingham under the name of Jews' glass; the coincidence
was at least curious, but facts were wanting to establish any connection
between the Jewish glass of the middle ages and the modern "Jews'
glass." It is known that the manufacture of glass was pursued extensively
by the Jews during the dark and middle ages. There were Jewish glass-
blowers at Constantinople between A.D. 531 and 565. This is proved
incidentally by the following narrative, related in the ' History of the
Jews:'†—

    " It was the custom of the Church to distribute the crumbs of the conse-
crated host which might remain to children summoned for that purpose

---

[1] It contained nearly 7000 pearls, besides diamonds and rubies, and was
valued at 200,000 crowns.

[2] Archæological Journal for 1845, p. xlii.

[3] See Secreti di Don Alessio, Part ii., p. 35.   Bol. MS., Nos. 246,
264, 320.

---

    * P. 245.   † Hist. of the Jews, vol. iii. p. 230.

from their schools. While Menas was Bishop of Constantinople, the child of a Jewish glass-blower went to the church with the rest, and partook of the sacred elements. The father, inquiring the cause of his delay, discovered what he had done. In his fury he seized him and shut him up in the blazing furnace. The mother went wandering about the city, wailing and seeking her lost offspring. The third day she sat down by the door of the workshop, still weeping, and calling on the name of her child. The child answered from the furnace, the doors were forced open, and the child was discovered sitting unhurt amid the red-hot ashes. His account was, that a lady in a purple robe, of course the Blessed Virgin, had appeared, and poured water on the coals that were immediately around him. The unnatural father was put to death, the mother and child baptized."

Filiasi * relates, that in 687 many Greek workmen went to France for the purpose of working in glass. It is probable that these persons practised the art after the same methods as the Jews, and that they made the processes known in France. It appears that the Jews carried on the art in Syria also. Benjamin of Tudela, whose ' Travels ' bear date from 1160 to 1173, states that he found 400 Jews resident in Tyre, who were glass-blowers. This fact certainly shows a great trade in this branch of industry, and may be considered a confirmation of the assertion that the soda found at Tyre was peculiarly fitted for the manufacture of glass.† The glass-works in Syria do not appear to have been confined to Tyre, for Miss Martineau relates,‡ that a glass-house still exists at Hebron. The glass made here, however, appears to be of the most ordinary description, and it seems that the workmen are Arabs, and not Jews.

At the beginning of the ninth century the Venetians traded with the ports of Egypt and Syria; and when, in 1122, the King of Jerusalem requested the Venetian navy to assist him at the siege of Tyre, the Venetians stipulated for the possession of a third part of the city, and the payment of an annual sum of 300 besants. In the fourteenth century the Venetians had still a colony at Tyre.§ The art of glass-making, therefore, with which the Venetians are supposed to have been acquainted as early as the eleventh century, may have been communicated to them by the Tyrian Jews. It appears certain that they acquired it in the East.

It was in the eleventh century that a leaden glaze was, as I have mentioned (p. 177), first found on European pottery. The recipes in the MS. of Eraclius prove that lead-glass was known in some parts of Europe

---

* Saggio sull' antico Commercio, &c., p. 148, n.

† Neri, Arte Vetraria, lib. i. cap. 1, and lib. vii. cap. 117, and Merret's notes on these chapters. The Venetians and Genoese had both settlements at Tyre in the 12th century.

‡ " Next we were conducted to a glass-house, of all odd places to see in Hebron. I would recommend a Newcastle one in preference, as there the glass is not greenish and thin, and the articles made can stand upright. We thought here as before, however, that the Arabs are expert enough at manual arts if they had fair play with tools and materials."—Eastern Life, vol. iii. p. 64.

§ Depping, Histoire du Commerce, &c., vol. i., p. 153, quoting Navigero, Storia della Republ. Veneziana, 819; in vol. xxiii. of Murat., Script. Rer. Ital., and And. Dandolo, Chronic. Venet., ann 828, in vol. xii. of the same work.

at least as early as the thirteenth century; but it appears that it was not generally known even at a later period,* for Neri, who published his ' Arte Vetraria' in 1612, says (lib. iv. cap. lxi.) it was a secret known to but few glass-workers, " Cosa nota a pochi dell' arte vetraria." Merret, the commentator on Neri, in a note to this passage, remarks, that it was not in use in England on account of its want of durability. Both writers speak of the extreme beauty of the colours of the factitious gems made of this kind of glass, and Neri says " that it is the most beautiful and noble kind of glass that is made, for real oriental jewels may be imitated with it; which cannot be done so well with crystal or any other kind of glass; but if great care is not taken, it is so extremely fusible, that it will run through the glass-pots, and be lost among the coals used in heating the furnace." From these facts, therefore, it is considered that there may be some reason for ascribing the invention, or at least the introduction, of glass containing lead, &c., to the Jews, and at the same time of supposing that the correct reading of the above passage in Eraclius has been given.

---

* A peculiar kind of Venetian glass, containing lead, was used in Italy as a dryer for certain colours. See Mr. Eastlake's 'Materials,' &c., p. 351.

CHAPTER V.

GILDING AND OTHER ARTS.

§ 1. On Gilding.

THE frequent and profuse employment of gilding in every kind of decorative work in the middle ages cannot have escaped the observation of the most superficial observer. The grounds of the most ancient mosaics were of gold, so were those of the pictures of the Byzantine and early Italian schools. The early Italian frescoes, as they are called, were adorned with gold leaf; the same decoration was extended to miniatures, and afterwards to painting in oil, and the use of gilding in pictures was universal, until Domenico Ghirlandaio discovered the method of imitating gold with colours.[1] The directions, therefore, of all old MSS. on painting are diffuse and minute on this head, and although the recipes are alike in principle, there is some variety in the details. The grounds of the ancient gildings were of two kinds; one of which was for miniatures and places not exposed to damp; the other consisted of an oil mordant, which was employed on walls and places exposed to humidity. As the gilding on many old mural paintings is in a remarkable state of preservation, it becomes important to ascertain the manner in which it was executed; and where there is no precise documentary evidence to demonstrate this, it is desirable to have recourse to chemical analysis.

Under this impression, Professor Branchi, of Pisa,

---

[1] Vasari, Vita di Domenico Ghirlandaio.

analysed some portions of the gold ground of the mural pictures by Benozzo Gozzoli and Buffalmacco in that noble relic of the arts and genius of the middle ages, the Campo Santo at Pisa. Professor Branchi relates in the following words the result of his experiments on this subject.[1]

"With regard to the ancient method of gilding in Pisa, I must observe that my experiments have not enabled me to discover any essential difference between the gilding in Pisa and that of the picture by Taddeo Gaddi, which is still to be seen in the suppressed church of St. Francesco.

" The intonaco is, however, white, fine, and of a thicker consistence. One denaro (grammi 1·779) contained gr. 11¾ (grammi 0·576) of a fine white sand, mixed with a little argillaceous earth.

" The gilding of the fragments of a picture by Buffalmacco in our magnificent Campo Santo, is spread upon a layer of wax of the thickness of about half a line. This yields to the action of the nail, is slightly transparent, inflammable, and lighter than water; it liquefies at a low heat, is soluble in boiling alcohol, from which it separates on cooling in the form of a white and bulky mass; it gives a lustre to wood, and being thrown upon burning charcoal, it diffuses sensibly the odour of wax, which cannot be mistaken for any other substance.[2] It is true that in some parts the gold is seen on both sides; from this I conjecture that this gilding was executed by Buffalmacco, either to repair some part already gilded, and with which he was not satisfied, or it was a reparation made at a subsequent period.

---

[1] Lettera del Prof. Branchi al Prof. Ciampi, &c., p. 18.

[2] " In making the above experiments I had no indication that a fixed drying oil was mixed with the wax. Among the various mordants which painters were accustomed to use in illuminating with gold, is that which is composed chiefly of the above-mentioned substances." [Note by Prof. Branchi.]

" The gilding of those small fragments which were removed from one of the numerous pictures painted by the celebrated Benozzo Gozzoli in the same Campo Santo is in excellent preservation. The gold being removed with a sharp instrument, discovers a thin layer, not opaque, which may be scraped like wax, and which, like that substance, gives a lustre to wood on which it is rubbed. Below this appears a yellowish tint, which penetrates into the intonaco to a small, but not always uniform depth. When the gold leaf was separated from the fragments by immersion in boiling distilled water, a pellicle of wax appeared on the surface.

" The liquid being filtered, and afterwards slightly evaporated, acquired a yellowish colour, and then formed a pellicle which differed from the preceding, and by complete evaporation left a small quantity of combustible matter—so small that I could not determine its nature.

" From these experiments it appears that our ancient gilding was executed, 1st, by applying on the smooth intonaco a kind of size, that is a liquid and tenacious substance, soluble in water, and coloured yellow; 2ndly, by applying on this a thin coating of wax; 3rdly, and finally, by affixing on this the gold leaf.

" It should here be remarked that the gold leaves being detached without having suffered any alteration in consequence of the liquefaction of the wax, gave me an opportunity of observing how much thicker they were at that period than they are at present. From the time of the Romans until now the art of gold-beating has been continually progressing towards perfection. From one ounce of this metal they were accustomed to obtain 750 square leaves and upwards, four fingers broad on each side,[1] which is certainly

---

[1] Pliny, lib. xxxiii. cap. 3. Modern goldbeaters now make 1200

below the number of those of equal dimension which our best goldbeaters now produce from the same quantity of gold. And as to the wax, which Benozzo applied to the intonaco in order to serve as a mordant, I shall observe that it must have been dissolved either in a volatile or in a fixed drying oil. From its characters I am inclined more towards the volatile than the fixed oil ; but in order to form an accurate decision on this point, it would be necessary to have at my disposal a larger quantity of the gilding. I am induced to believe from the experiments which I made on some ancient pictures in 1791 for my particular friend Signor Alessandro Morrona, the author of the celebrated work entitled ' Pisa Illustrata,' that the first of these oils was formerly added to the above-named substance." [1]

Some estimate of the extent to which gold was used on paintings in the fifteenth century may be formed from the document relative to the expenses of painting the chapel of S. Jacopo di Pistoia, which records that 7000 leaves of gold were used for this purpose.

§ 2. Auripetrum and Porporino.

When the parties for whom pictures were painted were unable or unwilling to pay for gold (which was always supplied by the persons who ordered the pictures), it was usual to substitute for it on mural paintings leaves of tin-foil, covered with a yellow varnish.

---

leaves from the same quantity. Cennino (cap. 139) complains that in his time 145 leaves were obtained from the ducat instead of 100 ; and it appears from Vasari, that in his time 435 leaves of gold were made from three ducats. The size of the leaves is described by Vasari to have been the eighth of a braccio square. Cennino does not mention their size.

[1] Vol. ii. p. 162. " Sig. Giov. Fabbroni has proved (Vantaggi e Metodi della Pittura Encausta) that in encaustic paintings the ancients did not unite the wax with mastic as Requeno asserts, nor with an alkali as Lorgna pretends, nor with gums and honey as Astori asserts, but with a volatile oil-like naphtha, or spirit of turpentine." [Note by Prof. Branchi.]

The method of applying and varnishing the tin-foil is
fully described in the MS. of S. Audemar, and many
other old works on painting. Its actual employment
on mural pictures is proved by the above-mentioned
document[1] relative to the expenses of the paintings
executed in the chapel of S. Jacopo di Pistoia, in
which 37 pieces of tin are mentioned. At the time
Professor Branchi made his experiments on the gilding and pigments employed on these paintings, ancient
treatises on art appear to have been but little studied.
Branchi, it is true, mentions the work of Theophilus,
which had been published by Lessing and Raspe ; but
his acquaintance with it must have been superficial, or
he would have recollected that Theophilus describes[2]
the leaves of tin, and the method of using them on
pictures and on books. If he had read this part of the
work, he would also have seen that the tin-foil was
varnished, and he would then have understood the
probable use of the varnish mentioned in the document,
for the employment of which he could not satisfactorily
account,[3] since he says that the fragments of the gilding, and of the pictures which he had analysed, gave
no indication of varnish.[4]

In order to economize gold, the old masters had
another invention called "porporino," a composition
made of quicksilver, tin, and sulphur, which produced
a yellow metallic powder that was employed instead of
gold.[5] The Bolognese MS. devotes a whole chapter to
this subject. A substance of a similar nature is now in

---

[1] Ciampi, Notizie, &c., p. 145.

[2] Lib. i. ch. 26 and 32, E. ed. The varnish for the tin leaves is fully
described in the MS. of S. Audemar, p. 163, 165.

[3] The small quantity of sandarac (one pound) mentioned in the document
published by Ciampi was evidently insufficient to varnish the pictures,
which, judging from the large quantity of colours supplied, must have been
very large or very numerous.

[4] Lettera di Branchi, p. 18.

[5] See Cennino Cennini, Trattato, cap. 159 ; Bol. MS., cap. 6.

use in England, and is employed as a substitute for gold on coloured woodcuts and chromolithographs.

§ 3. On the use of Wax in Painting.

The subject of wax-painting during the middle ages has been so fully and ably treated by Mr. Eastlake in his recent work,[1] that but little remains to be added.

It may, however, be remarked that, in addition to the use of wax as a mordant for gilding, in the manner before mentioned, it was employed as a varnish for paintings,[2] for which purpose it is supposed to have been dissolved in an essential oil. That it was also used as a vehicle for painting is established by the two recipes quoted by Mr. Eastlake from the Byzantine MS., and from that of Le Begue. The principle of these two recipes (the solution of wax in caustic potash[3]) is the same in both MSS., but the latter recipe contains mastic in addition to glue and wax. The last-mentioned vehicle must have resembled somewhat the cement, or *cera colla*, which was in use in England about the year 1385, and of which Mr. Hartshorne found the following notice among the documents preserved in Rochester Castle :[4]—"For 3½ lbs. of wax bought for cement (ad cimentum), 21*d*., at 6*d*. a lb. In 2 lbs. of frankincense, 6*d*. In 5 lbs. of lees (coda) and 1 lb. of pitch, 6½*d*." [5] It will be observed that glue is not mentioned in the above entry. Neither does it appear in the varnish used for painting on glass described in the Venetian MS.[6] This varnish

---

[1] Materials, &c., chap. 6.   [2] Ibid., p. 163, and n.

[3] In the Le Begue MS. (p. 307) the word "flandres" has been erroneously substituted for "cendres"—ashes, which, when boiled with water, made a lixivium, which was rendered caustic by the addition of lime, exactly in the manner now employed by soap-boilers.

[4] See Arch. Journ., Jan. 1845, p. 373.

[5] The Marciana MS. (p. 626) has a recipe for a cement of this kind, composed of wax, liquid varnish, and black naval pitch.

[6] Sloane MSS., No. 416. See Mr. Eastlake's 'Materials,' &c., p. 172, n.

consisted of wax, white turpentine, and mastic, and
was of the same nature as the cement employed by
Agnolo Gaddi in repairing the mosaics in S. Giovanni
at Florence, which varied from the above in being
composed of mastic and wax only; its object was to
exclude damp.

One of the very few medieval pictures reputed to be
painted with wax at present known to connoisseurs,
is the Martyrdom of St. Simon the Younger, by Andrea Mantegna, whose name is inscribed on the painting.   It is in the possession of Signor Giuseppe
Vallardi at Milan, and belonged formerly to the
Abbate Boni, of Venice.[1] The picture is very perfect,
the colours bright, and the touches sharp. The darks
are laid on very thick, but the paint appears to have
run into spots or streaks, as if it had been touched with
something which had disturbed the surface.   It is
said, however, that it has never been repaired, and its
authenticity is stated to be undoubted. It is evident
that the wax has been used liquid, for if the colours had
been fused by the application of heat, the sharpness and
precision of touch for which this picture, in common
with other paintings of this period, is remarkable, would
have been lost and melted down. The vehicle, whatever it was, appeared to me to have been as manage-
able as that of Van Eyck. This picture was painted
late in life by Mantegna.

The same collection also contains a modern picture,
which may with propriety be said to be in encaustic,
since the colours are melted in by the application of a
hot iron. This is a small picture of a sleeping Cupid
by Appiani, painted by way of experiment on a brick,
the surface of which was properly prepared. The
colours of this picture were dull, and the effect like
that of a fresco; it seemed to be better adapted for

---

[1] See Catalogo dei Quadri di Giuseppe Vallardi. Milano, 1830.

decorative effect than for cabinet pictures. The lights were poor, and did not bear out well.

Wax painting is now practised at Parma. An apartment of the Museo di Antichità, and another in the public library of that city, are now being painted with a wax vehicle, and after a process invented by an artist of that city, which he freely and obligingly communicated to me.

The vehicle used consists of wax and resin dissolved in spirit of turpentine. The mixture is fluid, and of the colour of milk. In this the colours are ground, and are then preserved in small glasses, and spirit of turpentine is poured *upon* them to preserve them. To close these glasses conveniently, the painter employs a cushion of leather larger than the glass, with a button on the top for a handle, and this contrivance effectually defends the colours from the air and dust.

All colours may be used indiscriminately, Prussian blue, orpiment, and others which are not permanent in oil.

For the ground, the wall or ceiling is plastered in the usual way with lime, and is not quite smooth, but is left with a kind of grain or tooth. The painting is executed on this ground when dry, without other preparation.

The method is said to require some practice, as the colours dry fast. When working, the colours are diluted with spirit of turpentine.

This kind of painting has great brilliancy and transparency, and can be seen well from any point of view. If durable, it seems well adapted for decorative purposes. The method has been in use for about six years.

§ 4. On Painting Statues.

The practice of painting statues was common during the middle ages.[1] The proofs of this are numerous.

---

[1] Ciampi, Notizie, &c., p. 118, 142.

The documents recording the wax vehicle, or varnish, called *cera colla*, furnished to Andrea Pisano for painting and varnishing a marble statue over the principal door in the façade of the Cathedral of Orvieto, has been mentioned by Mr. Eastlake.[1] This practice is alluded to more than once in the MS. of Le Begue,[2] and in the Tabula Imperfecta[3] is a reference to some directions contained in Theophilus[4] for painting round images, " ymagines rotundas,"[5] and other sculptured articles which are not covered with leather, cloth, or parchment. The most remarkable example, probably now in existence, of the union of painting with statuary, is in the baptistery near the Cathedral of Novara. The building is circular, and supported by ancient columns: the recesses between the columns contain the events of the Passion. The figures in plastic work are as large as life, coloured ; and in some cases the resemblance to life is completed by the addition of real hair. The wall behind the figures, which is painted in fresco, serves as a background to the figures; and the light aërial tone of the painting contributes much to the effect of the figures. The remarks on these groups, in a MS. Journal, quoted by the author of the ' Handbook for North Italy,' are so appropriate and judicious, that I shall make no apology for introducing them here. " They are," he says, " probably by Gaudenzio Ferrari,[6] who excelled in this branch of art; and many of the figures are of exquisite workmanship. The two finest groups are the Garden of Olives, and the Scourging of our Lord, which last, without being in the least disgusting or painful, is most deeply affecting. One of the

---

[1] Materials, &c., p. 170.

[2] See No. 180 (p. 145), and No. 344 (p. 315).   [3] P. 40.

[4] Lib. i. cap. 23, E. ed.   [5] The word " rotundas " is not in Theophilus.

[6] Gaudenzio Ferrari was born in 1484, and died in 1550. He was one of the principal painters of the Milanese school, and his merits, which have been overlooked by Vasari, have been justly appreciated and warmly eulogized by Lomazzo and Lanzi.

executioners is sitting down, tired with his work; the
Roman soldier looks on with pity; the other can no
longer look, and turns away. These representations
are so entirely at variance with our conventional rules,
that it requires a considerable degree of mental exertion
to appreciate them. The first step in this, and many
similar occasions, must be for the observer to forget all
that he has read upon the theory of the fine arts; and
to form his opinion, as the judge tells the jury, not to
mind what they have heard out of court, but to give
their verdict upon the evidence before them. In so
doing, you must recollect that the only valid plea by
which the introduction of images into churches is
attempted to be justified by the Romanists, is, that
they are books of instruction to the common people;
and certainly neither mere painting, nor mere sculpture, can realise the events of Scripture to the mind in
a manner so vivid as this union of form and colour.
You will rarely enter this baptistery without finding
individuals employed in acts of devotion before these
scenes; some reading appropriate selections from Scripture, some engaged in prayer, but not praying to the
images, for the circumstance of their forming entire
groups prevents any one being singled out as the object
of worship; and let us repeat, that the independent
judgment which we have ventured to advise the traveller to assert in Italy, will be much strengthened by
his asserting it in the baptistery of Novara." In
the Life of Andrea Verrocchio, Vasari gives a description of some curious effigies of Lorenzo de' Medicis,
which were modelled in wax and afterwards painted in
oil. His account is as follows:—" On the occasion of
the murder of Giuliano de' Medicis, and the narrow
escape of Lorenzo his brother, who was wounded at
the same time, in the Church of Sta. Maria del Fiore,
the friends of Lorenzo ordered several effigies of him
to be made in commemoration of this event. Among

others, Orsini, a celebrated modeller in wax, with the assistance and under the direction of Andrea Ver-rocchio, modelled three images as large as life. Within these was a kind of skeleton of wood, and split canes, which was covered with waxed cloth, disposed in such well-arranged folds, that it was impossible anything could more nearly resemble the reality. The heads, hands, and feet, which were of wax, were hollow within, and modelled from the life, and then painted in oil, real hair being added, and all appropriate ornaments. "These," says Vasari, "represented not waxen effigies, but living men, as may be seen in all three figures, one of which is in the church of the nuns of Chiarito, in the Via di S. Gallo. This figure is habited in the very dress which Lorenzo wore when, wounded in the throat and bandaged, he appeared at a window of his house, that he might be seen by the people, who had collected there to ascertain whether he was alive, as they wished him to be, or dead; and if dead, that they might avenge him." The second figure is in the church of the Servites, at Lucca, in the civil costume worn by the Florentines. The third image was sent to S$^{ta.}$ Maria degli Angeli, at Assisi. There were other wax figures by Orsini in the Church of the Servites. These were distinguished by a large O, within which was an R, with a cross above it. They were all fine works of art, and Vasari remarks that they have been equalled by few. He adds that the art was practised in his time, but whether from want of devotion, or other causes, it was then declining.

The custom of painting figures extended also to the colouring, with a kind of enamel, of figures and bassi rilievi in terra cotta; and the numerous specimens of this kind of decoration which still remain, prove the estimation in which this art was once held.

The most distinguished artist in this line was Luca della Robbia, to whom many improvements in the art are ascribed.

In Spain the art of colouring wooden statues was continued to a comparatively late period. Pacheco[1] gives instructions for painting statues, and it appears that he did not disdain to practise the art himself, and that he even claimed the honour of having introduced a better style of painting sculpture. Alonzo Cano and Montañes are said to have frequently stipulated that none but themselves should paint the images which they had carved.[2]

The practice of painting "ymagines rotundas" was not confined to those carved in wood; it extended also to stone statues, and was frequently employed on the sepulchral effigies of kings and nobles. In this case the dress of the sculptured figure exactly resembled that worn by the person whom it was intended to represent. Among the Germans and English a general custom prevailed of painting monumental effigies. A remarkable instance of this occurs in the effigy of Henry II. of England, at Fontevraud, in Normandy, described by Mr. Stothard in his work entitled 'The Monumental Effigies of Great Britain.' The beard of the figure is painted and stippled like a miniature, to represent its being closely shaven in the Norman fashion. The mantle, Mr. Stothard ascertained by scraping, had been painted several times; it was originally of a deep reddish chocolate.[3] The Dalmatica, or tunic, was of crimson, covered with gold stars. The boots were green, with gold spurs, fastened by red leathers. The gloves have jewels on the centre of the back of the hand, a mark of royalty or high ecclesiastical rank. The crown and the right hand are broken, but the latter still retains the sceptre. The sword lies on the bier by

---

[1] Tratado della Pintura, p. 402, &c.

[2] For additional information on this subject, see Ford's Hand-book for Spain, p. 110.

[3] Probably the deep red colour found on old frescoes, apparently produced by the red hæmatite.

the left side.   With the exception of the position of the
sword, it will be seen that this description agrees with
the account of the burial of Henry II., extracted by
Mr. Stothard from the History of Matthew Paris, who
says, " the king was arrayed in the royal investments,
having a golden crown on his head, and gloves on the
hands, boots wrought with gold on the feet, and spurs,
and a great ring on the finger, with the sceptre in the
hand, and girt with a sword: he lay with his face
uncovered."   Mr. Stothard continues, " It therefore
appears that the tomb was literally a representation of
the deceased king, as if he still lay in state.   Nor can
we, without supposing such was the custom, otherwise
account for the singular coincidence between the effigy
of King John on the lid of his coffin and his body
within it, when discovered a few years since." [1]

§ 5. Implements used in Painting.

The wood-cut, copied originally from a miniature of
the fifteenth century, in the Bibliothèque Royale at
Paris, appeared in the before-mentioned interesting
work of M. Aimé Champollion-Figeac; it exhibits a
female artist in the act of painting a statue of the
Virgin holding the infant Saviour.   The subject is
highly interesting in another point of view, because it
shows the implements used at that period in painting.
The artist holds a pencil or brush in her right hand,
and a palette with a handle in her left, thus affording
incontestable evidence that the palette was used in
France during the fifteenth century.   This is, perhaps,
the earliest notice of this implement with which we are
acquainted.   The colours, mixed in shells, as described
by Alcherius and other writers, are placed on a small
bench by her side, near which are the brushes in a tray,
and a second palette, also furnished with a handle.

---

[1] King John was buried in Worcester Cathedral.

Another illustration of the work of M. Champollion, copied from a miniature of the same period, represents the atelier of a painter of the fifteenth century. He is sitting on a folding stool, holding in his left hand a palette, similar in its form to those represented in the last cut. In his right hand he holds a brush, with which he is painting a picture of the Virgin and Child,

which, from being framed, suggests the idea of being painted on canvass. The picture is placed on an easel, supported by three legs. In the background is a man grinding colours, with a jar by his side. In the foreground is a low table, on which are shells of various kinds holding colours, and a tray full of brushes. The long and flowing sleeves of the painter, and the pointed shoes of the man grinding the colours, will assist in fixing the date of this drawing.

§ 6. Leather.

It has been mentioned that during the age of Frederick Barbarossa, the clothes of men were of leather, unlined. There is reason, however, to believe, from the recipes contained in the Lucca MS., and repeated in the Mappæ Clavicula, that the skins were frequently dyed. During the dark and middle ages, the preparation of leather appears to have been carried on chiefly in the south of Europe, and in the countries inhabited by the Saracens and Moors. The leather of Marseilles was particularly valued at this period; and one quarter of the city, called "La Cuiraterie," was especially set apart for the preparation of this article, with which the markets of Spain and Italy were supplied. In the twelfth, thirteenth, and fourteenth centuries, skins and leather were also imported from Africa into Barcelona, and the merchants of this city occupied, conjointly with those of Marseilles, a certain quarter of the city of Troyes, where they carried on a trade principally in Morocco leather.[1] From the ninth to the middle of the thirteenth century, the city of Cordova, in Spain, was celebrated for the leather called " Cordovan," which was manufactured there by the Moors.

The use of leather was not limited to articles of dress, but as men became more luxurious, the fashion

---

[1] Depping, Histoire du Commerce, vol. i. p. 249, 263, 294.

of hanging rooms with leather, painted linen-cloth,[1] or tapestry, was introduced. The walls of apartments were formerly left bare, and on the introduction of leather hangings or tapestry, they were confined to that part of the room which was immediately behind the seats occupied by the owners of the house. These hangings were suspended from hooks fixed in the wall, and, like the glass windows, were removed when the family changed their residence. Frequent examples of these partial hangings of apartments may be seen in miniatures and pictures of the thirteenth and fourteenth centuries. In the fifteenth century, the hangings were continued round the apartment, and the leather was frequently stamped and gilt, or ornamented with tin-foil, and afterwards varnished with a yellow varnish. Descriptions of this varnish are to be found in all technical works relating to art, from the Lucca MS. to the Treatise of Pacheco, inclusive.

Filiasi[2] observes that " the art of gilding skins and leather has been exercised from time immemorial in the [Venetian] lagoon, and to such an extent was the commerce in this merchandise carried on with Spain and the Levant, that, one year with another, the trade in gilt leather brought into Venice a clear profit of about 100,000 ducats and more." Apartments hung with this stamped and gilt leather may still be seen in some of the palaces at Venice. The Barbarigo Palace has more than one room decorated in this manner. Leather hangings were also in use in our own country; the best specimens are at Nonsuch Palace, in Surrey; Hinchinbrook House, near Huntingdon; Ruffor Abbey, in Nottinghamshire; and at Blenheim.[3]

Gilt leather was also applied to other purposes. It

---

1 See Mr. Eastlake's ' Materials,' p. 97.

2 Saggio sull' Antico Commercio, sull' Arti, e sulla Marina de' Veneziani, appended to the 7th volume of his Memorie Storiche de' Veneti, p. 153.

3 See a paper on this subject in the Art Union for August, 1847.

was used for the covers of books, and for frames
of mirrors. Examples of both may be seen in the
museum in the Hôtel de Cluny at Paris. Pictures
were also frequently painted on plain leather, stretched
on a panel. The circumstance is alluded to by
Eraclius. Marco Rizzi sometimes painted in tempera
on kid-skins;[1] and in the Fondaco de' Tedeschi an
apartment is decorated with historical pictures by Paolo
Veronese, painted on the gilt leather for, which Venice
was so famous.[2]

In the commencement of this Introduction full credit
has been given to the monks for the preservation of
literature and the arts; but it must be allowed that if
they have been the cause of the preservation of learning
during the dark ages, they have also actually destroyed
the writings of many classic authors in order to tran-
scribe on the parchment on which they were written
the works of the fathers or the legends of the saints.
Some of the lost works of antiquity have been
brought to light by the labours of Cardinal Angelo
Mai and other learned men; but alas! the ingenious
monks had discovered another and more effectual
method of destroying the literary treasures of antiquity.
This method is revealed in the Bolognese MS.,[3] where
we find a recipe "To make chamois leather with sheep
or goat-skin *parchment, which has been written on!*"
Who shall say how many classic works have been made
into leather waistcoats for the warriors of the middle
ages or cut into sandals for the sleek and well-fed
monks? Who shall even say how many works were
obliterated before the destroying process was brought
to perfection, and the grand discovery made that parchment which had been written on would make as good
leather as that which had never been touched by a pen?

---

[1] Zanetti, della Pittura Veneziana, p. 442, n.
[2] Ibid., p. 194.   [3] Ibid., p. 375.

§ 7. Niello.

Among the arts formerly practised and now fallen into disuse, there is perhaps none which has led to such important results as the ancient nigellum or niello, for to this we are indebted for the invention of engraving. The art was known to the ancients and was practised during the middle ages, as we find from the 'Mappæ Clavicula,' the MSS. of Eraclius, Theophilus, and Le Begue, as well as from specimens of the art still existing in different museums. These examples are extremely rare.

That the art was practised by the Byzantine Greeks is proved by the specimens in the Pala d'Oro, which was made at Constantinople in 976, by order of the Doge Pietro Orseolo, for the church of S. Mark at Venice, where it may now be seen. The material is silver-gilt ornamented with gems and enamels. Some of the inscriptions are in Greek and some in Latin, but the letters are all in niello. The Pala d'Oro was repaired in 1105, in 1209, and in 1345, but it is highly probable that the nielli formed part of the original design. Some fragments of it are now in England. The Marquess Trivulzio of Milan has a collection of about forty nielli, among which I saw a very fine specimen by Maso Finiguerra and another by Peregrino, besides others highly interesting.

This art was much cultivated by the early Milanese goldsmiths, who applied it to the decoration of arms and armour, as well as to religious purposes.[1]

Benvenuto Cellini remarks[2] that the art of executing nielli was nearly forgotten at Florence in the year 1515, when he began to learn the craft of the goldsmith. But, he proceeds, as he was continually

---

[1] Milano e il suo Territorio, vol. ii. p. 244.
[2] Dell' Arte del Niellare, e del Modo di fare il Niello.

hearing from the goldsmiths of the beauty of the nielli, and particularly of the skill of Maso Finiguerra in this art, he applied himself with great diligence to follow the traces of these skilful goldsmiths ; but not content with learning to engrave on the silver only, he learned also the mode of executing the nielli, in order to work with more facility and certainty. Cellini has left us the most precise description of the mode of working nielli which is extant. It has been published with his other works.[1]

The art consisted [2] in drawing the design on gold or silver with a style and then engraving it with the burin ; a black composition was then made of copper, lead, silver, and sulphur, incorporated together by heat. When cold the composition was pounded and laid on the engraved silver plate, a little borax was sprinkled over it, and the plate was then placed over a charcoal fire until the composition, being dissolved, flowed into all the lines of the design. When cold, the work was scraped and burnished, and the niello presented the effect of a drawing in black on gold or silver.

§ 8. Dyeing.

During the dark ages the Jews appear to have monopolised the trade of dyeing. Benjamin of Tudela relates that when he visited Jerusalem (between 1160 and 1173) he found only two hundred Jews resident in that city, who were all dyers of wool, and who had purchased a monopoly of the trade. Beckmann [3] has shown that the art of dyeing was principally carried on by this people during the same period in Italy. Dye-houses were established in the duchy of Benevento as early as the eleventh century, and in Sicily at the com-

---

[1] The Life and Writings of Cellini were published in 3 vols. 8vo., in 1806, at Milan.

[2] See Vasari, Int., cap. xxxiii.   [3] Inventions, Title *Indigo*.

mencement of the thirteenth. From the Jews resident in Italy the art soon spread to the Italians, who carried it to a greater degree of perfection than the other nations of Europe.

In Venice there appear to have been distinct establishments for dyeing in the thirteenth century,[1] for this city was then celebrated for its purple dyes. The scarlet dyes prepared from the kermes (*grana*) at Florence were particularly prized. About the year 1338 this city contained nearly two hundred of these factories.[2] In the year 1300 the art of dyeing with the purple colour obtained from the lichen Roccella or Oricello was introduced from the Levant; but the secret of preparing the dye was for a long period confined to a single family, who acquired a large fortune by cultivating this branch of industry, and who for this reason received the name of " Ruccellai."

Previous to this period Marseilles, Arles, Montpellier, and other parts of the South of France, were famous for red, blue, and rose-coloured dyes. The statutes of these cities contain regulations relative to the use of madder, kermes, and brasil wood in dyeing.[3]

The date of the introduction of the art of dyeing into England seems uncertain. Hume remarks that "in the reign of Henry III. woollen cloth, which the English had not then the art of dyeing, was worn by them white, and without receiving the last hand of the manufacturer;" and it is certain that as late as the year 1284[4] the English were in the habit of contracting with the Florentine merchants for the sale of their fleeces for a period of one year or more. Mr. Hallam[5] has, however, shown that a woollen-manufactory existed

---

[1] Filiasi, Saggio, &c., p. 153.

[2] Depping, Histoire du Commerce, &c., vol. i. p. 235.

[3] Ibid., vol. ii. p. 293, 300.

[4] Ibid., vol. i. p. 337, quoting Pagnini ' Della Decima e delle altre Gravezze.' [5] History of the Middle Ages, vol. iii. p. 378.

in England under Henry II., which was noticed in the regulations of Richard I., and which, by the importation of woad under John, may be considered to have been then flourishing. From the importation of woad it may certainly be inferred that the English understood and practised the art of dyeing as early as the time of John. The MS. of S. Audemar alludes to a substance called folium,[1] which was used by the English to dye wool red or purple. The date of this MS. is uncertain, but it is probably not later than the beginning of the thirteenth century.

From the frequent occurrence of treatises on dyeing in old MSS. relative to the arts, it seems probable that this art was formerly practised in monasteries conjointly with painting and medicine. The older MSS., such as that of Lucca and the 'Mappæ Clavicula,' contain recipes for dyeing skins and leather only. The Bolognese MS. contains a long treatise on dyeing, in which various methods of dyeing skins and leather of all kinds, as well as silk, thread, and woollen stuffs, are circumstantially detailed. The Sloane MS., No. 1754, contains also a treatise " de Tincturis," which seems to have been written principally for the use of the monks, the dyeing of the dresses worn by them being described in it. These treatises are generally accompanied by recipes for removing stains from cloth. In the introduction to the MSS. of Le Begue a practice is noticed[2] which prevailed in England, previous to the introduction of printing with blocks, of painting linen cloth intended for wearing-apparel with figures, flowers, and various devices in imitation of embroidery. Recipes of a similar kind are contained in the Sloane MS. above mentioned, and also in the Bolognese MS.[3]

---

[1] A vegetable colour employed also in painting, prepared from the juice of the Croton tinctorium.

[2] Page 7.   [3] Page 491.

CHAPTER VI.

PAINTING IN OIL.

THE fact that in Italy colours were mixed with oil in painting long before the alleged introduction of oil painting by Antonello da Messina, has been established by the clearest evidence; but the method adopted by these early artists was rude and imperfect; and it was only after the middle of the fifteenth century that the process, which had been perfected by the genius and skill of the brothers Van Eyck, was introduced into Italy by their pupils and followers.

In the course of years the Flemish process underwent various modifications, some of the old practices were altered, and new ones introduced, until the example of Titian and Paolo Veronese occasioned a radical change in the technical methods of the Italian painters. After their time the new methods were again modified and changed by succeeding painters, until not only the original Flemish process, but those of the Venetian painters, had fallen into oblivion, and but few traces of the old practices remained. Some of these have been handed down traditionally from master to pupil; others may be collected from works on painting.

It was with a view to collect these scattered reminiscences of art that the present work was principally undertaken.

As traditionary practices might possibly preserve the remembrance of technical processes not recorded in books, or at least serve to confirm those which have been described by writers on art, it appeared to me most desirable to learn as many of them as I could. With this view, I applied for information to several eminent artists and restorers of pictures in the north of Italy. Nothing can exceed the kindness and frankness with which they answered my inquiries, and communicated all they knew respecting the old methods of painting. On one occasion only was there the slightest degree of reserve.

The information contained in the treatises published in these volumes, and in other works on art, relative to technical details, is frequently concise and incomplete, and sometimes merely incidental. Extensive reading is, therefore, necessary to enable one to form a just idea of the early methods of oil-painting. As many of the processes are described in books which are so rare as to be scarcely accessible to the general reader, I have endeavoured to collect from them, as well as from the communications of Italian artists, such information as will give the reader some slight notions of the Italian practice of oil-painting.

The materials I have collected may be arranged under the following heads:—1st. The communications made by foreign professors of painting. 2ndly. An explanation of the colours used in painting, with some account of the manner in which they are employed. 3rdly. A description of the mode of preparing oils and varnishes, and of the resins of which the latter are composed; and, 4thly, A short account of the process of painting.

§ 1. Opinions of eminent Italian Artists as to the Practice of the Old Masters.

The following particulars relative to old methods of painting were communicated to me by Signor A., an artist who had practised many years at Milan, and is esteemed as a skilful restorer of pictures.

The Society of Painters in the Italian States were

governed by certain rules and regulations among themselves, and when a young man wished to become a
painter, he was placed with one of established reputation, with whom he was to continue one year on trial.
If at the end of that period the master was dissatisfied
with the boy's progress, he returned him to his parents;
if he approved of him, the boy was bound to him for
twelve years,[1] the first six or seven of which were spent
in learning to grind colours, and all the other mechanical parts of the art, as well as in painting "Madon-
nine," which were sent to the fairs for sale, and the
proceeds helped to pay the expenses of the boy's board
and lodging. The pupil was sworn never to divulge
the secrets[2] of the art until he became a master himself, when he was allowed to teach his own pupils, first
binding them to secrecy. Signor A. remarked that a
master could not execute large works properly unless
he had half a dozen pupils at least, and the object of
the long apprenticeship was, that the pupil might by
his services repay the master who had maintained and
taught him, for in those days pupils did not pay
apprentice fees.

He observed that Titian painted on a ground of thin
"gesso marcio,"[3] taking especial care not to put too
much glue,[4] and this slightly absorbent ground was
useful in getting rid of the superfluous oil. He next
stated that the two great faults of the moderns were the
use of white lead in their grounds, and the little care
they took in purifying their colours. He said that any

---

[1] Cennini (cap. civ.) mentions a similar term of apprenticeship. He
says the first year was spent in studying drawing; the next six in learning
to grind colours, to make glue, to prepare grounds, and to gild; and the
remaining six years in learning to paint.

[2] Compare with the Statutes of Sienese Painters, s. xiii. xl. Carteggio
Inedito, vol. ii.

[3] See Zanetti, della Pittura Veneziana, p. 101.

[4] Strong glue would have hardened the ground and rendered it non-
absorbent. See p. 888.

picture in which white lead was used in the ground
would inevitably crack within fifty years after it was
painted, and that pictures painted with oil on a white
lead ground would moreover turn brown.[1] This practice, he said, was observed by Mengs, who in other
respects painted with the true method. He also said
that the colours were always *ground* with oil, but that
oil was not used to paint with. The colours, he said,
were of the most common description, as we read in
Lanzi and others,[2] but they were carefully purified
and washed. Signor A. told me, that when he was at
Venice he made a point of going to the Piazza San
Salvatore,[3] where Titian used to purchase his colours,
to see whether there were any "speziali"[4] there still.
He found one, and inquired of him if he had any old
colours, such as were used by the old painters, and he
was shown an orange-coloured pigment, which resembled a colour frequently found on Venetian pictures.
Signor A. gave me an ounce or more of this colour.

He said the blue used by Titian, Correggio, Paul
Veronese, and others, was " bleu minerale," (he pro-
nounced this word in the Italian manner;) he showed
me his bottle of this blue, and told me I could purchase it for one soldo an ounce, for it was now used for
the most common purposes ; but that it could not be
used with oil, or in any method but his, on oil paintings. He said the Venetians never used ultramarine,[5]
which inclined too much to the violet.

As to Titian's method of painting, he said the whole
subject was painted in chiaroscuro with this same blue,
mixed with white and terra rossa, as if painting with

---

[1] Vasari (Int., cap. xxi.) and Armenini mention that white lead was
used in the grounds.

[2] Zanetti, della Pittura Veneziana, p. 100.

[3] Titian is said to have purchased his colours in Rialto ; San Salvatore is
on the other side of the Canal Grande.

[4] Apothecaries or druggists who sold colours.

[5] There is proof that the Venetians did occasionally use ultramarine.

Indian ink; that the lights were laid on with flesh-colour (red and white); the picture was then laid aside for several months (say five or six); afterwards the flesh-colour, consisting of terra rossa, or whatever you please, was glazed over the flesh, and then the picture was again laid by to dry. I think Signor A. said the shades and half tints were then painted, and the picture again dried. The glazing was then repeated until the painter was satisfied with his work, setting the picture aside between every glazing, until quite dry and hard.[1] That the picture was invariably first painted in cold colours, and that the warm colours were afterwards glazed upon them. That the whole surface of the picture, when the painting was completed, was glazed over with asphaltum ("spalto bianco, bitume Hebraico "). " But," I remarked, " if asphaltum is now used, it is almost sure to crack." He answered, " That is because you do not know how to use it." He added, that all Titian's pictures were glazed with it. The effect of daylight discernible in Titian's pictures was, he observed, produced by his studying after the life in the public gardens and the open air, and never in the darkened studio.[2]

I asked whether placing the picture in the sun made any difference: he hesitated. I then related the passage from the letters of Rubens,[3] giving the authority; and he admitted this was necessary to prevent the picture becoming yellow.[4]

He also said it is reported that Correggio was a

---

[1] The subject was resumed at another interview, and is more clearly explained in p. cxxiii.

[2] See Zanetti, della Pittura Veneziana, p. 99.

[3] See Gachet, Lettres inédites de P. P. Rubens, 1840, p. 234.

[4] I had been previously informed that it was the custom in Italy to place pictures in the air, and to expose them to the heavy dew, and then to suffer them to dry thoroughly in the sun, that this process was carried on after every coat of paint, and that it was owing to this process that the oil of old pictures did not become yellow. I have myself seen pictures so exposed at Milan.

pupil of Mantegna's, but that he was certain from the manner in which his pictures were painted, that he was a pupil of Giorgione's or Pordenone's. He said it was more difficult to imitate Correggio than any other painter. He spoke of his (Correggio's) St. Jerome, at Parma, which he said was the finest picture ever painted, and stated that Correggio had painted the figure of St. Jerome in two days. The first day he painted the head and half the body, passing from the top of the shoulder to the wrist with one stroke of the brush. The next day, he said, he began at the hips and finished at the toes with one stroke of the brush. "This facility," said he, "he obtained from painting in fresco."

I noticed that some of his own pictures had in places that shrivelled look which is sometimes found on Titian's and Palma Vecchio's pictures, which Merimée mentions [1] as a proof that oil or an oleo-resinous varnish had been used.

With regard to the darks being raised above the surface, he said that in Correggio's St. Jerome beforementioned, the blue drapery was the thickness of a five franc piece above the rest of the picture. He showed me a copy he was painting of Correggio's Marriage of St. Catherine, which was unfinished and without the glazings. The paint seemed to be dry and hard as he rapped it with his fingers, and did not shine, excepting a portion of the drapery. A part of the Virgin's red drapery was glazed; the glazing shone like varnish, and was higher than the lights — that is, it stood up with an edge where it joined the lights. I have reason to think that the vehicle used was amber varnish. I inquired what he thought of Lionardo da Vinci's different processes as related by Lomazzo and others; he said they were "niente, niente." That he (Lionardo) was always experimenting ("soffisticare"),

---

[1] De la Peinture à l'Huile, p. 31.

taking up his oils with little bits of cotton, and so on, *but the oil was of little consequence* ; that when Titian was asked about his oil, he said, " If you have good oil, you can make a good picture ; if you have *bad* oil, you can still make a good picture."

He observed, " the Englishman Laurent (Sir T. Lawrence) thought the secret consisted in wax ; but before his death he discovered his error." He also observed, " some use litharge and the oxides of lead with their oils ; but nothing can be worse for the pictures than oxides of lead, for they will always darken the colours." Signor A. also remarked that the difference between the methods of Titian and Rubens consisted in the former glazing the whole picture, while Rubens only glazed parts. The numerous sketches, however, left by Rubens, and the testimony of various writers,[1] show that Rubens painted his pictures in a different manner, Rubens beginning his pictures with rich browns, then the silver gray shades, then the various flesh tints ; while, according to Signor A., Titian began with the cold colours and finished with the warm ; each attaining transparency by a different road.

He also observed that the old painters never used a mahl-stick on large pictures : that Rubens mentions being obliged to have recourse to one in his old age and in declining health.[2] He allowed that the Dutch used them on small easel pictures ;[3] and he said that the great painters used brushes with long handles, and stood at a great distance from their pictures ;[4] that the

---

[1] Rubens' method of colouring is described at some length by Mr. Eastlake, ' Materials,' &c., 408, 409, 483, 494—508, 516—528.

[2] If I am not mistaken, this fact is related by Rubens in one of his letters.

[3] Cespides mentions a mahl-stick among the implements necessary for a painter. See Pacheco, p. 395.

[4] This is said to have been the case with Velasquez, and in modern times with our own Gainsborough. Vasari recommends that the cartoon should be drawn with a piece of charcoal fixed into a long cane.

practice of keeping a youth drawing for years with a hard point (a pencil) was very injurious to his progress as a painter; that he should be taught to draw with his brush, which was flexible and elastic at the point, and which gives freedom and facility of execution ; and that there was no practice so good to form a painter as fresco painting. He added, if a man is not a good painter at the age of 18 or 20, he never will be, because he will be too timid to work with proper boldness.

Signor A. called on me again, and I inquired further respecting the method of Titian. He told me that Titian began by painting in the flesh in chiaroscuro with a mixed tint, formed of biadetto, biacca, and a very little terra rossa. He then painted the lights with flesh colour, and laid by the picture to dry. After 5 or 6 months he glazed the flesh with terra rossa and let it dry. He then painted in the shades transparently (that is, without any white in the shadows), using a great deal of asphaltum with them. Signor A. then stated that Titian always represented his subjects surrounded by daylight, and reflected upon by surrounding objects. He also said that in a blue drapery he painted the shades with lake, and then laid on the lights [with white]. That these colours were laid on with great body, and when dry he took a large brush and spread the biadetto over the whole.[1] Signor A. also told me that the beautiful green used by the Venetian painters was an artificial pigment formed of copper and vitriol (he said he could not describe it

---

[1] Sig. Palmaroli (note to Marcucci, p. 230 n.) states that he succeeded in imitating certain blue tints in draperies by Titian and Paolo Veronese, by drawing and painting the shadows very transparently with the usual brown tint, broken with lake, next to these the blue tint composed of smaltino and a little verdigris. The lights were painted with white and ultramarine and a little verdigris, and when dry the whole was glazed with ultramarine mixed with varnish.

more accurately because he did not understand chemistry), called verde lavita, or verde vita, which was
sold so cheap that it might almost be said to be worth
nothing.[1] He added, that all the colours used by the
Venetians were cheap and common ; but that they
were made valuable by their mode of using them. He
said, " You may use the biadetto as I have directed
you with all the Venetian impasto, but in two years
it will become green"[2] (meaning to say it could only be
used with his vehicle, which he did not describe). I
said that in England painters mixed varnish with the
colours, and that the pictures cracked. He replied,
" that was because they painted with the colours mixed
with varnish before the under colours were dry ;" but,
he added, painters did not all adopt Titian's manner ;
some could paint a picture in four hours; Rubens
painted his Descent in nine days ; and painters could
so temper their colours that they could complete a
picture as fast as their hands could execute it ; that
their vehicle gave them complete command over their
materials, and that every one added more or less of
" certe droghe " (certain drugs), according to their
convenience and manner of working.

Sig. A. has an accurate and most extensive knowledge of all the writers on painting, and seems to know
every thing in these authors that bears on technical
points. He quoted passages from Vasari, Ridolfi,
Bellori, Zanetti, Guarienti's 'Abecedario,' &c. I asked
him whether he knew anything of Errante's paintings
at Rome, and of the work he had written,[3] the object
of which was to recommend the addition of ground

---

[1] The Venetians used " verde eterno," which is crystallised or purified verdigris, sometimes called distilled verdigris.

[2] It is well known that biadetto and other blues from copper cannot be
used with oil without turning green. See Palomino, vol. ii. p. 52. Paolo
Veronese frequently mixed them with size instead of oil. See Boschini,
Ricche Minere ; and Baldinucci, Vita di Paolo Veronese.

[3] Saggio sui Colori, del Cav. D. Giuseppe Errante, Roma, 1817.

rock-crystal and "smalti" to the colours. Sig. A.
replied, that it was "Niente, niente," and added, "see
what his pictures become in a few years." But he did
not explain in what respect the pictures had suffered.

Sig. A. showed me a picture by Bamboccio (Peter
Van Laer), and at the same time informed me he possessed a black mirror which was used by this artist
in painting, and in which the subject was reflected,
"exactly," he said, "like a Flemish landscape;" "and
then," he added, "they had only to paint what they
saw in the mirror."[1] This mirror was bequeathed by
Bamboccio to Gaspar Poussin; by the latter to some
other painter, until it ultimately came into the hands
of Sig. A.

In order to prevent insects from eating the panels,
Sig. A. stated that roche-alum should be mixed with
the grounds. He also told me that to destroy the
insects which had already got into the wood or ground of
pictures, some assafœtida and sulphur should be burnt
in an open vessel, over which the back of the picture
should be placed at a proper distance; the whole should
be then covered in, so as to enclose the smoke arising
from these ingredients, which will effectually destroy
the insects. The picture may afterwards be washed, if
necessary, but the sulphur will not injure the painting.
Assafœtida and garlic were both used by the old
masters for these purposes.[2]

Sig A. thinks the old masters used madder-lake, and
that they burned it to make it darker.

Verona.—We breakfasted this morning with Count
——, who had invited an artist, principally employed
in restoring pictures, to meet us. Among other things
this artist said that ultramarine was the only blue pig-

---

[1] See Du Fresnoy, de Arte Graphica, l. 286, and the Commentary of
De Piles.

[2] See Pacheco, Tratado, p. 382, &c. Palomino, vol. ii. p. 49.

ment used by the old masters. That they did not use red-lead, but other colours mixed to imitate it; that the Venetians used cochineal lakes. That if they laid oil upon oil,[1] they waited a year between each painting. That there are few painters who have painted so many times over their pictures as Titian; that he did not apply asphaltum over the surface of the picture, but that he used a yellow varnish; that the old masters did not use oil-varnish in painting; that if new pictures were exposed to the sun they would crack to a certainty, unless they were previously wetted, when the process might be repeated several times. (This reminds me of what I had been previously told about exposing pictures to the dew as well as to the sun.) That the canvass was never primed on both sides. He stated that he had found on a picture of Titian's a coat of thin gesso, then a coat of very strong glue, made from pig's-skin, very hard and shining, upon which the picture was painted.[2] I inquired whether the plan described by Sig. A., of getting in the chiaro-scuro with a blueish tint, was that of Titian? He said it was not. That he painted his pictures first with colours of great body, and then finished with glazings. Sig. A. also said he painted his colours with great body at first. This artist mentioned a kind of strong glue called *crocante*, the nature of which I have not been able to ascertain. He prepared his linseed-oil first by straining it; he then put white-lead into a sieve and filtered the oil through it, when all impurities remained behind in the lead, but he never boiled it. He always found that Guimet's ultramarine, mixed with this oil, turned black.

---

[1] To understand this expression, it is necessary to state that I had been previously informed that the Venetians painted the solid colours at once with oil, and finished with varnish, so that one layer of colour mixed with oil was not laid on another.

[2] That this coat of hard glue is frequently laid between the ground and the picture is proved by Edwards's Report, p. 888. This glue rendered the ground non-absorbent, of which he did not approve.

Venice.—I was introduced to Sig. B., an artist who had been long employed in restoring the public pictures. He had then just dead-coloured a copy he was making of a picture by Gian Bellino. The dead-colouring of the flesh was not so blue in the shades as Sig. A.'s. There was more red with it; indeed the dead-colouring seemed conducted exactly in the same manner as I have seen it done by artists in England The blue drapery was dead-coloured with bleu de Berlin. The following is a summary of the information I obtained from this artist.

1. The grounds consisted of nothing but gesso and glue, which absorbed the superfluous oil.

2. The dead-colouring was always painted with cold colours, the lights white, and the shades warm;[1] you may then make your picture any thing you please.

3. The warm colours were always glazed, over the more solid tints.

4. The vehicle he used for every part of the picture was linseed-oil, boiled on litharge, which was of a high colour, indeed almost black, and which he purchased in bottles imported from Germany. He also showed me another bottle containing linseed-oil thickened in the sun, and mixed with litharge; more than half the contents of this last bottle was a black sediment. He said he required nothing thinner to dilute the colours; he never used spirit of turpentine or varnish in painting. He used bladder-colours. The lake he mixed with his boiled oil, and it stood up on the palette, and when put on his nail did not flow. He said he exposed his pictures to the sun after every process of painting; that this never occasioned their cracking, and that he did not wet them before exposing them to the sun. He paints on the plan always observed in the Venetian

---

[1] The first shades in the picture he was copying were painted in cold colours. He must have meant that the shades when finished were to be warm.

school. He does not know the Flemish method, or
that of Rubens. He knows that his own method is
that pursued by the Venetians, from the frequent
opportunities he has had of observation when cleaning
their pictures. Sig. B. said that Titian *did* put red
shades under his blue draperies.[1] He also said, " If
you paint your half tints cold, your shades warm,
and your lights white, you may glaze your picture
to whatever tone you like."

Sig. B. observed that the Venetians used little
besides earths, and never orpiment; but that the
modern Romans use it in great quantity.

There was a most beautiful deep lake-coloured
drapery in an old picture in the room where he was
painting. I asked with what colour was that done?
He shook his head, and said he did not know, but that
the dead-colouring was done with much white, and
when dry it was glazed with lake until it was sufficiently dark.

I asked why in old pictures the darks were always
raised higher than the lights? He said it was because
the painters went over them a great many times. I
remarked that the *blues* are always more in relief than
any other colour. In this he agreed, but assigned no
further reason. His knowledge seemed entirely practical, and his practice derived from his restorations of
old pictures. He said Titian used asphaltum, and
that blue draperies were glazed with ultramarine.

Sig. C., another artist, who had been frequently
employed during the last thirty years in restoring the
public pictures at Venice, informed me that Titian
generally painted on a ground of glue and gesso, but
great care was necessary, when this ground was used on
canvass, to make it soft and pliant; the best means of

---

[1] See p. cxxiii., cxxix.

securing this was to add some *milk* to the glue and gesso. That the use of this gesso ground was to absorb the superfluous oil.

He also observed, that Titian sometimes used a ground composed of terra rossa, with oil. That he laid in the subject in the natural colours, or as nearly as he could to nature, only much fainter, and thin of colour, and when dry painted in the colours more solidly; but that he always painted the shades *cold*. He then put the picture by for a year, and corrected it by glazing. That Titian generally used nothing but oil; that he sometimes went seven, eight, or nine times over the same part,[1] with oil glazings, which is the reason why his paintings become more yellow than others; that he sometimes glazed with varnish. That he did not put red under the shades of his blue draperies; but that when this appearance was perceived it arose from his having used a red ground, and when the blue became thin by being rubbed off, the red ground appeared through. That the blue used formerly was called " Turchino," that it may still be purchased, that some old painters still use it, and that it is very apt to turn green. I mentioned that Baldinucci said that Paul Veronese laid on the blue in distemper. He said it was the fact, and that many restorers did not know it until they found it out by taking off the colour unintentionally in cleaning it. That some of Paul Veronese's blues turned green; but those that best retained their colour were found to have been painted in distemper.

Sig. C. observed that Titian and Paul Veronese both painted " con colori di corpo," that they suffered the colours to dry thoroughly before they painted on them again, and this hard, dry body of colours enabled them to apply the glazings and sfregazzi.[2]

---

[1] See Zanetti, della Pittura Veneziana, p. 102.   [2] See note, p. 879.

That the brilliant reds were obtained by glazing lake over terra rossa; that the terra rossa they had formerly is now lost; that the best is now brought from Spain.[1]

That for a green drapery, Titian began with terra verde, with, perhaps, giallolino for the lights. When dry he glazed the whole with verdigris, and the shades with asphaltum; both these colours might be rubbed in with the hand. Sometimes he glazed with asphaltum without the verdigris, when he required a warm rich green.

That asphaltum could be easily dissolved for use in spirit of turpentine.

That litharge mixed with oils was very bad for the picture; and that it corroded the paint, as well as darkened the colours.

I saw Sig. C. on the following day, when I again cross-examined him. The following is the substance of the replies elicited :—

That he had never heard of mixing powdered glass with oil or colours.

That he had heard of encaustic painting, but not of mixing wax with oil.

That he had never heard of dissolving resins in oil, and thus making an oil varnish.[2]

---

[1] I am inclined to believe that the red earth, called sinopia, was a finer colour than any of the iron ores now in use as pigments. I have frequently noticed a red of this description on old mural paintings in Italy, and I have also seen specimens of a fine red colour in a dry state in a volume of drawings by Lionardo da Vinci, in the possession of Sig. G. Vallardi, at Milan. Some of these drawings had been executed on the paper of which the books used for keeping leaf gold were made. Before the gold was laid in these books, the leaves were rubbed over with dry sinopia, as we read in Theophilus (lib. i. cap. 24), and the above instance proves that the custom was continued in Italy at least until the time of Lionardo da Vinci.

[2] As far as I could ascertain, oleo-resinous varnishes are not only obsolete in the north of Italy, but they appear to be almost entirely forgotten. When living artists mentioned the colours being mixed with oil and varnish, they always alluded to the mixture of an essential oil-varnish with linseed or nut-oil. In one instance only had I reason to think an oleo-resinous varnish was habitually employed by a living artist.

That he had never heard of placing pictures in the sun, unless it was for the purpose of cracking a new picture to make it look like an old one.

That the reason why old pictures cannot be repaired with oil colours, is that the oil in the old picture has undergone all its changes, that the new tints are made to match the old with oil that will change; and when this change takes place the colours darken, and cease to match the old paint.

That all restorations are now done with colours mixed with varnish; that Sig. Pietro Edwards was the first who introduced this practice.

Sig. C. then remarked that the reason why spirit of wine dissolved old oil paintings, and not new ones painted entirely in oil, was because the greater part of the oil was dried up, and no more remained in the picture than was sufficient to hold the paint together. In other words, that the oil of the old picture was converted into a resin, and, like other resins, was soluble in spirit of wine.

That the Venetians did not paint on gold grounds after the time of Titian.

That the Venetians sometimes laid a coat of white-lead and oil over the gesso ground.

With regard to the use of ultramarine, he observed that it was occasionally used by the Venetians, chiefly on easel pictures. That as this colour was a stone, and not a metal, it never changed colour; but that if used with oil, in time the oil would dry and leave it, and the colour would come off in powder. That it should be used in distemper, and then it would last; that all those painters whose blues have stood, have applied them in distemper.

He also stated that the lake used by the Venetian painters was called " *Lacca di Cambaneri o di Verzino*;"[1] that it may still be purchased at Venice; that

---

[1] If this lake was made of verzino, it should probably have been called " Lacca Colombina."

it was always glazed, and used with varnish ; that it will not stand with oil. That the blue tinge of the lake in old pictures was occasioned by adding blue to the lake.

That the Venetians and Titian glazed with varnish.

That red-lead might be used with boiled oil, because as the oil was already oxidised to the highest degree, it would not de-oxidise the red-lead (deut-oxide of lead), which would therefore not change.

He said also that Paolo Veronese had originally glazed his red-leads with giallolino, which had been removed in cleaning ; and that the rich bright yellow colour I had noticed in P. Veronese's picture was gamboge.

That the Venetians of the present day make great use of madder-lake ; and that the old Venetian school also possessed this pigment, because the madder-plant grows in the neighbourhood of Venice.[1]

Sig. C. also informed me that Titian glazed much with asphaltum, and that in glazing he used an essential oil varnish, such as aqua di ragia.[2]

He stated also, that the very fine hair-like cracks in old pictures were the effect of time only.[3]

He mentioned that distemper was frequently employed on early oil-pictures, particularly on parts that it was feared would turn yellow, such as white linen.

With regard to the method of Titian, he observed that Titian always softened the shades of flesh with his fingers ; and that he used sometimes nut-oil, and sometimes linseed-oil, and sometimes both together ; but that linseed-oil was the best, because the nut-oil soon became rancid, and when mixed with the colours underwent a sort of fermentation.

---

[1] This reasoning is not conclusive, and it is probable that the Venetian madder was not the best, since in 1565 madder was imported for dyeing by the Venetians from Flanders, under the name of "robbia o vero roza di Fiandra." See ' Libro intitolato Plicto,' Venezia, 1565.

[2] If this be true, whence arise the wrinkles so frequently observed on Titian's pictures, which can only take place on the tough surface of the oil ?

[3] If so, why do not those of Van Eyck, Lucas Van Leyden, Hammelink, Antonello da Messina, Francesco Francia, and others of that period crack also ?

From what this gentleman said I collect that he deems the rapid drying of the vehicle to be of the first importance to the permanence of the colours, which were not likely to change when once dry, and that it is better to use a dark-coloured oil which will *not* change than any of a lighter colour which will change.

Sig. D., an eminent artist, called on me this evening for the purpose of describing the methods of painting practised by Titian and others of the Venetian school.

He began by stating that the only artists to be considered as examples in the mechanical part of the art are Gian Bellino, Giorgione, Titian, Bonifazio, and the two Bassans. That the decline of the art is to be attributed to Tintoretto, who, to save expense, used bad colours in his immense pictures, and to Palma Giovane.

The following was the plan generally adopted by the first-mentioned artists:—

The grounds were made with gesso and a very thin glue; sometimes a little black was added to this by Gian Bellino and others. Over this one or two coats of glue were applied to prevent the ground being too absorbent.

The glue was made of parings of leather.

An analysis of some pictures by Gian Bellino showed they were painted in the following manner and order:—

The ground as above.

Then the outline with ink.

The chiaroscuro painted very thin with brown.

Then the first flesh colour, very rosy, the colour being spread thin.

Second coat of flesh colour made browner, with more yellow, also very thin.

Third coat thin, and with more white, to match the complexion.

This manner of painting keeps the flesh light and clear, because it permits the white grounds and the rosy tints to be seen through.[1]

These colours are all mixed with oil, but the coats of paint being so thin, the colours dry quickly and hard before the oil has had time to become rancid.

The flesh was finished with glazings of asphaltum.

Draperies.—The lights and shades strongly contrasted, the lights pure white or nearly so.

The darks consisted of the pure colour.

Then the glazings with the local transparent colours.

The whole figure, drapery, &c., finished with glazings of asphaltum and terra di Cologna,[2] not much burnt.

Asphaltum was mixed with olio di sasso (naphtha) or spirit of turpentine.

No part of paintings in oil was executed in distemper.

Titian generally began his pictures like Gian Bellino, but instead of painting the flesh three times only, he painted over it four, five, or six times; consequently the ground would not absorb all the superfluous oil, which rose to the top and darkened the picture.

That he frequently laid on the paint with his fingers.

That he did not paint with a thick coat of colour, but always used his colours thin, for the reason given above.

That he frequently covered the whole picture except the white linen with asphaltum.

He painted no part in distemper.

Bonifazio glazed more than any of the others.

Giorgione began like Gian Bellino and Titian. Did not lay in any part of the picture with distemper.

Paolo Veronese painted generally *alla prima* with

---

[1] As to the lights in early oil paintings being semi-opaque, see Mr. Eastlake's ' Materials,' &c., p. 408.

[2] I am not aware that Cologne earth is mentioned in Italian works, at least previous to the 17th century. The colour might have been terra di Campagna.

more body than Titian (whose patience he appeared to want), so that the finished picture was little more than the abbozzo ; that is, that he painted up his picture at once.

That he did not employ distemper on his pictures ; but with regard to the appearance of distemper observed on his pictures, it had been remarked that the pictures in the churches in Venice that had hung on south walls for a great many years had the appearance of tempera paintings *because the sun had dried up all the oil*, and that the colours of these pictures would wash off with water.

That the old Venetians always exposed their pictures to the sun, and the dew even, for five or six months, in order to prevent their becoming yellow ; that he himself had always done this, and without the least injury to his pictures.

That he had never found glue, &c., between the picture and the varnish in *old* pictures, but that this was the modern practice, because the varnish spread and adhered better on the glue than on the oil.

He said also that *Damara* varnish has been found in old pictures, and not *mastic*, which is modern.[1]

That varnish is found mixed with the paint and oil in old pictures.

That he had never heard of colours having been mixed with vernice liquida, as described by Caneparius,[2] and thinks this practice must have been introduced after the decline of the art.

Sig. D. also mentioned that Chilone, an old painter who died about seven or eight years ago, was acquainted with Canal and Canaletto, and that he had told Sig. D. that these artists used oil boiled on litharge, and re-

---

[1] It is almost unnecessary to remark that mastic was used by the old masters, and that Damara resin appears to be only recently introduced.

[2] Canepario was a Venetian physician. His work, De Atramentis, was published in London in 1660.

commended him to use it also, and that they frequently spread it over the whole picture.

That mastic varnish was sure to crack if used in painting pictures, but that Damara varnish was not so strong and would not crack.

The reason the darks stood higher than the lights on old pictures was because the painter went over them so often, and generally mixed varnish with them.

He said the oil always rose to the surface of the picture and dried dark; that they (the restorers of pictures) take off this crust of oil with potash.

That the green used by the Venetians was *verd' eterno*, and when used with oil the surface turns black; that when cleaning pictures the crust is scraped off and the green beneath is found as fine a colour as ever.

He told me also that he had made experiments by taking off some of the colours with a knife, and had had them analysed by a very skilful chemist (now dead).

The following are the colours he has found on Venetian pictures of the best period :—

White-lead, yellow, red, and other earths, ultramarine, native cinnabar,[1] cinabro d'Ollanda, verd' eterno, Cologne earth, asphaltum, lakes of kermes and madder; Naples yellow, very seldom used; orpiment, used by Bonifazio only; red-lead, very seldom used, and always with varnish; biadetto and verzino lake, used by Tintoretto only; verd' eterno and lake, always laid on with varnish.

Sig. D. stated that he had found no blue but ultramarine, and the reason this colour was raised so much above the surface of the pictures on draperies was that it was used very thick, because as it was coarsely ground it would otherwise look granular and show the white through.

---

[1] Probably the hard red hæmatite, which was called " cinabro minerale " by the Italians.

With regard to the grinding of the colours, he observed that the Venetians did not grind their colours fine, and that he has often picked out large grains of different colours which he has had analysed.

As to the propriety of early varnishing, he said that the Venetians did not varnish their pictures soon after finishing if they could avoid it, but that early varnishing was safer where the coats of colour had been thin than where they were laid on in great body.

He also remarked that many Venetian pictures which had hung in churches on northern walls had been destroyed by damp,[1] while those on south walls had, by the drying away of the oil, assumed the appearance of paintings in distemper.

In reply to my inquiry how he had ascertained the number of the coats of colour on pictures, he replied, " By taking them off one after another with a knife."

Sig. D. told me he generally used *fresh* linseed-oil unboiled; that he had once filtered the oil through animal charcoal, but that this rendered it too thin. The only preparation he used habitually was to filter the oil through four or five sheets of paper.

In consequence of what Sig. D. told me concerning the painting of Paolo, I inquired of Sig. C. whether colla (glue or size) had ever been found on the pictures of Paolo: he said, "Yes, certainly." But he did not *know* that it had been found on the oil-paintings of any other person.[2]

Having frequently observed in Paolo's pictures at

---

1 Extraordinary precautions were sometimes taken at Venice to defend oil-paintings from damp. See p. 880, n.

2 See Orsini, Elogio e Memorie di Pietro Perugino, 208, n., where it is stated that the blue in a picture by this artist at Montone was tempered with flour-paste, or starch (colla di farina). A part of Van Eyck's celebrated altar-piece at Ghent was painted in distemper. This discovery was made accidentally by some ignorant painters washing off the colour in cleaning it. See also Pacheco, Tratado de la Pintura, p. 373.

Venice that the colour appears laid on at once, the *dark* threads of the canvass being visible on great part of the picture without any appearance of a ground, I inquired the reason of this appearance, and why the white threads of the canvass should appear black. Sig. C. told me it was because Paolo frequently painted without any other ground than a little *colla*, just sufficient to bind the loose downy threads of the canvass and enable the brush to move freely; that this being absorbent the oil soaked into the canvass and turned it black, or nearly so.

It will perhaps be recollected that Pozzo, the Jesuit, generally painted without a ground, for he said the gesso caused the colours to change.[1] Callot, the Venetian, painted on the same kind of ground.

I mentioned having been informed that Titian had begun his pictures in chiaroscuro, and alluded to his early picture in the gallery Manfrin; but Sig. C. would not allow that it was painted in this manner, and he denied that Titian ever began his pictures in this way, but that he always laid in the abbozzo with the local colours, but very thinly and light in colour. In support of his opinion Sig. C. said there was an unfinished picture by Titian at Udine, in which part of the abbozzo may still be seen, having never been covered over. The S. Sebastian in the Barbarigo palace is another example by Titian of an abbozzo in his last manner. From the passage in Paolo Pino's Dialogue it appears that the practice of beginning pictures in chiaroscuro with brown was discontinued some time previous to 1548, the date of Pino's work. The probability is that Titian painted in his youth in the Flemish manner, but that he afterwards changed it to that usually ascribed to him.

In the Manfrini gallery is a picture said to have been painted by Titian when he was only sixteen years of

---

[1] See Lanzi, vol. ii. p. 228.

age. This picture is evidently painted in the manner described by Sig. D., that is, the chiaroscuro with brown and the flesh colours upon this ; the lights of the draperies are white, and the local colours glazed over it when dry : this is seen where the lake has been nearly all rubbed off.

I inquired of Sig. C. whether he had found the description given by Boschini [1] of Tintoretto's method of painting correct. He replied that Tintoretto did not begin his *pictures* in chiaroscuro, but that he made the *sketch* in water-colours in chiaroscuro, and then oiled it ; and when it was dry he painted in the local colours with oil. Several of these sketches, he told me, were in the possession of Sig. Bernardino Corniani.

I inquired of Sig. C. whether it was true that pictures which had been hung for a very long period of time (say 100 or 200 years) on a south wall were found in a different state from those which had hung on other walls. He answered "Yes: those which have been hung on north walls are always found destroyed by the damp, or at least much injured ; because the damp dissolves the glue of the ground and the picture scales off, while those on the south walls are always found dried up and burnt from the effects of the sun."

I also inquired his authority for saying that colours were frequently mixed with milk ; he replied, "It is an old tradition ; milk was much used by the ancients, and is mentioned by Pliny."

Another day I observed to the same professor, if the Venetians always required so long a period for their colours to dry before they laid on another coat of paint, how could those pictures be painted that were said to be executed in so short a time ? He replied

---

[1] See Ricche Minere. Boschini, speaking of Tintoretto, says, "Abbozzava il quadro tutto di chiaroscuro, havendo sempre oggetto principale di concertare tutta la massa come s' è detto," &c.

that Tintoretto had painted his Crucifixion entirely in twelve days, but that he had painted it up at once, without touching the same part twice, consequently without glazing. I asked whether this picture was in good preservation; his answer was "Benone" (excellent). Sig. C. told me also this picture was painted on a ground of flour-paste.[1]

Signor C. told me it had been found that Paolo Veronese's pictures were painted in the following manner and order:—

A ground of gesso.

The abbozzo.

The solid painting with colours mixed with oil.

A light coat of varnish.

Then the blues, vermilions, red lead, and white linen (biancheria), as well as the vermilion tints in flesh, were laid on in distemper, and over the whole picture was a coat of varnish. He added, the tints in distemper were so firmly united, that they would sometimes bear washing twice without being disturbed, and that the restorers were ignorant of the manner in which they were painted, until, having removed the varnish, they found the colours soluble in water.

I asked, how could the distemper colours be made to adhere upon oil colours? He said the distemper colours mixed with size and milk, adhered firmly to the thin coat of varnish, before mentioned.

Signor C. also said that Paolo used a general tint, composed of Cologne earth, or some other brown pigment, a little white lead, a little blue, and a very little terra rossa, which he spread thinly over the shadows,

---

[1] " La prontezza xè meterse davanti
Una gran tela, e de farina propia
Tamisar, e impastar figure in copia,
E senza natural, far casi tanti."
Boschini, La Carta del Navegar, p. 339.

(which had been previously prepared with a grey tint,) sometimes *a velatura*, sometimes *a sfregazzo*, and that he used this tint on every part of the picture, even on the heads.[1]

Speaking one day of the hardness of the old pictures, that when tried with the file, they scaled off, and presented almost a glassy surface, Signor C. said he had experienced this, but attributed it merely to the viscous nature of the oil, and the varnish with which it was mixed.

He also told me the pictures of Cima da Conegliano were painted with solid colours in a light key, and that the shades were laid on transparently with asphaltum. This also was discovered in the cleaning of his pictures; when the varnish was removed, the shades came away with it.[2]

Signor C. stated that the colour so much used by Titian in shading was not, as is generally supposed, terra rossa, but terra di Siena, burnt to different shades of colour, from yellowish brown to almost black.

I asked whether Titian had painted in tempera on his oil-paintings? Signor C. said No; Paolo Veronese being aware that oil darkened the colours, had employed tempera: but he did not know of any other who had done so. I inquired whether Paolo glazed much? He answered, " Very little, and in the shades only."

Did he use asphaltum? No, not that he was aware of. But Tintoretto used it extensively, and some few used *mommia*, but it was not generally approved of.

With regard to the use of oil, Signor C. said that Titian had used more oil than other artists of the same period; that he frequently glazed with oil, although he sometimes used varnish.

---

[1] See Zanetti, della Pittura Veneziana, p. 164.

[2] I observed that the blue draperies in the pictures of Tintoretto in the Scuola of S. Rocco were painted with a flat and uniform tint of colour, and that the shades had all disappeared, probably in cleaning.

He again mentioned that the Venetian school used little beside earths, and as few metallic colours as possible; and that the latter were used with varnish, except by Paolo Veronese, who applied them in distemper.

Speaking, again, of the practice of Titian, he observed he lived to a great age, and had time to improve, and he changed his methods several times; but those pictures best retain their colour which he painted in the manner of Gio. Bellino; he added, also, he had seen one picture by Titian the colours of which were very brilliant, and this was painted on a ground of terra rossa; and he added, "I think the terra rossa was laid on in distemper." He mentioned that this picture was on a ceiling.

Signor C. observed it was the same with Giorgione as with Titian; his early pictures were bright and clear, but the later ones were dark. He said that he had seen some pictures by the former as dark as could be. The same remark applied to Tintoretto; but he said Gian Bellino's were always transparent and bright.[1] Signor C. seemed to know nothing of the manner in which these pictures were painted; indeed he told me Gian Bellino did not begin his pictures in chiaroscuro. I then showed him the passage in Paolo Pino's 'Dialogue,'[2] "disegnare le tavole con tanta estrema diligenza, componendo il tutto di chiaro et scuro, come usava Giovan. Bellino, perchè è fatica gettata, havendosi à coprire il tutto con li colori," &c. Signor C. said this method was practised by the Roman school; but the restorers in the Venetian territories seem to know little or nothing of the practice of any but the Venetian school.

I called the attention of Signor C. to some passages in the Marquis Selvatico's work,[3] treating of the practice of oil-painting, where it is observed that the coat

---

[1] See Boschini, Ricche Minere. [2] Dialogo di Pittura, fo. 16.
[3] 'Sull' Educazione del Pittore storico odierno Italiano,' Padova, 1842.

of glue and gesso on the panels was, from the beginning to the end of the sixteenth century, covered with a coat of boiled oil. I asked, had he observed this? He replied he had frequently; but he always added the ground should be very absorbent to get rid of the oil.

He observed Titian never used white lead in the grounds. He also mentioned that Paolo Veronese always laid in the abbozzo with very little colour, so that only a faint impression of the colours should be left; and if the colour was too deep, that it was sometimes the practice to rub it down with pumice stone. On this abbozzo he laid the local colours solidly, but he seldom repeated his colours, or employed glazings; that many coats of paint were never found on any part of his pictures. In this respect his manner was entirely opposed to that of Titian, on whose pictures they frequently found seven, eight, or nine coats of colour.

Returning again to the subject of painting parts of the picture in tempera, Signor C. said that he had found the blue painted with varnish only, and that he had been assured that it was frequently painted in distemper, and that in this case there was no oil paint under it, but that where the skies in Paolo's pictures had turned green, they had been found to be painted in oil.

Speaking again of the old method, and of the different practice of modern artists in restoring pictures, Signor C. observed, "I think we have lost something. Every artist restores in his own way, and the present method of painting is very bad, much worse than it was in the last century." He added, that in restoring he had used oil with a small quantity of thin mastic varnish, in which a little honey was put, and that this had cracked *less* than other vehicles.

Signor C. said it was an error to paint with the colours *too dry*.[1] That this was the case with the

---

[1] See Requeno, Saggi sul Ristabilimento dell' Antica Arte de' Greci e Romani, vol. i. p. 163.

*

beautiful copy by Baroccio of Raphael's Transfiguration. When this picture was lined, the person en-
trusted with it neglected to secure the face of the
picture by pasting paper over it; the consequence was,
that when they attempted to raise the picture after
lining it, they found that, by wetting the back in order
to fix the new canvass, they had dissolved the ground,
and that the picture, which had become very dry, was
detached from it, and had dropped to pieces, and that
it could never be put together again properly.

He also told me that when he had been painting
with oil, and had found the oil penetrate through the
gesso ground, he had laid glue and gesso on the back
of that part where the oil had soaked through to absorb
it,[1] and when that was saturated, he had scraped it off,
and had laid on fresh gesso, and had repeated the
operation until all the superfluous oil was absorbed;
but this was only in cases where he had found it necessary to repeat the coats of oil colour. Everything
shows that the Venetians endeavoured to use as little
oil as possible.

Signor C. observed that another cause of the darkening of pictures has been the excessive use of asphaltum and mummy; that many used them as solid
colours (di corpo), whereas they should be used in
glazing only, and very thin, and that they should be
mixed with varnish only, and should not be ground
with oil or spirit of turpentine. He said, also, that
he believed mastic was not much used by the Italians
of the time of Titian, and that those who had analysed
Venetian pictures had never found wax in them.

He also observed that Paolo never painted the
abbozzo with colours tempered with water, and that yolk

---

[1] Merimée (de la Peinture à l'Huile, p. 31) mentions having seen a
picture by Sir Joshua Reynolds, in which the latter had employed a similar
contrivance to get rid of the superfluous oil, where he had found it necessary to repaint the head.

of egg had not been found on his pictures; that the
tempera vehicle used by Paolo consisted of animal glue.

Signor C. showed me a picture painted with boiled
oil which had not been varnished. I inquired how the
glossy surface was produced? he replied, "by polishing
it with a soft cloth."

I saw this morning Signor E., an artist who had
restored some pictures by Paolo Veronese. He told
me his plan, formed from observation of Titian's
pictures, is to lay on the canvass a thin ground of gesso
and glue, made of the primings of leather; over this
he spreads a coat of colour mixed with oil (the colour
is drab, made, I should think, of a little umber, white,
and a little black). The gesso ground absorbs the oil,
which makes the back of the canvass quite yellow. On
this ground the artist paints the whole picture with solid
colours, mixed with raw linseed oil, without any glazings. He says that glazings are never permanent, and
that nothing can make them so; and as a proof, he
told me there were in a certain palace several pictures
by Titian, which had always been covered by glasses.
That he was present when the glasses were removed for
the first time; when, to the surprise of every one
present, the glazings were found to have evaporated
from the pictures, and to have adhered to the inside of
the glass. I considered this incredible, and it certainly
appears to require proof, although it must be recollected that Lionardo da Vinci says, "Il verde fatto
dal rame, ancorchè tal color sia messo a olio, se ne va
in fumo," &c. If the colour evaporated from the picture, it would certainly be retained by the glass; and
this artist distinctly said that all the glazings were fixed
on the inside of the glass, exactly above the painting,
and that the effect of the different colours on the glass
was very singular. From that time, he added, that he
had left off glazing his pictures.

The same gentleman informed me that he had never found any colours in distemper on Titian's paintings; and that what people took for tempera painting on the pictures of Paolo Veronese was not really so, but was done in the following manner:—

The first painting was executed with colours mixed with oil, and the part to be painted on with metallic colours (or with such as darken with oil) was left to dry until it was *tacky*; the metallic colours were then applied, mixed with *water only*. The water evaporated, and the oil left on the picture in the first painting was sufficient to bind the upper layer of colours firmly to the picture.

Of the Grounds used by some of the principal Painters of Bologna.
[A communication from an eminent liner of pictures in that city.]

Panels were formerly prepared with gesso only, applied with the pencil in the same manner as is done by gilders; after this, the panels received a coat of glue or oil to prevent the colours from sinking in. In this way Francesco Francia prepared his panels, and Samacchini,[1] Sabbatini,[2] and Tibaldi[3] both their panels and canvass. Then came the Carracci. Ludovico[4] used no other priming than a thin coat of white lead and ochre mixed with oil, sufficiently thick to ensure a smooth surface, and he employed this priming as a shadow colour, which we know too well was the cause of the great change observable in his pictures. But Ludovico Carracci was not sufficiently remunerated for his pictures to enable him to incur great expenses in the priming. Annibale, his cousin, sometimes employed successfully on canvass, "creta,"[5] mixed with

---

[1] He died in 1577, aged 45.
[2] Also called Andrea di Salerno, was born about 1480, and died about 1545.
[3] Called also Pellegrini da Bologna, was born in 1527, died 1591.
[4] Born 1555, died 1619.
[5] Is this "creta" the same as "gesso Bolognese?"

white lead. Instead of "creta," Guercino generally adopted in his early pictures a thin priming of marble dust and size, and his pictures are thought to owe much of their brilliancy to this circumstance. In his second manner, the priming was thicker. When lining Guercino's pictures, it is generally found necessary to remove the ground as well as the canvass. The ground sometimes appears to be composed of hard and gritty terra rossa, and which is thought to have been procured outside the Porta Castiglione at Bologna. Grounds are now prepared extremely well at Bologna and at Rome. The canvass is all the produce of Bologna, which province produces hemp of the finest quality.

The most durable and unchangeable pictures are stated to be those painted on gesso. In the eighteenth century coarse open canvass, the holes of which were filled up with strong glue, was introduced; pictures painted on these canvasses were not durable, for in time the colours scaled off.

The following particulars relative to the method of painting in oil as practised by the Parmasan School were communicated to me by a distinguished painter of Parma :—

1st. That gesso grounds were used.

2nd. That neither size nor varnish was laid over this ground, which was suffered to absorb the oil.

3rd. That the picture was begun in chiaroscuro.

4th. That the first colours were painted with raw nut oil.

5th. That in the glazings and retouchings varnish was used.

I was informed that a professor of that city had devoted much time and attention to the study of the good method of oil-painting, and that he knew more about it than any other person.

The professor had been suffering from illness; but at

the request of the Cav. Pezzana, of the Ducal Library at Parma, he kindly permitted us to pay him a short visit. He perfectly recollected having sent a bottle of varnish to an English artist, and he said that the reason he had not written to him was because he had lost the use of his hand, and could not write legibly ; that he had written out the recipe for some person, but that it proved useless, for the varnish could not be made from this recipe on account of the difficulty of the manipulation.

I asked, could he tell me the ingredients ? He said it consisted of amber in the natural state, and the higher coloured the better, dissolved in oil of spike, and this was rendered slower in drying by the addition of oil (balsam) of copaiba.

I immediately inquired whether he had found any document showing it was used by Correggio ?

He said No ; it was the result of his own observation and study.

I asked whether he had ever analysed any of Correggio's pictures ?

He replied without hesitation, No, no ; and as I saw it was painful to him to talk, I took my leave.

On my return to the library, I was told that the professor *had* analysed parts of pictures by Raphael, and had found amber.

In one respect my informant was probably mistaken, —namely, as to the artist whose pictures had been analysed, since the professor had said the varnish he had made was that of *Correggio*. It appeared, however, quite clear that amber varnish had been found on the pictures of one or other of these great painters.

§ 2. Colours used in Painting.

The Italians appear generally to have exercised the same care in the purification and preparation of their pigments as the Flemish, Dutch, and French artists. This is apparent from the directions preserved in those

manuscripts which treat in an especial manner of the
manufacture of colours, but it is seldom alluded to in
the treatises on painting. The omission in the last-
named works is easily accounted for on the supposition
that the different processes of washing, purifying, and
grinding colours were taught to the students during the
first six years of their long apprenticeship. It is probable also that many studios possessed manuals or handbooks like those published in the following pages. The
Byzantine MS. of Mount Athos, the Treatise of Cennini,
and several MSS. now in the British Museum, are
works of this class. In the MS. of Le Begue several
instances are mentioned of the loan of MSS. of this description by different painters to Alcherius ; and Cennini
wrote his treatise, as he himself informs us, for the
benefit of all who studied the arts. It was, therefore,
less necessary to introduce such directions in works of
higher pretensions.

Next, perhaps, in importance to the purification and
preparation of the pigments was their agreement or
incompatibility with each other. This subject occupied
the attention of artists at a very early period ; it is
noticed in the third book of Eraclius,[1] and in the Marciana MS.[2] The subject is also alluded to in the
Paduan MS. and in the Treatise of Lomazzo ;[3] and
these passages are useful in showing what pigments
were actually mixed together by the old painters, and
what mixtures were to be avoided. Among the latter
were verdigris and white lead, orpiment and white lead,
indigo and cochineal lake, Indian lac lake and white
lead. In some cases the mixtures of pigments were
not such as would be recommended by modern professors of chemistry ; but it is possible that, as the old
masters were so select in the choice of vehicles for
certain colours, they could regulate the drying of

---

[1] Cap. lvii. p. 252.   [2] P. 609.
[3] Trattato, p. 193—195. See also De Piles' Elémens de Peinture, p. 110.

these pigments in such a manner as to prevent their exercising any chemical agency upon each other. Boschini[1] praises the colours used by Gian Bellino, especially the ultramarine, which, he says, compared with the moderns, put the latter to shame by their greater vivacity and beauty. Boschini attributes this not altogether to the goodness of the colours, but to the skill of Bellino in every part of the art.

The choice of good pigments was another point which engaged the attention of artists : a few hints on this subject may be collected from the work of Volpato.[2] The same work also contains directions[3] for burning earths of different colours.

The different drying properties of the several pigments were also studied by the old painters, and the desiccation of some which were too long in drying was assisted by the addition of pounded glass, white copperas, or verdigris, with or without boiled oil, as the nature of the colour required.

The action of oil on the pigments, and especially on mineral pigments, was also well understood by the old masters ; and where oil was known to be injurious, varnish, or, in some instances, size was substituted for it.

White Pigments.

Several white substances used as pigments and in the preparation of colours and grounds, are mentioned in the following treatises. The white pigment universally employed for oil painting is *white lead,* which is mentioned in the MSS. under its various synonymes of albus, blacha, bracha, blanchet, biacca, and ceruse. It was called albayalde by the Spaniards.

White lead is considered a good dryer, and is even used to render oil more drying ; it is, therefore, remarkable that it should be classed in the Brussels MS.[4]

---

[1] Ricche Minere.   [2] P. 745.   [3] P. 745, 747.   [4] P. 818.

among the colours which do not dry well. De Piles,
however, states[1] that it dries with difficulty, especially
in winter, if ground with new oil, or if it has been
recently ground. The 'Traité de Mignature' of Christophe Ballard[2] contains "a great secret to make white
lead dry without changing." This consists in tempering it with oil of turpentine.

The Italians, and especially the Venetians, were extremely careful in the preparation of their white lead,[3]
which was generally purified by washing. Fra Fortunato of Rovigo, in his 'Raccolta di Secreti,' gives the
following recipe "for rendering white lead extraordi-
narily white. Take white lead in scales, select the
finest quality, grind it well on marble with vinegar and
it will become black, then take an earthen vessel full of
water and wash your white well, and let it settle to the
bottom, and pour off the water. Grind it again with
vinegar and again wash it, and when you have repeated
the operation three or four times, you will have white
lead which will be as excellent for miniature painting
as for painting in oil."[4]

There is scarcely a doubt that the pigment called
" *lime* " was the preparation of lime mentioned by
Cennini[5] and Imperato,[6] under the name of Bianco
San Giovanni. The lime was prepared by macerating it
in water until it had lost all causticity. According to
Imperato, pulverized white marble was added to the

---

[1] Elémens de Peinture, p. 140.

[2] Lyon, 1693, 6th Ed., p. 216. The first edition was published in 1682.

[3] " Lindo alvayalde de Venecia"—" el meyor alvayalde que se hallare,
i lo es sobre todos el de Venecia." Pacheco, Tratado, pp. 354, 387.

[4] Per rendere la biacca più bianca straordinariamente. Prendete biacca
di piombo in scaglie, elegete la più bella, e macinatela bene sul marmo con
aceto, e diventarà nera, allora prendete un vaso di terra piena d'acqua, e
lavata il vostro bianco bene, poi lasciatelo bene dar in fondo, e verrate
l' acqua per inclinazione. Tornatela a macinare con aceto et a lavare ; e
fatta questa operatione med[a.] 3 o 4 volte, che havera una biacca che sarà
perfettam[te] bella tanto per miniare, quanto per dipingere a olio.

[5] Cap. 58.   [6] Istoria Naturale, lib. iv. cap. 13.

lime. This pigment was used in fresco painting. It is
known to later authors by the name of *biancho secco*.[1]

White chalk, marble dust, gesso, the *bone of cuttle
fish, alumen,* and *travertine,* were occasionally used as
white pigments. They were also frequently mixed with
transparent vegetable colours to give them body.

Calcined hart's-horn or *bones* were used occasionally
as a white pigment.[2]

Egg-shell white was employed in fresco painting.
With reference to this pigment, Lomazzo[3] says, that
" there is another thing which, in fresco painting, causes
the colours to remain unchanged as when first applied
on the damp lime ; and this, which is one of the rare
inventions belonging to the technical part of the art,
consists of the shells of eggs finely ground, and mixed
in greater or less proportion with all the colours."

Terra di cava, terra da boccali, or *terretta,* a white
earth used by potters. It is mentioned by Volpato[4]
and Baldinucci[5] to have been employed in the priming
for oil paintings.

The pigment called *alumen* by Eraclius[6] appears to
have been allume scagliuola, a kind of stone resembling
talc, of which, when calcined, is made the "gesso da
oro," or gesso of the gilders, which is also used for the
grounds of pictures. According to Eraclius[7] it was
prepared for painting by grinding with gum and water,
and was distempered when required with white of egg.

Travertine is a calcareous stone, sometimes light and
porous, sometimes dense and heavy. It is of various
colours, white, grey, yellowish, reddish yellow, and
variegated. It is found at Pisa and Tivoli. The travertine from Tivoli is white. It was used by painters
to give a body to lake made from verzino.

---

[1] Lomazzo, Trattato, pp. 192, 194.
[2] Sloane MS., No. 1754 ; Strasburg MS., cited by Mr. Eastlake, 'Materials,' p. 133.   [3] Trattato, p. 191.
[4] P. 730.   [5] Voc. Dis.   [6] P. 245.   [7] P. 232.

White marble is mentioned as a pigment for tempera painting by Palomino.[1]

" A most beautiful white pigment," probably for miniature painting, is described in the Paduan MS.[2] It is composed of powdered Venetian glass (cristallo) and sulphur, and is precisely similar to the opaque white glass used for painting pottery, for which recipes are given in the second and third books of Eraclius.[3]

Yellow Pigments.

Arzica.—Two pigments are known by this name in medieval MSS.

The first kind of *arzica* is mentioned by Cennini (cap. 50), who says that it was much used at Florence for miniature painting. With regard to the nature of the pigment, he observes merely that it is an artificial colour. The Bolognese MS., written about the time of Cennini, or soon after, proves[4] that it was a yellow lake made from the herb " gualda," which is the Spanish and Provençal name for the Reseda luteola. The plant has been used as a yellow dye not only in England but in all Europe, from a very early period. This yellow lake was known to the Spanish painters under the name of ancorca[5] or encorca, and when used for the kind of painting called " estofado," was mixed with lemon juice and weak size.

The second kind of *arzica* is stated to be a yellow earth for painting, of which the moulds for casting brass are formed.[6] A yellow loam is still used for this purpose in the foundries at Brighton. It is brought by sea from Woolwich, and when washed and dried it yields an ochreous pigment of a pale yellow colour.

---

[1] Museo Pictorico, vol. ii. p. 113, 152.

[2] P. 704.   [3] P. 201, 205.   [4] P. 483.

[5] Indice de los Terminos Primativos de la Pintura, appended to Palomino's Museo Pictorico.

[6] Table of Synonymes, p. 19, 23.

When burnt it changes to an orange colour, which is likely to prove valuable in painting.

Arzicon, or *Arsicon*.—In the Table of Synonymes arzicon is considered synonymous with *arzica*. This is not the case. Le Begue is, however, correct in saying that it is the same as orpiment. It is undoubtedly a contraction or corruption of *arsenicon*, which Vitruvius (lib. vii. cap. vii.) says was the Greek name for orpiment. The term arzicon must not be confounded with *azarcon*, the Spanish name for *red lead*.

Auripigmentum or *Orpiment*.—There was a native as well as an artificial pigment known by this name. The former is found in masses in the neighbourhood of Naples, and in other volcanic countries. It has the great advantage over the artificial pigment of being less poisonous. The artificial pigment only seems to have been known to Cennini.[1] Being difficult to grind, powdered glass was mixed with it, as we are expressly told, for this purpose.[2] And Pacheco directs[3] that orpiment should be mixed with linseed oil, made drying by boiling it with red lead or copperas in powder.[4] For miniature painting it was tempered with gum-water and white of egg. Its brilliant yellow colour renders it a desirable pigment for draperies in oil painting, but it is not durable when mixed with oil, and dries very slowly. The author of the third book of Eraclius says,[5] " If you mix oil with it, it will never dry." Lebrun remarks,[6] that " fat oil should be added to orpiment to make it dry, otherwise it will never dry." Lomazzo also mentions[7] that it was mixed with pulverized glass, but he does not state for what purpose the latter was added. De Mayerne, however, states[8] that Vandyck was accustomed to mix powdered glass with orpiment

---

[1] Cap. 47. [2] P. 503. [3] Tratado, p. 388.
[4] He was evidently unacquainted with the fact that lead decomposes orpiment. [5] P. 234. [6] P. 813. [7] Trattato, p. 192.
[8] See Mr. Eastlake's ' Materials,' &c., p. 534.

to make it dry.   Pacheco[1] recommends it for the same
purpose; but there is some doubt as to the propriety of
this mixture.

In the third book of Eraclius it is directed[2] that
orpiment should be crushed in a leather bag, and then
ground upon marble with a little calcined bone; in this
respect the directions resemble those given in the Strassburg[3] and also in the Sloane MSS., No. 1754, where
calcined hartshorn is said to be the only substance
which can be safely mixed with orpiment to lighten it.

Orpiment is mentioned by Biondo[4] among the pigments used by the Venetians; and Boschini states[5] that
it was employed by Pordenone and by Paolo Veronese.
A professor of painting at Venice informed me that he
had found it, by analysis, on the pictures of Bonifazio
only.   It is generally asserted, and there appears every
reason to think justly, that orpiment should not be
mixed with any other colour, and especially with white
lead, the bad effects of which were well known to the
Italians.[6]   But there is evidence that the Italians were
in the habit of mixing it with ultramarine or with
indigo to make a brilliant green.[7]   The Marciana MS.[8]
recommends that white lead should be laid under orpiment, because it has no body.

This pigment was called jalde, or oropimente, by the
Spaniards.   Pacheco directs,[9] that for the second or
half tints of draperies the orpiment should be burnt in
an iron shovel over the fire.   Palomino, after describing
the method of painting draperies with orpiment, remarks,[10] that he did not approve of the colour, which
dried very badly and required many precautions in
using it, and that it was, moreover, liable to turn black;

---

[1] Tratado, p. 388.   [2] P. 239.   [3] Materials, &c., p. 133, 438.
[4] Della Pittura, cap. 24, f. 20.   [5] Ricche Minere.
[6] See p. 609, and Armenini, lib. ii. cap. 8.
[7] Cennini, cap. 53, 55; Borghini, Riposo, p. 170; Marciana MS.,
p. 611.   [8] P. 611.   [9] Tratado, p. 388.   [10] Vol. ii. p. 252.

this, he adds, may be prevented by varnishing it as soon as it is dry.

Giallolino, Giallorino, or *Gialdolino,* strictly signifies a pale yellow. It is a diminutive of *giallo.*

There appears to be so much confusion in the accounts of this colour by different writers, that it will be necessary to treat of it at some length.

According to Borghini[1] and Baldinucci[2] there were two kinds of Giallolino : the first, called " Giallolino fino," which was brought from Flanders, was used in painting in oil, and contained lead ; the other, which was brought from Venice, was composed of " Giallo di vetro " and " Giallolino fino " above mentioned. Lomazzo[3] speaks of three kinds of Giallolino, which, he says, are artificial pigments, but the terms in which he mentions them are not sufficiently precise to determine exactly their names or composition.

Sig. Branchi[4] found on analysis that the giallolino of the old pictures at Pistoia, mentioned in the documents published by Ciampi, consisted of the yellow oxide of lead, which, he said, was known by this name in the sixteenth century. In support of this he quotes Cesalpino, who mentions a pigment then prepared from burnt or calcined lead, which was commonly called giallolino—" pigmentum pictoribus . . . quod hodie arte paratur ex plumbo usto, vulgoque giallolinum vocant."[5] And again, Cesalpino[6] says, " the ashes (calx) of burnt lead assume a yellow colour, on account of the black soot mixed with the white ; tin, however, gives a white calx.[7] Painters use the former for lights and for representing flame, calling it giallolino. Potters use the

---

[1] Riposo, p. 166. [2] Voc. Dis.
[3] Trattato, p. 192. [4] Lettera di Branchi, &c., p. 13.
[5] De Metallicis, lib. ii. cap. 62. [6] Lib. iii. cap. vii.
[7] Thomson (Annals, &c., p. 166) says, that the grey oxide of tin, when brought to a full red heat, takes fire, and acquiring an excess of oxygen, passes to a yellow colour.

latter to give a white colour to their vessels." Professor Branchi adds, that this is confirmed by Ferrante Imperato,[1] a Neapolitan writer of the same century. This author says, " Giallolino, which is made of burnt ceruse (the first degree of alteration by fire), imitates the colour of the yellow broom."

Dr. Fabroni,[2] of Arezzo, analysed the colours of a miniature of the fourteenth or beginning of the fifteenth century, and he ascertained that the yellow pigment consisted of " massicot," which, he says, is the first gradation of the " cerussa usta " of the ancients.

In further confirmation of the above statements it may be observed, that neither Cennini, Borghini, Lionardo da Vinci, Lomazzo, Baldinucci, nor the Paduan MS., mention " massicot," while they all speak of giallolino.[3] It may also be observed, that Lebrun, the author of the Brussels MS., mentions[4] no yellows but ochre and *massicot*; the latter, he says, serves for the fine or bright yellows. Van Mander, Hoogstraten, De Bie, and Beurs,[5] in enumerating the yellow pigments used by the Flemings, mention ochre, massicot, and yellow lake, to which all but De Bie add orpiment. Bulengerus[6] also names massicot, which he calls " fin jaune."

As a further proof of the identity of these pigments, it may be observed, that Haydocke, the translator of Lomazzo's Treatise on Painting, published in 1598, translates *giallolino* by the word *massicot*.[7] The last au-

---

[1] Istoria Naturale, lib. iv. cap. 42.

[2] Ricerche Chimiche sopra le Miniature di un Manuscritto, Memoria del Dr. A. Fabroni di Arezzo, letta nelle Adunanze Accademiche de' 13 Genn. e 17 Febb. 1811.

[3] See Cennini, Trattato, cap. 46. Borghini, Riposo, p. 166. Lionardo da Vinci, Trattato, cap. 352, 353. Lomazzo, Trattato, p. 191, 192, 193, &c. Baldinucci, Voc. Dis.

[4] Cap. 1, No. 6 ; cap. 7, No. 5.

[5] See Mr. Eastlake's ' Materials,' &c., p. 438, 440.

[6] De Pictura, &c., lib. ii. cap. iii.

[7] A Tracte, containing the Artes of curious Painting, Carving, and Build-

thority is particularly valuable on account of the translation having been made so soon after the publication
of the original work.

Lomazzo mentions [1] " Giallolino di fornace di Fiandra e di Alamagna." From this it would appear that
two kinds of Giallolino were brought from the north
into Italy. These were probably the two kinds of
massicot mentioned by Félibien, who states [2] they were
made of calcined lead, " Le massicot jaune et le massicot blanc," or as they are called in Jombert's edition
of the Elémens de Peinture, " le massicot doré et le
massicot pâle." Haydocke translates the above-mentioned passage thus, " Yeallowe of the Flaunders fornace, and of Almany, commonly called *masticot* and
generall."

There is no doubt, therefore, that the " Giallolino
Fino " and " Giallolino di Fornace di Fiandra " was
massicot, or the yellow oxide of lead, the " Fin jaune "
of the French.

The yellow pigment prepared from lead is described
by Theophilus (cap. i.), who, however, does not give
it a name. The same pigment is mentioned in the
MS. of Le Begue.

We now come to the second kind of factitious giallolino which Baldinucci [3] states was brought from Venice,
and was composed of the giallolino di Fiandra and
giallo di vetro. Borghini says [4] nearly the same. In
the Bolognese MS. No. 272, is a recipe for " Vetrio
giallo per patrenostro o ambre," the ingredients of
which are lead 1 lb. and tin 2 lbs., melted and calcined.
The recipe which follows this, No. 273, is entitled " A
fare zallolino [5] per dipengiare," and the directions are to

ing, written first in Italian by Jo. Paul Lomatius, painter, of Milan, and
Englished by R. H. (Haydocke), student in physick, 1598, p. 99.
[1] Trattato, p. 191.   [2] Principes, &c., p. 299.
[3] Voc. Dis.   [4] Riposo, p. 166.
[5] It will not escape observation that the *gi* in this word are changed into
z, as was usual among the Venetians.

take 2 lbs. of the above-mentioned glass, 2½ lbs. of
minium, and ½ lb. of sand from the Val d'Arno: the
ingredients are to be pulverized finely, and then refined
in the furnace.   I can scarcely doubt that this is the
second kind of giallolino mentioned by Baldinucci and
Borghini.   It may also be the third variety mentioned
by Lomazzo.[1]

It must be observed that Marcucci does not mention giallolino among the modern Italian pigments;
he describes[2] three yellow pigments, namely, *giallo di
Napoli* (Naples yellow), which he says is composed of
the yellow oxide of lead and the oxide of antimony,
massicot, or the yellow oxide of lead, and *giallo minerale,*
which was composed of muriate of lead.

The earliest notice I have met with in Italian writers
of a pigment called Naples yellow, is in the work of
Pozzo the Jesuit.[3]   The name he applies to the pigment is "Luteolum Romæ dicitur Luteolum Napolitanum," and he enumerates it among the pigments to
be used in fresco.   He also gives a list of colours
improper for this kind of painting, among which we
find cerussa, minium, and luteolum Belgicum, which
can be no other than giallolino di Fiandra.   The conclusion then is unavoidable that the luteolum Napolitanum was not the yellow oxide of lead.   In the French
translation of Pozzo's Treatise on Fresco-painting [4] the
term luteolum Napolitanum is very properly translated
Jaune de Naples, and luteolum Belgicum by Jaune
de Flandres.   In other parts of Jombert's edition of the
' Elémens de Peinture,' [5] two kinds of massicot, the
yellow or golden and the pale or white, are mentioned;
but they are not identified with jaune de Naples, which

[1] Trattato, p. 192.   [2] Saggio, &c., p. 66.
[3] The Treatise on Fresco Painting, appended to his work on Perspective,
published at Rome, 1693—1702.
[4] See Jombert's ed. of the Elémens de Peinture, by De Piles, Paris, 1766.
[5] Elémens de Peinture, pp. 252, 286, &c.

is mentioned as a distinct colour. The Italian translator of Pozzo's treatise [1] renders luteolum Napolitanum
by giallolino di fornace, which he says is called giallolino di Napoli, and luteolum Belgicum by giallolino di
Francia. This writer does not appear to have been
aware that giallolino di fornace and giallolino di
Fiandra were synonymous. Giallolino di Francia appears to be a mistake for giallolino di Fiandra.

Félibien, [2] Pomet, [3] Pozzo, [4] and the author of the
article "Fresque" in the Encyclopédie describe the
pigment jaune de Naples as a natural production found
near mines of sulphur, which is used in fresco-painting,
although it is not so good as the colour formed of
ochre and white. M. d'Arclais de Montamy, in his
Treatise on the Colours for Enamel Painting, describes
it as a stone of a pale or deep yellow colour, which appears to be composed of a species of yellow sand, loosely
combined. He believes it to be the production of a
volcano. He adds that Naples yellow may be considered as saffron of Mars, first produced by a volcano,
and that then the colour was brought to perfection by
remaining in the earth, or as a ferruginous substance,
the vitrification of which was afterwards decomposed.[5]
Cennini's description [6] of this pigment is as follows:—
" There is a yellow colour called giallolino, which is
artificial and very compact. It is as heavy as a stone,
and difficult to break. This colour is used in fresco,
and lasts for ever (that is on walls and on tempera
pictures). It must be ground like the preceding with
water. It is difficult to grind ; and before grinding,

---

[1] At the end of the Abecedario Pittorico (Naples, 1788).

[2] De l'Architecture, &c., 1697, p. 292.

[3] Histoire Générale des Drogues.

[4] See the French translation of this Treatise in Jombert's edition of the
Elémens de Peinture, by De Piles, p. 191.

[5] Treatise on Painting and the Composition of Colours, translated from
the French of M. Constant de Massoul. London, 1797. P. 137.

[6] Trattato, cap. xlvi.

as it is very difficult to pulverize, it should be broken in a bronze mortar, in the same way as the lapis amatito. When employed in painting, it is a very beautiful yellow ; and with this colour and other mixtures which I will describe to you, you may paint beautiful foliage and herbage. And I have been informed that this colour is a real stone, produced in volcanoes ; and it is for this reason that I said it is formed artificially, but not in the chemical laboratory."

From this account it is evident that Cennini is describing a native mineral which he considers to be produced by volcanic agency—" Però ti dico sia color artificiato, ma non di archimia." The accordance of this description with that of the jaune de Naples just mentioned is apparent. It is therefore certain that there was a native yellow pigment found in the neighbourhood of volcanoes, the nature of which was not well understood, which was known by the name of giallolino or giallolino di Napoli and jaune de Naples. This is the opinion also of Branchi and Watin.[1] In this case therefore giallolino and giallolino di Napoli (Naples yellow) were really synonymous. There is also an artificial pigment called Naples yellow or jaune de Naples, which, by some authors, has been considered to consist of an earth coloured with weld (gaude, Reseda luteola) and by others to be composed of the oxides of lead and antimony with other ingredients. The last is the general opinion, and there appears to be no doubt the modern pigment of this name is composed of these oxides.[2] The vegetable pigment above mentioned is the *arzica* of Cennini, the Le Begue, the Bolognese MS., and Borghini, and the *ancorca* of Palomino.[3]

---

[1] Lettera di Branchi, p. 12.

[2] See Merimée, de la Peinture à l'Huile, p. 110 ; Marcucci, Saggio Analitico de' Colori, p. 66; Lettera di Branchi, p. 12; Bachhoffner, Chemistry as applied to the Arts, &c.

[3] Indice de los Terminos Primativos de la Pintura—appended to Palomino's Museo Pictorico.

I consider it therefore established that there were three kinds of giallolino employed by the old Italian Masters, namely :—

1. A native mineral yellow pigment known by the names of giallolino, giallolino di Napoli, jaune de Naples, luteolum Napolitanum.

2. An artificial pigment which was composed of the yellow protoxide of lead, and which was called giallolino, giallolino fino, giallolino di fornace di Fiandra, giallolino di fornace, giallolino di Fiandra, luteolum Belgicum, genuli (the last is a Spanish term) and massicot, of which there were two varieties; namely, the golden or yellow and the white or pale massicot.

3. An artificial pigment made at Venice composed of giallolino fino and a certain kind of "giallo di vetro," or vitreous yellow, for which a recipe is given in the Bolognese MS. No. 273, in the Venetian dialect, and which appears to have been the hornaza of the Spaniards.

I consider it also established that there are two kinds of Naples yellow, namely :—

1. A native mineral pigment found in the neighbourhood of volcanoes, the nature of which is not accurately known, and which was called giallolino, giallolino di Napoli, and jaune de Naples, and which is synonymous with the first kind of giallolino above mentioned.

2. An artificial pigment now in use composed of the oxides of lead and antimony, called also giallo di Napoli, jaune de Naples, and Naples yellow, which was not known to the old Italian artists.

From the above statements it will be seen that it is scarcely possible to determine which of the three pigments called "giallolino" is alluded to when the term occurs alone in writers on art. It is certain, however, that one or other of these pigments was much used by the Italian masters. Giallolino was recommended by Lionardo da Vinci [1] to be mixed with white lead and

---

[1] Trattato, cap. 353.

lake for flesh tints. There is reason to suppose it was also used by Raphael, since it is mentioned in an account of payments for colours found on the back of a drawing by the great painter preserved in the Academy at Venice, and supposed to be in his hand-writing.

It was seldom found among the colours of Venetian pictures which have been analysed. It is stated on the authority of Boschini [1] (who mentions that the pigment was not generally approved by the Venetians) to have been used by Giacomo Bassano and Paolo Veronese, and it is also enumerated among the pigments named by Biondo.[2]

Massicot is however frequently disapproved as a pigment, especially when mixed with white.[3] We have the evidence of Cennini that the native pigment called giallolino was a durable colour. Pacheco remarks that he has employed *genuli,* which has surpassed in brilliancy and beauty the best orpiment, excelling it in durability ; he adds that it is preserved in water like white, and is very drying.

Giallo in Vetro, or Giallo di Vetro.—Borghini states[4] that this pigment, which is used in fresco, is made in the glass furnaces, and he recommends that it should be purchased ready made. It is probable, as has been before observed, that this pigment was of the same nature as the vetrio giallo mentioned in the Bolognese MS. No. 272 to have been composed of tin and lead calcined.

The *ochres,* so remarkable for their durability and variety, will always be among the most valuable yellow pigments. Many varieties are enumerated by writers on art, among which may be mentioned arzica, ochre de ru, mottée de sil, &c. The best kinds are sold in Italy in the lump, and Volpato recommends [5] that such

---

[1] Ricche Minere.   [2] Della Pittura.

[3] See Mr. Eastlake's ' Materials,' p. 440.   [4] Riposo, p. 166.

[5] P. 745.

should be preferred to those which are sold in powder, because the first are in the natural state and no other material is mixed with them ; " for," he continues, " the vendors are accustomed to falsify everything."

During the middle ages, an imitation of the Attic ochre of Pliny was in use. This pigment, to which the name of "Sillacetus" was given, was a preparation of white chalk or gesso, saturated with the colour extracted from the wall-flower [1] (Viola lutea).

Vegetable yellow pigments were of two kinds—those which were precipitated on a white earth, such as the different kinds of yellow lake, and those which were used as transparent colours, without any other preparation than that of expressing and inspissating the juice of certain plants. Of the latter kind were *saffron*, the *zafferano* of Cennini, and aloes; the latter was chiefly used for colouring varnishes, or for heightening the colour of verdigris in the manner recommended by Lionardo da Vinci.[2]

Giallo santo was a kind of yellow lake, which was made from various plants. It was sometimes prepared from the berries of the buckthorn [3] (spincervino), sometimes from the flowers of the yellow goat's-beard (barba di becco), sometimes from the flowers of the yellow broom, sometimes from weld or dyer's weed: the latter is the arzica of Cennini and the Bolognese MS. The sillacetus of the Table of Synonymes was a yellow lake.

The French call pigments of this description "*stil de grain*," and include under them not only those pigments which are of a pure yellow colour, but such as incline to green. The English term for this class of pigments is or was "*pink.*" Thus we have "*Dutch pink,*" "*Italian pink,*" "*brown pink,*" &c.

Volpato observes [4] that giallo santo should be of a

---

[1] Table of Synonymes, p. 36.   [2] Trattato, cap. 120.   [3] P. 708.   [4] P. 744.

fine colour, that in grinding it should become very liquid, so as to require but very little oil to temper it, and that it should dry very quickly, which is a sign that it is pure ; but if it hardens and requires a great deal of oil in grinding, this is a proof that it contains dust and other impurities, and in this case it dries slowly and fades on the pictures.

As another test, he directs[1] that the colour should be exposed to the sun; if it faded, it was bad. He also mentions that it should not be kept in water. Giallo santo appears to have been extensively used by the Italians, and although it is included among the colours which Boschini says the Venetians "detested like the plague," it appears, on his own evidence, that it was employed by Giacomo Bassano in shading yellow drapery. The pigment is also mentioned by Biondo, by Armenini, by Borghini, and in the Paduan MS. Malvasia says that it was used by Tiarini and Cavedone.

Saffron, zafferano, the crocus of the middle ages, is produced from the flowers of the crocus.   Peter de S. Audemar informs us that saffron was produced in France in his time; but he says the French saffron was not good; he mentions that this drug was imported from Spain and Italy, and that the best kind was brought from Sicily, and was called *coriscos.* The plant is cultivated extensively in England in the neighbourhood of Saffron-Walden, and the name of the place is derived from this circumstance.   It was brought into England from the Levant in the reign of Edward III., and the manner in which it was introduced is thus described by Hakluyt:[2]—"It is reported at Saffron-Walden, that a pilgrim, purposing to do good to his country, stole a head of saffron, and hid the same in his palmer's staff, which he had made hollow before on purpose, and so he brought this root into this realm with venture of his

---

[1] P. 744.   [2] See Beckmann's Inventions, vol. i. p. 179, n.

life ; for if he had been taken, by the law of the country
from whence it came, he had died for the fact."

To these vegetable pigments may be added *gamboge*,
which is a gum resin that flows from the Hebradendron
Cambogioides. It derives its name from Kamboia, a
river in Siam, in the vicinity of which the gum is obtained in abundance. It was certainly in use in the
Venetian territories at the period when the Paduan
MS. was written, and is believed to have been employed
by Paolo Veronese. It was sometimes purified by being
ground up with lemon juice and roche alum.[1]

Gamboge is prepared for painting in oil by depriving
it of its gum. Marcucci recommends[2] the following
method :—" Gamboge of the finest colour is to be
ground with water ; it is then to be put into a china
cup, and a sufficient quantity of water is to be poured
on it to cover it twice its own height ; after being left
thus two days, the supernatant water is to be decanted,
and the resin which remains at the bottom of the water
is to be dried. When quite dry, a quantity of spirit of
turpentine sufficient to cover it is to be poured over it,
and the cup is to be placed upon warm ashes until the
resin is quite dissolved and incorporated with the turpentine. A little nut oil is then to be added, and it is
to be preserved for use." Marcucci adds, "this is
excellent for glazing yellow and green draperies ; for
the latter it must be mixed with ultramarine." Other
modes of preparation are mentioned by Mr. Eastlake
in his recent work.[3]

It appears from the Brussels MS.[4] that gamboge
was in use in France in 1635. Palomino remarks[5] that this pigment, which he calls "Gutiambar,"
was employed to glaze yellow draperies, and that it
dried so badly as to require the addition of the common drying oil.

---

[1] P. 660.   [2] Saggio, &c., p. 135.   [3] Materials, &c., p. 442.
       [4] P. 784.   [5] Museo Pictorico, vol. ii. p. 53.

A recipe for an artificial pigment somewhat analogous to the modern pigment called "Gallstone" appears in the second book of Eraclius. It consisted of the gall of a large fish precipitated on a white earth. It was said to have resembled orpiment in colour.

Aloes.—The inspissated juice of the aloë spicata. The plant is a native of Africa. The finest kind of aloes has a brilliant reddish-brown colour, and is translucent at the edges of the fragmented pieces; its fracture is smooth and conchoidal, its odour aromatic and rather agreeable, its powder deep gold colour, its taste intensely bitter and nauseous. But such is rarely found in trade; it is generally opaque, of a dull brown, when it is called *Hepatic aloes*, often passing into black, when it is denominated *Caballine aloes*. It appears to be a mixture of gum, extractive, and a little resin. It is nearly soluble in boiling water, but as the solution cools, some resin and altered extractive are thrown down; the alkalies and their carbonates form with it permanent solutions, and proof spirit dissolves and retains it with only a slight precipitation of resin. Caballine aloes are mentioned by Lionardo da Vinci[1] as an improvement to the colour of verdigris, and he recommends its solution in warm spirit (aqua vitæ).

Orange-coloured Pigments.

The ochreous pigment called *Arzica* in the Table of Synonymes, affords, when burnt, an orange-coloured pigment, which is likely to prove a valuable addition to the palette.

Orange or *red orpiment—realgar.*—This pigment, as well as yellow orpiment, is sometimes found native. It is also prepared artificially by melting it in a crucible over a charcoal fire, and when cool, grinding it.[2]

Burnt or orange orpiment is mentioned by Borghini[3]

---

[1] Trattato, cap. 120.   [2] Paduan MS., p. 662.   [3] Riposo, p. 166.

and by Lomazzo,[1] who observes with regard to this
pigment, which was said to be of the colour of gold,
" and this is the alchemy of the Venetian painters."
Matthioli makes a similar remark; after describing the
manner of converting the yellow orpiment into red by
burning it, he says, that every one may provide himself
with the latter by inquiring for it in the "calle" (lanes
or narrow streets) of Venice, where colours are sold.
It is probable that red orpiment was used by some of
the Venetian artists,[2] since a colour resembling it is
frequently seen on pictures of this school, particularly
on those of Bonifazio. A few ounces of a pigment of
the colour of orange orpiment was given to me at
Milan by an artist who told me it was used by Titian,
and that he had procured it at an old colour-shop in
Venice. He called the colour *rauschel minerale*, and
said that he had shown the pigment to a colourman at
Bergamo who knew it by that name. From the name,
therefore, it may be conjectured, that the pigment was
native red orpiment or realgar, and that the name by
which it was known to this artist was intended for
rüschegel or *rauschgelb*. This pigment was called *jalde*
or *oropimente quemado* by the Spaniards,[3] and *sandaraca* by the Greeks.[4] It is considered to be less durable
than yellow orpiment, and extremely corrosive, for
Merimée relates[5] that where it had been employed on
flower-pieces, it appears to have corroded the priming.
The term *sandaraca* was also applied during the middle
ages to *red lead*, or *minium*.[6] With the artists of this
period it must have been a favourite colour; if we may
judge from the numerous recipes for preparing it which

[1] Trattato, p. 191.
[2] Marcucci is of this opinion : see Saggio, &c., p. 226—228. According
to this writer, it was also used by Fra Bartolomeo : see Saggio, &c., p. 215.
[3] Palomino, vol. ii. p. 66.
[4] Diosc., lib. v. cap. 80, by Matt., p. 1428.
[5] De la Peinture à l'Huile, p. 124.
[6] See Table of Synonymes, p. 36.   S. Audemar, p. 141.

occur in old MSS. on art, and from its being mentioned so much more frequently than vermilion. It was purified by washing it in a horn with wine and water.[1] When to be used on walls it was to be mixed with gum water, when on parchment with egg, but when on wood with oil. For illuminating books it was frequently mixed with vermilion.[2]

It is mentioned by many Italian writers on painting,[3] and has been found on Venetian pictures of the best period. Boschini informs[4] us that it was used by Pordenone, by Paolo Veronese,[5] and by Maffeo Verona. Sig. Pietro Palmaroli states[6] that it was employed by Titian. According to Marcucci, it was also used by Fra Bartolomeo.[7]

Lomazzo states[8] that it was sometimes mixed with lake. Lebrun recommends[9] it in painting flesh, and says, " If some minium be mixed with white lead and a little fine lake, a most beautiful carnation tint will be formed, as I know from experience." Bisagno also observes[10] that in order to make vermilion dry, a little minium may be mixed with it. The general opinion seems to be that minium should be used alone, and according to the observations of the Venetian restorers of pictures always with varnish.

Palomino alludes[11] more than once to its want of durability; he says that, " after a time it throws upon the surface a kind of salt which destroys the juice of the picture." Perhaps this defect may be corrected by purifying the red lead in the manner described by De Mayerne,[12] who observes, " If you extract the salt from

---

[1] Le Begue, p. 143, 295.   [2] Ibid., p. 141, 297.
[3] Biondo, c. 20. Lomazzo, Trattato, pp. 191, 193. Borghini, p. 166. Volpato, p. 745. Paduan MS., p. 655.
[4] Ricche Minere.   [5] See also Marcucci, Saggio, &c., p. 228.
[6] Note to Marcucci, p. 226.   [7] Saggio, &c., p. 217.
[8] Trattato, p. 195.   [9] Brussels MS., p. 820, 822.
[10] Trattato della Pittura, p. 206.   [11] Vol. i. p. 56; vol. ii. p. 52.
[12] See Mr. Eastlake's ' Materials,' &c., p. 452.

minium by washing it with distilled vinegar the remainder does not fade and dries very well." When
minium is thus purified, it appears to resemble the
pigment formerly known by the name of Saturnine red ;
which consisted merely of minium washed in large vessels of distilled water, which was changed every forty-four
hours, till the surface was quite free from extraneous
matter, and the colour ceased to blacken at the edge of
the vessel. The colour was afterwards purified with
spirits of wine.[1] Pacheco mentions[2] that native red
lead (azarcon de la tierra) was used in his time in
tempera painting.

Red Pigments.

A great variety of native red pigments have always
been used in painting. They all owe their colour to
iron.[3] Of this kind were the *sinopia* of Pliny and
Cennini, the *terra rossa d'Inghilterra, terra rossa di
Spagna, Majolica, ferretta di Spagna, almagre, Pa-
vonazo, Indian red, light red, Venetian red, hœmatite,
lapis amatito, sanguine, terra rubea, brunus, brown red,
mottée de sil, red ochres.*

The *terra rossa d'Inghilterra*, so frequently mentioned by Italian writers, is still sold in Italy, where it
is imported from England.

The colour called *Venetian red* is procured from
Verona. Besides its use in painting, this earth was
formerly much employed in making the bricks of
which many of the old buildings in Venice are constructed. The fine colour of these bricks, heightened
perhaps by their contrast with the green waters of the

---

[1] Constant de Massoul, p. 205.

[2] Tratado, p. 345. Native minium occurs amorphous and pulverulent,
but when examined by the lens exhibits a crystalline structure. It is supposed to be an oxide of lead, and to arise from the decomposition of galena,
in which it commonly occurs. Phillips, Min., p. 337.

[3] The different kinds of red earth used in painting are fully described
in the Introduction to my work on Fresco Painting, pp. xiii.—xxxiv.

narrow canals, can scarcely have escaped the observation
of travellers.

Hill, the translator of Theophrastus, mentions that
what is sold in the shops as *Indian red* is a native red
earth [hæmatite] found in England. He states (p. 122,
n. 9), " I have a specimen of some from the Forest of
Dean in Gloucestershire, very little inferior to the sort
brought from Ormuz in the Persian Gulf, which is so
much esteemed and used by our painters under the
name of Indian red. It is indeed so like, both in
colour and quality, that it is used for it, as the people
employed in taking it up informed me, and sent to
London to be sold under its name. On comparing it
with some of the true Persian kind, which I had from
the East Indies, I find it of a paler colour, but of a much
finer texture." The real Indian red has also a sparkling
appearance, which is wanting in the common sort.

The *Sinopia* of Pliny and Cennini was, as has been
before mentioned, a red earth originally brought from
Sinope, but medieval writers north of the Alps gave
the name of *Sinopia*, or *Sinopis de Mellana*, to a kind
of lake made either of the gum of the ivy ground with
vinegar and mixed with wheat flour, or of the gum of
ivy and madder.[1] Sinopis is sometimes written for
cinnabar, as in p. 68, where it is said to be made of
mercury. The term *Vermiculus* is used by Le Begue[2]
to denote the red colour called " coccus," which was
undoubtedly the coccus of the ancients. It is synonymous with kermes.[3] In the Bolognese MS. it is put for
vermilion.[4] *Cinnabar*, or *vermilion*, is of two kinds,
natural and artificial. Both are stated to have been
used by the Italians and Spaniards in painting, but
the former was preferred for fresco-painting, although
the latter was of a much finer colour. If we may
judge from the recipes in old treatises, the medieval

---

[1] Le Begue, p. 145.   [2] Table of Synonymes, p. 38.
[3] Matth. 1085.   [4] P. 449.

artists employed the latter only. Directions for refining and purifying it are given in the Bolognese MS.,
the Paduan MS.,[1] and in the recipes at the end of the
Abecedario Pittorico.

Lebrun observes,[2] that vermilion is frequently adulterated with lime ; to detect this he recommends that
some should be put on the blade of a knife and heated ;
if good, it would, when cold, be of the same colour as
before ; but if one side of the knife remained black, and
then became brown and dark, this would be a proof of
its impurity.

Native cinnabar does not appear to be mentioned by
writers on art previous to the latter part of the 16th
century, when it is spoken of together with the artificial
by Lomazzo[3] and Borghini.[4]   It is also mentioned and
described by the Spanish writers Cespides, Pacheco,[5] and
Palomino,[6] and by Félibien.[7]   I was informed by a
Venetian artist that both native and artificial, or, as he
called the latter, Dutch cinnabar, had been found among
the colours of Venetian pictures which he had procured to be analysed.   It is difficult to imagine how
native cinnabar can be distinguished by chemical
analysis from artificial, since mercury combines with
sulphur in two proportions only, forming the protosulphuret which is black, and the bisulphuret (vermilion
or cinnabar) which is red.[8]   The difficulty may perhaps
be explained by a knowledge of the fact that the name
of " mineral cinnabar" was given by the Italians to the
hard red hæmatite.   Agricola says, that the stone

---

[1] See pp. 500, 660, and 664.

[2] Brussels MS., p. 814.   [3] Trattato, p. 191, 192.

[4] Riposo, p. 167.   [5] Tratado, p. 342.

[6] Museo Pictorico, vol. i. p. 359 ; vol. ii. pp. 53, 149, 340.

[7] De la Peinture, p. 299.

[8] The atomic composition is stated to be as follows :

The protosulphuret—1 atom mercury 200+1 atom sulphur 16=216.

The bisulphuret—1 atom mercury 200+2 atoms sulphur 32=232.

According to Phillips (Min., p. 358), the composition of native cinnabar
is quicksilver 84·5—sulphur 14·75.

which he calls schist (after Pliny) resembled in appearance *minium*, and that the painters called it *cinnabar*; that when calcined it imitated the colour of cinnabar. This is confirmed by Borghini,[1] who states that lapis amatita (the hæmatite) is called by some persons "mineral cinnabar." Baldinucci[2] and Alberti[3] make the same remark; and Pungelone[4] mentions a design by Correggio, in which may be seen several "pentimenti" drawn with "matita, comunemente detta cinabro minerale." It is not, therefore, unreasonable to conclude, that the mineral cinnabar said to have been found on Venetian pictures may have been the colour procured from the hard red hæmatite burnt; at the same time it must be acknowledged, that if the pigment so called had actually been subjected to analysis, its composition must have been settled beyond a doubt, since no chemist could have mistaken a combination of mercury and sulphur for an ore of iron. Vermilion has been used by all Italian and Spanish painters. Lomazzo[5] and Pacheco[6] direct it to be sometimes employed in flesh tints. Its use by Flemish writers in painting has been mentioned by Mr. Eastlake.[7] Cennini recommends[8] that cinnabar should be purchased in the mass and never bruised or ground, because it was frequently adulterated with minium or pounded bricks.

Lakes.—The red lakes used by the Italian painters were either of animal or of vegetable origin, or a mixture of both kinds.

To the first class belonged the lake produced from kermes or grana, the most common form of which was the lacca di cimatura, lac lake, and cochineal lake. To the second class belonged the lake made from Brazil

[1] Riposo, p. 168.   [2] Voc. Dis.
[3] Diz. Enc., tit. *Cinabro minerale*, and *Lapis*.
[4] Life of Correggio, vol. i. p. 174.
[5] Trattato, p. 312.   [6] Tratado, p. 386.   [7] 'Materials,' &c., p. 443.
[8] Trattato, cap. xl.

wood or verzino. The third description was composed
of a mixture of the first and second kinds of lake.

Kermes or *Grana*.—The dead bodies of the female
insect of the coccus ilicis, which lives upon the leaves
of the prickly oak. It appears to have been known
from the time of Moses, and has been employed from
an early period in India to dye silk. It was called by
the Greeks *coccus baphica*, by the Latins *granum in-
fectorium*, by Pliny *coccigranum*, by the Arabs *charmen*,
kermes, and *chermes*, by the Germans *scharlack ber*, by
the Spaniards *grana para teñir* and *grana in grano*, by
the French *vermillon*, and by the Italians *grana* or
grana da tentori.[1]

The kermes grains or berries, whence the name
grana, are mentioned (probably as a dye) in the Lucca
MS. and the Clavicula[2] under the name of coccarin, and
in the latter MS. they are identified with cinnaberin
and vermiculum : " Vermiculi tereni qui in foliis ceri
nascitur—coccarin nascitur, sicut supra dictum est, in
foliis ceri." They are constantly to be traced as a dye
during the middle ages in the South of Europe, and
are noticed in a commercial agreement between Bologna
and Ferrara as early as 1193, and in the Statutes of
Marseilles for the year 1287. At Montpellier no other
dye was permitted to be used for the finest red stuffs.[3]
In the fourteenth century Florence[4] and Venice[5] were
celebrated for their red stuffs dyed with kermes, which
the latter city exported to other parts of Italy. The

[1] See Matthioli, p. 1085.   [2] See Mappæ Clavicula, p. 41.
[3] Depping, vol. i. pp. 241, 293, 300.   [4] Ibid., vol. i. pp. 234, 235.
[5] Filiasi, Saggio, &c., pp. 153, 154 n.   Hellot (L'Art de Teinture,
Paris, 1701, pp. 244, 264) said this red colour was called " Ecarlatte de
graine," formerly " Ecarlatte de France," and now " Ecarlatte de Venise,"
because it was much used there, and more was made there than any other
place. He adds, " the red draperies of the figures in the old Brussels
tapestries were dyed with this ingredient, and their colour, which in some
of these tapestries is 200 years old, has lost nothing of its vivacity." In
his time kermes was only used to dye wool for tapestry.

red stuffs dyed with kermes or grana found their way
into the towns of the North of Europe.   Pierce Plow-
man (whose 'Vision' is supposed to have been written in
1350), in describing the dress of a lady richly clad,
says that her robe was of "scarlet in grain;" that is,
scarlet dyed with grana, the best and most durable red
dye.   The import of the words "in grain" was afterwards changed, and the term was applied generally to
all colours with which cloths were dyed which were considered to be permanent; in this sense it is still used.

The idea of preparing a pigment directly from the
kermes grains appears not to have suggested itself to
the early painters, who employed the rather indirect
process of boiling the clippings or shearings[1] of cloth
dyed with kermes in ley, and then precipitating the
colour with alum.   The colouring matter, combined
with alumina, was well washed to remove the salts, and
after being dried on a porous stone or brick was preserved in small cakes.   The pigment so produced was
the "lacca di cimatura di grana da rosato," commonly
called "lacca di cimatura," which appears to have been
in common use as a red pigment until the seventeenth
century.[2]   Neri is probably the first author who gives a
recipe for a red pigment prepared directly from the
kermes.   The method he recommends was, he said,
invented by himself at Pisa.[3]   Other recipes for lake
from the kermes berries are contained in the Paduan
MS.[4]   Lake from "quermes" was used in France for
oil and miniature painting in 1682.[5]

As a dye the kermes was considered among the most
durable of all colours.   M. Hellot says,[6] " From the

---

[1] These consisted of the loose wool, which was removed from the face
of the cloth, in order to produce a smooth surface.

[2] See Cennini, Trattato, cap. 44; Le Begue, p. 91; Bol. MS., p. 433,
&c.; Secreti di D. Alessio, part i. p. 103; Caneparo, p. 335.

[3] Arte Vetraria, lib. vii. cap. 119.   [4] P. 703.

[5] See Traité de Mignature de C. Ballard, p. 14.

[6] L'Art de Teinture, p. 264.

experiments which have been made with the scarlet dye from kermes, as well by exposure to the sun as by different re-agents, it has been found that there is neither a better nor more durable colour, and yet it is used nowhere but at Venice." This author attributes the solidity of the colour of the kermes to its being nourished on a shrub possessing astringent properties, which have been communicated to the insect; for he remarks " that all barks, roots, woods, fruits, and other substances of an astringent nature, furnish durable colours for dyeing."[1] The Italian painters were aware of this property possessed by astringent substances of rendering colours more durable, and we find accordingly that assafœtida,[2] a handful of the bark of the white beech, or three or four small branches of the Lombardy poplar, were boiled with the lake in order to make the colour more permanent.[3] The bark of the white beech was considered best for rose colours; the practice was not confined to the red from kermes, but extended also to madder lake.

Cremisi, Cremisino.—Although there appears to be no doubt that *chermes* and *grana* were really synonymous, yet it also appears that the term cremisino was applied in Italy during the time of Matthioli to the colour procured from certain berries or grains attached to the roots of the pimpinella,[4] as well as to cochineal. Matthioli adds,[5] " There is now brought from the West Indies by way of Spain a new kind of *cremisino;* and as great quantities of it are made in Italy, it has lowered the price of silks of this colour." This cremisino from the West Indies, brought by way of Spain, can be no other than cochineal; it is therefore certain that it was well known and abundant in Italy at least as early as

---

[1] L'Art de Teinture, p. 271. [2] Bol. MS., pp. 435, 442.
[3] Traité de la Peinture au Pastel. Paris, 1788.
[4] Poterium sanguisorba. The Burnet, probably the Bruneta of the Sloane MS. No. 1754. [5] Matt., p. 1085.

1549, the date of Matthioli's work. This may also be considered to be proved by the 'Tariffa Perpetua di Zuane Mariani,'[1] in which *cremese* is mentioned as well as "grana" and "polvere di grana." Both are also spoken of in the 'Plicto.'[2] These notices are certainly evidence that the terms were not synonymous. Matthioli further states that at the time his work was written a lake was made for painters from the cremese or cremisino, and Canepario[3] carefully distinguishes *grana* from *karbisini* or *cremesi*. Cochineal lake is mentioned in the Paduan MS.[4] In this treatise it is stated to have been prepared for painting by boiling it with lemon-juice, garlic-juice, and burnt alum ; this treatment would probably communicate to it a scarlet tint. The anonymous author of the 'Trattato di Miniatura'[5] states that the colour called "lacca fina di Venezia" was made from cochineal after the carmine had been extracted, and that this pigment was made at Paris.

The cochineal insect is produced on different species of cactus. The most perfect variety is that which breeds on the cactus coccinillifer. When the Spaniards first arrived in Mexico they saw the cochineal employed by the native inhabitants in communicating colours to some ornaments and in dyeing cloth. Struck with its beautiful colour, they transmitted accounts of it to the Spanish ministry, who, about the year 1523, ordered Cortes to direct his attention to the propagation of this substance. The pigment prepared from cochineal, though extremely beautiful, is not so durable as those from lac and kermes. It is, however, worthy of trial whether it may not be rendered more durable by

---

[1] Published at Venezia, 1567.   [2] Venice, 1557.

[3] De Atramentis diversi Coloribus, pp. 326, 336.

[4] Pp. 661, 699, 703, 709.

[5] This work, which was published at Turin in 1758, appears to be a translation of Ballard's Traité de Mignature. In this last work, carmino is stated to be made of cochineal and rocou (Bixa orellana, an American plant).

boiling it with some astringent bark, as recommended
with regard to kermes lake.

Lac, Lacca.—The term *lacca* occurs in the Lucca
MS., and also in the Clavicula; but it does not appear
whether it is used to signify gum lac or the juice of the
ivy, which is described by Eraclius in the chapter entitled "De Edera et Lacca." These notices appear rather
to refer to a dye than to a colour for painting. In 1220
the Catalans and Provençals imported lac into their
ports for the purpose of dyeing.[1] As a pigment lac
was known in Italy at least as early as 1409, since
recipes for making lake from it are given in the book
lent by Fra Dionisio to Alcherius. Other recipes are
contained in the Bolognese and Paduan MSS. and in
that of Fra Fortunato of Rovigo.

Lac does not appear to have been mentioned in the
'Tariffa Perpetua' of Mariani, but it was used in dyeing
at Venice in 1557, when the 'Plicto' was published; and
it is among the articles enumerated in the 'Tariffa' of
Bartolommeo del Paxi de Venezia.[2] Lac lake was in
use at Venice in Matthioli's time, and even as late as that
of Caneparius.[3] It was also in use at Naples in 1733.[4]

*Madder, Rubea Tinctoria, Robbia overo Roza di
Fiandra, Sandis, Granza, Garancia, Warantia,
" Rubea Major, id est Waranz."*—A red pigment prepared from this root is mentioned in the Sloane MS.,
No. 1754, and in that of S. Audemar,[5] the same recipe
being introduced into both treatises. In the former
work it appears also to be alluded to under the term
gorma:—" Gorma quedam herba est que trahit in pur-
puram et affertur de quadam regione et hec *rosa*
dicitur." Rosa, as has been already mentioned, is sy-

---

[1] Capmany, Memorias, &c.; and Statuts de Marseille, cited by Depping, vol. i. p. 144.

[2] Venezia, 1503.

[3] De Atramentis, p. 331. This work was published in 1660.

[4] See recipes at the end of the Abecedario, published at Naples.

[5] Le Begue, p. 145.

nonymous with Robbia.[1] It is possible that the *menesch* of Theophilus may have been madder, since *mnitsch* is the Indian name for this plant.[2] In the third book of Eraclius[3] madder is enumerated among colours for painting; it is also mentioned in the Table of Synonymes.[4] From the time the latter work was written until that of Neri all traces of madder as a pigment seem to be lost. This author gives[5] a recipe for madder and verzino lake; he remarks that in making these lakes a larger proportion of madder or verzino must be allowed than of the cimatura, because the colour afforded by the two former is not so deep as the latter. He concludes by observing, "In this manner you will obtain very fine lake for painters at less expense than that made from 'chermisi;' the madder lake especially is very beautiful and pleasing to the eye." From these expressions it may almost be inferred that Neri was recommending what he considered to be a new pigment; had it been known to painters, it would have been unnecessary to advert to the beauty of the colour. With the exception of Neri the pigment does not appear to be mentioned by Italian writers until 1733, when madder lake is noticed among other lakes in the recipes for colours at the end of the 'Abecedario Pittorico.' The French writers are equally silent on this subject until 1788, when the anonymous author of the 'Traité de la Peinture au Pastel' observes, "Madder is, of all the plants known in our climates, that which yields the most durable red, and the addition of the juice of the poplar makes it still more permanent. The juice of the bark of the white beech is still better for rose colours." Constant de Massoul[6] also mentions madder lake, which he says is less likely to change than any other.

---

[1] See the 'Plicto.'   [2] Nemnich, Polyglotten Lexicon.
[3] P. 249, 251.   [4] P. 34.
[5] Arte Vetraria, Firenze, 1612, lib. vii. cap. 118.
[6] Art of Painting, p. 208.

Madder is enumerated among the pigments which it is stated were used by the great Venetian painters.

Madder has been used in dyeing from time immemorial, and by the Orientals as well as the inhabitants of Europe. It was cultivated and used extensively for dyeing in the neighbourhood of Avignon and Marseilles, and it is mentioned in the statutes of the latter city as early as 1287.[1] It grew wild all over Italy, and that produced in the neighbourhood of Rome was at one time much esteemed. In the middle of the sixteenth century Dutch or Flemish madder was preferred to the Italian,[2] since the former only was imported into Venice.

Verzino Lake, or Lake from Brazil Wood.—The identity of these pigments is fully proved from various passages in these MSS.,[3] and the numerous recipes which have been transmitted to us by writers on the arts show the extent to which verzino lake was formerly used. The dyewood from which the pigment was prepared was known to the Hebrews, as appears from the dictionary of the Rabbi David Kimchi, entitled 'Book of Roots,' and was called by the Arabs "albakim" or "bacam."[4]

Verzino Colombino.—Marco Polo states that the best verzino grew in the island of Ceylon, whence Depping supposes that the term "Verzino Colombino" was derived from Colombo, the capital of that island. The colour to which Pierre Pomet[5] and Marcucci[6] give this name was composed not of verzino, but of the clippings of scarlet cloth; the former author remarks that the preparation of this lake is attended with much

---

[1] Depping, Histoire, &c., vol. i. p. 293.   [2] See 'Plicto.'

[3] See Le Begue, p. 53.   Bol. MS., p. 441.   See also Mr. Eastlake's 'Materials,' &c., p. 114, and Caneparius, p. 297.

[4] Dict. Universel, Français et Latin, vulgairement appelé Dictionnaire de Trevoux, Art. Brésil.   Paris, 1732.

[5] Histoire Générale des Drogues, vol. i. p. 34.

[6] Saggio, &c., p. 125; and see also Trattato di Miniatura, p. 29.

difficulty, and that it is seldom conducted successfully out of Venice, because the Venetians add to the alumina a very white earth, which causes the lake to become very light (in weight). A pigment of this description is still sold at Venice in masses of a pink colour and powdery texture, which breaks easily and is remarkably light in weight. It is said this pigment should be well burnt. A recipe for " Laque Colombine," composed of Brazil or other dyewood, will be found in Ballard's ' Traité de Mignature.' Verzino or Brazil wood is not the only wood mentioned in these MSS. which furnished red colouring matter. Red sandal-wood,[1] Campeachy or logwood, are also mentioned ; and it appears from Ballard's ' Traité de Mignature ' that when that work was published the Brazil wood of America called by the French " le Brésillet de Fernambouc" (*cæsalpinia Brasiliensis*) was used in making lake instead of the Oriental Brazil wood, or verzino (*cæsalpinia Sappan*).

Venetian Lake.—It is difficult to say what this pigment really was. The anonymous author of the ' Trattato di Miniatura ' before mentioned states that the "lacca fina di Venezia " was composed of cochineal after the carmine had been extracted. Pierre Pomet[2] says that it was made of cochineal, Brésil of Fernambouc, burnt alum, arsenic, and Egyptian natron, or white soda. According to Palomino[3] Venetian lake was composed of gum lac and grana, or cochineal.

Florentine Lake.—The old pigment was probably the same as lacca di cimatura, since this was the principal kind of lake described by Neri,[4] whose work was published at Florence, although he appears to have resided at Pisa. The modern pigment of this name is made of cochineal and other ingredients.[5]

---

[1] P. 517.   [2] Histoire Générale des Drogues, vol. i. p. 33.
[3] Museo Pictorico, vol. ii. p. 340.   [4] Arte Vetraria, lib. vii. c. 116.
[5] Dizionario delle Droghe, di Chevalier e Richard, Tradizione da F. du Pré, Venezia, 1830.

Lake from Ivy.—The medieval painters were accustomed to prepare a red colour from the juice or gum which in warm countries flowed from the ivy in the month of March. This colour differed from the lakes before described, inasmuch as the juice or gum was inspissated by boiling, and not precipitated upon a white earth.

The Purple of the Ancients is mentioned in the Table of Synonymes.[1] It is also mentioned in the passages borrowed from Vitruvius in the third book of Eraclius.[2]

It has been observed that the characteristic of the Venetian school was the free and unsparing use of a powerful blue, I would add of a very beautiful and cool lake colour also, which in all pictures of the Venetian school, from the Vivarini to Tintoretto, invariably retains its colour. The Venetian lakes always incline to blue — an effect which was probably produced by the mixture of blue with the lake. Tassi, in his ' Lives of the Bergamasque Painters,' speaking of the beautiful blues and lakes found on the cinque-cento pictures, says: " Where will you find such colours now?"[3] These considerations make it most important to ascertain, if possible, what kind of lakes were used.

The lakes of Florence and Venice were particularly celebrated. We have seen that in both cities the lacca di cimatura was most common. Cennini[4] gives the preference to the pigment prepared from gum lac, and it is generally believed that the latter was the lake most frequently employed by the old masters, especially by those of the Venetian school:[5] the colour of the lake in pictures of this school favours this supposition.

Pacheco, on the contrary, prefers the Florentine to

---

[1] P. 25, 33.　　　　[2] P. 251.

[3] He published in 1793.　　　[4] Trattato, cap. 44.

[5] Note by Tambroni to Cennini, Trattato, cap. 44.

the lac lake, as more durable, but he says lake of Honduras is not bad. By the last term he probably meant the lake from cochineal or American Brazil wood. Matthioli states [1] that in his time four kinds of lake were made; namely, 1st, that from *cremesi* or *cremisino*, which was undoubtedly cochineal; 2nd, that made from *grana* or *kermes*; 3rd, that from gum lac; and 4th, that from verzino, which was the worst and least valued of all the others. Lomazzo mentions more than once, in enumerating the colours used, "le lacche tutte," which is a proof that several kinds of lake were used in his time; and in another place he speaks of "grano," whence we may infer that the kermes lake was among the number.

Florentine lake must have had considerable reputation in Venice, since Leandro Bassano contracted to employ it in his picture of the ' Combat of the Angels,' painted for the church of S. Giorgio Maggiore at Venice in 1597.[2]

A Venetian artist told me that the Venetians used kermes (grana) and madder lakes, and that verzino lake was employed by Tintoret only. Another artist, on the contrary, said that the Venetian painters used chiefly verzino lake. A painter and restorer of pictures at Verona believed they used cochineal lake, and, as we have seen, he may be right as far as regards the painters who lived after the middle of the sixteenth century.

From the preceding authorities it will be seen that previous to the middle of the sixteenth century the best lake pigments employed by the Italian painters must have been either the lacca di cimatura or lac lake, or a mixture of one of these with verzino, and that after this period cochineal lake might have been in use. At present there is no evidence which of the two

---

[1] Matt. 75.   [2] Iscriz. Venet., vol. iv. p. 349.

former was generally preferred: judging from the greater number of the recipes for lacca di cimatura, we should perhaps decide that this was the pigment generally adopted; but if an opinion may be formed from the colour of the lake on Italian, and especially on Venetian pictures, we should say that the lac lake was preferred.

Chemical analysis does not diminish the difficulty; the lake-coloured pigments of a miniature of the end of the fourteenth or beginning of the fifteenth century have been analysed by Dr. Antonio Fabroni of Arezzo, who, after stating [1] that the tint where it was mixed with white was of a bright blood colour, draws the following conclusions from his experiments: "The behaviour of this pigment with re-agents proves that this colour is a combination of a terrene base, and probably of very fine white chalk with a red juice, or perhaps with several juices, either of a vegetable or animal nature. It is, in fact, a composition analogous to our modern lakes, or rather to the 'stils de grain' of the French. . . . From chemical experiments I should be inclined to believe that the dark red colour of the miniature was produced from verzino, if, besides the chronological difficulty,[2] the depth and inalterability of the colour, which are incompatible with the nature of Brazil wood, did not oblige me to abandon this conjecture.

"Carthamus, gum-lac, and madder appear to me excluded by experiment, and by the appearance of the colour to the eye. I think then, that this lake colour can only be attributed to the kermes (the coccus of the ancients) modified by some indigenous vegetable juice."

Perhaps it may be safe to conjecture that where lake-coloured draperies are of the colour of blood they

---

[1] Ricerche Chimiche sopra le Miniature di un Manuscritto.

[2] Sig. Fabroni probably considered that Brazil gave its name to the wood, whereas it is supposed that the name of the wood was transferred to the country.

have been painted with kermes, and where they incline to the rose-colour, or pink, that lac-lake has been used for them, if painted previous to the middle of the sixteenth century; but if after that period, that either lac, cochineal, or madder may have been employed.

The price of lake does not often appear in old documents, although it is frequently stipulated in contracts that it should be provided by the person who ordered the picture. It is however stated[1] that the lake supplied for the altar-piece, painted in 1521, by Fra Marco Pensaben, at Treviso, was 6 lire the ounce, exactly double the price of the azzurro.

When Guercino was painting the picture called " L'Amore Virtuoso," 25 oz. of lake, besides 21 oz. of lapis-lazuli to make ultramarine, were given to him.[2]

Volpato remarks[3] that lakes should not only be of beautiful colour, but in grinding they should have body, and not become liquid; and De Mayerne observes,[4] " Lake for glazing should be mixed with but a small quantity of oil, and should be ground as thick as butter, so that it may be cut, otherwise it will have no body, and be good for nothing." Lake that is left on the palette cannot be preserved, like other colours, by placing it in water, for that would spoil it.[5] Lakes being slow dryers, the addition of boiled oil or pulverized glass is necessary to promote their desiccation.[6] Palomino[7] observes that the colour which in Spain is called ' Laca de Francia,' and in France 'Carmin,' although very beautiful for illuminations and miniatures, is not durable in oil; for besides losing its beautiful colour, and becoming dark, it dries so badly,

---

[1] Memorie Trevigiane.

[2] See the Account Book of Guercino, published in the new edition of the Felsina Pittrice.   [3] P. 745.

[4] MS., quoted by Mr. Eastlake, ' Materials,' &c., p. 451 n.

[5] Volpato, p. 741.

[6] Bald., Voc. Dis., Tit. *Olio cotto.* Paduan MS., p. 666.   Pacheco, p. 390.   [7] Museo Pictorico, vol. ii. p. 53.

that after being to all appearance dry, if the picture be washed even six years after it has been painted, the lake will wash off." It was remarked to me at Venice that verzino lake was always applied as a glazing colour, and with varnish.

In painting lake or rose-coloured draperies, the Venetians generally painted the lights with pure white, and glazed with lake until the colour was sufficiently dark. With lac-lake this was a wise precaution; for Mr. Field remarks,[1] that white-lead destroys this colour. We find that it was sometimes the practice to mix the bone of the cuttle-fish, or white chalk, with lake, in order to give it body. The peculiar kind of lake now made at Venice is an example of this.[2]

Dragons'-blood, a resin of a dark red colour, which drops in tears from the tree called Pterocarpus draco. It has been used from a very early period in miniature painting, but is not considered a durable colour. Its tint was varied by adding to it an alkali, or soap, when it was called "carmine," or "ponso." When a large quantity of soap was added, it was called "cremesino."

Pavonazzo, Purple, and Mulberry colours.

Morello di ferro.—Probably some ore of iron, burnt until it assumes a morello or murrey colour; or it might have been the hard red hæmatite, ground without being calcined. It was used for painting in oil.[3]

Vitriuolo Romano abbruciato.—*Burnt Roman Vitriol.* —An artificial pigment, prepared by calcining sulphate of iron, by which process it acquires a red colour.

Morello di Sale.—The nature of this pigment has not been well ascertained. It is distinguished by Lomazzo[4] from morello di ferro, and from burnt Roman

---

[1] Chromatography, p. 185.

[2] And see Félibien, de la Peinture, &c., p. 299.

[3] Lomazzo, Trattato, p. 192.

[4] Ibid., p. 191, " Il morello di ferro, e quello di sale, fanno il morello, e oltre di ciò il vetriuolo cotto," &c.

vitriol. The same author also places it among the
colours used in fresco painting. Borghini calls[1] it
Pagonazzo di sale, and says it was used for painting in
fresco and in tempera. Haydocke, the translator of
Lomazzo, took much pains to ascertain the nature of
this pigment. He says,[2] " But as for morello di sale, it
must needes be the rust of salte, called flos salis, whereof
Mathiolus, l. 5, c. 88, uppon Dioscorides writing saith,
that it is of a saffron colour, in these words: ' There is
a reddish colour, like unto rust, digged out of the German salt-mines, much desired of the painters, which,
peradventure, is ipse flos salis, the flower itselfe of
salt; for it is like it in colour and tast; and is commonly called morello di sale.' Wherefore I rather
think that it is the rust of iron, and the rust of salte,
making naturally a bay colour; for which cause I have
still translated them the rust of iron and salte; though
in some places they agree not in colour as they are
named in the mixture. So that I imagine there is
some errour crept into the booke, which by mine owne
paines I cannot yet finde, nor by my conference with
many good painters and chemists."

I have been unable to find the passage quoted by
Haydocke in Matthioli's translation of Dioscorides, lib.
5, cap. 88, or cap. 87, in which he treats of the various
kinds of salts. Matthioli says, in speaking of " fiore di
sale," that " it is of a red colour, like rust of salt—that
it is very deliquescent, and that by suffering it to repose,
the sediment subsides, and the upper portion remains
liquid." This description agrees somewhat with the
information I received at Venice, namely, that morello
di sale is the sediment which subsides from rock-salt
when it is purified.

Phillips[3] describes rock-salt as of various colours,

---

[1] Riposo, p. 174.
[2] Translation of Lomazzo's Treatise on Painting, p. 100.
[3] Mineralogy, p. 193.

namely, white, grey, reddish-brown, brick-red, violet, and green; when coloured it is always more or less impure. He says that red or greyish clay frequently alternates in beds with rock-salt.

It seems probable that morello di sale was the same as the morellen salz of the Germans. From an analysis, made by a friend, the latter pigment is found to consist of peroxide of iron, with a small quantity of silica and alumina. I am informed that there is nothing in these ingredients which militates against the opinion of the Venetians that morello di sale is the sediment formed in the purification of rock-salt. This purification generally takes place in iron vessels, some portions of which may be dissolved and precipitated together with the clay which usually accompanies the salt.

Vasari, it seems, did not approve of this colour in fresco-painting. Speaking of the frescoes of Buffalmacco, he says,[1] "It was the custom of Buffalmacco, in order to paint the flesh with greater facility, to spread a coat of morello di sale over the whole, which in time caused a salt to form, which consumed the white and other colours; whence it is not surprising that these works are spoiled and destroyed, while others which he painted long before are in good preservation. And I, who thought that these pictures had been injured by the damp, have since proved by experience, and by comparing them with other works of this artist, that the injury did not arise from damp, but it was entirely owing to this habit of Buffalmacco that some of them are so ruined, that not even the design is visible; and where the flesh tints were formerly, nothing now remains but the pavonazzo. This method of painting should not be adopted by any one who wishes his pictures to last."

Folium, Turnsol.—Theophilus[2] and S. Audemar[3] describe three kinds of folium, namely, red, purple,

---

[1] Vita di Buffalmacco.   [2] Theoph. lib. i. cap. xxxv.   [3] P. 132.

and blue, which were prepared from a plant used in England to dye wool. According to these authors, the purple folium was procured artificially by the addition of other ingredients to the red folium.

S. Audemar gives the English name for the plant from which folium was produced; but the word appears to have been so disguised by the French transcriber, Le Begue, that it is quite unintelligible.

Fortunately, however, Mr. Hendrie has ascertained[1] that the name of the plant from which folium was produced, has been preserved in two MSS., one of which is of the fourteenth century, and the other of the fifteenth. In the first of these[2] the plant which is called "morella" is described as growing in the country of St. Giles, and as producing seeds consisting of three grains or berries, with the juice of which were dyed pieces of cloth, which yield a mulberry colour called folium.

The second description of folium, which differs but little from the first, is from a MS. belonging to the Bibliothèque Royale at Montpellier. The directions for the preparation of the colours resemble those in Theophilus and S. Audemar.

From these MSS. it appears that the colour called folium was produced from a plant called "morella," the seeds of which were formed in groups of three berries in a cluster, and that the plant grew "in terra Sancti Egidii." The Venetian MS. in the Sloane Collection (No. 416) describes a plant,[3] from the pulpy

---

[1] Theoph., p. 59.   [2] Sloane MS., No. 1754.

[3] A fare peçolla azurra la quale e molto fina. R. una erba la quale se chiama torna sole che e grande uno braço e la foia sua e fatta chomo lortiga e da il colore a modo de tera v̄de de quela che vende i spiçiali e le semençe soe sono fate al modo che e el mira—solle el so cholore de le dite semençe e verde schuro e la gamba sie bianchaça e se voi a chognossiere la dita ēba tola ī mano e tochate el chollo īcontinente te bruxa e piçara e queste semençe sono quele de le q̄le se fa el color arecholgi queste semençe la maitina p̣ tempo īnāti che lo sole se lieva e volsse arecholgiere a la ussita de Zug°, &c.

seeds of which blue and purple colours were obtained; but this plant is called " tornasole," and not " morella. " The description[1] is accompanied by a drawing of a plant which bears three berries, and it is followed by an account of the process of preparing the colour, which corresponds with those given by Theophilus, S. Audemar, and the Montpellier MS.

Now there are two plants mentioned by medieval writers under the name of " morella," one of which is the solanum nigrum, the solatro nero, or ortense, the morella, or herba morella of the Italians, the morelle des jardins, morelle au fruit noir of the French, the black nightshade of the English.[2] Red, green, and blue dyes were prepared from the seeds of this plant, as we find from the MS. of Le Begue, Nos. 94, 338; the Bolognese MS., No. 91; and Paduan MS., Nos. 35 and 100; but on referring to the figure of this plant in Matthioli, we see that the berries grew in bunches of four, and not in three, and that in other respects it differed from the description of the plant in the Venetian MS.

The other plant called " morella " is the croton tinctorium, or crozophora tinctoria, the heliotropium minus tricoccum, which is called in French *tournesole*, but at Montpellier "maurelle."[3] The term *tricoccum* will not escape observation as agreeing with the old descriptions, and the name " tornasole " given to the acrid plant described in the Venetian MS. sufficiently identifies it with the croton tinctorium, the corrosive properties of which are well known.

And now with regard to the place where it grows. The heliotropium tricoccum grows in marshy places, and is a native of the Levant and south of Europe, Provence and Languedoc, especially of Galarques,

---

[1] For this recipe from the Venetian MS. I am indebted to Mr. Eastlake.
[2] Nemnich, Polyglotten Lexicon.   [3] Ibid.

where a colour is still prepared by steeping rags in the juice of this plant,[1] and the neighbourhood of Nismes and Montpellier. The Montpellier and Sloane MSS., it will be recollected, state that it grew in "terra Sancti Egidii," and Egidius is the Latin name for Gilles, or Giles: now about thirteen miles due south of Nismes is *St. Gilles*, a town of great antiquity, the Rhoda Rhodiorum of Pliny, chiefly remarkable at present for its magnificent abbey (which dates from the twelfth century), and other medieval remains. This then is the "terra Sancti Egidii" of the MSS., and the plant morella is the "maurelle" of Montpellier, the modern turnsol. Montpellier and its neighbourhood have always been celebrated for the dyes prepared there, and this city was at one time the centre of the commerce of Languedoc.[2] At the present time it carries on extensive dye and chemical works, and manufactories of colours, some of which are nearly peculiar to itself and neighbourhood.

Having now determined the name and species of the plant from which folium was procured, and the country where it grew, it remains to account for the appellation folium, which, at first sight, appears inapplicable to the juice of a berry. I consider that this is explained by the Montpellier and the Venetian MSS. The directions in the former for preparing the colour are rather indefinite, but the Venetian MS. is more explicit. It directs[3] that pieces of cloth or rag are to be dyed with the juice pressed from the pulp surrounding the seeds; and then dried in the shade, and preserved by laying them between the leaves of a book, like leaves of gold,

---

[1] Marcucci, Saggio, &c., p. 132.

[2] Depping, Histoire du Commerce, &c., vol. i. p. 302.

[3] —" e quando serano seche le dite peçe mitele ī uno libro de charta bōbaxina e tine lo libro soto lo chavezale aço che nō pia umiditad e quando ne voi adoverar taiane uno puocho e mitelo amoio la sira ī uno chaparaço con uno puocho de aqᵃ la maitina sera fato e lo cholore foro de la peça."

and when required for use, the colour was discharged
from the rag by steeping it in water. I imagine the
dye derived its name of " folium" from this practice
of preserving the pieces of cloth in books.

Some little difficulty has been thrown on this subject,
from the statement of Theophilus and S. Audemar,
that red, blue, and purple colours were obtained from
the same plant. In the Sloane MS. the colour is said
to be mulberry. Pierre Pomet says that turnsole en
drapeau consists of nothing but rags dyed *red* with the
juice of the heliotropium tricoccum, or tornesol, the fruit
of which makes a very fine *blue*, but that the least acid
turns it red. In the Table of Synonymes it is mentioned
among the *red* colours. Nemnich,[1] De Candolle,[2]
Léméri,[3] the author of the Paduan MS., and the
translators of ' Beckmann's Inventions,' speak of it as
producing a *blue* dye. Clusius,[4] De l'Abel,[5] and Merret,[6]
who follows Libavius, say it dyes cloth a bright *green*,
which changes to *blue* and *purple*. Gerarde[7] mentions
a *purple* colour only. Constant de Massoul[8] says, a
paste is prepared from the fruit of the heliotropium
tricoccum, that grows in gardens in France. This
paste being steeped in water, takes a beautiful *blue*
tint. It will sometimes appear of a *red* colour, but by
adding a little lime-water it will return to its *blue* colour.

All these authors speak of the colour being preserved
by dyeing rags in it. It may be considered then that
the colour, when fresh, was green, that it became blue
on drying, and afterwards purple and red, according to
the ingredients used in the preparation.

The rags thus tinged with the juice of the Croton

---

[1] Polyglotten Lexicon.   [2] Flore Française.
[3] Histoire des Drogues.   [4] Rariorum Plant. Hist., 1501.
[5] Plantarum seu Stirpium Hist., 1576, and Adversaria, 1576.
[6] Notes to Neri, cap. 110.
[7] The Herball, or Generall Historie of Plantes, 1597.
[8] Treatise on the Art of Painting, London, 1797, p. 186.

Tinctorium or Turnsol were called in Italian Pezzette, literally, small pieces, or as we should say, rags; for soft, fine, and worn-out linen cloth was used for this purpose. In Italy the pezzette were of various colours. Cennini speaks [1] of "pezzette di Levante." Don Alessio states, that they were made from "cimatura di grana," or verzino; Pomet and Léméri say that the "tournesole en drapeau" of Constantinople was fine linen or crape, dyed with an acid preparation of cochineal. "Pezzette morelle" were made from the juice of the wild elder; "pezzette pavonaze" from the juice of the myrtle. "Pezzette" of different colours are described in the Bolognese MS.[2]

I have little doubt that the bezette of the Germans was the pezzette of the Italians, and the bisetus of the middle ages.

The folium of Theophilus and S. Audemar must not be confounded with the folium described by St. Isidore, in the passage quoted by M. de l'Escalopier in his 'Theophilus,' p. 293—" Folium dictum, quod sine ulla radice innatans in Indiæ litoribus colligitur. Quod lino perforatum, siccant Indi, atque reponunt. Fertur autem Paradisi esse herba, gustu nardum referens."

The Catholicon gives a nearly similar description of folium, and adds, that the precious ointment called "foliatum" was made from it. The passage evidently relates to the Malabathrum of Dioscorides, which Matthioli [3] says was called "Folio Indiano," and which was valued for its perfume, and not for its colour.

Indigo appears also to have been called "folium Indicum," as may be understood from the following passage from Du Cange, also quoted by M. de l'Escalopier:[4]— "Peto, ut nobis mittas ad decorandos parietes colores diversos, qui ad manum habentur, videlicet auripigmentum, folium Indicum, minium, lazur."

---

[1] Cap. x.   [2] Pp. 443, 427, 439, 443.   [3] Matt., p. 47.
[4] Théophile, p. 293, n.

Bisetus, or Biseth Folii.—There is some difficulty in
reconciling the few notices I have been able to collect
respecting this pigment. It is mentioned in Eraclius,[1]
who says "Folium incide de bruno; matiza di *biseto
folii.*" Again, "misces brunum cum albo, fietque pulcra
rosa; incide de bruno, matiza di albo vel de *biseto
folii.*" "Viride incide de nigro, et matizabis de *biseto.*"
"Indicum incide de nigro; matiza de azurio, vel de
vergaut, aut *biseth.*" "Misce auripigmentum cum azurio
vel indico, aut ocrum cum indico, vel viride, et erit
bonum vergaut; inde de bruno, aut di nigro, undabis;
auripigmentum aut de biseth matizabis."

The only information to be collected from these passages is, that it was a colour which served for heightening the others, consequently that it was lighter than
they were. In the first case, it was used for the lights
of a red, purple, or blue drapery; in the second, of a
red drapery; in the third and fifth, of a green drapery;
and in the fourth, of a blue drapery.

These passages, therefore, are no guide to the colour;
and as Eraclius gives directions for painting changeable
draperies in this chapter, it is by no means necessary that
the lights should be of the same colour as the shades.

The next notice of bisetus is in the Table of Synonymes,[2] where it is described as being less red than
folium, and is said to be taken from that portion which
swims on the surface. Le Begue adds, "I believe that
this term is applicable in the same sense to the lighter tint
of any colour, when tempered in shells (such lighter tint
rising to the surface), after the colour has settled a little."[3]

Merret, in his notes to Neri's 'Arte Vetraria' (cap.
cx.), mentions bezetta as a synonyme of turnsol, "bezetta
seu tornasolis;" this, it will be observed, agrees with the
description in the Table of Synonymes. In speaking of this

---

[1] P. 253.   [2] P. 21.
[3] I have adopted Mr. Eastlake's translation. See 'Materials,' &c., p. 425.

colour, Merret quotes a passage from the 'Wormianum,' in which Wormius relates that a piece of cloth tinged with a bright and beautiful red colour was given to him by Christopher Herfert (apothecary to Christian V.), who did not know how it was produced; that it appeared to have been coloured with red sandal wood, and was used to give a red colour to food in the same way as the common turnsol; but that it was far superior to it; that it was fit for rouge, and had this peculiarity, that it communicated its colour to water, and with some difficulty to wine, but not to spirit of wine. From this it would appear that Merret considered this piece of red cloth might be included under the general term bezzetta, and that the term was not applicable solely to cloth dyed with turnsole.

My opinion is strengthened by a remark of Nemnich, who says,[1] that cloths dyed with the juice of the turnsol were called in the Levant and at Venice "pezzette," and not "bezzette," as it is usually written. An eminent German chemist informed me that in the laboratory in Berlin, where he studied chemistry, there were several old boxes marked with the word "bezzette," which contained coloured rags. It is probable, therefore, that bisetus or biseth is a Latin term for bezzette, which is a corruption of the Italian pezzette; and that these pezzette might be of different colours; hence the opinion expressed by Le Begue in the Table of Synonymes was probably correct. Whether it is practicable to obtain two tints from folium, that is to say, one from the juice itself and another from the scum which arises on it, and whether this lighter tint was of a pale red only, or sometimes purple or blue, can only be determined by experiment.

With regard to the use of bisetus on the lights in the manner mentioned by Eraclius, it must be observed,

---

[1] Polyglotten Lexicon, tit. Croton Tinctorium.

that the colour with which the rags were saturated being transparent, might be made to appear as light as it was necessary, by being much diluted, and that the strength of the colour would depend on the quantity of water with which it was mixed, and the repetition of the colour.

Palomino mentions a colour which he calls "*urchilla*;"[1] he states that it is of a morello colour, and known only to a few persons; that it is excellent for illuminating and for shading sketches (or subjects in chiaroscuro); he adds, that although he "could describe the mode of preparation from the juice of morello-coloured lilies and alum, it was not his intention so to do, but merely to mention a beautiful transformation which it undergoes, for by throwing into it lemon-juice instead of water, it changes its colour to that of carmine or dragon's blood; so that, from being one colour only, it becomes two, and both may be used for illuminating, for miniatures, and for sketches." It is unnecessary to observe that if this colour were really made of the juice of blue lilies, it could not have been the oricello of the Italians. Pacheco says[2] that in illuminating, blues were shaded with this colour.

Blue Pigments.

AZZURRO.—By this term the early Italian painters appear to have understood Azzurro della Magna.

Azzurro della Magna, Azzurro Todesco, Azzurro Spagnuolo, Azzurro de Anglia, Azzurro de Lombardia,[3] *Lazurstein, Citramarinum.*—I have stated my opinion (supported by what appeared to me satisfactory evidence) in a former work,[4] that this German azure was a native blue ore of copper. I

---

[1] Vol. ii. p. 343. [2] Tratado, p. 354.

[3] Cennini states (cap. lx.) that Azzurro della Magna was found near Siena. It is also stated to be produced at Striscia, in the district of Volterra. See Ricett. Fiorent. [4] Art of Fresco Painting, p. xxxiv.—li.

have since ascertained that the fact has been settled beyond a doubt by Professor Branchi of Pisa.[1] This gentleman analysed a portion of the blue pigment from one of the pictures formerly in the chapel of S. Jacopo di Pistoia. For this purpose he poured a sufficient quantity of concentrated sulphuric acid on the blue pigment, which he afterwards evaporated to dryness ; the residue then being dissolved in distilled water, gave a blue colour with ammonia, and a bluish-green precipitate with carbonate of potash. An iron knife-blade being immersed in the liquor, metallic copper was deposited on it. The Professor also obtained the same results from the analyses of the blue pigments of other ancient pictures, especially that from the ground of the very ancient Madonna in the Lunette of the lateral door of the Duomo of Pisa, for which, as appears from the account-roll preserved in the archives, azzurro d'Alemagna was provided. Dr. A. Fabroni, of Arezzo, also analysed a portion of the blue colour of a MS. of the beginning of the fifteenth century. After describing[2] the effects of different chemical re-agents on this pigment, he observes, "At first sight this colour resembles ultramarine, or at least the finest smaltino. Nevertheless it is clearly shown by analysis to be an oxide of copper, and I have satisfied myself by ocular examination, as well as by the comparative effects of re-agents, that it is identical with our *biadetto* (cendre bleue of the French), although it is much deeper in colour. It is to be observed that I have seen the same colour on some ancient fresco paintings which existed in the suppressed monastery of S.S. Flora and Lucilla in our city, which for some centuries have been exposed to the injuries of the air, and yet the colour is very bright." Sig. Fabroni conjectured that the colour was " moun-

---

[1] Lettera di Branchi, &c., pp. 7, 8, 9.

[2] See Ricerche Chimiche sopra le Miniature di un Manuscritto, published in the Acts of the Soc. of Arts, &c., of Arezzo, 1843, vol. i. p. 3.

tain blue heightened by some acid or saline preparation."
But it appears quite possible for the colour to have been
produced by the indurated blue carbonate of copper,
which is of as deep and fine a colour as ultramarine
when first prepared and used, although it differs from
the latter in being more easily affected by re-agents,
and in fact by being generally less permanent. Professor
Petrini has written several articles in the 'Antologia'[1]
respecting the pigment azzurro della magna. In one
of these, dated August, 1821, after mentioning the
experiments of Branchi on the old pictures in S. Jacopo
di Pistoia, he says, "the same experiments have been
tried with similar success on a great number of pictures of
the thirteenth and fourteenth centuries, whence it appears
that the painters of that period knew no other mineral
azures than ultramarine and azzurro della magna."

De Boot[2] distinguishes two kinds of azure, that which
was fixed in the fire, and that which was not fixed. The
former was the real ultramarine, which was always
brought from the East; the latter was found in Germany, and was commonly called *lazurstein*, and this, he
observes, "occupies a mean place between the Armenian stone, which is friable, and the lapis lazuli, which
it resembles in hardness. The colour prepared from
the lazurstein is called *asurblau*, but many painters do
not distinguish between this mineral and the Armenian
stone, which they confound together, because the colours
extracted from both are alike. Nevertheless, the stones
differ in hardness, and the colour prepared from that
which is not fixed in the fire is generally more beautiful than that prepared from the Armenian stone. I
possess colours prepared by my own hand, which are so
fine that they bear comparison with ultramarine."

The above description, as well as those of Cennini[3]

---

[1] Published at Florence.

[2] Le parfaict Joaillier, p. 351.   [3] Trattato, cap. lx.

and the Bolognese MS.,[1] corresponds with the charac-
teristics of the indurated native blue carbonate of
copper. The difficulty of distinguishing between these
two minerals has always been felt, and there appears
to be no test but that of fire, which was known at a
very early period.[2]

The mode of preparing this mineral as a pigment is
described by Cennini, and in the Bolognese MS.[3]
Having shown that the blue pigment in several old
paintings, both mural and on miniatures, has been ascertained to be copper, I shall now give a few extracts
from documents, proving that it was used on pictures
also. The stipulation in the contract to use azzurro
della magna must be considered evidence of the esteem
in which it was held.

" 1453, 10 August . . . . . . Padua.

" Agreement made between the monastery of Sta. Giustina and
me, Andrea Mantegna, painter, relative to the painting of an altar-
piece to be placed over the altar of S. Luca in the church of Sta.
Giustina, by which I, Andrea Mantegna, agree to paint all the
figures at my own expense, including the colours, for the price of
50 ducats in Venetian gold, and to inlay with *azzurro Todesco* all
the carvings and ornaments of the said altar-piece," &c.[4]

This picture, observes Moschini in 1826, is now
fresh and intact at Milan. On my second visit to
Milan, Conte Pompeo Litta obligingly procured me an
order, which enabled me to obtain a private view of
this picture (which, with many others, had been removed

---

[1] P. 343. Both kinds of carbonate of copper appear to be described in
this chapter.   [2] See pp. 247, 341, 385.   [3] P. 365.

[4] " 1453, adi 10 Agosto . . . . . . Padova.

" Pati fati con el Monastero di Sta. Giustina e mi Andrea Mantegna pen-
tor cerca el penger de una so pala da altare da esser mesa a l'altar de San
Luca in la dita Gesia di Sta. Giustina soe de depenger tutte le figure a mie
spese e colori per prexio de ducati cinquanta doro veniciani con questo che
debo campizar dazuro todesco tuti li intagi e adornamenti de la dita pala,"
&c. Copied from the original contract in the possession of the Conte
Francesco de' Lazara, at Padua. The contract has been published by Moschini in his work entitled ' Dell' Origine e delle Vicende della Pittura in
Padova,' p. 34 n.

from the gallery of Brera, for the purpose of re-laying the floors). The picture is divided into twelve compartments, separated by columns. In the centre is an evangelist, and in the other compartments are saints; those in the upper row are half-figures, while those in the lower are whole lengths. The figures are painted on gold grounds, and there are several dark-blue draperies, but the blue has turned black. All the colours appear to have darkened, except the lakes, which are as good as ever. The carvings and ornaments inlaid with blue are no longer with the picture. Andrea Mantegna was in his 22nd year when he painted this altar-piece.

By a contract, dated 22nd February, 1474, Giacomo Filipo, a painter of Ferrara, agreed with Fra Ludovico da Forlì, Prior of the old Church of S. Salvatore at Bologna, to paint certain pictures, "de boni coluri a modo stia bene," on a ground of "azuro todesco," of the price of 10 bolognini the ounce.[1]

In the documents respecting the celebrated altar-piece by Fra Marco Pensaben at Treviso, published in the 'Memorie Trevigiane,' a blue colour, which from its price could not have been ultramarine, is mentioned in the following terms:—" 1521, 13: Ott. Dati per oncie 10 e mezza d'azzurro, a lire tre l'onza."

Azzurro di Terra, Azzurro di Spagna, Biadetto, Cenere Azzurre, Ceneretta, la Cendrée, Cendres bleues, Cenizas azules, Bleu de Montagne, Bice, Terra biaua, Sanders blue, Ongaro, Bleu minerale, Turchino, Berglblau. —A blue pigment, prepared from carbonate of copper, has been known to artists under the above names from a very early period. It appears to have been of a paler colour than the pigment called azzurro della magna,[2] and in fact not to have exceeded in depth of colour the blue of the sky. It is probable that the azzurro di terra was produced from the earthy blue

[1] Gualandi, Memorie di Belle Arti, Ser. iv. p. 91.
[2] See Caneparius, p. 360.

carbonate of copper; but when the latter was of a bluish-green colour it was employed for preparing the pigment called verde azzurro.

It will be seen from the following MSS., that artificial blue pigments prepared from copper were common at an early period. As these azures were easily and cheaply made, and as they were, when freshly prepared, but little inferior in colour to the natural pigments, they found a ready sale, and were not easily distinguishable from the native pigments; indeed it appears from more than one writer of the seventeenth and eighteenth centuries, that it was not generally known whether "cenere azzurre" were natural or artificial productions. The author of the 'Trattato di Miniatura' remarks (p. 52), "It is not known exactly what the 'cenere azzurre' of England really are, or how they are made. They are brought from Dantzic by the English and Dutch, who export them to France and other places, whence they are called 'cenere d'Inghilterra.'" Pierre Pomet says [1] that "cendre bleue" is a composition, or pulverized stone, brought from England or Rouen, whence it is imported into France by the Swedes, Hamburghers, and Danes. Notwithstanding the diligent inquiries I have made, I have found it impossible to ascertain the nature of the "cendre bleue:" some tell me it is a composition made at Rouen; but as those who make it keep it a secret, I could not learn how it is made. The author of the 'Traité de la Peinture au Pastel' appears to have been better informed; he says, "à l'égard de la cendre bleue, c'est une terre chargée d'une certaine quantité de chaux minérale de cuivre; le ton de ce minéral est d'un bleu naissant très agréable."

It is almost unnecessary to observe that sanders blue is a corruption of "cendre bleue."

A blue pigment prepared from the native ore of

---

[1] Hist. Générale des Drogues, vol. ii. p. 385.

copper was in use in Italy at the time of Lomazzo under the name of "Ongaro."[1] This is the pigment which, it is stated on the authority of Pacheco, Michael Coxie obtained from Titian for the purpose of painting the mantle of the Virgin in the copy he was making of the celebrated altar-piece of the Van Eycks at Ghent.[2] Ongaro is mentioned in the Paduan MS.

Biadetto.—This term, which occurs so frequently in technical works on painting, has been applied both to the native and to the artificial pigment prepared from copper. There is no doubt that at an early period of art the natural pigment (which was of a much finer colour than the factitious) was much used.[3] Mr. Eastlake[4] has discovered the true derivation of the term "biadetto" in the 'Bladetus de Inde' of the Venetian MS., which is identified by De Mayerne with "la cendrée," and *beis* or *bice*. "La cendrée" is described to be "made of the blue stone which comes from India, and which is found in silver mines."

The "azzurro di biadetti" of Borghini and Baldinucci was the artificial pigment. The native mineral pigment is mentioned under the term azzurro di vena naturale, and both these are distinguished from azzurro della magna. The biadetto now sold in Italy is the artificial pigment which is imported from England; but I could not ascertain the commercial name. The modern biadetto is described in the 'Secreti' of Fra Fortunato to be composed of verdigris, sal-ammoniac, and tartar.

The name *turchino* is stated to have been applied to this class of pigments in consequence of their being imported at one time into Italy in large quantities by the Turks;[5] others trace the name to the resemblance of the colour of the pigment to the blue stone called turquoise, a mineral which also owes its colour to copper.

---

[1] See Trattato, p. 191.   [2] See Pacheco, p. 373.   [3] Lettera di Branchi.
[4] Materials, &c., p. 121.   [5] See Ciampi, Notizie, &c., p. 57.

A modern blue pigment, known under the name of *copper, mountain, English, Hambro', lime, kassler, mineral,* and *Neuwieder blue,* is prepared from carbonate of copper, with hydrated oxide of copper and lime. "It is obtained by a particular process (which at present is kept in part secret), by decomposing subchloride of copper by a solution of caustic potash, and afterwards mixing the mass with caustic lime, and exposing the mixture for some time to the air. When the greenish-blue colour has become a pure blue, the mass is dried and ground into a rather coarse, crumbling, or dust-like powder. The darker sorts contain only a small percentage of quick lime; but the lighter sorts, on the contrary, from 20 to 70 per cent. Mountain blue is used as a lime colour, but chiefly for colouring rooms, on account of its unchangeability on lime grounds; sometimes as enamel colour instead of oxide of copper." [1]

Although Boschini affirms that biadetto was one of those colours which the Venetians "abhorred like the plague," there is evidence to show that blue pigments from copper were used by Venetian painters. The fact of Titian having in his possession some of the colour called "ongaro" has been already mentioned. Paolo Veronese is stated by Signor Pietro Edwards to have employed "a certain mineral azure which is no longer in use;" and Paolo's well-known practice of mixing his blues with size may be considered a confirmation of this assertion, since the copper blues if used with oil were certain to change. A Venetian artist, whose family have always been painters, and who doubtless possesses much traditionary knowledge, also stated that the Venetians used a "terra azzurra" [2] which is now lost; but he added, that on analysis biadetto had been found on the pictures of Tintoretto only. The 'Tariffa'

---

[1] Pharmaceutical Journal, vol. vi. p. 82.

[2] Caneparius also mentions (p. 360, 362) a "terra cerulea."

of Zuane Mariana proves that a terra biaua was in
1567 imported into Venice in such quantities as to be
sold by the *peso grosso*; and when we consider the
immense quantity of blue found on the paintings of the
Venetian school, we are obliged to conclude either that
ultramarine was much more plentiful than it is at
present, or that some other blue pigment has been
used. To the above instances must be added the
opinion current in Venice that biadetto is the pigment
which best matches the blue found in Venetian pictures.

The use of blue pigments from copper appears to
have prevailed in other schools of the North of Italy.
I was informed at Milan that the blue in the drapery
of the Virgin in the St. Jerome of Correggio, at Parma,
was painted with biadetto. It appears that either
biadetto or azzurro della magna was used by Lionardo
da Vinci, since there are the following entries in his
MS. book of drawings in the Ambrogiana Library at
Milan : " di spesa tra azurro, oro, biaca, giesso, indacho,
et cholla ; lire 3 . . . . fra smalto, azurro, e altri colori,
lire 1½, fra azurro e oro, lire 3½, un' oncia d'azuro, soldi
10." Here we have the exact price of the " azuro,"
which could not have been ultramarine, and which
appears to have been too cheap for azzurro della magna.[1]

With regard to the manner in which these pigments
were employed—in the first place it is clear that they
cannot be used with oil without turning green.[2] It is
true that Borghini, Baldinucci, and Lomazzo state that
they may be used with oil ; but Bisagno remarks " la
ceneretta is but little adapted for painting skies, because it becomes green in time :" and the author of the
'Traité de la Peinture au Pastel' observes that cendres
bleues might be employed in tempera painting and in

---

[1] The price of this pigment at Florence, in 1459, was 3 great florins the
oz. ; see a letter from Benozzo Gozzoli in the Carteggio Inedito, vol. i.
p. 193. The author of the Bol. MS. states that azzurro della magna was
sold from 10 to 30 bolognini the oz.

[2] See Palomino, vol. ii. p. 52.

unimportant works, that cupreous earths might be used for *peinturage* (by which he probably meant common decorative effects), but never for painting, even in fresco.

Paolo Veronese is stated to have generally painted the blues in his pictures with size; Signor Pietro Edwards mentions [1] that in the picture by Paolo in the ceiling of the Collegio in the Ducal Palace at Venice, the blue sky was painted in tempera, and the clouds with oil.

As the grounds employed by Paolo consisted generally of a thin coating of glue and gesso only, no preparation was necessary before applying the blue of the sky with size. But when the blue was required to be laid upon oil colours, it was necessary to apply a thin coat of varnish, or to rub the surface with juice of garlic.[2] The colour was afterwards varnished. Fra Fortunato of Rovigo states, that to prepare biadetto for miniature painting, so that it should spread well, it should be ground with burnt roche alum, or with a little tartar or sandarac. He adds, biadetto should be ground very fine, and used with varnish made of spirit of turpentine and clear mastic; it will then spread well, glaze brilliantly, and be of a beautiful colour. Blue was sometimes applied in powder. De Boot mentions [3] that "on account of the excessive price of ultramarine, painters were accustomed to dead colour the parts of their pictures intended to be blue with Armenian stone, or a blue glass called smalt, to which white was added for the lights. When this preparation was quite dry, ultramarine, mixed with nut oil and spirit of turpentine, or varnish, was glazed over it. By this means the colours spread beneath, as if under a glass, became brilliant and splendid, borrowing through this veil from the ultramarine, not only beauty but durability; so

---

[1] In a document addressed to Sig. Savio Cassier, dated the 25th of Aug., 1780, and now preserved in the Academy at Venice, where I saw it.

[2] See Mr. Eastlake's 'Materials,' &c., p. 455.

[3] Le parfaict Joaillier, &c., p. 372.

that in two hundred years they lost but little of their brightness and beauty." Volpato directs [1] that azzurro di Spagna should be tempered as firmly as possible with nut oil, and that it should be made to flow with spirit of turpentine.

Bisagno remarks that ceneretta must not be mixed with smaltino, because these colours are inimical to each other,[2] and Constant de Massoul [3] makes the same remark with regard to cendre bleue and orpiment.

There is one peculiarity attending the blue pigments in Italian pictures, which was first pointed out to me by a Milanese artist, and this is that the blues invariably are raised above the surface of the other colours, and that in some cases (and he particularly instanced Correggio's S. Jerome at Parma) they stand up as high as a five franc piece above the canvass. I have myself seen them on some pictures raised to the height of an English shilling. This artist ascribed the effect to the difficulty of using the blue, and to the necessity of repeating the colour several times.

Pacheco's method of using blue pigments has been described briefly by Mr. Eastlake.[4]

Smalto and Smaltini, Email, Azur à poudrer.— There were two kinds of pigment of this name, one of which was a preparation of zaffre, the other was a glass composed of sand, nitre, and copper filings. The latter is the Vestorian azure described by Vitruvius, which was called also azzurro di Pozzuoli. It was chiefly used in fresco painting.[5] The smalto made at Venice in the time of Caneparius seems to have been of the latter kind, since this author describes the first under the term zaphara.

---

[1] P. 747.   [2] Pacheco, however, recommends that azul de Santo Domingo should be shaded with good smalti. Tratado, p. 391.

[3] Art of Painting, p. 176.

[4] Materials, &c., p. 431 ; and see Pacheco, p. 361.

[5] See translations of Vitruvius by Orsini, published in 1822 ; and by Galliani, published at Naples in 1758.

It is not always easy to decide which pigment is
intended when these terms are employed, for there is
evidence that they were both in use at the same time
in Italy. Lomazzo mentions "gli smalti, come quello
di Fiandra che è il migliore de gl'altri tutti;" from the
last words it might almost be inferred that other vitrified pigments of this kind were known, besides the two
above-mentioned. There is little doubt that the "smalto
di Fiandra" was *zaffre*, and that it was very similar to
the pigment we now call "smalt." The smaltino of
the 'Abecedario' was also a preparation of zaffre.

One kind of azzurro di smalto only is mentioned by
Borghini;[1] this he states was composed of glass, and
was used in fresco, in tempera, and in oil.

Lionardi da Vinci mentions "smalto" among the
colours provided for the decoration of the apartments
in the castle in which Lodovico il Moro resided;[2] but
at the period when these paintings were executed
(1492), it is scarcely probable that zaffre was known in
Italy. In the absence, therefore, of evidence to the
contrary, we must believe that the smalto mentioned
by him was of the same nature as the smaltino used by
his contemporary Pietro Perugino for the mantle of the
Virgin in his picture at Montone. Baldassare Orsini
states that the smaltino in this picture was painted in
distemper on a ground of black; and to modify the
brightness of this blue Pietro had stippled the whole
drapery with lake. With regard to the composition of
the smaltino, Orsini states that he had analysed this
colour, and had found that it was a vitrified pigment
like that described by Vitruvius in powder, and that it
was tempered with flour paste.[3]

Smaltino appears also to have been occasionally employed in oil-paintings, as we learn from Borghini, and
from Bisagno; the latter says it should not be mixed

---

[1] Riposo, p. 173.   [2] Amoretti, Memorie Storiche di L. da Vinci, p. 38.
[3] Elogio e Memorie di Pietro Perugino, p. 208, and n.

with " ceneretta," and that for painting skies it should
be mixed with white lead, and tempered with nut oil.
This pigment is called " *cerulée* " in the Brussels MS.[1]
Lebrun states[2] that very beautiful blue draperies are
made with " azur à poudrer " (smalt) :[3] they must be
first painted with black and white, the lights being
bright (that is to say, very white), and the shades being
very dark, and then sprinkled with " azur à poudrer."
Mr. Eastlake gives[4] several instances of blue being
painted in this manner.   Christophe Ballard recommends[5] that email (smalt) should be mixed with oil
of turpentine, in order that it may dry and not flow,
email, he states, " being very difficult to use ; for if it be
made too liquid it will flow ; and if too thick and firm
you will not be able to use it ; but by mixing it with
spirit of turpentine it may be easily used ; for the oil of
turpentine evaporates in the air."   This author gives
the following directions for preventing the colour from
flowing (qu'elle ne coule) :—" When you have painted
your drapery, you will place your picture upon the
ground, or upon a table ; then you will take some
crumpled paper, such as the grey paper used by merchants, tear it into small pieces, and let it fall upon
your work.   The paper will absorb all the oil ; and
when the blue is nearly dry, and, as we say, ' embu,'
even although it should not be quite dry, the paper will
prevent the colour from flowing.   To remove the
paper, you must strike the picture upon a corner, and
all the paper will fall off : and note, that you must not
suffer it to dry, or you will not be able to remove the
paper ; neither must the pieces of paper be too large, or
they will mark the drapery."[6]

---

[1] P. 804.   [2] P. 821.

[3] Pierre Pomet, Hist. des Drogues, vol. i. p. 192, 193.

[4] Materials, &c., p. 431, 455.   [5] Traité de Mignature, p. 216, 217.

[6] For other methods of using smalt, see also Mr. Eastlake's ' Materials,'
&c., p. 427—432.

In 1676, "the finest ground smalt that ever came into England" was valued at 8s. a pound.[1]

The early history of cobalt and zaffre is involved in so much obscurity, and the evidence respecting it appears so conflicting, that it is considered useless to enter into the subject in the present work.[2] The same remark applies to the zaffirro of the middle ages, which, although it decidedly signifies in some cases ultra-marine, or lapis lazuli, is yet used so vaguely that it cannot be understood to be limited to this substance only. The difficulty of coming to any decision on this subject may be estimated by the consideration that the term zafirro, saffiro, or saphiro, was used to denote a precious stone of a blue colour as well as a blue mineral, which from its description must be lapis lazuli; that zaffera, saphra, or zaffre was a blue pigment prepared from cobalt, which is now known by the name of smalt, and that safar is the Moorish name for copper.[3] So little variation is there between the terms used to designate the three minerals from which the principal blue pigments are made.

Various kinds of artificial mineral azures were employed in Italy; many of these are described in the Bolognese MS. (cap. ii.). The pigment described at p. 388 is represented to be better than azzurro della magna, and in appearance and colour to be equal to ultramarine. Another of these azures is stated to be worth four ducats the pound;[4] and a third, five gold

---

[1] Walpole's Anecdotes, vol. iii. p. 137.

[2] It may be observed here that the Egyptians were acquainted with cobalt, but they used it only for colouring glass. The small blue figurines are coloured with copper, and neither M. Laurent, M. Malaguti, nor M. Salvetat, have been able to detect any cobalt in them. See De Brongniart, Traité des Arts Céramiques, p. 558, 563. The experiments of Prof. John, of Berlin, prove that the blues in the Egyptian paintings were oxides of copper, with a small intermixture of iron, and that none of them contain cobalt. See 'The Epochs of Painting characterised: a Sketch of the History of Painting, Ancient and Modern,' by Mr. Wornum.

[3] See Mr. Ford's Hand-book for Spain, p. 128.   [4] P. 391.

ducats the pound.[1] Borghini describes [2] several of these
artificial azures.   But of all the pigments of this class
there is none which is mentioned so frequently by all
writers on colours as the azure said to be prepared from
silver.[3] Yet, in spite of the most diligent inquiry, I have
been unable to ascertain that any salt of silver is ca-
pable of producing a blue colour. It is probable that the
composition of such a pigment may have been suggested
by the known fact, that the old bladetus de Inde before
mentioned was found in silver mines ; and it is very
probable that the medieval artists attributed to silver
the blue colour which was actually owing to the copper
with which the silver was mixed. Whenever a blue
colour was really produced from the solution of silver
plates in acetic acid, it may be concluded that the
colour was produced by the solution of the copper with
which the silver was alloyed ; and there appears to be
no evidence to support the assertion found in some
medieval MSS., that a blue colour could be produced
from pure silver. The blue pigment composed of sulphur, mercury, and sal ammoniac, has been called
Venetian azure.[4]

Bleu Minerale. — There is some doubt as to the
nature of the pigment known in Italy by this name.
Some persons consider it the same as turchino ; and
it seems a pigment prepared from copper and lime is
still sold under this name. Other persons state that it
was a preparation of cobalt, and was brought from Germany. In the Pharmaceutical Journal [5] it is stated to
be a cyanide of iron, produced by mixing a solution of
sulphate of iron with prussiate of potash, and carefully
heating the light precipitate, which is formed with nitric
acid, till it assumes a deep blue colour. The white
substances used for the finer sorts are alumina, gypsum,

---

[1] P. 403.   [2] Riposo, p. 173.
[3] Le Begue, p. 47, 49.   Bol. MS., p. 395, 399.   Theoph., E. ed., p. 422.
[4] See recipes at the end of the Abecedario Pittorico.   [5] Vol. vi. p. 82.

and heavy spar ; for the more common sorts, starch or clay. The same author also mentions that Prussian blue mixed with the oxide of zinc, was formerly sold under the name of bleu minerale.[1]

Ultramarine, Azur d'Acre.—The exact period when this fine pigment was introduced is not yet determined. There is no doubt, however, that the real lapis lazuli from Tartary was known in the thirteenth century, since it is mentioned in the work of Yousouf Jeifaschy, who appears to have been a jeweller of Cairo.[2] The term ultramarine must have been common in Italy at the beginning of the fourteenth century, since it occurs in the Italian MS. of Johannes de Modena,[3] and in the recipe given by Michelino de Vesuccio to Alcherius, both of which were copied in 1410. In some MSS. it is called " azurrum transmarinum," in contradistinction to azzurro della magna, which was called azzurrum citramarinum.[4] Ultramarine has always been occasionally used by the Italian painters, and so much was it esteemed that it was frequently the subject of a particular stipulation in contracts. It was generally supplied by the person who ordered the picture, but in some cases the artist himself agreed to employ it. Thus in 1501, Aloese Vivarino di Murano agreed to use ultramarine in his picture painted for the guardians of the Scuola della Carità.[5] It was employed by Paolo Veronese in the "Nozze di Cana;"[6] by Leandro Bassano, in his picture of the Battle of the good Angels with Lucifer, and in that of Sta. Lucia, painted for the church of S. Giorgio Maggiore at Venice;[7] by Pietro

[1] See Traité de la Peinture au Pastel, where this colour is said not to have been affected by the strongest vapours of liver of sulphur in effervescence with the mineral acids.

[2] Depping, Hist. du Commerce, vol. i. p. 147.   [3] P. 96, 102.

[4] P. 348 and n.

[5] For this notice, extracted from the Venetian archives, I am indebted to the Abbate Cadorin, the biographer of Titian.

[6] Iscriz. Venet., vol. iv. p. 253.   [7] Ibid., p. 349, 352.

Perugino, for his picture in the Duomo of Orvieto;[1] by
Palma Giovane, for the pictures he painted in S. Nicolò
at Treviso, in 1618;[2] by Gio. Batista Ponchino, for
the Pala d'Altare in the choir of the Archipresbiterale
at Treviso,[3] in 1551; by Denys Calvart, in 1601, and
by Francesco Albano, in 1639,[4] for their pictures in the
church of the Servites at Bologna; by Innocenza da
Imola, in his pictures in S. Michele in Bosco;[5] by
Felice Damiani, in 1593;[6] and by Ludovico Carracci,
in 1587,[7] in the picture of the Conversion of S. Paul.
It appears, from various entries in the account book
kept by Guercino[8] of the receipts for his pictures, that
he generally employed ultramarine which was furnished
by his employer. Sometimes the pigment, ready prepared, was given to him, and sometimes the lapis lazuli,
from which it appears he was to prepare the colour
himself. Thus, for the picture called "L'Amore Virtuoso," he received twenty-one ounces of lapis lazuli to
make ultramarine.

Contrary to the assertion of some modern artists,
Pungeleone states[9] that Correggio always made use of
ultramarine, although it appears that he employed
" azzurro " (probably azzurro della magna), which cost
but three lire the ounce, for the decoration of the " casa
del anchona de lo altare grando " at Correggio.[10]

Ultramarine is stated to have been found on Venetian
pictures; and although the artists of this school used also
the blue pigments from copper, there seems little doubt
that the greater part of the ultramarine imported into

---

[1] Orsini, Elogio di Pietro Perugino, p. 194 and n.

[2] Memorie Trevigiane, vol. ii. p. 59.

[3] Ibid., p. 76.

[4] Gualandi, Memorie, ser. i. p. 4, 19.   [5] Ibid., p. 61.

[6] Ibid., ser. ii. p. 4.   [7] Ibid., ser. ii. p. 132.

[8] The original account book is in the Ercolani Collection at Bologna.
It has been published in the new edition of the Felsina Pittrice, by Jacopo
Alesandro Calvi, at Bologna.

[9] Life of Correggio, vol. i. p. 248.   [10] Ibid., vol. ii. p. 68, 69.

Italy was introduced by way of Venice, which was the great emporium of Oriental commerce.

The price of ultramarine at different periods has been preserved by several writers. In 1437 it was sold at Florence for eight ducats the ounce.[1] In 1548 the price at Venice was sixty scudi the ounce.[2] In 1788 the price at Paris was one hundred francs, or even as much as fifty crowns the ounce.[3] The value of ultramarine is not stated in the Bolognese MS., but the price of a pound of lapis lazuli varied, according to the goodness of the specimen, from two to five ducats. De Boot mentions[4] that lapis lazuli was usually sold for eight or ten thalers the pound, and if the stone was good it would produce at least ten ounces of azure. One of the best specimens would yield five and a half ounces of the best colour, worth twenty thalers the ounce. The second quality was worth five or six thalers, the third only one thaler, or one and a half. The price paid by Lely for one ounce of ultramarine was 2*l*. 10*s*., but for the best kind he paid as much as 4*l*. 10*s*. the ounce.[5]

Pacheco states[6] that ultramarine was not used by the Spanish painters in his time, but it was introduced at a subsequent period, since he himself mentions the colour;[7] and Palomino gives directions[8] for using it. The latter remarks that it was never used in the first painting, because, as it had but little body, it did not cover well; and also because, as it was very dear, it would have been employed uselessly; it was therefore either glazed or worked upon some of the other blues. When employed in glazing it was only necessary to mix it with nut-oil, and to pass it over the drapery with a soft brush, moistened with nut-oil and a few drops of spirit of turpentine, so as to leave it smooth and even.

[1] Cennini, Trattato, cap. 62.   [2] Paolo Pino, Dialogo, p. 18.
[3] Traité de la Peinture au Pastel.   [4] Le parfaict Joaillier, p. 371.
[5] Walpole's Anecdotes, vol. iii. pp. 130, 132.   [6] Tratado, p. 391.
[7] Ibid., p. 392.   [8] Museo Pictorico, vol. ii. p. 68.

If the drapery was to be painted with ultramarine, the light and dark tints were to be mixed with white lead and nut-oil, and the shadows heightened with indigo, and if the drapery were previously glazed with ultramarine it would be more easy to execute. As a dryer, Palomino recommends pulverized smalt; but, he says, it must be used cautiously or it will spoil the colour of the ultramarine.[1]

De Piles also remarks,[2] that ultramarine should not be employed for the first painting, but that the lights and shades should be painted in very distinctly, the high lights consisting of pure white, with common colours; or that the first shade tints, and even the half tints, may be painted with charcoal of the willow, which inclines to blue, or with bone black, and then finished with ultramarine; but he adds, that this last method was not so good as the former, neither were the tints so fresh.

Ultramarine was employed by Simone Cantarini with terra verde in the shadows of flesh, and probably by Guido and some of his pupils,[3] and by Baroccio;[4] and Padre Francesco Lana recommends[5] that it should be mixed with all the flesh tints.

Blue pigments prepared from vegetables are not numerous; the principal are those procured from indigo and woad. Blue colours were also procured from the flowers of the cornflower,[6] from turnsol or folium, and other plants. The use of these pigments was limited to miniature painting. *Guato*, or more correctly *guado*, is the Italian name for the isatis tinctoria, called also glastum sativum—a plant which grows spontaneously in France, Germany, England, and other parts of Europe. It was called glastum by the Romans, and is now

---

[1] Museo Pictorico, vol. ii. p. 57.   [2] Elémens, pp. 108, 118.

[3] Malvasia, Fels. Pitt., vol. ii. pp. 80, 448.

[4] Bellori, Vite, &c., p. 118.   [5] P. 746.

[6] Constant de Massoul, p. 186.

known in France by the names of Pastel, Vouede, and Gaude.

There is sufficient evidence to show that indigo was known as a pigment in the time of the Romans, and that it was used as such during the middle ages in Italy, where it was sold under the name of indigo bagadel, indigo baccadeo or bandas, indacca detto buccaddeo, indaco del golfo.[1] But there is no doubt that the pigment called "indigo," so frequently mentioned by writers on colours in the thirteenth, fourteenth, and fifteenth centuries, was generally prepared from woad, and not from the real indigo. This will appear from various recipes in the Bolognese MS.,[2] in the whole of which woad is the principal ingredient.

It will be observed that the pigment is generally prepared from the blue or purple coloured scum which floats on the dyers' vats, and which is the produce of fermentation. This agrees with the account of Dioscorides, who says there were two kinds of indigo, the first of which was brought from India, but the second, which was made during the process of dyeing, was a purple scum which floated on the surface of the vats. In commenting on this passage, Matthioli observes,[3] " the indigo generally used by the painters was that made in dyehouses, which was procured from woad with which wool is dyed." This passage alone is sufficient to prove that the term "indigo" was applied to woad. Beckmann says,[4] that under the name *indigo* must be understood every kind of blue pigment separated from plants by fermentation, and converted into a friable substance by desiccation ; for those who should maintain that the real indigo must be made from those

---

[1] Depping, vol. i. p. 141. See Cennini, Trattato, cap. 61. Le Begue, pp. 86, 273.

[2] Pp. 412—416. See also Secreti di D. Alessio, parte ii. p. 34; Nuovo Plicto d'ogni sorte di Tinture ; and Paduan MS., p. 676.

[3] Trans. of Dioscorides, p. 1414.   [4] Inventions, tit. Indigo.

plants named in the botanical system *Indigofera tinctoria*, would confine the subject within too narrow limits; as the substance which our merchants and dyers consider as real indigo is prepared in different countries from so great a number of plants, that they are not even varieties of the same species." Although indigo was not considered a durable colour, it appears to have been occasionally used in oil.

The tints were made with white lead. Palomino says,[1] " that it is a fine colour for draperies, and works pleasantly, but that it is necessary to observe the following conditions: 1st, That the lights should not be too light, because the colour fades—therefore the tints should be sufficiently deep; the 2nd and most important, that the tints should not be too oily, but thick, and not tormented with the brush; and 3rdly, that the colour should be well purified." Different modes of purifying indigo are described by Palomino,[2] and in the recipes at the end of the Abecedario Pittorico, and also in the Paduan MS.[3] When carefully employed, Félibien states[4] that it is durable if properly used, but that too much oil must not be mixed with it, and allowance must be made for its tendency to fade.

Green Pigments.

Mineral green pigments, both natural and artificial, are produced from copper. The native green ores of this metal have always been used in painting under the names of *mountain green, Hungarian green, chrysocolla, malachite, cenere verde, verde de miniera, verde di Spagna, verdetto,* and *green bice.* To these colours must be added *terra verde,* which is said by some persons to owe its colour to copper;[5] others consider that

---

[1] Vol. ii. p. 67.   [2] Museo Pictorico, vol. ii. p. 67.

[3] P. 676.   [4] Des Principes, &c., p. 299.

[5] Marcucci, Saggio, &c., p. 71.   Pierre Pomet, Hist. des Drogues, vol. ii. p. 385.

it is a bluish or grey coaly clay, combined with yellow oxide of iron or yellow ochre.[1] It was sometimes called *Prasino* and *Theodote.* Pierre Pomet[2] states that mountain green was a greenish powder in small grains like sand, and that it was distinguished by this sandy appearance from the artificial, which consisted of pulverized verdigris mixed with a little white lead. It was also sometimes adulterated with cendre verte, of which there were many varieties.[3] Mountain green appears to have been but little used in oil painting.

Native carbonate of copper, although sometimes a pure blue and sometimes pure green, was frequently of a mixed colour, when it was called *verde azzurro.*

Prasino or *Prasminum.*—Isidorus gives this name to green earth [4] (terre verte). But in some cases the name has been applied to a white earth saturated with a vegetable juice of a green colour, as in the Bolognese MS., No. 88.

Verde Porro—Perhaps the same as the Prasino of the middle ages. It is mentioned in the Paduan MS., also by Pozzo in his instructions for painting in fresco, and by Baldinucci;[5] the latter states that it was a pigment of a whitish green colour, like that of the leek, whence it takes its name. It appears that during the middle ages the juice of the leek was actually used as a pigment.[6]

Various artificial green pigments were prepared from copper which were known to medieval painters under the names of *viride salsum, viride Hispanicum, viride Rothomagense,* and *viride Græcum.* In the last may be traced the verdigris (verd de Grèce)[7] of the moderns.

The best kind of verdigris was prepared at Marseilles by a process which has been frequently described.

---

[1] Field, Chromatography, p. 233; and see Merimée, p. 191.
[2] Hist. des Drogues, vol. ii. p. 286.   [3] Ibid., p. 385.
[4] See p. 244, n. 4; and Theophilus, E. ed., 101.   [5] Voc. Dis.
[6] See p. 156.   [7] See Mr. Eastlake's ' Materials,' &c., p. 118.

This pigment was known to the Spaniards by the names
of verdete and cardenillo. Verdigris was generally
purified by redissolving it in vinegar, and then suffering
it to crystallize in large crystals, by the evaporation of
the vinegar, when it was sold under the name of "distilled" or "crystallized verdigris" and "verde eterno."

Verdetto.—There are several pigments of this name.
1. A mineral green pigment which, according to Borghini and Baldinucci, is found in the mountains of Germany; this probably was mountain green or malachite,
the green carbonate of copper. 2. A vegetable pigment mentioned by Lomazzo and in the Paduan MS.,
which was of a yellowish colour, apparently of the
nature of brown pink; Haydocke called this colour
holy green. 3. An artificial green pigment prepared
from copper, called "Verdet" in the Brussels MS.,[1]
and Verdete by the Spanish. These two pigments
differ in the mode of preparation.

Verde eterno.—Another name for distilled or crystallized verdigris.[2] It is a neutral acetate of copper,
prepared by dissolving verdigris in hot acetic acid,
and leaving the filtered solution to cool. It forms
beautiful dark green crystals. It is said to have been
much used by the Venetian painters. This colour is
mentioned by Volpato, who remarks,[3] " Il verde eterno
si cristalino chiaro e di color vivace." Baldinucci says[4]
it was so called because it never lost its brightness, as
all other greens did. He adds that this was nothing
else but a glazing of purified verdigris spread thin over
silver leaf.[5]

Green pigments prepared from vegetables are numerous. The principal of these are *sap green*, the *verde di
vesicha* and *pasta verde* of the Italians, prepared from
the berries of the buckthorn (Spincervino—Rhamnus

[1] P. 806.   [2] Marcucci, Saggio, &c., p. 74.   [3] P. 744.
[4] Voc. Dis.   [5] See also Mr. Eastlake's ' Materials,' p. 458.

catharticus). The juice being boiled down was inspissated, and when dry was preserved in bladders.

Lily or *Iris* green (verde giglio).—This pigment was sometimes prepared for use by dipping pieces of linen (pezzette) into the juice and then preserving them dry. Green pigments were also prepared from rue, parsley, columbine, and from the black nightshade (the herba morella of the Italians, which must be distinguished from the " maurelle " or Croton tinctorium). The juice of this plant was incorporated with green earth ; in this respect it resembled the pigments called by the French stils de grain, prepared from the berries of the Rhamnus infectorius (grain d'Avignon). The colour of these pigments varied from a brownish green (brown pink) to yellow.

It was generally considered that mixed greens, composed of blue and yellow, were more permanent than any of the before-mentioned green pigments. They were frequently compounded of ultramarine and orpiment, of azzurro della magna and giallolino, of indigo and orpiment, and of one of the mineral blues with a yellow lake.[1]

Verdigris, and especially distilled verdigris, or verde eterno, was extensively employed by all the Italian schools for glazing, and especially by the Venetian, and the brilliant green draperies on the pictures of this school were produced by this colour.

Verdigris was sometimes added to black to make it dry,[2] but Le Brun remarks [3] that it must only be used in the shadows, for it is a poison in painting, and kills all the colours with which it is mixed. It appears, from the Paduan MS.[4] to have been sometimes mixed with vegetable greens and yellows, and also with umber

---

[1] See Cennini, cap. 53, 54, 55 ; Borghini, p. 170.   [2] Volpato, p. 747.
[3] P. 823, and see De Piles, Elémens, &c., p. 124. Félibien, Principes, &c., 300.   [4] P. 652.

and indigo for making dark green. It should, however, be used alone; and De Piles observes[1] that if the smallest particle of it enter into the priming of a picture, it is sufficient to ruin it. It is even necessary, he adds, to avoid using with other colours the brushes which have been employed for verdigris.

Lionardo da Vinci remarks[2] that it was liable not only to fade, but to be removed from the picture by washing it with water, unless a coat of varnish was passed over it.

Volpato also notices the solubility of this colour in water, and remarks that it must be removed from the palette before the latter is put into water to preserve the colours when the day's work is over. In the Venetian school it appears the colour was usually laid on with varnish.

Pacheco directs[3] that purified verdigris should be ground in oil for the first painting, but for the last glazing varnish should be added. Lebrun says[4] that to make a very beautiful green for glazing, verdigris should be used with varnish; it will then be very beautiful, and will not fade. In another place he observes,[5] "Verdigris is very good, if employed with fat oil."

Verdigris is liable to turn black in time, and when in this state the surface has been removed by a penknife, and the colour beneath was found to be perfectly fresh and bright.

Borghini states[6] that terra verde was used in all three (fresco, oil, and tempera) kinds of painting. Lebrun remarks:[7] "Verd de terre is used in the shades of flesh-colour, but it must be employed sparingly, for with age the colour appears crude, which would produce a bad effect." Merimée observes[8] that Rubens had made great use of this colour, not only in landscapes but

---

[1] Elémens, &c., p. 124.   [2] Trattato, cap. xcix.
[3] Tratado, p. 389.   [4] P. 813.   [5] P. 815.
[6] Riposo, p. 169.   [7] P. 813.   [8] De la Peinture à l'Huile, p. 192.

in his carnations. He concurs with Le Brun in the fact
of the colour deepening in time, and states that for this
reason terre verte should be employed cautiously.
There are frequent notices in Italian writers of terre
verte being employed in painting the shades of flesh,
but it is not always clear whether the pigment was
used raw or burnt. Thus Malvasia,[1] in speaking of
Simone Cantarini's method of painting flesh, remarks,
" He was therefore as partial to white lead as he was
inimical to lake and umber for his outlines and shades;
in which he used to employ plenty of ultramarine and
terra verde, learning from Guido the value of these
two colours in painting delicate shadows." It is very
possible that as the terra verde was used for the shadows, it might have been burnt. Lomazzo directs[2]
that the shadow colour for flesh should be made with
nero di campana and *burnt* terra verde, or with umber
and *burnt* terra verde; and the Paduan MS.[3] states
that umber, *burnt* terra verde, and asphaltum were
used for the same purpose.

Brown Pigments.

The brown pigments used in the middle ages were
very few; those employed by the Italians were not
numerous, and they are frequently classed with black
pigments. The principal were bistre, which is mentioned by medieval writers under the name of fuligo
and by Lomazzo under that of fuligine; umber, raw
and burnt; Cologne earth, burnt terra verde, and
asphaltum.

Umber is a hydrate of oxide of iron mixed with a
variable quantity of oxide of manganese and a small
proportion of clay.[4] Merimée says it contains silica and
alumina also. The best is reputed to be brought from
the Levant, although it is really the produce of

---

[1] Fels. Pitt., vol. ii. p. 448.   [2] Trattato, p. 302.   [3] P. 650.
[4] De Brongniart, Essaie des Arts Céramiques, p. 539.

Cyprus.[1] This was probably imported into Venice, and thence to other parts of Europe, particularly to Spain, where the Venetian umber was sold under the name of sombra di Venezia.[2]

Besides its use in painting as a shadow colour both in flesh[3] and yellow draperies[4] and for all colours lighter than itself,[5] it was sometimes boiled with oil as a drier both for painting and mordants.[6] It was also occasionally added to grounds,[7] but for this purpose it was not generally approved.[8] Umber was sometimes called falzalo by the Italians.[9] Mixed with fine lake, it was used as a glazing colour for shadows.

Cologne earth, a bituminous earth, which, although a powerful colour, has the disadvantage of fading and of drying very slowly. The former, according to Merimée, is prevented by mixing it with very durable pigments, the latter can only be remedied by the addition of a drier to the oil. This pigment does not appear to have been known to Lomazzo, Borghini, or the early Italian writers. Neither does the name occur in any of the treatises in this work, nor in the 'Principes de Peinture' of Félibien, nor the 'Elémens de Peinture' of De Piles. It seems to have been used principally by the Flemish and Dutch painters.[10] It is, however, stated to have been employed by the Venetian painters, but this appears to require confirmation.

When *terra verde* is burnt over a slow fire,[11] and the heat gradually increased until the pigment is roasted, it is converted into a fine warm brown, which was used, mixed with other colours, by the Italians for the shadows of flesh.[12] Modern writers do not mention this

---

[1] Merimée, p. 206. [2] Palomino, vol. ii. pp. 52, 149.
[3] Pp. 650, 654. Malvasia, Fels. Pitt., vol. ii. p. 448. Palomino, vol. ii. pp. 62—64. Lomazzo, Trattato, pp. 191, 312.
[4] Palomino, vol. ii. p. 66. [5] Lomazzo, Trattato, p. 197.
[6] Borghini, p. 176. Paduan MS., p. 740. [7] Volpato, pp. 730, 746, n.
[8] P. 813. Merimée, p. 206. [9] Lomazzo, Trattato, p. 191.
[10] Mr. Eastlake's 'Materials,' &c., p. 462. [11] P. 745.
[12] P. 650. Lomazzo, Trattato, p. 191.

colour, but the use of it has been revived by an eminent English artist, under the name of "Verona
brown."

Asphaltum, Bitume Giudaico, Nero di Spalto.—
Several kinds of asphaltum are used in the arts. The
best is considered to be the Egyptian. This will dissolve neither in oil, water, nor turpentine, but it must
be fused, and then mixed with linseed oil.[1] There is
little doubt from the descriptions of Borghini[2] and
Baldinucci,[3] that the old masters used the Egyptian
asphaltum, since they mention that it was brought from
the Lake of Sodom. Other kinds of asphaltum are
brought from China, France, Neufchâtel, and Naples.
That brought from Naples is reputed to be next in
goodness to the Egyptian. It will dissolve in oil, but
never yields that intense black to the same quantity of
oil as the real Egyptian. This is probably the kind
now employed by the Italians, who dissolve it in oil,
spirit of turpentine, and Venice turpentine. It is not
always easy to procure genuine asphaltum. Watin
remarks[4] that it was frequently adulterated with pitch,
and that what is generally sold for asphaltum in Hol-
land is nothing but the residuum left after the distillation of oil of amber. Mr. Wilson Neil states that
a similar kind of factitious asphaltum is now made in
London, which is not inferior to the best Egyptian.
This consists of the residuum left from burning linseed-
oil and resin. The mixture of resin with asphaltum
may be detected by spirit of wine, which dissolves the
resin, but not the asphaltum.[5]

Lomazzo says[6] that it was used to give brightness to
light and chesnut hair. Boschini states[7] that it was
much employed by Andrea Schiavone, who used it in

---

[1] Wilson Neil on the Manufacture of Varnishes, Trans. Soc. Arts, vol.
xlix. p. 57.   [2] Riposo, p. 164.   [3] Voc. Dis.
[4] L'Art du Vernisseur, p. 216.   [5] Marcucci, Saggio, &c., p. 95.
[6] Trattato, p. 198.   [7] Ricche Minere.

glazing the shades of the flesh in undraped figures,—
that Giacomo Bassano (il Vecchio) employed it mixed
with lake in the ultimate retouchings, and that he
glazed with this colour all the shadows indifferently,
whether of flesh, or drapery, or other things. In the
Paduan MS. it is stated to be used for the shadows of
flesh mixed with umber and burnt terra verde.[1]

Palomino[2] classes asphaltum among the useless
colours, and says its place may be supplied with bone
black, mixed with fine carmine and ancorca; that it is
a bad drier, and requires the addition of a mordant to
make it dry: he adds, that there is no doubt it was
used by the great colourists, especially in Seville and
Granada, although one may do miracles without it.
Volpato directs[3] that it should be mixed with boiled
oil and verdigris to make it dry.

The evidence of a modern Italian writer[4] and of
several restorers of pictures is decidedly in favour of its
having been used as a glazing colour only; according
to the latter it was dissolved in oil or spirit of turpentine, and applied, like other glazing colours, with the
hand, which insured its being thinly and evenly spread.
But even as a glazing colour, it grew darker in time,[5]
and the obscurity, so frequently observed and regretted,
of many Italian pictures, is attributed to the excessive
use of asphaltum. The fact that the Neapolitan asphaltum does not yield so intense a black to the same
quantity of oil as the Egyptian, with its known property
of darkening with age on paintings, would seem to
suggest the propriety of using the Egyptian asphaltum,
which being intensely black at first, would probably be
less likely to increase in colour. Its extreme blackness
would at least cause it to be employed sparingly and
very thinly as a shadow colour.

---

[1] P. 650.   [2] Museo Pictorico, vol. ii. p. 53.   [3] P. 747.
[4] Marcucci, pp. 95, 208.   [5] Bald., Voc. Dis.

Marcucci describes a liquid preparation of asphaltum composed in the following manner: one part of Venice turpentine and one and a half part of spirit of turpentine are put into a bottle which is to be placed in a sand-bath to liquefy; two parts of asphaltum are then to be added in powder, and the whole is to be stirred and left over the fire until it boils. When it has boiled for one hour, it is to be removed from the fire, and before it cools a little nut-oil is to be added to give it a proper consistence, and when it is used a small quantity of mastic varnish and some kind of drier are to be added. This, he says, is an excellent colour for glazing, but it must be used sparingly, as it deepens its colour with age.

Mummy is by some [1] considered to be the same as asphaltum, but Marcucci [2] states that the colour of the former is warmer, and the smell more aromatic, and that its external character is different. He remarks that it is a fine colour for glazing oil-paintings, especially in the carnations; it is ground with nut-oil, and is used with varnish and a drier.

Black Pigments.

The principal black pigments were terra nera, coal, terra nera di Campana, nero di schiuma di ferro, and charcoal of various kinds; namely, burnt ivory and bones, oak and vine branches, stones of peaches, shells of almonds, paper, smoke of resin, and of nut-oil.

Terra nera, which may certainly be considered synonymous with *terre noire*, is identified by De Mayerne with " *crayon noir*," or " *black chalke*." [3] The Italians procured terra nera from several places. Cennini [4] mentions a black stone brought from Piedmont, used for drawing and painting, which he describes as soft and unctuous. Later Italian writers mention terra

---

[1] Palomino, vol. ii. p. 53.   [2] Saggio, &c., p. 95.
[3] Mr. Eastlake's ' Materials,' &c., p. 466.   [4] Cap. 34.

nera di Roma and terra nera di Venezia; the latter was procured from Verona. Borghini says[1] that nero di terra is a native unctuous pigment, which may be used in fresco, oil, and tempera painting. The name of this pigment occurs in the Paduan MS.[2] Lomazzo[3] does not appear to distinguish it from nero di scaglia.

A black pigment from common coal (charbon de terre) does not appear to be mentioned by Italian writers, although it is said, on the authority of Lebrun,[4] to have been much used in Italy for external painting, because it was more durable than any other. Mr. Eastlake has shown[5] that it was frequently employed by the Flemish and Dutch painters. The tint furnished by coal mixed with oil is stated to be brownish.

Terra nera di Campana is made from a certain crust which forms on the moulds in which bells and artillery are cast. It is used in all three kinds of painting, but in a short time it fades and spoils the pictures. It is mentioned by Borghini,[6] by Baldinucci,[7] and by Lomazzo.[8]

Nero di Schiuma di Ferro was composed of scales of iron mixed with terra verde and finely ground. Borghini, Lomazzo, and Baldinucci mention this colour.

Ivory Black is distinguished by many writers from bone black. It is described as being intensely black, and very transparent. Lebrun remarks that if it is steeped in vinegar and dried in the sun, it cannot be effaced.

Bone Black was prepared from the bones of various animals, but Palomino states[9] that the best kind was prepared from the bones of pigs, although the bones of stags and oxen were sometimes used. Others employed mutton bones. It is represented to be of a reddish colour, which may even be converted into brown by

---

[1] Riposo, p. 164.   [2] P. 650.   [3] Trattato, p. 192.   [4] P. 812 and n.
[5] Materials, &c., p. 467.   [6] Riposo, p. 164.   [7] Voc. Dis.
[8] Trattato, p. 193.   [9] Museo Pictorico, vol. ii. p. 53.

arresting the carbonization before it is complete, and to
dry very slowly. In grinding it with oil it is necessary
to use more force than with any other colour, in order
to add with more facility the necessary quantity of fat
or drying oil.[1]

The blacks made from vegetable charcoal are not of
so intense a black as those of ivory and bone ;[2] of these
some painters preferred the black made from burnt
vine-branches, sometimes called *blue black*,[3] which Borghini says[4] is excellent for painting in oil. Other authors
mention the charcoal of burnt oak stripped of the bark,[5]
of the stones of peaches, and of the shells of almonds.[6]
The black of peach stones when mixed with white has a
blue tint. Lamp black is used in oil painting, although
not approved of by many writers.[7] It is always necessary
to calcine it before it is used in oil painting.[8] Ink, and
especially printing-ink, was formerly made of the soot
collected from burning resin or oil in a paper lantern.
This is the ink of which Cennini speaks in the early
part of his book. It was also used by Lionardo da
Vinci[9] mixed with lake for the darkest shades, and Vasari relates that Fra Bartolomeo wishing to imitate the
colouring of Lionardo on a certain picture, also employed this colour and burnt ivory, and that the picture
had darkened much in consequence. To the same cause
Vasari attributes the darkening of the colours in the
'Transfiguration' of Raphael.[10]

Another charcoal black was procured from the ashes
of paper, burnt in a closed iron tube and afterwards
ground with water.[11] This black pigment is mentioned

---

[1] Constant de Massoul, p. 215.   [2] Merimée, p. 208.
[3] Constant de Massoul, p. 215.
[4] Riposo, p. 164; and see Cennini, Trattato, cap. xxxvii.
[5] Palomino, vol. ii. p. 54. Borghini, p. 164.
[6] Cennini, cap. 37. Borghini, p. 164. Baldinucci, Voc. Dis.
[7] See p. 823.   [8] Marcucci, p. 167. Merimée, p. 209.
[9] Trattato, c. 353 ; and see Vasari, Vita di Fra Bartolomeo.
[10] Vasari, Vita di Raffaello da Urbino.   [11] Marcucci, p. 167.

by Borghini [1] and by Baldinucci, and appears to be still made in Italy. Marcucci [2] states that he had found it a very good black, and that it did not deepen in colour like some other blacks.

Black pigments are considered slow in drying. Volpato directs [3] that boiled oil and verdigris should be added to lamp-black to make it dry. [4] The Paduan MS. [5] recommends the addition of ground glass, which it is stated will make the colour dry in twenty-four hours. Baldinucci [6] says black earth, bone black, and lamp black require the addition of litharge or ground glass to the boiled oil.

From the preceding account of the principal colours used in painting it will be seen that, notwithstanding the numerous names by which pigments were known in different countries and at different periods, the real number was not in fact so great as might be at first imagined. This is exemplified in the various names by which the blue carbonate of copper and the red ores of iron were formerly known.

It will also be observed that the colours lost or fallen into disuse are the native mineral pigments, for which artificial preparations of a similar nature have been substituted. Thus the native yellow and red orpiment have been superseded by the artificial pigments which bear these names, and which, besides the usual defects of artificial as compared with natural pigments, have the additional disadvantage of being more poisonous. Instead of the native giallorino, or Naples yellow, we have the modern pigment composed of the oxides of lead and antimony, known under the name of Naples yellow. Instead of the native carbonates of copper we have the artificial preparations. Native minium and native cinnabar have also fallen into disuse. The only

---

[1] Riposo, p. 164.　　[2] Saggio, p. 208.　　[3] P. 747.　　[4] P. 822.
[5] P. 666.　　　　[6] Voc. Dis.

exception, perhaps, besides the natural yellow and red ochres, is ultramarine, for which no perfect substitute, possessing properties in every respect equally eligible, has yet been discovered. With the exception of these natural pigments, the colours lost are of little value.

It will be also observed that the more durable lakes prepared from kermes and lac have been superseded by the more brilliant, but less permanent, lake from cochineal.

Another source of confusion, and which has much increased the difficulty of identifying pigments, has arisen from giving the name of a well-known pigment to another which resembled it in colour, but which in other respects differed essentially. Among pigments of this description may be enumerated *sandarace, sandaraca,* which has been used to denote red orpiment, red lead, and massicot; *minium,* the ancient term for vermilion, and the modern term for red lead; *cinnabar,* used to signify a red earth and vermilion; *smalto, smaltino,* sometimes applied to a vitreous blue pigment coloured with smalt, sometimes to one coloured with copper; *indigo,* used to denote both woad and indigo; *arzica,* which signified both a yellow lake and a native ochreous pigment; *verdetto,* which denoted sometimes a native mineral green pigment, sometimes an artificial mineral pigment of the same colour, and sometimes a vegetable green pigment.

Finally, the confusion has been increased by adopting foreign names instead of the original term; thus one of the old pigments called giallorino is now known in Italy under the term massicot, and the original appellation is almost lost.

Of Grinding and Diluting the Colours.

The universal testimony of all writers who have
treated on the technical part of painting establishes the
fact that the colours (excepting some which were kept
in powder) were ground in oil.[1] Vasari, Armenini,
Bisagno, Borghini, and Gasparo Colombino[2] give the
preference to nut-oil, which, it is stated, is less apt to
become yellow. Borghini says,[3] "Let him who would
paint in oil on panel . . . . colour it with colours tempered with nut-oil only, and nothing else " (senza più).
Volpato directs[4] that white lead should be ground with
nut-oil; verde eterno, indigo, and all other blues, charcoal, and other colours with linseed oil. The Marciana
MS. also directs[5] that all the colours were to be ground
with oil as stiffly as possible, that is, with very little oil,
and that they were to be ground so finely that on being
felt with the fingers no hard grains could be perceived.
This is in accordance with the old Italian practice, as
described by Cennini, who repeatedly inculcates the
perfect levigation of the colours; and with the example
of Michael Angelo, who is said to have ground his own
colours,[6] and also with the practice of the Flemish
school.[7] But it appears that the later Italians, and
especially the Venetians, did not consider this point of
importance as far as regards the under colours. If
there were any doubt of the colours of the Venetians
being coarsely ground, it would be sufficiently proved
by the assertion of a professor of painting at Venice
that he had with his penknife picked out of Venetian

---

[1] Félibien, Principes, &c., p. 295. Bulengerus, De Pictura, &c. Bald.,
Voc. Dis.   Lebrun, p. 771.

[2] Discorso del Disegno, &c. Padova, 1623.

[3] Riposo, p. 138.   [4] P. 739.   [5] P. 627.

[6] See Lanzi, Storia Pittorica, vol. i. p. 114.

[7] " Les peintres Flamands ne prennent que la créme des couleurs, après
les avoir délayées et noyées dans une grande quantité d'eau."—Traité de la
Peinture au Pastel, &c.

pictures of the best period grains of colour sufficiently large to have them analysed.

The recommendation in the Marciana MS. before mentioned to grind the colours with as little oil as possible is insisted upon by most writers on art.[1] Borghini gives[2] as a reason for this practice that the oil in drying would become dark (nero). Again, he remarks, "If the colours are made liquid with too much oil, it lessens considerably their brilliancy." The use of too much oil is frequently condemned by Malvasia[3] and by Lanzi. The latter attributes[4] to this cause the ruin of so many paintings by the Carracci, by Lo Spagnuolo, and by Pasignano. Armenini also concurs in stating that oil renders the colours dark.

After directing how the colours are to be ground the Marciana MS. continues, "Also, while you are painting, if you find the colours too stiff, dip your pencil into a little oil and stir it well into the colour." The same MS. also directs that the "vernice comune," which might be mixed with colours, was, when too thick, to be diluted with oil. It may be considered certain, then, that during the first half of the sixteenth century it was the practice in Italy to dilute the colours with nut or linseed oil, and not with an essential oil. The anecdote related by Ridolfi, who wrote a century later than this MS., proves that this practice was preserved, traditionally at least, in his time. But although this may have been the general practice, it by no means follows that all colours were thus diluted; and the specification that certain colours were to be made to flow by dipping the brush in an essential oil, is at once an admission that it was the general custom to use linseed or nut oil for this purpose, and also that these oils were not equally adapted

---

1 Félibien, Principes, &c., p. 298. Requenos, Saggio, &c., vol. i. p. 163. Verri, Saggio Elementare, &c., p. 116. Marcucci, Saggio, &c., p. 201.

2 Riposo, p. 175. 3 Fels. Pitt., vol. ii. p. 450.

4 Storia Pittorica, vol. v. pp. 70, 161 ; vol. i. p. 196.

for all colours. Thus Volpato observes[1] that painters were accustomed to make Spanish blue flow by dipping their brushes in spirit of turpentine, and ultramarine with naphtha. Pacheco, whose whites and blues were the admiration of Cespedes, and of those Italian painters who had seen them, relates[2] that he dipped his brush in oil of spike when painting to make the colours flow. It appears, however, that the practice of diluting the colours with naphtha was sometimes carried to excess by the Bolognese painters; this was the case with Flaminio Torre, the irrecoverable decay of whose pictures is attributed by Malvasia[3] and Lanzi[4] to the constant use of naphtha. Félibien,[5] who appears to have been well acquainted with the Italian practice, remarks that "those who wish their pictures to remain fresh use as little oil as possible, and keep their colours firmer by mixing a little oil of spike with them; this soon evaporates, but it makes the colours flow and work more easily." From a passage in the Brussels MS.[6] it may be concluded that oil of chamomile was sometimes used for the same purpose.

On the Purification and Bleaching of Oil.

There appears to be no doubt that oil was always purified and bleached before the colours were ground with it. It is, however, somewhat extraordinary that neither Armenini, Vasari, Borghini, nor Bisagno allude to this fact. The precautions taken by Lionardo da Vinci[7] for the preparation of his oils are, however, well known, and incidental allusions to the purification of oil may also be found in Vasari[8] and other authors. The remark of the Gesuato, at the end of his directions

---

[1] P. 749.   [2] Tratado, p. 392.   [3] Fels. Pitt., vol. ii. p. 450.

[4] Storia Pittorica, vol. v. p. 105.   [5] Principes, &c , p. 297.   [6] P. 814.

[7] Amoretti, Memorie Storiche, &c., di Lionardo da Vinci, p. 149.

[8] See account of Giovan Francesco Caroti, in the Life of Fra Giocondo.

for purifying oil—"Observe that, whenever you find oil mentioned, this purified oil is meant"—may be considered proof of the importance attached to this fact. The recipe of the Gesuato forms part of the directions for preparing ultramarine,[1] and the oil was used in making the resinous pastille into which the powdered ultramarine was kneaded, and the colour worked out into the water. If it was necessary to employ purified oil for this purpose, it was much more important to procure such an oil to mix with colours.

The Marciana MS. directs[2] that purified oil should be used for mordants, and at the end of the recipe gives the following directions for purifying it:—" Boil it over the fire with water for three or four hours, then let it settle, and separate it from the water." In another recipe it is said,[3]—" Take linseed-oil, boiled in the usual way;" from which it appears that the method just described was that which was usually adopted. In the same MS. it is remarked,[4] that if the nut or linseed-oil is inspissated by exposure to the sun, the varnish made with it will be clearer.

Palomino states[5] that all colours were generally ground with linseed-oil, because it was more drying than nut-oil, which was reserved solely for the blues and whites in finishing, and especially for ultramarine; " but," he adds, " if nut-oil cannot be obtained, linseed-oil may be clarified by putting it into a vessel with white-lead in powder, stirring it well until it is quite white, and exposing it to the sun and dew, stirring it up every day, for three days, then let it be used, because if it is kept longer it will become fat. Pacheco's method of preparing bleached linseed-oil, which might be used with white and blue, was as follows:[6]—" Take a glass vessel, and to one pound of limpid and clear

---

[1] Secreti di Don Alessio, parte ii. f. 62; and see Mr. Eastlake's ' Materials,' p. 327.   [2] P. 621.   [3] Ibid.

[4] P. 635.   [5] Museo Pictorico, vol. ii. p. 55.   [6] Tratado, p. 393.

linseed-oil, add three ounces of spirit of wine, and two ounces of lavender flowers, place it in the sun for fifteen days, shaking it twice every day, and in this manner it will be purified and clear. Then pouring it into another vessel, it may be used for whites, blues, and flesh tints." Some time since I tried this recipe, and found that in proportion as the oil lost its colour, the spirit of wine acquired it, and the mucilage separating, was carried to the bottom of the bottle with the lavender flowers. The yellow colour of the spirit of wine may, perhaps, be accounted for by the fact, that a small quantity of linseed oil is soluble in spirit of wine; four ounce measures of spirit of wine dissolve one drachm of linseed-oil.[1]

Joannes Zahn recommends[2] the following process for the clarification and bleaching of oil for painting:— " Take the acetous herb, which in German is called ' Sauerampffer' (sorrel), cut it into tolerably sized pieces, and boil it in water over the fire ; then strain it through a linen cloth, put it into a tin vessel, or into a vase made of iron, tinned, which must be prepared so as to be long and broad, but not deep. This being done, pour on to this water the oil which is to be clarified and bleached, and then put the vase, with the water and supernatant oil, into a place free from dust, and exposed to the hottest rays of the sun in summer for a few days; in a short time the oil will deposit all its impurities, and be wonderfully clarified and bleached by this process, in the same manner as wax and linen are bleached. The oil thus prepared may be used by painters, not only for making their colours more lively, but also for the preparation of the clearer and more brilliant varnishes." This method of purifying linseed-oil I have also tried, and found it very successful in removing the mucilage, which is thrown down in a few

---

[1] Henry's Chemistry, vol. ii. p. 226.   [2] Oculus Artificialis, p. 625.

days, and the oil remains very clear and bright, and of a golden colour: it may afterwards be bleached by exposure to the sun.

The purification and preparation of oil for painting, by exposure to heat and washing with water, has been so fully treated by Mr. Eastlake, that it will be unnecessary to cite the authorities or repeat the processes he has described. It may, however, be interesting to state, that I have bleached and clarified linseed-oil by the following process, suggested by the directions of the Gesuato [1] and those of Dreme. [2] A bottle was filled, about one third with oil, another third with water; it was then corked and shaken, until the water and oil were mixed like an emulsion, when the cork was removed, and a piece of muslin tied over the bottle, which was placed on the boiler of a kitchen-range, [3] and kept in a moderate heat day and night. The oil was shaken every day (the muslin being first removed and the cork inserted in the bottle) for a few days, and then suffered to clear. In about a week the oil was removed from the water into another bottle, and the process was repeated for several weeks until the water below the oil ceased to appear milky, and the oil itself was clear and colourless. During this experiment I observed that the mucilage was thrown down sooner if warm water was added to the oil instead of cold, and that the oil separated more rapidly from the water when the bottle was exposed to a gentle and regular heat, although in a dark situation, than when it was placed in the variable warmth of a sunny window. The addition of salt or sand accelerates the clarification of the oil. Many weeks are necessary to complete the process of bleaching and purification. If the oil is intended to remain fluid, it should be preserved in bottles well stopped. [4]

---

[1] See 'Materials,' &c., p. 327.   [2] Der Virniss-u Kittmacher, &c.
[3] Dreme recommends that the bottle should be suspended in an oven moderately heated.   [4] See Mr. Eastlake's 'Materials,' &c., p. 341.

The purification of oil will always be attended with much waste. It may be considered that, with the greatest care, nearly half will be lost in the process. The mucilage alone frequently forms one-third of the oil.

Dryers and Drying Oils.

The necessity of the colours drying quickly, and the circumstance of some drying more rapidly than others, led to the addition of other ingredients to the oil.

The following observations will be limited to the drying ingredients mentioned in the Treatises contained in this work, and to those adopted by the Italian and Spanish painters.

The earliest notice of drying oil which occurs in the following works is to be found in the MS. of Eraclius.[1] In this recipe the oil was boiled with lime,[2] and ceruse being then added, it was placed in the sun for a month or more, and frequently stirred. The use of white-lead as a dryer has been continued to the present day. It was sometimes stirred into the oil, which was then exposed to the sun and dew, and well stirred every day for three days, when it was ready for use.[3] If suffered to remain longer than the time specified, it would become fat. By some modern Italian artists white-lead

---

[1] P. 232.

[2] The most powerful of all dryers is perhaps chloride of lime in a dry state : a small quantity of this added to clarified oil will convert it into a solid; for this reason it must be employed very cautiously. If too much be used, it may burn the brushes, and injure the colours. It has the advantage of not darkening the oil, and its drying property appears to arise from its absorbing the watery particles of the oil. Chloride of calcium is equally efficacious as a dryer ; but the small quantity of iron which it contains dissolves in the oil, and darkens it. It seems probable that if the chloride of lime were judiciously employed, it might prove serviceable as a dryer ; but as I am not aware that it has been tried as such by any person but myself, the utmost caution would be required, and some experiments would be necessary in order to ascertain the smallest possible quantity which would answer the purpose intended. As a dryer for house paint it may perhaps be found useful.

[3] Palomino, vol. ii. p. 55.

is placed on a strainer, and the oil is suffered to filter through it, when it is ready for use.

The preparation of oil for painting is not mentioned in the Bolognese MS.; but in two of the recipes for making " vernice liquida" directions are given for rendering the oil drying previous to the addition of the resin. In No. 207,[1] the oil is directed to be boiled with burnt roche alum in powder, and minium or vermilion; and after boiling a proper time it is to be set fire to, and allowed to burn for a short time, when it is to be extinguished, and again placed over the fire and burnt as before.

This is, probably, the only recipe for drying oil in which vermilion is mentioned; but as that pigment is not known to possess any peculiarly siccative properties, it may be supposed that it was considered by the writer as synonymous with minium (the cinnabar of the ancients), the term applied to red-lead during the middle ages throughout Europe, and from that time to the present in Italy.

The burning of the oil, recommended in this recipe, was for the purpose of depriving it of its unctuosity, and with this view it is still resorted to by the makers of printing ink.

In the recipe No. 262, in the Bolognese MS.,[2] 2 lbs. of common oil, that is, olive-oil, and 2 lbs. of linseed-oil are boiled with 30 or 40 cloves of garlic, until, on dipping a hen's feather into the oil, it is found to be burnt. This trial with the feather is still the common test of the oil's being sufficiently boiled. The use of the garlic was probably to supply moisture to the oil, and thus prevent its carbonization. Garlic is mentioned as an ingredient in drying oil or fat oil by Pacheco and Palomino; and according to the former the oil was boiled until the garlic was burnt or toasted.[3]

---

[1] P. 489.   [2] P. 521.   [3] Tratado, p. 404.

Garlic yields a gelatinous juice, which does not appear to be miscible with oil. Pacheco also mentions as dryers, minium and white lead, which if added to oil, and placed in a glass vessel in the sun in summer, for fifteen days, stirring it every day, and then straining it, would be very good.

According to Lebrun,[1] drying oil was prepared by suspending a piece of rag containing umber and minium in a vessel with nut-oil, and boiling it. The mordants described in the Paduan MS.,[2] and in the 'Riposo' of Borghini (p. 176), greatly resemble this drying oil. In the first, ochre is added to the other ingredients; in the second, giallorino, calcined bones, and burnt vitriol; which Borghini says is to be "calcined in the fire until it is red; and this vitriol makes all colours which are naturally bad dryers siccative, although it discolours them."[3]

Besides white-lead and minium, litharge, the semi-vitrified oxide of lead, was employed as a dryer for oil. Volpato gives[4] directions for preparing *olio cotto*, by boiling it on litharge, but he does not specify the proportion of litharge. The Jesuit, Father Lana,[5] recommends, for this purpose, two ounces of litharge for each pound of oil. Lebrun calls[6] this preparation "huile grasse," fat oil, which he distinguishes from drying oil.

Lebrun also remarks, that the litharge might be ground on the porphyry with oil, made into a little ball and dried When required for use it was to be boiled until the litharge was dissolved, and, when cold, the oil was said to become as clear as rock-water. This oil was considered very good as a siccative for those colours which did not dry well, such as lakes, black,[7] &c. When used for painting on glass, the proportion of litharge was much increased: thus the Paduan MS.[8]

---

[1] P. 816.   [2] P. 692.

[3] Burnt vitriol is sulphate of iron calcined. Iron is to a certain extent soluble in oil, which it renders dark.   [4] P. 741.   [5] P. 746, n.

[6] P. 816.   [7] P. 818.   [8] P. 692.

prescribes half a pound of this ingredient to a pound of
oil; but for pictures this cannot be recommended. The
recipe for " olio cotto," given by Fra Fortunato, differs
from these recipes in directing the addition of water,
which is to be boiled with the litharge and oil, which
he says will cause the oil to become as clear (colourless)
as water itself.[1]

In the appendix to the Italian edition of ' L'Idée du
Peintre Parfait' of De Piles, drying oil is described as
composed of nut-oil boiled with litharge and sandarac.
This composition is in fact identical with the old " vernice liquida." It differs but little from the mordant of
Cennini,[2] which consisted of linseed oil, vernice (dry
sandarac), and white lead. In the former, the dryer
was litharge; in the latter, white lead.

In the time of Baldinucci, *olio cotto* was prepared by
boiling linseed or nut-oil, either alone, or with litharge
or glass, finely ground with water. It is stated by this
author to have been used to temper those colours which
are slow in drying, such as lake, terra nera, bone, and
other blacks, because both litharge and ground glass
have the property of making them dry quickly. Oil,
boiled without either of these ingredients, was used to
accelerate the drying of those colours, which dry well
of themselves, such as white lead, minium, terra verde,
umber, cinnabar, smalti, and others; but if used with
white lead it would become yellow. " Pure boiled oil,"
continues Baldinucci, " when it is prepared with very
clear oil, is also used by painters instead of varnish in
the darkest shades, and where the colours have sunk in.
And remember, that raw nut and linseed oil are by
nature drying, but they do not dry so soon as when

---

[1] " Per far l' olio cotto da Pittore, che sia chiaro, come acqua. Metti il
solito piumazzolo col litargirio, et altro come si usa dentro l' oglio di noce, o
di lino, a bollire, e con esso mettivi seco dell' acqua a bollire, che questa la
fara rimaner chiaro, come l' acqua medesima."

[2] Trattato, cap. 151.

boiled, and especially as when mixed with ground glass and litharge." [1]

Volpato also recommends [2] that " olio cotto " and verdigris should be mixed with asphaltum and black to make them dry.

An eminent professor of painting at Venice stated that Chilone, an old Venetian painter, who died about the year 1834 or 1836, was acquainted with Canal [3] and Canaletto, [4] and that Chilone said these two artists used oil boiled on litharge, which they recommended him to use also, and that they frequently spread it over the whole picture.

It appears certain then from the above evidence, that the preparations of lead were the dryers most approved in Italy, but it may be collected from an expression of Padre Lana's that some doubts had been raised as to their eligibility for this purpose.   Speaking of oil boiled on litharge, Lana says, "This application is not so injurious as some persons have imagined ; and the advantage is, that it dries quickly, for raw oil is a long time in drying."   There can be no doubt, however, that litharge is injurious to those colours which are incompatible with lead, such as Indian lake and orpiment.

The mixture of ground glass with colours as a dryer is not, that I am aware of, mentioned in Italian works written earlier than the seventeenth century : the Paduan MS. [5] and Baldinucci's ' Vocabulary of Design ' appear to be the only Italian authorities for it, although it may have been common at the time these works were written.   The practice probably originated in the ancient custom of mixing pulverised glass with orpiment, with the object, as some authors say, of making it grind more easily ; others say, of making it dry

---

[1] Vocabolario del Disegno.   [2] P. 747.

[3] Fabio Canal was born in 1703, and died in 1767.

[4] The real name of Canaletto was Antonio Canal.   He died in 1768, aged 71.   [5] P. 666.

better. For the latter purpose it was employed by
Pacheco, who remarks [1] that when orpiment was ground
with linseed oil, it required a dryer, and that some
persons added to it glass ground with water ; others
added linseed oil which has been suffered to fatten by
mixing with it red lead in powder. Others, he adds,
use a proper quantity of white copperas in powder ; but
he warns his readers to beware of verdigris, which is its
greatest enemy. Pacheco also recommends,[2] as a dryer
for carmine, either ground glass or litharge in powder,
or a little of the fat oil (with minium) before mentioned,
or white copperas tempered with oil, or added in powder.

Ground glass appears to have been a favourite dryer
with Palomino, who says [3] that it was excellent for all
colours, and that it might be ground with nut or linseed
oil like one of the colours, and preserved in a bladder,
and a little put on the palette when necessary. This
author describes [4] a drying oil for blues and whites,
composed of ground glass, litharge, white lead, and red
lead, of each one ounce, and half a pound of oil, boiled
for a short time together in a water bath. Ground
glass also forms one of the ingredients in a recipe
given by the same author for drying oil, which, from
being boiled longer, appears to have been of a darker
colour.

The mixture of pulverized glass with colours is scarcely
to be recommended, because a part of the alkali, which
is free, is liable to be acted on by the air and other
causes.[5] That the alkali is free, may be ascertained by
merely boiling some powdered glass in water ; on dipping turmeric paper into the water, the paper will be
found to have acquired a brown stain. The ill effects

---

[1] Tratado, p. 388.   [2] Ibid., p. 390.
[3] Vol. ii. p. 56.   [4] Vol. ii. p. 55.
[5] See an article in the Magazine of Science, vol. iv. p. 67, " On the action
of water on powdered glass."

liable to ensue from the presence of salts in pictures
have been described by Mr. Smith in the First Report
of the Commissioners of the Fine Arts: they are also
alluded to by De Piles,[1] by Lanzi[2] in a note on Correggio's method of painting, and by Mr. Eastlake.[3]
The glass made in Venice contained lead; when this
glass was ground and mixed with colours, the lead
probably acted on the oil as a dryer, and would affect
the colours in the same way as other preparations of
lead. In this point of view, therefore, glass can scarcely
be an eligible dryer for orpiment, which is decomposed
by lead. Manganese was another ingredient in Italian
glass; but as the native oxide of manganese is not
found pure, but is contaminated with iron, lead, and
copper, it may be conjectured that these metals formed
part of the glass. The manganese of Piedmont was
considered by Neri to be purer than that of Tuscany and Liguria; the latter contained much iron,
which gave the glass a dark hue, but it is still probable
that the manganese of Piedmont contained the other
metals, which cannot be a desirable addition to colours,
especially as oils are known to act on copper and iron.
If pounded glass has really any drying property (and it
must be supposed that it was not classed among dryers
without due consideration), this property may be attributed to the metals it contains, which are in the state
of oxides.

There is good reason to suppose that white copperas
(sulphate of zinc), which is mentioned as a dryer by
Flemish and German writers of the fifteenth century,
was the dryer of Van Eyck. We owe this discovery
to the research of Mr. Eastlake.[4]

With the exception of Padre Vincente Coronelli,
white copperas does not appear to be mentioned by any

---

[1] Elémens, p. 141.   [2] Vol. iv. p. 71, n.   [3] Materials, &c., p. 424, n.
[4] See Materials, &c., p. 130, 136, 284, 299, 311, 365-367.

Italian author as an ingredient in drying oil; but it was employed in Italy in the composition of a mordant for painting on glass by a Venetian friar,[1] about 150 years previous to the date of Coronelli's work. This mordant is described in the Marciana MS.:[2] it consisted of white copperas, mastic, dry sandarac, and roche-alum, ground in purified linseed oil. As a mordant for gold, the effects of this composition could not have been very durable, since it is recommended that vessels on which it was applied should be washed with cold water only, and rubbed or wiped very gently. Copperas is mentioned as an ingredient in a mordant for gilding, and as a dryer, by Pacheco,[3] who recommends it for orpiment and carmine; and by Palomino,[4] who remarks that it may be ground with oil, and placed on the palette like a colour: he says that burnt alum may be added to it, but that he has not tried this dryer. De Piles also states[5] that copperas ground in oil was used as a dryer for lake and ultramarine, but he expresses a doubt whether, on account of its being a salt, it may not, in drying, cover the picture with a white efflorescence, especially in damp situations. There can be little doubt that the objection of De Piles was well founded. It has been already observed that the introduction of any salt into the colours must always be prejudicial, and there seems no reason to make an exception in favour of sulphate of zinc. The same objection does not apply to the addition of this substance to drying-oil: on the contrary, there is reason to believe that calcined sulphate of zinc and the oxide of zinc are the safest of all metallic dryers.[6]

---

[1] It is very probable, as was suggested to me by a friend, that this "fratre Veneziano" was Fra Sebastian del Piombo, who was a native of Venice. If this be the fact, it affords additional reason for considering that copperas was the dryer of Van Eyck, inasmuch as Fra Sebastian was the pupil of Gian Bellino, who was contemporary with Antonello da Messina.

[2] P. 621.   [3] Tratado, p. 388, 390, 418.   [4] Vol. ii. p. 56.

[5] Elémens, p. 140.   [6] See Mr. Eastlake's ' Materials,' &c., p. 349.

Verdigris is one of the most powerful dryers, and its effects have long been known. Cennini mentions [1] it as promoting the drying of mordants. Armenini, and his copyist Bisagno, and De Piles,[2] recommend its being added to black, Volpato [3] to black and asphaltum, and Palomino [4] to black and carmine. But its drying properties appear to be more than counterbalanced by others which are highly injurious to many pigments, and cautions may be found in several writers against the injudicious use of it. De Piles [5] remarks that it is the plague of all the colours, and that if the smallest particle were to be mixed with the priming, it might destroy the whole picture.

There is another dryer mentioned by Italian writers which can only be used in dark primings or mordants: this is the dirty oil pressed from the brushes into a tin vessel kept for this purpose. Volpato says,[6] " this dries like a mordant even in winter." Lebrun remarks [7] that this oil may be used for the dead-colouring or for the priming ; Borghini mentions [8] it as an ingredient in a mordant.

Calcined bones, which were so much used by the Flemish painters, do not appear to have been employed to promote the drying of oil by the Italians, although they are mentioned as an ingredient in a mordant by Borghini.[9]

It will be seen, therefore, from the above-mentioned authorities, that the dryers named in works of art as most commonly used in Italy, from the earliest period until the present time, were preparations of lead.

Mastic, which has always been so much used in varnish, has from a very early period been considered a dryer. Mr. Eastlake gives [10] two instances, one of

---

[1] Trattato, cap. 151, 152.   [2] Elémens, p. 125.
[3] P. 747.   [4] Vol. ii. p. 56.   [5] Elémens, p. 124.
[6] P. 732.   [7] P. 770.   [8] Riposo, p. 176.   [9] Ibid., p. 176.
[10] Materials, &c., p. 172, n.

which is from the Lucca MS., the other from the Venetian MS.   A solution of mastic in nut oil is recommended by Errante [1] as the only eligible dryer.   This
fact naturally leads to the consideration of the varnishes
used with colours in Italy, and of the resins of which
they were composed.   Before entering on this subject,
I shall offer a few observations on some of the essential
oils used in painting.

Essential Oils.

The purity of the essential oils is not less requisite
than that of the other materials.   Mr. Eastlake observes [2] that " their drying property is in proportion to
their rectification, and that the lasting purity of their
tint may partly depend on the same circumstance."

Essential oils should be kept in close vessels, and
excluded from light.   By long exposure to air and
light, volatile oils become thick, and darker in colour,
and assume the appearance of resins.

The essential oils commonly used in painting were
naphtha, spirit or oil of turpentine, and oil of spike.
The first of these is considered to have been employed
in painting by the ancient Egyptians.[3]

Oil of spike should be the foreign oil of lavender ;
but what is usually sold as such is a mixture of three
parts oil of turpentine and one part oil of spike.[4]
These ingredients are sometimes rectified together.
English oil of lavender is sold for a guinea a pound,
while oil of spike may be purchased for twelve or
fourteen shillings the pound.

The naphtha, used by the Italian painters for diluting their colours and varnishes, was a natural production of many parts of Italy, particularly of the territories of Modena and Parma.   It is also found in

---

[1] Saggio sui Colori, &c.   [2] Materials, &c., p. 313.
[3] See D'Agincourt, vol. ii. p. 2.
[4] See Rennie's Supplement to the Pharmacopœias.

Bohemia, Persia, and in Colebrooke Dale in Shrop-
shire; but the finest specimens are furnished by Italy.
Naphtha, like turpentine, should be rectified before it
is used for painting or varnishes.[1] The naphtha of the
shops is distilled from wood; but it probably differs
considerably from the native naphtha, which is used
by chemists for the purpose of keeping potassium, for
which the wood naphtha is entirely unfit. The native
naphtha, therefore, should be procured for painting.
It is said to be the purest and most unchangeable of the
essential oils.[2]

While mentioning essential oils, it will be proper to
allude briefly to the volatile oil of linseed or nuts, which
was occasionally used in diluting varnishes.

The earliest notice of distilled linseed oil is probably
that which occurs in the old part of the Bolognese
MS.,[3] (written previously to the introduction of the
Flemish process of oil-painting into Italy,) in a recipe
for making artificial stones for rings. It will be observed that although the distilled oil in this case was
not used for painting, yet it is stated by the author that
any pigment put into it will retain its colour for ever.

Vasari's account of the singular experiments, as he
calls them, of Lionardo da Vinci on oils and varnish,
is not conclusive evidence that he distilled linseed and
nut oils, or either of them; he merely states that he
distilled oils and herbs to make varnishes;[4] and this may
be true with regard to the olio di trementina and olio
di spigo, as well as to linseed and nut oil. The passage
in Lomazzo's 'Tempio della Pittura'[5] is rather more
definite; but even this is not conclusive. In speaking
of Lionardo, he says, "della tempera, passò all' olio,
il quale usava di assotigliar con i lambicchi, onde è

---

[1] Verri, Saggio, &c., p. 138.
[2] Mr. Eastlake's 'Materials,' &c., p. 314.   [3] P. 507.
[4] "Cominciò a stillare oli ed erbe per fare la vernice." See Life of
Lionardo da Vinci.   [5] P. 49.

causato che quasi tutte le opere sue si sono spiccate dai muri, siccome fra l'altre si vede nel consiglio di Fiorenza la mirabile battaglia, e in Milano la Cena di Christo in Sta. Maria delle Gratie che sono guaste per l'imprematura che egli gli diede sotto."

Besides the passages in Vasari and Lomazzo, which attribute to Lionardo the use of distilled oil, there is the recipe in the 'Secreti' of Alessio,[1] which is conclusive as to the fact that linseed oil was distilled and used to dilute amber varnish. This recipe has been copied by Wecker,[2] by Bonanni, and by Salmon in his 'Polygraphices.' It is stated that this varnish was to be applied on pictures or figures, "sopra alle figure."

Another notice of linseed oil, distilled with other ingredients, occurs in the 'Nuovo Plicto.'[3] In this recipe linseed oil, vernice liquida, roche-alum, nitre, Roman vitriol, and mastic are boiled together, and afterwards distilled. The water which comes over is said to be good for tempering colours in miniature-painting, and for staining or dyeing linen and other things. It must be kept closely corked, otherwise it will evaporate.

The fact, therefore, of linseed and nut oil being used in painting, except for miniatures, appears to rest on the inconclusive testimony of Vasari and Lomazzo that it was used by Lionardo da Vinci; at the same time it will not escape notice that both these authors, who were painters, and undoubtedly acquainted with the method practised at the time they lived, disapproved of the processes of Lionardo, which they evidently considered unusual. As a mere diluent, distilled linseed or nut oil when rectified, and no longer subject to crystallise at a low temperature,[4] may not be more objectionable than spirit of turpentine, oil of spike, or

---

[1] Part ii. p. 74.   [2] De Secretis, lib. xvi. p. 643.   [3] P. 76, 77.
[4] At the temperature of 40° of Fahrenheit distilled linseed oil is converted into a mass of needle-shaped crystals.

naphtha; but the circumstance of its being so rarely mentioned by writers on painting, when so many must have been acquainted with it, suggests the idea that it was not in general use.

Some caution is necessary in using these essential oils either with varnish or colours upon paint that is not thoroughly dry, lest they should disturb the colours,[1] for they are all powerful solvents. Oil of spike and oil of turpentine are frequently used by picture cleaners to dissolve dirty varnishes, and they often bring away the glazings which have been applied with an essential oil varnish, as well as the varnish itself.

Resins.

Turpentine and Resin.—By turpentine, trementina, and terebinthina is understood the resinous liquid which flows from many kinds of trees; when this liquid is hardened by the sun, or by fire, it is called *resin, ragia,* or *colophony.*

The turpentine of Dioscorides appears to have been what is now called Chio turpentine, the produce of the Pistacia terebinthus of Linnæus; the Terebinthina pistacina, Off. We have no means of ascertaining whether this was the turpentine mentioned in mediæval MSS., for Matthioli relates[2] that in his time the importation of it had ceased for so long a period that the remembrance of it was almost lost, and the resin of the larch had been introduced in its place, and had usurped its name. This author, however, states that the real turpentine tree grew plentifully at Trent, and in several parts of Italy. He also remarks that, although this was the best kind of turpentine, it had only recently (Matthioli's work was published in 1549) been brought to Venice. It was first imported in the dry state, but it was afterwards brought in abundance liquid as it

---

[1] See De Piles, Elémens de Peinture, p. 167. De Massoul, Art of Painting, p. 25. [2] Diosc., p. 126.

exuded from the tree.   Laguna mentions [1] that Venice was supplied with the best kind of turpentine from Cyprus; but it was so much adulterated that out of one barrel were made twenty.   When, therefore, turpentine and larch resin are both mentioned in early medieval MSS., as in the chapter *de Lucide ad Lucidas* in the Lucca MS., the turpentine may be considered to have been of the kind mentioned by Dioscorides ; but where turpentine only is spoken of, the point is doubtful.   At a later period, and until a few years previous to 1549, trementina may be understood in the works of Italian writers to signify the turpentine of the larch. In this sense, perhaps, the trementina and terebinthina of the Bolognese MS. (in which larch resin is not mentioned) are to be understood.

Venice Turpentine.—Matthioli states that the produce of the Pinus larix (larice of the Italians, mélèze of the French, the larch), called *turpentine of the larch* and Venice turpentine, was formerly called " *laricina.*" His account of this resin is as follows:—

" There is also extracted from the larch that liquid and excellent resin which is called ' terebinthina ' in all the druggists' shops in Italy, because it superseded that which is extracted from the terebinthino; for the merchants having ceased to import the terebinthina, the physicians brought into use instead of it that which is produced by the larch, whence it acquired the name of *turpentine* (terebinthina).   Nevertheless Fuchsio, in his last book on the Composition of Medicines, was mistaken when he wrote that the apothecaries now use instead of the true terebinthina nothing but the liquid resin of the abeto (Pinus picea of Linnæus), which we call tears (lagrime), for it is known to all the world that the common terebinthina now in use is not extracted from any other tree but the larch. . . . . . The

[1] Diosc. ilustrado por el Doct. Laguna.   Salamanca, 1570.

peasants inhabiting those mountains call this liquor *largà*, from the larch (larice), whence it exudes.[1] This kind of turpentine is called "largata" by Zuane Mariani,[2] and it appears to have been the only sort of turpentine imported into Venice in 1567.

The liquid resin which was sold in France under the name of térébenthine de Venise, was procured in the neighbourhood of Lyons; and Pomet says[3] that it should rather be called " térébenthine fine du bois de Pilatre ou de Lyon." The Lyonnais called it *bijon*; but at Rouen it was called *berniz*. At the present time much of this resin is brought from the confines of Briançon.[4]

Olio di Abezzo, Strassburg Turpentine, Gomme du Sapin.—The resin which exudes from the Terebinthina abietina, Off., the Pinus picea of Linnæus, the abete of the Italians, the sapin of the French, is the Resina sapini of the Lucca MS. and Clavicula (p. 54). "The abete produces that most excellent liquor commonly called tears (lagrime), or olio di abezzo. . . . . . It is frequently adulterated with the resin of the larch, which is not so dear as the olio di abezzo, and sometimes when the larch resin is very clear and limpid it is sold for the real olio di abezzo; for few apothecaries know one from the other. But the fraud may be detected, first, because the olio di abezzo is much more liquid, and also because it has an agreeable odour, and is much more bitter to the taste than the larch resin; and when it is more than a year old, it acquires a yellowish colour, and becomes somewhat solid."[5] The Marciana MS. mentions[6] that genuine olio di abezzo may be distinguished by its drying rapidly; but when it is mixed with turpentine it dries very slowly.

[1] Matthioli, p. 118.

[2] See Tariffa Perpetua di Zuane Mariani, Venetia, 1567.

[3] Histoire des Drogues, vol. ii. p. 62.

[4] Diz. delle Droghe di Chevalier e Richard. Venezia, 1831.

[5] Matthioli, p. 120.   [6] P. 635.

Resin, Resin of the Pine, Gomme de Pin, Bordeaux Turpentine.—This is the produce of the Terebinthina pinea, the Pinus maritima, a variety of the Pinus sylvestris, the Pinus abies of Linnæus.[1] Whenever the word "ragia" occurs in Italian writers, the resin of the pine is always to be understood.[2] This resin is firmer and more solid than that of the larch or the abete. When this resin has been purified by melting it in the sun, and suffering it to run through the small holes perforated in the bottom of the vessel containing it, it is considered equal in quality to Strassburg turpentine. When it is purified by melting it over the fire, and straining it through straw, it is called "yellow pitch or resin," "white pitch," and "Burgundy pitch." If the residuum left after the distillation of spirit of turpentine be stirred briskly with water, it loses its transparency, and acquires a dark yellow colour. In this state it is called "yellow resin or pitch."[3]

Pierre Pomet states that it was called in France "barras," or "galipot," and that there were two kinds, one of which was called "encens blanc," the other "encens marbré." The incense usually burnt in churches is the produce of the Pinus abies.[4]

Pece Greca, or Greek Pitch, Pece Spagnuola, or di Spagna, Pegola di Spagna, Colophony.—The signification of these terms cannot be better explained than in the words of Matthioli :[5]— "What is commonly called pece di Spagna, pece Greca, and colophonia by the apothecaries is nothing but resin boiled in the manner described by Dioscorides. These names were derived from the places whence they were brought. But there was another kind of colophonia described by Dioscorides, which was liquid, and which was called, *par excellence*, colophonia. This was very scarce and

---

[1] Trattato delle Droghe Semplici, da Guibourt, iii. p. 412.   [2] Ricett. Fior.
[3] Trattato delle Droghe, da Guibourt, p. 415.
[4] Humboldt's Kosmos, ii. 441.   [5] Trans. of Diosc., p. 126.

dear." Matthioli thinks that the latter was the olio di abezzo, which is not mentioned either by Dioscorides or Pliny.

The hardest of all the resins is colophonia;[1] the terebinthina continues liquid a long time, and the olio di abezzo remains in a moderately liquid state. The best "pece di Spagna" was brought from the island of Pityusa, on the coast of Spain.

In the Greek MS. of Mount Athos, pece Greca is called Pégoula.[2] It appears that it was also known by this name in Italy. Thus Fioravanti states,[3] in his 'Secreti,' "La vernice commune è una compositione, la quale si fa di olio di lino e di pece Greca, con una parte del olio, e tre di *pegola*," &c.

Olibanum, Thus album, Incenso, Frankincense, are synonymous terms in works on art. Under the first name this resin appears to be included among the ingredients in the chapters of the Lucca MS. and Mappæ Clavicula (p. 54, 55), entitled " De Petalo Aureo," and " Lucida quomodo fiant super Colores." This resin is mentioned in the commercial treaty between Bologna and Ferrara in 1193.[4] The best kind was formerly imported by way of Tauris (now Tabreez), whence it was called " Torisino."[5] The tree which produced the Arabian frankincense of Hadhramaut, so famous from the most ancient times, has not yet been discovered and determined by any botanist. There is a similar product in the East Indies, which, according to Colebrooke, has been obtained from the Boswellia thurifera, or serrata. The olibanum of our druggists is the produce of an American plant, the Icica guyanensis, of the same family (Burseraceæ) as the Boswellia.[6] Frankincense was used by the old

---

[1] Trans. of Diosc., p. 127. [2] Manuel d'Iconographie, p. 40.
[3] Secreti di S. Leonard. Fioravanti, lib. iii. cap. 95. [4] Depping, i. 241.
[5] See the work of Pegoletti and Uzzano, cited by Depping, i. 142.
[6] Humboldt's Kosmos, Sabine's translation, London, 1848, vol. ii. p. 440.

painters in the composition of the pastille with which
ultramarine was mixed, as well as in varnishes;[1] and
we learn from the Bolognese MS.[2] that when it was
dissolved in linseed-oil, the composition was sometimes
called "vernice liquida." From the scarcity of oriental olibanum, it was frequently adulterated with gum
and resin. The resin held in most esteem in the East
for burning as incense was, according to Agricola,[3]
amber; but it is probable that for amber we should read
oriental copal.[4]

Sandarac.—This resin is brought from the southern
provinces of Morocco. In the language of the country
it is called "el Grassa;"[5] and by this name it has
always been known in Spain. Thus Pacheco says,
"Grassa . . . . which is the gum of the juniper,
which the Arabs call sandarac."[6] Palomino mentions
this resin under the name "grasilla." It was generally
believed that sandarac was the gum of the juniper, and
as such it is described by Matthioli, Laguna,[7] Bulengerus,[8] and other writers; but it is now known to exude
from the Thuya articulata (African arbor vitæ), a
dwarf tree somewhat resembling the juniper.[9] In its
dry state, sandarac was called vernix, vernice grossa,[10]
vernice in grana,[11] vernice da scrivere.[12] The last name
was derived from the pulverized sandarac being formerly
rubbed over cotton paper to prepare it for writing.

---

[1] Pp. 165, 630.   [2] P. 489.   [3] De Metallicis, p. 243.
[4] See Pharmaceutical Journal, vol. v. part iv.
[5] Encyc. Brit., tit. Sandarac.
[6] "Grassa, que es la goma del enepro que los Arabes llaman Sandaraca."
Tratado, 410.
[7] Diosc. ilustr. por el Doct. Laguna, p. 62.   [8] De Pictura, &c.
[9] Mr. Eastlake's 'Materials,' &c., p. 232.
[10] Borghini (Riposo, p. 175) says "sandaraca ovvero vernice grossa."
[11] "Vernice di sandaraca o vernice in grana," Secreti di S. Leonard.
Fioravanti, Torino, 1580, lib. iii. cap. 68. Marciana MS., pp. 609, 621, 631.
[12] "Vernice da scrivere, cioè sandracha, cioè gomma di ginepro." Secreti
di D. Alessio, part ii. f. 57.

When sandarac was dissolved in linseed-oil, it constituted the "vernice liquida" of the Italians.[1]

Mastic.—This is a resin obtained from the Pistacia
lentiscus, a tree which grows in the Levant, and particularly in the island of Chios. Mastic appears to have
been always used in the arts as a varnish; and in the
Lucca MS.[2] it is recommended to be added to a varnish
or mordant composed of linseed-oil, with resins and
gums of various kinds, as a dryer. Mastic and mastic-
varnish are also mentioned as dryers by Italian writers
on art.[3]

Amber, Succinum, Carabe, Glassa, Glas.—The vegetable origin of amber is now universally admitted. On
this subject Humboldt remarks:[4]—"Goeppert's excellent researches, which, it is hoped, will soon appear
illustrated with plates, inform us 'that all the Baltic
amber is derived from a coniferous tree, which, as
proclaimed by the extant remains of the wood and bark,
were obviously of different ages, came nearest to our
white and red pine timber, but still constituted a particular species.' The amber-tree of the former world
(Pinites succifer) had a richness in resin with which
none of the coniferous tribes of the present world will
bear comparison, inasmuch as great masses of amber are
contained not only within and upon the bark, but also
between the rings of the wood, and in the direction of
the medullary rays, which, as well as the cells, are seen
under the microscope to be filled with ambreous resin,
of a whiter or yellower colour in different places.
Amongst the vegetable matters inclosed in amber we
find both male and female flowers of indigenous, aci-

---

[1] Bol. MS., pp. 489, 521. Secreti di D. Alessio, part ii. f. 57, 160.
Caneparius, de Atramentis, pp. 260, 341, 378, 379. Bulengerus de
Pictura, &c., lib. ii. cap. ii. Other authorities are cited by Mr. Eastlake,
'Materials,' &c., p. 238.

[2] De Confectio Lucidæ; and see Clavicula, p. 53.

[3] See Errante, Saggio sui Colori; Armenini, de' Veri Precetti; and Bisagno, Trattato, &c.   [4] Kosmos, vol. i. p. 303, and see vol. ii. p. 412.

cular-leaved, and cupuliferous trees; but distinct fragments of Thuja, Cupressus, Ephedera, and Castania
vesca, mingled with others of junipers and firs, indicate
a vegetation which is different from that of the present
coasts and plains of the Baltic."

Amber, according to Berzelius, " contains *five*
substances:—1. An odoriferous oil, in small quantity.—2. A yellow resin, intimately combined with this
oil, dissolving freely in alcohol, ether, and alkalis, very
fusible, and resembling ordinary vegetable resins.—3. A
resin soluble with difficulty in cold alcohol, more freely
in hot alcohol, from which it separates on cooling, as a
white powder soluble in ether and alkalis. These two
resins and the volatile oil, if removed from amber by
ether, and then obtained by evaporation of the latter in
water, form a natural viscid balsam, very odorous, of a
clear yellow colour, and which gradually becomes hard,
but retains some odour. There is every reason for
supposing this to be precisely the substance from
which amber originates, but rather poorer in essential oil than at first; and that the insoluble
substances in amber have been gradually formed by a
spontaneous alteration of this balsam, but at the same
time have enveloped one part of it, and so preserved it
from entire decomposition or change.—4. Succinic acid,
dissolved with the preceding bodies by ether, alcohol,
and alkalis.—5. A body insoluble in alcohol, ether, and
alkalis, analogous in some points to the substance found
by Dr. John in lac, and called by him the *principle of
lac.* This is formed in large quantity when a solution
of lac in alkali is precipitated by chlorine."[1]

Amber was formerly found on the coasts of the
Baltic, also near the Po and Adriatic: and it is stated
by Depping[2] to have been imported from the Maldives.

---

[1] Ure's Dictionary of Chemistry, p. 147.

[2] Histoire du Commerce, vol. i. p. 142.

The amber found on the shores of the Baltic was known
to the inhabitants of those countries under the name of
glessum, whence *glasse, glassa, glas.* The fact of
amber having been found near the Po, and on the
shores of the Adriatic, is mentioned by Agricola,[1] and
by Matthioli, merely as a report, which they considered
to have originated from the circumstance that amber
necklaces were commonly worn by the peasant women
of these countries;[2] and both authors carefully distinguish amber or succino from the gum or resin which
exudes from the black and white poplars growing on
the banks of the Po. The latter writer, especially, is
very precise in this respect. In quoting the following
passage from Serapion, "Et dicitur quod gummi Haur
Romi,[3] quod nascitur circa fluvium, qui dicitur Eri-
danus, quando distillat in flumine illo, coagulatur ibi, et
est illud, quod dicitur Alipton, id est electrum; et
sunt qui nominant ipsum Arsopodon, et est charabe,"
and a similar passage from Avicenna, he remarks, they
do not affirm that charabe is the gum of the black
poplar, but merely that it is said to be. Conder,[4] however, mentions that amber is found in earth impregnated
with petroleum, beneath the vineyards and corn-fields
in the territory of Modena; and it will also be recollected that in the book lent by Fra Dionisio to
Alcherius, a certain gum, Andrianum, which had attractive powers similar to those possessed by amber and
resins generally, is stated to have been found on Monte
Buono (Bene).[5] Phillips[6] states that amber is actually
found in Italy and on the coast of the Adriatic.

---

[1] De Metallicis, f. 238. Trans. of Diosc., pp. 155, 156.

[2] "The Etrurians carried on considerable trade through the north of
Italy and across the Alps, where 'the Sacred Road' led to the distant amber
countries." (See Humboldt's Kosmos, vol. ii. p. 164.) These traders probably supplied the Italian women with amber.

[3] Haur Romi is the Arab name for the black poplar. See Matt., p. 155.

[4] Italy, vol. ii. p. 46.   [5] See p. 82.   [6] Mineralogy, p. 373.

It may be considered questionable whether the sub-stance reputed to have been imported from the Maldives during the middle ages, under the name of amber, was really amber or oriental copal. Mr. Eastlake has shown[1] that these substances were scarcely distinguished in ancient recipes. Old writers mention two kinds of amber, the white and the yellow ; and the only distinctive property they assign to amber is, that of attracting straws, which proves to be common to resins generally, and cannot therefore be considered as decisive. Agri-cola asserts[2] that amber was certainly found in Africa, but he knew not in what parts: he says it was also found in Syria, in India, and, according to Marco Polo, the Venetian traveller, in the Island of Mada-gascar. It appears that copal is found in Abyssinia, in Palestine, and in the East Indies; and it is sold in the bazaars of Jerusalem, Mecca, and other places, as a choice specimen of incense.[3] In this respect it agrees with what Agricola says[4] of amber; namely, that the odour of the smoke of amber was more agreeable to the Indians than that of incense. Copal is also brought from Madagascar.[5] There are some grounds then for considering that the amber stated to have been procured from Africa and Asia may have been oriental copal; and that although amber was actually found in some parts of Italy, European nations were principally sup-plied with it from Germany.

There are two kinds of amber: the best, which is imported from Prussia and Poland, is hard and trans-parent, and the surface is frequently marked in a peculiar manner, as if, when in a fluid state, it had been enclosed in wood, and had then taken and retained the impression of the fibres of the wood and bark. This kind

---

[1] Materials, &c., p. 233, 234.   [2] De Metallicis, f. 243.
[3] Pharmaceutical Journal, vol. v. No. iv.   [4] De Metallicis, f. 243.
[5] Guibourt, Histoire des Drogues, vol. ii. p. 526.

of amber makes the best varnish, and dissolves perfectly
in oil. The other sort of amber is called sea-amber,
and is of the size of coffee-beans, but irregular in shape,
darker than the first kind, and much less transparent.
Mr. Wilson Neil says,[1] " it is harder to fuse, has less
fluidity, and contains more salt, gas, and impurities."

Copal.—A very white transparent resin, used formerly by the aborigines of Spanish America as incense.
In the language of these people it signified all kinds of
resin exuding from trees.[2] Under the name of copal,
therefore, it is useless to look for this resin in works
written previous to the period of the introduction of
American produce into Europe. At present three
varieties are known in commerce, viz., Brazilian, West
Indian, and East Indian or Levantine copal. The
former, which is called soft copal, exudes from one of
the Hymenææ; the latter, or hard copal, is the produce
of the Vateria Indica.[3] The last variety was probably the same substance which was called *amber* by
the Italians, and which was stated by Agricola and
Matthioli to have been imported from Syria and
India, and by Marco Polo from the Island of
Madagascar; and this supposition is rendered more
probable by the fact that the Levantine copal is now
brought from Palestine, Abyssinia, and Madagascar.
The South African copal is considered the finest in
quality, and the best samples which sometimes reach
Europe from India were originally procured from
Africa.[4] The white resin of Arabia, mentioned in the
Paduan MS.,[5] was perhaps African copal, which it
appears is sold in the bazaars of Jerusalem, Mecca, and
other places, as a species of choice incense, and is at the

[1] On the Manufacture of Varnishes, Trans. Soc. Arts, vol. xlix. part 2.
[2] Ray's History of Plants, p. 1846. [3] Pharm. Times, vol. iii. p. 603.
[4] See Mr. Eastlake's ' Materials,' &c., p. 234, citing Tripier-Deveaux,
' Traité Théorique et Pratique sur l'Art de faire les Vernis,' Paris, 1845,
p. 40; and Guibourt, Hist. des Drogues, vol. ii. p. 526, on the Copal of
Madagascar. [5] P. 695.

present time chiefly employed for this purpose on the altars of Mahomet.[1]

The earliest writer who mentions copal by this name as an ingredient in varnishes is probably Fra Fortunato of Rovigo, the recipes in whose 'Secreti' date from 1659 to 1711. The next author is Palomino, who gives[2] a recipe for varnish composed of copal dissolved in spirit of turpentine. As the solvent in both recipes is the same, it may be concluded that copal was at this period usually dissolved in spirits of turpentine. I have ascertained that copal is perfectly soluble in cold oil of spike, but the solution is not effected in less than five or six years. I possess a specimen of copal varnish prepared in this way, which is very clear and pale.

Black Poplar Resin.—It has been observed that this resin was considered by Serapion, Avicenna, and other writers as synonymous with carabe or amber, and that Agricola and Matthioli had shown that a resin actually exuded from both kinds of poplar, and that the black poplar was the tree known to the Arabs under the name of "haur Romi." Schrœder has, however, the reputation of having been the first who pointed out this resin, which he obtained not from the bark in the manner described by the ancients, but by boiling the buds of the black poplar in water and afterwards pressing them. The buds yield about one-fourth of their weight of resin, which is said to resemble Botany Bay resin.[3] But although new to the moderns, this resin was apparently not unknown to the medieval writers, since we find "flores populi" among the ingredients in two kinds of varnish, for which there are recipes in the Lucca MS., which are copied in the Clavicula.[4]

Lac.—There is some doubt whether the "lacca" of the Lucca MS. and the Clavicula was gum lac or the

[1] Pharmaceutical Journal, vol. iv. p. 4.   [2] Museo Pictorico, vol. ii. p. 328.
[3] See London Encyclop., art. Chemistry, p. 494.
[4] Mappæ Clavicula, p. 53, 54.

gum of the ivy, but it is certain that Indian gum lac
was imported into Spain and Provence as early as
1220.[1] Although the art of preparing a red pigment
from this resin was known at an early period, the resin
itself appears to have been considered useless, and it
was probably only towards the close of the seventeenth
century that it came into use as an ingredient in varnishes. The Paduan MS.[2] contains directions for separating the red colouring matter, so that the gum might
be used in japanning as a varnish with or without
colours. Lac varnish does not appear to have been used
for varnishing pictures or in painting until very recently.

Benzoin.—A solid balsam,[3] extracted from incisions
made in the Storax benzoe, a tree which grows in Su-
matra. According to Depping[4] it was imported at an
early period into Europe; but as an ingredient in
varnish it does not appear to have been used until the
middle of the sixteenth century. It was employed for
this purpose by the Italians and Spaniards, and the
earliest notices of it probably occur in the Marciana
MS.[5] and in the 'Secreti' of D. Alessio.[6] Varnish of
benzoin is also mentioned by Armenini,[7] and in the
Paduan MS.[8] The benzoin was dissolved in spirit of
turpentine or spirit of wine. Benzoin appears never to
have been an ingredient in oil varnishes. Palomino and
Pacheco mention this balsam under the name of *menjui.*

---

[1] Capmany, Memorias, &c.; and the Statutes of Marseilles, quoted by
Depping, vol. i. p. 147.   [2] P. 686, 688.

[3] "Balsams are mixtures of resins and volatile oils. They differ very
greatly in consistence, some being quite fluid, others solid and brittle. By
keeping, the softer kinds often become hard. Balsams may be conveniently
divided into two classes, viz., those which, like common and Venice turpentine, Canada balsam, Copaiba balsam, &c., are merely natural varnishes, or
solutions of resins, in volatile oils, and those which contain benzoic or cin-
namic acid in addition, as Peru and Tolu balsams, and the solid resinous
benzoin, commonly called gum-benzoin."—Fownes, Manual of Elementary
Chemistry, p. 501.

[4] Hist. du Commerce, vol. i. p. 142.   [5] P. 629.

[6] Secreti, part i. f. 115.   [7] De' Veri Precetti, lib. ii. cap. ix.   [8] P. 698.

Copaiva is obtained from incisions made in the trunk of the Copaifera officinalis, a tree which grows in South America and some of the West India islands. It is mentioned as an ingredient in amber varnish, in the Paduan MS., and appears to have been used by the later Venetians both in varnishes and in painting.[1]

Damara Resin. — Terebinta di Dammara is the produce of the Pinus dammara (Lambert), Agathis dammara (Rich., Conifère, tav. 19), a tree which grows in the Indian Archipelago. Its odour is strongly resinous and its taste very bitter.[2] At the present time this resin is much used in the Venetian territories as a varnish, and it is currently reputed to have been employed by the old masters ; but this opinion appears to be unsupported by evidence—indeed, its uses are described by Chevalier and Richard as being unknown. It has, however, been recently employed at Munich as a vehicle for painting, for which purpose it was dissolved in spirits of turpentine with a certain proportion of bleached wax.[3] For the following recipe for damara varnish for pictures, I am indebted to a painter of Verona :—Put two and a half ounces of damara resin finely powdered and six ounces of spirit of turpentine into a bottle ; shake occasionally until the resin is dissolved, and it will be a strong varnish. No heat is necessary.

Varnishes.

The earliest varnish and that which was most universally adopted in Italy was unquestionably the old vernice liquida, which was composed of linseed oil and pulverised sandarac, commonly called " vernice," " vernice da scrivere," and " gomma di gineparo." The varnishes of Theophilus are referred to under the name

---

[1] See Mr. Sheldrake's Essay, Trans. Soc. Arts, vol. xix. ; and Marcucci, p. 222.   [2] Diz. delle Droghe di Chevalier e Richard, &c.

[3] See Appendix to the Third Report of the Commissioners of the Fine Arts, p. 52.

of vernice liquida in the Tabula Imperfecta prefixed
to the Le Begue MS. In this table and under the
same head is another reference to the recipe of Le
Begue: " A faire bonne vernix liquide pour peintres,"[1]
which appears to have been compiled by him from
the two recipes of Theophilus, with a few additions
of his own. From this recipe it may be inferred that
Le Begue considered the materials in both the recipes
of Theophilus as identical, but a comparison of these
chapters of Theophilus with the three recipes in St.
Audemar, Nos. 207, 208, and 209, and that in Eraclius
(p. 241), make it highly probable that the resin in one
case was sandarac and in the other amber.[2] In addition
to linseed oil Le Begue mentions hemp-seed and nut
oils, which, he says, might be used instead of linseed
oil ; and it may be remarked that in making varnishes
linseed and nut oils were used indifferently.

There is still another reference in the Tabula Imperfecta to a recipe in the Le Begue MS. for " vernice
liquida," but as No. 210, the recipe referred to, does
not describe a varnish, one of those described in Nos.
207, 208, and 209, and probably the first, must be intended.

The term " vernice liquida " occurs frequently in the
early Italian recipes copied in 1409 from the book of
Fra Dionisio, and also in the treatise of St. Audemar.
It is also frequently mentioned in the Bolognese MS.,
which contains no less than three recipes for making it.
The first of these,[3] the old " vernice liquida," consisted
of linseed oil and sandarac, under the name of " gomma
di gineparo." The varnish described in the second
recipe was composed of linseed oil and incense. This
varnish was made clear by the addition of roche alum,
and was rendered drying by the addition of minium ;

---

[1] No. 341, p. 313.   [2] See Mr. Eastlake's ' Materials,' &c., p. 241—246.
[3] No. 206, p. 489.

the oil, moreover, was set on fire and burnt to deprive
it of its unctuosity.[1] From this recipe it is apparent
that the term "vernice liquida" was not always limited
to the original signification, but was sometimes extended
to a varnish composed of oil and incense. When, however, the materials of which the varnish is composed
are not specified, the old vernice liquida (linseed oil
and sandarac) is generally to be understood. The third
varnish was, like the first, composed of linseed oil,
sandarac, here called "vernice da scrivere," and thirty
or forty cloves of garlic; and when the varnish was
nearly cold the whites of several eggs were added to it
and well mixed, and the bottle was placed in the sun
for one day. Vernice liquida is also frequently mentioned by Cennini not only as a varnish for pictures[2]
and for tin,[3] but as an ingredient in cements,[4] and mordants,[5] and other works.

Although vernice liquida is not mentioned in the
Paduan MS. or by Volpato, Armenini, Bisagno, or
Borghini, the evidence of Matthioli, Caneparius, and
others is sufficient to establish the fact that the use of it
with colours was not entirely discontinued in the sixteenth and seventeenth centuries. By the Spanish
painters this varnish, which is described by Pacheco as
that of the "guadamacileros" (leather-gilders), was in
his time mixed with colours in a particular kind of oil
painting, which this writer calls[6] "las encarnaciones de
polimento."

The "drying oil" mentioned in the appendix to the
Italian edition of 'L'Idée du Peintre Parfait' of De
Piles consisted of vernice liquida made drying by the
addition of litharge.

In the course of time the old vernice liquida was
modified in various ways. It was sometimes combined

---

[1] P. 521.   [2] Cap. 155.   [3] Caps. 97, 98, 101.   [4] Cap. 107.
              [5] Cap. 151.   [6] Tratado, p. 404.

with incense, as in the recipe in the Marciana MS., approved by Sansovino,[1] and sometimes with pece Greca.[2]

Next in importance to the "vernice liquida" was the "vernice comune," or common varnish, of the Italians, which Armenini and Bisagno direct to be mixed with the priming, and with certain colours. There is no doubt that the term was first applied to the varnish of sandarac and oil, which Caneparius calls[3] "common liquid varnish;" but before Armenini's time the appellation "common" appears to have been applied to another varnish also.

Armenini and Bisagno give several recipes for varnish, and after describing one made of mastic and nut-oil, they add that "this varnish may be added to the finer kinds of azure, lakes, and other colours, that they may dry more quickly;" but neither of them states that this is the "vernice comune." A similar varnish is mentioned in the Marciana MS.[4] as a most excellent varnish for lutes, leather, paintings on panel, cloth, &c. In the recipe for making printing-ink the same author says,[5] "Take varnish made for varnishing, and the finer it is the better; but the *common varnish* which the apothecaries sell to varnish wood and other things will do." The composition of "the best vernice comune, which is good for varnishing whatever you please," is described at p. 637, where it is stated to consist of linseed oil and pece Greca. The statement that "vernice comune" was made of linseed oil and pece Greca is confirmed by Leonard Fioravanti,[6] who recommends one part oil and three parts pece Greca. It will be observed that the common Italian varnish corresponds with one of the varnishes in the Strassburg MS.,[7] with

---

[1] P. 631.   [2] P. 637. See also Venetian MS. in the Sloane Collection, No. 416, f. 139.   [3] De Atramentis, p. 260.

[4] P. 633.   [5] See p. 619.   [6] Secreti, lib. iii. caps. 67, 95.

[7] Quoted by Mr. Eastlake, ' Materials,' &c., p. 280.

one of those in the Venetian MS.,[1] and also with the varnish of "Péséri" of the Byzantine MS.[2]

Another varnish described in the Marciana MS.[3] "as a most excellent, clear, and drying varnish, proper for colours both in oil-painting and in other kinds of painting," consists of the "vernice comune," with the addition of mastic. This addition was probably made with the view of rendering the varnish more siccative, since mastic was placed among dryers as early as the date of the Lucca MS. The drying properties of mastic varnish are alluded to by Armenini[4] and Bisagno, and the varnish of mastic and nut-oil is recommended by Errante[5] as the safest of all dryers. It is not therefore improbable that this varnish may have borne the name of "vernice comune" as well as the varnish made of nut or linseed oil and pece Greca. It is probable that the varnishes composed of pece Greca, mastic, and incense were much lighter in colour than the "vernice liquida," and therefore were better adapted for mixing with light colours. It must be observed that the common varnish used by the Flemish painters employed by Charles I. in England consisted of Venice turpentine dissolved in oil of turpentine.[6] The "vernix commun" of the French resembled this.

According to Pierre Pomet[7] the latter was nothing more than the turpentine procured from the pine (Pinus abies) liquefied in spirit of turpentine. The same author also calls[8] this varnish "le vernis gros." Pierre Pomet wrote in the eighteenth century, and as a varnish

---

[1] Sloane MS., No. 416, p. 139.   [2] Manuel d'Iconographie, p. 40.

[3] P. 633. According to Bonanni this varnish is used by the Turks for bows, &c.

[4] Speaking of the varnish of mastic and nut-oil, Armenini says " e di questa se ne può mettere negli azzurri fini, nelle lacche e in altri colori, acciò si asciughino più presto."

[5] Saggio, &c.   [6] Mr. Eastlake, ' Materials,' 471—476.

[7] Hist. Générale des Drogues, ii. 106.   [8] Ib., p. 71.

composed of a balsam dissolved in an essential oil can
be traced in Italy as early as the date of the Marciana
MS.,[1] and was reputed to be in general use throughout
Lombardy about 1580,[2] there is reason to believe that
this kind of varnish was of Italian origin.[3] That it was
used in Spain is proved by Pacheco, who remarks[4] that
the Strassburg turpentine (trementina de veta de
Francia) should be used.

But the "gros vernis" of the French was not the
"vernice grossa" of the Italians. By the latter, the
term was applied sometimes to a dry substance and
sometimes to a liquid varnish. When Borghini[5] says,
"Prendasi . . . . un' oncia d' olio di spigo e un' oncia di
sandarac ovvero vernice grossa," it is probable that he
means sandarac in its dry state. Baldinucci defines
"vernice grossa" to be a varnish which serves as a preparation for painting in oil on walls (per intonacare a
olio), and which is also used in the composition of printing-ink. D. Alessio states[6] that the varnish used for
the latter purpose was "vernice liquida." Caneparius[7] is
still more precise ; he calls it "Common liquid varnish
. . . made of Arabian sandarac, which is the gum of the
juniper, and linseed-oil." It appears then that the term
"vernice grossa" was applied both to dry sandarac and
to the old vernice liquida. In the last sense we are
probably to understand the words of Vasari in speaking[8]
of preparing walls for painting in oil: "Make in a
pipkin a mixture of pece Greca, mastic, and vernice
grossa, and when this is boiled apply it with a large
brush."[9] It can scarcely be supposed that the resins

---

[1] P. 635.   [2] See Armenini, de' Veri Precetti, &c. Hackert states
that this varnish had been in use all over the north of Europe for upwards
of 200 years. See Lettera al Cav. Hamilton, sull' Uso della Vernice nella
Pittura. Perugia, 1788.   [3] See Mr. Eastlake's ' Materials,' &c., p. 470.
[4] Tratado, p. 412.   [5] Riposo, p. 175.   [6] Secreti, parte i. f. 118.
[7] De Atramentis, p. 260.   [8] Int., cap. xxii.
[9] Compare with Vasari's description of Sebastian del Piombo's method
of painting in oil on walls, in the ' Life' of that artist.

would spread if they were merely melted without being diluted with oil. In the 'Elémens de Peinture' of De Piles [1] this passage is translated "de poix Grecque, de mastic, et de gros vernis;" but the "gros vernis" of the French was, I have shown, not identical with the "vernice grossa" of the Italians. At a later period, the term "vernice grosse" was also used to denote the common oleo-resinous varnishes. Thus linseed-oil boiled with litharge is said to be of great use in house-painting and in the composition of "vernici grosse." [2]

Amber, the principal ingredient in the German varnish, [3] does not appear to be noticed as a varnish by Italian writers previous to the time of Lionardo da Vinci, [4] who directs that a picture to be painted according to certain directions given by him, should be varnished either with nut-oil and amber, or with nut-oil thickened in the sun. [5] As Lionardo was one of the earliest Italian artists who practised oil-painting upon its first diffusion in Italy, after its introduction by Antonello da Messina, and as the early Flemish painters are known to have used amber varnish, it may be supposed that this varnish of nut-oil and amber was one of the recent improvements introduced from Flanders [6] by Antonello da Messina and the German artists, pupils and followers of Van Eyck, [7] who visited Italy in the latter half of the fifteenth century.

---

[1] Jombert's edition, p. 133. Paris, 1766.

[2] Diz. delle Droghe di Chevalier e Richard, Traduzione da F. du Pré. Venezia, 1830.   [3] See Mr. Eastlake's 'Materials,' p. 288.

[4] Lionardo was a pupil of Andrea Verrocchio, who was probably acquainted with the art of oil painting, since Vasari relates that he painted certain wax effigies of Lorenzo de' Medici with oil colours. See Vasari, Life of Andrea Verrocchio.   [5] Trattato, cap. 352.

[6] It must not be forgotten that the Byzantine MS. of Mount Athos contains a recipe for varnish made of oil and "santalose," which was probably "amber;" amber varnish may therefore have been introduced into Italy by the Greeks; but of this there appears no evidence.

[7] Roger of Bruges, Memling, and Justus van Ghent. See Mr. Eastlake's 'Materials,' p. 217.

Notices of amber varnish are not of frequent occurrence in early Italian works on art. It appears, however, to be mentioned in the Marciana MS. under the term " carbone," which has undoubtedly been written instead of " carabe," [1] the Arabic and Persian term for amber. The varnish made according to the recipe in question would, like all the old varnishes, be very thick, the proportions being one part of amber to three of oil. It was, therefore, diluted with naphtha, oil, or spirit of wine, and was used warm.

The 'Secreti' of Alessio also describes [2] a varnish for pictures consisting of three parts of amber varnish and one of distilled linseed-oil; and another varnish composed of linseed-oil and amber is quoted by Mr. Eastlake from the 'Secreti' of Rossello. [3]

It appears from the MS. of Volpato [4] that amber varnish was in use in his time, and that it was purchased ready-made at the shops, whence it may be inferred that it was in common use. In the absence, however, of any precise recipe for this amber varnish of which Volpato speaks, it cannot be determined whether amber was actually an ingredient, or whether the so-called amber varnish was the old " vernice comune " (linseed-oil and pece Greca) which was known in Bonanni's time under the name of " amber varnish." [5] The ingredients of this varnish were linseed-oil one part, and pece Greca three parts, so that it was, in fact, the vernice comune of the Italians, before described. It is difficult, indeed without additional evidence it is impossible, to assign any reason for the new name given to this varnish. We may, perhaps, be allowed to hazard a conjecture, and

---

[1] See p. 628 and note.   [2] Part ii. p. 57.

[3] Published at Venice in 1575, quoted in ' Materials,' &c., p. 241.

[4] P. 743.

[5] Trattato sopra la Vernice detta comunemente Cinese, p. 42. The " new " edition was published in 1786.

to suppose that on account of the high price of amber, and the great difficulty of making pale amber varnish, it was customary to purchase it ready made, and that the dealers substituted for it the before-mentioned thick composition of linseed-oil and pece Greca.

In the before-mentioned recipes for amber varnish, the amber was dissolved in oil; but in those which are now to be described, a balsam was substituted for the oil. Such varnishes were perhaps more brilliant, but less solid than the first, which contained oil. In the recipe for amber varnish in the Paduan MS.[1] the amber is dissolved in turpentine liquefied over the fire. The mixture, which when cold is hard, is to be diluted with spirits of turpentine. Another recipe, which is stated by Mr. Sheldrake[2] to have been brought from Venice towards the close of the last century, resembled the amber varnish of the Paduan MS.[3] except that copal was used instead of amber. He tried the recipe and failed, because, as he afterwards found, the Venice turpentine of the shops was not the natural balsam, but common resin dissolved in spirit of turpentine. He tried the experiment a second time with Chio turpentine, and succeeded.

Nearly similar to this is the varnish used by Le Blond on his prints.[4] On this subject Mr. Sheldrake observes, " Le Blond's prints were long neglected, and are now forgotten. Whatever difference of opinion may prevail respecting them, there can be none respecting his varnish, as I have seen some of these prints in

---

[1] P. 688.   [2] See a paper by Mr. Sheldrake in the Transactions of the Society of Arts, vol. xix.   [3] P. 688.

[4] The recipe is as follows :—" Take 4 parts of balsam of copavi and one of copal. Powder and sift the copal, and throw it by degrees into the balsam of copavi, stirring it well each time it is put in ; I say each time, for the powdered copal must be put in by degrees, day after day, in at least 15 different parts. The vessel must be close stopped and exposed to the heat of the sun, or a similar degree of heat, during the whole time ; and when the whole is reduced uniformly to the consistence of honey, add a quantity of warm turpentine."

perfect condition, notwithstanding they had been
thrown carelessly about for nearly sixty years. Le
Blond was a pupil of Carlo Maratti. He died at a
very advanced age, leaving behind him the character of
an ingenious projector." Mr. Sheldrake's conjecture
respecting the Italian origin of this recipe appears to
be well founded.

It will be observed that these varnishes contained
neither linseed nor nut oil; and in this respect they
resembled a varnish which a professor of Parma considers to have been that of Correggio. The ingredients
of the latter varnish differed slightly from those in the
varnish last described; they consisted of amber dissolved in balsam of copaiba (an American production,
probably not in use in the time of Correggio), and
thinned with oil of spike. Sometimes, as in the receipts of the Paduan MS.,[1] mastic was substituted for
amber and copal, and sometimes sandarac and incense.
A varnish composed of these last ingredients with
Venice turpentine is described by D. Alessio[2] to dry as
soon as spread.

The transition is easy from these resinous varnishes
containing amber and copal to those composed only of
a balsam liquefied in an essential oil like that stated by
Armenini to have been adopted by Correggio, which
consisted of the olio di abezzo liquefied over the fire,
and thinned with naphtha. Count Carlo Verri attempted
several times unsuccessfully to make this varnish; at
length, having procured genuine olio di abezzo from the
Valtellina, and the naphtha having been rectified by a
chemist on whom he could depend, he succeeded perfectly.[3]

The above varnish of olio di abezzo and naphtha is

---

[1] Pp. 671, 673.   [2] Secreti, part ii. p. 57.

[3] Verri, Saggio Elementare sul Disegno della Figura Umana, p. 138.
The results of Count Carlo Verri's experiments with this varnish are stated
by Mr. Eastlake, ' Materials,' &c., p. 481.

mentioned in the Marciana MS.,[1] accompanied by a
statement that the olio di abezzo may be diluted with
linseed or nut oil inspissated by exposure to the sun, or
with naphtha. Count Carlo Verri's failure in making
this varnish was probably not the only one; for this MS.
requires that the olio di abezzo should be genuine; and
in order to test its purity, directs that olio di abezzo and
the oil with which it is tempered should be warmed, and
then spread over the work : if the olio di abezzo was not
genuine, it would be long in drying, which was a proof that
it had been mixed with turpentine; but if it dried
quickly and perfectly, this was a proof of its purity.
From this it appears that pure olio di abezzo was a good
drier. The above instances are sufficient to show the
importance of procuring the best materials for varnishes.

In addition to the varnishes above mentioned, those
composed of a resin or balsam dissolved in an essential
oil appear to have been used on pictures. Of these
the favourite varnish, if we may judge by the number of
the recipes, was benzoin dissolved in spirits of wine :
this is mentioned not only in the Marciana MS.[2] but in
the Paduan MS.[3] and by D. Alessio, Armenini, Bisagno,
Pacheco, and Palomino.

On referring to the recipes for making the varnishes
before mentioned, it will be observed that they were so
thick as to be sometimes solid on cooling. They were
therefore sometimes diluted, while warm, with a proper
quantity of purified linseed or nut oil, spirit of turpentine, naphtha, or oil of spike ; and, when thick, they were
applied on the picture previously warmed in the sun,
with the hand or with a sponge. It may be remarked
that the varnishes to be mixed with colours were not
required to be thin, because a small quantity only was
to be mixed with the colours already ground with oil.

With regard to the high colour of oleo-resinous var-

---

[1] P. 635.   [2] P. 629.   [3] P. 699.

nishes, it may be observed that it is the custom in Germany to keep these varnishes in a sunny window; amber varnish, thus exposed to the light, will, it is said, in three years become sufficiently pale for general use.

The use of amber varnish as a vehicle for painting was revived and recommended as long ago as 1801 by Mr. Sheldrake in a paper published in the 19th volume of the Transactions of the Society of Arts. In these papers Mr. Sheldrake endeavours to prove that this varnish was used by the Italian painters; and as his opinion has been in a great measure confirmed by documentary evidence, his papers acquire additional interest from his having recorded the experiments made by himself in painting with this varnish.

The result of Mr. Sheldrake's experiments is thus stated :—

" I dissolved it [amber] in each of the painter's oils, by Dr. Lewis's process, without injuring its colour; and this solution was made in the common way. It was much darker coloured in itself, but produced scarcely any difference in effect when mixed with colour. By experiments with each of these solutions I ascertained the following facts, viz. :—

" Every colour, and all the tints compounded from it, were more brilliant than corresponding tints and colours mixed with the best drying oils to be procured from the shops.

" Colours mixed with amber, after having been shut up in a drawer for several years, lost nothing of their original brilliancy. The same colours tempered with oils, and excluded from the air, were so much altered that they could scarcely be recognised.

" Colours tempered with amber were laid on plates of metal, and exposed (both in the air and close boxes) for a long time to different degrees of heat, from that of the sun in summer to the strong heat of a stove, without being injured. It is needless to observe that oil-colours cannot undergo the same trials without being destroyed.

" These colours, when perfectly dried in any way, were not acted upon by spirit of wine and spirit of turpentine united. They were washed with spirit of sal ammoniac and solutions of potash for a longer time than would destroy common oil-colours without being injured.

" They dry as well in damp as in dry weather, and without any skin upon the surface. They are not liable to crack, and are of a flinty hardness; whence it appears that this vehicle possesses every desirable property, and it is presumed may be a discovery of some importance to artists.

" Having succeeded thus far with amber, I tried the same experiments upon solutions of gum copal, which is nearly as hard and insoluble as amber itself. The result of these was the same as the former, except that with copal the colours were something brighter than with amber. As it is extremely troublesome to dissolve the copal and amber, I tried those solutions of them in oil which are sold in the shops. When good I found them to answer as well as my own. This is a great convenience, as many might be deterred by the difficulty of preparing this vehicle, who may willingly use it, as it is thus to be procured without that trouble."

Mr. Sheldrake also observes :—

" If my experiments have not misled me, I am entitled to draw the following conclusions from them :—wherever a picture was found possessing evidently superior brilliancy of colour, independent of what is produced by the painter's skill in colouring, that brilliancy is derived from the admixture of some resinous substance in the vehicle. If it does not yield on the application of spirit of turpentine and spirit of wine, separately or together, or to such alkalies as are known to dissolve oils in the same time, it is to be presumed that vehicle

contains amber or copal, because they are the only substances known to resist those menstrua.

" I have been told, and some experiments of my own
prove the information to be true, that the Venetian
pictures, considered with respect to vehicle, are of two
kinds: for some are extremely hard, and not at all
affected by any of the above menstrua;[1] others are
similar in colour, but so tender that it is scarcely possible to clean them without injury, and in that respect
are little superior to turpentine colours. The first,
in consequence of the data which I have laid down,
incur the suspicion of being painted with amber or
copal."

The correctness of Mr. Sheldrake's observations will
be acknowledged on comparing them with Mr. Eastlake's
remarks[2] on the advantages of amber varnish as a vehicle for painting. The firmest and most durable varnishes were undoubtedly those composed of amber and
oil ;[3] the next were those composed of other resins, such
as sandarac, mastic, and pece Greca, with oil, or of amber or copal dissolved in a balsam; and the last class,
which consisted only of resins dissolved in essential oils,
was decidedly the least durable.

---

[1] "By an attentive examination of pictures which belong to the first
epoch of painting in oil, one may be convinced that some of the Italians
have employed oil varnishes which are harder than those now used by the
Flemings, since they offer greater resistance to solvents."—Merimée, &c.,
p. 30.   [2] Materials, &c., pp. 290, 302, 303, 304 n., 306, 316, 486.
[3] See Mr. Wilson Neil on the Manufacture of Varnishes, Trans. Soc.
Arts, p. 69.   Dreme, Der Virniss-u. Kittmacher, &c.   Marcucci, Saggio,
&c., p. 163.   Merimée, p. 48.

Dr. Lewis, after describing the experiment of Hoffmann mentioned by
Mr. Eastlake,[*] shows that perfect solutions of amber in drying and other
oils may be obtained in the following manner :—" In Dr. Stockar's very
curious *Specimen Inaugurale de Succino*, printed at Leyden in 1760,
there are sundry more important experiments on the subject, made by
himself conjointly with my worthy correspondent Mr. Ziegler, of Win-
terthur. They found that by continuing a simmering heat twelve hours,

---

[*] Materials, p. 318.

On the use of Varnish with Colours in Painting.

It has been mentioned that in glazing, varnish was generally mixed with the colours. The practice, however, does not appear to have been universal, and the same artist is reputed to have employed different materials upon different pictures. Sometimes it is said that oil only was used to paint with, and sometimes the

---

and confining the vapour as much as stone-ware vessels would bear without bursting (the danger of which was avoided by making a small notch in the cork stoppers), powdered amber dissolved perfectly in expressed oils, in turpentine, and in balsam of copaiba. A strong copper vessel, with a cover screwed on it, seemed most eligible; and for the greater security a valve may be made in the cover, kept down by a spring that shall give way before the confined vapour is of sufficient force to be in any danger of bursting the vessel. Though such a heat as converts part of the oil into strong elastic vapours, and the forcible compressure of the vapour, are expedient for hastening the dissolution, they do not appear to be essentially necessary; for, by digestion for a week in close stopped glass vessels, in which the compressure could not be very great, solutions equally perfect were obtained.

" The solution in rape-seed oil, and in oil of almonds, was of a fine yellowish colour; in linseed oil, gold coloured; in oil of poppy-seeds, yellowish red; in oil of olive, of a beautiful red; in oil of nuts, deeper coloured; and in oil of bays, of a purplish red. It is observable that this last oil, which of itself, in the greatest common heat of the atmosphere, proves a thick butyraceous consistence, continued fluid when the amber was dissolved in it. The solutions made with turpentine and with balsam of copaiba were of a deep red colour, and on cooling hardened into a brittle mass of the same colour. All the solutions mingle perfectly with spirit of turpentine. Those made with the oils of linseed, bays, poppy-seeds, and nuts, and with the balsam of copaiba and turpentine, being diluted with four times their quantity of spirit of turpentine, formed hard, tenacious, glossy varnishes, which dried sufficiently quick, and appeared greatly preferable to those made in the common manner from melted amber.

" My worthy friend Mr. Ziegler, in an elegant German translation with which he had honoured this work, described a varnish, with the method of using it, which appeared from his experiments to be the best. Fine transparent amber reduced to powder is boiled in a brass vessel having a valve in its cover, with as much drying oil as will just cover it; generally in 5 or 6 hours the amber is perfectly dissolved. Dilute the solution with four or five times its quantity of oil of turpentine, and let it stand some days, that all the impurities may settle to the bottom."—Commercium Philosophico-Technicum, or the Philosophical Commerce of Arts, by W. Lewis, London, 1763, 4to., p. 366, &c.

colours are stated to have been mixed with varnish. The following instances and observations, referring chiefly to the Italian schools, will show that varnish was frequently used, not only in glazing, but in the priming, and with the shadow colours.

Armenini and Bisagno recommend the addition of common varnish to the priming, to those colours which dried with difficulty, and to the glazing colours. Baldinucci states [1] that boiled oil (olio cotto) was sometimes used in the darkest parts *instead* of varnish, and in other parts where the colours had sunk in. From this it appears that it was usual to mix varnish with the dark shades.

As an additional proof of the use of varnish in the dark parts of the picture, may be quoted the following description given by Vasari [2] of the method adopted by Giovan Francesco Caroti:—" He was of opinion, and in this he was not far from the truth, that varnishing was injurious to pictures, and that it caused them to appear old sooner than they would do otherwise; and for this reason, he used varnish and certain purified oils in the shades when painting." This is certainly an admission that varnish was necessary either in the picture or on the surface, and that the former was, by Caroti at least, considered preferable.

De Piles mentions that in painting on walls, varnish was mixed with the colours to prevent the necessity of varnishing afterwards; [3] and in the Italian edition of this work [4] it is stated that painting on wood was executed in the same manner as on walls; whence it may be inferred varnish was mixed with the colours. Canepario, the Venetian physician, says, [5] "others are accustomed to mix colours with liquid varnish and

---

[1] Voc. Dis., tit. Olio Cotto.   [2] Vita di Fra Giocondo ed altri.
[3] These instructions are as old as Vasari. See Int., cap. xix.
[4] Published at Turin in 1769.   [5] De Atramentis, p. 304.

linseed or nut oil, instead of white of egg and gum-water; for a liquid and oily varnish binds the colours better together, &c." The Marciana MS.[1] describes "an excellent clear and drying varnish proper for colours, both in oil-painting and in other kinds of painting."

These direct proofs of the mixture of colours with varnish are from the works of authors describing the processes of their contemporaries.[2] As an indirect proof, but not the less valuable on that account, is the following anecdote related by Luigi Crespi[3] of his father Giuseppe Maria Crespi, called "Lo Spagnuolo." "One day Cardinal Lambertini was in our house sitting for his portrait, which my father was painting, when one of my brothers entered the room, bringing a letter, just arrived by post, from another brother who was at Modena on business. The Cardinal took the letter, and, on opening it, said to my father, 'Go on painting, and I will read it.' Having opened it, he began to read quickly, inventing an imaginary letter, in which the absent son, with the greatest expressions of shame and humiliation, prostrated himself at the feet of his father, begging his pardon, and saying that he had found it impossible to disengage himself from a stringent promise of marrying a certain Signora Apollonia, whence . . . . . but he had hardly proceeded thus far when my father leaped on to his feet, knocking over palette, pencils, and chair, *and upsetting oil, varnish, and everything else which was on the little bench,* and uttering all kinds of exclamations. The Cardinal jumped up at the same time to quiet and pacify him, telling him as well as he could for laughing, that it was all nonsense, and entirely an invention of his own. Meanwhile my father was running round the room in despair, the Cardinal following him; and thus pleasantly ended the

---

[1] P. 633.   [2] For additional proof see the work of Gerard Lairesse,
cap. v.   [3] Lives of the Bolognese Painters, p. 220.

morning's work. After this time, whenever his Eminence came to see my father, before getting out of the carriage, he would whisper, 'that he had no doubt Signora Apollonia was at home with him.'"

It is apparent from this passage, that Lo Spagnuolo was accustomed to use varnish in painting, or the varnish would not have been placed *with* the oil on the low bench by his side while painting a portrait, for which the Cardinal was actually then sitting; it may also be inferred that varnish was still used in painting by Luigi Crespi, his son, who related the anecdote. The period when this scene took place was between 1717 and 1732. Lo Spagnuolo studied first under Angelo Michele Toni, afterwards under Domenico Maria Canuti (who was a pupil of Guido), and lastly under Carlo Cignani; and it is fair to presume that he employed their technical processes. The use made by Sir Peter Lely of varnish mixed with colour, when painting the portrait of Tillotson,[1] may be considered another incidental proof of the use of varnish with colours.

To these proofs from contemporary writers may be added the evidence of those who have cleaned and experimented on old pictures. Among the earliest may be reckoned the declaration of Requeno[2] that some of the pictures of Guercino were painted with oil mixed with pece Greca (the vernice comune of the sixteenth century), others with gums and resins, and some with oil only; and the letter written by Hackert,[3] advocating the use of varnishes in painting. The reply to this letter[4] by a gentleman who at that period possessed the finest collection of Flemish pictures in Rome is equally conclusive. This gentleman

---

[1] Walpole's Anecdotes, vol. iii. p. 129.
[2] Saggi sul Ristabilimento, &c., vol. i. p. 169, n.
[3] Published at Perugia, 1788.
[4] Inserted in the Giornale di Roma, 20th December, 1788.

states that varnish was always used by those Italian schools most distinguished for colouring, and that the works of Domenichino, who used varnish, were in better preservation than those of other pupils of the Carracci. We may also mention the certificate, dated 1754, by Carlo Cesare Giovannini of Bologna,[1] respecting the state of preservation of the celebrated picture by Raphael called the Madonna di S. Sisto, which he says was until that period intact, and had never been touched with varnishes, or otherwise, since the day when it had been placed over the altar of S. Sisto, perhaps by Raphael himself, and on which the varnish used in retouching by Raphael is now visible on close examination in some rancid-looking spots on the body of the infant Jesus, where the varnish had accidentally been left rather thick by the pencil of the master. To these instances may be added the evidence of Marcucci,[2] of Palmaroli,[3] of Requeno,[4] of Merimée,[5] of Sampieri,[6] of the professor mentioned by Lanzi, who restored a picture by Correggio, and of the other professors now living who have been already mentioned in this work. While, however, these authorities appear to leave no doubt as to the adoption by the Italians, during the best period of the art, of varnish with colours on certain parts of the picture, the assertion of Boschini,[7] that in painting flesh the Venetians abhorred like the plague all lustrous or shining surfaces, must not be

---

[1] Gualandi, Memorie, ser. i. p. 29. This picture was purchased, with 62 other celebrated paintings, by Augustus III., King of Poland and Elector of Saxony, for 40,000 Roman scudi, and was taken to Dresden by Giovannini. It was restored by Sig. P. Palmaroli, the author of the Notes to Marcucci's Observations on the Practice of Painting in Oil of the Florentine, Venetian, and Flemish Schools of Painting in their best time.

[2] Saggio, &c., p. 222, &c.   [3] Notes to Marcucci, Saggio, &c.

[4] Saggio sul Ristabilimento dell' Antico Arte de' Greci e Romani Pittori, vol. i. p. 169, n.   [5] De la Peinture à l'Huile, p. xvii. n. xx.

[6] See Lanzi, Storia Pittorica, ed. of Pisa, 1823, note 15 by Boni.

[7] Ricche Minere.

overlooked. This assertion, as far as regards the solid painting, is generally supported by the direction in the Marciana MS.,[1] to grind and temper the colours with oil as stiff as possible, and if they were too stiff to dilute them by dipping the brush in oil, as well as by the evidence of the professors of the art now living at Venice. The latter appear to consider that oil only was used in the solid painting, and that the varnish was reserved for the glazing and finishing colours, and especially for such as would be injured by admixture with oil, such as red lead, cenere azzurre, and others.

The same may also be observed with regard to the later Bolognese school; and this appears to have been the opinion of Lanzi, who, in describing the manner of Lo Spagnuolo, says that "he used gums in painting (per colorire) in the same way as others used them in glazing." The Parmasan school are also stated to have painted in the same manner—namely, the solid colours with oil, and the glazing colours with varnish.

The present state of a picture by Tintoretto in the Casa Barbarigo at Venice is instructive as to the practice of this artist. The surface of the picture alluded to is generally dull, as if the varnish had been removed or worn off, with the exception of certain dark parts, and of the foliage, which are glossy, as if these colours had been mixed with varnish.

Of Varnishing Pictures.

Pictures painted in the Flemish manner, or finished with colours mixed with varnish, did not require the superposition of varnish when complete, and we find that even in the time of Lebrun and Lana the custom of varnishing finished pictures was not universal. The latter remarks (p. 165), " when the painting is finished, some painters are accustomed to varnish it, in

---

[1] P. 627.

order that the work may appear more smooth and
brilliant." And Lebrun,[1] after directing white of egg
to be spread over the picture to preserve it from dust
and fly-marks, adds, "when necessary, the picture may
be cleaned by passing a wet cloth over it, which easily
removes the white of egg, with the dust attached to it.[2]
This," he adds, "could not be done with varnish."
These passages, therefore, may be considered evidence
of the truth of Vasari's statement that pictures painted
according to the process invented by Van Eyck required no varnish. It may also be collected from an
expression of Vasari's, in his account of Giovan Francesco Caroti,[3] that the biographer disapproved of
varnishing pictures; he says, "Caroti was of opinion,
and in this he was not far from the truth, that varnishing pictures spoiled them, and made them appear
old sooner than they otherwise would do."

The fact that pictures were generally varnished is,
however, too well authenticated to require any proof.

On the Preparation of the Grounds.

There is nothing, perhaps, on which the durability of
a picture so much depends as on the goodness of the
ground; and at the same time there is, perhaps, no part
of a picture on which the opinions of artists have been
so much divided as on the manner of preparing the
grounds; some painters preferring white grounds, others
dark grounds; some electing to paint on absorbent
grounds, others on non-absorbent grounds; while others
reject all preparations but a coat or two of size to fill up
the pores of the wood, or the holes of the canvass.

The subject of the preparation of panels and canvass
forms an important part of most of the old treatises.

The earliest paintings in oil were generally executed

---

[1] P. 816.   [2] See the disadvantages of white of egg as a varnish
described in a letter by Hackert, 1788.   [3] Vita di Fra Giocondo ed altri.

on panels. The panels were composed of various pieces of wood cemented together with cheese glue, and this glue caused them to adhere so firmly together, that such panels were considered stronger than those which consisted of one piece of wood only. Strips of linen were usually glued over the joinings of the panels, and in some cases the panel was entirely covered with linen. Animal glue was used for this purpose.

Several coats of warm glue, which filled up the pores of the wood, were then to be applied.

The Italian name for the next process is *ingessare*.[1] This consisted in the application of several thin coats of size [2] and *gesso marcio*[3] over the surface of the panel, which when dry was carefully smoothed with a knife or pumice stone.

Upon this preparation the old tempera painters were accustomed to apply a coat of Armenian bole mixed with glue, on which they spread leaf gold; a practice which, though gradually discontinued, was sometimes adopted in oil-painting, and was occasionally practised in Italy.[4] In Flanders the practice was continued to a comparatively late period. The gold ground was considered to give great brilliancy to the colours.[5]

This practice, however, was not universal; the grounds were more frequently left white; but in this state they would absorb the oil from the colours applied

---

[1] See Bol. MS., p. 595. Vasari, Int., cap. xx., xxi. Cennini, cap. cxv.

[2] The durability of the painting depends much on the glue being employed of the proper strength. It is better that it should be too weak than too strong. See Volpato MS., p. 728, 732; Bol. MS., p. 595; Palomino, vol. ii. p. 47.

[3] Plaster of Paris stirred with water until it loses its power of setting.— Third Report of the Commissioners on the Fine Arts, p. 47, n. Cennini, cap. cxvi. Other writers call the plaster " gesso sottile."

[4] Zanetti states (Delle Pittura Veneziana, p. 194) that some pictures by Paolo Veronese, in the Fondaco de' Tedeschi at Venice, are executed on gilt leather.

[5] See Baldinucci, Vite de' Pittori, vol. vi. p. 262.

on them, unless prevented by the application of several coats of size, varnish, boiled oil,[1] or of colour mixed with oil [2]—practices which prevailed generally in Italy during the fifteenth, sixteenth, and seventeenth centuries, except in Venice, where some artists used absorbent grounds, as will be hereafter noticed; the painters of the other schools, however, adhered to the general practice of employing white and non-absorbent grounds.

The use of linen for grounds is considered to have been an invention of the Germans or Flemings, and by them introduced into Italy.[3] The canvass prepared by the Flemings was in great repute in the time of Borghini, for the facility with which it could be rolled without cracking.[4]

The Venetians are generally considered to have been the first among the Italians who adopted the custom of painting on canvass, on which they were able to execute larger paintings than they could on wood, and which combined the advantages of lightness, cheapness, and portability. The practice, however, necessarily caused an alteration in the nature of the ground, which on canvass was required to be composed of pliant and elastic materials, not liable to crack or be detached when the canvass was rolled up; and this has always been found a great difficulty.

Great diversity of opinion exists among writers on

---

[1] Merimée, de la Peinture à l'Huile, p. 15 ; Lanzi, vol. iv. p. 71 n.

[2] Vasari, Int., cap. xxi.   Armenini, lib. ii. cap. ix.   The colour usually employed for this purpose was a warm tint inclining to yellow or flesh colour ; it sometimes consisted of yellow ochre, or minium ground in oil. Fra Bartolomeo is said to have used sometimes one, and sometimes the other of these colours. See Marcucci, Saggio, &c., p. 213.

[3] Painted cloth as a substitute for window glass, and waters for painting on linen, silk, or woollen, are mentioned in the Bolognese MS., pp. 491, 493. It is probable that the latter were for articles of dress or the hanging of rooms.

Riposo, p. 136.

painting as to the most eligible mode of preparing canvass; and several processes are recorded as having been employed by good artists. In general the coats of gesso were omitted on cloth,[1] it being considered that they were liable to crack when the picture was rolled.

Vasari recommends that three or four coats of size should be applied, and upon them a mixture composed of flour paste with nut oil, and a little white lead, should be spread with a knife and smoothed with the hand, so as to fill up all the holes; then one or two other coats of weak size should be applied, and lastly the priming. Armenini also recommends several coats of glue, one of which was to be applied on the back of the canvass. The same author states[2] that "painters were in the habit of filling up the holes of the canvass with a mixture composed of flour paste, and a third part of white lead, before the glue was applied. On this preparation the priming, which consisted of white lead, giallolino, and terra di campane, or of verdigris, white lead, and umber, was spread. But the preparation he especially recommended was a light flesh colour inclining to the colour of flame, by means of the varnish, of which rather more than the usual quantity was to be added, because it was observed that "this added to the effect of the colours, especially the blues and reds, without causing them to change; for," continues Armenini, "it is known that oil darkens and sullies all the colours, which appear soiled and dirty in proportion to the darkness of the ground beneath them." He adds that those who were desirous that the colours should not change from the effects of time, made the grounds almost entirely of white lead, adding to them a sixth part of varnish, and a little red, and when this was dry they polished the surface, upon

---

[1] See Vasari, Int., cap. xxiii. Armenini, lib. ii. cap. viii.
[2] Lib. ii. cap. ix.

which they either drew or traced the outlines. In a note to this passage, Signor Palmaroli[1] observes that he has sometimes found in grounds ochre or red lead mixed with the gesso, upon which was laid a coat of oil diluted with spirit of turpentine, applied with a piece of cotton or a sponge.

Borghini states[2] that the Flemish canvass, which could be easily rolled and carried everywhere, was prepared simply with one or two coats of size, and that it was then coloured, taking care to fill the holes of the cloth with the colours. He also recommends[3] one coat of size and two of priming, particularly if the canvass was to be rolled and removed to another country. He mentions that canvass was sometimes prepared by applying a coat of gesso and flour, boiled in linseed oil. Other authors recommend a priming of potter's earth[4] mixed with oil, and applied upon a coat of size or flour paste.[5] Pacheco[6] mentions a mixture of flour paste, salad oil,[7] and a little honey; and when this application was quite dry, and had been smoothed with pumicestone, then a coat or two of priming was applied. Other painters, he states, first apply size made from the parings of leather, then a coat of sifted ashes instead of gesso, which after being smoothed with pumicestone was covered with the priming of almagra (a red earth), ground with linseed oil; these grounds, Pacheco says, were used at Madrid. Another kind of priming, according to the same author, was composed of white lead, red lead, charcoal black, and linseed oil upon the gesso ground. Pacheco, however, disapproved of all these methods: he says, " I know by experience that

---

[1] Notes to Marcucci, Saggio, &c., p. 207.   [2] Riposo, p. 136.

[3] Ibid., p. 138.   [4] This earth was called by the Italians Terretta, Terra di Cave, Terra da Boccale.

[5] Volpato, p. 730.   [6] Tratado, p. 383.

[7] Palomino (vol. ii. p. 46) says linseed oil should be used, and not salad oil, which is prejudicial to the picture.

flour-paste, gesso, and ashes are, in time, affected by damp, and that they decay, together with the canvass;" and he finally recommends the application of a few coats of size, and then two coats of priming, composed of the potter's clay [1] used at Seville, ground up with linseed oil, each coat being polished with pumice-stone when dry. Upon this was spread a third coat, to which a little white-lead might be added or not, at pleasure. He observes, that although weak size made the cloth more supple, it might be omitted. This, Pacheco states, is the best kind of priming, and that which he always used himself; because he had remarked that the six pictures which he began in 1600, in the cloisters belonging to the monastery of the Order of Mercy, on this kind of ground, were in good preservation when he wrote his work (which was published in 1649), and showed no symptoms of scaling off.

The directions given by Palomino [2] resemble so nearly those of Pacheco that it is useless to repeat them. It may, however, be observed that the former mentions that in Andalusia canvass was frequently primed with a kind of clay, washed up by the rivers when they rose; or, if this could not be had, with chalk, which was ground up with almagra: adding to it, when ground, some old colours (those which are cleaned from the palette and brushes[3]), if they could be obtained, or in default of this a dark colour, called sombre del Viejo, should be added to assist the drying, the clay and chalk being bad dryers.

The custom of using gesso grounds on cloth was, however, never entirely abandoned,[4] and, among other artists, they were used by Bassano. With regard to the

---

[1] Called at Madrid " Tierra de Esquivias" (Palomino, vol. ii. p. 48), probably similar to the Terra da Boccale of the Italians.

[2] Vol. ii. p. 46—48.   [3] See Volpato, p. 733.

[4] See Armenini, lib. ii. cap. viii.   Borghini, p. 138.   Pacheco, p. 383, 384.

pictures of this artist, Volpato mentions having remarked that those painted on grounds prepared with a
small quantity of gesso were in good condition, while
the colours scaled off those pictures on which much had
been used. The directions given by Volpato [1] as to the
preparation of grounds need not be alluded to here, as
they are contained in the work.

To return to the gesso grounds: it is asserted that
they were used also by the Bolognése painters, Samacchini, Sabbatini, and Tibaldi, both on canvass and
panels. Correggio also is said to have prepared his
canvass with a very thin coat of size and gesso, over
which he laid a coat of boiled oil.[2]

As to the colour of the priming, the weight of authority is in favour of white grounds.[3] Mr. Eastlake
observes (Goethe on Colours, p. 378), " the secret of
Van Eyck and his contemporaries is always assumed to
consist in the vehicle (varnish or oils) he employed;
but a far more important condition of the splendour of
colour of the works of those masters was the careful
preservation of internal light by painting thinly, but
ultimately with great force, on white grounds." As an
additional argument in favour of white grounds, it may
be stated that modern Italian artists are now so convinced of the propriety of employing them, that they
have almost all returned to the use of them. When I
was in Italy, I was informed that the Academy of
Parma had recently decided against the authenticity of
a picture attributed to Correggio, because it was painted
on a red ground; the Academicians considering that
none but white grounds were in use during the life of

---

[1] Volpato, p. 729—733.   [2] Lanzi, vol. iv. p. 71 and n.

[3] See Lionardo da Vinci, Trattato, cap. c.; Du Fresnoy, Art of Painting, with the Commentary of De Piles; Orsini, Vita di Pietro Perugino; Algarotti, Lettere sopra la Pittura, vol. viii. p. 50, 51, Venezia, 1792;
Delaval on Colours; and Quatremère de Quincy, Life of Raffaelle.

this artist. There is, however, some diversity of opinion as to the expediency of their being non-absorbent.

Sometimes the grounds were prepared by giving the canvass a few coats of glue only, without other priming.[1] The paintings by Callot, at Venice, are prepared in this way; and a picture by Lionardo da Vinci, or one of his scholars, mentioned by Amoretti, and in the possession of Signor Mussi, is executed on canvass prepared with size only.[2] Pictures so prepared stand well. Pozzo, the Jesuit, also painted on the same grounds, but his pictures are much changed, probably from other causes; for Félibien remarks[3] that if the canvass were not primed at all, but painted on at once, the colours would bear out better and remain more brilliant.

Various grounds were in use in the Venetian school. A Venetian professor communicated, among other particulars, the following information as the result of his experiments on the grounds of the old Venetian pictures:—" The grounds were made of gesso and very weak size; sometimes a little black[4] was added by Gian Bellino and others. Over this were laid one or two coats of glue to prevent the ground being too absorbent; the glue was made of the parings of leather." This information was confirmed by other professors of Venice and Verona.

With respect to the grounds used by Titian, I was informed that this great artist employed a ground of " gesso marcio,"[5] taking especial care not to use too much glue, and that this slightly absorbent ground was useful in getting rid of some of the oil. It is certain,

---

[1] Palomino, vol. ii. p. 45.

[2] Amoretti, Memorie Storiche di Lionardo da Vinci, p. 165.

[3] Principes, &c., p. 297.

[4] These grey grounds were also used in the Flemish school. The series of pictures by Rubens of the life of Mary de' Medicis are painted on a grey preparation.

[5] Compare Merimée, de la Peinture à l'Huile, p. 241; De Piles, Elémens de Peinture, p. 130.

however, that Titian sometimes employed a non-absorbent ground, since a restorer of pictures at Verona stated that he had found on the gesso-ground a coat of strong glue, made of pig's skin (much used in the Venetian territories), which was very hard and shining, and on which the picture was painted. This was probably the case with Titian's picture of S. Pietro Martire, which, when at Paris, was transferred from panel to canvass. The author of the 'Histoire de la Peinture en Italie,'[1] who was present at the operation, remarks, "I observed that the ground and the painting were not consolidated together, but were laid one upon the other."

Titian is said sometimes to have used a red ground made of terra rossa with size, and Merimée mentions that, on analysing the ground of a picture by Titian, he found flour-paste and gesso, but no glue.[2]

Tintoretto is stated to have painted his celebrated Crucifixion in the Scuola of S. Rocco on a simple preparation of flour-paste, and this picture is in excellent preservation. Many painters, and especially Volpato, Pacheco, and Palomino, object to the flour paste. The reason assigned by Volpato is, that if the paste is too stiff, it causes the colour to scale off; and if too weak, the picture is liable to decay from damp. He states, also, that it was frequently used by those who primed bad canvass, which would decay in a few years, because it was useful in filling up the threads of the canvass.

Paul Veronese generally painted on a twilled canvass,

---

[1] M. B. A. A., Paris, 1817.

[2] Merimée, de la Peinture à l'Huile, p. 241.   On this subject Boschini (La Carta del Navegar, &c. p. 339) says—

<blockquote>
"La prontezza xe meterse davanti
Una gran tela, e de farina propria
Tamisar, e impastar figure in copia,
E senza natural, far casi tanti."
</blockquote>

called in Venice "terlise," which he prepared with a very thin coat of glue and gesso; so thin as to show the texture of the cloth through the paint. This coat, being absorbent,[1] imbibed the superfluous oil which darkened the threads of the canvass.

Sig. Pietro Edwards, whose opportunities of examining pictures of the Venetian school were perhaps greater than ever fell to the lot of any other person, has recorded his opinion that these grounds were best adapted to ensure the durability of paintings; and in support of this opinion he instances the three pictures by Paolo Veronese, representing the legend of Sta. Cristina, which were executed, with very few repaintings, either on a ground of gesso not hardened by strong size, or on canvass, with a thin coating of gesso, the colours of which were, he says, so fresh that they appeared to have been painted but two days instead of two hundred years.[2]

The same favourable opinion of white tempera grounds is expressed by De Piles;[3] but he adds that they have the disadvantage of being liable to crack when rolled up. This was the case with the celebrated Nozze di Cana by Paolo Veronese, which, on its arrival at Paris, was found to be in such a state as to render it necessary to line it with great care in order to prevent its scaling entirely from the canvass. This operation, with some necessary reparations, was performed at the Louvre with all requisite care and attention. But when, in 1815, the picture was about to be restored to Venice, according to the treaty, it was perceived that the colours crumbled off and fell into dust at the slightest movement. To continue the operation, therefore, was to expose one of the finest works of the Venetian school to certain destruction; and the committee decided that the picture

---

[1] See the Dissertation of Sig. Pietro Edwards, p. 887, 888.
[2] See p. 888.   [3] Elémens, p. 131.

of Paolo should remain at Paris, and that a painting of Lebrun's should be sent to Venice in its stead.[1]

Absorbent grounds of size and gesso are considered to have been employed by the Parmasan school.

Various contrivances were resorted to in order to prevent the cracking of pictures when the canvass was rolled. Some artists added honey and oil to the preparation of size and gesso ;[2] but the Venetian artists are stated traditionally to have used milk for this purpose. All writers speak of the necessity of the grounds on canvass being thin, as a means of preventing their cracking.

With regard to the use of white lead in the priming, the general opinion seems to be that it is injurious. It has been stated that any picture in which white lead was used in the grounds would infallibly crack in less than fifty years ; and that pictures painted on a ground of white lead and oil would moreover turn brown. The pictures of Longhi (born in 1702, and living in 1762) are in good preservation, with the exception of the grounds, which are full of large cracks, attributed by the Italian restorers to the use of white lead in the grounds. Neither Palomino, Pacheco, Borghini, Volpato, nor Lebrun recommend white lead in the preparation of the grounds. Vasari and Armenini and some few modern painters, on the contrary, are in favour of it.

---

[1] This account was given by the French painter M. Camille Rogier to Sig. Cigogna, who inserted it in his ' Iscrizioni Veneziane,' vol. iv. p. 328.

It may not be uninteresting to the reader to know that the sum received by Paolo for painting this picture was 324 ducats, and not 90, as asserted by Algarotti. The original contract, with the signature of Paolo, is preserved among the papers belonging to the Monastery of S. Giorgio Maggiore at Venice. It has been copied and published by Sig. E. A. Cigogna in the 4th volume of the ' Iscrizioni Veneziane.' It may also be interesting to know that the date of the contract was the 6th of June, 1562 ; and the day on which Paolo gave his receipt for the money, on the completion of the picture, was the 6th of October, 1563 : so that the picture was begun and finished in 16 months.

[2] Pacheco, p. 383 ; Palomino, vol. ii. p. 47 ; and see Ballard's Traité de Mignature, p. 220. Salmon's Polygraphices, p. 80. Marcucci, Saggio, &c., p. 205, n.

The Carracci are said to have used white lead in their grounds. " The only priming used by Ludovico was a slight coat of white lead and ochre, with sufficient oil to ensure a smooth surface, and he made use of this priming as a shadow colour. Annibale, his cousin, sometimes used a mixture of ' creta ' and white lead for his grounds. Guercino instead of ' creta ' employed marble dust; and with this his pictures in his first manner are thinly primed; in the second manner the priming is thicker."

Some artists, and especially Guido, painted occasionally on silk, which was thought to be more durable than linen cloth. It was frequently prepared for painting by applying a coat of size, to which a little honey was added to prevent its cracking, and on this the priming was laid.[1]

Pictures were frequently painted on copper, and in this case the only preparation necessary was a coat of glue, which prevented the oil from acting on the colours.

The introduction of dark grounds into Bologna is attributed to the Carracci. They were introduced into Venice by Palma Giovane, who has been called the last of the good Venetian painters, and the first of the bad.

On a careful examination of the different authorities, it appears that pictures painted on a ground of gesso are the most durable, but that when this material is used on canvass the greatest care is necessary to prevent its cracking. It also appears that when the surface of the gesso ground has been polished quite smooth with pumice-stone, one or two coats of glue made from pig's skin, and perhaps a coat of varnish or oil, if the picture is to be painted in the Flemish manner, should be applied to prevent absorption. But if the Venetian manner of painting is pursued, the thin distemper ground used by Paolo Veronese is considered best adapted to

---

[1] Ballard's Traité de Mignature, p. 229.

promote the durability of the picture. The great re-
quisites in grounds for canvass are thinness, whiteness,
and flexibility, and a perfectly smooth surface.

Methods of Painting.

In examining the technical processes of oil-painting
in the North of Italy, it will be seen that they arrange
themselves under two great divisions: in the first, which
may be called the Flemish process, the picture was
begun in chiaroscuro, and finished with the local colours;
in the second, or Italian process, which was introduced
in the beginning of the sixteenth century, the picture
was commenced with the local colours painted solidly
with oil, white being introduced into the cool grey or
bluish shadows, and was finished with warm glazings.
The former system was generally adopted in Lombardy
and Bologna; the latter in Venice, where it originated:
but this arrangement was not without exceptions, and in
later times the Venetian method was preferred to the
Flemish, which has almost fallen into disuse and oblivion in Italy. Both methods, however, underwent
various modifications according to the genius or the
caprice of the different professors of painting, and so
great was the diversity in the technical habits of the
Italian painters, that the pictures of the same artist are
frequently found to have been painted in various manners and with different materials. Thus Titian is said
to have changed his method several times, and Requeno
relates [1] that he has seen pictures by Guercino in some
of which oil only had been used, in others oil and pece
Greca, and in others resins and gums. The funda-
mental principle in all may, however, be traced to one
or other of the above-mentioned sources.

In the early period of painting in oil the same pro-

---

[1] Saggi sul Ristabilimento, &c., vol. i. p. 169, n.

cess of painting was observed throughout Italy, as well as in Flanders and Germany. The process may be thus briefly described :—

The ground being properly prepared, the next process was to draw the subject of the picture. This was frequently done with black chalk or black-lead pencil, but in order to insure greater correctness the subject was frequently traced in the usual way from a drawing on paper. Baroccio always adopted the latter method,[1] and the outlines deeply indented, as if with a style, may be seen in a large unfinished picture by him in the library of the Archiginnasio at Bologna. The outline was then secured by marking over it with a brown colour (as in the unfinished picture by Lionardo da Vinci in the gallery of Brera at Milan), or with a tint composed of carmine and dark ochre.[2]

When describing the different kinds of grounds used in painting, I have mentioned that a coat of size, of varnish, or of boiled oil was applied upon the gesso ground to render it non-absorbent;[3] but Mr. Eastlake has proved[4] that the outline was occasionally, at least, drawn before this last application, and the coating of size or the warm transparent oil priming was spread over the outline. It is probable that this plan was adopted in the Venetian school, and it may be observed that sketches by Tintoretto are still in existence which were begun in chiaroscuro with water colours, and then oiled, the local colours being afterwards painted in their places with oil. To this instance may be added the passage quoted by Walpole[5] from the Pocket-book of Mr. Beale, in which it is mentioned that Lely "ap-

---

[1] See Bellori, Vite de' Pittori, p. 117. Lanzi, vol. ii. p. 124.

[2] Palomino, vol. ii. p. 57, 59.

[3] The present state of many of the pictures of Luini and other artists proves beyond a doubt that the ground on which they were painted was non-absorbent. The colours having in some parts scaled off, leave visible the white ground unstained with oil, and of dazzling whiteness.

[4] 'Materials,' &c., p. 384. [5] Anecdotes, vol. iii. p. 129.

prehending the colour of the cloth on which he painted was too light, before he began to lay on the flesh colour, he glazed the whole place where the face and haire were drawn in a colour over thin, with Cullen's earth, and a little bone black (as he told us) made very thin with varnish." The practice does not, however, appear to have been universal in Italy, especially when the priming was opaque or nearly so, since Vasari, Borghini, Armenini, and his copyist Bisagno direct the design to be traced or drawn *upon* the priming. Perhaps it may not be far from the truth to suppose that when the priming was transparent it was spread over the outline; but when it was opaque the outline was drawn on it.

The subject having been outlined with ink, or black and lake, or brown, the picture was begun in chiaroscuro by washing in the shadows lightly with the same colour, like a drawing in Indian ink, and it was suffered to dry. This practice is alluded to incidentally by writers on painting, and especially by Paolo Pino,[1] where he objects to painters designing their pictures with such extreme diligence, composing the whole in chiaroscuro according to the custom of Gian Bellino, for this, he observes, was labour thrown away, as the whole had afterwards to be covered with colours, &c. Vasari mentions[2] that Fra Bartolomeo di S. Marco was partial to this method of painting, and Malvasia,[3] speaking of Tiarini, relates that he commenced his pictures in chiaroscuro with white lead and bone black, and then covered them with colours and finished with glazings. The custom is also mentioned by Pacheco,[4] who did not approve of it.

When the chiaroscuro had been painted with black, or when the white ground had been covered with a grey

---

[1] Dialogo, f. 16.   [2] Vita di Fra Bartolomeo di S. Marco.
[3] Felsina Pittrice, vol. ii. p. 206.   [4] Tratado, p. 386.

preparation, as in some of the pictures of Gian Bellino and Rubens, the artist proceeded to paint the flesh tints.[1] But where the chiaroscuro was of a rich brown, it was necessary to interpose grey tints between the shades and the flesh tints. The latter, which were made more rosy than nature, were then laid on very thinly, beginning with the lights and proceeding gradually with deeper and redder tints into the shades,[2] laying each tint in its place and not tormenting it with the brush.

The next tints, which were also very thin, had more yellow in them, and the last coat of colours was also thin, and contained more white, and with this the flesh was toned to match the complexion. The number of coats of colour is not to be understood as limited to three.[3] Titian is said to have repeated his colours nine or ten times; the same has been said of Correggio ; and it is mentioned on the authority of Mr. Beale,[4] that Lely said he believed Vandyck had painted over a portrait fourteen times. This method of painting keeps the flesh light and clear, because it permits the white grounds to appear through it.[5] Different colours were used for the shadows of flesh: some artists employed a mixed tint of black, lake, and some transparent yellow, or yellow varnish. Armenini says that asphaltum, mummy, and the smoke of pece Greca were commonly used for this purpose. Lomazzo names[6] terra di cam-

---

[1] Even where the chiaroscuro has been dark brown, the scumbling of the thin flesh tints over it has produced the effect of grey.—See Mr. Sheldrake's Paper, in the Transactions of the Soc. of Arts, vol. xvi. For the effect of darkness seen through a semi-transparent medium, see Goethe on Colours, by Mr. Eastlake, Nos. 151, 160.

[2] See Lomazzo, Trattato, lib. vi. cap. vi.

[3] Vasari mentions incidentally that Pietro Perugino had laid three coats of colour on some pictures in the Church of the Servi at Florence. See Life of Pietro Perugino.

[4] See Extracts from Mr. Beale's Pocket-books, quoted by Walpole, Anecdotes, vol. iii. p. 125.

[5] As to the lights in early oil paintings being semi-opaque, see Mr. Eastlake's ' Materials,' &c., p. 408.   [6] Trattato, p. 191.

pana, umber (which he calls also falzalo), burnt terra
verde, asphaltum, and mummy. The Paduan MS.[1]
mentions umber, burnt terra verde, and asphaltum; and
in another place,[2] lake, minium, and umber. Other
artists used for the outlines and shadows umber and
lake.[3] Pacheco mentions [4] bone-black, umber, charcoal-
black, or smoke [of burnt resin], asphaltum, almagra,
and carmine. In this method of painting it will be
observed that the shadows are transparent, and that the
white-lead is reserved for the lights, which are semi-
opaque.

It appears to have been the general practice of the
Italian painters, from Giotto to Lomazzo, to mix their
tints before beginning to paint. The instructions of
Cennini [5] and Lomazzo [6] are full and precise on this
point. The custom of mixing tints on the palette was
not, however, universal, and instances of the opposite
practice may be found in works on art.[7]

The method of painting above described appears to
have been followed by the Florentine, the Roman, the
Lombard, the early Bolognese,[8] and the early Venetian
schools. Titian's earliest pictures were painted in this
manner, and the process may be seen on some unfinished
pictures by Rubens, Vandyck, Fra Bartolomeo, and
others.

The beauty of this method of painting consisted in
its transparency, every coat of colour being so thin as to
show those laid beneath.

The most perfect outline is necessary when pictures
are painted in the method just described, because if a
part be shaded that ought to be light, the dark colour

---

[1] P. 650.   [2] P. 654.

[3] See Malvasia, Felsina Pittrice, vol. ii. p. 448; Lomazzo, Trattato,
p. 198.   [4] Tratado, p. 386.   [5] Caps. 67, 71—85, 93, 145.

[6] Trattato, lib. vi. cap. vi.   [7] See Zanetti, della Pittura, &c., p. 401.

[8] See Marcucci, Saggio, &c., p. 213. Malvasia, Fels. Pitt., vol. ii.
p. 206. Merimée, de la Peinture à l'Huile, p. 15, 16.

will always be visible through the light tints over it, and the colour will look opaque.[1]

The unfinished picture by Lionardo da Vinci in the Gallery of Brera, before mentioned, shows that it was not always customary to complete the chiaroscuro before beginning the painting. In this picture, some parts are finished, or nearly so, while parts of the ground are left white.[2]

---

[1] See Marcucci, Saggio, &c., p. 213 and n.; and see Mr. Eastlake's 'Materials,' &c., p. 397, 398.

[2] This very interesting picture has been mentioned by Mr. Eastlake ('Materials,' p. 392), but as I have alluded to it several times, I shall give a description of it from my own memoranda:—The picture represents the Virgin and Child with the Lamb. It is painted on a white ground, which has a yellowish tint, apparently from being covered with varnish. The ground is full of small hair-like cracks. The subject is drawn with a black pencil. The sky and distance are finished with blue and white, with a slight greenish tint. There is a rock behind the figures, the colour of which, with the earth around, is of a very dark brown, probably formed of black and majorica and a little lake.[*] A space between the distance and rocky ground is left quite blank, the white ground appearing. The face of the Virgin is more finished than the rest of the picture; it was apparently begun in chiaroscuro with the usual brown—the gray shades incline to black, the lights on the face to lake. The face of the Infant is nearly finished. The hands are just sketched in lightly with the same brown, and the first flesh tints are laid on almost as thin as a first wash of water colours. The same may be observed with respect to the toes: the black pencil-marks are visible on the nails. The drapery, which is scarlet, appears to be formed of earthy reds, with vermilion on the lights. The outer drapery is red also, and is lined with a yellowish green, or perhaps this was to be a changeable drapery, since the shades are red and the lights green. These were Lionardo's favourite colours for drapery. The sleeves of the Virgin, part of the mantle, indeed all that part covering her knees, part of the Infant's drapery, and the whole of the Lamb are left quite blank, excepting that the outline of her knee is marked in pencil. This shows that Lionardo sometimes finished portions of his pictures, leaving the rest untouched, instead of beginning on all parts equally, or even of painting the subject in chiaroscuro. The darks are raised higher than the lights, and the foliage is minutely worked on the dark background. My impression is that this picture was begun upon a non-absorbent white

---

[*] See Lionardo da Vinci, Trattato della Pittura, cap. 353. Vasari shows that the black used by Lionardo was the lamp black used by the printers, and ivory black. See Vita di Francesco Bartolomeo di S. Marco.

There is little doubt that the method of painting just described was discontinued in Venice in the early part of the sixteenth century. This is proved by the assertion of a professor of painting now residing at Venice, that Cima da Conegliano (of whom nothing is known after 1517 [1]) adopted the Venetian method of beginning his pictures with solid colours, and finishing with glazings. In Florence the latter method had been introduced previous to the completion of Vasari's work.[2]

In the earliest oil pictures the touches of the brush are not visible, the whole being softened and blended so as to convey the idea of real shadow, except the sharp touches, which stand up crisply and distinctly in a manner that cannot be imitated with oil alone. This is particularly apparent in the pictures of Van Eyck, Lucas Van Leyden, Lionardo da Vinci, Luini, and others of that time.

At a later period the touches of the brush were often suffered to remain unsoftened ; but, in both cases, it is remarkable that, on close observation, the darks will be seen to stand higher above the surface of the picture than the lights : this effect is universally attributed to the use of varnish in the shades.

Four different methods of painting in oil have, at different times, prevailed in Venice. The first was that just described, which was followed by the Bellini [3] and their pupils, and by Titian in the early part of his career; the second was that adopted by Titian in his best time, and by his pupils and followers; the third was that employed by Paolo Veronese; and the last that introduced, it is said, by Palma Giovane, of paint-

---

ground, and that the yellowish tint is owing to the varnish with which it has been covered.

[1] See Ridolfi, vol. i. p. 101.   [2] See Vasari, Life of Fra Bartolomeo.
[3] See ante, p. cxxxiii.

ing on dark grounds, to which, as it is considered to have led to the decline of the art, it will be unnecessary to advert.

The pictures of Titian are not all painted in the same manner, but the method he frequently adopted was nearly as follows:—When the subject was drawn, the local colours were laid in lightly and thinly with colours mixed with oil,[1] the shades being left very cold. The picture was then exposed to the sun and the dew until perfectly dry and hard; a smooth surface was then given to it by rubbing it down with pumice-stone until quite smooth.

After many months the dead or first colouring or *abbozzo*, as it is called in Italian, was examined and corrected, and fresh colours were laid on;[2] finishing colours were then applied, and the tints were frequently repeated seven, eight, or nine times,[3] until the artist was satisfied with his work, always however suffering a long period to elapse between each layer of colour, and exposing the picture to the sun and dew between each painting. The coats of colour being very thin, the colours dried quickly and hard, and, as the Venetians express it, before the oil had had time to become rancid.[4] Titian, it is said, frequently laid on the paint with his fingers, particularly on the flesh and in glazing.

---

[1] Lanzi, vol. v. p. 89, 90; and see Boschini, Ricche Minere, &c.; Verri, Saggio sul Disegno, &c., p. 121, 127. Compare also Marcucci, Saggio, p. 213, n.   [2] Boschini, Ricche Minere.

[3] Soleva dir el nostro gran Tician "

.   .   .   .   .   .

" Che per formar el vivo colorito,
No' se possa a la prima (come hò dito),
Fenir le carne con intendimento;
Ma ben con replicar diverse tente."

Boschini, La Carta del Navegar, &c., p. 341.

[4] It is related that Bombelli, the Venetian painter, said that he wished his pictures to dry as fast as possible, that the oil in them might not have time to rise to the surface and turn yellow. See Trans. Soc. Arts, vol. xix. p. 329.

When large surfaces were to be glazed, the colour was frequently rubbed on with all the fingers or the flat of the hand, so as to fill the interstices left by the brush, and to cover the surface thinly and evenly.   Another way of applying the colour with the finger, frequently used for the soft shadows of flesh, was to dip the finger into the colour and draw it *once* along the surface to be painted with an even movement.   These touches were called *sfregazzi*,[1] and were distinguished from the process first described, which was called "velatura." Trial will show that there is no other method by which soft shadows can be so easily produced.   The reason given by the Venetians why the fingers are preferable to the brush for this purpose, is because the colour can be laid on thinner in this way, and it has the effect of filling up all the interstices caused by the strokes of the brush.   The thinness of the paint also contributed to the durability of the colours, because as the varnish or oil dried more quickly from the thinness of the layer of paint, the colours were preserved from being changed by the action of the air upon them.   The shadows were glazed with asphaltum and lake, and Titian is said to have frequently glazed the whole surface of the picture, except the white linen, with asphaltum, or, as others say, with a yellow varnish.   The glazings were generally laid on with varnish, although it is said that Titian sometimes used oil for this purpose, which is the reason that his paintings become more yellow than those of other painters.

There is no doubt, however, that Titian used frequently an oleo-resinous varnish in glazing, and to this

---

[1] " Quei rossi, e macadure de colori,
       Quei sfregazzi co' i' dei, quel spegazzar
       Fà le figure vive bulegar;
       Quei le fà luser con mile splendori."
                Boschini, La Carta del Navegar, &c., p. 340.

is attributed the shrivelled surface so often seen on his pictures.[1]

Paolo Veronese laid in the abbozzo with the local colours thinly on a tempera ground; some say the colours were mixed with oil, others that they were applied in distemper.[2] When these were dry and hard the surface was rasped and smoothed, so as to leave only a thin coat of colour.[3] On this he painted the solid colours, availing himself of a general colour for all the half tints, as well in the flesh as in the draperies and architecture.[4] After this he covered the whole with a very thin coat of varnish to bring out the colours, and then retouched the lights and shades with brilliant and resolute touches, using varnish for vermilion, red-lead,

---

[1] Merimée, de la Peinture à l'Huile, p. 31. Mr. Eastlake's ' Materials,' &c., p. 37.

At the public library at Brescia I was shown, among other curiosities, two small miniatures by Titian, painted one on each side of a piece of lapis lazuli, which served for the ground of the painting, a head of Christ on one side, and of the Madonna on the other. Two slight injuries on the painting showed that there was no ground laid under the figures, but the surface round the parts injured looked like glue or resin semitransparent at the edges. I examined the painting with a powerful magnifying glass, and the surface, which was perfect, except in these two places, showed the oil shrivelled as in many of Titian's large pictures, the wrinkles in this picture bearing the same proportionate size to the miniature as those I have observed in his larger pictures.

I observed also in the head of our Saviour another remarkable appearance when examined with the magnifying glass. This was the impression or appearance (for we could not tell which) of threads of silk, so that I almost fancied it had been painted on silk, and cut out and then fixed to the lapis lazuli. The surface of the painting had the usual yellowish brown cast, so frequently observed in Titian's paintings.

[2] See Appendix to the Italian edition of the ' Idée du Peintre Parfait,' p. 163; and Félibien, Principes, &c., p. 297. Merimée (de la Peinture à l'Huile, p. 249) says that Paul Veronese, and before him other painters, who lived at the period when artists began to leave tempera for oil painting, were accustomed to begin their pictures with size colours on absorbent grounds. All traditions of oil paintings having been begun in tempera appear to be now lost in Venice.

[3] Compare Armenini as to the general practice in Italy, lib. ii. cap. ix. ; Bisagno, Trattato, &c.

[4] Boschini, Ricche Minere ; Zanetti, della Pittura, &c., p. 164.

blues, the tints used in painting white linen, and for the vermilion tints in flesh. He frequently painted the blues in tempera, as in the picture in the Soffitto of the Collegio of the Ducal Palace,[1] in which the blue sky was painted in tempera, and the clouds with oil. These tempera colours are said to adhere so firmly that they will bear being twice washed without being disturbed. The method of Paolo is opposed to that of Titian. The former usually painted " alla prima," seldom repeating his colours; and with few glazings.[2] Titian on the contrary frequently painted over the same part seven, eight, or nine times. His pictures are neither so fresh nor so well preserved as those of Paolo.[3]

After the time of Titian the art rapidly declined in Venice; large pictures and rapidity of execution superseded the more sterling qualities of the art; and the practice of glazing to an almost unlimited extent with asphaltum (for which Tintoretto is greatly blamed), the introduction of dark grounds,[4] and the excessive use of oil, caused the pictures of succeeding painters to become dark.

The honour of having re-discovered and made known some of the early processes of painting in oil, and of the principles which regulated the practice of the old masters, belongs to an Englishman, Mr. Sheldrake, whose Essays,[5] little known in his own country, are

---

[1] This is proved by a document in the Accademia at Venice addressed by Sig. P. Edwards to Sig. Savio Cassier, dated the 25th of August, 1780.

[2] Bald., Life of Paolo Veronese ; Boschini, Ricche Minere.

[3] See p. 888.

[4] Marcucci (p. 201) attributes the darkening of the later Italian pictures to three causes, namely—first, the badness of the priming, either from being too absorbent or from the use of dark grounds ; secondly, the too free employment of " olio cotto ;" thirdly, the use of certain black pigments, which deepen in colour in a very short time. See also Zanetti, della Pittura, &c., pp. 374, 401, 438, 528.

[5] These essays were entitled ' A Dissertation on Painting in Oil in a manner similar to that practised in the ancient Venetian Schools '—' On the Nature and Properties of Drying Oils '—' On the Use of Amber Var-

appreciated and quoted by foreigners. It is unnecessary to analyse these Essays; it will be sufficient to recommend them strongly to the perusal of the reader, and to state generally, that Mr. Sheldrake considered that the method adopted by the Venetian masters was as follows:—The chiaroscuro was painted with umber on a tempera preparation, composed of umber, broken with red, yellow, or blue, diluted with chalk or whitening to the proper degree of strength. A coat of varnish was then applied, and on this, when dry, the lights were painted solidly with pure white, scumbling it thinner by degrees until it united with the shadows. In this manner the chiaroscuro was finished as much as possible, and the local colour of every object glazed over it. The picture was then varnished.

The general resemblance between this method and that first described as the Flemish or early Italian process is apparent. The principal variation consisted in the absorbent ground, and the solid painting with white on the lights, which was rendered necessary by the coloured priming.

The method of Titian was, with certain modifications, adopted by the other schools of Italy; some artists, however, still continued to adhere to the older method. It is probable that the method of Titian was commonly adopted at Florence in the time of Vasari, for he mentions[1] that Fra Bartolomeo delighted in beginning his pictures in chiaroscuro, as if this custom of his was an exception to the general rule. This supposition is strengthened by the short description of

---

nish with Colours, and the Method of Dissolving Amber and Copal '—' Conjectures tending to show that these Vehicles were similar in Principle, if not identically the same as that used by several of the older Painters who were eminent for their skill in Colouring '—' An Account of the Process used to separate the Mucilage from Linseed Oil,' &c. These Essays, written between 1797 and 1801, were published in the Transactions of the Society of Arts, vols. xvi., xvii., and xix.

[1] Vita di Fra Bartolomeo di S. Marco.

the process of oil-painting by Borghini, who was a
Florentine, and who may be supposed to have been
well acquainted with the works of that school. This
author directs[1] that when the first colours were laid in
with as little oil as possible (for the oil in drying would,
he says, cause the colours to darken), the picture
should be laid aside for a long time, until the colours
were perfectly dry; it was then to be rigorously examined, and the necessary corrections made, and then
was to be applied the last coat of the finest colours
tempered with very little oil, which would remain
bright and lively; for if the (fresh) colours were laid
upon the dry dead colouring, the former would retain
when dry all their beauty; but if they were applied on
the dead colouring before it was dry, the first and last
colours would mix together, and the whole would be
dusky and darkened, especially when the colours were
made liquid with much oil, which detracts much from
the brightness of the colours. It will be observed
this author does not allude to the use of varnish in
glazing.

There is another reason why one layer of colours
should be suffered to dry perfectly before another
was applied; namely, to prevent their cracking. Some
of the early Italian artists, and particularly Pietro
Perugino, appear to have bought their experience in this
respect. Several of the pictures of Pietro are stated to
have suffered from this cause. With reference to some
of these pictures, Vasari remarks, "These three pictures[2] are much injured, and the dark parts and shadows
are everywhere cracked; and the reason of this is,
because when they were painted, the first colour laid on
the priming (for three coats of colour were laid one

---

[1] Riposo, p. 174.
[2] The Christ in the Garden, the Pietà, and the Crucifixion, with Mary
Magdalen and Saints, at Florence.

upon the other) was not dry, so that the under colours shrunk in drying, and thus occasioned those cracks on the surface; but Pietro could not have known that this would happen, because in his time artists were only beginning to paint well in oil."[1]

The precaution of waiting long between the dead colouring and the finishing was observed generally by the Italians; Boschini relates that it was the practice of Titian, and its universality may be inferred from the common custom of rubbing down the surface of the picture with pumice-stone, or even scraping it with a knife, as related by Armenini—a process which could not take place until the painting was perfectly dry. This practice seems to have been common to all the later schools, and some unfinished pictures by Guido and Guercino at Bologna present the appearance of having undergone this operation.

But it was necessary that the painting should be quite dry and hard before the surface was thus rendered smooth; and for this reason, as well as to prevent the yellowing of the oil, the painting was exposed to the sun at intervals until it was dry. This last process was repeated after every layer of colour.

During the winter the colours dried more slowly,[2] and when the heat of the sun was insufficient to dry them, or the weather particularly damp, they were exposed to the heat of a stove, which Errante says[3] was the custom of the best colourists. The practice has the sanction of Lionardo da Vinci.[4]

Painters had another reason for exposing their pictures to the sun in the various stages of the painting,

---

[1] Life of Pietro Perugino.

[2] Gachet, Lettres Inédites de P. P. Rubens; De Piles, Elémens, p. 142.

[3] Saggio sui Colori. Rome, 1817.

[4] Trattato, cap. 352. The experiments of Mr. Sheldrake prove that paintings executed with amber varnish were not injured by exposure to the strong heat of a stove.

and this was to remove by evaporation the yellow coat of oil which always rose to the surface, and which if not removed by this process darkened the colours. A letter of Rubens,[1] addressed to Peiresc, mentions this defect to which new pictures are subject, and prescribes the only remedy. The letter was written in Italian, and is thus translated by Mr. Eastlake:[2]—" If I knew that my portrait was still at Antwerp, I would cause it to be detained and the case to be opened, in order to see if it is not spoiled after having been so long shut up without air; and whether, as commonly happens to fresh colours [under such circumstances], it has not turned yellow, so as to be no longer in appearance what it was at first. The remedy, however, if it should happen to be in so bad a state, will be to place it several times in the sun, as the sun can dissipate the superfluity of oil which causes this alteration. And, if at any time it should again become brown, it should again be exposed to the sun's rays, which are the only antidote for this disease of the heart."

The perusal of this letter and other evidence which, as it has been given by Mr. Eastlake, it is unnecessary to repeat, induced me about three years since to try and restore by exposure to the sun, the colour of some grounds on canvass which had been made for a particular purpose, of white-lead and marble-dust mixed with oil. They had been turned towards the wall, or otherwise excluded from light and air for some years, and were nearly of the colour of yellow ochre. One of these was placed in a balcony exposed to the afternoon sun. In two days there was a perceptible difference, and in a fortnight the yellow hue had nearly disappeared. A long loop of riband, by which the canvass

---

[1] Dated London, Aug. 9, 1629, published by Gachet.
[2] For much additional information on this subject, see the ' Materials,' &c., pp. 509—519.

(which was old) had formerly hung against the wall, was accidentally suffered to hang over the face of the canvass; on raising the riband it was found that the ground was not bleached where the riband had lain, and this circumstance afforded the means of judging correctly of the effect of the exposure to the sun.[1]

The opinion of Rubens and other evidence of a similar nature suggested the importance of ascertaining whether the custom of exposing pictures to the sun still existed in Italy; and from the inquiries I made, I am induced to believe that the practice of exposing pictures freshly painted in oil to the sun has always existed in Italy, and has descended traditionally from the early ages of oil-painting to the present time;[2] that the custom is now observed by several eminent professors and restorers of pictures at Milan and Venice, and that the picture is by some artists exposed to the dew and then dried thoroughly in the hot sun between every coat of paint; in short, that the great principle in painting is to make the paint dry *rapidly* and *perfectly* between every coat of colour, in order to prevent the pigments being acted on by each other and by the air.[3] The tradition in Venice is that the oil always rises to the surface of the picture and dries dark; and if the colours are long in drying, the oil with which they are mixed becomes rancid and has a deleterious influence on the colours. For this purpose the pigments are to be mixed with as little oil as possible, and the tints laid on extremely thin, where it is intended to repeat the colours fre-

---

[1] In the directions given by Pacheco for cleaning and refreshing old oil paintings, darkened by smoke and varnish, without danger to the picture, he recommends that if they are on cloth, they should be placed in the sun for half a day; but if on panel, they should be exposed to the dew for two nights previous to being washed. Tratado, p. 394.

[2] See Cennini, Trattato, cap. 155; and Ridolfi, Vita di Maffeo Verona.

[3] See the remark of Bombelli (a Venetian painter) quoted by Mr. Sheldrake, Trans. Soc. Arts, vol. xix. p. 329. See also an extract from the letter of an eminent foreign Professor in Mr. Eastlake's ‘Materials,’ &c., p. 365.

quently, especially in glazing, when the hand is to be used instead of the pencil, for the express reason that the colours can be laid on by it more thinly than with a brush.

With regard to employing colours mixed with size on oil pictures, it was the opinion of Merimée [1] that Paolo Veronese sometimes began his pictures in tempera and finished them in oil. I cannot discover that any Italian author mentions this fact, nor have I met with any traditionary account of such a practice. But the fact that some parts of oil paintings were at times painted with size-colours, is established beyond a doubt, as the practice not only of the Venetians, but of artists belonging to the other schools; and as it is alleged [2] that some part of the celebrated altar-piece of the Van Eycks at Ghent was painted in tempera, it appears probable that the practice has existed from the earliest period of the introduction of oil painting in Italy. Besides this picture of the Van Eycks, it has been ascertained [3] that the blue sky of a picture by Pietro Perugino (the first who practised the Flemish method of oil painting in Perugia) was painted with smaltino tempered with starch or flour paste (colla di farina). There is sufficient evidence to prove that Paolo Veronese frequently painted the blue sky in tempera, and it has been asserted that he applied the more delicate finishing colours in the same manner, but this requires confirmation.

In the Flemish system of painting, which adopted by the early Italian schools, varnish was added to the oil colours, so that the full effect of the colours was always visible; and as the layers of colour were thin and the colours always finely ground, there was no

---

[1] De la Peinture à l'Huile, p. 249—251.   [2] Pacheco, Tratado, p. 373.
[3] See ' La Vita, Elogio, e Memorie dell' egregio Pittore Pietro Perugino, e degli Scolari di esso.' Da B. Orsini. Perugia, 1804, p. 208, n.

necessity for rasping the surface. But where the local colours were laid on solidly, and not finely ground as in the Venetian school, it was necessary, when the abbozzo was perfectly dry and hard, in order to secure an even surface for the finishing colours, to rub down the surface with pumice-stone.[1]

In the Venetian manner the colours of the abbozzo having been painted with oil only, were dull; and as the difficulty of retouching a picture "in secco," that is with a perfectly dry surface, was felt by all artists,[2] it was considered necessary by some to apply a thin coat of varnish in order to bring out the colours in all their force, as well as to enable the finishing colours to adhere more firmly.[3] This is said to have been the practice of Paolo Veronese, and is still observed by some Venetian artists. Volpato states[4] that white of egg was some- times used for this purpose, and sometimes varnish or oil. Lana recommends[5] boiled oil to which litharge has been added in preference to raw oil, and De Piles[6] prefers oil to varnish. Armenini and Bisagno direct that a thin coat of oil should be passed over the picture, or at least over the parts to be retouched, and then wiped off immediately, leaving only a slight degree of moisture on the surface.[7] This process is technically called " oiling out."

To conclude, I might have indulged in expressing the feelings of delight with which I contemplated the works of the great Masters of the Italian School; but I feel that this would not have accorded with the techni- cal and practical details of the various subjects treated

---

[1] Mengs is said to have adopted this practice.

[2] Goethe on Colours, by Eastlake, p. 407. n.

[3] Lairesse, le Grand Livre des Peintres, vol. i. cap. v.

[4] Pp. 747, 749. [5] P. 746, n. [6] Elémens, pp. 114, 118.

[7] See generally Mr. Eastlake's ' Materials,' &c., pp. 476, 304 n. ; and see Verri, Saggio Elementare, &c., p. 115.

of in these volumes. It has been my object to support the statements I have made, and the opinions I have expressed, by the authorities quoted, or to which I have referred. From the commencement to the conclusion, the pleasing expectation of discovery has alleviated the labour of research, and smoothed the path of inquiry ; and although I have not succeeded to the full extent of my wishes, I indulge the hope that my labours, which have been devoted entirely to this object for upwards of three years, may be found useful, and not altogether uninteresting.

NOTE ON A MANUSCRIPT

Entitled ' Raccolti di Secreti, Specifici, Remedj, &c. ; ora adesso di Fra Fortunato da Rovigo, Laico Capucino, Infermiere nel Convento dei Capucini di Verona.'

This MS., which is in two thick volumes in 8vo., is in the possession of the Canon Ramelli, of Rovigo. The MS. consists of several treatises on medicine, and of collections of recipes for colours, with directions for miniature painting. Many of the former are translations from the French, and were probably used by Fra Fortunato in his character of superintendent of the infirmary of the convent. The recipes date from 1659 (soon after the profession of Fra Fortunato) to 1711. A copy from the books of the convent, of the register of his profession, is inscribed in the first page of the MS.

The recipes for painting resemble so closely those in other MSS. of Secreti, that it appeared unnecessary to copy the whole. I have transcribed a few only, which show the colours and methods in use during the time of Fra Fortunato. From these we find that lake was prepared from "grana tinctoria " or " grana di kermes," " cimatura di scarlato," " cremisi" (probably cochineal), " verzino," and " gomma lacca."—" Lacca fina" was made from " cimatura di scarlato overo grana fina, cochiniglia, and gomma lacca."

Among the blue pigments, azzurro di Germania is stated to be composed of mercury, sulphur, and sal ammoniac. " The blue colour made at Pozzuoli " is the old vestorian azure ; it was made of sand, " fior di nitro," and copper filings. " Biadetto " was composed of verdigris, sal ammoniac, and tartar. These blue pigments appear to have been difficult to use, since there are especial directions for tempering them. Sometimes a varnish composed of spirit of turpentine and mastic was employed for this purpose. " Biadetto " was to be ground with a little burnt roche alum, or tartar, or sandarac ; it was to be ground very fine, and in miniature painting was to be used with a clear varnish of spirit of turpentine and mastic ; it would then spread extremely well, glaze brilliantly, and be a most beautiful colour.*

---

* *Biadetto fare, che bene si possi stendere, miniando.*—Si macina bene con un

" Boiled oil for painters, as clear (colourless ?) as water," was prepared in the following manner :—" Put the usual piece of rag containing litharge and other customary things in linseed or nut oil, add water, and boil, and this will cause it [the oil] to be clear (colourless ?) as water itself."*

The recipes for varnish are not numerous. A recipe for one which is ascribed to P. Bonaventura, a monk of Cento, dated 3rd of April, 1707, for paper, wood, and other things, consisted of spirits of wine 6 oz., sandarac 2 oz., olio d'abezzo ¾ oz. Another varnish, which is not injured by hot water, consists of linseed oil and resin ; this was the Italian " vernice comune." Another varnish was composed of spirit of turpentine, sandarac, and (concrete) turpentine ; and another of " gomma copale" dissolved in spirit of turpentine.

The directions for " painting in fresco on lime with colours that are not mineral (such as lake), and to enable them to resist for a long period the effects of the air," are comprised in a few words, namely, to apply a coat of " gesso da sarto" upon the lime spread on the wall, and then paint on it.

The short instructions for miniature painting contain but little that is new. Fra Fortunato, however, recommends that the gum should be added to the colours, only when required for use, because if the colours were suffered to remain long mixed with gum, they would become dry, and the addition of water to them would cause the more delicate colours, such as lake, giallolino, cinnabar, and azure, to change. From this it appears that it was the common practice to keep the colours for miniature painting ready mixed with gum.

---

poco di alume di rocco, bruciato, o vero con un poco di tartaro, o pure con sandracca. Vedi qui sotto.

Il biadetto macinato ben sottile, e adoprato miniando con vernice fatta con acqua di ragia e mastice, che sia ben chiara, si stende benissimo, vela pulito, e fa colore bellissimo.

* Per far l' olio cotto da pittore, che sia chiaro come acqua.—Metti il solito piumazzolo col litargirio, et altro come si usa dentro l' oglio di noce o di lino a bollire, e con esso mettivi seco dell' acqua a bollire, che questa lo fara rimaner chiara, come l' acqua medesima.

MANUSCRIPTS OF JEHAN LE BEGUE.

PRELIMINARY OBSERVATIONS.

In the year 1431, Jehan le Begue, a licentiate in the law and Notary of the Masters of the Mint at Paris, being then in the sixty-third year of his age,[1] composed, or rather compiled, the following manuscript,[2] from a collection of works on painting made by one

---

[1] See end of manuscript of Le Begue.

[2] The original manuscript of Jehan le Begue is preserved in the Bibliothèque Royale at Paris. It is on paper, and is numbered 6741. For the first information concerning this manuscript we are indebted to Lessing, who mentions it in his Treatise, ' Dom Alter der Oelmalerey aus dem Theophilus Presbyter,' 1774. Lessing, however, did not know the work, but quoted the title only from the Catalogue of Manuscripts in the above-mentioned library, because he believed it contained a copy of the manuscript of Theophilus. It does, in fact, contain great part of the first book of this author. Raspe[a] and Emeric David[b] both mention the manuscript, but with reference to the copy of Theophilus only ; the remainder and greater part of the manuscript seems to have been unknown until 1842 or 1843, when M. le Comte Charles de l'Escalopier procured a copy of the whole for the purpose of completing his edition of Theophilus. In the autumn of 1844 I went to Paris to procure a copy of the manuscript, which I obtained after some unavoidable delay. Some extracts from the work have been recently published by Mr. Eastlake, in his ' Materials for Painting in Oil,' and by Mr. Hendrie, in his edition of Theophilus ; but the whole work has never yet been published.

---

[a] Critical Essay on Oil Painting, Lond. 1781, p. 38.

[b] Biographie Universelle—Art. Théophile.

Jehan Alcherius, or Alcerius.   The motive that induced Jehan le Begue to undertake the work does
not appear.   He himself tells us that he was unaccus-
tomed to such writing;[1] and the numerous mistakes
throughout the manuscript prove that he told the truth.
But, whatever might have been his inducements, the
zeal with which he undertook the work, and the manner in which he executed his task, show his attachment
to the arts, and his desire to obtain information on all
subjects connected with it.   The formation and alphabetical arrangement of the Table of Synonymes at the
commencement of the work, at a period when the art
of printing was unknown,[2] and the sources of information from books must have been very limited, was no
small proof of his industry and perseverance.   His
authorities seem to have been the works collected by
Alcherius, and the Catholicon, which was then in manuscript, and which was not printed until twenty-nine
years after Jehan le Begue completed his work.[3]

---

[1] See [No. 303a].   These numbers refer to the recipes in the text.

[2] The first essay of Laurentius, the inventor of printing with separate
wooden types, was about the year 1430.

[3] The ‘ Catholicon’ was a Latin Dictionary, composed in the year 1286,
by Fra. Giovan. Baldi, a Genoese.   It was printed at Mentz in 1460,
nearly thirty years after it was quoted by Jehan le Begue ; and Bettinelli remarks it was the fourth book after the Bible which was printed with moveable
types of fused metal, but the author of the article ‘ Printing’ in the ‘ Encyclopædia Britannica’ says it was printed by Guttemberg with types of cut
metal, and that Guttemberg used none but wood or cut metal types until the
year 1462.   Previous to the ‘ Catholicon,’ two other Latin vocabularies
had been composed in Italy, the first of which was entitled ‘ Glossario
della Lingua Latina ;’ this was written by Papia, a Lombard, and, as it is
believed, a native of Milan, who was one of the most learned Greek scholars
of his age : he flourished about A.D. 1060.   This was followed by the Dictionary of Uguccione Pisano, Bishop of Ferrara, in 1190.   See Bettinelli’s
‘ Risorgimento d’ Italia,’ vol. i. p. 110 n.

My reasons for supposing this Table of Synonymes to have been composed by Le Begue are, that the recipes in old French at the end (which the table of contents[1] informs us were added by Le Begue) are referred to in the Table of Synonymes, and also because this Table is full of errors, and contains many statements which Alcherius must have known to be incorrect.

After the Table of Synonymes are two fragments of alphabetical indices, the first of which begins at the letter Q, and concludes with W; the other comprises the letter A only. These fragments, I consider, are both the work of Le Begue, because they contain references to the recipes in old French at the end of the manuscript.

Of the early life and profession of Jehan Alcherius, or Archerius, the manuscript gives no indications. It does not actually appear that he was a painter, but his attachment to the art is unquestionable, or he would not have taken the pains he did to become acquainted with the technical processes, and to write down so many recipes from the dictation of others. In all that related to the art he was superior to Jehan le Begue; he also possessed the additional advantage of understanding Italian, which he acquired in Italy during his occasional visits to that country. The object of these visits does not transpire; it is, however, certain that he frequented the company of painters, and that he neglected no means of obtaining information relative to the art.

The earliest biographical notice of Alcherius is dated

---

[1] I am of opinion this table of contents is not in the hand-writing of Le Begue.

March, 1382,[1] at which time he left Milan for Paris,
taking with him a recipe for making writing-ink, which
had been given to him by Alberto Porzello, "who was
most perfect in all kinds of writing and forms of letters,
and who, while he lived, kept a school at Milan, and
taught boys and young men to write." In 1398
Alcherius was at Paris. On the 28th of July, in that
year, he wrote his treatise ' De Coloribus diversis
modis tractatur,'[2] from the dictation of Jacob Cona, a
Flemish painter, then living at Paris. This treatise
relates chiefly to miniature painting, and its usual
accompaniment gilding. On the 8th of August following he wrote another short treatise, which also relates
to the same subject, entitled ' De diversis Coloribus,'[3]
from the dictation of Antonio di Compendio, "an illuminator of books, and an old man," who had tried all
the recipes himself. These recipes therefore may be
considered to date from the middle of the fourteenth
century, at least. In October, 1398, he was still at
Paris.[4] Nothing more is known of him from that time
until the month of March, 1409, when it appears he
was again at Milan, where he copied the recipes at the
commencement of the work as far as No. 88, from a
book lent to him by Fra Dionisio, a Servite, or, as it is
expressed in the manuscript, "of the order of the Servants of St. Mary, which order in Milan is called ' Del
Sacho.' "[5] These recipes, from Nos. 1 to 47 inclusive,
are for colours of various kinds for painting and writing,
and other things belonging to the art of miniature

---

[1] See Preface to No. 302.   [2] See Preface to No. 291.
[3] See Preface to No. 297.   [4] See Preface to No. 303.
[5] See Preface to No. 47.

painting. Nos. 47 to 88 contain various recipes for working in metals; for hardening iron; for a kind of nigellum; for making a sort of pyrophorus—namely, a light which should burn under water, and which could be extinguished with oil only; and also a candle which should burn with water and without fire. In No. 86 a kind of gum is mentioned, which was said to have attractive powers somewhat like the loadstone. It is possible that this gum Andrianum, the name by which it is called in the manuscript, may be another name for amber (of which this attractive power is a known attribute), which is found embedded in stones in various parts of Europe, and in Italy on the coast of the Adriatic.[1] From the description, however, and from a consideration of the locality where it was found, it seems equally probable that it was a sort of native bitumen.

The mountain where the gum is found is called in the text Monte Bono or Buono; it should be Monte Bene. This mountain is on the high road from Bologna to Florence, and is covered with scattered rocks of breccia, and is remarkable for its fine scenery, and for the singular natural phenomena which are found in its vicinity. The height is above 4000 feet. The fires of Pietra Mala, a village near this mountain, are known to all tourists. These extraordinary fires are constantly issuing from a spot of ground three or four yards across. When the air is calm they are seen at a great distance, rising about a foot from the ground, and in

---

[1] See Agricola, ' De Metallicis,' f. 238. See also Eastlake, ' Materials,' &c., 234 n.

damp weather are very bright and luminous. They are extinguished by a high wind, but light again spontaneously on the air becoming calm. They resemble the flame of alcohol; and Volta ascertained that the gas emitted is a composition of carbon and hydrogen—probably produced by the decomposition of vegetable remains in the subjacent sand-rock. Between Monte Bene and Montoggioli is a singular spring, which is frequently dry. If a lighted match be brought near the mud of this spring, the gases exhaled from it immediately take fire, burning with a lambent flame.[1]

On the 2nd of February, 1410, Johannes Alcherius wrote a description of'the process of preparing ultramarine from the instruction given him by one Master Johannes, a Norman, residing in the house of Pietro da Verona.[2] This Pietro da Verona was probably a painter; and the researches of the Abbate Moschoni have shown that a painter of this name was at Padua in 1398, and that his son Antonia da Verona was also at Padua in 1393.[3] We may therefore suppose that the former was the contemporary of Johannes Alcherius.

On the 11th February, 1410, Johannes Alcherius was at Bologna, where he became acquainted with one Theodore, a native of Flanders and an embroiderer, who had been employed at Pavia by Gian Galeazzo Visconti, and who gave him certain recipes and directions for preparing and using coloured waters, which Theo-

---

[1] See Murray's ' Guide to North Italy.'

[2] See Preface to No. 118.

[3] See Moschini ' della Origine e delle Vicende della Pittura in Padova.' Padova, 1826, p. 9.

dore stated he had procured at London in England.[1]
These recipes, which, it appears from the Note to No.
96, were given in writing, were written in French.

It is certain that these passages relate to the preparation of transparent colours for painting;[2] but I
think that they refer also to the art of dyeing, and to
the decoration of wearing apparel. No. 92 is evidently
a mordant, and was used both to prepare the cloth to
receive the colours, and to bleach certain parts of coloured cloths, by which a regular pattern might be given
to them. The note of the author attached to this recipe
certainly alludes to this operation of the art of dyeing,
in which it is expressly stated white letters and figures
could be drawn upon a coloured ground; for it is well
known if figures, &c., be drawn with the mordant on
cloth, and then suffered to dry, and if, when dry, the
cloth be dipped into a coloured dye and afterwards
dried, it will appear one uniform colour; but if the cloth
so coloured be then washed in plain water, the colour
will be discharged from those parts on which the mordant was not applied, and the cloth will be marked with
a coloured figure on a white ground. This appears to
be the process alluded to in the text, No. 92.

An additional reason for supposing that these recipes relate also to the process of dyeing arises from the
fact that the stuff to be stained was sometimes made of
wool expressed by the French word "drap," and the

---

[1] See Preface to No. 89. Gian Galeazzo died in 1402. He had the
glory of commencing the ' Duomo' of Milan in 1386, and the ' Certosa' of
Pavia in 1396. He was succeeded by Gian Maria Visconti.

[2] See Eastlake, ' Materials,' &c., cap. 5. See also Eraclius, lib. iii.
No. 26.

Latin " *drapis* coloricis *lane*;" and I am not aware that
woollen cloth has ever been used for the purpose of
serving as a ground for pictures. The word "tellis,"
which occurs in the note after No. 99, shows that the
staining or painting was not limited to woollen cloths,
but extended also to those made of linen. This supposition receives more weight from a passage in the
manuscript of St. Audemar (No. 195), where he says,
" If you wish to gild leather, or purple cloth, or linen,
or silk, stir it (the mordant) up altogether and draw
beasts, birds, and flowers upon it; then lay on the
gold." This passage can only be understood as applicable to articles of dress, unless indeed the painted or
gilded cloths should have been used as altar-cloths or
for the hangings of apartments.

The view I have taken of this subject is, I think,
confirmed by the fact that the English in the fourteenth
century actually wore garments painted with various
colours, or in the words of the manuscript chronicle
quoted by Mr. Planché, in his 'History of British
Costume,' "All that time the Englishmen were clothed
all in cootes and hoodes peynted with letters and
flowers, and seemly with long beards."

The practice is further illustrated by the epigram
which, in 1327, was affixed to the church-door of St.
Peter Stangate :—

> " Long beirds hertiless,
> *Peynted hoods* witless,
> Gay cotes graceless,
> Maketh Englonde thriftless."

Nor does it appear to me any objection that the
words "lavorare" and "depingere" are used, because
it does not appear that at this period blocks for calico-

printing were invented, and consequently the letters
and figures were necessarily painted on the cloth by
hand.   It seems to me very natural that an embroiderer should have learnt the particulars of an invention which must materially have interfered with his
own trade.

On the 13th of February, 1410, Johannes caused
the recipes numbered 100 to 116, inclusive, to be
copied from a book lent to him by "Johannes de
Modena, a painter living at Bologna."[1]   These are
the recipes which, being written in Italian, Jehan le
Begue could not read; he, however, procured a Latin
translation of them to be made by a friend of his "who
was skilled in both languages."   They relate chiefly to
colours and to mordants for laying on gold.   Among
the latter is one which will not be affected by the
weather, and which consisted of minium, ceruse, verdigris, bole, and ochre ground up with linseed oil and
"liquid varnish."   There is also a recipe for preparing
"gesso sottile" for a ground for the gold.

There is reason to believe that the Giovanni da
Modena, the painter mentioned in this manuscript,
and Giovanni Rossi da Modena, who was called "Il
Negro," the architect, were identical.

Giovanni da Modena is mentioned for the first time
as a painter in 1410, when it appears from the manuscript of Le Begue and from some documents preserved in Bologna, that he was then resident in that
city.

In 1408, Bartolommeo Bolognini directed by his will

---

[1] 'Guida di Bologna,' p. 112.

that certain pictures were to be painted in the chapel of S. Giorgio (now S. Abbondio, in the church of S. Petronio in Bologna), which belonged to him, and which he described, as well as the subjects of the pictures to be painted. It appears, from the archives of S. Petronio, that in 1420 Giovanni da Modena was selected to paint some pictures illustrative of stories from the Old Testament in this chapel, and as the subjects of the paintings now there correspond with those ordered by Bartolommeo Bolognini, it is conjectured that some of these paintings are by Giovanni da Modena.[1] His name again occurs as a painter in 1451 in some documents preserved at Bologna, but his works are not mentioned; and from this time until 1455 we hear nothing more of Giovanni da Modena; but about that time Giovanni Rossi executed, for the Duke Borso, the beautiful miniatures in the Bible of the House of Este, now preserved in the Ducal Library at Modena.[2] Lanzi says this Giovanni Rossi exercised his art at Mantua. From the few historical notices of Giovanni Rossi da Modena, the architect, called 'Il Negro,' it appears that he was the son of Martino de Rubeis de Mutina; that he was living at Bologna in 1410,[3] and the archives of S. Petronio

---

[1] 'Guida di Bologna,' p. 265.

[2] Marchese, 'Memorie dei Pittori Domenicani,' vol. i. p. 174. Lanzi, vol. iv. p. 6.

[3] While I was preparing these notes, I received the following note (which I translate literally) from Sig. Michaelangelo Gualandi of Bologna, whose archæological researches in the cause of the fine arts are well known and appreciated :—

"We have met with the name of one *Giovanni da Modena*, a painter, between the years 1410 and 1451, but none of his works are named. As to the architect of S. Petronio in Bologna, by name *Giovanni da Modena*,

show that he succeeded Paolo Tibaldi as the architect of that edifice in 1454.[1] His name may now be seen on some architectural designs preserved in S. Petronio. He was living in 1470.

From these facts there appears scarcely a doubt of the identity of the painter and architect; for it has been shown that Giovanni Rossi, or Russi, was an architect in 1454, and that about 1455 a Giovanni Rossi, a painter, executed some miniatures for the Duke of Modena. The identity is further confirmed by the circumstance that both painter and architect resided, at least occasionally, in Bologna from 1410, when Alcherius visited that city, until 1454 or 1455. In addition to these facts it must be remembered that the old masters frequently exercised both professions, to which they sometimes added also that of sculptor. Giotto, the reformer of the Florentine school of painting, was the architect of the beautiful Campanile of Florence. Michael Angelo painted in the Sistine Chapel, and was the architect of St. Peter's. Bramante also was a painter and an architect: there is nothing singular, therefore,

---

I am going to publish some interesting notices respecting him; among others, that dated from Rome, 22nd February, 1454, in which he is described as follows :—' Providum vir *Magistrum Johannem* quondam *Martini de Rubeis de Mutina*, Muratorem Bonon commorantem qui comuniter dicitur M. Johane Negro.' He is styled ' Architecto Magistrum et Ingeniorum.' He lived until 1470, whence it is scarcely probable (supposing him also to have been a painter) that he should have been the same individual who worked in 1410, when he must at least have been twenty-five years of age.''

This fact is certainly sufficient to raise a doubt as to the identity of the painter and architect, but instances of longevity are so common among painters, that there is nothing unreasonable in supposing Giovanni da Modena to have attained the age of eighty or eighty-five years.

[1] ' Guida di Bologna,' p. 97.

in Giovanni da Modena being at the same time a painter and an architect.

Giovanni de' Rossi had a son named Antonio, who became a Dominican in the convent of Sta. Maria Novella, at Florence, and who being afflicted with a tedious and incurable malady which rendered him unfit for other studies, occupied himself entirely in writing and illuminating the choral books of the convent. He died of the plague in 1495.[1] The name of Antonio da Modena also occurs among the names of the artists in the book belonging to the Society of Painters in Padua during the year 1441 :[2] this was probably Antonio, the son of Giovanni de' Rossi above mentioned.

From Bologna, it appears, Johannes Alcherius went to Venice, where, on the 4th of May, 1410, he procured a recipe for preparing ultramarine from " Michelino di Vesuccio, the most excellent painter among all the painters of the world." [3] The high opinion entertained by Alcherius for the skill of Michelino was general among his contemporaries. Pietro Candido Dicembrio asserts that he was one of the most famous painters of his time—*inter cæteres ætatis suæ illustris.*

The Conte Gaetano Melzi informed me that Michelino was a native of Besuzzo (a village in the province of Milan), which forms part of the estates of the Borromeo family, by whom he was much employed. The present representative of this noble house possessed, until very

---

1 Marchese, ' Memorie,' &c., vol. i. p. 174.
2 See Moschini ' della Pittura in Padova,' p. 23.
3 See Preface to No. 117.

lately, a picture, now entirely decayed, by this artist. Conte Giberto Borromeo was polite enough to search for the picture in order to show it to me, but it was so dilapidated that I could not see it. The following biographical notice respecting this painter is translated from a manuscript volume of Memoirs of the early Milanese Painters, Architects, and Sculptors, kindly lent me by Conte Gaetano Melzi of Milan, a nobleman distinguished for his literary attainments and possessing an excellent library:—

" We may reasonably conclude that this is the Michelino of Milan who is named by Vasari among the disciples of Taddeo Gaddi. He is mentioned by Lomazzo, who says he was a very old Milanese painter who lived a hundred and fifty years before his time; [1] and that he was one of the best of that period, judging from his works, some of which exist to this day. He added that he was ' stupendissimo nel far figure di animali;' and he gives us a description of a picture or drawing in which are represented some peasants in the act of joking and laughing, which was really an extraordinary work of the kind. Pietro Candido Dicembrio, who was a contemporary of this same Michelino, mentions another of his pictures, which was the portrait of Gian Maria Visconti, Duke of Milan. It is also asserted that Michelino was not less skilful in architecture, and that he took a prominent part in the academy instituted by the Duke Gian Galeazzo about the year 1380."

---

[1] Lomazzo published his Treatise in 1584; this would bring the date of Michelino at least as far back as 1434.

Michelino, therefore, is another instance of a painter exercising the profession of architect conjointly with his own.

Lanzi (vol. iv. p. 139), after repeating what Lomazzo had said in praise of Michelino, adds, that it appears he was esteemed even by foreigners, for it is mentioned by Morelli (*Notizie, &c.*, p. 81) that the Vendramini family in Venice possessed a small parchment book in quarto, containing animals painted by this artist. The note of Alcherius shows that Michelino was at Venice in 1410. Lanzi says he was living in 1435.

Johannes Alcherius returned to Paris in 1410; and in December, 1411, a year after his return from Italy, he employed himself in recopying and correcting the manuscripts he had collected on painting.[1] This appears to have been his last labour in the service of the arts. From this time nothing more is known of this indefatigable collector of manuscripts on art, whose labours extended over a space of thirty years. Twenty years after we find his manuscripts in the hands of Jehan le Begue, who copied them "with his own hand into one volume," and who probably arranged them in their present form.

I have entered into these particulars because they give authority to the recipes, and authenticity to the manuscripts.

Besides these manuscripts which I have mentioned, the volume of Le Begue contains also a copy of part of the first book of Theophilus; a Treatise on the Com-

---

[1] See Prefaces to Nos. 290, 297, 302.

position of Colours, by Petrus de Sancto Audemaro; and three books by Eraclius, entitled " De Artibus Romanorum."

The whole of the treatise of Theophilus has recently been published, with an excellent English translation and notes, by Mr. Hendrie.

TABLE OF CONTENTS.

Table of the synonymous names of colours, and of the qualities and accidents of colours, and things pertaining to the art of painting ; also of the works and exercises proper and incident to them.

Another table imperfect, and without a beginning.

Experiments on colours.

Divers experiments not upon colours.

The work of Theophilus, a most admirable and learned master of the whole science of the art of painting.

The work of Master Peter, of St. Audemar, on making colours.

The first and metrical book of Eraclius (a most learned man), on the colours and arts of the Romans.

The second book by the same author, also metrical.

The third book, in prose, on the aforesaid colours and arts.

Chapters written by John Archerius, or Alcherius, in the year of our Lord 1398, on colours for painting, as he received them from Jacob Cona, a Flemish painter, then living in Paris.

Chapters on the colours used for illuminating books, written and noted by the same Alcherius in the year 1398, as he received them from Antonio de Compendio, an illuminator of books in Paris ; and from Master Alberto Porzello, a schoolmaster at Milan, who was most skilful in all kinds of writing.

Other recipes in Latin and French by Master John, surnamed Le Begue, a licentiate in law, and secretary of the general magistrates of the king's mint at Paris ; who wrote the present work, or the chapters collected in this volume, with his own hand, in the year of our Lord 1431, and in the 63rd year of his age.

Illustra Deus oculum.

CONTINENTUR HOC VOLUMINE.

TABULA de vocabulis synonymis et equivocis colorum rerumque et accidentium colorum ipsisque omni arti pictorie conferentium nec non operum exercitiorumque propitiorum ac contingentium eorum.

Alia tabula licet imperfecta et sine initio.

Experimenta de coloribus.

Experimenta diversa alia quam de coloribus.

Liber Theophili admirabilis et doctissimi magistri de omni scientia picturæ artis.

Liber Magistri Petri de Sancto Audemaro de coloribus faciendis.

Eraclii sapientissimi viri liber primus et metricus de coloribus et de artibus Romanorum.

    Ejusdem liber secundus, item metricus.

    Ejusdem liber tertius sed prosaicus de coloribus et artibus prædictis.

De coloribus ad pingendum capitula scripta et notata a Johanne Archerio seu Alcherio anno Domini 1398 ut accepit a Jacobo Cona flamingo pictore commorante tunc Parisiis.

Capitula de coloribus ad illuminandum libros ab eodem Archerio sive Alcherio scripta et notata anno 1398 ut accepit ab Antonio de compendio illuminatore librorum in Parisiis et a magistro Alberto Porzello perfectissimo in omnibus modis scribendi, mediolani scholas tenente.

Aultres receptes en Latin et en François per Magistrum Johannem dit Le Begue Licentiatum in legibus et generalium magistrorum monetæ regis greffarium Parisiis. Qui præsens opus seu capitula in hoc volumine aggregata propria manu scripsit anno Domini 1431. Ætatis vero suæ 63.

    Illustra Deus oculum.

TABULA de VOCABULIS SINONIMIS et EQUIVOCIS COLORUM, rerumque, et accidencium colorum, ipsisque et arti pictorie conferentium, nec non operum exerciciorumque propiciorum ac contingencium eorum.

[Habitis per presentem tabulam declaracionibus nominum, colorum, rerumque, et accidencium eorum et artis pictorie, et eis conferencium, nec non operum et exerciciorum propiciorum ac contingencium eorum, querantur ipsorum et ipsorum effectus et operaciones in hoc libro, et in capitulis ejus, per primam ex tabulis sequentibus.]

Albus est color, aliter, secundum Grecos, dicitur leucos et secundum Catholiconem dicitur glaucus ; et est cerusa, aliter album Hispanie, et aliter album plumbum dicitur, et aliter bracha seu blacha.[1]

Azurium vel lazurium est color ; aliter celestis vel celestinus, aliter blauccus, aliter persus, et aliter ethereus dicitur.

Aurum est nobilius metallum croceum [2] colorem habens et tenuatur in petulis, quo carentes utuntur stanno attenuato, et colorito colore croceo, et in petulis tenuato.

Argentum est nobile metallum album colorem habens, quo qui caret utitur ejus loco de dicto stanno tenuato, non colorito.

Auripigmentum est color croceus qui aliter arsicon dicitur.

Aureola [3] est color qui aliter pictura translucida vocatur ; et omnis pictura, cujuslibet coloris, in stanno attenuato facta, si

---

NOTE.—The technical nature of the terms, and the obscurity of many of the explanations, render a translation impracticable.

---

[1] *Albus* appears to signify *white lead*. Blacha was probably written *biacha* (biacca).

[2] *Crocus, Croceum* is used for yellow. See Croceum.

[3] Aureola. This appears to be the auripetrum of Pietro di S. Audemar, No. 202, and the Clavicula.

ipsa liniatur, per eam transparet, et pulcra fit, precipue si in stanno tenuato polito sit.

Attramentum est color niger quo scribitur, aliter incaustum dicitur, et vide in incausto, et de ipso quoque utitur pingendo dum fit de fuligine ardentis candele vel lampadis vel carbone mollis ligni vel vitis.[1]

Auripentrum[2] est color croceus qui stanno lucido suppositus et linitus speciem auri procul intuentibus mentitur.

Auripigmento similis est color qui vocatur (*sic*) et fit de felle piscis magni marini, credo balene, mixto cum creta alba seu gersa et modico aceto.

Arsicon vel *arxica*[3] sicut est auripigmentum, est color croceus, et miscendo succo herbe que scalda bassa dicitur fit viridis et succi gratia quarumdam aliarum herbarum ad hoc boni sunt.

Anguillaria herba facit colorem (*sic*) cum miscetur vitro.

Alba creta est gipsus, aliter gersa dicta, et fit de lapide quodam in fornace usque ad dealbacionem decocto, et de subtiliore ipsius dealbantur tabule altarium. Alii plastrum vocant.

Arxica est quedam terra crocea ad pingendum apta ac etiam ad formas operum cupri fundendorum fiendas utilima.

Alumen glacie[4] quod alibi, precipue in Parisiis glassa dicitur, et si color non sit, tamen pluribus coloribus ad picturam et illuminaturam aptis nimis conveniens est.

Assisiam auri faciendo intrat moniculum[5] quod est quedam (*sic*).

---

1 Atramentum, then, is charcoal or lamp-black, No. 172.

2 Auripentrum, called auripetrum by Petrus di S. Audemar, No. 202; by Eraclius, No. xliv.; and in the Clavicula. This appears to be the same as Aureola.

3 Arzicon and Arzica are here considered synonymous, but they are not so in fact: the former is declared by Eraclius, No. l., to be the same as orpiment, but the latter is shown by the Bolognese manuscript to have been a yellow lake, made from the Reseda Luteola, Dyers' weed, or, as it is generally called, Weld. Arzicon appears to be a corruption of *Arsenicon*, which Vitruvius (lib. vii. cap. vii.) says was the Greek name for Auripigmentum.

4 Alumen glacie appears to be common alum, see Nos. 42, 299, 313.

5 Gum ammoniac.

Aurare seu deaurare chrisare dicitur, ut dicit Catholicon.

Argilla dicitur creta alba, et aliis modis vocatur ut sequenter in creta dicetur.

Albi colores seu materie et metalla eorum sunt et nominantur, ut et in hac tabula reperies in locis suis, cerusa, blacha, argentum et stannum tenuatum, gipsus, creta alba, candidus calx, gersa, tavertinus.

Bracha seu *Blacha* [1] est color albus, et fit de plumbo vel de ejus corrupcione, sicut rubigo fit de ferro; aliter vocatur cerusa, album plumbum, et aliter glaucus.

Blauccus [2] est color, aliter lazurium vel azurum aliter celestis vel celestinus, aliter persus, aliter ethereus dictus.

Brunus [3] est color quem puto esse bularminium alibi ponitur pro sanguine drachonis qui quasi coloris bularminici est.

Bures [4] est liquor qui in licivio de cinere fabarum coctus facit colorem   (*sic*) credo viridem, per ea que continentur in capitulo 247.

---

[1] It is probable this word was originally written biacha, the old Italian way of spelling biacca.

[2] *Blauccus*, or, as it is written in No. 294, *Blauctus*, and in No. 314 *blauet*, signifies Blue.

[3] *Brunus*. Probably Bruno di Spagna, which Haydocke, the translator of Lomazzo's Treatise on Painting (p. 99), identifies with Majolica, and which there is no reason to doubt is the soft red hæmatite, called also Bruno d'Inhilterra. This colour is mentioned by Eraclius, Nos. 282, 286.

[4] There is scarcely a doubt that this should be written *Borax*, and not Bures. The word Borax is derived in the first place from the Hebrew Borith, and more immediately from the Arabic Baurach, and was so corrupted by the different nations who practised the arts in which it was used, that it is seldom found in old MSS. written twice alike. By Theophilus it is called " parahas," or " barabas ;" in the Montpelier MS. described by Mr. Hendrie (Theoph. p. 429) it is written " Boraxa ;" in the Clavicula, Burrago, Borras, Borrax, and Borac. It was also known to the Arabs under another name, derived from Tincal, its denomination in India, whence it was brought to Europe, namely Tincar, whence the Spanish name Atincar. It is a native borate of soda, and is found at the bottom of lakes in Persia, the Mogul territory, in Thibet, China, and Japan.

Bisetus, vel *Biseth* folii,[1] est color minus rubeus quam folium, et de eodem folio cum supernatat acceptus, et credo per hoc etiam potest intelligi quilibet clarescens color supernatans cuilibet ex coloribus cum in conchillis temperati sunt ad pingendum et aliquantulum quieverunt.

Bularminium[2] est color rubeus nigrescens, ut morellus, vel ut sanguis drachonis.

Blacha seu *Bracha*[3] est color albus, aliter cerusa, aliter album Hispanie, aliter album plumbum, et aliter glaucus dicitur.

Braxilium vel *Brexilium*[4] est lignum rubeum a quo cum pistus rixus sit in lixivio forti vel urina cum albumine commiscetur exit color roxeus vel purpureus.

Blaca, dicit Catholicon, est purpura cujusdem animalis colorem mutans; et qui blateus dicitur, purpureus, vel talis coloris, scilicet blauius dicitur ipse.

Blondus est color albo et rubeo mixtus, aliter cerulus vel ceruleus; et ceruleus color alibi ponitur pro colore ex albo et viridi mixto; et facto vel ex viridi, albo, et croceo.

Berettinus[5] color, Lombardice sic vocatus, est color medius inter album et nigrum, qui Latine elbus vel elbidus dicitur, ut in Catholicone scilicet; Gallice grisus appellatur.

Birsus[6] est color rufus vel niger, ut dicit Catholicon.

Blaui[7] colores, seu materie eorum sunt et nominantur ut in

---

[1] See Folium. Bisetus, or Biseth folii, a Latin form of "Bezette," which is a corruption of the Italian word "Pezzette." See the note to "Succus."

[2] Bularmenium—Armenian Bole.

[3] Blacha, or bracha. This should probably be written *biacha* (biacca), Nos. 1, 18.

[4] Braxilium, or brexilium, the verzino of the Italians.

[5] This colour, which is a true grey, is the veneda of Theophilus.

[6] Birsus. This appears to be a dark purple colour. See Cennino Cennini, chap. cxiv., note by Tambroni.

[7] *Blaui* colores, that is blue colours. See *ante,* Blauccus. This term occurs in the extracts from the Archivio delle Riformazione di Firenze, published by Gaye, Carteggio inedito, vol. i. p. 449, and in Venetian tariffs. Mr. Hendrie says the word is of Byzantine origin. The resemblance to the German *Blau* is striking.

hac tabula in locis suis reperies, azurium seu lazurium, viola, herbe flos, persicus, persus, indicus, silacetus, safirecus, rubigo argenti finissimi.

Chriso, Chrisas, id est deaurare vel aurare ut in Catholicon dicitur.

Citrinus color aliquantulum differt a duobus coloribus, id est, croceo, et punico vel puniceo, et citrinus est color ex croceo et rubeo mixtus seu factus.[1]

Croceus[2] color aliquantulum differt a coloribus duobus, puniceo videlicet et citrino.

Carnatura,[3] alia membrana, alia cedra, alia holcus vel olcus, alia lumina, alia veneda seu veneda, alia fulvus, menesch, prasis, posech, cerusa, purpureus, folium, sinopis, ruscus, rosa, rubi, succus, menech, exedra.

Cedra[4] est color qui fit de rubeo, mixto cum pauco nigri coloris, ad nuda ymaginum humanarum operanda ; aliter dicitur exedra.

Coccicus,[5] *ci,* color est rubeus, seu sanguineus ; vel etiam genus est tincture coloris medii inter rubeum et croceum : alii coccinum illud vocant, ut, in passione Christi, de colore vestis ejus.

Coccus dicunt Greci, nos vero coccicum, seu cortinum aut coccinum, rubeum colorem qui fit et est ex diversis ut sunt frondes silvestres, flores rose rubee, vel creta, que et terra rubea, et alii colores rubei artificiali ; aliter dicitur vernilculus vel vermiletus, et aliter sanguineus.

---

[1] Orange colour.

[2] Yellow.

[3] Under this term the author has included all the tints used in painting flesh, as well the flesh tints as those for shadows.

[4] Cedra. The shadow-colour for flesh. See Theophilus, lib. i. chap. xiii., where it is called Excedra or Exedra.

[5] Coccicus or Coccicum. By this term was meant the colour called by the Italians " Grana," and which the Arabs called " Alkermes," and we Kermes.

Cortex[1] secundus nigra prunii, si decoquatur facit colorem croceum.

Crocea terra, vel creta crocea, est ad pingendum apta ; aliter ocra vel ogra dicitur. Alia terra crocea est que arxica[2] dicitur qua forme operum fusilium cupri fiunt.

Cerulus vel *ceruleus*,[3] dicit Catholicon, id est fulvus ad instar cere viridis, niger, glaucus, et est prope blondus ; sed alibi idem Catholicon dicit quod fulvus est aliquantulum rubeus vel cum nigro rubeus mixtus, et, ut idem Catholicon, flavus, albus, rubeus, aut blondus albo et rubeo factus.

Celestinus vel *celestis* est color aliter azurium, aliter blaucus, aliter persus, aliter ethereus dictus.

Cerusa est color albus qui fit de plumbo ; aliter vocatur bracha seu blacha, et aliter glaucus et alibi dicitur que cerusa fit de cupro adusto.[4]

Croma Grece, Latine color, secundum Catholiconem, quod est vocabulum universale pro omnibus coloribus.

Color similiter est vocabulum universale pro omnibus coloribus, et Grece croma dicitur, et quot sunt planete, tot sunt colores, videlicet septem, qui sunt, primo duo extremi, albus et niger, et reliqui quinque qui intermedii dicuntur, videlicet, celestis seu Lazurius, rubeus, croceus seu aureus, viridis, et sanguineus seu purpureus aut violetus vel fulvus de quorum singulis reperies in hac tabula in locis suis secundum litteras alphabeti primas nominum eorum et materias quibus fiunt, et de quorum etiam interunpcionibus ad invicem infinite diversitates colorum ad placitum humani ingenii distinguuntur.

Crocus vel *Crocum*[5] est color exiens de saffranno madefacto,

---

1 Cortex. See Nos. 206, 208, 209. This appears to have been used in making yellow varnishes which, being spread over tin, caused it to appear like gold.

2 Is this the " Terra di Matton bianchi " mentioned by Baldinucci ? Voc. Dis.

3 Cerulus. This is quite unintelligible.

4 See Eraclius, No. liv.

5 Crocus or Crocum. The zafarano of the Italians. See Cennini, cap. 49.

vel est idem saffrannus ; et melior est cicilianus qui coriscos vocatur.

Croceus [1] est color idem exiens de saffranno, et est qui fit ex mixtura fellis et crete albe, et est ocra vel ogra terra quedam, et est color auri, et est auripigmentum, et est etiam quedam terra crocea que arxica dicitur apta ad formas operum cupri fiendas, et alii dicunt ipsam argillam.

Candidus est color albus differens ab albo.

Calx [2] calcis est color albus, videlicet lapis durus in igne usque ad ejus dealbacionem decoctus, de quo lathomi cementum ad muros edificandos faciunt.

Carminium [3] est color rubeus, aliter cinobrium vel sinopis dictus ; alibi dicitur quod fit de albo et ocro mixtis.

Cerosius est color viridis, alibi capitur pro quodam succo in 159, et alibi pro   (*sic*).

Coriscos est crocus, id est, saffranus perfectissimus, ut ait Ysidorus, nascens in Cicilia insula.

Caligo [4] est color, videlicet, materia illa crocea obscura, quam fumus ignis generat sub caminatis sub quibus continue fit ignis decoquendo fercula.

Caprifolium [5] est herba in Anglico dicta "gaterice," cujus grana in vino trita et bulita si emitatur ferrum eruginatum color viridis fulgentis efficitur, et si addatur atramentum, niger efficitur.

Creta alba, dicitur argilla, est color albus factus de lapide in fornace cocto, qui aliter plastrum dicitur, et aliter gersa, et aliter gipsus, et utuntur ipsa pelliparii ; alia est rubea, alia viridis et alia nigra, que terra nigra seu lapis niger vocatur, et alia crocea.

---

[1] Croceus may here be considered a general name for yellow pigments.

[2] Lime.

[3] See Eraclius, No. lvi.

[4] This appears to be the colour we call Bistre.

[5] Sir Thomas Phillips says, in his Introduction to the Clavicula, that for Gaterice we should read gate-tree, *i. e.* goat-tree.

Creta viridis,[1] cujus melior nascitur in creta cirina insula, et vocatur Grece theodote ; alia creta reperitur rubea, et alia alba, et alia nigra, que appellata est lapis niger.

Crisicula[2] est color   (*sic*) veniens a Macedonia, et foditur ex metallis ærariis.

Ceruleus color fit ex succo de lutea herba expresso, alibi dicitur quod viridissimum colorem facit, ipsa herba seu succus ejus, precipue si alicui substancioso colori albo admisceatur, ut crete aut cerusie ; et alibi ceruseus est color blondus ex albo et rubeo factus.

Carbo[3] est color niger factus de lignis mollibus ustis, ut salix, populus, vitis, et similia.

Cinobrium[4] vel cinopis aliter carminium dicitur.

Conchile[5] vel concile maris circonscise sanguinem purpureum colorem habentem emittunt, quo tinctura purpurea fit pro lanis.

Crocei colores seu materie, et metalla eorum sunt et nominantur ut in hac tabula reperies in locis suis : aurum, auripigmentum, auripigmento similis color, arsica, suffranus, coriscos, caligo, decoctio secundi corticis nigri pruni, ocra vel ogra, fel, grecumspect, stannum tenuatum croce colore in hoc convenienti coloritum.

Celare a celo, celas, id est lanire, sculpere, pingere, figurare, protrahere, designare ; et inde celatura, celature, etc.

Drachonis sanguis[6] est color morellus seu rubeus obscurus.

Deaurare, id est, auro aurare, chrisare dicitur, ut in Catholicon.

---

[1] This creta viridis seems to be our terra verte.

[2] Chrysocolla. This is the native green carbonate of copper.

[3] Carbo, that is, charcoal black.

[4] Cinnabar or vermilion. The writers of these old MSS. speak of the artificial cinnabar only.

[5] This was the purpura of Pliny and the ancients, from which the celebrated Tyrian dye was prepared, and which was procured from a fish of the genus Buccinum found in the Mediterranean.

[6] Dragon's blood.

Designare, protrahere, pingere, sculpere, figurare, lanire, celare, quasi idem significant.

Exedra[1] est color ex mixtura rubea et modico nigri ad nuda corporum humanorum fienda aliter dicta cedra.

Edera[2] est herba arboribus herendo, repens, que in Gallico dicitur "yene" vel "lierre," cujus rami ex sobula perforati, vel hinc inde infra eos incisi, ad medium videlicet de mense Marcii emittunt liquorem sanguineum, qui, cum urina coctus, lacca est, qua tinguntur pelles parcium.

Ethereus color aliter dicitur lazurium seu azurium, et aliter persus, aliter blauctus, et aliter celestinus seu celestis.

Elbus,[3]-ba,-bum, vel elbidus,-da,-dum, color est medius inter album et nigrum, ut ait Catholicon, et Gallice dicitur Grisus, set Lombardice Berretinus nominatur.

Flavus[4] color fit de cerusa combusta.

Folium[5] est pro tingendo lanas, et est color rubeus, et quidam alter est purpureus, et alter saphireus, scilicet est quidam alter qui fit miscendo ipsi rubeo cinerem vel lexivium cinerum ligni ulmi, et vocatur folium scampnense.

Fel[6] est liquor croceus, seu color, quo si cuprum cultello rasum et dente politum ungatur quociens conveniat, splendificatur tanquam si deauratum esset, et si ipsum fel misceatur cum creta seu gersa alba, et modico aceto, efficitur color auripigmento similis, videlicet croceus.

Fuscus est color niger, ex carbone, vel ex fumo lampadis

---

[1] Exedra. See Theophilus, lib. i. cap. xiii. ; and Le Begue, No. 345.

[2] Edera, the ivy.

[3] In English, *Grey*.

[4] Flavus. This appears to be the colour we now call massacot, the protoxide of lead.

[5] Folium. See Vocabulary of Colours, *supra*.

[6] A similar colour is in use at the present day, called Gallstone. It is a beautiful and very transparent yellow, but it is not permanent. It is used in water-colours.

aut candele ardentis factus, et aliter dicitur fuligo,[1] dicitur aliter fuscus sanctonicus dicitur.

Fuligo est color niger vel quasi niger, ad croceum tendens, et veniens a camino ignis, aliter dicta caligo, et est etiam fumus candele et lampadis nigerrimus recollectus ad scutellam vel aliud vas ferreum, vel cupreum, vel terreum.

Fumus[2] est color niger, si cum ab igne candele sepi vel cere, vel a lampadis lumine exit, colligatur, qui aliter fuscus, et aliter fuligo nominatur.

Fulvus, dicit Catholicon, est rubeus aliquantulum, vel cum nigro rubeus ; et vide sequenter in R. littera super verbo *ravus*, quod ibi aliter dicitur.

Fenix, seu phenix, vel feniceus color rubeus est et feniceon Grece Latine rubeum colori rosarum rubearum similatus.

Ferula,[3] aliter galbanum dicta, est genus, et lac herbe, et est quidem color inde de succo ex palmitibus ejus expresso factus ut dicit Catholicon.

Figurare, pingere, sculpere, protrahere, designare, lanire, celare, quasi idem significant.

Galbanum[4] est genus et lac herbe, que dicitur ferula, et est quidem color inde de succo ex palmitibus ejus factus, et sic dicit Catholicon.

Grisus color, Gallice sic dictus, est color inter album et nigrum, qui Latine elbus vel elbidus dicitur ut in Catholicon, set Lombardice vocatur beretinus.

Grenuspect[5] herba, cujus decoctio vini aut cervisie crocea est, de qua, si temperetur et teretur viride Grecum, fit pulcrum viride, quod credo esse viridegris.

---

[1] The colour here described is Bistre.

[2] Fumus—Lamp black.

[3] Ferula—See Galbanum.

[4] Galbanum, a liquor or gum produced by a species of ferula in Africa and Turkey, called Ferula Galbanifera.

[5] Grenuspect. Sir Thomas Phillips thinks this should be written " Greningwert."

Gersa[1] est color albus, de quadam terra, vel lapide non duro, cocto in fornace factus, qui aliter gipsus vel creta alba vocatur, et ipsa utuntur pelliparii, et aliter plastra dicitur. Set etiam pelliparii pocius utuntur alia creta alba, que fit de quodam meliori lapide absque coctione albissimo pulverizato, Gallice " croye."

Glades[2] vel *glacies*, cum ex metallis primum exciduntur, gutas argenti vivi exprimunt, pro usu artificum, et sine ipsis es neque argentum inaurari possunt.

Garancia[3] herba est ad faciendum tincturas lanarum et lineorum, et in Ytalico gadus dicitur.

Gadus[4] herba est, in Gallico garancia dicta, ad faciendum tincturas lanarum et lineorum.

Glassa[5] credo quod sit alumen glasse seu glacie.

Gipsus[6] est color albus, aliter gersa, et aliter alba creta dictus, et est terra seu lapis in fornace usque ad dealbacionem decoctus, quo tabule altarium dealbantur ut depingantur.

Granetus est color de albo et viridi factus.

Gladius[7] viridis est color viridis factus de auripigmento et indico mixtus.

---

[1] This is plaster of Paris, the gesso of the Italians. The other stone is our English chalk.

[2] I believe this passage is from Pliny. See Eraclius, No. 241.

[3] Garancia is certainly madder, but its Italian name is Robbia, and not gadus.

[4] Gadus. This is a mistake: the French term is Gaude; the Italian, Guado; the English, Woad—*Isatis Tinctoria*.

[5] Glassa. In these manuscripts of Le Begue the word Glassa is used in two significations: first, it is used to denote Sandarac or Amber, as in Nos. 208 and 341; and, secondly, it is used in conjunction with Alumen, and appears to mean crystallized alum simply, or Roche alum, as in Nos. 42 and 299.

[6] Gipsus. Gesso—plaster of Paris.

[7] Gladius viridis. A vegetable green, prepared from the leaves of the Gladiolus communis; in Italian, Gladiolo; in French, Glayeul flambe; in English, the Corn-flag; in Sicilian, Spatulidda. This pigment was much used in Italy. See 'Secreti di Alessio,' part ii. p. 37 b. A blue colour was made from the flowers of the same plant.

Glaucus est color albus, ut cerusa, que aliter dicitur album plumbum, aliter blacha, et aliter album Hispanie.

Gaterice [1] Anglice est herba, cujus grana in vino trita et bullita, si immittatur ferrum eruginatum efficitur color viridis fulgentis et si addatur attramentum niger efficitur.

Gumma [2] edere, lacha est facta ex succo vel liquore exeunte in Marcio de ramis edere herbe arboribus inherentis et repentis, si aculeo ferro perforentur.

Holcus [3] vel olcus est color, qui aliter membrana dicitur, ex rubeo, et albo, et pauco viridis creta compositus ad nuda corpora et membra humana depingenda.

Herba morella, [4] trita cum gersa seu gipso, id est, creta alba, facit colorem viridem.

Herba sandix [5] vocata, est rubea, et de ipsa fit tinctura rubea aut sanguinea.

Herba vaccinium [6] vocata duplex est; una rubea, que temperata cum lacte purpureum colorem facit elegantem, reliqua vero croceum colorem facit.

Herba viola dicta, cujus flos persus seu blavus est, facit colorem blavum si ipse ejus flos misceatur crete albe et teratur.

Herba que *scalda lassa* vocatur in janua facit succum si pistetur et exprimatur, qui mixtus cum arxicon vel arxica, colore croceo, fit color viridis.

Iris est color   (*sic*).

Indicus vel indicum est color celestinus obscurus.

---

[1] See ante, Caprifolium.

[2] Gumma Edera.   Gum from the Ivy.

[3] See Theophilus, lib. i. cap. i. ; and Pietro di S. Audemar, No. 180.

[4] Herba Morella (Solanum Nigrum) is here, as in the Bol. manuscript, said to make a green colour.

[5] Herba sandix—the madder.   The word madder is derived from the Danish, Swedish, and Russian languages.

[6] Herba vaccinium, the violet.   That from which a yellow colour is made is the Viola lutea, the Wall-flower.

Incaustum est color quo scribitur, aliter attramentum dictum, vide in attramento, id est factum ex decoctione gallarum fractarum, et vitriolo et gummi Arabico, aut ex decoctione mirce que vulgariter genestra dicitur, et dictis vitriolo et gummi Arabico et decoctio etiam corticis hoene ligni aut ceresi ligni posset convenire, nec non cortex secundus nigri pruni arboris ad hoc per decoctionem adaptaretur cum addicione suprascriptorum vitrioli et gummi Arabici.

Jas viride dicitur, ut dicit Catholicon.

Lumina[1] est color ex mixtura membrane et ceruse factus ad illuminandum facies et nuda corpora humana in pictura, seu ad gibbositates in ipsis elevandos.

Lacca est gumma quedam, facta de liquore rubeo, qui exit de liquore edere, arboribus herente et repente, si rami ipsius in mense Marcii aculeo ferreo perforentur.

Lazurium vel azurium fit de lapide lazulli; dicitur aliter persus, aliter celestis vel celestinus, aliter blauctus seu blauus, et aliter ethereus.

Lucee[2] herbe succus coloris cerulei est, et alibi dicitur quod viridissimus est.

Lazuli lapis ⎫ reperitur in montibus vel partibus et est ce-
Lapis lazuli ⎭ lestis coloris seu persi vel blaui et de ipso fit pulver qui purificatur et postea est azurium.

Lapis niger[3] est, de quo, si satis mollis sit, utuntur pictores et carpentarii, protrahendo ad siccum; et de ipso pingitur terendo ad liquidum ; aliter terra nigra dicitur.

Lignum braxillii[4] rubeum seu purpureum colorem reddit si in lixivio vel urina aut in claro ovi cum alumine temperetur.

---

[1] Lumina. See Theophilus, lib. i.

[2] Herba Luzza, either the Erba lizza, the Tragopogon pratense, yellow goat's beard, or the Erba Lutea of Pliny, the Reseda Luteola, Dyer's weed, or weld.

[3] Black chalk, or graphite.

[4] The Verzino of the Italians.

Leucos Grece, Latine album, ut ait Catholicon, qui color et glaucus dicitur.

Lanire, celare, sculpere, pingere, figurare, protrahere, designare, quasi idem significant, etc.

Membrana[1] est color quo pinguntur facies et nuda corpora humana ; aliter olcus dicitur, vel holcus, et aliter carnatura.

Minium[2] est color non tam rubeus ut synopis, set magis pallidus, aliter dictus sendracum vel sendaraca.

Menesch ;[3] aliqui dicunt quod est color rubeus, minus clarus quam minicum, et magis clarus quam synopis ; alii ipsum vocant succum, et indici coloris est ; aliter dicitur esse succus sambuci, qui viridis est.

Mellana[4] est color cum quo ex lacha seu gumma edere et flore farine tritici in urina positus fit rubeus color synopis vocatus.

Morella[5] herba trita cum gersa seu creta alba est color viridis.

Mellinus est color metalli speciem habens.

Morellus est color ex rubeo et nigro factus.

Morus Grece, est arbor quam et Latini etiam sic appellant cujus fructus morum dicitur, et ejus succus, mixtus cum creta

---

[1] Membrana.   See Theophilus, lib. i. cap. 1, and Pietro di S. Audemar, No. 180.

[2] The term Sandaraca is sometimes applied to Red orpiment, and sometimes to Minium.

[3] Menesch.   Mr. Hendrie (Theoph. p. 81) says this is a Romaic word, signifying violet colour ; but I would suggest whether it may not signify " Madder," the Indian name for which is *Mnitsch*.   This construction is perfectly compatible with the directions of Theophilus ; and in this case it will also agree with the definition in the Table of Synonymes, on which, however, I acknowledge but little dependence can be placed.

[4] Mellana.   In the MS. of S. Audemar this colour is called Sinopis de Mellana.   It is a kind of lake.

[5] Morella.   This is one of the Italian names for the Solanum Nigrum, the Black nightshade.   It is also called in Italy Solatro Nero, and Cacabo. In French it is called " Morelle," " Morelle des Jardins ;" but it must be distinguished from the " Maurelle," the name which the Croton Tinctorium bears at Montpellier.

alba et aliis rebus convenientibus, simul et separatim, colorem roseum et sanguineum faciunt.

Mirca[1] est arbor vulgariter dicta genestra, que interponitur faciendo incaustum ad scribendum.

Moniculum[2] est   (*sic*), quod intrat ad faciendum assisiam auri.

Niger est color terre nigre, que lapis niger dicitur, satis mollis ad protrahendum, et color niger est etiam ex carbone molito, vel ex fumo lampadis aut candele factus; aliter fuscus dicitur, et aliter sanccenicus.

Neveda,[3] seu veneda est color ex mixtura nigri cum modico albo plumbo, et si poni vult in muro, ponatur calx loco dicti albi plumbi.

Nigri pruni cortex secundus, si decoquatur, facit colorem croceum, et si immittantur in ipsa decoctione debite quantitates vitrioli et gummi Arabici, fit attramentum seu incaustum ad scribendum.

Niger color et rufus color vocantur birsus, ut ait Catholicon, et vide in *rufus* et *ravus* quod ibi dicitur, ac etiam in *birsus*.

Nigri colores, seu materie eorum, sunt et nominantur ut et in hac tabula reperies in locis suis, attramentum, incaustum, fuligo, carbo, lapis niger, fuscus, fumus, sanctonicus.

Ocra,
Ogra, } est color terre crocee.

Olchus[4] color aliter appellatur membrana, ad facies et nuda corpora humana depingenda.

Oster[5] piscis est marinus, cujus sanguis color est rubeus; purpureus vocatus.

---

1 Mirca.   See note to MSS. of St. Audemar, No. 206.

2 Probably Gum ammoniac.

3 See Veneda.

4 Olchus.   See Pietro di S. Audemaro, No. 180, and Theophilus, lib. i. cap. i.

5 The purpura of the ancients.

Prasis[1] est creta viridis ut dicit Catholicon.

Prasinus[2] est color rubeus; alii dicunt quod habet similitudinem viridis coloris et nigri, set Catholicon dicit quod prasin Grece, latine dicitur viridis.

Posch[3] est color ex mixtura prasini, et rubei combusti, et ocre, et modico cenobrio, factus, ad distinguendas partes membrorum humani corporis in membrana colore, set alibi posch dicitur fieri ex ogra et viridi simul mixtis.

Purpureus, qui est color rubeus, aliter folium vocatur,— vide in *folium;* et Anglici, in quorum terra nascitur, ipsum vocant "unormam;" fit etiam color purpureus ex lapide silicis exusto, et in aceto dum callescit extincto, et oster est certum quid, id est, piscis maris, aut aliud, quo fit color purpureus, vel de sanguine ejus; et concule maris etiam circumcise purpureum colorem faciunt, et similiter creta alba infecta radice rubea, et sic herba que vaccinium dicitur facit purpureum colorem si cum lacte temperetur.

Pruni nigri secundus cortex facit ex decoctione colorem croceum.

Paratonium est color   (*Sic*).

Persus est color aliter celestis, aliter lazurium vel azurum, aliter ethereus, et aliter blauus dictus.

Pictura translucida,[4] aliter aureola dicta, est color seu liquor per quem omnes alii colores transparent, si cum in operibus siccaverint ipso liniantur, precipue in stanno attenuato et polito.

Pallidus est color non proprie albus, set declinans aliquantulum ad obscuritatem.

Plumlus albus est color ex plumbo factus, aliter albus hispanie, aliter glaucus, aliter cerusa, et aliter blacha dictus.

---

[1] Probably Terre Verte.

[2] Prasinus, the same as Prasis. See Theophilus, lib. i. cap. ii.

[3] Posch. See Theophilus, lib. i. cap. iii. and vii.; and Le Begue, No. 344.

[4] See the Chapters ' De Confectio Lucidæ' and ' De Lucide ad Lucidas' of the Lucca manuscript, and Clavicula.

Plastra est terra vel lapis, qui, decoctus fornaci, albissimus est, aliter gersa, aliter creta alba, et aliter gipsus.

Phenix color rubeus est, vel fenix ; et feniceon Grece, latine rubeum.

Pumiceus color seu puniceus, aliquantulum differt a duobus coloribus, id est, a croceo et citrino, que plus continet de croceo, et minus de rubeo, quam citrinno.

Puniceus vel pumiceus, dicit liber de proprietatibus rerum, est color circumdans rubeum colorem, aliter etiam dicitur citrinus, qui est color ab eo parum differens que puniceus plus continet de croceo et minus de rubeo quam citrinus.

Pingere, lanire, celare, sculpere, figurare, protrahere, designare, quasi idem significant.

Rubeus est color qui ex frondibus silvestribus et aliis materialibus diversis fit, et diversis in obscuritate, et claritate, et aliis varietatibus, ut sunt dicti frondes, et etiam flores, ac terra vel creta rubea, et alii colores rubei artificiati ; et Greci ipsum coctum dicunt, nos vero rubeum vel vermiletum.

Rosa est color ex mixtura membrane et modico cenobrii et modico minii factus ad rubricandas facies et membra humanorum corporum in pictura, et fit de vermiculo et albo plumbo, ac de brasilio et alumine cum urina.

Rubi sunt rubei fructus arborum qui apud Grecos morus dicuntur, et fructus ipse eorum morum dicitur, ex quibus succus, mixtus aliis rebus materialibus, ut crete, seu gipso, sanguinei vel rosei colores fiunt.

Rubea radix[1] est de qua rubeus color fit, miscendo cum
Radix rubea creta alba, id est, gipso.

Rubea terra, seu creta, ex qua trita pingitur.

Rava color niger est fulvo mixtus, dicit Catholicon.

Roseus est color rosarum rubearum colori similatus, et aliter vide in cocticus, coctus, fulvus, fenix seu phenix vel fenicus aut feniceus, per *p* et *h* vel *f* et *e* scribendo, et vide etiam in *purpureus* et in *folium.*

---

[1] Madder.

Rufus color et niger color vocantur birsus ut ait Catholicon.

Ravus, rava, ravum, id est, fulvi color, ut ait Catholicon, et vide ante in fulvus quod ibi aliter dicitur et in eodem Catholicone dicitur ravus talis color, videlicet niger fulvo mixtus, et vide advertenter in birsus quod ibi dicitur.

Rubei colores seu materie eorum sunt et nominantur ut et in hac tabula reperies in locis suis carminium, cinobrium, sinopis, coctinus, cocticus, coctus, vermiculus, herba sandix, herba vaccinium dicta, folium, succus luchet herbe, mellana, sandaraca, minium, sandix, terra seu creta rubea, fenix seu phenix, roseus, et sanguineus; set nota quod colores nominatim in fenix seu phenix in roseus et sanguineus differunt a rubeis, et est de ipsis coloribus sanguineis aliud capitulum generale factum in littera S. in fine.

Sinopis[1] est color magis rubeus quam vermiculus; aliter dicitur cenobrium, aliter mellana, et fit de warancia, et aliter est qui fit ex lacha vel gumma edere, et flore farine bullitis in urina; et aliter sinopis fit ex warancia et lacha suprascripta.

Saffranus, qui reddit colorem croceum, dicitur crocus, et perfectior qui sit Sicilianus, tam in colore quam in sapore, qui vocatur coriscos.

Succus[2] est color trahens ad indicum; alii dicunt esse rubeum minus clarum quam minium et magis clarum quam

---

[1] There was a natural pigment called Sinopia, which is described by Pliny and by Cennini (cap. 38), and which is also mentioned in the Bolognese MS. The sinopis of the text was a red lake.

[2] Succus. In the ' Secreti di Don Alessio Piemontese,' part 2, p. 37, is a recipe for making " Pezzette morelle " from the berries of the Ebuli, or Sambuco Salvatico (Dwarf Elder). The pezzette were pieces of rag which were dipped into the coloured juice of the elder, and other plants, until they absorbed the juice. They were then dried in the shade ; when dry, they were then dipped in a solution of alum and again dried. When they were required for use, a piece was put into a shell, and a little gum-water being poured over it, it was stirred about until the colour was discharged, when the rag was thrown away : the colour left, which was transparent, was used for painting.

sinopis, et aliter vocatur menesch, quod aliter dicitur ipse menech esse succus sambuci.

Succus sambuci est color seu liquor viridis obscurus, qui aliter menech dicitur.

Succus herbarum est color viridis seu liquor cui sepe admiscentur alia ad virides colores faciendos.

Stannum attenuatum album utitur scilicet loco argenti, qui caret argento; et loco auri, qui auro caret, depingitur seu coloratur croce colore, et ipso utitur.

Sandaracum[1] seu sandaracha est color minus rubeus quam vermiculus, et est aliter minium dictus.

Scrupulum   (Sic).

Sandix[2] genus est herbe rubee de qua fit tinctura ut dicit Catholicon.

Sandalica est genus coloris.

Sanguis drachonis[3] est color rubeus obscurus seu est color morellus.

Sillacetus[4] color fit ex violis aridis decoctis, et, expressa aqua, tritis super lapide cum creta alba, id est, gersa.

Safireus color est color quilibet saphiri lapidis assimilans, videlicet proprie inter celestem et rubeum, plus ad celestem trahens colorem quam ad rubeum.

Sanctonicus color aliter fuscus dicitur, qui color niger est.

Sanguineus est color rosarum rubearum colori, ac etiam colorum sanguinis assimilatus, et aliter vide in *roseus* et in aliis locis ibi nominatis.

Scupere, lenire, celare, pingere, figurare, protrahere, designare, quasi idem significant, &c.

Sanguinei colores seu materie eorum sunt et nominantur ut et in hac tabula in locis suis reperies, bullarminium, sanguis

---

[1] Red orpiment is frequently understood by this term. It is used by S. Audemar in the terms mentioned in the text.

[2] Madder.

[3] Dragon's blood.

[4] This is a yellow colour, prepared from the Viola lutea, the Wall-flower, and white chalk or gesso. The name in the text is derived from Pliny.

drachonis, braxillii lignum, lacca, purpura, blacca, sanguis
conchillarum maris, coctus, vermiculus, liquor edere herbe,
gomma edere, sandix herba, vaccinium herba, mellana, morus,
oster maris, rosa, rubi, rubea radix, roseus ; et nota quod
sanguinei colores a rubeis differunt, ut in capitulo generali de
rubeis coloribus dictum est in littera R.

Terreus color fit de cerusa combusta.

Therdote (*sic*) Grece, latine est creta viridis, cujus melior
nascitur in creta cirina.

Terra nigra vel lapis niger mollis est, de quo terendo fit
color niger; et, non terendo, utuntur carpentarii et pictores
protrahendo ad siccum.

Terra seu creta *rubea,* ex qua trita pingitur.

Terra vel creta *viridis* ad pingendum est cujus melior nascitur in creta cirina, et in Greco dicitur Theodote.

Terra vel creta *crocea* est apta ad pingendum et aliter ocra
vel ogra dicitur.

Terra seu creta alba, aliter gersa, aliter gipsus, aliter plastra
dicitur, qua utuntur pelliparii ; et est alia rubea, alia crocea,
alia nigra que de terra vel lapide aut creta nigra trita fit, alia
viridis cujus melior nascitur in creta cirina, et ipsa in Greco
dicitur theodoce.

Tavertinus[1] albus color, seu lapis qui apte rubificatur, si in
ligno braxilii, cum urina, vel lexivio, et alumine misceatur.

Viridis vel viride est color ex diversis factus sicut creta vel
terra viridis et alii ex herbarum succis et metalli facti virides
artificiati.

Violaceus vel violetus color est, qui ex rubeo et nigro, aut
ex rubeo et perso vel lazurio, fit miscendo.

---

[1] Travertine. A stone dug in many parts of Italy, particularly in Siena,
Pisa, Lucca, and near the river Teverone at Tivoli. It is a peculiar kind
of limestone, formed by a deposit from the rivers in these districts. It was
much used in Italy for building, and for making lime. See 1st ' Report of
Commissioners of Fine Arts,' p. 39, and n

Warancia[1] est color seu materia coloris, quia cocta in aqua cum lacha seu gumma edere fit quidam color rubeus sinopis vocatus et etiam ex ipsa warancia fit color rubeus ad tingendum pelles parcium.

Viridis terra seu creta quedam est, cujus melior est que nascitur in creta cirina, et aliter, videlicet in Greco, theodoce dicitur.

Violetus est color, qui ex rubeo et perso, seu azurio, mixtus, maxime ex rubeo claro, id est, lacha, et azurio fino fit.

Vaccinium[2] est herba rubea que temperata cum lacte facit colorem purpureum elegantem, et est quedam alia herba similiter vaccinium vocata que croceum colorem facit.

Vergaut[3] est color qui est quasi ut azurium respectu coloris, non respectu materie.

Viola est flos cujusdem herbe persus seu blauus, quo cum creta alba fit color blauus, et aliter cilacetus color dictus est.

Vermiculus[4] color rubeus est, qui fit ex frondibus silvestribus, ut dicit Catholicon, et Grece ipsum dicunt coctum ; nos vero rubeum vel vermiletum.

Veneda[5] seu neveda est color factus ex mixtura nigri cum modico albi plumbi, et si poni vult in muro, ponatur calx loco dicti albi plumbi.

Vercanda[6] nominatur in capitulo libri colorum 342.

Verblea[7] nominatur in capitulo 345 libri colorum.

---

[1] Vuarantia. The name by which madder was generally known during the middle ages, especially in the western parts of Europe. It was called "Garance" in French, and "Granza" in Spanish, whence the term warantia is apparently derived.

[2] Vaccinium, the purple violet. The latter is the Viola lutea, or Wallflower.

[3] Vergaut. See Eraclius, No. 282. Perhaps Vertbleu.

[4] By Vermiculus is here meant the kermes, or coccus, the "grana" of the Italians.

[5] Veneda, a true grey. See Theophilus, lib. i. cap. vi.

[6] In the number referred to this word appears to be written "Vernide" and "Vercande," a proof that this part of the table of synonymes was written after Le Begue had added his recipes.

[7] Verblea. Probably Vert-bleu, the Verde Azzurro of the Italians, a native carbonate of copper, of a greenish-blue colour, the Armenian stone of Pliny.

Usticium, usticii, genus est coloris, ut dicit Catholicon.

Virides colores seu materie, et metalla eorum, sunt et nominantur ut et in hac tabula in locis suis reperies, arxica mixta succo viridi herbarum, cerosius, caprifolium, gaterice, ceruleus, succus luree herbe, gladius, herba morella, scalda bassa herba, prassis vel prassinus, succus herbarum diversarum, theodote terra vel creta viridis, jas, succus rute herbe mixtus cum viride eris.

Alia Tabula, licet imperfecta et sine inicio.

Quociens ponendi sunt colores in operibus, 147.

Rosam primam, scilicet colorem sic nominatum facere, 124.

Rosam secundam, id est, colorem sic dictum ad differentiam prime facere, 128.

Rosam colorem facere de ligno brixillii et creta alba, 289, 299, 304.

Rose colorem cum brexillio et creta alba, 293.

Rosam facere cum ligno brexillii absque creta alba set cum aliis, 14, 15, 16, 17, 334.

Roseum seu sanguineum colorem facere, 234, 14, 15, 16, 17, 184, 218, 289, 299, 304, 293.

Roseas litteras scribere, 16.

Roseam aquam facere de brexillo, 20.

Rubeam quam facere ad pingendum in telis, 91, 93.

Rubeum succum edere herbe arboribus repentis lacham dictum facere vel habere, 184, 218.

Rubeum minium ex cerusa facere, et cerusam etiam facere, 288.

Rubificare ossa ligna et alia materialia, 51, 335.

Safranum seu crocum finum eligere seu cognoscere et distemperare, 165, 331.

Sanguineus color qui lacha dicitur quomodo de ligno brexillii fit, 309.

Sanguineum vel roseum colorem qui lacha dicitur facere, 184, 218, 332, 11, 12, 13, 16, 37, 100, 181, 309, 332.

Sanguineum vel roseum colorem facere, 14, 15, 16, 17, 18, 218, 289, 299, 293, 334, 309.

Sanguine vel roseo colore tingere materialia, 42, 326.

Scribendo apti colores diversi quomodo de campestribus floribus fiunt, 212.

Scribere litteras aureas non cum auro set cum colore, 25.

Scripturam argenteam absque argento facere, 321.

Scripturam auream et argenteam absque auro et argento facere, 324.

Scribere litteras argenteas de petula argenti, 24, 320.

Scribere litteras auro molito, 217, 219, 320, 323, 328, 336, 339, 310.

Scripturas et picturas de auro molito facere, 310.

Scripturas auro, argento, et lotono mollitis facere, 312.

Scripturam stanneam de stanno molito facere, 185.

Scribere litteras roseas, 16.

Scribere virides litteras, 28, 199, 221.

Sculpa opera lignea que corio, panno, nec pergameno, cooperiuntur, ut rotunde ymagines, selle equestres, scabella, et alia talia opera pingere, 140.

Sellas equestres, scabellas, ymagines rotundas et alia opera lignea sculpa que pergameno nec drapo cooperiri possunt propter sculpturas in ipsis factas pingere, 140.

Senum decrepitorum et juvenum capillis et barbis colorem aptum facere, 132.

Sigilli formam facere, 49.

Sinopis quis color sit, 179.

Sinopidem de mellana colorem facere, 182.

Sinopidem ex lacha et Warancia facere, 183.

Spongia vitellum ovi parare, 270.

Stanneam scripturam de stanno molito facere, 185.

Stannum atenuatum, id est, petulas stanni facere, 143, 205.

Stannum atenuatum cum petula auri fini aurare, 105, 142.

Stanneas petulas in opere ponere et eas coloribus oleo temperatis pingere, 145.

Stannum tenuatum seu petulas stanni colore verzini seu brixilli pingere, 101.

Stanni petulas vel folia seu laminas colorare taliter quod aurate videantur, 144, 202, 205, 206, 207, 208, 209.

Stampnence folium colorem purpureum in Anglia Wormam dictum distemperare seu facere, 162, 164, 166.

Succum rubeum edre herbe arboribus repentis lacham dictum habere, 184, 218.

Tabulas seu laminas stagni tenuatas que petule vocantur facere, 143, 205.

Tabulas seu laminas stanni tenuatas que petule vocantur colorare taliter quod aurate videantur, 144, 202, 205, 206, 207, 208, 209.

Tabulas seu laminas stanni tenuatas que petule vocantur ponere in opere et eas coloribus oleo temperatis pingere, 145.

Tabulas et asseres ligneas et ligna aptare ad pingendum, 268, 269.

Tabulas altarium et alias pingere, 131.

Tabulas et ostia et alia lignea opera cum coloribus oleo temperatis pingere, 138.

Tellam lineam aut canapinam preparare ut possit in ipsa pingi et aurum poni, 280.

Tellas rubea aqua pingere, 91, 93.

Tellas violacea aqua pingere, 95.

Tellas aqua indica vel persea pingere, 97.

Tellas viridi aqua pingere, 90, 94, 98, 99, 110, 199.

Tellas aqua nigra pingere, 89.

Tingere quelibet materialia in quolibet colore, 326, 41, 40, 46, 199, 42.

Temperamenta colorum in libris ponendorum facere et de quibus liquoribus, 197, 306, 325, 346, 347.

Temperare colores qui cum goma seu aqua gomata tempe-
rari non possunt, quo modo fit, 146.

Terreas fialas preciosa pictura bituminis vitri facta ornare,
213.

Tingere in sanguineo colore materialia, 42, 326.

Tingere pelles in viride, 46, 199, 326.

Tingere in viridi ligna ossa tellam et alia materialia in quocumque colore, 41.

Tollere litteras de carta et papiro, 2, 17, 21, 34.

Translucidam picturam facere, 148.

Temperamentum colorum tam infectivorum seu transluci-
dorum quam corpulentorum vel simplicium seu materialium
facere ad eos ponendum in opere seu stampno et plumbo vel
super metallis aliis stampnatis vel plumbeatis aut simplicibus
per se videlicet non stampnatis nec plombeatis nec aliquo alio
ex metallis co-opertis, 368.[1]

Vasa figuli id est terrea plumbeare seu vitreare vitro plumbi,
259.

Vasorum fictilium pingendorum picturam vitri nigri facere,
230.

Vasorum fictilium, id est, terreorum pingendorum picturam
albi vitri facere, 229, 233.

Vasorum fictilium depingendorum picturam viridis vitri facere, 228, 232.

Vasorum fictilium pingendo picturam vitri nimis virentis
facere, 231, 234.

Vasa fracta terrea et lapides integrare, 8.

Venedam alibi venedam colorem facere, 126, 330.

Vernicem liquidam, id est glutinam pro pictoribus facere,
341, 138, 139, 210.

Viride eris facere, 8, 43, 44, 152, 155, 156, 157, 159, 201,
273, 287, 300, 331.

---

[1] Iste liber non est completus usque ad illum numerum.—[Marginal note
by author.]

Viride eris pulcherrimam facere, 45, 161.

Viride eris colorem cum sale facere, 150.

Viride eris distemperare et facere, 152, 331.

Viride eris subtiliare et liquidum facere, 160.

Viridi eris mixturas aliorum colorum in fine capituli seu post capitulum, 159.

Viridem colorem facere cum corpore et non corrosivum sed dulcem, quamvis in ipso sit de viride eris quod de se corrosivum est, 301, 331.

Virides litteras scribere cum colore cum viride eris facere, 28, 331.

Viridem aquam ex viride eris et aliis facere ad pingendum in tellis, 90, 94, 98, 99, 331.

Viridi eris tingere pelles, 46, 331.

Viridia cum viride eris et aliorum facere ligna ossa telam filum et alia materialia, 40, 81.

Viridem alium quam eris facere, 158, 199, 221, 227, 331, 395, 398.

Virides litteras scribere cum colore non de ere, 199, 221, 227, 331, 295, 158.

Viridem aquam vel colorem non eris ad scribendum facere, 199, 221, 227, 331, 395, 158.

Viridem aquam aliter quam de viride eris facere ad pingendum in telis, 110, 199, 221, 227, 331, 295, 158.

Viridem colorem aliter quam de ere facere ad detingendum pelles, 199, 110, 221.

Viridem colorem non de ere facere pro operando in diversis, 295, 331, 227, 199, 110, 221, 158.

Viridem colorem absque ere ad que volueris depingenda facere, 227, 295, 331, 227, 199, 110, 158, 221.

Viride terreum distemperare, 265.

Viride vitrum ad vasa fictilia depingenda facere, 228, 232.

Virentem nimis vitrum ad vasa fictilia depingenda facere, 231, 234.

Vitri invencio, 255.

Vitrum flexibilem facere invenit quidam qui ideo jussu imperatoris, decapitatus fuit, 256.[1]

Vitriare vitro plombi, id est, plombeare vasa figuli id est terrea, 259.

Vitri bitumine preciosa tinctura facta terreas fialas vitriare
et ornare, 213.

Vitrum album ad vasa fictilia pingenda facere, 229, 233.

Vitrum album et de diversis coloribus facere, 257.

Vitrum viride ad vasa fictilia, id est, figuli pingénda facere,
228, 232.

Vitrum nimis virentem ad vasa figuli seu fictilia depingenda
facere, 231, 234.

Vitrum nigrum ad vasa fictilia depingenda facere, 230.

Vitrum pingere, 272.

Vitrum coloribus colorare et ipsum de plumbo facere, 271.

Vitreas et terreas fialas auro decorare, 215.

Vermiculum facere quod est color rubeus, 174, 175.

Vermiculi mixto cum minio, 177.

Vernicium seu vernicem liquidam vel glutinam facere est
post numerum 138 ; item est in numero 139, 210.

Verniciare aurum ne perdat colorem, 267.

Verniciare opera depicta, 147.

Verzinum facere colorem, id est brixillii pro tenendo ad ponendum in opere quando necesse est, 202.

Verzini colorem facere proponendo super argento aut super
stanno tenuato, 101.

Violetam aquam facere ad pingendum in telis, 95.

Vitellum ovi spongia parare, 270.

Viscum seu gluten vel collam de corio bovis vel vacce facere, 186.

Viscum casei seu collam aut gluten facere, 127, 163.

Warencia colore rubeo pelles tingere, 258.

---

[1] Malum premium.—[Marginal note by author.]

Vultum et nudorum corporum colores, scilicet exedram vel posam et alios facere, 133, 317, 344.

Worniam colorem sic in Anglia nominatum qui est aptus ad tingendum lannas est purpureus, aliter folium dictus distemperare, 162, 164.

————

Tabula ad reperiendum quodlibet capitulum arcium fabulis et aurifabulis et rerum et accidencium illis conferencium nec non operum exerciciorum que et contingencium eorum.

Aqua cavans ferrum, 64.

Arma et alia ferramenta conservare a rubigine, 69, 348.

Attribucio cujuslibet ex metallis alicui ex septem planetis continetur post numerum, 46.

Aurare cuprum fellis pinguedine seu liquore, 226.

Aurare auricalcum, 249.

Aurare metalla fusilia, 252.

Aurare ferrum, 237, 238.

Auraturam facere, 253.

Auraturam metalli perditam recuperare.

Aurei coloris ferrum facere, 67.

Aureo colore metallos colorare, 66.

Auricalcum aurare, 249.

Auricalcum facere, 49.

Auricalcum seu lathonum solidare, 65.

Auricalcum seu lathonum pulcrum facere sicut aurum, 82.

Aurum et argentum fondere, 365.

Argentum et aurum fondere, 365.

Azarium et ferrum temperare, 57, 58, 61, 62, 83, 84, 223, 333, 364.

————

EXPERIMENTS UPON COLOURS.

1. Know that gold letters are thus written with the following water. Take of sulphur vivum, of the inner bark of the pomegranate, of alum, salt, and gold dust (?), as much as you like, and liquid gum water and a little saffron. Mix, and write.

2. *To erase black letters upon paper.*—Make a water from the following things. Take nitre, and Roman vitriol, of each one pound, and distil them in an alembic, and a clear water will be produced; with this water slightly moisten a sponge, and rub the letters with it.[1]

3. *To make fine azure.*—Take plates of fine silver, and put them into a new jar; cover the jar closely with a tile, and place it in the skins of the grapes for 40 days; then scrape off the efflorescence, which you will find upon the plates, and which is fine azure.

4. *Also azure which is not fine is made in another way.*—Put vinegar into a glass bottle, the mouth of which must be well covered with tenacious earth, and let it be buried in horse dung for a month, and afterwards dry it in the sun.

5. *To make azure.*—Take a vase of pure copper, and put into it a colour [pigment] made of white marble (some recipes say quicklime) so as to half fill it. Afterwards fill it up with very strong vinegar, cover it over, and put in a warm place, or under dung, for a month, and you will find a blue good both for panels and walls.

6. *For the same.*—Take a new glazed jar, or a vase of silver, and put into it plates of very pure silver, as many as you like, rubbed over[2] with good wine, and place the jar under the refuse

---

[1] The produce of this distillation is nitric acid.

[2] From *sborfato*, a Bolognese word.

EXPERIMENTA DE COLORIBUS.

————————

1. Nota quod auree littere scribuntur sic, cum ista aqua ; accipe sulphur vivum, et corticem interiorem mali granati, aluminis, saltis, et de pluvia auri, tantum quantum vis, et aquam gummi liquide, et modicum de croco, et misce, et scribe.

2. *Ad delendum litteras nigras de carta.*—Fac aquam de[1] infrascriptis rebus. Accipe salniterum, et vitriolum Romanum, de quolibet libram unam, et distilla per alembicum, et erit clara aqua, et cum ipsa aqua balnea spongiam modicum, et de ipsa frica litteras.

3. *Ad faciendum azurium finum.*—Recipe laminas argenti fini, et pone in olla nova, et cooperiatur bene cum tegula, et pone ollam in vinariis uvarum per dies xl[a], et flos quem repereris super laminas radde, quod est azurium finum.

4. *Item aliter azurum non finum fit.*—Ponatur acetum in ampulla vitrea, cujus orificium bene cooperiatur cum terra tenaci, et sepeliatur in fimo equino per unum mensem, et postea siccetur ad solem.

5. *Ad faciendum azurrum.*—Recipe ampullam de puro cupro et pone intus colorem de albo marmore, ita ut sit dimedia ; et in aliis receptis dicitur calx viva. Postea imple de aceto fortissimo, et cooperiri, et pone in loco calido, vel sub fimo, per mensem, et invenies azurrum bonum, in ligno, et in pariete.

6. *Ad idem.*—Habeas ollam novam incretatam, vel vas argenti, et immitte laminas argenti purissimi, quot vis, brofatas bono vino ; et mitte vas in profundo viaziarum,[2] per dies

———————————————————————————————

[1] Id est infrascriptum et scribitur ut supra causa brevitatis.—[Marginal note by author.] [2] Vindemiarum ?

of the grapes for 36 or 40 days ; and afterwards scrape or shake off into a clean vase the efflorescence which you find round and about the plates, which efflorescence is preserved upon the plates, in the same manner as rust upon iron, and verdigris upon plates or in vases of brass.

7. *To make azure.*—Take very thin plates of fine silver, as many as you like.   You must also have a glazed earthen jar, with a cover; and on the middle of the under part of this cover there must be a small hook, to which you must hang the silver plates with a silver thread, so that they may not touch each other ; and put very strong vinegar into the said jar, so as not to touch the plates, but to reach near them ; and close carefully the said cover with a piece of linen and with glue, and put the jar for 15 days under dung, or over a slow fire or under the refuse of grapes.   Afterwards scrape off the azure which you find upon the plates, and if you want more azure, do the same with the plates as you did before.

8. *Green from copper* or brass is made in the same manner with plates of brass, as was directed to be done with silver plates to make blue.

9. *To make perfect azure.*—Take an earthen jar with a cover similar to that in which ceruse is made, and take sheets or plates of fine tin, wetted with strong vinegar, and sprinkled over with powdered white quicklime, place the vase, with the aforesaid plates, in the dung of sheep or horses, for 10 days, and then scrape off the efflorescence which you find on the tin plates, and if you want more of it, put back the jar with the plates as before.

10. *To make perfect ultramarine azure.*—Take of lapis lazuli as much as you like, and grind it very fine upon a porphyry slab. Then make a cake or pastille of the following ingredients, namely, if there is one pound of lapis lazuli, take vi. oz. of Greek pitch, ij. oz. of mastic, ij. oz. of wax, ij. oz. of black pitch, ij. oz. of gum from the pine, 1 oz. of oil of spike or of linseed, and ½ oz. of turpentine.   All these things must boil in a pipkin until they are nearly liquefied, afterwards strain them into cold water, and take what drops into the water through the strainer, and knead

xxxvi. vel xl^{ta}; postea excucias seu raddas in vas mundum
florem quem inveneris in cercuita laminarum, qui flos conser-
vatur super ipsis laminis, sicut fit rubigo super ferro, et viride
eris super laminas vel in vasis eris.

7. *Ad faciendum azurrum.*—Recipe laminas argenti fini quot
vis subtilissimas, et habeas vas terre vitriatum cum coperculo,
et in parte inferiori dicti coperculi sit unus uncinellus in medio,
cui suspendas laminas suprascriptas cum filo argenteo, taliter
quod lamine non se tangant invicem; et in vase mitte acetum
fortissimum, tantum quod non tangat ipsas laminas, set stet
prope; et optura bene dictum coperculum cum pecia lini, et
cum cola, et pone vas sub fimo per xv^{cim} dies, vel ad ignem
temperatum, vel sub vinariis; postea radde azurum quod inveneris super laminas, et, si plus velis, fac iterum de ipsis laminis ut fecisti.

8. *Ad viride rami seu eris.*—Fiat eo modo de laminis eris, ut
supra dictum est de argenteis pro azurro.

9. *Ad faciendum azurrum perfectum.*—Accipe vas terrenum,
cum coperculo tali, ut illud de quo fit cerusia, et habe laminas
seu plactas fini stagni, balneatas aceto forti, et sparsas alba calce
viva pulverizata, et pone vas, cum laminis suprascriptis in ipso,
in fimo pecorum vel equorum, per decem dies; postea radde
florem quem invenies super laminis, et, si plus vis, repone vas
cum laminis, ut prius.

10. *Ad faciendum azurrum ultramarinum perfectum.*—Recipe de lapide lazulli quantum vis, et teres super lapide porfirico
subtilissime, et fac massam seu pastilum ex rebus insertis;
videlicet, si dictus lapis est libra una accipe oncias vj. picis
Grece, oncias ij. masticis, oncias ij. cere, oncias ij. picis nigre,
oncias ij. gummi pini, onciam j. olei spici vel lini, et onciam ½
trementinæ, que omnia buliant in uno pignatello, usque dum
quasi sint strinta [strutta?], et postea cola in aqua frigida, et tolle
quod cadit in aqua, quod est celatum, et deducas, et misces bene

*

and mix it well with the powder of the lapis lazuli until it is
well incorporated ; and so let it stand for viij. days ; and the
longer it stands, the better and finer will be the azure.   Afterwards work this paste in your hands, throwing it into water, and
keep the first water by itself, and the second by itself, and the
third also by itself.   And when you see the azure sink to the
bottom, pour off the water, and keep the azure.

11. *To make fine lake.*—Take the ashes of oak,[1] and make
a ley, and boil in it clippings of fine scarlet of rubea de grana[2]
until the colour is extracted from the clippings, and then strain
the ley with the colour through a linen cloth.   Afterwards take
some more ley, similar to what you first took, and heat it, and
put into it some finely powdered roche alum, and let it stand
until the alum is dissolved.   Then strain it through the strainer
with the other liquor or ley in which the clippings were put, and
immediately the ley will be coagulated, and make a lump or
mass, which you must stir well.   Remove it afterwards from the
vase, and lay it on a new hollow brick, which will absorb the
ley, and the lake will be left dry.   You must afterwards take
it off the brick and keep it for use.

12. *Also to make lake.*—Take 1 oz. of lac, which is a certain
gum called lac, or take some of the grana with which scarlet
cloths are dyed, and steep it in ley, or in urine, so as to
cover over the lac, or the grana, and let it boil for half an
hour on a moderate fire without smoke, namely, with smith's
charcoal, stirring it continually with a stick whilst it boils.   Afterwards take $\frac{1}{2}$ an oz. of roche alum and $\frac{1}{2}$ an oz. of sal gem,
and grind them well with ley, and put them into the vase before
it ceases to boil.   Then remove the vase from the fire, and let
it cool.   Afterwards take a glazed jar, and a little urine, or
strong ley, and empty the before-mentioned jar into it, and stir
or shake it every evening and every morning, and after 15 days

---

[1] The Turkey oak, the Cerro of the Italians.
[2] Strictly speaking, " Rubea " means madder, and " Grana " kermes ;
but as it appears that at this period the kermes was generally used in

illud per dictum pulverem lapidis lazuli, donec bene incorporentur omnia, et sic stent per viii° dies, et, quanto plus stete-
rint, tanta azurrum erit melius, et magis finum ; et postea deduc hanc massam per manus, proiciendo cum aqua, et primam
aquam serva per se, et secundam per se, et tertiam per se.   Et,
postquam videris azurrum descensum ad fundum, proice aquam
et retine azurrum.

11. *Ad faciendum lacham finam.*—Tolle cineres ligni cerri,
vel roboris, et fac lecivium, et in ipso fac bulire cimaturam
scarlate fine rubee de grana, tantum quod ex dicta cimatura
extractus sit color ; postea ipsum lessivium, cum dicta cimatura, colla per pannum lineum ; postea accipe de alio lexivio
simili suprascripti quod prius accepisti, et calefac, et pone in
ipso de alumine roche trito subtiliter, et permitte donec alumen
sit fusum, postea cum dicto colatorio cola ipsum in dicta alia
collatura vel lexivio, in quo stetit cymatura, et subito dictum
lessivium stringetur, et faciet unam bussaturam seu massam,
quam mistica bene, et postea trahe ipsam de vase, et pone in
madono concavo novo, qui bibet lessivium, et remanebit sicca
dicta lacha, quam postea trahe de madone et serva usui.

12. *Item ad faciendum lacham.*—Tolle unciam unam lache,
que est quedam gumma dicta lacha, vel accipe de grana de qua
tinguntur scarlate, et pone in lissivio vel urina viri, tanta que
coperiat lacham seu granam, et fac bullire per mediam horam
ad ignem temperatum, absque fumo, videlicet cum carbonibus
fabrorum, deducendo cum baculo semper dum bulit.   Postea
tolle onciam $\frac{1}{2}$ aluminis roche, et onciam $\frac{1}{2}$ salis geme, et mole
bene cum lexivio, et postea pone in vase suprascripto antequam
cesset bulire.   Postea leva vas ab igne, et permitte frigidari.
Postea tolle unum vas vitriatum, et unum paucum urini hominis, vel de lessivio fortissimo, et mitte simul de super vase, et
deduc vel agita omni sero et omni mane, et post xv^{cim} dies cola

---

dyeing scarlet, and as the recipes for making this " Lacca di Cimatura"
generally direct the clippings of cloth dyed with kermes to be used, it is
probable that the kermes was meant in the present case, and not madder.
*

strain it by means of a linen bag placed upon a new tile, which
will immediately dry the lake, which will remain in the bag,
and which you may keep for use, and when you wish to use it,
grind it well upon a slab, and work with it.   And if you like
strain the water again, as before directed ; and, if you wish to
make more lake, boil the said water, and take more of the
before-mentioned ingredients, and do as before, and it will be
finer than the first mentioned above.

13. *To make very fine lake.*—Take clippings of very fine
scarlet of rubea de grana, and put them into a vase, with sufficient urine to cover the clippings to the depth of one or
two fingers' breadths, and let it stand for some days, until
the clippings are decomposed, which you may know by touching
them with your hand or your fingers.   Afterwards take them
out of the vase, without squeezing them, and put them on a
clean stone, and allow the liquor to flow out by itself.   Then
grind it well upon a stone, and strain it through a thin piece of
linen, and you will have fine lake, to use upon paper, parchment, and upon primed wooden panels, but not on walls.

14. *To make a fine rose colour.*—Take fine brexillium, and
scrape it fine, and take strong ley made with the ashes of oak,
and make it boil, and pour it over the said verzino into a glazed
earthen saucer, so as to cover the brexillium, and let it stand
for an hour.   Then take egg-shells, pound them well, and
grind them very fine on a porphyry slab with clear water, and
lay them on a new hollow brick, that the water may be absorbed.   Afterwards put them into a glazed earthen jar, and
pound up some roche alum, and mix with the powdered egg-
shells ; afterwards strain the ley in which the verxillium is put,
and pour the ley which is dyed red with the verzilium upon
the egg-shells, and mix, that the whole may be incorporated
together ; and afterwards dry the lake, not in the sun, but on
a hollow brick, straining it through a linen cloth, and you will
have a perfect rose colour.

15. *Also, to make a colour deeper than rose colour.*—Take
1 oz. of scraped verzino and put it in a glazed saucer, with

cum saculo telle lini, posito super tegula nova, que subito sicca-
bit lacham, que remansit in saculo, quam serva ad usum ; et
cum voles uti, mole bene super lapide, et operare. Et, si vis,
recola dictam aquam, prout dictum est ; et si plus volueris
facere, fac bulire dictam aquam, et accipe de novo de rebus
supradictis, et fac ut prius, et erit ista finior quam suprascripta.

13. *Ad faciendum lacham finissimam.*—Accipe cimaturam
scarlate fine rubee de grana, et pone in vase cum tanta urina
hominis, que cooperiat cimaturam quantum est grossitudo digiti
unius vel duorum, et stet per plures dies, donec dicta cimatura
sit bene putrefacta, cujus putrefactionem cognosces tangendo
cum manu vel digitis. Postea trahe ipsam de vase absque
ipsam exprimere, et pone super mondo lapide et dimitte ipsam
per se excolare. Postea mole ipsam bene super lapide, postea
cola per peciam subtilem lini, et habebis lacham finam pro
operendo in cartis et in tabulis gissatis, set non in muro.

14. *Ad faciendum colorem rosete fine.*—Accipe berxillium
finum, et rade subtiliter, et accipe de lessivio forti facto de
cineribus cerri, quod fac bullire, et ipsum mitte desuper dicto
versino, in una scutella terre vitreata tantum quod cooperiat
verxillium, et stet per horam ; postea accipe corticas ovorum,
et trita bene, et molle super lapide porfirico cum aqua clara
subtiliter, et pone super madono concavo novo ut aqua de-
cicetur. Postea pone in scutella vitriata, deinde pista de
alumine roche, et misce cum dictis corticis tritis, et postea cola
lissivium in quo est verxillium, et lessivium illud rubefactum
a verzilio mitte desuper dictas corticas, et misce ut incorporentur omnia, et postea desica, non ad solem, set super madono
concavo, colando per tellam, et habebis perfectam rosetam.

15. *Ad faciendum etiam colorem plusquam de roxeta.*—Accipe
onciam ½ verzini rasi, et pone in scutella vitriata cum tanta

*

sufficient urine to cover it, and make it boil, on a charcoal fire, for an hour; then, before you take it off the fire,
add 1 oz. of honey, and mix it; then remove it from the fire,
and leave it so until the next morning, and you will have a fine
rose colour.

16. *To make a rose colour for drawing letters.*—Take red
brexillium, and roche alum ground upon a stone, and put them
both together in whipped white of egg, and let it stand for a
day and a night, and you will have what was mentioned.

17. *Item, to make a rose colour.*—Put into a glazed saucer
1 oz. of scraped verzino, and pour in enough urine to cover
the verzino and the ingredients which are to be added afterwards. Then add 1 oz. of white marble, ground upon a stone
with water, and dried, and ½ oz. of roche alum in powder;
and when putting the before-mentioned ingredients into the
saucer, let the last thing which is added be the marble dust.
Do not mix it until it has stood in the sun long enough for the
marble to imbibe the colour; and if it should dry in the sun
before the marble has absorbed the colour, add to it some
more of the same urine as before, and let it stand in the sun
until the marble is sufficiently coloured, and it will become
red, or rose coloured. Afterwards strain it through a linen
cloth, and dry it upon a baked stone or brick, and keep it
for use.

18. *To make flowers and letters of gold.*—Take sal ammoniac, and temper with pure water; then write with that water
and draw flowers, and, when they are dry, lay gold leaf upon
them.

19. *To make the colour purpurinus.*—Take of sal ammoniac
1 oz., quicksilver 1 oz., sulphur vivum 1 oz., tin 1 oz.; melt the
tin over the fire, then pour the quicksilver into it, and allow it
to stand for a short time; next grind the sal ammoniac and
sulphur together, and add them to the melted tin and quicksilver; put them all together into a glass flask, so that it may
be filled only up to the neck, and then cover the flask all over
with chalk, of the thickness of one finger's breadth; place it

urina hominis que cooperiatur, et fac bulire ad ignem carbonum per horam ; postea, antequam leves ab igne, onciamque
j. mellis, et misce, et leva ab igne, et dimitte sic usque de
mane sequenti, et habebis colorem rosete fine.

16. *Ad faciendum colorem roxeum pro scribendo litteras.*—
Accipe vexilium roxeum, et alumen roxie tritum super lapide,
et pone omnia in clara ovi spongiata, et stet per diem et noctem, et habebis quod dictum est.

17. *Item ad faciendum colorem roxaceum.*—Pone in scutella
vitriata onciam i. verzini rasi, et pone tantam urinam pueri
que cooperiri possit dictum verzinum, et alia que secuntur ;
postea impone onciam i. marboris albi, triti super lapide cum
aqua clara, et siccati, et onciam ½ aluminis roche triti, et ultimum quod ponetur in dicta scutella, ponendo in ipsa ea que
dicta sunt, sit dictus marmor tritus ; et non misceas, donec
steterit ad solem tantum quod marmor ceperit colorem, et si
sicaretur ad solem antequam marmor cepisset colorem, pone
iterum de simili urina ut prius, et stet ad solem donec marmor
ceperit colorem, et devenerit rubeus seu roxaceus. Postea
cola per pannum lineum, et fac siccari cum lapide cocto seu
madono, et serva ad usum.

18. *Ad faciendum flores et litteras auri.*— Accipe sal armoniacum, et distempera in aqua pura, et de illa aqua scribe, et
fac flores, et cum desicate sint, pone desuper folium auri.

19. *Ad faciendum purpurinum colorem.*—Accipe sal armoniacum onciam i., argentum vivium onciam i., sulphur vivium
onciam i., Stangnum onciam i., et fonde dictum Stagnum ad
ignem, et in ipso mitte argentum vivum, et dimitte stare aliquantulum, et mole dictum sal armoniacum et sulphur simul ;
et pone in dicto stagno liquefacto, in quo est argentum vivum,
et omnia pone in ampula vitri, quod ex ipsis impleatur solum
usque ad collum, et sic ipsa ampula, circumlinita de creta

in a small furnace, in a hole at the top of the furnace made for this purpose, so that the flask may only be half way through the hole, and then, by means of a hole made in the side of the furnace, make a strong fire in it, and cover the mouth of the flask with a plate of iron, pierced, in order that the vapour may escape from the flask, and continue the fire strongly until the fumes cease to come from the flask. Then remove it from the fire, let it cool, break the flask, and take your purpurinus; and when you want to use it, temper it with gum-water or with whipped white of egg.

20. *To make a rose-coloured water for shading figures and other things.*—Put scraped verzino into whipped white of egg, and let it stand for a day. Then strain and squeeze through a cloth, and temper what passes through with pure water: shade whatever you like with it, both on parchment and on paper I think that the colour will not be extracted from the said brexillium or verzino, unless a little roche alum be added.

21. *To erase letters on parchment without injury to the paper.* —Take a hare's skin and dress it, and salt it down, afterwards dry it over the smoke of a fire, and reduce it to powder; put some of this powder upon the letters which you wish to erase, and rub them with pumice-stone, and the letters will be erased without injury to the paper.

22. *To make letters which will seem to be of gold.*—Make a small hole in a hen's egg, and take out the white only, and fill the egg with quicksilver; close up the opening carefully, place it under hot dung for 40 days. Then remove the quicksilver, and take 1 oz. of crystal and reduce it to a very fine powder, and incorporate it with the yolk of the egg. Then, with this composition smear the paper, or whatever else you want, and when it is dry rub gold or silver upon it, and it will remain of the colour of gold or silver.

23. *That letters may seem to be of gold.*—Mix sal nitrinum with water and write upon parchment, and illuminate it with juice of celandine and warm the paper, and the letters will appear like gold.

grossa, per grosseciam unius digiti, quam pone in parva fornace per foramen fornacis superius, propter hoc factum, ita quod dicta ampula descendat in dicto foramine solum usque ad medium ampule; et postea, per aliud foramen factum a latere dicte fornacis, immitte, et fac ignem fortem, et cooperi orificium ampule cum lamina ferri forata, ut exeat fumus ampule, et continua fortem ignem usque quo fumus ampule cessaverit exire, et tunc leva ab igne, et dimitte frigidari, et rumpe ampulam, et accipe purpurinum, et ipsum, cum vis operari, distempera cum aqua gummata, vel cum clara ovi spongiata.

20. *Ad faciendum aquam roxeaceam pro umbrando ymagines et alia.*—Pone de verxino raso, in albumine ovi spongiato, et stet per diem. Postea cola per telam, stringendo, et quod exierit distempera cum aqua pura, et umbra quod vis, in carta, et papiro. Credo quod color non exibit a dicto brexillo, seu verzino, nisi ponatur de alumine roze.

21. *Ad delendum litteras de carta absque lesione carte.*—Accipe cossam leporis, et decoria ipsam, et postea in salla, et desicca ad fumum ignis, et pulveriza, et posito de ipso pulvere super litteris quas raddere vis, trahe desuper pumicem, et radetur absque lesione carte.

22. *Ad faciendum litteras, que videantur esse de auro.*—Fac in ovo galine foramen parvum, et extrahe albumen solum, et postea reple ovum argento vivo, et claude bene foramen ovi, et ipsum pone sub fimo calido per dies xl[a]; postea extrahe argentum vivum, et accipe onciam i. cristalli, et pulveris subtilissime, et incorpora cum dicto vitello. Dein cum dicta pasta unge cartam aut quidquid vis, et, cum siccaverit, frica desuper cum auro vel argento, et remanebunt coloris auri vel argenti.

23. *Ut littere videantur de auro.*—Incorpora salnitrinum cum aqua, et scribe in carta, et inlumina cum suco celidonie, et calefac, et videbuntur de auro.

24. *To make gold or silver letters.*—Take sal ammoniac, the juice of pounded vervain mallows, and gum arabic, mix all these together, temper them with urine so as to make them rather liquid; afterwards make the mixture liquid with gum-arabic. Then write whatever you like with this liquid and let it dry. Then breathe upon it well with your mouth, so that the surface of it may be rather damp, and lay gold leaf upon it, and press it on lightly with a piece of cotton.

25. *To make letters of silver.*—Take three parts of quick-silver and a fourth part of tin, melt them together, and let the mixture cool; then grind it on a stone and temper it with a solution of gum-arabic; write with it and let it dry, and polish it with the tooth of a dog or other animal, fit for the purpose, and the letters will be beautiful and brilliant.

26. *To make letters appear like gold.*—Take the horn of a goat, cut it into very small pieces, and distil it in an alembic, and keep the water which comes over, in a glazed jar, in the sun for some days; afterwards write with this water, and the letters will appear like gold.

27. *To erase letters from parchment.*—Take the juice of an orange and dip cotton or sponge in it, and rub it lightly upon the letters, and it will erase them perfectly. But as the parchment will be wetted and made soft, it must be rendered dry and white in the following manner :—Take white lime in powder and mix it with clear water, and afterwards strain through a piece of white linen, dip cotton in the water which has been strained and dab it upon the parchment where it is soft, and it will become white and firm. I think it would be better to dip the cotton in dry lime, and not to wet it.

28. *To make a green ink for writing.*—Take of good vinegar oz. ij., sal ammoniac oz. ij., common salt oz. ij., brass filings oz. ij., put them all together in a glass flask for six days, and it will make a green ink, which you must strain and keep for use.

24. *Ad faciendum litteras aureas vel argenteas.*—Accipe sal armoniacum, et succum alci pisti, et gumirabicum, et hec simul distempera, et postea distempera cum urina, ut sit liquida aliquantulum ; postea perfecte liquidam facies cum aqua gumirabici, postea scribe cum hoc que vis, et permitas sicari, et postea flaa desuper cum ore multum bene, ut aliquantulum humectetur superficies, et pone desuper folium auri, super quo deduc leviter bombacem.[1]

25. *Ad faciendum litteras argenti.*—Accipe argentum vivum per tres partes, et per quartam de stagno, et fonde simul, et permitte frigidari, et molle super lapide, et distempera cum aqua gumi arabici, et scribe cum hoc, et permitte siccari, et polias cum dente canis vel alterius animalis ad hoc apto, et erunt pulcre littere et lucentes.

26. *Ut littere videantur de auro.*—Accipe cornu yrci, et ipsum incide minutissime, et distilla per alembicum, et aquam que exibit tene in vase vitriato ad solem per aliquot dies, et postea cum ipsa aqua scribe et littere videbuntur de auro.

27. *Ad delendum litteras de carta.*—Accipe succum pomi ranzii, et in ipso balnea bombacem vel spongiam, et frica leviter super litteras, et optime dellet, et quia carta libri balneatur, et efficitur mollis, remediari debet isto modo, ut sit sicca et alba. Accipe florem calcis, distemperate cum aqua clara, postea cola cum pecia lini alba, et de aqua alba que exibit balnea bombacem, quam ducas super cartam ubi mollis erat, et fiet alba et solida. Credo quod melius esset intingere bombacem in calce sicca et non madida.

28. *Ad faciendum aquam viridem ad scribendum.*—Accipe bonum acetum oncias ii., salis armoniaci ii., salis communis oncias ii., limature eris oncias ii., pone omnia in ampula vitrea per vj. dies, et fiet aqua viridis, quam cola et reserva.

[1] Bombacem, id est spongiam ut jam supra vel lanam. [Marginal note by author.]

29. *To make excellent azure.*—Take of sal ammoniac oz. iij., and of verdigris oz. vi., mix them together and make them into a paste with solution of tartar, and put them into a glass jar, which you must stop up, and lute, and place in warm dung, and let it stand there for some days, and when you take it up you will find the green changed to excellent azure.

30. *For the same.*—Take of alum scagliola one part, of vinegar two parts ; grind them together upon a slab, and make them boil a little in a glass or other vase, and put them into a glass flask and bury them in dung for five days or more, until you see it is become of a blue colour.[1]

31. *Good ink is thus made.*—Take 1½ lb. of pounded galls, soak them in warm rain water, or warm wine or vinegar, of the quantity of 10 phials, and so let it stand for a day or more ; then boil it until the said water, wine, or vinegar is reduced to one-third, and let it be taken off the fire and a phial or two of wine or vinegar be immediately added, and let so much water be added as was boiled away from the said mixture, and let them all be put on the fire again. When the mixture begins to boil let it be removed from the fire ; when it is only just warm strain it, and add to it 1½ lb. of gum-arabic in powder and 1 lb. of Roman vitriol, and mix the whole together.

32. *If you wish to make a gold or silver colour for writing.*—Take talc and put it into a glass vase, and pour over it good vinegar made from white wine, and add mercury to it, namely half an oz., and 1 oz. of fish-glue, and put it on the fire, that it may become liquid like water, and write with it, and it will make silver letters. If you wish to make golden letters, add a little saffron.

33. *Cement for joining parchment is thus made.*—Take gum-arabic and whipped white of egg, dissolve the gum in this white of egg and let it dry in the sun, and when you wish to use it wet the edge of the piece with your tongue and lips and

---

[1] The colouring ingredient seems wanting in this recipe.

29. *Ad faciendum azurrum optimum.*—Accipe salis armoniaci oncias iii., viridis eris oncias vi., et misce simul, et con-
ficiantur cum aqua tartari ad modum unguenti, et ponantur in
ampula vitrea, que obturetur, et luctetur, et ponatur in fimo
calido, et stet per aliquos dies, et accipe que invenies, viridem
conversum in optimum azurrum.

30. *Ad idem.*—Accipe aluminis scarole partem unam, aceti
partes duas, tere simul super lapide, et bulire facias parum in
vase vitreo vel alio vase, et pone in ampula vitrea, et sepelias
in fimo per dies v., vel plures, donec videas devenisse azurri
colores.

31. *Attramentum optimum sic fit.* — Recipe galle fracte
libram 1½, et pone in aqua pluviali tepida, vel in aceto, aut
vino tepido, ad x. fialarum quantitatem, et sic stet per unum
diem vel plus, et postea buliantur donec remaneant ad terciam
partem dicte aque, seu vini, aut aceti, et deponantur ab igne,
et statim super addatur fiala una vel due aceti vel vini; et
ponatur tantum de aqua, quantum consummata fuerit ipsa
mixtura, et iterum omnia ponantur ad ignem, et cum inceperit
bulire deponatur ab igne, et cum ad tepiditatem reductum erit,
coletur, et ponatur in ipso libra 1½ gumi arabici pulverizati, et
libram 1 vitrioli romani, et simul misceantur omnia.

32. *Si vis facere colorem aureum vel argenteum ad scribendum.*
—Accipe talch, et pone in vase vitreo, et superpone acetum
de vernazia perfectum, et pone cum ipso mercurium, videlicet
onciam ½, et colam piscis onciam i., et pone super ignem ut
liquefiat ut aqua, et scribe, et fient littere argentee; et si vis
quod faciat litteras aureas, pone cum ipso parum croci.

33. *Colla ad jungendum cartas sic fit.*—Accipe gummi arabici, et clarum ovi spongiati, et dissolvatur gumi in ipsa clara
ovi, et siccentur ad solem, et cum operari volueris, balnea caput
ipsius masse cum lingua et labiis oris, et trahe desuper cartis

*

apply it to the parchment where the pieces are to be joined, and let it dry in the shade, and the pieces will adhere firmly together. But if you wish to join paper only and not parchment, wheat-flour or powdered bread-crumbs mixed with pure water and slightly boiled is very good for paper. But if you mix a little gum-arabic or whipped white of egg with it, it will do for parchment.

34. *If you wish to erase letters from paper*, take roche alum, and grind it, and make it into a paste with the juice of an orange, and expose it to the wind, and let it dry; afterwards rub it upon the letters, and it will erase them from the paper.

35. *If you wish to make letters of the colour of brass, silver, or gold*, take crystal, and grind it very fine upon a marble or porphyry slab, with white of egg, and write what you like with it; and when the letters are dry, rub them with the metal whose colour you wish them to take, and they will take the colour. Powdered glass will do instead of powdered crystal.

36. *To make lake.*—Take urine, and keep it for a long while, and afterwards make it boil until half of it is evaporated upon a slow and clear fire, skimming it continually, until it is perfectly purified. Then strain it through a linen cloth, and put 4 lbs. of it into a glazed jar of the said urine, and 1 lb. of raw lac well ground, and add to it a sufficient quantity of alumine zuccarino, and put it by and keep it for use.

37. *For the same purpose.*—Take of gum lac, ground very fine, as much as you like, and put it into clear urine for three days, and afterwards make it boil on the fire, and skim it. Add a little Roman vitriol to it, and strain it through a linen cloth of loose texture; then add some urine, and make it boil, always stirring it with the ladle, until one fourth part or more is evaporated; then put it in the sun and let it dry, and keep it for use.

38. *If you wish to remove oil from parchment or letters*, take bones of chicken or capons, and burn them until they are white, and reduce them to powder. Lay some of this powder on the

in locis juncture, et junge, et permitte siccari ad umbram, et
tenebunt se simul fortiter. Set si non cartam, set solum papirum, jungere velis, farina frumenti, vel tritura panis subti-
liata, et distemperata cum aqua clara, et modicum bulita,
optima est pro papiro; set si immisceris parum gumi arabici,
vel clare ovi spongiate, valebit pro cartis.

34. *Si vis elevare litteras de carta.*—Accipe aluminis roche,
et tere et impasta cum succo pomi aranzii, et pone ad auram,
et dimitte siccari; postea frica super litteras, et levabit eas a
carta.

35. *Si vis facere litteras coloris erei, argentei, aut aurei.*—
Accipe cristallum, et tere subtiliter super lapide marmoris vel
porfirici, cum clara ovi, et scribe quod vis de ipso bitumine, et,
siccatis litteris, frica desuper metallum illud, cujus colorem vis
quod recipiant littere, et accipient; pulver vitri esset bona loco
cristalli triti.

36. *Ut facias lacham.*—Accipe urinam hominis bibentis
bonum vinum, et diu serva, et postea bullire facias usque ad con-
sumpcionem medietatis, semper despumendo, super lentum et
clarum ignem, donec sit optime purgata; postea cola per telam,
et pone in vase vitriato libras iiii^{or} dicte urine, et libram unam
lache crude, bene trite, et pone de alumine Zucarino quantum
sufficit, et repone servando ad opus.

37. *Ad idem.*—Accipe gumam lache quantum vis tritam subtiliter, et pone in urina nitida per tres dies; postea fac bulire
ad ignem, et spuma, postea pone in ipsa parum vitrioli romani,
postea cola per pannum lineum rarum. Postea adde de urina,
et fac bulire agitando semper cum spatula, donec consumatur
circa quarta pars vel plus. Postea pone ad solem, et dimittas
siccari, et serva ad usum.

38. *Si vis oleum de cartis vel litteris extrahere.*—Accipe
ossa pullorum vel castroni, et arde usque ad albedinem, et pulveriza, et de ipso pulvere super pone ubi est oleum, et per-

place where the oil is, and let it stand, in summer in the shade, and in the sun in winter. If necessary, repeat this two or three times. Lime also is good for this purpose.

39. *To make the colour purpurinus as beautiful as gold.*— Take quicksilver and tin, and melt them together; then take sulphur vivum and sal ammoniac, and grind these two together, and mix them with the before-mentioned ingredients, grinding the whole very fine upon a stone, with   [1] Then put them into a glass flask well luted, so as not to be quite full of the aforesaid things, and put them on the fire, and let the mouth of the flask be uncovered, and let it stand on the fire until the vapour ceases to issue from the mouth of the flask. Afterwards let it cool, and break the flask, and collect and keep all that is above the dregs, and it will be an excellent colour for using on books and parchment.

40. *If you wish to stain, of a green colour, bones, wood, tablets, or pannels of wood, knife-handles, thread, and linen cloth,* take strong red vinegar, in a glass vase, with brass filings, a little Roman vitriol, and some roche alum, and make all boil together for a short time, and allow it to stand for a few days; and when you wish to stain anything, put it into this mixture, and let it boil a little, and it will become of a good and lasting colour.

41. *To make a water for staining anything of any colour.*— Take of sal ammoniac 1 lb., and of nitre ½ lb., and distil it in an alembic; and if you take 1 oz. of this water, and put into it the weight of two florins of calcined gold, it will make a yellow water; if calcined silver, it will make a blue; if mercury, a black; if calcined copper, a green; if calcined lead, a white water; and if calcined iron, a water of a red colour.[2]

42. *If you wish to dye anything a blood colour,* take a very strong lye, and soak in it shavings of brazillium, and ground

---

[1] So in original.

[2] This water, which dissolves gold, must be Nitro-Muriatic Acid (Aqua Regia).—See Henry's 'Chemistry,' vol. ii. p. 131. The recipe proves that the solvent power of this acid on gold was generally known as early

mitte stare in estate ad umbram, in yeme ad solem, donec
oleum exierit a carta. Et, si necesse fuerit, facias hoc bis vel
ter ; et calx etiam est bonum ad hoc faciendum.

39. *Ad faciendum purpureum colorem pulcrum et aurum.*—
Accipe argenti vivi et stagni, et fonde simul ; postea accipe
sulphuris vivi, salis armoniaci, et tere simul hec duo, et pone
cum predictis, terendo super lapide subtiliter cum   (*sic*),
postea pone in ampula vitrea bene luctata, que de predictis non
sit plena, et pone ad ignem, et ampula sit discoperta ad orificium, et stet ad ignem tam diu quod fumus cesset exire de
orificio ampule ; postea dimitte frigidari, et frange ampullam,
et totum quod super feces fuerit collige, et serva, et est color
optimus ad ponendum super libris et cartis.

40. *Si vis in colore viridi tingere ossa, ligna, tabulas, seu
telas ligni, manubria cutellorum, filum, et pannum lini.*—
Accipe de aceto rubeo et forti, in vase vitreo, cum limatura
eris, parum vitrioli romani, et de alumine roche, et fac aliquantulum bulire omnia simul, et permitte stare per aliquos dies,
et, cum vis aliqua tingere, pone in ipsa mistura, et fac aliquantulum bulire, et fient coloris optimi perdurantis.

41. *Ad faciendum aquam ad tingendum aliquid in quocumque
colore.*—Accipe salis armoniaci libram 1, salis nitri libram ½,
et distilla per alembicum, et si de ista aqua acceperis onciam
unam, et in ipsa posueris pondus duorum florenorum auri
calcinati, fiet aqua crocea; si argenti calcinati, fiet aqua celestis ; si mercurii, fiet aqua nigra ; si cupri calcinati, fiet aqua
viridis ; si plumbi calcinati, fiet aqua alba ; et si ferri calcinati,
fiet aqua coloris rubei.

42. *Si vis aliqua tingere in colore sanguineo.*—Accipe lessivium fortissimum, et in ipso pone rasuram Brazillii, Alumen

---

as 1409.   Mr. Hendrie (*Theoph.*, p. 427) shows that it was known to
Geber (*De Alchem.*, Norimb., 1545, cap. xxiii.), who lived during the
ninth century.

alumen glaciæ; and let it stand for five days or more, and it
will be of a blood colour. Whatever you mean to dye, you
must soak in it for three days, and then boil it until what you
have put in it is properly dyed.

43. *If you wish to make verdigris*, take a brass vase, and put
urine into it to the depth of one finger's breadth. Add a little
sal ammoniac to it, and expose it to very strong sunshine until
it is dry, when you must scrape off whatever you find in the
vase, and it will be very good verdigris.

44. *For the same purpose.*—Take of alum zuccarino oz. vi ;
of brass filings 1 lb. ; of common salt 2 lbs. ; of nitre ij oz. ; of
roche alum, burnt and bleached, iij oz. Reduce all these things
to a very fine powder, and smear brass plates with it. Place
the brass plates in a well-covered glazed jar ; and then, through
a hole made in the side of the jar, pour in hot urine or hot
vinegar, and close up the hole, and place the vase under warm
dung, and let it remain there 40 days. Then take it out, and
scrape the brass plates, and you will have a green colour. You
can repeat this several times, if you wish to have more colour.

45. *If you wish to make a very deep and beautiful green*, take
the herb rue, or parsley, when fresh, and extract the juice from
it, and with this juice mix verdigris, and grind it upon a stone ;
then put it into a shell, adding to it a little strong vinegar coloured with saffron, and it will do even without the saffron.
Make it liquid as if for writing, and use it.

46. *If you wish to make a very green colour for dyeing skins*,
take of filings of Venus, or copper, 1 part, and of sal ammoniac 2
parts, and temper it with urine. Stretch the skins which you wish
to dry upon a hoop, and paint them on the side next the flesh with
this colour, and let them dry, and the colour will pass through to
the other side.
_____

Whereas in the preceding recipes mention is made of five metals, giving
them the names of the planets to which they are appropriated, the following remarks are necessary in order to understand them.

Sol is put for gold, the colour of which is yellow.

Luna for silver, the rust of which is azure.

glacie tritum, et stet per dies quinque vel plus, et erit sanguinea, et quod tingere vis pona in ipsa per tres dies, et postea
fac bulire, donec quod in ipsa ad tingendum posueris tinctum
sit.

43. *Si vis facere viridem ramum.*—Accipe vas ereum, et
pone in ipso urinam, usque ad altitudinem grossesiei unius
digiti, et in ipsa pone parum salis armoniaci, et mitte ad fortissimum solem, quousque siccetur, et quod postea inveneris, in
vase rade, et erit optimum rami viride.

44. *Ad idem.* — Accipe aluminis zucarini onciam vi., et
limature eris libram j., salis communis libras ii., nitri oncias
ij., aluminis roche combusti et dealbati oncias iij., pulverisentur
hec omnia subtilissime, et unge laminas ereas, quas pone in
vase vitriato bene coperto ; postea per foramen quoddam,
factum a latere vasis, proice urinam calidam vel acetum calidum, postea claude dictum foramen, et pone vas sub fimo
calido, et stet ibi per xl dies ; postea tolle et radde tabulas,
seu laminas, et habebis viridem colorem ; et potes hoc pluries
reiterare, pro habendo plus de colore.

45. *Si vis coloratissimum et pulcherrimum viridem facere.*—
Accipe herbam rute, vel petroxellii, recentem, et ex ipsa trahe
siccum, cum quo misce viride eris, et tere super lapide, postea
pone in conchilla, et adde de forti aceto aliquantulum, quod sit
coloratum cum croco ; et etiam absque croco potest fieri ; et
distempera ut liquidum sicut ad scribendum, et operare de ipso.

46. *Si vis facere viridissimum colorem pro pellibus tingendis.*
—Accipe limaturam veneris seu rami, partem unam, et de sale
armoniaco, partes duas, et distempera cum urina, et pelles quas
vis colorare tende in circulo, et perunge ex ipso colore ex parte
carnis, et dimitte siccari ad umbram, et color transibit ad aliam
partem.

————————————

Quia in precedentibus quinque dicuntur metalla, nominando ea per
nomina planetarum quibus appropriantur, ideo ut intelligantur, nota ut
sequitur.

Pro sole, aurum, cujus color croceus est.

Pro luna, argentum, cujus rubigo color lazuli est.

Mars for iron, the rust of which is violet, rather inclining to
blackness.

Mercury for quicksilver, of which are made sinopis and minium, which are red.

Jupiter for tin.

Venus for copper or brass, the rust of which is green.

Saturn for lead, the rust of which is a white colour.

> Also, note, that in the MS. from which I copied the preceding
> recipes, it was thus written in this place. "The whole that is con-
> tained in this unbound book, namely, from the beginning of number
> 1 to this place, I copied 'in Janua' in the year 1409, in the month
> of June, having extracted it from an unbound book lent me by
> Brother Dionysius[1]   of the order of the servants of St. Mary,
> which order is called *del sacho* at Milan."
>
> Also, in the said MS., on the margin of the recipe immediately fol-
> lowing, where the number 47 begins, was written, "I had 'in
> Janua' this receipt on the 1st day of March, 1409."

47. *To make good ink for writing, particularly for books.*—
Take 4 bottles of good wine, white or red, and 1 lb. of galls,
slightly bruised, which must be put into the wine, and allowed
to stand in it for 12 days, and be stirred every day with a stick.
The twelfth day it must be strained through a strainer of fine
linen, and must be poured into a clean jar, and put on the fire
to get hot, until it almost boils.   Then remove it from the fire,
and when it has cooled so as only to be tepid, put into it 4 oz.
of gum-arabic, which must be very bright and clear, and stir
it with a stick, then add ½ lb. of Roman vitriol, and stir it continually with the stick, until all things are well incorporated
together, and let it cool and keep it for use.   And note, that
ink made with wine is good for writing books upon the sciences,
because, when books are written with it, the letters do not fade,
and can hardly be scraped out or discharged from parchment
or paper.   But if they are written with ink made with water, it
is not so, for they can easily be scraped out, and it may happen
that the letters written with it will fade.

---

[1] So in original.

Pro marte, ferrum, cujus rubigo violacea est, et pocius nigredini comparata.

Pro Mercurio, argentum vivum, de quo fiunt sinopis, et minium, qui rubei sunt.

Pro jove, stagnum.

Pro venere, ramum, seu es, cujus rubigo viridis est.

Pro saturno, plumbum, cujus rubigo albus color est.

Item, nota, quod in exemplari a quo prescripta sumpsi, in hoc loco, scriptum sic erat, " totum quod continetur in isto quaterno, scilicet a principio numeri 1, usque hic, scripsi in Janua, anno 1409, de mense Junii, extrahendo ab uno quaterno michi prestato per Fratem Dionisium de   (*sic*), ordinis Servorum Sancte Marie, qui ordo in Mediolano dicitur ' del sacho.' "

Item, in eodem exemplari, super margine recepte immediate sequentis, qua incipit numerus 47, scribebatur sic, " habui in Janua istam receptam die primo Marcii, 1409."

47. *Ad faciendum optimum attramentum pro scribendo, precipue libros.*—Recipe bocales iiii^{or} optimi vini vermigii vel albi, et libram i. galle modicum fracte, que ponatur in dicto vino, et stet in ipso per duodecim dies, et agitetur omni die cum baculo, ultima vero die colletur bene subtiliter per colatorium tele linee ; postea ponatur in vase mondo ad ignem, et callefiat usque dum quasi bulliat ; deinde deponatur ab igne, et cum refrigidatum sit, taliter quod sit tepidum, ponantur in ipso onzie iiii^{or} gummi arabici bene lucidi et clari, et agitetur cum baculo ; deinde ponatur libra ½ vitrioli romani, et semper misceatur cum baculo, donec bene incorporentur omnia simul, et infrigidetur et usui servetur.   Et nota quod attramentum factum cum vino est bonum ad scribendum libros scienciarum, que cum de ipso scripti sunt libri, non cadunt littere, neque quasi raddi possunt, nec expelli de carta, nec de papiro.   Set si scripti sunt de attramento, seu incausto, facto de aqua, non est sic, que bene radi possunt leviter, et accidere potest quod littere de ipso scripte caduce sint.

*

4 bottles of wine, or water, or half of each.

1 pound of galls of xij. oz. to the pound.

4 oz. of gum arabic.

6 oz. of Roman vitriol.

And if you took equal parts of each, galls, gum, and vitriol, as much of one as of the other, by weight, it would still be good ; as, for instance, 6 oz. of each, which would be sufficient for the said 4 lbs. of wine or water, or of wine and water mixed as before.

OTHER EXPERIMENTS NOT UPON COLOURS.

48. *The preparation of Tucia.*—Take as much as you please of Alexandrine tucia, pulverize it well, put it in an iron ladle, and distemper it over the fire until the tucia becomes red. Then take vinegar and urine, and stir it in well with a rod until the tucia becomes of a citrine colour.

49. *To make brass.*—Take thin plates of copper, clean them well with salt, urine, and honey, and when they become red, and are well cleansed, take red honey, and rub it over the plates ; then sprinkle powdered tucia on the honey and liquefy it in a shell with   [1] (?) of holly, it will then be very good brass.

50. *To write with black on gold or silver.*—Take burnt lead and sulphur, distemper them together, and write on the gold or silver ; then heat it with fire, and the desired effect will be produced.

51. *To redden white bones.*—Distemper sal ammoniac with pure water, put any bones into the water and leave them for 2 days. Add some Brazil wood raspings, and a little ley, and leave them for 2 days more. Then take them out, and if they

------

[1] The word is illegible in the original.

Bocales iiii^{or} vini, vel aque, vel per medietatem de utroque.

Lipra i. gallarum, de onziis xii. pro lipra.

Onzie iiii^{or} gummi arabici.

Onzie vi. vitrioli romani.

Et qui caperet gallas, gummam, et vitriolum, quodlibet ad equale, videlicet totidem de uno quotidem de alio, ad pondus, ad huc bonum esset, videlicet ut onzie vi. de quolibet, quod satis esset pro dictis libris iiii^{or} vini, seu aque, vel aque et vini, ut supra.

EXPERIMENTA DIVERSA ALIA QUAM DE COLORIBUS.

48. *Preparacio tuchie.*—Recipe tucie alexandrine quantumvis, bene pulverizate, et pone in ramaiolo ferreo, et distempera ad ignem, tantum quod tucia rubescat. Postea accipe acetum, et urinam pueri, et imbibe, et misce cum baculo, tantum quod tucia deveniat ad modum citrini.

49. *Ad ottonem faciendum.*—Habeas laminas eris subtiles, et purga bene cum sale, et urina pueri, et melle, et quando fuerit rubeum, et bene purgatum, accipe mel rubeum, et unge dictas laminas, et super mel asperge pulverem tucie, et liquefac concham bomb . . . de aggrefolio, et erit optimum ottonum.

50. *Ad scribendum de nigro in auro vel argendo.*—Accipe plumbum ustum, et sulphur, et distempera simul, et scribe super aurum vel argentum, et calefac ad ignem, et feceris quod dictum est.

51. *Ad faciendum ossa alba fieri rubea.*—Distempera sal armoniacum in aqua pura, postea mitte in ipsa aqua osse que vis, et stent per duos dies, et postea adde de verxino raso cum modico lissivii, et stet per duos dies, postea extrahantur ossa, et,

are too red put them in water in which sal ammoniac has been dissolved, and if they are not sufficiently red, do not put them into a fresh solution of sal ammoniac but replace them in the first, containing the Brazil wood raspings, and add more Brazil wood; leave them for some time, and they will become sufficiently red.

52. *To blacken horns or bones of animals.*—Take 2 pints of rain water, 3 oz. of quicksilver, and 2 oz. of quicklime, boil them together for a short time; then take the mixture off the fire, and when it becomes tepid, steep horn or bone in it, and it will become black.

53. *A medicine for silvering divers things in a durable manner.*—Take Lupins, boil them in water until their virtue is imparted to the water. Then strain and boil until the water is reduced to the consistence of honey, and add a quantity of quicksilver equal in weight to the water, stirring it well until the quicksilver is no longer visible. With this you may wash wood, metals, and whatever you please. This will silver them, and this silvering will never separate or fall off.

54. *To make a durable silvering.*—Take clay, pig's blood, vine-wood ashes, and quicksilver, mix them well, then dry and pulverize them; rub anything with this powder and it will be silvered.

55. *To make gold worms, or worms which seem gilt, for gilding anything.*—Take bull's brains, put them in a marble vase, and leave them for 3 weeks, when you will find gold-making worms; preserve them carefully.

56. *To make a powder which shall light a candle without fire but with water.*—Take an ounce of loadstone and 4 ounces of quicklime. Put half of the lime into some strong pipkin, then add to it the loadstone, and fill the pipkin with the remainder of the lime; cover it well, and leave it in a brick-kiln for 9 days, then take it out of the kiln, and when it is cold uncover it entirely: then remove the lime gently, when you will find the loadstone in powder; keep it separately, and when you wish to light a candle take some of this powder, put it on a

si nimis sint rubea, reponantur in alia aqua salis armoniaci.
Et si parum, non ponantur in aqua nova salis armoniaci, set in
prima in qua prius fuerant, in qua est verxinum, et addatur de
verxino, et stent, et fient rubea ad sufficienciam.

52. *Ad nigrandum cornu vel osse animalis.*—Accipe duas
pintas aque pluvialis, uncias tres argenti vivi, et uncias duas
calcis vive, et fac bulire simul aliquantulum, et depone ab igne,
et cum devenerit ad tepiditatem, pone in ipso cornu vel osse
animalis, et denigrabitur.

53. *Medicina ad argentacionem perpetuam diversarum rerum
materialium.*—Accipe lupinos, et decoque in aqua, donec virtus
eorum transierit in aquam. Postea cola, et fac bulire usque
ad spisitudinem mellis, et pone intus de mercurio seu argento
vivo, ad pondus aque, et misce bene, ita quod in ea non appareat
argentum vivum, et de ipsa lignias ligna, metalla, et alia que
vis, et erunt de argentata, et ipsa de argentacio nunquam sepa-
rabitur seu cadet.

54. *Ad faciendum argentacionem durabilem.*—Accipe terram
tenacem, sanguinem porci, cineres de sermento, et argentum
vivum, et commisceantur bene, et postea siccentur, et pulveri-
zentur, et ex ipso pulvere frica que vis, et argentabuntur.

55. *Ad faciendum vermes auri, vel qui videantur deaurati,
pro deaurando que vis.*—Accipe cerebrum tauri, et pone in vase
marmoris, et stet per tres ebdomadas, et invenies intus vermes
facientes aurum, et custodi bene.

56. *Ad faciendum pulverem que candelam accendat, absque
igne, set cum aqua.*—Accipe calamitem masculum onziam i., et
calcem vivam onzias iiii^{or}, et pone medietatem dicte calcis in
aliquo pignatello forti, et postea pone in ipso dictam calamittam
integram, postea cooperiri pignaculum cum alia parte dicti
calcis, et obtura bene dictum pignatellum, et pone per novem
dies in fornace in qua cocuntur lateres. Postea leva dictum
vas de fornace, et cum frigidum sit apperi plane, et remove
moderate dictum calcem, donec inveneris calamittam pulveriza-

piece of paper or on the wick of a candle, and touch it with water or saliva, when the candle will be lighted. But take care you do not keep it in a damp or warm place.[1]

57. *To temper iron well.*—Take powdered glass and burnt goat's horn or stag's bone, well pulverized, heat the iron slightly, and grease it with mutton fat and sprinkle with the powders that part of the iron which is to be made hard. Then heat the iron or the part which you wish to harden and quench it in water which has been distilled from radish-roots and red earthworms which are found in damp places.

58. *To temper iron so that it will be hard enough to cut precious stones.*—Heat the iron in the fire to a convenient heat, and extinguish it in the blood of a goat in the month of March.

59. *To take the impression of seals and other things with engraved or raised surfaces.*—Take 2 parts of gypsum and 1 of flour, mix them together and make them into a paste with glue made of hartshorn and reduce them until they become of the consistence of soft wax. Then make two small tablets of this paste and before they dry press between them the seal or image or other form which must be wrapped in onion skins. Then take out the seal or image, let the tablets dry, then melt lead or wax and pour it into the mould. When cool remove it from the mould or tablets, and you will have what you desire.

60. *To make a perfect glue for fixing hard bodies, such as crystal, glass, and gems, together; or for fixing wood, horn, or other things on to stones.*—Take ceruse made from burnt bricks, that is to say, the powder of them, and finish by grinding it

---

[1] It appears from a passage in Beckmann's Inventions, vol. ii. p. 504, that this recipe was quoted by Cardan, who ascribed it to one Marcus

tam, quam serva per se ; et dum vis lumen accendere, accipe
de pulvere dicte calamite, et pone in papiro, seu licivo candele,
et tange cum aqua dictum licivum, vel cum sputo, et accendetur
candela ; set cave ne ipsum pulverem teneas in loco humido
nec calido.

57. *Ad temperandum ferrum optime.*—Accipe vitrum pulverizatum, et cornua yrci, vel ossa cervi, usta et pulverizata, et
calefac parum dictum ferrum, et ipsum unge cepo castrati, *i.e.*
muttonis, et asperge de dictis pulveribus simul mixtis, ab illa
parte ferri que expedit fieri dura, et calefac ipsum ferrum, seu
partem illam ejus quam vis duram facere, et extingue in aqua
distillata per alembicum, de radicibus raffanorum, et vermibus
terrestribus, seu bombricibus rubescentibus, nascentibus in locis
humidis.

58. *Ad temperandum ferrum, quod erit tam durum, quod de
ipso poterunt incidi duri lapides preciosi.*—Callefac ferrum ad
ignem ut convenit, et extingue in sanguine irci libidine amoris
inflammati, id est in marcio mense.

59. *Ad faciendum formam sigilli, et aliarum rerum sculptarum
vel levatarum, quas voles extrahere.*—Accipe partes duas gipsi,
farine unam, et misce, et fac pastam de ipsis cum cola cervina,
et deduc, et confice, donec fit sicut cera mollis ; postea fac de
ipsa duas tabuletas, et, antequam siccentur, stringe inter ipsas
sigillum, vel ymaginem, aut aliud, cujus formam facere vis, et
sit involutum in pelliculis ceparum, et postea extrahe sigillum
vel ymaginem, et permittas siccari dictas tabuletas, et cola
plumbum vel ceram ut vis, et immitte in dicta forma, et dimitte
frigidari, et apperi formam, id est dictas tabulas, et habebis
quod quesivisti.

60. *Ad faciendum collam perfectam, ad corpora dura fir-
manda, ut cristallum, vitrum, et gemmas, invicem, vel super
petras, ligna, cornua, aut alia.*—Accipe cerussam laterum coctorum, videlicet pulverem ipsorum, et confice subtiliando super

---

Græcus, who, according to some persons, lived in the ninth century, and,
according to others, in the thirteenth.

finely on the porphyry slab with painter's liquid varnish.   With
this preparation you may join anything you like, and then dry
it in the sun.   And if you have no liquid varnish, take linseed
oil with a little lime, and the said ceruse, or powder of bricks
burnt in the furnace, and well triturated and pulverized.[1]

61. *To temper iron.*—Take a sufficient quantity of the juice
of radish roots, then take earth-worms and put them in salt or
sea-water for an hour until they die, and in dying they will be
purified from their superfluous humours.   Then remove them
from the water without squeezing them, but only laying them
down and shaking the water from them.   Then put them in a
glass cucurbit, and pour the radish-juice on them so as just to
cover them.   Then fix an alembic on the said cucurbit, lute it,
place the cup in the ashes, give it a slow fire, and collect the
water, which will come off clear as spring water.   When your
iron is properly heated quench it in this.

62. *For the same purpose.*—Take the herb which is called
" famula "[2] and which is like " vidalia," but which has leaves
like the " elder," extract its juice, and when your iron is properly heated quench and temper it in this.

63. *To make a water which corrodes iron.*—Take 1 oz. of
sal ammoniac, 1 oz. of roche alum, 1 oz. of sublimed silver, and
1 oz. of Roman vitriol, pound them well, take a glazed earthen
vase, pour into it equal parts of vinegar and water, then throw
in the above-mentioned articles.   Boil the whole until reduced
to half a cup or a cup, apply it to such parts of the iron as you
may wish to hollow or corrode, and the water will corrode them.

64. *A water which corrodes iron, and takes away the spots on
all metals, and cleanses wounds.*—Take Roman vitriol and eu-

---

[1] There appears to be some error in this recipe.

[2] Probably " Flammula ;" in French, *Clématite flammule;* in Italian,
" Flamula ;" in English, the sweet-scented Clematis.   This is rendered
more probable by the comparison of this plant with another species of Cle-

lapide porfirico cum vernice liquida pictorum, et de hac confectione junge quod vis, et dimitte siccari ad solem.   Et si non
habes, accipe oleum lini, et aliquantulum calcis, cum dicta
cerrusa, seu pulvere laterum coctorum in fornace, atritorum, et
pulverizatorum subtiliter.

61. *Ad temperandum ferrum.*—Recipe radices rafani, extrahe
succum ita quod de eo habeas satis ad quod vis facere, et accipe
lombricos, aliter bombricos, terrestres, quos pone in aqua bene
salita, vel marina, per horam, donec moriantur, et moriendo
purgentur ab eorum humoribus superfluis.   Postea extrahe
ipsos de aqua absque eos exprimere, set solum jaciendo, et excuciendo aquam, et pone eos in cucurbita vitri, et superpone
dictum succum rafani, ita quod succum superet eos aliquantulum, et dicte cucurbite superpone alembicum, et luta, et loca
cucurbitam in cineribus, et da ignem lentum et recollige aquam,
que exiet clara ut aqua fontis, et in ipsa extingue ferrum debite
ignitum.

62. *Ad idem.*—Accipe herbam que vocatur famula, que est
ad modum vidalie.   Set scias quod habet folia ad modum sambuci ; et de ipsa trahe succum, in quo extingue, et tempera,
ferrum debite ignitum seu calefactum in igne.

63. *Ad faciendum aquam que cavat ferrum.*—Accipe onciam
i. salis armoniaci, et onciam i. aluminis roche, et onciam i. de
argento sublimato, et onciam i. vitrioli romani, et pista omnia
bene, et accipe unum vas terre vitriatum, et pone in ipso aquam
et acetum, de utroque equaliter, et immitte que dicta sunt, et
fac bulire, donec devenerit ad quantitatem medii ziatus, vel
unius ; et, hiis factis, de ipsa linias ferrum, modo quo vis ipsum
cavere, seu radere, et radebit ipsum dicta aqua.

64. *Aqua que cavat ferrum et levat maculas ab omnibus metallis et purgat putredinem vulneris.*—Accipe de vitriolo romano

matis, the Clematis Vitalba, the wild Clematis, or common Virgin's bower ;
the Vitalba and Clematite of the Italians ; La Clématite des Haies of the
French.

phorbia,[1] and distil them in an alembic.   Then take the water
which is distilled from them and apply it to the wound, and it
will purify it and remove the dead flesh without great pain.
If you write with this on iron or any other metal, the letters
will immediately be made and bitten into it.

65. *To fix one piece of brass to another.*—Take the scrapings
of a cask, that is, tartar, burn it until it no longer smokes, and
reduce it to powder ; then take a fourth part of borax, put it
in a small quantity of water, and stir it until it is dissolved ;
then add the tartar to it, until it makes, as it were, red bubbles,
when you must add a little water to make it more liquid : you
may then use it to fix anything you please, smearing the
article with the said water or mixture.   Then put a few copper
filings and powdered borax into the said water and smear this
mixture as before.   Then put what you join into the fire, and
when you see the copper filings run or melt, at that instant
throw water on the fire, take out whatever you have soldered,
and you will find it firmly fixed.

66. *If you wish to give a gold colour to any metal.*—Take
powdered red sulphur and red orpiment, heat them in a crucible
over the fire, stain your work with this composition, and it will
be of a gold colour.

67. *To give iron a golden colour.*—Take alum of Jameni,
grind it with urine so as to be of the consistence of ointment, and
spread it wherever you like on the plates of iron ; then heat it
over the lighted coals ; what you have spread will become of a
golden colour.

68 or 69. *To preserve arms and other iron utensils from rust.*
—Anoint them with chicken's grease.

70, 71, 72, 73, or 74. *To make fire which will burn under
water, and which cannot be extinguished with anything but oil.*—
Take equal parts of quicklime and sulphur, 1 oz. of wax, a

---

[1] Euphorbia, the spurge, of which there are many species, one of which
is mentioned in the Bolognese MS., No. 38, under the name of Turtumagli,
a derivation from the Latin Tithymalus, the Euphorbia Esula (Erba Latte,

et euforbiano, et distilla per alembicum, et de aqua que exierit
pone in plaga, et expurgabitur, et levabit carnem mortuam
absque dolore magno, et si de ipsa scripseris litteras in ferro,
vel alio metallo, statim fient et cavabuntur in ipso.

65. *Ad consolidandum unum latonem cum alio.*—Accipe rasuram vegetis, id est, tartarum, et combure donec fumum non
faciat, et pulveriza eam ; postea accipe quartam partem borratis,
quam mitte in modico aque, et misce, et agita eam, donec
liquefiat; postea mitte cum ea dictam rasuram, donec faciat bul-
las quasi rubeas, postea mitte parum aque, ut sit magis liquida,
postea de ipsa operare, et consolida que vis, et unge eas de
ipsa aqua seu mistura ; postea mitte in ipsa mistura aliquantulum limature cupri, et aliquantulum borracis pulverizate, et
de ipsa mistura unge ubi supra, et que jonxeris pone ad ignem,
donec videbis spargi, seu fondi, linituram dicte mixture positam
super jonctura duorum conjonctorum, et subito proice desuper
de aqua in igne, et extrahe de igne ea que jonxisti, quia con-
solidata erunt.

66. *Si vis dare aureum colorem alicui metallo.*—Accipe pulverem sulphuris rubei, auriplumenti rubei, et bulias ad ignem
in cruxibulo, et de tali confectione opus tuum intinge, et sus-
cipiet aureum colorem.

67. *Ad faciendum aureum colorem super ferrum.*—Accipe
aluminis jameni, et tere cum urina, ut sit quas unguentum,
et linias ex ea lamina ferrea ubi volueris, et calefac super carbones ignitos, et fiet linitura color aureus.

68 vel 69. *Ad conservandum arma et alia ferramenta a
rubigine.*—Ungantur asungia gallinarum.

70, 71, 72, 73, vel 74. *Ad faciendum ignem qui ardebit sub
aqua, nec poterit extingui, nisi cum oleo.*—Accipe calcis vive,
sulphuris vivi, ana, onziam i. cera, parum olei, parum petrolei,

Lattaroli ; Euphorbe à feuille de pin, La petite Esule, the Gromwell-
leaved spurge). All the species are acrid and poisonous.

little oil, and a little petroleum. Mix these things together, smear them over iron or wood, put this under water, and it will burn. If you wish to extinguish it, put it in oil.

75. *If you wish to keep a fire for some time.*—Put lighted coals or charcoal under the ashes of juniper wood, and they will not be extinguished for a long time.

76. *To make maggots and lice fall from your head.*—Anoint your head with the juice of rue.

77. *If you wish to take spots of oil, and so forth, out of woollen cloth.*—Distemper white, or gypsum, or marble dust ground with egg, lay it on the spot, dry it, and then wash it with cold water.

78. *To take stains out of scarlet, velvet, &c.*—Take roche alum, with a little common salt, and grind it, and make it into a paste with yolk of egg and a little vinegar; put this on the spots and dry it. The dried "mixture" may be removed by rubbing, and the cloth will remain free from the spot.

80.[1] *For the same purpose.*—Take burnt tartar of wine, and a little sulphur, grind them and make them into a paste with yolk of egg and water. Put this on the spots, dry it, and re-move it by rubbing and beating.

81. *If you wish to stain bones, wood, planks, wooden platters, knife-handles, thread, and linen cloths green,* put some strong red vinegar into a glass vase with brass filings, a little Roman vitriol, and roche alum, and boil all these things together for a short time, and then let them stand for a few days. When you desire to stain anything, put it into this mixture, boil it a little, and it will be of a beautiful and durable green colour.

82. *If you wish to make brass as beautiful as gold,* take 1 lb. of brass plates, ½ lb. of the best tuchia, melt them together in a crucible over the fire, add 2 oz. of tin, stir well, and let the mixture cool. Then melt it a second time, add 3 oz. of tuchia, stir it, and again set it aside to cool. Then melt it a third time, add 3 oz. more of tuchia, stir and cast it in the form of rods, strips, plates, or any other form, and it will be beautiful.

---

[1] 79 is missing in original.

et hec misce simul, et lignias de hoc ferrum vel lignum, et mittas sub aqua et ardebit; et si vis extinguere, mitte in oleo.

75. *Si vis conservare ignem maximum tempus ne extingatur.*— Pone carbones, seu calcicos accensos, sub cineribus ligni juniperi, et durabunt diu.

76. *Ut lendines et pediculi cadant de capite.*—Unge caput succo rute.

77. *Si vis extrahere de pannis lannarum maculas olei et aliorum.*—Distempera album, vel gessum, vel marmor, tritum cum ovo, et inunge ubi est macula, et dimitte siccari, postea lava cum aqua frigida.

78. *Ad extrahendum maculam de scarlata, et voluto, et talibus.* —Accipe de alumine roche, et parum salis communis, et tere, et impastentur cum vitello ovi, et pauco aceti, et superponatur macule, et siccetur, et confricando expellatur dictum bitumen siccum, et pannus remanebit liberatus a macula.

80. *Ad idem.*—Accipe alumen fecis, et parum sulphuris, et tridentur et impastentur cum vitello ovi et aqua, et superponantur macule et dimittantur siccari, et expellantur confricando et excuciendo.

81. *Si in colore viridi vis tingere ossa, ligna, tabulas, scutellas ligni, manubria cutellorum, filum, et pannum lini.*—Accipe de aceto rubeo et forti in vase vitreo cum limatura eris, parum vitrioli romani, et de alumine roche, et fac aliquantulum bulire omnia simul, et permitte sistare per aliquos dies, et cum vis aliqua tingere, pone in ipsa mistura, et fac aliquantulum bulire, et fient colores pulcri viridis optime perdurantes.

82. *Si vis facere lottonem pulcrum sicut aurum.*—Accipe laminas eris libram i, et optimam tuchiam libras s, et simul fonde in igne cum cruxibulo, et pone intus onzias ii stagni, et misce, et dimitte frigidari. Postea fonde secundo, et pone intus de tuchia onzias iii, et misce, et dimite frigidari. Postea tercio fonde, et mitte in ipso onzias iii tuchie, et misce, et jacta in virgis vel laminis platis, vel in qua forma vis, et erit pulcher.

83. *To make a good temper for iron utensils.*—Early in the morning collect a large quantity of celandine when it is wet or full of dew. Extract its juice by pounding, boiling it until one third is consumed, and the two parts remaining will be excellent. Then take the whole of the herb Lattaroli[1] (?), pounded, and extract its juice. Distil this, if possible, and sprinkle some finely powdered antimony on the iron, heat the iron, and quench it in the distilled water.

84. *For the same purpose.*—Take the leafstalks of briony, pound them, and extract the juice. Distil this, and quench the red-hot iron in the water which is distilled from it.

85. *To mend broken vases of earth, stone, and marble.*—Take the white earth of the fellmongers, that is, chalk, which is otherwise called gersa [gesso]; make it into a plaster with white of egg, grind it well on a stone, and use it.[2]

86. *If you wish to attract glass touched with some gum, as iron is attracted by the magnet,* take the gum Andrianum, which is found in the large rocks near Bologna towards Tuscany, in Monte Bono, or Buono, and besmear a stick with this gum. Touch the glass phials on the table with this stick, draw away the stick, and the phials will follow it, as iron follows the magnet.

87. *If you wish to turn black skins white,* take a mole, boil it, then take the water in which it has boiled, and smear a black horse with it, on any part. The black hairs will fall off, and white hairs will grow.

88. *For the same purpose.*—Take cheese, heat it by the fire, press it strongly on the forehead of a black horse, and it will make a star as you know.

> After the preceding, it was written in the MS., " All the things contained in this unbound book, namely, from number 47 unto this page, I wrote ' in Janua' in the year 1409, in the month of June, extracting them from a book lent to me by brother Dionysius de   (*sic*)   of

---

[1] The Euphorbia Esula. See ante, note to p. 78.

[2] This recipe appears to be copied from Pliny, who says quicklime should be used.

83. *Ad faciendum bonam temperam ferramentis.*—Collige summo mane bonam quantitatem celidonie, quando est plena seu madida rore, cujus succum pistendo extrahe, et fac bulire, donec consummata sit tertia pars ejus; due vero remanentes partes optime sunt; et accipe totidem herbam lateranniam, pista, et succum extrahe, et ipsum distilla per alembicum, si fieri poterit, et pulverem antimonii triti pulverizati proice super ferrum, et calefac ferrum, et extingue in dicta aqua distillata.

84. *Ad idem.*—Accipe radicem de foliis brionie, et pista, et extrahe succum, quem distilla per alembicum, et in aqua que exierit extingue ferrum ignitum.

85. *Ad reintegrandum vasa terrea, lapidea, et marmorea, fracta.*—Accipe terram albam pellipariorum, id est cretam, que aliter gersa vocatur, de qua fac emplastrum cum albumine ovi, et subtilia super lapide et utere.

86. *Si vis vitrum tactum de quadam guma attrahere, sicut ferrum attrahitur a calamita.*—Accipe gumam andrianam que invenitur in saxis maximis Bononie versus Tuscam in monte Bono seu Buono, et cum ipsa guma unge baculam, et cum ipso baculo tange fialas vitri positas super mensa, et deduc baculum per mensam, et fiale sequentur baculum, sicut ferrum sequiter calamitam.

87. *Si vis de pellibus nigris facere albas.*—Accipe talpam et fac bulire, et ex ipsa aqua in qua bulierit linias equum nigrum, ubi vis, et cadent pili nigri, et orientur albi.

88. *Ad idem.*—Accipe caseum et calefac ad ignem, et in fronte equi nigri imprime fortiter, et fiet stella sicut scis.

Post predicta scriptum erat in exemplari, " omnia contenta in presenti quaterno, id est, a numero 47, usque hic, scripsi in Janua, anno 1409, de mense Junii, extrahendo ab uno quaterno prestato michi per Fratrem Dyonisium de   (*sic*), ordinis Servorum Sancte

the order of the Servants of St. Mary, which order, in Milan, is
called Del Sacho; and from that same book I copied also many
experiments for making colours for illuminating books, which experiments I wrote in another quire which precedes this."

These are the experiments, Nos. 1 to 47 inclusive.

Also in the same MS., in another unbound book attached to the preceding, it was thus written: "On Tuesday the 11th day of February,
1410, I caused the following to be copied in Bologna from recipes lent
to me at that place by Theodore   (*sic*) of Flanders, an embroiderer, accustomed to work at Pavia during the life of the late
renowned Duke of Milan;[1] which recipes the said Theodore said he
had procured in London, in England, from the persons who work
with the waters hereinafter mentioned."

The following recipes were brought from England :—

89. *To make black water.*—Take a pint of water from under
the grindstone on which knives are ground,[2] and place it over
the fire, and throw into it a glass of vinegar and ii. oz. of
galls ; then take ½ an oz. of alum and an oz. of copperas, and
boil it until it is reduced by one-third, and then let it stand for
a day.

90. *To make green water.*—Take an ounce of verdigris, half
an ounce of alum, a little saffron, and a little parsley; grind
the whole well together, and distemper it with one glass of
vinegar ; then strain it through a cloth into a saucer, and let it
rest for a day.

91. *To make red water.*—Take an ounce of rags or clippings
of scarlet [cloth], and soak them in a jar in a pint of strong
ley; then put the jar over the fire, and throw into it a little
alum and gum arabic, and make it boil until it is reduced one-
half, and let it rest for a day.

92. *To make the water for staining cloth of all colours, and
to make it quite white.*—Take a pint of strong ley, and put it over
the fire, and throw into it an ounce of alum and an ounce of
saltpetre, and when it is melted take it off the fire and use it.

---

[1] Gian Galeazzo, who died in 1402.

[2] This water probably contained iron-dust. It is also mentioned in the
Bolognese MS., Nos. 134, 338.

Marie, qui in Mediolano dicitur ' del Sacho,' et ab ipso quaterno copiavi etiam multa experimenta ad faciendum colores pro illuminando libro, que experimenta scripsi super uno alio quaterno precedenti   (*sic*) finis quaterni." [Ista sunt experimenta que scribuntur a pre   (*sic*) numeri 1 usque ad numerum 47].

Item in eodem exemplari in quodam alio quaterno precedentibus contiguo scribebatur sic " 1410 Die Martis xi Februarii, feci copiari in Bononia, a receptis ibi mihi prestatis per Thedericum   (*sic*) de Flandria, rachamatorem solitum operari in castro papie, in vita condam incliti ducis Mediolani, quas receptas idem Thedericus dixit habuisse in Londonia in Anglia, ab operariis infrascriptarum aquarum."

Ab Anglia venerunt recepte sequentes :—

89. *Pour faire l'eau noire.*—Prenez une pinte de l'yaue de dessoulz la meule sur quoy on meult les couteaulx, et la mettez sur le feu, et gettez ung voire de vin aigre, et ii onces de galles, et prenez demie onche d'alon, et une onche de coperose, et le faitez tant boulir, qu'il apetice du tiers, et puis le laissier reposer un jour.

90. *Pour faire l'eaue verte.*—Prenez une once de vert de gris, et demie once d'alon, et un petit de safren, et un petit de persil, et broyez bien tout ensemble, et puis le destrempez en j voire de vin aigre, et puis le coulez parmi un drapel dedens une escuelle, et le laissiez reposer i jour.

91. *Pour faire l'eaue rouge.*—Prenez une once de bourre d'escarlate, ou tondure, et le destrempez dedens une olle, en une pinte de la forte lexive, et puis le mettez sur le feu, et gettez dedens un po d'alun, et de gomme arabique, et le faites tant boulir qu'il apetice de la moitié, et puis le laissiez reposer un jour.

92. *Pour faire l'eaue a destaindre drap de toutes couleurs, et faire devenir tout blanc.*—Prenez une pinte de la forte lessive, et la mettez sur le feu, et gettez dedens une once d'alun, et une once de salepetre, et quant il est fondu mettez le jus du feu et en ouvrez.

Note.—It seems also possible to draw, with the said water, on coloured woollen cloths, any letters and other drawings, the parts within the outlines of which only, where the water has touched, will be bleached ; and thus there will be white letters and figures ; the ground, where it has not been touched by the water, still retaining its own colour.

93. *To make the red water.*—Take an ounce of Brazil in powder and a 6th part of alun de glace, and make it boil well in a vessel of clear water until it is reduced to one half, and then use it.

94. *To make the green water.*—Take an ounce of water of the leaves of the black nightshade,[1] and ½ an ounce of alum and the worth of a blanc[2] of saffron, and ij. oz. of verdigris ; grind all together as well as you can, and distemper with a chopine[3] of strong vinegar, and then use it.

95. *To make the violet water.*—Take an ounce of turnsole and soak it in a chopine of strong and tepid ley, and then use it.

What is here called turnsole is to be understood " Bresil."

96. *To make the blue water.*—Take an ounce of indigo of Bandas, that is to say, Baguedel,[4] and reduce it to powder, and then distemper it with ½ a "lot"[5] of strong lessive fondisse, and put it on the fire ; and just before it boils, throw into it a 6th part of quicklime, and the same quantity of "meltrac" (?), and then take it off the fire and stir it well, and when it is tepid use it.

Also in the said MS., over the recipe immediately following, was written—" At the beginning of this are wanting several words which had been cut off, as appeared when I caused this to be copied from the MS. ; but I think it is for making a water of an azure colour, or a blue or indigo water."

97. Take the worth of a blanc of quicklime, and the same quantity of calcined lees of wine, and of calx of tin, and some " creeres " of indigo, and boil all together in two lots of clear

---

[1] Morelle. The herba Morella, Solanum Nigrum, Black Nightshade.

[2] A blanc was equivalent to 5 deniers.

[3] Chopine, a half pint. The old French " pinte " was equivalent to 1 quart English.

[4] This was the real Indigo.

[5] Lot, a liquid measure, perhaps what was afterwards called " Litre."

Addicio.—Debent etiam posse cum dicta aqua protrahi in drapis coloricis lane quelibet littere, et alie protractiones, in quarum solis continenciis, quantum aqua eadem tetigerit, albificatio fiet, et sic habebuntur ibi protractiones et littere albe, remanente campo in suo colore ubi a qua ipsa non tetigerit.

93. *Pour faire l'eaue rouge.*—Prenez une once de brezil en poudre, et un sisain d'alun de glace, et le faites bien cuire, en desmerlant d'yaue clere, tant qu'il appetice de la moitie, et puiz en ouvrez.

94. *Pour faire l'iaue verte.*—Prenez une once d'eaue de morelle de la feuille, et demi once d'alun, et pour un blanc de saffren, et ij onces de vert de gris, et broyez tout ensemble si bien comme vous porrez, et puis le destrempez d'une chopine de fort vin aigre, et puis en œuvrez.

95. *Pour faire l'eaue violete.*—Prenez une once de tornesel, et le met tremper en une chopine de forte lessive fondisse, et que elle soit tiede, et puis en œuvre.

Nota.—Quod ubi dicitur tornesel vult dicere Bresil.

96. *Pour faire l'eaue perse.*—Prenez une once de inde de Bandas, c'est à dire, Baguedel, et le met en pouldre, et puis le destrempe en demi lot de forte lessive fondisse, et puis le met sur le feu, et quant il voudra boulir, gette dedens un sisain de chaulx vive, et autant de meltrac, e puis le met jus du feu, et le remue bien, et quant il est tede s'en œuvre.

Item in eodem exemplari et supra receptam immediate sequentem sic erat scriptum. "Hic, in principio, deficiunt plura verba, que ab exemplari erant abscisa, ut apparebat, quando feci hoc copiari ab ipso exemplari; set credo quod sit ad faciendum aquam coloris celestini, aut aquam persam vel indicam."

97. Pren pour un blanc de chaulx vive, et un blanc de cendre de lie de vin, et un blanc de la cendre d'estaing creeres de Inde, et fait tout boulir ensemble en ij lotz d'iaue clere une

water for an instant, and stir it well, and then take it off the
fire, and throw into it a glass of cold water; and when it is
settled you can use it.

> Also in the same MS., over the two paragraphs following, it was thus
> written—" I think that the following recipes are for making two
> green waters, as I collect from the contents, and the names and
> things which are mentioned in them."

98. One oz. of tartar of white wine, 1 oz. of sal gem, 1 oz.
of alun de glace, ½ an oz. of alun de plume, 6 esterlins[1] of
verdigris, 1 chopine of common salt.

99. 1 oz. of copperas, ½ an oz. of verdigris, 1 oz. of saltpetre, ½ an oz. of rhubarb.

Take a chopine of water and put it into a new earthen jar,
and when you see that the water begins to boil put in your
powder, and take it off the fire and stir it with a skewer, and
let it cool.

> I think these words of the above written paragraph relate to both the
> articles marked 98 and 99.
> After the aforesaid, it was thus written in the before-mentioned
> MS.:—
> " The true method of working in England with [coloured] waters.—
> The aforesaid [2] Theodore, from whom I had the above-written recipes
> for the aforesaid waters, told me that in England the painters work
> with these waters upon closely woven cloths, wetted with gum-water
> made with gum-arabic, and then dried, and afterwards stretched out
> on the floor of the soler, upon thick woollen and frieze cloths; and
> the painters, walking with their clean feet over the said cloths, work
> and paint upon them figures, stories, and other things. And because
> these cloths lie stretched out on a flat surface, the coloured waters do
> not flow or spread in painting upon them, but remain where they are
> placed, and the watery moisture sinks into the woollen cloth, which
> absorbs it; and even the touches of the paint-brush made with these
> waters do not spread, because the gum with which, as already men-

---

[1] Esterlins, 18½ grains, a goldsmith's weight. According to Spelman
(*Gloss.* 203) and Dufresne (3, 165), the word was derived from the Ester-
lings or Easterlings, as those Saxons were anciently called who inhabited
the district in Germany now occupied by the Hanse Towns and their ap-
pendages, the earliest traders in Europe. See Tomlin's *Law Dict.*, art.
Coin.

[2] Who is mentioned before in page 84, previous to No. 89.

onde, et le remuer bien, et puis le met jus du feu, et gette dedens un godet d'yaue froide, et quant elle sera rassisse tu en puez ouvrer.

Item in eodem exemplari super ij partes sequentes sic erat, "credo quod hec verba sequencia sint ad faciendum aquas duas virides, ut comprehendo per contentus verborum ac rerum in ipsis verbis nominatarum."

98. Une once de gravelle de vin blanc, une once de sal gemme, une once d'alun de glace, demie once d'alun de plume, vi esterlins de vert de gris, un estrelin de sel commun.

99. Une once de coperose, demie once de vert de gris, une once de salpetre, demie once de rubarbe.

Prenez une chopine d'yaue et la metez en 1 pot de terre neuf, et quant vous verrez que l'iaue commencera a boulir, si metez vostre pouldre, et ne l'ostez hors du feu, et la remuez a une brochete, et laissiez refroider.

Credo quod ipsa verba suprascripti capituli serviant articulis signatis uno 98 alio 99.

Vero modum operandi in Anglia cum aquis.

Post supradicta scriptum sic erat in prefato exemplari, "Antedictus[1] Thedericus, a quo habui ante scriptas receptas prescriptarum aquarum, dixit quod in Anglia operantur operarii pictores cum ipsis aquis, super tellis bene contextis, et belneatis cum aqua gummata de gummi arabico, et siccatis, et postea extensis super solario[2] per terram, super drappis grossis lanne et frixia, incedentes cum pedibus nitidis ipsi qui operantur, iunt, inde per super ipsas telas, operando et depingendo super ipsis imagines, historias, et alia. Et quodque ipse telle sedent et stant in planicie extense, ut dictum est, et super dictis drapis dicte aque colorate pingendo non fluunt, se spargentes, set stant ut ponuntur, et humitidas aquea descendit in drapo lanne, qui eam bibit, ac etiam non sparguntur tractus pincellorum facti ex ipsis aquis, quea gumacio tele facta ut dictum est, prohibet sparsionem

---

[1] De quo supra in 2ª· pagina folii precedentis ante numerum 89.

[2] Solario—the *soler*, or upper story of a house. See Illustrations of Domestic Architecture from popular Medieval writers. By Mr. Wright. Published in the Archæological Journal, September, 1844, p. 218.

tioned, the cloth is wetted, prevents their spreading. And when the
cloths are thus painted, their texture is not thickened or darkened
any more than if they had not been painted, because the aforesaid
watery colours have not sufficient body to thicken the cloth."

Also in the beginning of the following quire in the same MS. it was thus
written—" On Thursday, the 13th day of February, 1410, I caused
the following to be copied at Bologna, by the hand of Dom Johannes
de diversis, from a certain book of Magister Johannes de Modena, a
painter living at Bologna."

It must also be remarked that the articles which follow, namely, from
the article 100 to the article 116 inclusive, were in the book from
which I, John Le Begue, copied, as has been already said, the
present articles; and that this book was written in the Italian language; and as I did not understand that language, I caused it to be
translated into Latin by a certain friend of mine, who was skilled in
both languages.

100. *To make lake.*—Take ashes of oak, and boil them in a
boiler full of water, namely, in one containing 6 small cups of
water, and one parasis, i. e. a large [saucer or] basin full of the
ashes, and boil it until it is reduced to three cups. Then let
it settle, and when it is clear, pour it into a glazed earthen
basin; then take a woollen cloth, and strain the said water,
and when it is strained it will be a ley. Put into the said ley
a sufficient quantity of the clippings, that is, cuttings of scarlet
cloth of rubeum de grana, to be perfectly covered by the ley.
Then put it into a glazed earthen jar, and let it rest for twelve
hours. Next take that ley, together with the clippings, and
put it into a glazed earthen pipkin, and set it by the fire, and
let it simmer gently for an hour. After that try it, by putting
it on your nail, and if it stands up well on your nail, it is
done; then remove it from the fire and strain it through a
thick woollen cloth. You must then have a new glazed
earthen pot, and pour into it what was strained through the
said cloth; add to it vi oz. of roche alum, and stir it together
until it is dissolved. Then take a spoon and skim off all the
froth that forms over the top of it, and throw away this scum,
for it is not good. But the other part is good, and should be
put into a glazed earthen vase, and suffered to stand until it

ipsam tractuum pincellorum ; et cum telle ipse operate sunt, tamen
raritas ipsarum non est inspisata, nec ob fuscata, plus quam si non
picte fuissent, quia aquei colores suprascripti non habent tantum
corpus, quod possent inspicare raritatem telle."

Item in principio quaterni sequentis in eodem exemplari sicut erat
scriptum, "1410, die Jovis xiiiᵃ Februarii, feci copiari que sequuntur in Bononia, de manu domini Johannis de diversis, a quodam
libello magistri Johannis de Modena, pictoris habitantis iu Bononia."

Et autem sciendum, quod articuli qui sequuntur, scilicet ab articulo 100
usque ad articulum 116 inclusive, erant in libro a quo ego, Johannes
le Begue, presencium articulorum, ut supra dictum est, in ytalico
sermone conscripsi, quem sermonem, cum non intelligerem, feci per
quemdam amicum meum, utriusque lingue peritum, in latinum vertii,
eo qui sequitur modo.

100. *Ad faciendum lacha.*—Ad faciendum lacha, accipe
cinerem de quercu, et fac bulire in una patella plena aque,
videlicet quod sint intus sex cassete aque, et una parasis de
dicta cinere, videlicet una magna scutella, et fac tantum bullire
quod reveniant ad tres cassetas tantum modo. Postea sine
clarificare, et, quando est clarificata, ponas in una patella de
terra vitreata ; postea habeas pannum de lanna, et per ipsum
fac colare dictam aquam, et, cum fuerit clarefacta, tum erit
lessivium ; ponas in dicto lessivio tantum cimature, videlicet
burre de panno scarlato rubeo in grana, quod super habundet
aliqualiter lessivium dictam cimaturam. Postea ponas totum
in uno vase de terra vitriato, et sine morari intus per xij horas.
Postea capias illud lessivium una cum cimatura, et ponas in
una olla de terra vitreata, quam pones juxta ignem, et fac
bulire paulatim per unam horam. Et postea experimentes, et
ponas supra unguem, et si teneat se super unguem, tunc est
coctum, et hoc facto amovebis ab igne, et fac colorare per
pannum grossum de lana. Postea habebis unum potum de
terra vitreatum novum, et ponas intus illud quod colaverit per
dictum pannum, et accipe vi oncias de alumine de Roch, et
ponas intus, et misce ad invicem, usque quo liquefacerit.
Postea accipe unum coclearium, et collige tantum illam

has become somewhat dry, when it must be formed into small grains, and be put in the sun.

101. *To make verzino for painting on silver.*—To make verzino for painting on silver or tin-foil, so that the brilliancy of the silver or tin may shine and appear through it, put a piece of white lime about the size of an egg into water to dissolve, and let it stand in the water for three days and three nights. Then rasp or scrape verzino, and add it to the lime-water, and let it stand for an hour ; then put it on the fire in a small jar, and let it boil until, when you put it upon your nail, it remains upon it. Then take isinglass, or, as some say, turpentine, a piece about the size of a bean, and put into it, and remove it from the fire. Take a little roche alum, which you must stick in the end of a small stick and tie it there, and dip it into the said mixture, and let it remain there until you see that it is dissolved. Then take a strainer, and strain or filter the water through it.

102. *To make* [*a liquid*] *for dyeing.*—Take the whites of six eggs, and put them in a glazed basin, and break or beat them well with a sponge. Then take an ounce of verzino and scrape it, and add it to this white of egg, and let it remain in it for three days. Then take a little roche alum and scrape into it, and set it to strain or filter through a strainer. Then place it in the sun, and let it stand until it dries. Temper it with a little weak gum, that is, gum-water, made with gum arabic, having but little gum in it, on account of the viscosity of the white of egg, which is sufficient for it.

103. *To make gesso sottile.*—Take fine gesso sifted, that is, passed through a sieve, and put it into water to dissolve, and change the water every day, and stir it together every day, and

spumam que veniet desuper, et illud quod remanet desuper separes, quod non est bonum. Alterum vero est bonum, et ipsum ponas in uno vaso de terra vitreato, et sinas stare intus usque quo aliqualiter desiccetur, et, quando desiccatum fuerit, fac de ipso parva grana, et ponas ad solem.

101. *Ad faciendum verzin super argento ponendo.*—Ad faciendum verzin super argento vel stagno verberato, ponendo taliter quod splendor argenti et stagni splendeat et lucescat, accipe calcem albam tantum, quantum est unum ovum, et ponas in aqua ad liquefaciendum, et sine stare in dicta aqua per tres dies et tres noctes. Postea habeas feltrum, et per ipsum cola dictam aquam. Postea ratices sive radas verzin, et ponas in dicta aqua de calce, et sine stare intus per unam horam, postea ponas super ignem in una parva olla, et sinas tantum bulire, quod si posueris super unguem, ibi remaneat. Postea habeas de cola piscium, et aliqui volunt dicere de Trementina, tantum quantum unum granum fabe, et pone intus et removeas ab igne, et habeas parumper de alumine de roch, quod ponas in summitate unius parvi baculi, et liges ipsum, et emerge in dicta aqua commixtionata, et sine stare usquequo videris esse liquefactum. Postea habeas unam stamineam, et per ipsam fac penetrare sive colare dictam aquam.

102. *Ad faciendum pro tingendo.*—Accipe clarum sex ovorum, et ponas in una scutella vitreata et deducas, sive percussias, bene cum una spungia. Postea habeas unam onciam de verzin, et ratices, et ponas in isto claro ovorum, et sinas stare intus per tres dies. Postea habeas aliquantum de alumine de roch, et ratices desuper, et pone ad colandum, sive penetrandum, in una staminea. Postea ponas ad solem, et sine stare tantum quod sit siccum. Postea tempera ipsum cum aliquantum de gumma debili, id est de aqua gommata de gummi arabico, que parum gumme in se habet, causa viscositatis clari ovi jam impositi, que sufficit.

103. *Ad faciendum gessum subtile.*—Accipe de gesso subtili sedassato, id est, penetrato per aliquam stamineam, et pone in aqua ad liquefaciendum, et cotidie renoves aquam, et cothidie

do this for a month. Then strain or filter off the water, and take the part that remains behind and put it into a fresh vase, in which you must let it remain till it has settled properly; then make it into a cake, and let it dry.

104. *To lay burnished gold upon paper.*—Take gesso sottile and grind it on a stone with water. Then let it dry, and when it is dry take some glue, not very strong, and mix with it, and add a little minium and ceruse—*i. e.* blanchet—and lay the gesso on the paper, and let it dry. Then scrape it, and lay over it Armenian bole well ground with white of egg, and when it is dry, lay gold upon it with white of egg, and burnish it in proper time.

105. *To lay fine gold upon gilt tin.*—Take white of egg, and whip or beat it well with a sponge, with which wet also the tin, but the sponge must not be too wet. Then take fine gold, and lay it on the tin, and let it stand until it is fit to burnish.

106. *To make a mordant with garlic.*—Take garlic, and pound or grind it very fine, and strain or sift it through a very fine sieve. Then take what passed through, and put it on a stone with a little minium and ceruse, viz., blanchet and a little bole, and grind and mix all these together, and let the mixture stand till it becomes tacky.

107. *To make a mordant which will not be affected by the weather.*—Take a little minium and ceruse, viz., blanchet, also verdigris, bole, and ochre, and grind all together with water, and let them dry until the water is completely evaporated. Then take what remains and grind it with oil and linseed, and add a little liquid varnish to it, and a little gold size, and grind all these things well together, and apply the mordant, and when you have applied it lay on the gold.

108. *To make lake.*—Take verzino and rasp it with glass, and take travertine rasped to powder, and a little roche alum, and grind it, and soak all these things in a ley, and let them

commisceas ad invicem, et in tali statu sine morari usque ad
unum mensem ; postea cola sive penetra aquam, et abstrahe
illud quod remanserit, et ponas in uno vase novo, ubi sinas
morari usque quo fuerit bene repausatum, postea fac panem,
et sine siccari.

104. *Ad ponendum aurum bornitum in carta.*—Accipe gessum subtile, et tere super petra cum aqua. Postea sine siccari, et quando erit siccum, habeto de cola non valde forti, et
extempera cum ipso et pone aliquantulum de minio, et de
ceruza, videlicet blanchet, et pone istud gessum super carta,
et sine siccari. Postea radas et ponas super bolarminum, bene
tritum cum claro ovi, et quando est siccum, pone super aurum
cum claro ovi. Postea bornisce quando tempus est.

105. *Ad ponendum aurum finum super stagno aurato.*—
Accipe clarum ovi, et deducas sive percutias bene cum spungiä,
et balne stagnum de dicta aqua cum spungia, et non valde ;
postea accipias aurum finum, et vade ponendo super stanno, et
sinas tantum quod sit ydoneum ad borniendum.

106. *Ad faciendum mordentem de aleo.*—Accipe de aleo, et
pista, sive tere, bene nitide, et cola, sive penetra, bene nitide
per unam pessiam. Postea collige illud quod penetraverit, et
ponas supra petra cum aliquantum de minio, et de cerusa,
videlicet Blanchet, et aliquantum de bolo, et omnia ista tere et
commisce ad invicem, et sine tantum quod efficiatur conglu-
tinosus.

107. *Ad faciendum mordentem qui stet ad aerem.*—Accipe
parumper de minio, et cerusa, videlicet blanchet, et de ver-
deramo, et de bolo, et de ocrea, et tere omnia ista ad invicem
cum aqua. Postea sine siccari usquequo aqua exiverit. Postea
accipe illud quod remanserit, et tere cum oleo et semine lini,
et pone intus cum aliquanto vernicis liquide, et aliquantum de
auratura ; et omnia ista tere bene invicem, et ponas in opere,
et quando pungit pone super aurum.

108. *Ad faciendum lacha.*—Accipe verzin, et ratices cum
aliquantum de vitreo, et accipe tevertini raticatum in pulvere,
et accipe alume de roch, et tere. Et omnia ista pone ad lique-

stand for a day. Then mix the whole well together, and put
the mixture in a new earthen jar, and make it boil for a quarter
of an hour. Then take a small bag, and pour the whole into
it, and let it remain until the moisture has passed or run
through, and let it fall into a saucer or stone basin.

109. *To make a yellow colour.*—Take an ounce of orpiment,
and an ounce of sulphur vivum, and temper this colour with
the milk of a fig-tree, and it is done.

110. *To make a green water.*—Take buckthorn berries, and
mix them in the same way as is done with wine or raisins when
they are boiled in a cauldron to make wine, and cover them
up, and let them remain for six days. Then squeeze them
into a parasis, viz., a basin of glazed earthenware, and add to
it a little   ' alum, lest it should be spoiled. Proportion the
alum to the quantity of the liquid, and place it in the sun to
dry. And when you wish to use it add a little ley to it; and
if you wish to have a beautiful green take some fine azure and
mix with this water; and note, that for this purpose azurrum
de Alemannia, provided it is good and perfect, is better than
ultramarine.

111. *To make ultramarine azure.*—Take 3 lbs. of lapis
lazuli, and pound finely in a copper mortar, and afterwards sift
it with a sieve such as perfumers use when they sift their perfumes after having pounded them. Then take 3 lbs. of turpentine, and put into a glazed earthen saucer, and place it on
the hot ashes. Then put into it a little olive oil, and when
you see that it begins to boil take it from the fire, and immediately put in the powdered lapis lazuli, little by little, stirring
it well with a stick, so that the turpentine may be well incorporated with the said powder. Then keep the saucer, with the
pastille thus made, for three days, and the longer it stands
the better. Afterwards take another larger saucer, and put
the pastille into it, and take some clean tepid water, and pour

---

' So in original.

faciendum cum lexivio, et sine morari per unum diem. Postea
misce omnia ista bene, et pone in una olla de terra nova, et
fac bulire per quartam partem unius hore. Postea habeas
unum parvum succum, et pone intus omnia ista, et sine morari
usquequo succus penetraverit, sive colaverit, et fac cadere in
una paraside, sive catino, de petra.

109. *Ad faciendum colorem croceum.*—Accipe unam unciam
de orpimento, et unam unciam de sulfure vivo, et distempera
istum colorem cum lacte de figu, et est factum.

110. *Ad faciendum aquam viridem.*—Accipe grana de spino
cervino, et ammusces sicut fit de vino sive raisinis, quando fit
bullire in cuva pro vino faciendo, et tege et sine morari usque
ad vj dies. Postea premas in una paraside, videlicet, in uno
catino de terra vitriato, et pone intus aliquantulum de alume de
(*sic*), ne corrumpatur, et ponas de dicto alume secundum
quantitatem dicti liquoris, et pone ad solem, et sine siccari.
Et quando vis de ipso operari, accipe aliquantum liscivii, et
mitte intus; et si vis facere pulcrum colorem viridem, fac quod
habeas pulcrum azurrum, et misce cum ista aqua; et scias
quod ad istud negotium melius est azurrum de Alemannia,
quam ultramarinum, dum modo sit bonum in perfectione.

111. *Ad faciendum azurium ultramarinum.*—Accipe libras
tres lapides lazuli, et pistes valde bene in uno mortario de
cupro, et fac postea penetrare per unam stamignam, qua
utuntur aromatarii, quando faciunt penetrare aromata postquam pestaverint. Postea habeas libras tres de trementina, et
ponas in una scutella vitreata, quam pones super cinerem
caldum. Postea pone intus aliquantum de oleo olivarum, et
si tu vides quod inceperit bulire, removeas ab igne, et statim
pone intus dictum pulverem lapidis lazulli, paulatim, miscendo,
et bene incorporando cum uno baculo, per modum quod illa
trementina sit bene incorporata cum dicto pulvere. Postea
conserva dictam scutellam cum dicto pastillo taliter confecto
per tres dies, et si plus staret, melius valeret. Postea habeto

over the pastille as much as would fill a small saucer of the size of the saucer in which the pastille was kept, and wash the pastille well with your hands in the water, and then strain the water through the cloth; and having strained the water from the pastille in that manner three times, keep it in another larger saucer, for in it you will have the flower of the azure. Also pour water again over the pastille in quantity about three saucers' full, pouring it over three times, one saucer full at a time, and do as you did before, and you will have good azure, but not so perfect as the first. Also pour water on the pastille a third time, and do as you did before, and you will then have another azure, yet not so perfect as the first or the second.

112. *To make the pastille with which the azure is prepared.*— Take 3 oz. of olive oil, also 2 oz. of turpentine, also ½ oz. of liquid varnish, also 2 sagii[1] of good incense; and, in my opinion, each sagium makes 1 sterling and a half. Afterwards prepare the oil in the following way:—Take a glazed jar, and first put some of the oil into it, and next the two ounces of turpentine, and place it on a clear fire, and let them boil together for so long as it would take to say a Paternoster and Ave Maria. Then put in the said 2 sagii of incense, and let them boil together for as long as it would take to say the *miserere mei Deus* twice. Then add the half ounce of liquid varnish, and let them boil together for as long as it would take to say the *miserere mei Deus* twice. Lastly, pour in the remainder of the oil, and afterwards strain it through a clean closely-woven linen cloth, and preserve it in a clean jar.

113. *To extract the azure from the pastille.*—Put the pastille into an earthen vase, and rub it very well with linseed oil, and afterwards make the said pastille into a round cake. Then

[1] A Sagium, or scruple, according to the Ricettario, weighed 24 grains. The saggio mercantile weighed 24 grains.—*Ricett. Fior.*, p. 126.

unam aliam scutellam majorem, et in dicta pone dictum pastillum, et habeas de aqua nitida et clara tepide, et in dicto
pastillo pone quantitatem unius parve scutelle, que scutella sit
quantitatis que erat prima scutella, in qua prius conservasti
dictum pastillum, et cum manibus lava bene dictum pastillum
in dicta aqua, et tunc cola dictam aquam in dicto panno, et
illam aquam, taliter colatam de pastillo, tribus vicibus reserva
in una alia majori scutella, quia in ista tu habebis florem azurii.
Item altera vice ponas aquam in metipso pastillo, in quantitate
trium scutellarum, ponendo per tres vices, et qualibet vice
unam scutellam, et fac sicut fecisti prius, et habebis azurum
bonum, set non tam perfectum sicut primum. Iterum, tercia
vice, ponas aquam in metipso pastillo, et fac sicut fecisti alteris
duabus vicibus, et tunc habebis alium azurum, set non erit in
perfectione sicut primum nec secundum.

112. *Ad faciendum pastillum de quo fit azurrum.*—Accipe
tres oncias de oleo olivarum, item duas oncias de trementina,
item dimidiam onciam vernicis liquide, item duos sagios boni
incensi ; et, secundum opinionem meam, quodlibet sagium facit
unum sterlingum cum dimidio. Postea confice dictum oleum
isto modo : in primis accipe unam ollam vitriatam, in qua pones
prius de dicto oleo, postea duas oncias de dicta trementina,
postea pones juxta ignem clarum, et sine bulire ad invicem,
tantum quod diceretur semel pater noster et ave Maria.
Postea pones dictos duos sagios incensi, et dimitte bullire invicem tantum, quod bis diceretur " *miserere mei Deus.*" Postea
pone dictam dimidiam unciam de vernice liquida, et sine bulire
tantum, quod diceretur bis *miserere mei Deus.* Postea finaliter
pone residuum de dicto oleo, et postea cola per unum pannum
lineum nitidum bene intextum, et ponas in uno vaso nitido.

113. *Ad trahendum azurrum de pastillo.*—Pone dictum pastillum in uno vaso de terra, et frica valde bene cum oleo de
semine lini, et postea fac de dicto pastillo unum panem ro-

take warm ley, well strained and clear, and pour it on the
pastille, and do the same thing a second and a third time, and
thus you will have three sorts of azure.   Then remove the ley
as well as you can, and put it afresh into another ley, and
make it boil slowly and gently, and skim it.   Then let it
boil for an hour, and remove it from the fire, and pour off the
ley, and wash and strain it well.   Make every three portions
boil in this way, and also each by itself; and also, if you wish
to strain it together with the ley you can do it.

114. *To make the pastille from which the ultramarine is
made.*—Take 1 lb. of lapis lazuli and grind it well, and take
three sagii of new wax.   In my opinion these sagii are equal to
1 sterling and a half each.   Also three sagii of mastic, also one
sagius of coarse incense, also one ounce of the before-mentioned
prepared oil, and then make a pastille in the following manner.
First take the wax, and chew it well with your teeth, and put
it into a glazed jar.   Then place it on the fire, and let it melt.
Next add the incense, and let it melt; and then add the mastic,
and let it boil slowly and gently for so long as it would take
you to say the *miserere mei Deus* once.   Then add half an ounce
of the oil, and let it stand by the fire until it boils.   Then remove it from the fire, and keep stirring it till it is cold, or
nearly so, when you must add the powder of lapis lazuli, and
stir it until it becomes hard.   Then take water that is slightly
warmed, and put the pastille into it, and mix it until the water
is well coloured.   Then put it into a parasis or basin of glazed
stoneware, and the perfect azure will immediately sink to the
bottom of the basin, and you must then pour off the water carefully; or, you may keep it, if you wish to do so, and then pour
off the water: add cold water, and wash the said azure well,
mixing it with a stick.   Then strain it through a closely-textured
linen cloth, and pour off the water and dry it, and you will
thus have perfect azure.

115. *To extract perfect azure.*—First take a phial of cold ley,
and put into it one drachm of the stone tuzia, well ground with
the said ley, then wash the azure in it, and afterwards wash it

tundum; postea habeas lessivium tepidum bene colatum et
clarum, et pone in dicto pastillo, et simili modo iterum facies
bina et trina vice, et sic habebis de tribus maneriebus azurri.
Postea atrahes lixivium quam melius poteris, et de uno pone in
alio lexivio, et fac bulire paulatim et plane, et schiumabis [from
schiumare] desuper; postea sine bulire per unam horam, et retrahe ab igne, et abstrahe lexivium, et lava bene, et similiter bene
colabis, et fac omnibus tribus vicibus sic bullire, et qualibet vice
pro se; et etiam, si velis colare una cum lessivio, facere poteris.

114. *Ad faciendum pastillum de quo fit azurum ultramarinum.*
—Accipe unam libram de petra vel lapide lazuli, et tere bene,
et accipe tres sagios de cera nova, qui sagii faciunt, videre meo,
quilibet unum sterlingum cum dimidio. Item tres sagios de
mastich, item unum sagium large incensi, item unam onciam
de oleo supradicto confecto, et postea fit pastillum tali modo.
In primis accipe ceram, et mastica bene cum dentibus, et pone
in una olla vitriata. Postea pone juxta ignem et sine liquefieri.
Postea ponas dictum incensum, et sine liquefieri; postea ponas
dictum mastich, et sine bullire paulatim et plane, tantum quod
diceretur semel " *miserere mei Deus.*" Postea ponas dimidiam
onciam de dicto oleo, et sine tantum stare juxta ignem quod
buliat. Postea remove ab igne, et commisce tantum quod sit
refrigeratum, vel quasi; postea pone dictum pulverem de lapide
lazulli, et misce tantum quod veniat dura; postea accipe de
aqua parumper calida, et pone supradictum pastillum, et tantum
misceas, quod aqua sit bene colorata. Postea ponas in una
paraside, sive catino, de lapide vitreato, et statim azurrum perfectum submergetur in profundo cathini; postea diligenter
abstrahe aquam, et, si vis ipsam reservare, potes, et abstrahe
dictam aquam, et ponas de aqua frigida, et laves bene dictum
azurrum, miscendo bene cum uno ligno. Postea cola per
panum lineum bene intextum, et abstrahe illam aquam, et
siccabis, et sic habebis azurrum perfectum.

115. *Ad abstrahendum azurrum perfectum.*—In primis accipe
unam fiolam de lissivio frigido, in qua pones intus unam drag-
mam de lapide tuzia bene trita cum dicto lixivio, postea lavabis

with cold water, until it remains pure and brilliant, and thus you will have a perfect blue.

116. *To obtain a blue, not quite so perfect.*—If you like you may also make up the pastille again, as before directed, except that you must not add to it any of the before-mentioned lapis lazuli, and you must keep and knead this second pastille as before directed with regard to the first, and thus you will have a second and a third kind of azure not so perfect.

> Whoever wishes to try all these experiments must observe and note that the pounds mentioned here must be understood as of twelve ounces each, according to the Italian mode of reckoning.
>
> Also in the said MS. it was thus written—" I received the following receipt at Venice, on Tuesday the 4th day of May, 1410, from Michelino di Vesuccio, the most excellent painter among all the painters of the world."

117. *Azure is thus made.*—Take 1 lb. of lapis lazuli and grind it well upon a porphyry slab; then wash it with water and dry it, and reduce it to powder. The pastille is thus made :—To each pound of powdered lapis lazuli take 1 lb. of Greek pitch, ij. oz. of liquid varnish, j. oz. of mastic ; put into a rough jar iij. oz. of good common oil, *i. e.* linseed or olive oil, and make it boil ; then put the mastic and varnish in powder into the oil, and stir it well with a stick, and when you see that they are dissolved add the Greek pitch in powder, and let it boil a little, until the whole is incorporated. Then strain it through a cloth into cold water and knead it with your hands greased with common oil, and then incorporate the powdered lapis lazuli very carefully upon a slab with the pastille, and let it stand for three days with the pastille. Afterwards extract the azure from the pastille in this way :—Stir it about with a stick in water that is a little more than tepid, and keep it in as long as any colour flows out; but if you cannot extract the colour put hotter water to it, and so keep adding water hotter and hotter by degrees until it brings out the colour. Lastly, pour off the water when it is at the hottest, and having extracted all the azure and separated it from the water, make a very strong ley, and put the azure into smooth vases, and pour

azurrum, postea etiam lavabis cum aqua frigida, tantum quod remaneat purum et nitidum, et sic habebis perfectum azurrum.

116. *Ad habendum azurrum non adeo perfectum.*—Si vis, fac pastillum etiam de novo, sicut dictum est de super, excepto quod tu non debes ponere aliquid de dicto lapide lazullino, et istud secundum pastillum debes custodire et incorporare, sicut dictum est de super in primo, et sic habebis azurrum in secundo et tercio modo non adeo perfectum.

> Sit autem monitus, vel advertat, quicumque habet omnia ista experiri, quod libre, de quibus in eis fit mencio, intelligantur de duodecim unciis quelibet libra, secundum morem italicum.
>
> Item in eodem exemplari sic erat scriptum, "hoc sequens experimentum hujusmodi, in Veneciis, die martis, IIII maii, anni 1410, a Michelino de Vesucio, pictore excellentissimo inter omnes pictores mundi."

117. *Azurrum sic fit.*—Recipe libram unam lapidis lazuli, et tere bene in lapide porfirico. Postea ablue ipsum cum aqua clara, deinde desica et reduce ipsum in pulverem. Pastillum sic fit; ad libram unam pulveris lapidis, pone libram unam picis grece, oncias ij. vernicis liquide, onc. i. masticis; ponantur in olla rudi onc. iij. olei communis, id est lini, vel olive, et boni, et fac bullire, et tunc mastice et vernicem pulverizatam pone in oleo, et bene moveas cum ligno. Et cum videas resoluta, pone piscem pulverizatam, et permitte parum bullire, donec omnia fuerunt bene incorporata. Postea cola per pannum in aqua frigida, et manicetur manibus oleo communi, et postea pulver lazulli incorporetur super lapidem cum dicto pastillo, et optime, et dimittatur per tres dies in dicto pastillo. Postea extrahatur azurrum de pastillo hoc modo; misceatur cum baculo in aqua calida, parum plusquam tepida, et taliter teneatur, quousque aliquid exiverit. Si vero non exiret, ponatur aqua magis calida, et sic gradatim, mittendo aquam calidiorem, et miscendo, donec aliquid exiverit; ultimo ponatur aqua quando magis fervet, et extracto toto azurro, et separato ab aqua, et sicato, fiat lexivium fortissimum, et ponatur azurrum in planis vasis, et superius ponatur lexivium, sicut nosti, ut exeant immondicii pastilli, quo purgato, dulcifica cum aqua clara, etc.

the ley upon it, in order, as you know, to get rid of the impurities of the pastille. Having thus purified it, wash it with clean water, &c.

> In the year of the Circumcision of Christ, 1410, on the 2nd day of February, after that Master Johannes de (^{1}) (a Norman, who was residing in the house of Master Petrus de Verona, who knows how to refine or make ultramarine azure, and does refine or make the said azure when he wants it) had told me, Johannes Alcherius, at Paris, the process which is used in-making the said ultramarine azure, I noted down and made the present writing, according to my opinion, and according to the things which I heard from him, and also according to the things which I saw in divers treatises concerning this, and as I heard from divers other persons.

118. *To clean, refine, or make ultramarine azure with a pastille; or to make it with lapis lazuli ground to powder, and to purify the powder with a pastille.*—Pound and grind very fine and dry in a copper mortar fine ultramarine lapis lazuli, which is the better in proportion as it is of a deeper and more brilliant sky blue, namely when the colour is not too pale or whitish, and the stone itself is not mixed with parts that are not of a blue colour, but of a yellow or earthy and whitish colour. And if, as it sometimes happens, the stone cannot be obtained in pieces, but the powder of it, which the salesmen call azure, can be obtained, although not refined or purified, take it and try whether it is fine, by heating it in the fire upon an iron plate. If it does not change its colour or get dull it is good. Then grind this powder excessively fine, upon a hard and smooth stone, with clean water, in the same way that colours are ground. Then dry it, and reduce it to powder, and make the pastille for purifying the said powder or azure, of the following things, in this manner :—

Put into a glazed earthen vase, 8 oz. of turpentine. This must be softened by warming, so that it may be stirred and washed ; and it must be washed several times with pure warm water, stirring the water and the turpentine with a stick, and

---

^{1} So in original.

Anno circoncisionis 1411, die ij Februarii, post quam magister
Johannes de   (*sic*), Normanus, commorans in domo magistri
Petri de Verona, qui sit afinare vel facere azurrum ultramarinum, et
afinat diatim, seu facit, cum expedit, dixit mihi Johanni Alcherio, in
Parisiis, modum quo utitur afiniando, seu faciendo ipsum azurrum,
notavi, et feci presentem scripturam, secundum avisum meum, et
juxta eaque ab ipso audivi, et juxta eaque per diversas scripturas
vidi de hoc, et a diversis aliis personis audivi.

118. *Ad purgandum, vel afinandum, seu faciendum, azurrum*
ultramarinum cum pastillo, seu ad faciendum illud de lapide
lazulli, trito in pulvere, et purgando pulverem cum pastillo.—
Pulverizatur et teritur subtilissime ad siccum, in mortario
cupri, lapis lazulli ultramarinus finus, cujus bonitatis est major,
quanto est magis celestis coloris, et vivi, videlicet quod non sit
nimis clarus color et albescens, seu quod lapis ipse non sit im-
mixtus de partibus non celestini coloris, set crocei, vel terrestis,
et albescentis ; et si, ut quandoque accidit, non invenitur lapis,
et inveniatur pulver de ipso factus, quem vendentes appellant
azurium, dato quod non sit afinatus seu purgatus, accipiatur et
probetur si fit finum, ponendo ipsum ad ignem super lamina
ferri, et si non mutat colorem, vel pejorat, est bonum ; deinde
pulver illud teratur super lapide duro, plano, bene subtiliter
cum aqua clara, ut teruntur colores, postea siccetur, et redigatur in pulverem, et fiat postea pastillus, pro purgando dictum
pulverem seu azurium, de rebus sequentibus, hoc modo.
Accipiantur in vase terreo vitreato uncie octo tormentine, que
si vel sic intepidetur, ut sit aliquantulum mollis, ut possit agitari lavando eam, et lavetur pluries cum aqua clara tepida,
agitando aquam et tormentinam simul cum baculo, et jactando
aquam, ita quod termentina fiat bene alba, clara, et purgata,

then throwing away the water, so that the turpentine may be bleached, cleaned, and purified. This is my own advice, although Master Johannes did not say that it would be better. Then add to it 2 oz. of pine resin, or Greek pitch, and 2 oz. of new wax, and melt or liquefy all these things together over the fire, and mix them well, and it will make the pastille, which must afterwards be allowed to cool a little, so that it may be just tepid and soft, and not liquid, but rather solid.

Then add viij., x., or xij. oz. of the said powdered lapis lazuli, putting it in by degrees, and mixing the pastille and the powder with a stick, so that the powder may be well incorporated with the pastille, and let it rest for about a day and a night or longer.

Then pour over it a quantity of warm water sufficient to cover the pastille, and let it stand for a short time, so that it may not be melted, but only warmed and softened sufficiently to allow it to be kneaded and stirred with the stick. Afterwards, if the water has become too cold, add more hot water, which thus being added to the former becomes and also causes the pastille to become of a convenient heat. It would therefore be more convenient in summer than in winter on account of the heat. Stir the pastille gently with a stick or a wooden spoon, and pour off the water, and the azure that is extracted with it, into another glazed earthen jar. And because the azure on account of its weight sinks presently to the bottom of the water, the water must be immediately poured off into another glazed earthen jar, lest any yellowish or white and earthy impurities, which are not so heavy as the azure, and which therefore do not sink to the bottom so soon, should, perhaps, render the water turbid ; and if the water should be turbid, these impurities will sink to the bottom along with the azure, which it will contaminate by being mixed with it. Afterwards wash the said pastille again several times in the same manner with warm water, not allowing it to cool or harden, but keeping it at a proper degree of heat and softness ; always pouring off the water of each washing, together with the azure which

quod advisavi ego, dato quod ipse magister Johannes non
dixerit erit melius. Postea ponantur in ipsa oncie due picis
rase, seu grece, et oncie due cere nove, et fundantur seu
liquefiant hec omnia simul ad ignem, et misceantur bene, et iste
erit pastillus, qui postea dimittatur aliquantulum infrigidari,
ita quod sit solum tepidus et mollis, et non liquidus, set aliquantulum obduratus. Deinde ponantur in ipso oncie viii°,
vel x^{cem}, vel xii^{cim}, dicti pulveris lazulli lapidis, paulatim im-
ponendo, et cum baculo pastillum cum pulvere miscendo, ita
quod bene incorporetur pulver cum pastillo ; postea dimitatur
per circa diem et noctem, vel plus, deinde ponatur de aqua
calida, ita quod pastillus cooperiatur, et stet paucum, ut efficiatur non liquefactus, sed tepidus et mollis, ut possit cum baculo
agitari et misceri. Postea, si aqua erit nimis infrigidata, et
suponatur de alia calida, que sic fit alteri adita remaneat, et
pastillus cum ea ad tepiditatem convenientem reducatur.
Igitur melius fit hoc in estate, pro calido, quam in hieme ; et
misceatur pastillus cum baculo, vel spatula ligni, moderato
modo, et azurrium, quod exibit cum aqua, immittatur, cum ipsa
aqua lavature sue, in alio vase terreo vitriato. Et quia azurium
subito, pro ejus ponderositate, descendit ad fondum aque, est
cito post ejus descensum proficienda est aliquo alio vase terreo
vitreato, ne aliqualis turpitudo albescens, vel crocea, et terrestris, que non est tam ponderosa, ut azurrium, et igitur nec tam
cito descendit ad fundum, et qua turpedine forte ipsa aqua es
aliqualiter turbida, si aliqualiter ex ea turbida erit, descendat
ad fondum cum azurrio, et ipsum deturpet se sibi immiscendo ;
et postea iterum relavetur simili modo dictus pastillus pluribus
vicibus cum aqua tepida, non dimittendo ipsum pastillum infrigidari nec indurari, set tenendo ipsum in tepiditate et mollicie
debita, et semper aquam, ad quamlibet lavaturam cum azurro
exeuntem quem secum traxerit et dixerit, mittendo in dicto
vase, in qua prima missa erit, donec videatur quod azurrium
incipiat exire a pastillo tanto minus bonum, seu minus pulcrum
in colore ejus, quam primum, quod ex nimia differencia conveniat non plus ipsum ulterius ex aliis lavaturis exeuntem

comes off with it and is mixed with it, into the vase in which
the first was put, until you see the azure come out of the pastille so much inferior in colour that on account of the too great
difference of colour it is not proper to mix this last with the
azure proceeding from the former washings, but it should be kept
separate. You must then put what comes off with the subsequent waters into another vase, separate from the first, and
pour off in a similar manner the water of the washings into the
same vase in which you put the water of the former washings.
And afterwards wash the azure again secondly as many times
as you were directed to wash the first sort aforesaid, namely
until the colour changes so materially for the worse, and then,
on account of the too great change in the colour, let the subsequent waters be poured off into another third vase, until the
whole pastille is washed in such manner that all the colour
which can be extracted from the pastille is obtained. There
will thus be three sorts of azure.

Next, pour off the water of all these different washings into
the other vase, which contains the rest of the water of the said
washings, and let the azure, which was thus made and refined,
dry, and keep it for use in painting pictures. Then stir the
aforesaid water, consisting of a mixture of all the washings of
the three sorts of azure, well from the bottom with a stick, so
as to mix up the grounds of the azure and the earthy parts,
and so that the water may be as turbid as possible ; let it stand
for a very, very short time, and then immediately pour the
water quickly off, with all the earthy impurities mixed with it,
leaving in the bottom of the vase any azure which may sink to
the bottom, if there should have been any portion of it with the
water, as there usually is in this manner of refining the azure,
namely with the water which is poured off from the three sorts
of azure.

And note that when it is wished to use the ultramarine
azure, which is made from the three sorts of waters above
mentioned, it must not be ground upon a stone, as is done with
sinobrium and other colours, because the grinding which it had

miscere cum primo, set teneri separate; et tunc quod exibit
ad alias sequentes lavaturas pastilli suprascripti ponatur in alio
vase, separatim a primo, et similiter mittendo aquam dictarum
lavaturarum in dicto vase, in quo alia aliarum lavaturarum
missa erit. Et postea iterum secundo per tot vices lavetur,
quod similiter ut de suprascripto primo dictum est, videatur
quod nimis mutet colorem in minori pulcritudine; et tunc,
ab ipsa nimia mutatione coloris antedicta, ponantur tertio
sequentes lavature in alio vase, donec pastillus totus sit taliter
lavatus, quod extractum sit de ipso totum azurium quod ex-
trahi poterit; et sic erunt tres sortes azurii, de quibus dictis
lavaturis similiter iniciatur aqua in predicto alio vase, cum alia
aqua omnium aliarum lavaturarum predictarum, et postea desiccari permittatur azurium, quod sic erit afinatum et factum,
et servetur ad usum operum fiendorum, et qua predicta, acu-
mulata de omnibus dictis lavaturis dictarum trium sortarum
azurii, agitetur fortiter cum baculo usque ad fondum, ut fecies
azurii et pars terrestris commoveatur, et turbidetur aqua
quantum poterit; deinde valde parum stet, et postea proiciatur
cito ipsa aqua, cum tota turpedine suprascripta terrestri in ipsa
immixta, et retineatur in fundo vasis illa aliqua pars azurii que
in ipso fondo erit descensa, si aliqua pars adherit, ut esse solet,
in talibus affinaturiis azurrii de dependenciis, scilicet dictarum
trium sortarum azurii; et nota, quod cum dicto azurrio ultra-
marino dictarum lavaturarum ipsarum trium sortarum in opere
ponere volueris, non debet teri super lapide, nec aliter, prout
fit de sinobrio et aliis coloribus, quia suffisit de prima suprascripta tritione facta, et etiam quia azurii color fortiter pejaretur
et vastaretur, sed debet sic ut est destempari cum aqua gomata,
seu cum clara ovi, vel cum cola liquefacta, aut cum oleo semi-
num lini, prout volet operari, et pertinebit operi fiendo; postea
si voluerit lavari de alio azurrio, accipiatur totidem de tormen-
tina, et pice, et cera, ut antea est dictum, et fiat alter pastillus,
et fiat ut prius, et tociens quociens fieri voluerit, semper re-
faciendo novos pastillos, secundum quantitatem que expedit
volenti facere et purgare azurrium.   Set credo quod, pro

at first is sufficient for it, and also because the colour of the
azure would very likely be spoilt or deteriorated, but it should
be tempered just as it is with gum-water, or with white of egg,
or melted glue, or with linseed oil, according to the choice of
the artist and the nature of the work which is to be done.
Afterwards if any more azure is to be washed, the same quantities of turpentine, pitch, and wax as were mentioned before
must be taken and another pastille must be made as before,
and the same method adopted ; and this may be done as often
as is wished, always making up new pastilles, according to the
quantity convenient to the person who wishes to wash or refine
the azure.

But I think, that in order to diminish the expense, the former
pastille might be cleansed from all the impurities which it has
contracted in the operation for which it was used, if it is put
over the fire to boil and liquefy in clear water, because the
pastille, being melted by the heat of the boiling water, would
liquefy and float upon it. It should then be stirred with a stick
or a wooden spoon, beating it up violently and quickly in the
water with the stick, so that the pastille may be well mixed
with the water and that the impurities of it may be dissolved
by the water, and leave the pastille and enter into the water,
and that when the stirring has ceased the melted pastille may
separate and float upon the top of the boiling water, entirely
cleansed from all earthy and other impurities, which by their
weight will sink to the bottom. If it is afterwards taken off the
fire and allowed to cool, the pastille being allowed to remain as
it is in the said water, when the water is cold and the pastille has
become hard, it can be taken out of the water, and the water
with the impurities can be thrown away ; and having been thus
renewed, it may be used again for the same purpose as before,
and thus it would be useless to incur any expense in making
fresh pastilles; but the labour of washing the azure might
be repeated as often as convenient, until the whole of the
washing necessary for the quantity of the azure has been completed.

faciendo minorem expensam, posset primus pastillus purgari
ab omni sorde in ipso inserta, pro operatione de ipso facta, si
poneretur ad ignem, ad bulliendum in aqua clara, et liquide
faciendum ; quia cum ex caliditate bullientis aque esset fusus
et liquidus, supernataret ipse pastillus in ipsa aqua bullienti ;
et, si agitaretur cum baculo vel spatula ligni, cum veloci stre-
pitu agitando cum ipso baculo usque ad aquam, ita quod im-
misceretur pastillus cum aqua, turpedo ipsius dilueretur, et
exiret ab ipso, et intraret in aquam ; et, cum cessaretur a dicta
agitacione, adunaretur ipse pastillus liquefactus, supernatatando
in superficie dicte aque bullientis, totus purgatus ab omni sorde
terrestri, et a quacumque alia, que, ut ponderosa, ad fondum
descendasset ; et postea, si levaretur ab igne, et permitteretur
infrigidari sic, ipso pastillo stante in dicta aqua, cum frigidatus
esset et durus, posset levari ab aqua, et abici aqua cum sorde,
et de ipso iterato refici opus primo de ipso factum, et sic non
expediret fieri expensa, pro aliis pastillis novis fiendis, set, quociens expediret, posset opus predictum lavacionis azurii eodem
dicto modo reiterari et refici, usque ad totalem expedicionem
lavende necessarie quantitatis azurrii.

OF THE MS. OF PETRUS DE S. AUDEMAR.

PRELIMINARY OBSERVATIONS.

This MS. affords internal proof that Petrus de S. Audemar (Pierre de St. Omer?) was a native of or a resident in the northern part of France. Many passages in the MS. prove that it is of French origin; among these I may mention that in which is described the Rothomagensian green, which derived its name from Rothomagus, the Latin name for Rouen on the Seine. Madder also, which is called in French Garance, is mentioned under the term Warancia, and in No. 201 a recipe is given for making a green colour after the Norman manner. There are indications also of some of the recipes being derived from English or Anglo-Saxon sources, and thence communicated to their fellow-subjects in Normandy. In No. 162 the English name for Folium is mentioned, and in Nos. 199 and 201 two other English plants are named. These last recipes are to be found in the Mappæ Clavicula, but without the addition, in No. 201, of the words "according to the Normans." Several other recipes belonging to this MS. are also in the Clavicula; some are found in the 1st book of Theophilus, and some in the Sloane MS., No. 1754.

The date of the MS. is doubtful. Mr. Eastlake (Materials for a History of Painting in Oil, p. 45) says it cannot be placed later than the end of the thirteenth or beginning of the fourteenth century. The fact of some of the recipes being in the Clavicula, which is supposed to be of the twelfth century, affords no evidence of the age of the MS., because some of them are comprised in the body of the work, but the greater part are to be found in the very beginning, even before the table of contents, and these seem to have been an addition to the original work. It is by no means improbable that these recipes were selected in both cases from some well-known originals as yet undiscovered.

The MS. contains the usual recipes for colours, for ink, and for gilding. Among the colours we find *greens* prepared in different ways from copper and vegetables; *white* from lead, *black* from charcoal, *blue* from silver, from copper, and from flowers. Ultramarine does not appear to have been known to our author. It seems from the description of the mode of purifying the blue pigment in No. 168, that it was a natural blue ore of copper, the Azzurro della Magna of Cennini (chap. lx.), which was extensively used both before and after the introduction of ultramarine, and which was produced in great abundance in the mines of Chessy, near Lyons. This mine was worked for a long period, and continued to produce great quantities of the blue ores of copper. It is now, however, closed. In the year 1845 I saw many specimens of these ores exposed for sale at Lyons.

The *red* pigments consisted of artificial vermilion, red lead, which the author calls " minium " and " sandaraca," and lake made from the gum of the ivy. It will be observed that the latter is also called "Sinopis de Mellana."

The only yellow pigment is saffron, but the principal use of this colour appears to have been in colouring varnishes, the yellow in old pictures being more frequently represented by gold.

Like Cennini, Peter de S. Audemar teaches what vehicles should be used with each colour, and from these instructions we learn that the colours were applied on walls in secco, tempered with egg or gum; in books, that is, miniatures with gum or egg; and on wood with oil—thus affording certain proof of the use of oil in painting at this period in France.

That varnish was used, is incidentally mentioned in the recipe for making auripetrum, which was a varnish to which a golden colour was imparted by saffron, and which, when spread over tinfoil, was employed to imitate gold. A similar recipe is given in Eraclius, and another will be found in the Lucca MS., which has been copied into the Clavicula, a proof of the extent to which it was used. A gold colour was also given to tin by applying over it several coats of gall (see No. 203), and also by applying a solution of aloes, No. 206. Other varnishes are described in Nos. 207, 208, and 209; and it seems these also must have been highly coloured, because they were to be used like the auripetrum, for colouring tin to imitate gold, the price of which placed it beyond the reach of all but the rich. As to the materials of the varnishes, one was composed of linseed oil, resin, and *vernix*, that is, sandarac; another of linseed oil boiled with the inner bark of the black plum, *glassa*, alum, and dragon's blood; and the third of the same linseed oil previously boiled with the inner bark of the black plum, resin, and *frankincense*. We must therefore suppose that three different ingredients were used for varnishes, for it is as reasonable to conclude from the text that they were *all* synonymous, as that *vernix* and *glassa* were the same in this instance, for it can scarcely be supposed that Peter de S. Audemar, who must have been in the habit of making these varnishes, should have used a different term, if any two had been synonymous.

It will also be observed, that there is no allusion in this MS. to the application of varnish upon colours or pictures, or to any other preparation of oil, except boiling it with the inner bark of the black plum (the object of which, if we may believe the Table of Synonymes, was to give the oil a yellow colour) before it was mixed with the resins; at the same time there is nothing to show that this boiled oil was not used in painting. The fact of " liquid varnish" being mentioned in the recipe for Auripetrum, No. 202, is sufficient proof that it was in use at this period, and that the drying effect produced on oils by boiling was known, because sandarac is not soluble in raw oils, and distilled oils were not used at this period. The recipes Nos. 208 and 209 much resemble those in the Paris MS. of Eraclius, No. 274.

BOOK OF MASTER PETER OF ST. AUDEMAR ON MAKING COLOURS,

AND FIRST THE

INTRODUCTION.

BY the assistance of God, of whom are all things that are good, I will explain to you (at whose request, as you know, I undertook this work) how to make colours for painters and illuminators of books, and the vehicles for them, and other things appertaining thereto, as faithfully as I can in the following chapters.

---

150. *The way to make a green colour with salt.*—First hear how to make a green colour with salt :—Stir some salt together in a jar or in a ladle, and heat it, stirring it frequently until it loses its former colour and becomes dusky—*i.e.* darkish. Then pound it, and, if necessary, pass it through a sieve, shaking it with your hand, in the same way that boys are accustomed to shake dust in a bottle ; sift it into a jar, or any other vase which will hold it, in order that, if by chance any hairs or other impurities be mixed with it, they may be separated ; as otherwise, if it continue white, or if any impurities remain in it, the colour will be dirty. Afterwards crush it well, dry as it is, upon a flat slab, either of marble or wood, with a smooth wooden block made for this purpose, or with a stone. Then temper some soap with wine or vinegar. Vinegar is made as follows.

151. *How to make vinegar.*—Take good wine, or wine as sour as you can get it, and put it into a jar or any other vase,

MAGISTRI PETRI DE SANCTO AUDEMARO DE COLORIBUS FACIENDIS,

ET PRIMO

PROHEMIUM.

Deo opitulante, cujus sunt omnia que bona sunt, tibi, sicut novisti, cujus rogatu hoc opus sum aggressus, de coloribus pictorum et illuminatorum librorum faciendis, de temperamentis que eorum, et de aliis hiis convenientibus, quam fidelius potere in sequentibus explicabo.

---

150. *De modo faciendi viridem colorem de sale.*—Primo quo modo ex sale fiat intellige ; salem igitur commiscens in olla seu patella torribis, sæpius movendo, usque quo primum colorem amittat, et fuscus fit, id est subniger. Deinde pulverizabis, et, si opus fuerit, induces cum stamino, et manu movendo, sicut pueri pulverem in catrasia positum agitare solent, et transire facies in ollam, vel in aliud quodcumque vas, illud recipiens ut si forte pili, vel aliæ sordes, ei commixtæ fuerint, seque ferentur alioquin, si albus remanserit, aut aliquod turpe in ipso remanserit, turpis color erit. Postea super tabulam æqualis superficiei, vel marmoream, vel ligneam, bene subtiliter ita siccum conteres cum ligno ad hoc parato equali, vel cum lapide. Deinde savonem cum vino vel aceto distemperabis. Acetum vero sic fit.

151. *Quomodo fit acetum.*—Sume vinum optimum, vel quantum acrius habere potes, et in ollam positum, seu vase alio,

and let it stand for 5 or 8 days, or for as many days as you like, in a vase covered with a plank or a stone, and not entirely closed, in order that it may feel the changes of the air, which cause it to turn sour; and let it acidify by exposing it to the sun, or suspending it over the fire. You can then put it by, and preserve it as long as you like.

If you have no soap, never mind; yet, nevertheless, wet plates of copper or basins,[1] cut into pieces or strips, all over with pure wine, without water, or else with the vinegar. Afterwards spread salt well and evenly over the metal, so that the copper may be entirely covered, but very thinly and evenly, because, if it be covered too thick, the colour will not be good. You must have a vase prepared for the purpose, either of earth or of wood, in the bottom of which you must pour a little wine or beer, or stale urine, which is better than fresh, and place the copper, salted as before directed, inside the vase. But, in order that it may not slip into the wine or urine, let it be supported by putting a piece of wood over the jar, to which the said slips or curved pieces (if formed by cutting up basins or cups) must be suspended side by side, so as not to touch one another. Then stop up the mouth of the jar, lest any dung should fall into it, and put plenty of horse-dung all round it, and under it and over it, and leave it in that manner to heat in the dung for 8 or 9 days, and you will then find your salt turned green, and of an excellent colour. The hotter the dung is, the sooner it will be done. You may, if you like, wait for 17 or 18 days before you uncover it and remove the colour. And in winter and summer, according as you find the heat of the dung greater or less, you will so time your work; and also according to whether the plates are made of copper or brass, as aforesaid, knowing that if they are of copper the work will be done—i.e. the colour will be made sooner; but if they are made of brass it will be longer before it is made. Heat accelerates the formation of the colour, cool weather retards it, and

---

[1] When the word "basin" is used alone, a vessel of copper or brass should be understood.

quinque, vel octo, vel quot volueris diebus, vase cooperto asce
vel lapide, et non obturato, ut aeris mutaciones sentiat, quæ
acuere facit, et ad solem, vel super ignem, suspensum, acui
permitte, et sic quantum diu volueris repositum servare poteris.

Si autem savonem non habueris, non sit tibi cure, nihilominus
tamen ex vino puro absque aqua, si vel ex dicto aceto, laminas
cupreas ex omni parte humectabis, vel bacinos decisos per
pecias seu laminas.   Et postea ex ipso sale asperge bene et
equaliter per totum, ita ut cuprum totum coopertum sit, tamen
tenuissime et equaliter, quia si spissum fuerit non habebit
optimum colorem.   Unum vero vas habebis ad hoc paratum,
vel ligneum, vel fictile, in cujus fundo pones parum vini, vel
cervisiæ, aut aceti, vel urinam, nihilominus vetustam, quæ
melior ad hoc probatur, et desuper in ipso vase pones cuprum,
sicut jam dixi, salitum.   Sed ne labatur in vino vel urina, sus-
tineatur ligno superposito, cui suspendantur dictæ laminæ in
aere, sive autem recte sint laminæ, seu curvæ, ut de de bacinis,
vel patellis incisis, sint juxta se alia post aliam, non se tangente.
Postea os ipsius olle obtures, ne fimus introcadat, et fimum
equinum habundanter, et sub vase, et in circuita, et superpones, et sic isto modo, in dicto fimo califactum, octava vel
nona die salem viridem recipies, et optimum.   Et quanto fer-
vencius callescet fimus, tanto fiat citius.   Et tum nihilominus,
si volueris, usque ad xvii. vel xviii. dies expectabis, antequam
discoperias vas, et recipias colorem.   Et in estate, et in hyeme,
sicut senseris calorem stercoris vel fimi majorem vel minorem,
ita tuum laborem moderabis; et tam de æneis, quam cupreis
tabulis, sicut dixi, sciens que si cupreæ fuerint, citius fiet
opus—i. e. colorabitur—si vere æneæ, tardius.   Calor ejus ac-
celerat colorem, sed tepiditas tardat; frigiditas vero nil agit;
et notandum est, quod si dictum vas cooperieris in fimo existenti
in stabulo equi, in alio secreto et calido loco, melius valet, et
opus acceleratur, quia interius calefit.   Hoc idem agere potes
in cumulo vinciarum, ad pressorium vini.   Hunc autem colo-

cold stops it altogether : it must also be remarked, that if the
vase is covered with dung in a horse-stable, or in some other
warm and close space, it is better, and the work will progress
more rapidly, because it is better warmed. The same thing
can be done in the heaps of grape-skins by the wine-presses.
You must then scrape and shave off the colour with a knife, or
any other instrument, from the aforesaid plates, and if you find
that any white salt has remained mixed with the green colour,
you need not be vexed at it, but just pick it out with a knife or
with your hand ; and you must afterwards wash these tablets
with water, preserving the water, if necessary. Then wash,
scour, and clean them a second time, with wood-ashes, rubbing
them down with a linen cloth before you put fresh salt upon
them, lest, if any of the old remained upon it, it should be a
hindrance. You must allow the water of the first washing,
which was done without the ashes, to remain quiet, so that you
may collect the colour which sinks to the bottom, throwing
away the supernatant water. This colour may be distempered
and mixed with water, or still better, with vinegar, and also
with linseed-oil, or even with white of egg.

152. *How to make and temper white and green.*—White and
green colours, without salt, are made and tempered as follows :
Pour very strong vinegar into a vase, and place twigs of trees
across it inside the vase, and then place strips of lead, and other
strips of copper or brass, suspended in the air by means of the
twigs, so as not to touch the vinegar or each other. Then close
the vase very carefully, and lute it with clay or cement, or
wax, so that there may not be the least hole through which the
vinegar may exhale. Then cover it with horse-dung, and, after
30 days, on account of the acidity of the vinegar or the wine—
for the wine, on account of the heat of the dung, will become
vinegar—on account, I say, of the acidity of the wine or vinegar,
the copper or brass will be found to be turned green, and the
lead white. Take the white, dry it, and grind it, and temper
it with wine, and use it for painting on parchment, and mix it
with oil for painting on wood and on walls. In the same manner

rem postea cum cultello, vel alio instrumento, a laminis predictis extirpere et radere debes, et si aliquantulum de albo sale
cum viridi remansisse invenies, non sit tibi curæ, sed caute cum
cultello vel manu separa, et projice.   Viridem autem reservan-
dum excipe, et postea ipsas tabulas debes primo cum aqua
lavare, si opus fuerit, servando aquam.   Deinde secundo etiam
cum cinere, et panno lineo fricando, lavabis, detergas, et
nitidas, antequam super ipsas alterum salem ponas, ne si quid
ex veteri remansit, impedimento fiat.   Cujus lavationis primæ
aquam, quæ absque cinere erit, quiescere dimitte, ut colorem,
qui in fundo remanet, colligas, projiciendo aquam.   Hic color
cum aqua, vel melius cum aceto, et etiam cum oleo lini, distemperatur, et mollitur, nec non et cum vitello ovi.

152. *De albo et viridi colore quomodo fiunt et distemperantur.*
—Albus autem et viridis color, absque sale, hoc modo fit et
distemperatur.   In vase aceto acerrimo imposito, et desuper
virgulas ligneas, intra vas, et sic tabulas plumbeas, et alias
æneas, vel cupreas, pones virgulis suspensas in aere, ne tangant
acetum, nec se invicem.   Deinde vas diligentissime claudes,
liniesque de argilla, vel cemento, vel cera, ne aliquod spiracu-
lum remaneat, per quod exalatio fiat.   Deinde co-operiatur in
fimo equino calido ; post dies autem xxx. vas aperiatur, et ex
fortitudine aceti vel vini, quod vinum excalore fimi devenerit
acetum, et ex fortitudine ipsius vini vel aceti, cuprum vel æs
virideum, plumbum vero album invenientur.   Sumptum autem
et arefactum album, teratur, et temperetur cum vino, et pinge-
tur in pergamenis, et cum oleo in lignis et in materiis.   Similiter virideum cum oleo teres, et distemperabis, et operaberis in
lignis, sed in materia cum vino, vel, si mavis, cum oleo.   In

grind and temper the green with oil, and use it for painting on wood; but on walls with wine, or, if you prefer it, with oil. On parchment, however, you must not grind it with oil, but you must temper it with very clear and good wine, or with vinegar.

153. *Of a green water, or colour, for writing.*—But if you wish to write letters, put the green powder of brass in wine or vinegar as aforesaid, and then stir it round a little with your finger only, and immediately the whole of the wine or vinegar will be green. If the wine, before it has cleared itself from the dregs of the said green powder, is very green, you may know that it has enough of the powder of brass. If it seems of a dirty colour, appearing contaminated by the admixture of yellow impurities, you must know that this is because a sufficient quantity of the green powder has not been added to it: you must therefore add a little more, and stir it again with your finger, and again let it rest; and if it is not yet of a beautiful colour, add more of the powder, and stir it again with your finger, and, if necessary, do this a third time. But if you wish it to be very beautiful, add a little saffron; and when it has settled so that the impurities have sunk to the bottom, pour off the clear green liquid which stands uppermost in the vase, and you will thus separate it from the impurities and gross substance of the saffron that was put into it. If you wish to write with it immediately, you cannot do so unless you first let it boil over the fire to make it thicker; or you may let it stand in the shade, or in the mild breeze of the evening or morning; but it must be done when the wind blows gently, and must not be put in the sun.

154. *To make minium out of the before-mentioned white colour.* —The white colour which we mentioned before, is called, I believe, by the armourers ceruse, and you may convert it into minium by putting it into a jar and torrefying it over the fire for two days and two nights, stirring it frequently in the vase or jar with any instrument; and this is the way to make minium. Take care not to let any flame get inside the jar, but make the fire of charcoal only without flame; you must heap the charcoal

perchamenis vero non teres cum oleo, sed in vino clarissimo et
bono, seu aceto, temperare debes.

153. *De aqua vel viridi colore ad scribendum.*—Si vero litteras scribere volueris, pone viridem pulverem æris in vino vel
aceto, ut dictum est, et sic digito tantum fricabis, et statim
totum vinum vel acetum virideum erit ; quod si valde virideum
fuerit illud vinum, cum necdum a fece sua dicte pulveris viridea
sit purgatum, scias quod sufficienter habet depulvere eris super-
scripto. Si vero turpem colorem videatur habere, et quasi
crocei, turpidis commixtione corruptum, scias esse hoc habere
parum pulveris ipsius viridis. Et ideo aliquantulum adde, et
digito iterum commisce, et postea paululum quiescere sines, et
si non ad huc pulchrum colorem habet, iterum adde de pulvere,
et iterum digito fricabis, et postea adhuc sines quiescere, et, si
necesse fuerit, fac similiter tercio. Et si vis quod miræ pul-
critudinis fiat, adde aliquantulum de croco et cum quieverit, ita
quod feces ad fundum decensa sint, mitte clarissimum virideum
desuper stantem in vasculo, et sic ipsum separabis a fecibus, et
a substancia grossa crossi imposite ; et si ex ipso statim scribere
volueris, non poteris, nisi prius ad ignem ipsum fervere permiseris, ut spissior fiat, vel in umbra solis, vel mane, vel vespere,
ad auram dulcem ; quando sed ventus suaviter flat ponendus
est, non autem in sole.

154. *Di minio faciendo de albo colore ante dicto.*—Album
autem colorem de quo supra diximus, scutarii, sicut puto, cerusam vocant, quem in minium vertes, si in olla posueris duobus
diebus noctibus que, eandem sæpe movendo, in vase, seu olla,
ipsa cum aliquo instrumento ad ignem torrueris, et sic minium
facies. Cave autem ne in olla flamma nullo modo tangat, sed
tantum carbones, verum absque flamma ; de quibus fac con-
geriem albam, usque ad medietatem ollæ, et eam ore aperto in

round the jar, so as to reach half-way up the jar, which must be put in the middle. The charcoal should be large, so that the air may pass through the spaces of it, and keep up the heat; it should not be small, for it would then be useless. When it begins to get hot, stir the colour which is inside it with a spoon, or with a strip of iron or brass, or a stick : so that the hot colour, which is next the side of the vase, may be mixed with the tepid part in the middle ; for this stirring is the principal cause of the perfect preparation of all which is thus torrefied ; and this stirring must be repeated four or five times in the space of every two or three hours. This process must be continued, as I said before, for two days and two nights following : not sleeping all the time, unless you have another person to supply your place and to continue stirring it, as well as to take care of the fire, and to manage the operation, other-wise your labour will be in vain. When the large charcoal is all consumed, take the jar off the fire with a blacksmith's pincers, or a twisted stick, or any other instrument, and throw away the small coal and ashes, and put fresh charcoal. We shall mention this colour frequently hereafter.

155. *How to make the green from brass which is called Greek or common green.*[1]—If you wish to make the copper-green which is called Greek, take a new jar, or any other concave vase, and put into it the strongest or most acid vinegar, so as not to fill it, and put strips of very clean copper or brass over the vinegar, so that they may not touch the vinegar or each other, being suspended to a stick placed across the vase. Then cover the vase and seal it, and put it into a warm place, or in dung, or under ground, and leave it so for six months, and then open the vase and scrape and shake out what you find in it, and on the strips of metal, into a clean vase, and put it in the sun to dry.

156. *To make Rothomagensian green.*[2]—If you wish to make Rothomagensian green, take strips of very pure copper or brass,

---

[1] This recipe and the next are in the Clavicula.

[2] Rothomagus, Rouen on the Seine. This recipe is in the Clavicula, and the Sloane MS., No. 1754.

medio compone, carbones autem sint magni, et per rimas eorum, ventus entret, et calorem exerceat ; non minuti vero, quod non perficerent. Cum autem torreri cœperit, colorem, qui intus est, cum cocleari, vel lamula ferrea, vel ærea, vel lignea, commove, ut qui circa testam seu ollam calet, illi qui in medio loco tepet, misceatur. Nam commotio hæc est principalis causa omnibus que coquuntur, ad perfectionem decoctionis ipsorum ; hoc autem per duarum vel trium horarum spatium, quater vel quinquies. Duobus enim diebus ac noctibus continuis est agendum, sicut dixi, non dormiendo nisi alter accedat, qui hoc ipsum procuret, et commociones ipsas, et ignis curam, et manutenaciones agat ; alioquin frustra laborabis. Cum autem carbones grossi con- sumpti fuerint, vel forcisibus ferieris, vel virga conterata, vel alio quodum insðrumento, ollam a foco extrahe, et minutos car- bones et cineres abjicies, et alios adhibe. De hoc eodem colore aliquanti spei in sequentibus loquimur.

155. *Quomodo fit viride eris quod Grecum dicitur seu com- mune.*—Si vis facere viride eris quod Grecum dicitur, accipe ollam novam, aut aliquod aliud vas concavum, et mitte in eo acetum fortissimum seu acerrimum, ita quod vas non sit ple- num, et laminas cupri mundissime, vel æris, pones supra acetum, ita ut non tangant acetum, aut se invicem, suspendendo eas ad aliquod lignum, in vase extranverso positum, et ita cooperi vas, et sigilla. Et sic pone illud in calido loco, aut in fimo, aut in terra, et ita dimitte usque ad sex menses, et tunc aperies illud vas, et quod in eo et circa dictas laminas inveneris, rade, et excute in vase mundo, et mitte ad solem siccare.

156. *De viride Rothomagense faciendo.* — Si vis viridem Rothomagensem facere, accipe laminas purissimi cupri, vel

smear them over with good soap, and put them into a clean vase made for this purpose, and pour into it some pure vinegar; then suspend the strips of copper or brass in the vase to a stick stretched across it, which should be placed as high up as possible, so that the strips may not touch each other or the vinegar. Then cover up the vase and seal it, and put it into a warm place, such as horse-dung, or the refuse of the wine-press; or, in winter, cover up and bury the vase in a deep hole under ground, and thus leave it for one month; then open it, and shake and scrape off what you find upon the strips, putting it in a bason or an earthen vase; place it in the sun to dry, and preserve it for use.

157. *Also, how to make verdigris for writing.*—Whoever wishes to make a green colour for writing, let him pour into a copper or brass vessel equal quantities by weight of honey well mixed with vinegar, and then bury the vessel in horse-dung, in the hottest part of the heap. After 12 days are passed, he may take the colour out of the vase, scraping it out; then dry it in the sun, and keep it for use.

158. *Also, how to make green without brass.*—If you wish to make earth-green, take, in the middle of May, a bunch of the flowers of the herb columbine; pound them well in a mortar, and strain the juice through a linen cloth. Then put this juice into a vase, and place it in the sun until it is hard. This must be tempered, first with water, and then with egg, on wood or on walls; but on parchment it must be used like ceruse.

159. *Also to make green.*—If you wish to make a green colour, take urine, or vinegar, and put it into a vase, and make a plate of brass, and place it over the liquid in the said vase so as not to touch the urine, and afterwards set the vase in a warm place and cover it up for 9 days, then take it out and collect the colour which is produced. This is tempered first with water, and afterwards with egg on wood or on walls. When you put verdigris upon paper, put cherry juice [or cervisia?] in it. If it is not of a fine green, mix *viride terrenum*. If it is too green, so as to be too dark, mix pure orpiment with it.

160. *Also verdigris is thus made.*—Take vinegar and put it

æris, et liniis ipsas in circuitu de optimo savone, et mitte ipsas in vase mundo ac hoc facto, et pone in ipso de puro aceto, et superpone in ipso vase dictas laminas cupreas vel æreas, suspensas ad virgulam in vase ex transverso, altius quam poteris, sitam ita ut lamine non se invicem, nec acetum tangant. Postea cooperies vas, et sigilla, et in calido loco, ut in fimo equino, aut in vinaciis pressorii vinarii, aut in hyeme sub terra, in profundo loco cooperias, et sepelias, dictum vas. Et sic dimittas uno mense, et postea aperies, et quod inveneris in circuitu laminarum excuties et rades, et mittendo in bacino vel vase terreo, et pones ad solem siccare, et usui reserva.

157. *Item de viridi eris, quo modo fit pro scribendo.*—Colorem viridem qui vult ad suum usum scribendi facere mel cum aceto valde mixtum equo pondere infundat ac deinde in sterquilinio equorum ubi plus calet in vase cuprea vel æreo cooperto positum sepeliat. Postea bis senis diebus transactis illud recipiet de vase ipsum colorem radendo et ad solum siccet et reservet pro usu.

158. *Item de fiendo viridi aliter quam eris.*—Si vis facere terreum viride in medio maio accipe massam florum herbæ quæ vocatur aquileia et pila in mortario optime et cola succum per pannum lineum. Deinde pone ipsum succum in vase et pone ad solem siccare usque quo durum sit. Hoc distemperatur primum cum aqua, deinde cum ovo ad lignum vel murum, in carta pone sicut cerosium.

159. *Item de viridi faciendo.*—Si vis facere colorem viridem, accipe mictum hominis, *i. e.* urinam, vel acetum et mitte in vas, et fac laminam eream, et pone desuper in dicto vase ita ut mictum non tangat et pone postea vas in calido loco et cooperi per novem dies postea trahe foris et colorem exortum execute. Hoc distemperatur primum cum aqua post cum ovo ad lignum vel murum. In cartam dum ponit viride eris pone succum cerosium in ipso si non bene est viridis misce terrenum viridem. Si nimium est viride ita ut nigrescat misce auripigmentum purum.

160. *Item eris viride sic fit.*—Accipe acetum et pone in vaso

into a brass or copper vase, and place it on the coals so as to
boil strongly, skim it well, and grind it with a little alum upon
a marble slab.   Afterwards put it in a brass vase, and then
leave it to settle for a day or two.   Then pour off the supernatant liquor which floats over the dregs at the bottom into another vase, separating it from the before-mentioned impurities,
and put it away and keep it for use.   Then pour more vinegar
into the aforesaid sediment, and mix it well.   Leave it so for
four days, so that everything may settle, and it will then be good
green.   But if it is too clear or liquid, put it upon lighted
charcoal without flame, so that it may boil a little and thicken,
and then put it into the vase, and keep it for use.

161. *How to make a beautiful green.*—Mix Spanish green
with saffron, and distemper them both together, and the colour
will be of wonderful beauty.

162. *Of folium, how it is distempered.*—The purple colour
called *folium* by the laity, by whom (or rather by the English,
in whose country it is prepared, and who call it *worina*) it is
used in dyeing wool, is not always tempered in the same manner ;
for some persons distemper it with urine, or with ley made from
the ashes of ash-trees, and particularly on walls ; while others,
on parchment, distemper it with cheese-glue, made as follows.

163. *How glue is made from cheese.*—Fresh cheese is first to
be washed in hot water, until the milk is washed out, and then
ground with lime and water, in a little mortar or on a marble
slab ; and a little before this is done—namely, while the cheese
is being ground—the colour is soaked in water again.   Then,
when the cement is prepared, so as to be as white, clear, and
shining as milk, it is put into a small vase, and the colour is
scraped into it with a knife, and care must be taken not to let
the air have access to the mixture ; and when the colour is seen
to be good, it may be used for writing at pleasure.

164. *Of folium stamipiensi, a purple colour, how it is tempered or made.*—Take the wood of the tree which is called
elm and burn it in the fire, and collect such a quantity of that
flowery ash which appears upon the coals as you think will be

æreo vel cupreo et super carbones pone ut fortiter bulliat et spuma illud optime et ex eo cum alumine modico super marmorem tere viridem. Postea in vase æreo mitte et sic uno die vel duobus dimitte ut resideat. Illud autem quod super feces in fundo descensas nataverit in aliud vas a dictis fecibus separando, mitte et reserva deinde acetum iterum mitte in fecibus superscriptis, et misce bene. Postea dimitte sic per quatuor dies ut quicquid quiescat et tunc forte bonum viride erit. Si vero nimium clarum seu liquidem fuerit pone super carbones ignitos absque flammis ut modicum bulliat et spissum fiet tunc mitte in prædicto vase ad servandum usui.

161. *Quomodo pulchrum fiat viride.*—Viridi Hispanico admisce crocum et distempera simul et miræ pulchritudinis erit.

162. *De folio quomodo distemperatur.*—Purpureus color quem folium vocant laici qui lanam inde tingunt vel potius Anglici in quorum terra conficitur worina vocant non uno semper modo distemperatur. Nam aliqui cum urina vel lexivia de cinere fraxini facta ut in parietibus precipue alii in pergamenis cum visco de caseo ita facto.

163. *Quomodo viscum de caseo fiat.*—Primum recentum caseum in aqua calida lavant, donec lac eliciatur et sic illum in mortariolo vel super marmorem terunt cum calce et aqua et paulo antequam hoc agant dum scilicet teritur caseus, iterum ipsum colorem in aqua temperare permittunt. Deinde cum viscum preparatum habent, sic album et nitidum et clarum velut lac. Inducunt in vasculo et super incidunt cultello ipsum colorem jam temperatum in aqua et tunc cavent ne ventus tangat ipsam confectionem et si cum viderit colorem esse bonum scribunt inde prout ipsis placuerit.

164. *De folio Stamipiensi* (sic) *purpureo colore quomodo distemperatur seu fit.*—Sume tibi ligna arboris quæ ulmus vocatur et arde in ignem, illum vero florem cineris qui super carbones apparet tolles et in unum pones quantum tibi sufficere putas et in

sufficient for you, grind it in a mortar, and distemper it with
urine so that it may be as thick as dough ; make it into cakes as
thick as you like, and put these cakes upon two trays or plates
of iron, or baked bricks, in order that they may burn for a day
and a half. Then take them out of the fire and put them into a
mortar and pound them until they are reduced to powder. Then
sift this powder through a sieve, or make it pass through a
sifter.   Again, while you are doing this, you must have a jar
prepared full of urine, and let it boil over the fire three or four
times ; then remove it from the fire, and add to it of fresh urine
one half or less, until it is tepid, and then stir them together.
Afterwards take the colour, which is called folium, and put it
into a vase, and wash it with this prepared urine, rubbing it
between your hands, and hold it against one side of the jar and
throw away the urine ; then take the above-mentioned ashes
and fill one ladle with them, and take another ladleful of
folium, and lay one couch of ashes in that vase by sprinkling
them, and then one of folium, and do so until the folium and
the ashes are all mixed.   Then again rub them between
your hands, and so leave them for three days, well covered
up by the fire, that they may keep warm.   But the best colour
will of itself, when it begins to get warm, be covered all over
with a purple bloom. If you wish to dye anything, put the
water into a vessel ; but if you have nothing to dye, let the
water and the folium cool, so that you may make it into small
cakes, and you may keep it as long as you like, and put it into
an oven.

165. *Of the different sorts of saffron.*—You must not take
all kinds of saffron for painting or writing with, for you must
know that that which grows in our country of Gaul, as well as
throughout the whole of France, is not good ; and although it
has some resemblance to the good sort, yet it has not the exact
colour, smell, or taste of the perfect sort ; for there is a certain
herb with whitish leaves and roots, the flowers of which we call
crocus, but which the laity call *saffron*.   When you see these
flowers have a certain whiteness at the top of one side, you

mortariolo fortiter teres, cum urina distemperabis ita ut panis crudus spissum sit, facies que de ea tortellos quantum grossos volueris quos super duas dolatiles seu laminas ferreas vel lateres coctos pones ut ibi super carbones usque ad dimidium diem ardeant. Dein trahe ab igne item que in mortariolo pones et multum fortiter usquedum pulvis fiat. Pestabis; postea attenuabis per satacium vel per staminiam, transire facias. Iterum dum hoc facies, habebis ollam paratam plenam urina et cum tribus vel quatuor vicibus bullire permittes. Postea ab igne retrahes et cum ea de urina cruda, medietatem vel minus, usque dum tepida fuerit vel fiat similiter misces. Posthæc accipies illum colorem qui folium vocatur et in uno vase pones abluesque de illa mixta urina inter manus tuas fricando, attrahes que in unam partem et feces urinæ projicies foris. Tunc accipies illum suprascriptum cinerem et unam scutellam de eo implebis et de folio aliam facies que in illo vase de cinere pulverando unum lettum et unum desuper de folio sic que facies usque dum folium et cinis mixta sint. Iterumque inter manus tuas fricabis et sic dimittes usque tribus diebus bene coopertum juxta ignem ut calefiat. Ipse vero optimus color de se ipso emittet colorem purpureum super se cum cepit calescere. Si vero aliquid tingere volueris pones aquam in sartagine. Si vero tingere non habes dimittes aquam et folium sic refrigerari ita ut possis ex eo parvos tortellos facere et servare poteris quantum volueris et in forulo pone.

165. *De croco et de diversitatibus ejus.*—Omnem crocum ad pingendum assumere non oportet vel ad scribendum. Illum enim qui in hac nostra patria galliæ ut in toto Francia crescit bonum non esse non nescias. Et quamvis aliquam similitudinem boni habeat tamen vere colorem nec odorem nec saporem illius perfecte habet et enim quedam herba albo silis foliis et radicibus cujus flores nos crocum laici vero safran vocant. Quos flores cum videris gestare quandam candorem ex una parte in summittate scias quod non est bonus cum duos digitos saliva

may know that they are good. When you wet two of your
fingers with saliva, and rub the saffron a little between your
fingers, if your fingers immediately become yellow, you may
know that the saffron comes from Italy or Spain, and is good ;
but in Sicily, as a certain Ysidius [Isidorus] says, the best is
that which is called *coriscos ;* and a great deal of excellent
saffron comes from thence, very fragrant to the smell, and of a
colour superior to gold. Some temper this with egg ; others
both grind and temper it with egg, or mix it with water, and
strain it through a linen cloth, and then they paint with it.
However, I do none of these things, but only put clear water
into a very clean vase ; I then sprinkle the saffron over it, and,
after a little while, when I see the water well impregnated with
it, I put it on the coals for a short time, leaving the saffron in
it, and then, with a pencil or pen prepared for this purpose, I
paint upon skins and other things, and upon box-wood, in order
to colour it yellow, or to redden it, by mixing the saffron with
wine, and then laying it on the box-wood. If you wish to make
the wood shine, let the saffron dry, and then lay on some more
with oil.

166. *That there are three kinds of folium, and of the way to
temper the purple folium.*[1]—There are three kinds of folium ;
one purple, another red, and a third sapphire blue, which you
must temper as follows. Take ashes, and sift them through a
cloth, pour cold water over them, make them into cakes like
loaves of bread, and put them into the fire until they are quite
white hot. When they have been burnt for a long time, and
have afterwards cooled, put part of them into an earthen vase,
and pour urine over, stir them with a stick, and, when they have
settled clear, pour the liquor on the red folium, and grind it a
little on a stone, adding to it one-fourth part of quicklime,
and when it is ground and sufficiently moistened, strain it
through a cloth, and lay it with a pencil wherever you like,
first thinly, and afterwards more thickly. And if you wish to

---

[1] This is a transcript of chap. xxxv. of the first book of Theophilus.

humectabis et florem inter eos paululum fricabis et statim crocos
habueris inde digitos scias quod ex Italia vel Expania venit et
bonus est.   In Sicilia autem, ut Ysidius ait quidam, melior est
qui coriscos dicitur, unde crocum plurimum et optimum venit.
Spiramine flagrantius et colore pulchrius auro.   Hunc cum ovo
distemperant, alii etiam cum ovo terunt et distemperant vel
cum aqua per lineum pannum transire faciunt et sic isti pin-
gunt.   Ego vero nichil horum facio sed tantum in mundissimo
vasculo claram aquam mitto, Dein crocum desuper spargo et
post modicum cum videro aquam totam inde confectam super
carbones paululum simulque crocum permitto et deinde cum
pincello vel pennula ad id parata in pellibus pingo et alibi et
super buxum ut croceus fiat vel rubicundior ubi crocus cum
vino distemperandus est et sic buxo superponendus est quod si
volueris ut ipsum lignum luceat permitte prius crocum siccari.
Postea cum oleo eum super illum pone.

166. *Quod folii tria sunt genera, et de modo distemperandi
purpureum.*—Tria sunt folii genera ; unum purpureum, aliud
rubeum, turcium saphirum que sic temperabis.   Tolle cineres
et crebra eos per pannum ; Perfondes eos aqua frigida fac inde
tortulas ad similitudinem panis mittes que ea in igne donec omnino candescant.   Postquam diutissime canduerint et postea
friguerint mitte partem in vas fictile perfunde urina, move ligno,
cum que resident lucide perfunde rubeum folium et teres illud
modice super lapidem addens ei quartam partem vivæ calcis, et
cum tritum fuerit, et sufficienter perfusum cola per pannum et
trahe cum pincello ubi volueris tenue deinde spissius et si placet
in similitudinem palii in pagina facere purpureo folio eodem
temperamento absque calce profuso pinge penna vel pincello.

represent a robe on the page [of a book], paint it with purple folium, moistened with the same vehicle, but without lime, with a pen or a hair pencil.

167. *Of azure ; how and with what vehicles it is tempered.*— Of the etherial colour, or, to speak in common language, the azure or blue colour, I have nothing very certain to say, as some grind and temper it with goat's milk, others with woman's milk, and others with white of egg ; and either of these is sufficiently good.

168. *How azure is prepared and purified.*—But I shall not conceal how I purify it when it comes to my hands. I first pour it into a bason, and put a little water along with it, and rub it with my finger until it is thoroughly moistened, and then I pour in more water and stir it well, and let it rest. When it has settled, I pour off the water, turbid from the impurities, into another vase, keeping the precious colour which remains at the bottom of the vase, for its nature is such that the finer and purer the colour is the heavier it is, and therefore the sooner it reaches the bottom ; and the impurities, or the whitish or yellowish parts, which are lighter, float or remain above it in the water. And, if necessary, I repeat this process several times, pouring water out and in until it is purified ; and when it is well purified and ground with water, after I have put it into a horn, I pour in very clear whipped white of egg, and paint upon the places in which I wish to paint anything ; and I afterwards throw away the same white of egg within the space of one hour, for if it remains in it any longer it spoils the colour by depriving it of its fine appearance and beauty. And after I have thrown away the white of egg, I immediately fill the horn with cold water and stir up the colour, and wash it with water, throwing away the same water after an hour, while the colour settles and sinks to the bottom ; for, as I said, if the egg, or the said water impregnated with the said egg by the washing of the colour were to remain any longer, the colour would be deteriorated. This colour is used on walls with egg and with water ; but on wood it is ground with oil, like other colours.

167. *De azurio quomodo distemperatur et cum quibus liquori-*
bus.—De etherio colore, vel ut juxta vulgare loquar lazurio vel
perso quid certius dicam non habeo quia alii cum lacte caprino
alii cum lacte mulieris alii cum glarea ovi molunt ac distemperant et satis utrumque bonum est.

168. *Quo modo preparetur et purgetur azurium.*—Sed quo
modo cum admanus meas venerit illum preparare non tacebo.
In primis fundo id opus in bacino simulque cum eo, paululum
aquæ mitto, et cum digito, tamdiu frico quousque totus made-
factus sit, ac deinde habundancius aquam infundo et bene misceo et quiescere permitto. Postquam quieverit eamdem aquam
sic turbatam ex emundicia in alio vase recipio reservaturque colorem preciosumqui in fundo remanet vasis, nam hujus modi
naturæ est ut quanto pulchrior et purior est tanto ponderosior
et ideo tanto ad fundum labatur ; et immundicea seu pars albescentis vel croceantis coloris qui nimis gravis est superius natet
vel maneat et si necesse fuerit id ipsum sæpius repeto aquam
sæpe infundendo et effundendo donec pergatus sit. Et jambene
purgatum et cum aqua tritum postquam in cornu reposuero
postea loca in quibus inde aliquid facere voluero glaream ovi
multum clarum immitto et operor. Postea glaream eamdem
prius unius hore spacium jecturus nam si diutius intus remanserit corrumpet colorem illi precipuam speciem et pulchritudinem
auferendo. Et postquam glaream ejecero statim illud cornu
aqua frigida repleo et misceo colorem et lavo cum aqua, eandem
aquam post horam dum color ad fundum quescendo descendit
rejecturus. Nam ut dixi si diutius remaneret ovum vel dicta
aqua, de dicto ovo ex ipsa lavatione coloris infecta color corrum-
peretur. Hunc colorem cum aqua et cum ovo in materia ponet
in ligno vero cum oleo ut tritos colores.

169. *How azure is made.*[1]—If you wish to make azure, take a new jar that has never been used, and put into it strips of very pure silver, as many as you like, and so cover it up, and seal it, and put the jar among the grape-skins, and keep it well for 14 days and then open the jar, and scrape into a very clean vase the efflorescence which you find on the silver, which will be a perfect azure, and of a blue colour, provided that the silver contains no alloy or mixture of any other metal, but only consists of the purest and finest silver. If it contains any brass, you will obtain a colour which is rather green, than blue or azure. If you afterwards want any more of it, do again as before directed.

170. *To make azure not so good* [*as the last*].[2]—If you wish to make another azure, take a jar of very pure copper, and put lime into it until it is half full, and then fill the jar with very strong vinegar, and so cover it up and seal it. Then place the jar under ground, if it is in winter, that it may be warm there, or among the grape-skins, or in hot horse-dung, or in any other hot place, and so leave it for one month. Afterwards, open the jar, and scrape off what you find upon it, and put it in the sun to dry. This azure is not so good as the last, but it is useful for wood or walls.

171. *Also of another way of making blue with the juice of blue flowers.*—If you wish to make a third kind of azure, take blue flowers, that is, of an azure colour, and grind them, and press out the juice, straining it through a cloth into a very clean vase. And you must first make the ground of your work, whether on wood or on parchment, with white lead, which is called ceruse, and put over it three or four, or five coats of this expressed blue juice or colour, and repeat this until you find the colour appears like azure, letting it dry each time you lay it on, before you apply a fresh coat.

---

[1] This recipe is in the Appendix to the MS. of Theophilus in the British Museum, and in the Mappæ Clavicula, p. 7.

[2] This recipe and the next are also in the Mappæ Clavicula, p. 7.

169.—*De azurio quo modo efficitur.*—Si vis facere azurrium
optimum accipe ollam novam que nunquam in opus fuerit et
mitte in eas laminas purissimi argenti quantas vis et sic cooperi
eam et sigilla et mitte ipsam ollam in vindemia et serva bene
usque ad quindecim dies et sic aperies illam ollam et illum
florem qui erit in circuitu laminarum argentearum excucies in
mundissimo vase.   Quod perfectum azurium erit et celestini
coloris dum tamen argentum laminarum mullum alligamentum
vel mixturam alterius cujus que metalli in se continuerit pre-
terquam purissimum ac finissimum argentum.   Quid si in se
aliquid eris continuerit viridatis potius quam celestis vel azurii
colorem obtinebis et si postea amplius volueris habere, iterum
fac ut superscriptum est.

170. *De azurio alio non tam bono faciendo.*—De alio azurio
si vis facere, accipe ampullam purissimi cupri, et mitte in eam
calcem usque ad medium, et sic imple ampulam fortissimo
aceto et ita cooperi et sigilla.   Et tunc mitte ipsam ampulam
in profundo terræ si erit in hyeme ut ibi calidum sit aut in
vindemia aut in fimo equimo calido, aut in alio calido loco, et
ita dimitte usque ad unum mensem et postea aperies ampulam
et ex ea rade quod in ipsa inveneris et mittes ad solem siccare.
Illud azureum non est ita bonum sicut aliud, tamen valet ad
lignum vel materiam.

171. *Item aliter modo fiendo azurio cum succo florum persa-
rum.*—Tertium azurium si vis facere, accipe flores blauos id
est celestini coloris et teres et exprime colando per telam in
mundissimo vase et fac prius campum tui operis sit in ligno vel
sit in pergameno, De albo plumbo quod cerusa dicitur et mitte
desuper tries aut quatuor aut quinque lectos de ipso succo seu
colore blauo expresso, et tantum ita fac usque quo videas ipsum
colorem similem esse azurio permittendo qualibet vice quam
posueris siccare antequam reponas.

172. *How to make a black colour in various manners.*—Every black colour which is used in painting on skins, we know to be atramentum, distempered in various manners, except that with which we stain the skin, which is commonly called *corduanum* (cordovan). But that black colour is made of oil and scales of iron, boiled together for a very long time, and it is laid on the skin, not with a pen or a brush, but with a very sharp piece of wood, namely boxwood. But on walls, or on wood, we take charcoal, made of leather, or of hay, or of wood of any kind, except oak, which, on account of its hardness, can scarcely ever be sufficiently ground. If you wish to lay black over other colours on parchment, you must not put incaustum, but know that you must take charcoal distempered with egg, and the same on walls either with water or with egg, and on wood with oil; and whoever takes the soot of rushes and oil, where they are burnt together over a lamp, and calcines it in a jar upon coals, and grinds it with water or with egg, or with oil, will find it a very excellent colour wherever he wants it.

173. *Also of another mode of making black.*—Take the bark of the wood which is called elm, and cut it into small pieces, and put it into a vessel to boil with water; and take the rust which is at the bottom of the water under a workman's grindstone, and mix it with the said bark, in order that they may boil over the fire together; and add to them atramentum distempered with the aforesaid water of the bark. Afterwards, if you wish to dye anything, put it in while the water boils, and so leave it from morning until the third hour of the day (*i.e.* from 6 to 9 A.M.), until it is diminished to a third of the quantity. And if what was put into it is not well dyed, put it in again, and add a little atramentum, in order that that which is put into the composition may be better dyed.

174. *To make vermilion.*[1]—If you wish to make very good vermilion, take a glass flask, and lute it outside. Then take one part by weight of quicksilver, and two parts of sulphur of a

---

[1] This recipe is also in the Clavicula.

172. *De nigro colore quomodo fit diversi mode.*—Omne atrum colorem unde pingitur in pellibus scimus attramentum esse variis modis distemperatum præter illum de quo tingimus illam pellem, quam vulgus corduanum vocat. Illud autem nigrum ex olio paleaque ferri diutissime simul coctis fit et in eadem pelle non cum penna nec cum pincello sed cum ligno acutissimo scilicet buxeo pingitur. In parietibus vero vel in lignis assumimus carbones scilicet de lignis cujus libet generis, vel de corio vel de feno factos præter querqueos que vix un-quam pro eorum duritie suffienter teri possunt. Sed si in per-gamenis supra ceteros colores ponere volueris nigrum non pones incaustum sed scias quod carbones cum ovo distemperatos assumes, in materiis similiter, vel cum aqua, vel cum ovo, et in lignis cum oleo. Fuligine quoque junci et olei ubi simul in lampade ardent qui ceperit si in testa super carbones torruerit et cum aqua vel cum ovo vel oleo triverit valde optimum colo-rem ubique voluerit comprobabit.

173. *Item, alio modo de nigro faciendo.*—Accipe corticem ligni quod elna vocatur et per particulas incides mittes que in sartaginem *i. e.* patellam cum aqua bullire. Accipies que fer-ruginem que est in fundo cum aqua subtus in ollam fabri. Et mitte cum dicto cortice ut simul ad ignem bulliat ponesque cum eis attramentum de illa supradicta aqua dicti corticis ligni distemperatum. Postea in volueris aliquid tingere mittes intus dum aqua bullierit et sic id dimittes a mane usque ad terciam. Et si bene tinctum non fuerit, quod intus positum fuerit, iterum intus reponatur adjiciatur que parumper de attramento ut me-lius tingatur id quod in compositione mittetur.

174. *De vermiculo faciendo.*—Si vis facere vermiculum opti-mum accipe ampulam vitream et lini de foris luto. Et sic accipe unum pondus argenti vivi et duo pondera sulphuris albi

white or yellow colour, and put them into the aforesaid flask, which you must afterwards place upon four stones, and make a very slow fire of charcoal piled round the flask, and cover up the mouth of the flask with a tile; and when you see a blue vapour come out of the mouth of the flask, cover it up; and if a yellow vapour comes out, cover it up also. But when there comes out a vapour nearly as red as vermilion, then take it away from the fire, and you will have excellent vermilion in the flask.

175. *Another way of making vermilion.*—Take a glass jar, and quicksilver and sulphur, and weigh them, so that two parts may be of sulphur, and the third of quicksilver, and fill the flask with them up to the neck. But first cover the flask with three coats of very good clay, then put in the aforesaid articles, so that the sulphur may be underneath, and the quicksilver above, and put red tile, well pounded, from the neck to the top of it, and place it upon three stones over a charcoal fire, and let it burn until a blue vapour comes off, and then it will suffice.

176. *How to make minium, otherwise called sandaraca.*—If I am not mistaken, minium, that is sandaraca, and white lead, that is ceruse, are of one nature. If you put ceruse into the fire it takes a new name, and colour, and strength; because, the more it is burnt the redder it is, and the less it is burnt the more it retains its former colour, that is, its whiteness or its paleness; and in laying it upon walls, it is ground with gum-water, but never with egg. It can, however, be laid upon parchment, distempered with egg; but on wood, with oil.

177. *How minium is mixed with vermilion.*—If any one wishes to illuminate a manuscript he must not do that with minium only, because, although the letters may be well formed yet they would not be beautiful, for they would be too pale; he must therefore mix minium with vermilion, that the colour may be brighter. But as I have certainly known some persons who are ignorant about this mixture, not knowing how much to put of one sort, or how much of the other, if they will give their

aut crocei coloris, et mitte in ampulam suprascriptam quam
postea pones super quatuor petras et ignem lentissimum de
carbonibus in circuitu ampullæ positis facias cooperto ore ampullæ tegula et quando videris fumum ex ore ampulæ exire
blauum, cooperi ; si vero fumus crocei coloris, iterum cooperi ;
quando autem exierit fumus rubeus quasi ut est vermiculum,
sic tolle ab igne et habebis vermiculum optimum in ipsa ampula.

175. *Alio modo ad faciendum vermiculum.*—Accipe ampull-
lam vitream et vivum argentum et sulphur, et libra ita ut duæ
partes sint de sulphure et tertia de argento vivo, et intus pone
ut veniat usque collum ampullæ et primitus lini ampulam de
argilla optima tribus vicibus et intus pone supradictas partes,
ita ut sulfuris pars subtus sit bene diminuta et argenti vivi pars
supersit et rubeam tegulam bene diminutam a collo usque ad
summum mitte et super tres lapides ampulam in igne de carbonibus et dimitte combuere donec ignis inde exeat glaucus et
tunc satis est.

176. *De minio faciendo aliter sandaraco dicto.*—Nisi fallor minium id est sandaracum et album plumbum id est cerusa unius
naturæ sunt, si in ignem mittas cerusam, nomen et colorem et
fortitudinem accipit quia quanto plus ustum fuerit plus rubet,
et quo minus ustum plus pristinum colorem retinet, id est albo-
rem vel pallorem et ponendo ipsum in materiis teritur cum
aqua gummata numquam vero cum ovo. In pergamenis vero
poni potest cum ovo distemperatum, sed in lignis cum oleo.

177. *Quomodo misceatur minium cum vermiculo.* — Si quis
codicem illuminare satagit non id de sole minio debet facere
quia quamvis litteræ forent bene formate pulchre tamen non
essent quia nimio pallore essent obfuscate, ideo minium cum
vermiculo misceat ut pulchriores sint. Verum tamen quia
aliquos de hac commixtione novi certe, nescientes quantum ex
uno nec quantum ex altero mittere deberent si mihi assint ani-
mo de hoc intimabo, quod mihi notum est, ut teneant. Si ipsum

attention to me I will teach them all that is known to me, that they may remember it. If the vermilion is very good and new, I put two parts of it, and scarcely the third part of minium. But if the minium is dusky and very old, put a half or a third part of the vermilion, and make the remainder of minium ; and you must know, that the older the vermilion is by nature, the darker and the less useful it is ; and the darker it is, the less of it must be added to the minium. When you have ground this minium thus cautiously mixed with vermilion well in clear water, if you wish to write with it immediately, allow it to dry completely, and then distemper the same with stale white of egg, namely, three or four days old. And if you wish to write or paint with this minium, which will shine with a sort of varnishy brilliancy, you must mix but a little clear water, or nothing at all, with the above-mentioned white of egg, with which you distemper the minium ; and then lay it sufficiently thickly on the parchment while you are writing, that is to say, you must paint the letter thick ; and if, after this, it should happen that the work does not shine, you may know that this is to be imputed to the quality of the air, or the weather, if it be damp. And you must know this also, that if it is dried at the fire, it will undoubtedly shine ; but it will turn black in the sun. The minium may be either fresh or have been prepared for some time.

178. *How minium is to be washed.*—But if, when you are illuminating any book, the minium is old, and of a dirty colour, you must wash it thus. Take water and wine, so that the third or the fourth part may be of wine, and put it into a horn with the minium, and mix it well, stirring it. Afterwards let it rest. When it has settled and is fallen to the bottom, throw out the water and the wine, and pour in a sufficient quantity of white of egg, and use it.

179. *Of sinopis.*—Sinopis, as I have heard, is a certain colour redder than vermilion, so that when the vermilion itself is very precious on account of its beauty, the heralds praising it call it sinopis, although the vermilion only resembles it on account of its redness.

vermiculum valde optimum et novum fuerit duas partes ex illo
et vix tertiam partem ex minio.   Si vero minium fuscum et
vetussimum fuerit dimediam seu tertiam partem ex illo vermiculo mitte et reliquas de minio facito.   Et sciendum est quod
vermiculum natura quanto vetustior tanto nigrior et minus utilis
et quanto nigrior est tanto minus de illo mittendum est in minio.
Quod minium sic ex vermiculo caute mixtium postquam bene
triveris cum aqua clara.   Si statim ex inde scribere volueris
permitte penitus prius exsiccare deinde cum vetusta glarea ovi
trium scilicet aut quatuor dierum ipsum idem distempera.   Et si
tibi accidat scripturam vel picturam ex eodem minio facere velle
quasi que verniciata nitore subluceat glarea suprascriptæ qua
ipsum minium distemperas parum aquæ claræ vel nil omnino
commisceas et exinde inter scribendum sufficienter pergameno
suppone crassam scilicet litteram debes facere.   Sane si post hoc
opus ipsum non lucere contingerit noveris hoc imputandum quali-
tati vel auræ vel tempori si humidum sit.   Hoc autem scire debes
quod si ad ignem exsiccetur procul dubio venitescet.   Sole vero
fuscabitur minium potest esse vel noviter vel ex multo tempore
paratum sit.

178. *Quomodo lavatur minium.* — Si autem cum aliquem
librum illuminas minium vetus sit et turpis coloris.   Debes ita
lavari.   Sume aquam et vinum, et ita ut tertia vel quarta pars
sit vinum et mitte in cornu cum minio et commove bene miscendo.   Postea permitte quiescere.   Cum autem sedatum et ad
fundum deductum erit eice aquam et vinum et mitte glaream
quantum opus sit et operetur.

179. *De sinopide.*—Sinopis est quidam color magis rubeus
ut didici quam vermiculum.   Unde et ipsum vermiculum sit
valde preciosum in pulchritudine fuerit quasi laudando scutarii
sinopidem vocant cum tantum modo vermiculum in rubeo teneat ejus similitudinem.

180. *How the colour olchus, otherwise membrana, is made.*—
The colour olchus, otherwise membrana, is so called from its
appearing like the human flesh on the face, the hands, and the
other parts of the body. It is made of red or vermilion, and
white or ceruse, and he who has no vermilion, must make it of
minium and white mixed together in proper proportions of each,
according to the greater or less ruddiness, or paleness, or whiteness, which he wishes to give to the naked figure, in painting it.
And because a greenish colour is proper for it, mix a little green
with it, in proper proportion as you may think proper.   And if
you have no green, mix orpiment with lazur, and you will
have a green which you may use.   Others also collect the
flowers of a certain herb, the name of which has escaped me,
which they grind or mix with the olchus, and thus make the
colour.

181. *How lake is made.*—Take filings or scrapings of Brazil
wood, and let them boil over the fire in a clean vase with red
wine.   Then add lake distempered with urine, and let them
boil together, and having done this, strain and squeeze them.
Then take alum and mix with the other ingredients in the vase
over the fire, and stir it a little.   Then remove it from the fire,
and pour the contents into a basin.   Then grind it well upon
a stone, and collect the lake together and let it dry in the sun.
Afterwards preserve it in a box.

182. *Item.—How to make sinopis de mellana.*—If you wish
to make sinopis de mellana, take lac, that is, the gum of ivy,
with which parcium is dyed, and grind it very fine, and temper
it with vinegar or urine.   Then, adding wheat flour well cleansed
from the bran, make it into little cakes, and bake it in an un-
glazed jar; and, while it is being baked, put a little of it upon
a stick with a twig, until you see that it is of a very good colour.
If you wish to have it very red, bake it but little; if less red,
bake it more.

183. *As before.— To make the same sinopis in a different manner.*—If you wish to make excellent sinopis, take lac, that is,
the gum of ivy, and madder, and boil it for a short time in a

180. *Quomodo componitur olchus color seu membrana.*—Olchus color aliter membrana vocatur qui sicuti humana caro in
facie in manibus et aliis partibus et membris corporis demon-
stratur.   Componitur ex rubeo seu vermiculo et albo seu cerusa.   Et qui non haberet vermiculum componeret ex minio
et albo simul ad proportionatas quantitates utriusque ipsorum
juxta majorem vel minorem rubedinem vel palliditatem, vel
albedinem quam dare voluerit nudo ymagini pingens ipsam.
Et quia virideus color in ipso convenit aliquantulum viridis per
debitam portionem sicut placuerit.   Et si viride non habetur
auripigmentum cum lazurio misceat et viride habebit quo uti
poterit alii colligunt colligunt (*sic*) etiam cujusdem herbe flores
cujus nomen excidit quos cum olcho terunt seu miscent et colorem inde facit.

181. *Quomodo efficitur lacha.*—Accipe Brasilis ligni limaturam vel rasuram, et in uno vase mundo cum vino rubeo permitte ad ignem bullire.   Deinde lacham cum urina distemper-
atam cum ea pone et simul bulliant et hoc facto colantur et
exprimantur.   Postea alumen accipe et misce cum eis in vase
ad ignem existente et move parumper.   Tunc ab igne tolle et
in scutella mitte.   Deinde super petram fortiter tere et collige
et ad solem siccare permitte.   Postea ad servandum in forulo vel
pixide pone.

182. *Item de faciendo sinopide de mellana.*—Si vis facere
sinopidem de mellana.   Accipe de lacca id est gumma ederæ
de qua parcium tingitur et optime tere et distempera cum aceto
vel urina.   Deinde farinam triticeam bene a furfure mundatam
adjungens, fac quasi pastulas et coque in olla rudi et frequenter
cum coquetur ex eo cum festuca super virgulam tuam pone,
donec videas optimi chloris esse et si multum rubeum volueris
minus coque si minus rubeum magis coque.

183. *Sicut supra de eodem synopide aliter faciendo.*—Si vis
facere optimum sinopidem, accipe laccam id est gummam ederæ
et Waranciam et coque in ollam aliquantulum cum aqua postea

jar with water, and afterwards take it out of the jar, and let it
cool a little. Then grind it well in a mortar, and strain it
through a cloth, squeezing it well out, and afterwards heat it
carefully in a basin or saucer, taking care not to let it boil, but
only simmer. And while it is on the fire put it frequently with
a twig upon your rod to try it; if it is thick enough, remove it
from the fire, and let it cool and harden, so that you may be able
to make it into cakes. Having made it into cakes, cut it up, and
put it into a small hole, and keep it for use.

184. *Of lake.*—In the month of March, cut branches of ivy
crosswise in various places, or pierce them with a bodkin, and
there will exude a liquid, which you must collect every third
day. This is boiled with urine, and turns to a blood colour,
which is also called lacha, with which the skins, commonly called
parcie, are dyed with alum. The above-mentioned liquid is
useful for many purposes.

185. *Of writing, or painting, with tin.*—When you are going
to make gold or silver writing or painting, if you have neither
of them, that is to say, neither gold nor silver, you must make
use of the following process. Cast very pure tin into strips of
half a foot or little more in length, namely, like those of which
glass windows are made. Then scrape with a knife one or
more of them, as many as you like, into very small pieces,
until they, or it, are, or is, entirely scraped away; and then put
the shavings into a mortar made of very hard metal, namely, of
that of which bells are made, which must be prepared for this
purpose, and fixed in a plank. You must also have a muller or
pestle of the same metal, which must revolve in the mortar.
Afterwards put these clippings into the mortar, and pour water
upon them, and grind them by pulling a thong backwards and
forwards; but when the muller begins to stick a little, so that
it will not turn, take it out, and pour or tip out the water and
tin into a very clean vase; and then, letting the tin remain in
the vase, pour the water cautiously off, without pouring away
the tin. Afterwards let the tin dry by the fire or in the sun.
Then put it on a very thick linen cloth, and make the fine parts

extrahes ab olla et aliquantulum refrigerari permitte.   Deinde
in mortariolo fortiter tere et per pannum extorquendo cola, et
postea in bacina vel in testa coque cum diligentia cavens ne
bulliat sed tantum fremat.   Et dum coquitur frequenter cum
festuca super virgulam tuam pone temptando ; si satis spissum
ab igne tolle et permitte frigescere et durescere.   Itaque inde
possis pastillos facere.   Et factis pastillis excisea et pone in
forulo et serva usui.

184. *De lacca.*—Mense Marcio ramas in diversis locis incide
de edera extransverso vel cum aculeo perfora et egredietur
liquor quem de tertio in tercium diem collige qui cum urina
coquitur et in sanguineum colorem vertetur, qui et lacha dicitur ex qua pelles alutine tingentur que vulgo parcie dicuntur.
Liquor superdictum ad multa valet.

185. *De stannea scriptura vel pictura.*—Auream seu argenteam scripturam vel picturam facturus, si neutrum habeas,
scilicet nec aurum nec argentum hac utere compositura.   Stannum purissimum funde in laminas quas dimidii pedis vel paulo
plus longitudinis fac ad instar scilicet earum ex quibus fenestre
vitree componuntur.   Deinde unam earum vel plures quot vis
cum cultello vel quo instrumento necesse fuerit minutatum
erade vel errade quo ad usque tota consumpta vel consumptæ
sint.   Et deinceps ipsas encisuras in mortariolo pone quod de
metallo durissimo sit, quo scilicet campanæ fiunt ad hoc opus
parato et in ligno infixo.   Habeas simulque molam seu pistil-
lam qui in mortariolo vertitur, de eodem metallo.   Postea in
ipso mortario pone ipsas incisuras.   Et super ipsas infunde
aquam et sic eas mole trahendo corrigiam et retrahendo seu
relaxendo.   Ubi autem mola stare ceperit paululum nec jam
posse verti extrahe illam et aquam et stannum in mundissimo
vase rejecta vel reversa.   Et ipsum stannum retinendo in ipso
vase eice caute aquam absque ejiciendo stannum.   Et postea
permitte ipsum stannum siccari ad ignem vel ad solem.   Deinde
panno lineo valde spisso indue ac fac transire subtiles minucias ;

pass through ; but the coarser parts, which will not pass through
the cloth, put back into the mortar, and grind as you did before :
and you must always make the finer parts pass through a cloth
as before, and then put them with the other similar parts ; and
so, when you have reduced the tin to a very clean powder, draw
upon the parchment and upon the cloth flowers and images, and
whatever else you like.   And in painting you must put glue
upon the places which you wish to gild or silver, with a brush
of ass's hair, which glue you must thus make from ox-skins :—

186. *How to make glue from the skin of an ox or a cow.*—
Take the skin of an ox or a cow, as thick as you can find it,
which has already been tanned for shoes, and put it in a jar
and pour water upon it, and make it boil over the fire from
daybreak on a summer's day until nearly the third hour of the
day, pouring water into it when necessary, or, when it is much
diminished, pour off the water, which has boiled so long, and
pour in clean water, and make it boil again until the sixth
hour.   Then pour off this water, which will be nearly all evaporated, and again pour clean water into the jar over the same
leather, and do not renew it more than once or twice more.
And take great care not to let it boil over, and then, having
boiled it down to one-third, pour it into a vase, and leave it to
cool all that day and night.   In the morning of the next day,
if it is coagulated in the vase, put your finger upon it.   If any
part of it remains sticking to your finger, you may know that it
is not good, and may throw it away as refuse.   Afterwards fill
up the jar with water as before, in order to boil it with the
leather ; and you must not fill it up any more, but take all
possible care not to let it boil over.   You will know when it is
good by (after you have boiled it sufficiently and let it cool)
putting your finger upon it as before, to see whether it is hard ;
and the harder you find it, the better you may know it to be.
Afterwards putting a small portion of it into an earthen vase,
set it on the coals and make it rather warm.   Then, removing
the vase from the fire, keep it at a moderate heat over a slow
fire made of a few pieces of charcoal, lest it should be con-

grossiores vero quæ per pannum transire non poterunt iterum in ipso mortario mitte et molle sicut antea feceras. Et semper minutiorem partem per pannum transire facias sicut dictum est et repone cum similibus minutiis et sic postquam in mundissimum pulverem redegeris stannum protrahe super pergamenum et super pannum flores et imagines et quodcumque opus volueris. Et in ipso opere per loca que de aurare vel argenteare voles, pones viscum cum pincello asinino quod viscum sic facies de corio bovis.

186. *Quomodo viscum vel gluten fit de corio bovis vel vaccæ.*—Corium bovis vel vaccæ quod spissius invenire poteris jam ad calcimaenta instinctum mitte in ollam simul que aquam et a primo deluculo usque ad horam pene tertiam temporis æstatis fervere fac ad ignem, aquam infundendo cum opus erit vel cum comminuta fuerit. Postea projicies ipsarum aquam que tandiu fervuerit et infundas claram aquam et iterum fervere facies usque ad horam sextam. Postea ipsam aquam pene consumptum projice atque iterum in olla cum corio eodem aquam claram mitte nec augeas plusquam semel aut bis sed diligenter observa ne ex inundando exiliat tunc usque ad tertiam partem coctam ipsam in vase recipe et refrigerari permitte tota die illa et nocte. Mane die altera si coagulatur invanis digitum suppone. Si digito aliqua pars adhærens remanserit, scias non esse bonam et projice illud velut stercora. Post hoc iterum aqua ollam implebis similiter ut cum eodem corio excoquatur, nec augebis amplius sed cum qua possis diligencia custodi ne exiliat sciens quod bona erit si digitum, postquam sufficienter bullierit et frigidari permiseris, supposueris ut supra et durum inveneris, et quanto duriorem senseris tanto meliorem esse scias. Postea sic aliquam partem de ea sumptam in testeo vasculo pone eo super carbones aliquantulum fac fervere. Ex igne autem in vasculum quem ad levem ignem paucorum carbonum ad moderatam caliditatem tunc ne congelitur pincellum minimum ad hoc paratum ea intinge et super pergamenum et super pannum quidquid protrahendo vel de protractis volueris fac et linias atque statim ut

gealed, and dip into it a very small paint-brush made for this purpose, and draw on the parchment or canvas whatever you like, or fill in any former drawings ; and as soon as you have drawn your paint-brush over a few places, before the glue is congealed, quickly, and without delay, in order that the tin may adhere before the glue dries, sprinkle plenty of the powdered tin over it, so that none whatever of those parts, which you spread over with the paint-brush full of glue or cement, may remain bare, or not covered with the powdered tin. And so go on by degrees with the remaining parts of the work, until you have completely filled in all that you intended to colour with it. Lastly, collect and put by the superfluous powder of the tin which is lying scattered about here and there on the paper, not adhering to the work, and leave your work until the next day to dry.

188. *How to know good tin.*[1]—Good tin is known as follows. Put a plate of tin to your ear, and bend it to and fro several times with both hands, as if you wished to know whether it was broken, and if it rings, that is, creaks or crackles, it is good. Also, if you cut a strip from the plate with a knife, and do not entirely separate it, but bend it to and fro six or seven times, as if you were going to break it off, and if it does not break, you will by that means prove the said tin to be very good.

189. *How to make ink.*[2]—If you wish to make ink, you must take, they say, the bark of blackthorn, and when you have torn it off clean from the wood, you must fill a vase with it, mixed also with plenty of water, which must not be renewed, and put it on the fire, and let the bark boil down over the fire like beef, and then take it out, and squeeze out of it the water which it has soaked up, and let the water boil quickly over the fire till it is reduced to one-half. Afterwards, pour it into the first vase, and let it boil still, and when it is reduced, pour it back into the other vase, and make it boil away.

---

1 No. 187 is missing in the original.

2 The word atramentum is written in the margin of this chapter in the original.

aliquantulum in aliquibus locis pincellum traxeris priusque
congeletur glutem cito non tardando ut stannum tenere possit
et antequam siccetur, habundanter stannum pulverisatum super
spargas et ita ut nil omnino de his quæ cum pincello de ipso
visco vel glutine linieris vacuum remaneat quin stanno pulverizato cooperiatur.   Deinde sic fac paulatim procedendo ad
reliquas partes operis usquequo intoto compleveris quod per-
ficere ex eo decreverit.   Demum stanni pulverem quod super
habundaverit et hac illuc dispersum erit non adherens operi,
colligas et recipe et opus tuum usque in crastinum siccari
permitte.

188. *De cognitione boni stanni.*—Sic autem bonum stannum
cognoscitur.   Accipe lamina stanni juxta aurem tuam et cum
utraque manu plices sepius illam quasi qui velis scire an facta sit
et osculta diligenter et si tinuit id est stridet vel crisnat bonum
est, et si de lamina cum cultello crispam sceveris nec tamen
omnino abrumperis sed quasi qui velis eam frangere, sexcies
vel septies plicueris et sine fractura remanserit optimum fore
dictum stannum isto modo comprobaverit.

189. *De incausto quo modo efficitur.*—Quisquis igitur incaustum conficere voluerit sumens ut aiunt corticem nigræ
spinæ quam cum de ligno ad purum evulserit impleat inde vas
mixta pariter habundantissime et semel tantum cum aqua qua
imposita igni sinat corticem dequoqui more carnis vaccinæ eo
que extracto extorqueat ab eoquam ebiberat aquam et ipsam
aquam igni prestolatur excoqui ad medietatem.   Postea ipsam
transfundat in vas primus et adhuc bullire permittat et cum
comminuta fuerit refundat in aliud vas et ebullire faciat.   Et
cum ad ultimum iterum comminuta erit evacuet in minimo

And when lastly it is again reduced, empty it into a very small vase, and make it boil away. And when the ink has become thick like porridge, take it off the fire, because it is sufficiently boiled. But when you wish to prepare it for writing, take some part of it, and put it into an earthen vessel with double the quantity of wine, and take great care, when it begins to get hot, to throw away the impurities which sink to the bottom, separating them from the ink by straining through a cloth. But what cannot be omitted is, that care must be taken not to let it run over the edge of the vase, for otherwise you will lose a great part of your labour. But when, as I had begun to say, it is still hot, mix up with it two pieces of burnt atramentum, and after four days or a week you will be able to write with it. And if the ink should remain pale, or soak the parchment like water, put it on the fire again, mixing with it a little incaustum and atramentum. But do not throw it away while it is still hot, for it is atramentum.

190. *How to lay gold on a wall, or on parchments.*—If you wish to lay gold on a wall, or on paper, or on wood, or upon a block of marble, grind gypsum by itself separately. Then grind brown separately in the same manner, and take three parts of gypsum and one of brown, and take glue made from parchment or leather, and distemper them together, mixing the said parts, and lay upon it [the object to be gilded] one coat of this mixture with a paint-brush, and then another; and so lay three or four coats. And when the last is dry, scrape it with a knife or other iron instrument fitted for the purpose, so that it may be very smooth; and then burnish it with a tooth or a stone, and lay over it, with the paint-brush, only one very thin coat of the gypsum, and let it dry. When it is dry, lay the gold upon that mordant, as you have been taught. Afterwards lay upon the gold a very fine cloth that has been two or three times warmed; or apply it as I do, not so warm, in order that the gold may be the better polished.

191. *Also how to lay on gold.*—Take gypsum and grind it

vase et ebullire faciat.   Cum que ipsum incaustum in modum
pultium densatum fuerit extrahat illud ab igne, quia ad ple-
num est decoctum, cum vero ad scribendum volueris aptare
tolles ab eo aliquam portionem pones in vas fictile, duplum que
vini, solicitate que procaveat ut cum ceperit fervere sordes in
fundo immergentes rejiciat separando eas ab incausto colando
ipsum per telam.   Hoc vero quod pone preteriri poterit ob-
servet ne vel tunc vel quando confectatur in caloris ora vasis
transeat.   Alioquin magna parte quassabitur suo labore.   Cum
vero ut dicere ceperam ad huc calet attramenti duo frustra
cremata commisceat quatuor que diebus vel ebdomada exacta
inde scribere poterit.   Et si in pallore perduraverit vel pergamenum transierit more aque appone iterum igni miscendo
aliquantulum incausti et attramenti sed tunc cum ad huc effer-
fuerit non abiciat quod attramentum est.

190. *Quomodo in muro vel in pergameno ponitur aurum.*—Si
vis aurum ponere in muro vel in carta vel in ligno vel super
petra marmorea, tere fortiter gypsum per se separatim.
Deinde brunum similiter teris separatim facies que de gypso
tres partes et quatuor de bruno.   Accipies que colam de pergamenis vel de corio factum et distemperes simul, miscendo
illas supradictas partes, facies que de ipsa mixtura unum
lectum de super cum pincello et ad huc de super alium.   Et
sic facies tres vel quatuor linitiones : cum vero siccum fuerit
rades cultello vel alio ferro ad hoc parato ita quod sit bene
adequatum deinde burnias dente vel petra et cum pincello de
super tantum una vice trahe de ipso gypso postea siccabitur.
Postquam siccatum fuerit pones de super ea distemperatura
tua aurum sicut doctus es.   Postea pannum delicatissimum
super aurum duabus vel tribus vicibus calefactam pones, vel
sicut ego facio minus calefactum, ad modum vel melius poliatur, super eum pone.

191. *Item de ponendo auro.*—Accipe gypsum et mola eum

well with water.   Then take your glue which is made of bull-
skin and mix with it a little white of egg, and distemper the
gypsum.   But when you wish to lay on the gold, cover the
place with gypsum with a paint-brush, and let it dry.   Do
this three times.   Then scrape it, that it may be smooth, and
burnish it, and again lay another coat of the glue or mordant
upon it, and then your gold upon that, and remove the dirt
gently with cotton, and then let it dry.   But if you wish to
polish it, do so with hæmatite, or with a dog's-tooth.

192. *Also how to lay on gold.*—Take *brasilium*, newly distempered with white of egg, well whipped with a sponge or
otherwise, and draw and paint with it whatever you like on
vellum or on any other thing you wish to gild, and immediately lay the gold upon it, and remove the dirt with cotton,
scarcely touching it, and leave it to dry for half a day or a
whole day if you like.   Then take a dog's-tooth, and begin to
burnish at first gently, lest you should spoil it all, and then
harder, and afterwards so hard that your forehead is wet with
perspiration.   And if you wish to lay gold on parchment made
of sheep's-skin, add a little plum-tree gum, otherwise gum
arabic, which is excellent for working on any kind of parchment, namely, from calf-skin, sheep-skin, and goat-skin, as we
shall declare in the following [recipe].   And either kind of
gum must be distempered as follows :—

193. *The mode of tempering the gums for laying on gold.*—
Take whichever of these gums you like, and tie it up in a very
clean linen cloth, and put it in a glass vase, and let it lie in
water for a whole day and night, although indeed, if you want
to make haste, you may stir up the water with your finger.
Then draw whatever you like on the parchment, and lay the
gold on it as before mentioned.

194. *Of the precautions required in gilding.*—But take notice
that you ought to work in gold and colours in a damp place
on account of the hot weather, which, as it is often injurious in
burnishing gold, both to the colours on which the gold is laid
and in [the operation] of gilding, if the work is done on parch-

fortiter cum aqua. Deinde accipe gluten tuum quod fit de
taurino pinguedine et misce cum eo parumper de glarea ovi,
et distempera gypsum. Ubi vero aurum ponere volueris ibi
cum pincello de gypso trahes, dimittes que siccare. Hæc facies
tribus vicibus; postea raddes eum ut sit planum et burnies;
iterum de dicto glutine seu cola de super trahes et illico aurum
tuum pones et de cotho suaviter turpedines ipsum et ita dimitte
siccare si vero polire eum vis de emate vel dente canino polies
ipsum.

192. *Item ad ponendum aurum.*—Accipe brasilium noviter
distemperatum cum glarea ovi optime fracta cum spungia vel
aliter et de ipso protrahe et pinge quæ vis in pergameno
vitulino vel alio ubi ponere aurum volueris et statim aurum de
super pone et de cotho quasi non tangens turpedine, dimittesque dimidium diem siccare vel per totum diem si vis.
Postea accipe dentem caninum et brunire incipias primum
quidem suaviter ne totum dissipes, deinde fortius postea tam
fortiter ut frons tua sudore madescat. Et si aurum in pergameno de ariete ponere volueris addes parumper de gumma
cinea aliter gumma arabica quæ mirabilis est ad operandum
in utroque pergameno scilicet vitulino, arietino et capretino
sicut in sequenti declarabimus utrumque etenim gummam distemperabis sic.

193. *Modus distemperandi gummas ad ponendum aurum.*—
Accipies gummam qualem vis unam de duabus hiis et ligabis
in pannum lineum nitissimum ponesque in vitreo vase tota die
et nocte in aqua jacere vel certe si festinare vis, distemperabis
eam digito tuo cum ipsa aqua. Sic que in pergamenum penna
protrahe omne quod vis et illico pone aurum ut suprascriptum
est.

194. *De advertentiis habendis in ponendo aurum.*—Sed inde
adverte quomodo operari te oportet de auro, et coloribus in
humido loco propter calidum tempus quod sicut sepe nocet ad
bruniendum aurum et ad colores de quibus aurum ponitur et
de auro operari si opus fiat in minus humido et nimis sicco

ment that is too dry and not sufficiently moist; so also it is injurious when the weather is too dry and arid, or too damp, while applying colours or gilding.

195. *Also how to lay on gold.*—Take gum arabic and distemper it as aforesaid. Then take gum ammoniac distempered with hot water over the fire, and mix it with the gum arabic, and stir it with your finger, and put it in the sun, that it may be well mixed and liquefied. Next, take gypsum, and distemper it with white of egg, and mix it with gum ammoniac and gum arabic. And when you wish to gild leather or purple cloth, or linen or silk cloths, stir it up altogether, and draw beasts and birds and flowers upon them with a very sharp stick, and let them dry. Then take the gold, and blow gently on the flowers, and lay on the gold directly, and press it down with a burnishing tooth or stone, and burnish it as before.

196. *Of certain kinds of gum or glue.*[1]—If you have not the air-bladder of a sea-fish, cut up thick vellum in the same manner, and wash it. Also wash carefully three times in warm water the dried bones of the head of a pike, and boil them. Whichever of these you boil, add to them one-third part of very clear gum, that is, gum arabic, and boil a little; and you may keep this as long as you will.

197. *How and with what vehicles to temper colours for painting in books.* —When mixing colours for painting in books, make a vehicle of the clearest gum arabic and water, as before, and mix with it all colours except green and ceruse, minium, and carmine. Salt green is of no use in a book. Spanish green you must temper with wine, and if you wish to shade it, add a little of the juice of sword grass, or cabbage, or leek. You must mix minium and ceruse, and carminium, with white of egg. Grind azure with soap, and wash it, and mix it with white of egg.

198. *How that various tints are made by the mixture of the*

---

[1] This chapter is a paraphrase of chap. xxxiii. of the first book of Theophilus, English ed.

[2] See Theophilus, lib. i. cap. xxxiv. (Eng. ed.), of which this is a para-

pergameno. Sic de coloribus vero operari et ponendo aurum
in tempus nimis rigidum vel siccum ac etiam minus humidum.

195. *Item ad ipsum aurum ponendum.*—Accipe gummam
arabicam et distempera ut dictum est. Accipiesque moniacu-
lum distemperatum cum aqua calida ad ignem et misces cum
arabica, distemperabis que digito tuo et pones ad solem ut
bene distemperetur et liquefiat. Postea accipe gypsum et distempera cum glarea ovi et clarum misce cum moniculo et arabica. Et quando aurum in corio vel in purpura vel in pellis
lineis vel siricis ponere volueris movebis omnia simul et facies
bestias et volucres et flores cum baculo acutissime de super
dimittesque siccum. Postea accipe illud et super flores modice
suffla et statim aurum impones et imprima dente vel lapide ad
bruniendum, et brunias ut supra.

196. *De quibusdam generibus gummi vel glutinis.*— Si vesicam
non habueris piscis marrini pergamenum vituli spissum eodem
modo incide, lava quoque ossa etiam capitis lupi piscis sicca,
diligenter lota in calida aqua ter illa coque; qualemcumque
horum coxeris. Adde eis terciam partem gummi lucidissimi,
i. e. arabici et modice coque et poteris servare quam diu volueris.

197. *Quomodo temperantur colores in libris ponendis et de
quibus liquoribus.*—Temperando colores in libris ponendos fac
temperamentum ex gummi arabico lucidissimo et aqua ut
supra et tempera omnes colores excepto viridi et cerusa et
minio et carminio; viride salsum non valet in libro, viride
hispanicum temperabis vino et si volueris umbras facere adde
modicum succi gladioli vel caulis vel porri; minium et cerusam
et carminium temperabis claro ovi. Azur mole cum sapone
et lava et distempera claro ovi.

198. *Qui ex mixturis colorum ad invicem plurimæ ipsorum*

---

phrase; the last sentence excepted, which is not in Theophilus, but part of
it will be found in the Clavicula, p. 61.

colours with one another.—All colours whatever are diversified
and varied in various ways and manners, by mixtures being
made with them or laid over them, of other colours, that agree
with them in proper manners and quantities. If you require
these mixtures for painting figures and other things, mix and
temper them as before for books. And all colours are to be
laid on twice, in books, and on parchment, first very thin, and
then thicker; but in letters only once.[1]

199. *Of black, and ink, and of a black and green colour.*[2]—
Take ripe berries of honeysuckle, that is, in English, galetrice,
and pound them well in a mortar. Afterwards boil them carefully in wine, adding also some rust of iron to the decoction.
This is a green and brilliant ink. If you wish to colour a cloth
or a skin green, paint it over with a paintbrush. But if you
wish it to be black, add ink to the composition, as usual.

200. *Gum prevents the ink from running.*—If you wish to
prevent the above written, or any other ink from running when
you are using it, add the gum of a plum-tree or of an apple, in
the boiling, and boil it together.

201. *Also how to make green, according to the Normans.*[3]—
Take the herb which is called grenuspett [or gremispett], and
boil it with beer or wine, so that the beer may be coloured
yellow by the herb. Then strain it. Then grind sufficiently
some Greek green with the beer, and afterwards let it stand in
a basin or a copper vase in the sun to ripen.

202. *How to make auripetrum.*—Spanish saffron, distempered
with very clear glue or liquid varnish, and laid over very clear,
that is, very bright and well polished tin, assumes the appearance of gold to those that look on it, for it receives its colour
from the sun, and its brilliancy from the tin, and thus may be
made excellent auripetrum.

---

[1] The latter part of this chapter is from Theophilus, lib. i. cap. xxxiv.

[2] This recipe and the next are in the Mappæ Clavicula, p. 43.

[3] This recipe is also in the Clavicula (p. 43), without, however, the remarkable addition "according to the Normans."

varietates fiunt.—Omnes et quicumque colores ex mixturis aliorum eis convenientium debitis modis et quantitatibus eis adhibitis et impositis diversificantur et variantur plurimis modis et differenciis. Quas mixturas si indigueris ad pingendum imagines et alia, compone et distempera in libris ut supra. Et omnes colores bis ponendi sunt in libris et pergamenis in primus tenuissime, Deinde spissius in literis vero semel.

199. *De attramento et incausto et de negro et viridi colore.*—Accipe grana matura caprifolii hoc est anglice galetrice et in mortario bene contere. Post vino diligenter fac bullire ferrum aruginatum decoctione similiter addiciens. Hoc est viride et fulgens incaustum et si vis pannum vel corium habere viride, pincello desuper linias. Si vero vis ut niger sit huic compositioni adde solito attramentum.

200. *Quod gumma cum prohibet fluxum incausti.*—Si vis facere quod superscriptum incaustum vel aliud non decurrat cum de ipso operatur, pone gummam cini vel pomi in coctione et simul coque.

201. *Item de viridi faciendo secundum normannos.*—Accipe herbam que dicitur gremispect et bulli cum cervesia aut vino adeo ut cervisia crocea sit de herba. Postea cola Deinde pulverem de viridi Greco mola cum ipsa cervisia ut satis sit, postea stet in baccino vel cupreo vase contra solem ad maturandum.

202. *Quomodo efficitur auripetrum.*—Crocus hispanicus cum lucidissimo glutine seu vernicio liquido distemperatur et stanno limpidissimo, *i.e.* pene polito et claro, superpositas speciem auri intuentibus mentitur quod a sole colorem et stanno accipit fulgorem et inde optimum fit auripetrum.

203. *Also, in the same manner, a coat of gall gives the appearance of gold to copper vases.*[1]—By scraping copper with a knife, and burnishing it with a bear's tooth, it is polished. Then lay gall evenly over every part of it with a paintbrush; and, when it is dry, lay on more and more coats of gall, and it imitates the colour of gold.

204. *How to colour copper.*—Take copper that has been well filed and polished and afterwards varnished over, and warm it frequently before the fire, and it will turn of a red colour. Afterwards scrape it with a sharp knife in several places and cover it again with some colour, and then the fire will turn it of a different colour; and so in proportion to the warmth.

205. *Also, the manner of beating out tin-plates, so as to appear gilt, to use in painting, on account of the price of gold.*—If you wish to make [imitate] gold leaf, take pure tin or silver and make it into very thin plates; and take dry saffron flowers, and wrap them up in a linen cloth and lay them in gum water, and leave them there until they are soft. Then take them out, being careful not to squeeze them. But if the saffron which you intend to soak in water is fresh, you must first put the flowers in the sun in a linen cloth by themselves, to dry, and when they are dry soak them in water as before directed. Afterwards take the beforementioned water and lay it thinly once over the plates and let them dry. Then take the flowers, dried as before directed, and soak them in white of egg, which has been whipped a little, and stir it with your finger, and let the plates lie in it a short time, until each piece has been dipped three times, letting the pieces dry separately between each of these three times, and afterwards polish them with an onyx stone; and if you have no onyx, grease the tin with the oil which is made from linseed, and let it dry, and put it on paper or on wood in this manner. Take the above mentioned gum and put it in tepid water, and allow it to remain for so long as it takes to sing a mass.[2] Afterwards lay pure white colour in

---

[1] See Eraclius, lib. ii. No. XVI.   [2] About a quarter of an hour.

203. *Itemque sic vasa cuprea linicio fellis deauraturam men-*
titur.—Cuprum raddendo cum cultello et bruniendo dente
ursino splendificatur. Deinde cum felle linies pincello per
omnes ejus partes tracto equaliter; quo siccato iterum atque
iterum fel superpone et auri mentitur colorem.

204. *Ad colorandum cuprum.*—Cuprum bene limatum et
planatum postea vernicio tinctum ad ignem sepe calefaciat et
contrahet colorem rubeum. Postea cum acuto cultello radde
in diversis locis et iterum illini aliquo colore et ibi alium
colorem habebit ad ignem et quanto plus calefiet.

205. *Item de modo attenuandi laminas stanni ut auratæ*
videantur ex carentia auri utendas in operibus.—Si vis facere
petonas de auro accipe stannum purum vel argentum et fac
laminas multum tenuas et accipe crocum florem siccum et involve in panno lineo et pone in aqua ubi gumma est et dimitte
ibi usquequo mollescat. Postea tolles eum et cave ne con-
stringas eum; si autem crocus recens est quum ipsam accipis
pro ponendo in aqua debes prius ponere ad solem in panno
lineo florem separatim siccare et dum siccus fuerit mitte in
aquam temperare ut dictum est superius. Post hec accipe
aquam supradictam et tinge laminas subtiliter semel et admitte
siccari. Dehinc accipe florem siccatam sicut dixi et pone in
glaream ovi aliquantulum vapulum et cum digito fricabis. Et
laminas dimitte jacere aliquantulum in ea donec omnes laminæ
infusæ sint ter. Ita tamen ut unaquaque vice exipsis tribus
permittas eas sigillatim siccari, postea liccabis eas cum onchino,
si non habes onchinum unge laminas de oleo quod fit de lini
semine et permitte siccari, et eas pones in carta vel in ligno
hoc modo. Accipies gummam supradictam et pones aquam
tepidam et iterum tantum permittes jacere, quantum spatii est
cantare missam. Postea pone purum album colorem sicut
ponere debes in locis in quibus ponere vis laminas et dum

a proper manner on those places on which you wish to apply
the tin, and, when they are dry, polish them with an onyx
stone ; then lay the gum water upon the white colour, and let it
dry.   Then polish it as before ; after this cut the tin according
to the form required, lay it on with the said gum-water, and
let it dry ; and clean it with a sponge dipped in cold water;
then rub it down with a linen cloth well wrung out, and rub
the tin, and afterwards polish it, as before mentioned.

206. *Also as before, how to gild leaves or beaten plates of
tin.*—Take the herb which is called myrrh,[1] and aloes, of each
equal weights, and having mixed them together, put them in
a proper quantity of water.   Then boil them well, and after
they have been boiled, pour the water into a vessel, and take
the leaves of tin well covered on one side with varnish, immerse it in the liquor as long as necessary.   Then boil the
middle bark of the black plum well in a vessel, and afterwards
dip the same tin in this water.   Then lay it on a table to dry.

207. *Also as before.*—Mix linseed oil and resin, an equal
weight of each, and add the same measure of vernix, put these
ingredients into a jar and boil them well.   Then dip leaves of
tin well varnished into it [the jar], and afterwards dry them in
the sun.

208. *Also as above.*—Put linseed-oil and the inner bark of
the black plum into a new jar, and boil it well for a short time
upon charcoal or upon a clear fire.   Then clean your glassa, by
weight as much as you like, and put it into another jar, and
take about half the quantity of alum, and of dragon's blood,
and put it all into the jar, and lastly add a little resin, and
melt the whole well together, and as soon as all the ingredients

---

[1] It seems probable that the gum-resin myrrh is meant, particularly as
myrrh is named among other gums and resins in the recipe entitled " Lucida quo modo fiant super colores," in the Clavicula, p. 53, and in the
Lucca MS., published by Muratori.   At the same time it must be observed,
that the author writes " the herb which is called myrrh ;" and in the Table
of Synonymes myrrh is said to be the " tree vulgarly called genestra."
The plant called " myrrha," myrrhis, &c., is the Scandix odorato,

siccum fuerit licca eum onichino et sic pones aquam in qua
gumma est super album colorem et dimitte siccare.   Item
licca ut supra; post hoc incide laminas secundum modum loci
ubi ponere volueris, et pone eas cum dicta aqua gummata, et
permitte siccari et cum spongia intincta in aqua frigida purga
postea ipsas laminas ubi posuisti eas, postea cum panno lineo
extersa optime et frica ipsas laminas et postea licca ut supra
scriptum est.

206. *Item ut supra de modo deaurandi folia seu laminas
stanni attenuatas.*—Accipe herbam que dicitur myrra et aloem
uno pondere ambas et commixtas simul pone in illam aquam
secundum modum appositam.   Deinde fac bullire bene, et post
coctionem herbarum mitte aquam in sartaginem et folia stanni
bene illinita una parte de vernix appone et bene merge quantum opus fuerit.   Deinde medianam corticis pruni nigri fac
bullire, in sartaginem bene et postea mitte eadem folia in hac
aqua.   Deinde appone folia super tabulam ad siccandum.

207. *Item ut supra.*—Oleum de lini semine et picem uno
pondere mixtum et eamdem mensuram de vernix pone in ollam
et fac bullire bene.   Deinde mitte folia stanni bene verniciata
intus et post modum siccata ad solem.

208. *Item ut supra.*—Oleum lineum et medianam corticem
nigri pruni mitte in ollam novam ac fac bene bullire super carbones vel claro igne paulatim, deinde munda glassam tuam
quantum volueris cum pondere et pone in alteram ollam et
aluminis quasi mediam partem et sanguinem drachonis et
omnia hæc mitte in ollam et ad ultimum mixtum picem ad-
junge et bene funde et quam citius hec omnia fondentur appone

---

Myrrhis magno semine longo sulcato, Myrrhis major cicutaria odorato.
Myrrhenkerbel, Aniskerbel.   In English, the sweet-scented Cicely, or
myrrh.   Cerfeuil odorant ou musqué, Cerfeuil d'Espagne, Fr. Cerfoglio
odoroso, Miroide, Ital.   Matthioli and Laguna say that the Cerfeuil of the
French was synonymous with the Gingidio of the Greeks (the Scandix cere-
folium): therefore, instead of "Genestra," we ought perhaps to read
"Gingidio."

are melted, add the abovementioned oil, and, as if you were
making a compound ointment, let them boil well together, and
stir them frequently, and afterwards dip your nail into the composition and try whether it is good or not.

209. *Also as before.*—Collect twigs of black plum, and put
them in the sun for a week or a fortnight, and then throw away
the outer bark, and take the inner bark, and put it into a
rough jar, so as to fill it.   Then take linseed or hempseed-oil,
and pour into the jar as much of it as it will hold, and heat
it slowly over the fire, until the bark is reduced to charcoal.
Then throw away the bark, and strain the remainder of the oil
through linen, and take resin and white frankincense, and clean
the jar well, and then put all the ingredients into it again, and
heat it as long as you please.

supradictum oleum et secundum unctionem confectionis et sine
bene bullire simul et sæpe move et post modum intinges ungu-
lam tuam et temptabis utrum bonum sit an non.

209. *Item ut antea.*—Collige virgulas de nigro pruno et
pone ad solem per octo dies aut quindecim et postea primum
projicies corticem accipies que secundum et pones in olla rudi
ita ut plena sit. Deinde accipies oleum de lino vel de canapo,
et in olla quantum intrare poteris impones et lente igne tam
diu coques donec ipse cortex in carbonem redigatur et tunc
projicies et per lintheum quod remanserit oleum colabis et
postea accipies picem et thus album et ipsam que ollulam fortiter mundabis, totum que simul repones iterum intus et quantum tibi placuerit coques.

MANUSCRIPTS OF ERACLIUS.

PRELIMINARY OBSERVATIONS.

Two ancient copies only of the MS. of Eraclius have been hitherto discovered, and it is somewhat singular that both are bound up with MSS. of Theophilus.

The most ancient of these is that discovered by Raspe in the library of Trinity College, Cambridge, and which he afterwards published in his work on Painting in Oil (London, 1801). This MS. is written on vellum, and is of the latter half of the thirteenth century.[1] It is now in the British Museum.[2] The first two books are in verse; the last, which consists of twenty-four or twenty-five chapters, is in prose.

The MS. next in point of antiquity is that which forms part of the MS. of Le Begue. It is written on paper, and was transcribed in the year 1431, probably from an older MS., the property of John Alcherius, which passed with his other MSS. into the hands of Le Begue. The third book of this copy contains a great many additional chapters, and the whole of those published by Raspe, with the exception of one chapter, " De probatione auri et argenti."[3]

---

[1] Raspe, ' On Painting in Oil,' p. 42; Eastlake, ' Materials for a History of Painting in Oil,' p. 33.

[2] Egerton MSS., 840, A.

[3] Raspe, p. 117.

There is reason, however, to suppose that many copies of this MS. existed formerly, and that they were as widely scattered as the copies of the MS. of Theophilus. That this was the case is, I think, proved by the fact that fragments of the Treatise of Eraclius are found in other works, although they are ascribed not unfrequently to other authors. I shall mention, in the first place, those works in which the metrical chapters are to be found.

The most ancient work in which this occurs is the Treatise of Theophilus, the copy of which in the British Museum contains fifteen chapters of the first and second books of Eraclius, some of which, like the original, are metrical, while the others are paraphrases in prose ; and this is certainly a proof that this part of the Treatise of Eraclius was written before that copy of Theophilus.[1]

---

[1] The mere fact of one MS. containing parts of another, is not of itself sufficient to prove the age of a MS. : as these old writers borrowed from each other without acknowledging their obligations, it is impossible to say which is the oldest, unless other circumstances assist in determining the age. In the case of Theophilus it is apparent that the poetical parts are borrowed, because they form part of another work written entirely in verse, while no part of Theophilus is in verse except the commencement, and the measure of the latter verses differs from those of Eraclius, for the former are Leonines, which is not the case with the latter. If this proof be insufficient, the passage in Theophilus, lib. iii. cap. cvi., will be quite conclusive. He says, " Ex vitro si quis depingere vascula quærit, et te verte ad hanc artem quæ in primo libro scripta est. Hæc enim ita se habet." The chapter referred to is not in Theophilus, but in the first book of Eraclius. In the case of the Clavicula, it is not so easy to determine whether it is older than Eraclius, because both contain copies of certain chapters which perhaps belonged to a third work, for some of them are repeated two or three times in the Clavicula. The age of the MS. must be settled by the consideration of other circumstances, and these favour the presumption that the Clavicula preceded the third book of Eraclius.

The earliest writer, after Theophilus, whose name I
have yet found attached to the verses of Eraclius is
Arnold de Villeneuve.[1]   The verses ascribed to him
occur in the Secreti of Wecker,[2] published at Basle in
1598, pp. 428 and 449. They relate to precious stones
and crystal.

Other metrical chapters of Eraclius, eight in number,
will be found in the same edition of Wecker (p. 643-
645); but these chapters, instead of being ascribed to
Arnold de Villeneuve, have the name of Marcellus
Palingenius attached to them.[3]

---

[1] Arnold de Villeneuve, a physician and alchemist.   He travelled in
Italy and Germany.   He was born A.D. 1245, and died previous to 1311.

[2] The work of J. J. Wecker, ' De Secretis,' was originally a translation
of the secrets of Don Alessio Piemontese ; the first edition was, according
to Haller, printed at Basle in 1559. " Every edition," says Beckmann,
" seems to differ from the preceding ; many things are omitted, and the
new editions are, for the most part, of little importance. I have the edition of Basle, 1592, 8vo., in which there is a great deal not to be found in
that of 1662, and which wants some things contained in the edition of 1582.
The latest editions are printed from that improved by Theod. Zuringer,
Basle, 1701, 8vo. The last edition by Zuringer was published at Basle in
1753." The edition of 1598, the preface of which is dated 1582, is the
only one to which I have had access ; I cannot say, therefore, whether the
extracts from Eraclius are contained in other editions.

[3] The real name of this Marcellus Palingenius was Manzelli, or Manzoli ;
he was a native of the neighbourhood of Ferrara, and being a reformer, he
narrowly escaped being put to death by the Inquisition. He published a
Latin poem, called the Zodiac ; the first edition of which was published
not prior to 1534. The measure of these verses is different from that of
Eraclius, and I could not discover that the work of the latter formed a part
of it. Another work has also been ascribed to Marcellus, entitled ' De
Corallorum Tinctura.' (See Potts' ' Chemical Dissertations,' translated by
Demachy.) The fragment from Eraclius may have formed part of this
work, for which I have inquired in vain in many public libraries. When I
was at Ferrara I inquired for this and other works of Marcellus Palingenius
of the Abb. Antonelli, the learned librarian of the public library of that
city, and I showed him the verses in Wecker, but he could give me no
information, except that the King of Prussia, when he was at Ferrara, had

With regard to the chapters of the third book contained in other MSS., I shall at present mention only that some of them are to be found in the Clavicula. These have been collated with the MS. of Eraclius, and the variations are inserted in the present work. It is probable that many more chapters may be incorporated into some of the works entitled "Secrets;" but there appears to be no inducement to undertake the labour of searching these works, since they would neither add to the practical knowledge of the arts they describe, nor make us acquainted with the history of Eraclius or of his works, since they do not bear his name.

Of the biography of Eraclius nothing is known: his country and the date of his work are equally uncertain. The same uncertainty attends the work; for there is some doubt whether the whole of the MS. ascribed to him in the Le Begue collection was actually written by him or not. I shall first offer some remarks on the work itself, and shall then state the conclusions I have drawn from a careful consideration of it.

With regard to the composition of the work itself, it appears to consist *primâ facie* of three books, the first two of which are metrical; the third is in prose.

The metrical part consists of twenty-one stanzas or

---

appeared to take a personal interest in Palingenius, and had procured such of his works as he could collect. On my return to England, Sir Henry Ellis was so obliging as to give me a letter of introduction to Dr. Pertz, the librarian of the King of Prussia, to whom I wrote, requesting to know whether he could inform me if these verses, of which I inclosed a copy, formed part of any work of Palingenius which might be preserved in the Royal Library at Berlin. Dr. Pertz very kindly searched both the Royal Library and the King's private library, but without success.

chapters. It commences with a prologue, which is preceded in the Cambridge MS. by these words, " Incipit
Liber Eraclii sapientissimi viri de coloribus et artibus
Romanorum." The commencement of the second book
in the same MS. is " Incipit Lib. II. de colore auripigmento simili;" while in the Paris MS. the word " metricus " is inserted in the title of both books after
" primus " and " secundus." The third book in the
Cambridge MS. has no heading; but in the Paris MS.
it is headed " Incipit tertius liber et prosaicus Eraclii
antedicti de coloribus et artibus prædictis." These
various readings certainly suggest the idea that the
headings of the chapters were not written by Eraclius
himself, and that the work consisted originally of the
metrical parts only; and this supposition gains ground
from a consideration of the difference of style observable
between the first and second books and the third part,
and from the fact that the metrical parts contain frequent allusions to the arts of the Romans, which is not
the case in the third book, with the exception, perhaps,
of the extracts from Vitruvius and Isidore. The chapter
" De edere et lacca " is singular, and seems to indicate
that the author was a native of Italy.   Eraclius says,

" Hujus enim frondem nimium coluere *priores*,
    Ad titulum laudis ; erat ipsa corona poetis."

while the parallel chapter in Theophilus (E. Ed. p.
394) runs thus : " Poetarum enim carmina cum reci-
tarentur in theatro ante conventum *romanorum* corona-
bantur hederâ." From this it may be inferred, not
only that Eraclius was a native of Italy, and that
Theophilus (supposing the *whole* of the MS. in the

British Museum ascribed to Theophilus to have been included in his work)[1] was aware of the fact, but also that the latter was not an Italian, otherwise he would not have changed the phraseology of Eraclius.

The first chapter of the second book describes a yellow colour, composed of the gall of a large fish, called " Huso," mixed with chalk, which produced a colour like orpiment. A similar recipe, which is entitled " colore aureo Lombardico," is contained in a small MS. in the Bibliothèque Royale at Paris.[2] This is another intimation of an Italian origin.

Although the name of Eraclius appears to be Greek,[3] and not Latin, I am induced to suppose that Eraclius, the author of the first two books, was an Italian, a native perhaps of some part of the Lombard dukedom of Benevento, which, says Sismondi, " had preserved, under independent princes and surrounded by the Greeks and Saracens, a degree of civilization which in the earlier part of the middle ages was unexampled throughout the rest of Italy. Many of the fine arts and some branches of science were cultivated there with success. The schools of Salerno communicated to the West the medical skill of the Arabs, and the commerce of Amalfi introduced into those fertile provinces not only wealth, but knowledge. From the eighth to the tenth century

---

[1] I have before observed, that the copy of the MS. of Theophilus in the British Museum contains no less than fifteen chapters taken from the first and second books of Eraclius. Some of these are transcripts, others are paraphrases. It is impossible to say whether these additions to the work of Theophilus were actually made by himself, or by one of his transcribers. The former appears to me probable, because I think it is evident that Theophilus was well acquainted with the MS. ascribed to Eraclius.

[2] No. vi. MDCCXLIX., B. No. 9.

[3] Raspe, p. 44.

various historical works, written, it is true, in Latin,
but distinguished for their fidelity, their spirit, and their
fire, proceeded from the pen of several men of talent,
natives of that district, some of whom clothed their
compositions in hexameter verses, which, compared
with others of the same period, display superior facility
and fancy."

The custom alluded to of composing works in hexameter verses, will not fail to recal to the mind of the
reader the metrical work of Eraclius, the literary merit
of which, however, certainly does not entitle it to rank
among the works alluded to by Sismondi.

It appears to have been also the custom in Italy
during the twelfth and thirteenth centuries, to place
inscriptions in Latin verse on works of art, as well of
architecture, as of sculpture and painting, and even in
mosaics. Many of these inscriptions have been published by Ciampi.[1] The verses were sometimes hex-
ameters, and sometimes leonines. It is not improbable,
therefore, that the first two books of Eraclius were
written during the prevalence of this custom.

The last book of the Cambridge MS. which follows
the metrical chapters without any title, contains about
twenty-five chapters which are arranged with some regard to order. Nos. I.—IV. relate to pottery ; two of
these I have before observed are versified in the second
book. Nos. V.—XII. treat of glass and precious stones.
In these chapters is given a narration, taken from
Isidore, who had copied Pliny, of the discovery of the
art of making glass, with the marvellous legend of the

---

[1] Notizie inedite della Sagrestia Pistoiese, &c., pp. 27, 37, 38, 43, 46, 48.

cup of flexible glass which, it is said, cost the inventor his life; to which are added from other sources the method of making glass of various colours and of cutting and polishing precious stones. Nos. XIII.— XXIII. relate to gilding on metals, and the last two chapters relate to painting. There is reason to suppose that this third book of the Cambridge MS. is incomplete, because there is a reference in one of the chapters to auripetrum, the composition of which is not described in this MS., but in that of Le Begue.

The third book in the Le Begue MS. contains all the chapters enumerated above, with the exception of one "De probatione auri et argenti," to which are added above thirty other chapters which treat chiefly of painting. The arrangement, however, observable in the Cambridge MS. is not the same in the MS. of Le Begue, in which the different recipes appear to be thrown together at random without any regard to the subject. As it was therefore necessary to select between the arrangement of the Cambridge MS. and that of Le Begue, I have adopted the former as the most methodical, and have arranged the remaining chapters of the third book as systematically as it was possible. I have however retained the numbers of the Le Begue MS. for the convenience of reference, and have attached to them other numbers which commence with the third book. As the last chapters of the Cambridge MS. treat of preparing wood and colours for painting, the chapters which relate to the preparation of grounds and vehicles are placed next. After this is a recipe for dyeing Cordovan leather, followed by recipes for colours, for gilding on pictures, and then for executing Nielli. Next follow several chapters relative to colours which are extracted principally from Vitruvius, and lastly three chapters on painting which have evidently formed part of some Byzantine MS.

While preparing this MS. for publication, I have had occasion to remark, that several chapters in the third book, contain words and expressions and allusions to arts, which appear to belong to the twelfth or thirteenth centuries. From these expressions it also appears to me quite clear, that the author of certain portions of the third book was neither a Greek nor an Italian; on the contrary it seems to me extremely probable, from the fact of some of the foreign words introduced being of French origin, while others occur in French MSS., that this part of the work was written by a Frenchman, under which term I include also the Normans, who were at that period English subjects.

I shall first notice the word " cerasin," which appears to me to be derived from the French, and if this could be proved it would at once fix the country of the author, for he says " quod *nos* Cerasin vocamus." If this be the fact, " Galienum " may also be considered a French term, for although it is mentioned in the Index of the second book of Theophilus (who calls it " Gallien " [1] and not " Galienum "), yet it will be recollected that this author professes to teach " quicquid in Fenestrarum preciosa varietate diligit *Francia*," and in lib. ii. cap. xii., he again mentions the skill of the French in this art. Besides, the term " Gali colour, red,"

---

[1] " De vitro quod vocatur Gallien." See the Wolfenbüttel MS. of Theophilus, published by Lessing. There is a reprint of this work in the 8vo. edition of Lessing's works, published in 1839.

occurs in the MS. of Mayerne in an extract from the book of "Mr. Colladon" entitled "Couleurs des Esmaulx ou Vernix de la Poterie de Faience; Copie de l'original d'un Maistre potier Anglais." [1]

The term "Grossinum," which occurs in No. VIII. and No. XLIX., appears to denote a gros, which was a French weight equal to 1 drachm or the 8th of an ounce; it may also denote a small German coin, but in the present case the former may be fairly considered to express its real signification.

Among the terms which are peculiar to the north and west of Europe may be enumerated "Cervisia," also "Warancia," which is mentioned in the recipe for Cordovan leather No. XXXII., and which in the extracts from Isidore No. LIII., is written "Garancia," [2] and is identified with Sandis (madder); "Glassam" called in German "Glas," and in French MSS. "Glasse," amber, and several others.

It is to be observed that several recipes occur in the

---

[1] It is observed by all writers on glass-painting, that the colours used for one art are always applicable to the other. See Le Vieil, de la Peinture sur Verre, p. 113.

Le Vieil (p. 25) observes, "A great many of our French churches, which date from the twelfth century, contain coloured glass windows, which consist only of different compartments of glass, the ground of which is generally red, and this red glass was so common then, and is now so rare, that it is only with regard to this fine red colour that we can truly consider the art of painting on glass as a secret now lost."

[2] Granza is the Spanish for madder; and Isidore, from whose work the passage in question was copied, was Bishop of Seville in the seventh century. Madder is called in French, Garance. In medieval MSS. the term Warantia is generally used.

The fact of the madder plant being mentioned under four different terms, two only of which are mentioned to be synonymous, is certainly a proof that the recipes were written by different persons. In No. XXXII. the term "Warancia" occurs; in No. LIII. we find "Sandis, id est Garancia;" and in No. LV. the plant is called "Rubea."

third book, which are merely variations of some in the first book. This occurs so frequently in old MSS., that no conclusions can be drawn from this fact alone, as to the antiquity or originality of those of the first book. No. XVIII. in the first book is a metrical version of No. I. in the third book; No. XIX. of the first book, of No. II. in the third book; No. XXI. of the first book, of No. IV. in the third book. There is no evidence to show which of these are the most ancient.

The same thing may be observed of the recipes for sculpturing or engraving gems and hardening iron, three of which occur in the first book; a similar number are contained in the third book. The recipes are all somewhat different, but they are alike in principle, and Eraclius informs us (Lib. i. No. VI.) that they were derived in the first instance from Pliny. Several of these are found to be in the Clavicula.

As to the date of the third book of Eraclius, it appears to me that it must not be considered earlier than the twelfth, or later than the thirteenth century.

The allusions to the arts of the Saracens or Arabians, in Nos. IX., XXXII., XLVI., and XLVII., prove that the work could not have been earlier than the ninth century, and the recipe for dyeing cordovan leather [1] (No. XXXII.), in which the word "Warancia"

---

[1] Cordova was taken by the Moors A.D. 711, and in the year 759 Abdurrahman established his royal residence there. From that time Cordova became the centre of the arts, of industry, and of genius. It was distinguished for the excellence of its manufactures, and was especially celebrated for its leather, hence called " Cordovan." The remains of the tan-pits employed in the process, which are still to be seen on the north side of the Guadalquivir, prove that the art was of Moorish origin, for they were formed of baked earth, a material, says Mr. Murphy, much used by the

occurs, affords a strong presumption that it was much later, in order to give time for the Moorish art to become known in those countries where madder was called by the above name.

The lead glaze mentioned in No. III. will, however, probably enable us to fix the earliest date at which this third book could have been written, for De Brongniart, the director of the manufactory at Sèvres, who certainly may be considered good authority on this subject, remarks in his Traité des Arts Céramiques, p. 304, "J'ai déjà dit que jusqu'à présent on n'avait reconnu aucune potterie Européenne qui avant le xiie siècle eut reçu une glaçure plombifère."[1] He also says that lead glazing was applied to pottery at Pesaro about 1100 ; that it had been found on pottery in a tomb at Jumièges, the date of which was 1120. He also remarks, that pottery with a lead glaze was found at Alsace in the thirteenth century.

The directions given by Eraclius for the preparation of oils and varnishes, and for painting generally, correspond with the practice of the thirteenth century, especially in England, as Mr. Eastlake[2] has shown from various documents preserved in the public records. I should also observe, that the real Lapis Lazuli is mentioned in No. LI., with the test by which it was distinguished from the Azzurro della Magna, which certainly does not occur in Theophilus, the Lucca MS., the Clavicula, or

---

Moors in Spain. The prospects of Cordova continued to increase until the dissensions which distracted the Moorish power in Spain, towards the close of the tenth century. After that period it continued to decline until the expulsion of the Moors in 1236. The trade in Cordovan leather was then nearly destroyed, and the Moors carried it with them to Morocco.

[1] See also pp. 96, 97, 98.

[2] ' Materials for a History of Painting in Oil,' pp. 49–57, and 552–561.

S. Audemar, and I think not in the first or second
books[1] of Eraclius.   Brazil wood also is mentioned in
the third book of Eraclius, and in S. Audemar, but
not in Theophilus, the Lucca MS., or the Clavicula.

The probability is, that the third part was written
after the Clavicula,[2] and shortly before the MS. of
Theophilus, who appears not only to have introduced
some of the metrical parts of the work into his own;
but it seems probable that he had the third book before
him when he composed his own second book, although
he has enlarged, and I must say, very much improved
upon his original, which I think I can trace in several chapters of the second book of Theophilus, and
I also think that three of the missing chapters mentioned in the table of contents of the second book of
Theophilus will be found in the MS. of Eraclius.   Red
glass, called " Gallienum," and green glass, are described in No. VII., and blue glass in No. VIII.
and No. XLIX. of Eraclius.[3]

The extracts from Isidore relative to glass are
contained in both MSS., those relating to pigments
are in the Le Begue MS. only.   Some of these are
abstracted in so imperfect a manner, as to be scarcely

---

[1] The lazur mentioned in the second book seems to have been native
carbonate of copper, and not lapis lazuli, because it turned *black in the fire.*

[2] The date of Sir T. Phillips's copy of the Clavicula (the only one
known) is of the twelfth century, but the earliest copies of Eraclius and
Theophilus are of the thirteenth century.   There is, however, internal
evidence of the Clavicula being older than the third book of Eraclius, especially those parts which relate to painting in oil, and which are found in the
Paris MS. only.

[3] The fourth of the missing chapters (De Coloribus qui fiunt ex cupro et
plumbo et sale) seems to be contained in cap. xxxi. of the second book of
Theophilus, entitled ' De Anulis,' where we find the following words :—
" Deinde acquire tibi cineres, sal, pulverem cupri, et plumbum."

intelligible. It is easy, however, to perceive that Nos. L. to LV. inclusive, are an abridgment of Chapters VII.—XIV. of the 7th book of Vitruvius, interspersed occasionally with a few original observations relative to colours generally, and to a few pigments which were employed during the middle ages.

Chapters LVI. and LVIII. appear to be translations from some MS. of Byzantine Art, which was current wherever painting was practised at this time, and parts of which also appear, with the variations likely to be met with in translations by different persons, and perhaps by persons of different nations, from the same original, in the Clavicula, in the MS. of S. Audemar, in the appendix to the Theophilus of the British Museum, and at the greatest length in the Sloane MS., No. 1754.

From the fact of all these translations appearing in MSS. of northern origin (always supposing Theophilus to have been a German), and of the white pigment so frequently mentioned being called Album de Pullia, or Apuleya, I have formed the opinion that the original MS. of Byzantine art was written by a Greco-Italian of the Duchy of Benevento (which included Apulia), and that the MS. was perhaps communicated by some descendant of the Norman followers of Robert Guiscard [1] to the Normans settled in the west of Europe.

---

[1] In 1002 or 1003 the Normans first landed in the Neapolitan territory : in 1015 they made their first settlement there. In 1019 the Normans under Raynulf, uniting with the Lombards and Greeks, drove the Saracens out of Sicily ; and the Greeks, who, on the arrival of the Normans, were in possession of about two-thirds of the kingdom of Naples, re-established themselves, and made a distinct province in the western part of Apulia, under the name of Capitanata. In 1056 Robert Guiscard, the Norman, was made Duke of Apulia, and his successors continued to enjoy the dignity until 1195, when the Normans submitted to the Emperor.

After a careful perusal of the MS. attributed to Eraclius, I have formed the following conclusions :—

That it is a collection of works on art, somewhat of
the same nature as the MS. of Le Begue.

That the metrical parts only constituted the Treatise
de Coloribus et Artibus Romanorum of Eraclius, and
that this part is more ancient than great part of the
third book.

That the third book consists of a miscellaneous collection of works on art, which may be arranged under
three heads : first of an abridgment or paraphrase from
Vitruvius and Isidore on making glass and on colours ;
secondly, of some translations of a Greek or Byzantine
MS. ; and thirdly, of original matter, or of recipes
collected from contemporary artists, many of which
appear to be of French origin.

That these MSS. fell into the hands of some person
who did for them what Le Begue did for the collection
of Alcherius, namely, united them into one work, and
who also extended to the whole work the title which
was probably intended for the first and second books
only.   I think there is some proof of this in the epithet
added in both MSS. to the name of Eraclius, " Vir sa-
pientissimus," which, whatever might have been the
opinion of Eraclius relative to his own abilities—and
he certainly did not underrate them—he would scarcely
have ventured to place there himself.

I think it of some importance to the arts that the
time of Eraclius should be fixed.   If my reasons are
not satisfactory, I shall probably be corrected by those
more skilled than myself on this subject.

EXPLANATION OF SYMBOLS

P. denotes the MS. in the Royal Library at Paris.

R. the MS. published by Raspe.

W. the chapters printed by Wecker, and by him ascribed to Arnaldus de Villanova and Marcellus Palingenius.

T. the chapters of Eraclius found in the MS. of Theophilus in the Harleian Collection at the British Museum.

(T.) those chapters of which a prose version is given in the last-mentioned MS.

S. the chapters of the third book of Eraclius contained in the MS. No. 1754, of the Sloane Collection at the British Museum.

C. the chapters of the third book of Eraclius contained in the treatise called ' Mappæ Clavicula.'

Cant. The MS. formerly at Cambridge, but now in the British Museum.

HERE BEGINS THE

FIRST AND METRICAL BOOK OF ERACLIUS,

A VERY WISE MAN,

ON THE COLOURS AND ARTS OF THE ROMANS.

AND FIRST THE

INTRODUCTION.

I have described, brother, various flowers for your use, as I best could. I have added to the flowers the arts which relate to, and are proper for writing; to which, if you pay attention, you will find them true in practice. I indeed write nothing to you, which I have not first tried myself. The greatness of intellect, for which the Roman people was once so eminent, has faded, and the care of the wise senate has perished. Who can now investigate these arts? Who is now able to show us what these artificers, powerful by their immense intellect, discovered for themselves? He who, by his powerful virtue, holds the keys of the mind, divides the pious hearts of men among various arts.

PRIMUS ET METRICUS[1] LIBER ERACLII,

SAPIENTISSIMI VIRI,

DE COLORIBUS ET ARTIBUS ROMANORUM.

ET PRIMO

PROHEMIUM.[2]

Ut potui levius varios tibi frater ad usus
Descripsi flores, adjeci floribus artes,
Congrua scripturis quæ sunt, et idonea[3] scriptis,
Que si perpendis, utendo vera probabis.
Nil tibi scribo quidem, quod[4] non prius ipse probassem.
Jam decus ingenii quod[4] plebs Romana probatur
Decidit, ut periit sapientum cura senatum.
Quis nunc has artes investigare valebit,
Quas isti artifices, immensa mente[5] potentes,
Invenere sibi, potens est ostendere nobis ?
Qui tenet ingenii claves virtute potenti
In varias artes resecat pia corda virorum.

---

[1] *Primus et metricus* omittit R.   [2] *Et primo prohemium* omittit R.
[3] *Idone* R.   [4] *Quæ* R.   [5] *Meree* R.

II. *How various colours fit for writing are made from wild flowers.*[1]

He who wishes to convert flowers into the various colours which, for the purpose of writing, the page of the book demands, must wander over the corn-fields early in the morning, and then he will find various flowers fresh sprung up. Let him make haste to pluck them for himself; and when he gets home, let him take care not to mix them together, but let him do what this art demands [namely], grind these flowers upon a smooth stone, and grind raw gypsum along with them. So you can preserve these colours dry. And if you wish to change the colour to green, mix lime with the flowers. You will then see what I have bid you [do], which is as I have already tried it myself.

[1] See Theoph., E. Ed., p. 392. Wecker, p. 643.

The early painters were accustomed to prepare many vegetable pigments for painting in miniature. Indeed there are scarcely any plants which yield colouring juices, which have not, at some period, been used for this purpose. The process employed in the text was simple enough : it consisted in grinding the flowers first by themselves and then with sulphate of lime, which, while it gave body to the vegetable pigments, did not affect the colours. The text shows that the effects of lime in changing vegetable blues to greens, even at that early period, were well understood.

III. *To paint earthen vases.*[1]

If any one wishes to paint vases with glass, [let him grind Roman glass well on marble, and when it is like dust, let him paint earthen vases with it, with the clear fatness of gum, mixed with spring water; and when dry, send them to the furnace. Let the earth [clay] be good, so as to stand the fire ; and at length he will take out of the furnace shining vases good enough for kings.] Let him choose for himself two stones of red marble, between which let him grind the Roman glass, and when it is

[1] See Theoph., E. Ed., p. 398; and Wecker, p. 644.

II. *Quomodo fiant diversi colores de floribus campestri-bus ad scribendum apti.*[1]

Flores in varios qui vult mutare colores,
Causa scribendi quos[2] libri pagina poscit,
Est opus ut segetes in summo mane pererret,
Et tunc[3] diversos flores ortuque recentes
Inveniet properetque sibi[4] decerpere eosdem.
Cumque domum[5] fuerit,[6] caveat ne ponat in unum
Illos, sed faciat quod[7] talis res[8] sibi poscit[9]
Desuper[10] equalem petram contriveris istos
Flores ; incoctum pariter tum[11] contere[12] gypsum[13]
Sic tibi siccatos poteris servare colores.
Ex quibus in viridem si vis mutare colorem,[14]
Calcem commisce cum floribus ; inde videbis[15]
Quod tibi mandavi, veluti prius ipse[16] probavi.

[1] Sic P. ; R. et T. habent *de floribus ad scribendum;* W. *Carmen de floribus seu coloribus, ad scribendum, pingendum,* &c.   [2] *Quis* P.   [3] *Et inter* R.   [4] *Sibi* omittunt P. R.   [5] *Domi* W. T.   [6] *Fuerint* T.   [7] *Quæ* P. R.   [8] *Quis* W.   [9] *Poscit vel quærit* T.   [10] *Dum super* W. T.   [11] *Tu* P. R.   [12] *Congere* T.   [13] Sic W. T. ; *Gipsum* P. R.   [14] *Recentem* W.   [15] Hanc lineam omittit W., errore forsan typographico.   [16] *Veluti prius ipse* W. ; *verum velut ipse* P. R. ; *veluti ipse* T.

III. *Ad vasa fictilia depingenda.*[1]

E vitro[2] si quis depingere vascula[3] quærit,
[Vitrum[4] Romanum bene marmore conterat, et cum
Ut pulvis fuerit, claro pinguedine gummi,
Fontis aqua mista, figulorum vascula pingat,
Siccaque fornaci mandes : sit terra probata
Quæ valeat flammis obstare, nitentia tandem
Regibus apta satis ex furno vascula tollet.]
Eligat ipse duas rufo de[5] marmore petras

[1] Sic W. ; *De preciosa pictura vitri* R. ; *De pictura ex vitro* T. ; *Quomodo fialæ terreæ ex preciosa pictura de vitri bitumine facta ornantur* P.   [2] *Ex vitro* T. ; *De vitro* W. ; *De vitro fialas* P.   [3] *Vascula* omittit P.   [4] In [ ] inclusa in W. solum continentur.   [5] *De rufo* T.

pulverized as fine as the dust of the earth, let him make it liquid with the clear fatness of gum. After this let him paint the vessels, which the workman has finely moulded in clay, and when they are dry, let him put them into the furnace. And let him take care to put them into [vessels of[1]] good clay, that they may thus be able to check the heat, and make them shining with perfect beauty.

[1] Compare with the last sentence in No. III. lib. iii.

IV. *Of sculpturing glass.*[1]

O all you artists, who wish to engrave in a beautiful manner on glass, I will now show you what I myself have tried. I sought fat worms, which the plough turns up from the earth; and the art useful in these things bid me at the same time seek vinegar, and the warm blood of a large he-goat, which I had cunningly fed for a short time on strong ivy, tied up under cover. After this, I threw the worms and vinegar into the warm blood, and anointed all the bright shining vessel, after which I tried to carve the glass with the hard stone called pyrites.

[1] See Theoph., E. Ed., p. 396; and Wecker, p. 644.

V. *Of phials decorated with gold.*

The Romans made themselves phials of glass, artfully varied with gold, very precious, to which I gave great pains and atten-

Inter quas vitrum Romanum conterat,[1] et cum
Ut pulvis terræ fuerit pariter resolutum,
Hoc faciat[2] liquidum clara pinguedine gummi
Post hæc[3] depingat petulas[4] quas finxit honeste
Figulus. Hoc facto succensæ imponat[5] easdem
Fornaci, caveatque simul quod[6] terra probata
Has teneat, quo[7] sic valeat[8] obstare calori[9]
Illas que faciat[10] plena virtute nitentes.

[1] *Conteret* P. R. W.   [2] *Faciet* P. R.   [3] *Post hoc* P. W.   [4] Sic P. R.
Paginas T.; *Peculas* W.   [5] *Figulus e terra; siccatas ponat* W.   [6] *Quæ*
P. R.; *quo* T.   [7] *Qua* W.   [8] *Valeant* W. T.   [9] *Colori* P. R.   [10] Sic T.;
Illasque faciet W. P.; *Illas qui facies* R.

IV. *De sculptura vitri.*[1]

O vos artifices qui sculpere vultis honeste[2]
Vitrum, nunc vobis pandam,[3] velut ipse probavi,
Vermes quæsivi pingues quos vertit aratrum
Ex terra,[4] atque simul me quærere jussit[5] acetum
Utilis ars istis rebus, calidum que[6] cruorem
Ex hirco[7] ingenti, quem sollers[8] tempore parvo
Ex hedera[9] forti pavi tecto religatum.
Sanguine cum calido; post hæc[10] vermes et acetum
Infudi,[11] ac totam fialam clare renitentem
Unxi; quo facto, temptavi[12] sculpere vitrum
Cum duro lapide piritis[13] nomine dicto.

[1] Sic R. and T.; *De Sculptura vitri, quomodo fit* P.; *Modus pingendi
vasa, et vitra* W.   [2] *Honesti* W.   [3] *Pandam vobis* W.   [4] *E terra* P. R.;
Per terram T.   [5] Sic W.; *Jussit me quærere* alii.   [6] *Atque* W.   [7] *Hyrco* T.
[8] *Solito quem* W.   [9] *Ex Hedera* W.; *ex herba* P. R.; *herba ex hedera* T.
[10] *Posthoc* P.   [11] *Infondi* P.   [12] *Quo pacto tentavi* W.   [13] *Piritis,* sic R.
P. T.; *Smerilli* W.

---

v. *De fialis auro decoratis.*[1]

Romani fialas, auro caute variatas,
Ex vitro fecere sibi, nimium preciosas;

[1] *De fialis vitri auro decorandis* P.

tion, and had my mind's eye fixed upon them day and night, that I might thus attain the art by which the phials shone so bright; I at length discovered what I will explain to you, my dearest friend. I found gold-leaf carefully inclosed between the double glass.[1] When I had often knowingly looked at it, being more and more troubled about it, I obtained some phials shining with clear glass, which I anointed with the fatness of gum with a paint-brush. Having done this, I began to lay leaf-gold upon them, and when they were dry I engraved birds and men and lions upon them, as I thought proper. Having done this, I placed over them glass made thin with fire by skilful blowing. After they had felt the heat thoroughly, the thinned glass adhered properly to the phials.

[1] A small design in gold and silver is mentioned by Count Caylus in his work entitled 'Recueil d'Antiquités,' tom. iii. p. 193, which is thought to be enclosed between two strata of glass, probably in the manner described in the text. One stratum of the glass mentioned by Caylus was blue, the other was colourless. From the recipe in the text, it may be conjectured that this method of gilding on glass was followed by the Romans, and early Italian school, which existed contemporaneously, although independently of the Byzantine school, at the time when the MS. of Eraclius was written. The process taught by Theophilus (lib. ii. cap. xiii.), and usually adopted in the Florentine school of Mosaic painters, who were taught by the Byzantine Greeks, appears to have been different. See Lettera di Branchi al Prof. Ciampi, Notizie Inedite, &c., p. 25, n.

VI. *Of engraving precious stones.*[1]

Whoever wishes to cut with iron the precious stones in which the kings of the Roman city (who anciently held the arts in high estimation) much delighted, upon gold, let him learn the discovery which I made with profound thought, for it is very precious. I procured urine, with the fresh blood of a huge he-goat, fed for a short time upon ivy, which being done, I cut the gems in the warm blood, as directed by Pliny, the author who wrote upon the arts which the Roman people put to proof, and who also well described the virtues of stones; of which he

[1] See Theoph., E. Ed., p. 402; and Wecker, p. 428.

Erga quas gessi cum summa mente laborem,
Atque oculos cordis super has noctuque dieque [1]
Intentos habui, quo sic attingere possem
Hanc artem, per quam fialæ valde renitebant; [2]
Tandem perfexi tibi quod Carissime pandam.
Inveni petulas[3] inter vitrum duplicatum
Inclusas caute. Cum sollers sepius illud
Visu lustrassem, super hoc magis et magis ipse
Commotus, quasdam claro vitro renitentes
Quæsivi fialas mihi,[4] quas pinguedine gummi
Unxi pincello. Quo facto[5] imponere cepi
Ex auro petulas super illas ; utque[6] fuere
Siccatæ volucres homines pariterque leones
Inscripsi ut sensi ; quo facto desuper ipsas
Armavi[7] vitrum docto flatu tenuatum
Ignis ; sed postquam pariter sensere calorem
Se vitrum fialis[8] tenuatum junxit honeste.

[1] *Diebus* P.   [2] *Nitebant* P.   [3] *Paculas* P.   [4] *Michi* P.   [5] *Ex auro* male supplet R.   [6] *Atque* P.   [7] *Ornavi* P.   [8] *Fialæ* R.

---

vi. *De preciosorum lapidum incisione.*[1]

Qui cupit egregios [2] lapides irrumpere ferro
Quos dilexerunt nimium reges [3] super aurum
Urbis Romanæ, qui celsas jam tenuere
Artes,[4] ingenium quod ego sub mente profunda
Inveni, accipiat[5] quoniam valde est[6] preciosum.
Urinam [7] mihi quæsivi, pariterque cruorem
Ex hirco ingenti, modico sub tempore pasto
Herba, quo facto, calefacto sanguine gemmas
Incidi, veluti monstravit[8] Plinius [9] auctor.
Artes qui scripsit quas plebs Romana probavit,

[1] Sic P. R.   *De sculpendis gemmis* T.   *Gemmarum sectio* W.   [2] *Egregio* W.   [3] *Reges nimium* W. T.   [4] *Arces* W.   [5] *Capiant* W.   [6] Sic P. ; *est* omittet R. ; T. habet *quem valde est ;* et W., *quoniam nimis est.*   [7] *Uriciam* R.   [8] *Monstrante* R.   [9] *Plenius* P.

who knows the powers, esteems them most.   For the first kings, who anciently held the city, adorned with gems their garments, gleaming with gold ; of these the most remarkable was Aurelian, who interwove his own robes with gems and gold.

VII. *Of golden writing.*[1]

Whoever wishes to execute beautiful writing with gold, let him read what I say in lowly verse.   Let him grind gold with pure wine, until it is well dissolved.   Then let him wash it frequently, for the white page of the book demands this, and then make it [liquid] with the fatness of ox [gall, if he pleases, or with the clear fatness of gum] ; and I also request him to stir it with a reed when he uses the gold, if he wishes to write beautifully.   When the writing is dry, let him make it very brilliant with the tooth of a savage bear.

[1] See Theoph., E. Ed., p. 392.

VIII. *Of ivy and lake.*[1]

The strong ivy is very useful for these purposes.   Our ancestors were very fond of its leaves as a mark of honour : it was used as a crown for poets.   In the spring all things rejoice,

[1] See Theoph., E. Ed., p. 394.

It appears that the resinous juice exudes from the ivy in warm countries only.   See *Nemnich, Polyglotten-Lexicon, Tit.* Hedera.   It will be observed, that the juice, when it first flowed from the ivy, was not red, but that it gradually acquired that colour.

Atque simul lapidum virtutes scripsit honeste,
Quorum qui noscit[1] vires, plus[2] diligit illos.
Nam primi reges, urbem qui jam tenuerunt[3]
Gemmis ornarunt vestes auro renitentes.
Ex quibus insignis primus fuit Aurelianus
Qui proprias vestes gemmis contexit et auro.[4]

[1] Sic T. W. ; *nescit* R. P.   [2] *Minus* R. P.   [3] *Tenuere* R. P.   [4] Hos quatuor versus ultimos omittit W., et eorum loco ponit " *Primus ait versus quot habet sententia sensus.*"

VII. *De aurea scriptura.*

Scripturam pulcram quisquis bene scribere quærit,[1]
Ex auro, legat hoc quod[2] vili carmine dico.
Aurum cum puro mero[3] molat, usque solutum
Hoc[4] nimium fuerit.   Tunc sepius abluat illud ;[5]
Nam quia[6] deposcit hoc candens pagina libri.
Exin taurini faciat[7] pinguedine [fellis[8]
Hoc liquidum, si vult, seu cum pinguedine] gummi.
Atque rogo pariter calamo cum ceperit aurum
Illud[9] commoveat, pulchre si scribere quærit.
Hinc siccata sicut[10] fuerit scriptura, nitentem
Hanc[11] nimium faciat ursi cum dente feroci.

[1] *Si quis scripturam quærit sibi scribere pulcram* T.   [2] *Hic quæ* R.
[3] *Mero* T., *Menio* P. ; omittit R.   [4] *Hoc* T. ; omittunt R. P.   [5] Sic R. P.
Moneo quod sæpe lavet illud T.   [6] *Namque* R. P.   [7] *Faciet* R. P.   [8] Ex T.
In R. P. male omissum.   [9] *Illum* T.   [10] *Sed ut* T.   [11] *Hunc* T.

VIII. *De edera et lacca.*[1]

Propositis rebus edere satis utile robur.
Hujus enim[2] frondem nimium coluere priores
Ad titulum laudis ; erat ipsa corona poetis.
Vere novo, reduci cum gaudent[3] omnia succo,

[1] Sic R. ; in P. vero *De edera herba et lacca succo ejus rubeo ab ipsa exeunti.*   [2] *Ut* R.   [3] *Cum gaudent* P.   *Congaudent* R.

being refreshed with new sap; and the spring brings back the moisture to the trees, while the winter refuses them the power of growing. The ivy is similarly affected; for the offshoots of the branches, pushed into barren places, give out a juice, which, whoever collects, should put into a red vase of baked earth, and it will gradually assume a blood colour. This the painter loves, and the scribe equally delights in. Hence also is made the parcia dyed with a rose colour. It also serves to dye the skins of goats and sheep.

IX. *Of gold-leaf, how it is laid on ivory.*[1]

You will decorate carvings in ivory with gold-leaf. Now hear in what manner this thing is done. . Seek to obtain the fish which is called " huso,"[2] and keep its air-bladder liquefied by being boiled in water, and with this mark over the place where you wish to lay the gold; and you will thus easily be able to fasten it to the ivory.

[1] See Theoph., E. Ed., p. 404; and Wecker, p. 645.

[2] The Huso or Huson (Acipenser Huso) was the large sturgeon from which isinglass is procured. It was the Ichthyocolla of Pliny; the Ittiocolla, Usone, Colpesce, of the Italians; the Copese of the Venetians; the Isinglass fish of the English; the Huizenblasfisk of the Dutch; Der Hausen of the Germans; and the Bjeluga of the Russians. See Nemnich, Polyg. Lexicon.

X. *How gems are polished.*[1]

If you wish to give a shining splendour to gems, obtain for yourself a piece of smooth marble, and lest it may be injured by this, lay it on the gem and rub it gently, and a polish will be given to the stone. The harder it is, the brighter polish will it take.

[1] See Theoph., E. Ed., p. 402; and see Wecker, p. 645.

Arboribusque refert humor, quas bruma negabat
Crescendi vires, ederam talis probat ordo.
Nam subula rami, loca per deserta forati,
Emittunt viscum, quem qui sibi sumpserit illum,
Transferet in rubeam coctum prurigine [1] formam ;
Sanguineumque sibi leviter capit ille colorem.
Hunc sibi pictor amat et scriptor diligit eque.
Hinc etiam roseo fit parcia tincta [2] colore.
Quæ [3] quoque caprinas, quæ [3] pelles tingit ovinas.

[1] *Prurigine* P. ; in R. lacuna relicta sic—....*rigine.* [2] *Parva tinctura*
P. [3] *Quam* R.

IX. *De petula auri, quomodo in ebore mittatur.*[1]

Sculpturas eboris auri petulis [2] decorabis
Quo tamen ipsa tibi [3] res ordine congruat audi.
Quære tibi piscem qui dicitur usa [4] liquentem
Vesicam tamen [5] serva cum flumine coctam
Inde locum petulam cui [6] vis componere signa
Sic ebori facile poteris ipsam consolidare.

[1] Sic R. ; *Quomodo petula auri in ebore mittatur, et cum quo visco* P. ;
De pictura eboris W., qui hunc versum cæteris premittit—"*Pingere si quis
ebur vult sic procedere debet.*" [2] *Pecula* W. [3] *Tibi* omittunt R. P. [4] Sic
P. ; *Husa* W. ; R. lacunam habet. [5] *Tantum* P. ; W. vero habet *Vesicam serva decoctam fluminis unda.* [6] *Petulam quem* P. ; *Pecula quem* W.,
qui sequentem versum omittit.

X. *De gemmis quomodo lucidæ fiunt.*[1]

Si vis splendentem gemmis inferre nitorem [2]
Partem quære tibi tantummodo marmoris æqui
Gemma superposita petræ, sed flumine pauco
Hinc ne lædatur, tractu leviore limetur.[3]
Quanto durescit, tanto magis ipsa nitescit.[4]

[1] Sic P. ; *De gemmis quomodo luceant* R. ; *Gemmæ ut nitescant* W.
[2] *Colorem* P. R. [3] Sic emendavi. W. habet " *Gemma supposita petræ, sed
flumine pauco : sed ne lædatur, tractu leniore limetur.*" P. et R. vero "*Hinc
ne lædatur, tactu leviore limetur Gemma superposito, sed petre lumine tracto.*"
[4] *Nitescit* P. ; *Accescit* R. ; *Nitebit* W.

XI. *Of a green colour for writing.*[1]

If you wish to embellish your writing with a green colour,
mix vinegar together with strong honey, and then cover up the
vase itself in very hot dung; and so take it out after twelve
days shall have elapsed.

[1] See Theoph., E. Ed., p. 396.

The vase mentioned in this chapter must have been of copper or brass.
The colour produced in that case would have been verdigris, which is an
acetate of copper.

XII. *How to cut crystal.*[1]

Crystal can easily be cut by the following artifice :—Seek
for yourself a convenient plate of lead, and join two boards to
it, one on each side, with a centre piece of iron, so as to keep
the lead steady; for to the lead alone belongs the business of
cutting, and the outer plates are as guides to make it run
round evenly. But you would not be able to overcome such
great hardness by the unassisted softness of the lead, unless
you join to it some powder, such as the pulverized fragment of
a furnace, which you will be able to fasten to the tender plate,
for this addition will make the lead sharp, and the fragments
of brick also have equal force; you must cut it, adding to it a
little river water. But let the blood of a goat first temper it,
for this blood makes the iron so hard that even adamant is soft
compared with it.

[1] See Wecker, p. 449.

Compare with Theophilus, lib. iii. cap. xciv. (E. Ed., p. 387). Crystal
is defined by Theophilus to be " water hardened into ice." In this, Mr.
Hendrie observes, he has repeated the opinion of Pliny. The term " crystal " was also applied to glass made from pulverized quartz or sand fused
with an alkali. In an extract from the book of Mr. Colladon, quoted in
the Mayerne MS. and by Mr. Hendrie (Theoph., p. 180), crystal is defined to be " very clear glass of Venice."

XI. *De viridi colore ad scribendum.*[1]

Si quæris viridi scriptura[2] colore notari,
Acri commissum melli miscebis acetum ;
Hinc valde calido vas ipsum contege fimo.
Sic et bissenis hoc extrahe solibus[3] actis.

[1] Sic R.; *ad scribendum quomodo fit* P.   [2] *Scripta* R.   [3] *Talibus* R.

XII. *Quomodo cristallum possit secari.*[1]

Cristallum tali facile[2] valet arte secari.[3]
Opportuna[4] tibi quæratur[5] lamina plumbi ;[6]
Huic[7] etiam binæ claves[8] jungantur utrinque,[9]
Ex ferro medium, quæ firmant[10] undique plumbum ;[11]
Nam plumbo soli[12] tribuetur cura secandi.
Ipsi custodes laminæ sint exteriores,
Ut sibi dent rectum recto consumere[13] cursum.
Sed nec duritiem[14] poteris prærumpere[15] tantam
Mollitie plumbi, nisi quædam junxeris[16] illi
Tanquam pulverulas fornacis fragmine micas[17]
Quæ teneræ poteris laminæ connectere plumbi[18]
Hæc etenim plumbum conjunctio reddet[19] acutum.
At quum rursus[20] habent lateris fragmenta vigorem
Concidis adjuncta paulatim fluminis unda[21]
Sed[22] vim cristalli cruor antea temperet hirci
Sanguis enim facilem ferro facit hic adamantem.[23]

[1] Sic R.   *Quomodo cristallum possis secare* P.   *Cristalli sectio* W.
[2] *Cristallus tali durus* W.   [3] *Parari* P.   [4] *Oportuna* P. R.   [5] *Quæretur* W.   [6] *Ferri* P. R.   [7] Hinc ? P. R.   [8] Sic R.   *Bene clavos* P. ; *Bini clavi* W.   [9] *Utrumque* P.   [10] *Qui solito medium consument* W.   [11] *Plumbi* P.
[12] *Solo* P. R.   [13] *Conamine* P. R.   [14] *Duriciam* R. P.   [15] *Prorumpere* R. P.
[16] Ita emendavi.   *Nec quiddam junxeris* R. ; *Nisi quoddam junxeris* P. ; *Nisi quædam junxerit,* W.   [17] Sic P. R. ; *Tanquam pulvereas fornacis fragmine mittas* W.   [18] Sic W. ; *Contere, quas teneræ poteris [possis P.] connectere laminæ* P. R.   [19] Hunc versum omittit W.   *Reddit* P.   [20] *Et quum rursum* P. R.   [21] Hunc versum omittunt P. R.   [22] *Si* W.   [23] Sic P. W. ; Hunc versum omittit R.

XIII. *Of tempering iron* [*hard for cutting stones.*][1]

[You must thus make iron hard for sculpturing gems.] Whoever wishes to cut stones with the solid iron, must observe the following rules to temper its edge. At the time when the goat is in heat his fat alone is fit for this purpose. For if any one quenches the hot iron in its fat, it immediately becomes hard with a firm edge.

[1] See Theoph. p. 404. Wecker, 428.

XIV. *Of the gems which you wish to make from Roman Glass.*

You will thus be able to make beautiful shining gems of every sort with Roman glass. Hollow out some clay for yourself as a mould for the stone ; and put into it some glass broken into small pieces. You may easily prepare this [the mould] by this artifice. Let a certain reed be skilfully turned round and round, and when it [the clay] begins to harden, and the rod sticks tight, then fix it on the rod on both sides, and let the rod be held by the glass placed round it ; and then put the clay, guarded by a hollow iron, into the fire, and when the glass is thoroughly liquefied, press it into the hollow with a bright iron, so that you may have no bubble or flaw in it.

XIII. *De temperamento duro ferri ad incidendum lapides.*[1]

Qui quærit solido[2] lapides irrumpere ferro,
Hos habeat ritus, ut acumen temperet ejus.
Tempore quo solito magis uritur[3] hircus amore,
Solus adeps hujus fit ad istos aptior usus.
Hujus enim calidum[4] si quis pinguedine ferrum
Extinguit,[5] subito durescit acumine firmo.

[1] Sic P. ; *De temperamento ferri* R. ; *Gemmarum sculptura* W., qui hunc versum alteris præmittit—*Sic gemmis durum sculpendis effice ferrum.* [2] *Qui quæret solido* R., *quisquis vult solito* W. [3] *Uritur magis* P. [4] *Candens* W. [5] *Restinguet* R. ; *refrigeret* P.

XIV. *De Gemmis quas de Romano vitro facere quæris.*

Sic ex Romano poteris conficere vitro
Splendentes pulcros generis cujusque lapillos
Ad modulum lapidis cretam tibi quippe cavabis ;
Hic pones vitrum per quædam frusta minutum.
Hunc ergo facile poteris hac arte parare.
Subtiliter[1] quædam circumvolvatur arundo,
Qui dum durescit, dum virga firmius[2] hæret,
Tunc ipsi virgæ superimponetur utrinque,[3]
Et circumposito teneatur virgula vitro ;
Atque cavo tectam ferro post[4] insere cretam
Igni ; fit[5] vitrum ; cum fit[6] penitus liquefactum,
In fossam lato fulgenti[7] comprime ferro ;
Quo vesica sibi, quo lesio nulla supersit.

[1] *Subtilis* P. [2] *Durius* P. [3] *Utrumque* P. [4] *Ferro post* P. *Penitus* R [5] *Fit.* Sic emendavi ; codices *sit* habent. [6] *Fit.* Sic R. *Sit* P. [7] *F-genti* P.

HERE BEGINS

THE SECOND AND METRICAL BOOK,

AND FIRST

XV. *Of a colour resembling orpiment.*[1]

You will easily be able to make a colour resembling orpiment thus; preserve it carefully in your memory. The gall of a large fish is very useful for this art. The liquor of the gall must be received in a marble stone, and you must mix a little vinegar with it, and then add some white clay to the fatness of the gall, and this mixture will make the colour brilliant.

[1] A recipe similar to this is contained in the small Paris MS., No. vi. MDCCXLIX. B., where it is called " Colore aureo Lombardico."

XVI. *Of copper gilt with the fatness of gall.*[1]

If you wish to prepare copper with the fatness of gall, so as to appear gilt, you may do it in this way. Having scraped it with a knife, burnish it by rubbing it with a bear's tooth, and then sprinkle it with a pencil [dipped in] the liquor of the gall, and lay it evenly all over; afterwards give it another smooth coat, and upon this a third; and each time pass the quill evenly all over it, lest any scratch, or lump, or bubble should make the copper rough.

[1] See Theoph., E. Ed., p. 406. S. Audemar, No. 204.

INCIPIT

LIBER SECUNDUS [METRICUS,

ET PRIMO][1]

xv. *De colore auripigmento simili.*

Sic facile similem poteris servare colorem
Auripigmento ; memori tu mente teneto.
Hinc piscis magni fel multum congruit arti,
Marmorea cujus petra liquor excipiatur,
Cui vetus et paucum tamen[2] admiscebis acetum,
Fellis et hinc albam tum[3] cum pinguedine cretam.
Reddet splendentem commixtio tanta colorem.[4]

[1] In [ ] omittit R.   [2] *Tum* R.   [3] *Ter* P.   [4] *Liquorem* R.

xvi. *De cupro fellis pinguedine deaurato.*

Si velut auratum fellis pinguedine cuprum
Condere curabis, sic hoc implere valebis.
Cultello rasum splendens hoc effice tactum.
Ursi dente ; quidem calamo post[1] sperge liquorem
Fellis ; et hoc eque tamen[2] apponatur ubique.
Appones alium post[3] equo tramite.   Rursum
Huic alium junges ; vice tamen undique duces
Equali calamum, ne qua divisio cuprum
Ne quis monticulus vel ne tumor efferat[4] ullus.

[1] *Post* P. ; *penitus* R.   [2] *Tegmen* P.   [3] *Penitus* R.   [4] *Offerat* P.

XVII. *How to make a green colour for painting what you please.*[1]

Thus, O painter ! you may obtain for yourself a green colour! Grind white earth with the leaves of the black nightshade.[2] Grind them both evenly together on a marble slab until they become liquid for the use of the pen, and afterwards take this juice and try it with your paintbrush. Then adorn any writings you please with the colour; but take care previously not to add too much earth.

[1] See Theoph., E. Ed., p. 394.

[2] This chapter must have been written by a person who habitually spoke Italian or French, because the Solanum Nigrum is not known by the name of " Morella," or " Morelle," except in the countries where the Italian and French languages are spoken. The expression in the MS. of Theophilus runs thus: " herba quae vulgò morella nuncupatur." The term " morelle " occurs more than once in the MS. of Le Begue, and also in the Bolognese MS. It must not be confounded with " Maurelle," the name by which the Croton Tinctorium is known at Montpelier.

XVIII. *How green glass is to be made for painting earthen vases.*[1]

By these things the effect of precious glass is shown. Take sulphur burnt in the fire, and [burnt] copper, and grind shining glass with the powder of these, and take care to make it liquid for yourself with gum only, and then place the jar, painted over with this, into the fire, for the painting will assume a green colour, when the outside of the jar begins to turn red.

[1] See Theoph., E. Ed., p. 398.   Wecker, p. 644.

XIX. *Of white glass for painting earthen vessels.*[1]

You must thus make white glass fine enough for painting. Grind white glass mixed with sulphur. With these, ground

[1] See Theoph., E. Ed., p. 400. Wecker, p. 644. This probably describes an opaque white glass, resembling those threads of white glass which Theo-

XVII. *De viridi colore quomodo fieri possit ad quæ volueris depingere.*

Sic poteris viridem tibi pictor habere colorem.
Cum foliis albam morellæ[1] contere cretam ;
Hæc in marmorea pariter quoque contere petra,
Usus ad pennæ liquidum dum fiat utrumque.[2]
Et post[3] hunc succum pincello sume probandum.
Hinc quascunque cupis scripturas conde colori,[4]
Ne cretæ nimium ponas tamen ante caveto.

[1] *Morellam* male habet R.   [2] *Utrinque* R.   [3] *Penitus* R.   [4] Sic emendavi. *Coloribus* P. R.

XVIII. *De vitro viridi quomodo fieri debeat, ad vasa fictilia[1] depingenda.*

His rebus vitri patet effectus preciosi :
Igni combustum sulphur, quærasque cupellum,[2]
Atque teras horum splendens cum pulvere vitrum ;
Hoc cures solo liquidum tibi[3] reddere gummo.
Attamen inde litam post[4] ignibus injice testam,[5]
Assumet viridem quoniam[6] pictura colorem,
Exterior testæ cum cœperit ipsa rubere.[7]

[1] *Figuli* P.   [2] *Quærasque cupressum* P., *assum quare cuprum* W.   [3] *Ter* W.   [4] *Penitus* R.   [5] *Coctam* P. R.   [6] *Qualem* R.   [7] *Rubore* P.

XIX. *De vitro albo, ad vasa fictilia[1] depingenda.*

Album picturis vitrum sic[2] attenuabis[3]
Candens permixtum cum sulphure contere vitrum

[1] *Vasa figuli* P., *Fictilia vasa* W.   [2] *Sic vitrum* R.   [3] *Attenuabit* R.

---

philus (lib. ii. cap. 14) says were sometimes made to surround long-necked bottles.   Le Vieil (p. 27) says that white opaque glass was used for the windows in the churches belonging to the monasteries of the Bernardines and Cistercians.

together until they are like dust, you must paint a thick jar all over the outside. Then put it in to be baked by the flame of the furnace; and when it is red-hot, and the painting adheres to it, take it out; so also you may paint vases in the manner described in the first book.

---

xx. *Of black glass for painting earthen vases.*[1]

In the same manner also you may make black glass useful for painting. Grind the azure that is found in the earth with gum; and then breaking clear glass upon a marble slab, mix it up with it, and grind them again. This mixture will assume a blue colour, which, however, the force of the fire will turn to a beautiful black.

[1] See Wecker, p. 645.

---

xxi. *Of glass which is very green.*[1]

So also you may make glass of a very deep green. Take very small fragments of burnt copper, which you must afterwards mix with the rust of the same. Then grind it again, with an admixture of shining glass. Afterwards, put the jar, painted with this, into the furnace; and when the flame makes it white hot, take it out. It will not be of a beautiful appearance until it is cold; for while the glass is made intensely hot, the violence of the flame takes away the real beauty of the colour.

[1] See Wecker, p. 645. Theoph., E. Ed., p. 400.

His simul attritis, postquam[1] fuerint quasi pulvis
Exterius spissam depinges[2] undique testam.
Injice post ipsam fornacis ab igne coquendam.
Cum[3] simul ipsa rubet, sibi cum pictura coheret,
Extrahe. Sic etiam[4] pinges hinc vascula quædam,
Ars velut in primo notat insinuata libello.

[1] *Penitusque* R.   [2] *Depurges* P.   [3] *Quam* P. R.   [4] *Ea* W.

---

xx. *De vitro nigro ad vasa fictilia*[1] *depingenda.*

Sic etiam nigrum pingendi transfer in usum.
Qui terra capitur cum gummo[2] contere lazur ;
Et sic[3] perspicuum frangens in marmore vitrum,
Ipsi miscebis, rursumque terendo parabis.
Hæc quoque cæruleam sumet[4] commixtio formam
Quam[5] tamen in nigrum vertet vis ignia[6] vitrum.

[1] *Vasa figuli* P., *ea vasa* W.   [2] *Gummi* R.   [3] *Ut sit* W.   [4] *Sumat* W.
[5] *Quæ* W.   [6] Sic emendavi ; *vertetur insignia* P. R., *convertet singula* W.

---

xxi. *De vitro quod nimium viret.*[1]

Sic etiam nimium tu virens effice vitrum.
Accipies assi subtilia fragmina cupri,
Quæ tamen ejusdem post[2] cum rubigine mittes ;
Rursus et admixto splendenti contere vitro,
Protinus hinc[3] pictam fornacibus injice testam.[4]
Postquam lucentem dabit ipsi flamma colorem,
Accipe. Non[5] pulcram capiet nisi[6] frigida formam,
Nam dum fit vitrum nimis fervere, coloris[7]
Huic auffert propriam[8] flammæ violentia formam.

[1] Sic P. R. *De vitro valde virente* W.   [2] *Penitus* R.   [3] *Hic* R.   [4] *Flammam* R.   [5] *Nam* R. W.   [6] *Hinc* W.   [7] *Nimio fervore vaporis* W.   [8] *Propria* R.

THE THIRD AND PROSAIC BOOK OF THE AFORESAID ERACLIUS,

ON THE AFORESAID COLOURS AND ARTS,

AND FIRST

I. [232]¹ *On painting earthen vases with green glass.*²—Take green glass and burnt thunderbolts,³ and also burnt copper, in powder, and mix them with clear glass, previously ground on a smooth stone. And if you wish to paint a vase with it, temper it with the aforesaid gum water, and lay it on the vase with a paint-brush, and put it into the furnace until it appears thoroughly red hot. When cool it will be of the colour of green glass.

II. [233] *To whiten earthen vases with white glass.*⁴—If you wish to make white glass for the purpose of painting, grind hot sulphur carefully with white glass, and lay it on a thick piece of earthenware, and put it into the furnace. And when it has run together, take it out of the fire ; and if you wish to paint saucers and phials, made of earthenware, with it, grind it up as if for writing, and do as before directed for the green glass.

III. [259] *How earthenware vessels are glazed.*—Take the strongest potter's clay you can procure, and put it into the furnace with the other vases, or in any other fire, and bake it until it is quite red hot. When it is cool, put it into any vase, and

---

¹ The figures in [ ] refer to the numbers in the Le Begue MS. at Paris.
² See lib. ii. No. xviii.
³ The nodules of iron pyrites found about the chalk-rocks at Brighton and other parts of the coast of Sussex, are still called by the lower orders "thunderbolts." The same term is also applied to the fossils called "Belemnitæ ;" but I consider that, in the present case, it can apply only to one of the minerals called "pyrites."
⁴ See lib. ii. No. xix.

INCIPIT

TERCIUS LIBER ET PROSAICUS ERACLII, ANTEDICTI,

DE COLORIBUS ET ARTIBUS PREDICTIS,

ET PRIMO[1]

I. [232] *De vasis testeis depingendis ex viridi vitro.*[2]—Viridis
vitri et usti fulminis pulverem, item usti cupri, accipe, et misce
cum claro vitro[3] prius bene[4] super marmoream petram planam[5]
trito. Si ex eo testam ornare volueris,[6] cum gummi liquore
supradicto temperes, et cum[7] pincello testam ex his[8] intinges,
et in fornacem pones ut bene rubeat.[9] Refrigerata vitri viridis
representabit[10] colorem.

II. [233] *Ad vasa testea albo vitro dealbanda.*[11]—Album
vitrum si facere vis ad usum pingendi,[12] calidum sulphur cum
vitro albo diligenter tere, et super spissam testam pone, et in
fornacem mitte. Cum autem glutinatum fuerit, extrahe ab
igne, et si ex eo scutellas[13] arte figuli factas vis dipingere, illud
contere[14] ad usum scripturæ, et fac quemadmodum[15] ante dictum est de viridi vitro.

III. [259] *Quomodo vasa figuli*[16] *plumbeantur.* — Accipe
terram figulorum quantum[17] fortem poteris invenire, et in furno
cum aliis vasis mitte,[18] ubi tantum lento igne coques, vel in alio
igne, quousque tota sit rubea. Quando[19] frigida fuerit, mitte eam

---

[1] Ex P. [2] Ex P. *De vasis testeis pingendis* R. [3] *Cum claro misce* R.
[4] *Bene* omittit P. [5] *Planam* omittit R. [6] *Temperes* hic inserit P., et post
omittit. [7] *Cum* omittit R. [8] *Hic* R. [9] *Ut tantum rubea appareat* R.
[10] *Resplendabit.* Cant. [11] Ex P. *Item ut supra* R. [12] *Tere* hic inserit P., et
post omittit. [13] *Et fialas* inserit P. [14] *Contere illum* P. [15] *Scripturæ qualiter*
R. [16] *Fignul* R. [17] *Quantumvis* R. [18] *Mitte* omittit R. [19] *Et quando* P.

grind it until it is reduced to powder. Then take water and mix with it, and pour off the water into another vase, and let it remain so until the next day, and then throw away that water. Then take [some of] the clay that is left behind, and mix it with other clay without sand, and with two parts of the aforesaid very strong clay. Then pound it with a mallet, and make whatever kind of vase you like with it. Afterwards, take [some more of] that clay which you allowed to settle, and mix oil with it, and spread it all over the vase which you have made, before it is baked. Then put it away in a secret place until it is quite dry, and do not let the draught get to it. If you wish to glaze the vessel, take wheat flour, and boil it in a jar, and let it cool, and wash over the vessel with this water. Then take lead well dissolved. But if you wish to make the vase green, take copper or brass, which is better, and melt it with lead in the following manner. Take lead and melt it well in a vase. When it is quite liquid, shake it round the vase with your hands until it is reduced to powder, and then mix six parts of brass filings with it, and while the vase is wet with the flour paste, you must immediately dust the lead over it [that is, dust it over with the aforesaid filings]. But if you wish it to be yellow, dust it over with the powder of lead alone, without the filings. Then place this vase in another larger vase, and put it into the furnace, that it may be more brilliant and beautiful, but with a slow fire, so as to be neither too strong nor too weak.

IV. [234] *Also to finish earthenware vessels with green glass.*[1] —Grind rust of copper and copper filings with clear glass, and afterwards paint a jar with them as before, and put it into a very hot furnace. Then take it out of the furnace, and you will have a precious colour.

---

[1] See lib. ii. No. xxi.

in quodam vase, et tamdiu tere, quousque tota sit quasi pulvis.
Deinde accipe aquam, et misce cum ea, et in alio vase cola, et
usque ad alium diem sic eam dimittes. Postea illam aquam
projicies foras. Deinde accipe illas feces, et cum alia terra
quæ sine sabulo est misces, cum duabus partibus illius fortis-
simæ terræ supradictæ. Postea tere eam cum malleo. Deinde
qualecunque vas volueris facies. Postea accipe illam fecem
quam sivisti quiescere, et cum oleo misces, et illud vas quod
fecisti, antequam coquatur, per totum linies. Deinde pones
eum in secreto loco quoadusque totum siccetur, et ne ventus ei
contrarius sit. Si vero eum plumbeum facere volueris, accipias[1] farinam de frumento, et in ollam bullire eam facies, et
refrigerari permittes, et de ipsa aqua eam per totum in circuitu linies. Postea accipe plumbum bene solutum. Si tamen
viride eum volueris[2] facere, accipe cuprum, vel auricalcum,
quod melius est, et cum plumbo misce sic. Accipe plumbum,
et in vase eum optime funde. Quando totum liquefactum
fuerit, circumvolve manibus tuis illud in vas usque dum pulvis
fiat et ita[3] VI partes limaturæ auricalci[4] cum eo misces.
Cum vas illud de aqua farinæ humefactum fuerit, statim pulverabis de plumbo [id[5] est, suprascripta limatura pulverabis].
Si vero vis ut croceus sit, de puro plumbo,[6] et sine[7] limatura,
pulverabis. Deinde in majori vase intus vas illud repone, et
in furno mitte ut sit plus splendidum et pulcrum, lento tamen
igni, ut non nimis fortiter nec nimis flebiliter.[8]

IV. [234] *Item, [ad[9] testea vasa, id est, figuli, viridi vitro
perficienda.]*—Rubiginem cupri et pulverem ejusdem,[10] cum
vitro claro tere, et postea ex hoc[11] testam ut supra pinge, et in
fornacem valde succensam mitte. Deinde a fornace extrahe,[12]
et preciosum habebis colorem.[13]

---

[1] *Accipies* P. [2] *Virideum volueris eum* P. [3] *Ita,* sic P. ; R. lacunam
habet. [4] *Auricalci limature* P. [5] Ex P. [6] *Deinde pones plumbo.* Cant.
[7] *Suprascripta.* Cant. [8] *Nimus fortiter nec minus flebis* R. [9] Ex P.
[10] *Rubiginem vitri* R. [11] *Ex hoc* omittit R. [12] *Abstrahe* R. [13] *Preciosum
colorem habeas viridem* P.

V. [255] *How and when glass was invented.*—Glass is so called, as Isidorus says, because it has the property of being transparent to the sight; for with regard to other metals, whatever is inclosed in them is concealed. But with regard to glass, whatever liquid or substance is contained in it, appears inside just as it appears outside, and is visible, however it may be inclosed. Its origin was as follows : In the part of Syria which is called Phœnicia, and which borders on Judea, at the foot of Mount Carmel, there is a swamp, in which the river Belus rises, which after a course of 5 miles flows into the sea just by Tholomaïs [Ptolemaïs], the sands of which are washed by the water flowing over them. At this place, as it is reported, a vessel of nitre-merchants was wrecked, and when they were preparing their food here and there upon the sands, having no stones to support their [cooking] vessels, they placed lumps of nitre [natron] under them; which being ignited, and mixed with the sand of the shore, streams of a new and transparent liquor began to flow, and this is asserted to have been the origin of glass.

Then as the ingenious skill of men was not contented with the glass alone, endeavours were made to extend and improve this art, with other mixtures; for it is heated with light and dry wood, together with copper and nitre, and is melted in constant furnaces like brass, and is made into lumps. Afterwards these lumps are again melted in the workshops, and some is formed into shape by blowing, some is ground on a lathe, and some is sculptured like silver. It is also tinged in many ways so as to imitate hyacinths and green sapphires and onyx stones, and other colours of gems. And there is no material fitter for mirrors, or for pictures especially, than the white glass, and particularly that which is made like crystal; so that for drinking cups it has driven gold and silver quite out of use. Glass was formerly made in Italy, and throughout Gaul, and in Spain. Very soft white sand was triturated with a pestle and mill. It was then mixed with three parts of nitre, by weight or measure, and when melted was transferred to other

V. [255] *Quomodo et quando inventum fuerit vitrum.*—Vitrum dictum,[1] ut ait Ysidorus,[2] quod visui perspecuitate transluceat. In aliis enim metallis quicquid intrinsecus continetur absconditur. In vitro vero,[3] quilibet liquor vel species[4] interius, talis[5] exterius declaratur, et quodam modo clausus[6] patet.[7] Cujus origo hæc fuit. In parte Syriæ quæ Fenicis vocatur, finitima Judeæ, circa radicem montis Carmeli, palus est, ex qua nascitur Belus amnis,[8] V millium passuum spatio in mare fluens, juxta Tholomaida, cujus arenæ, decurrente[9] fluctu, sordibus eluuntur. Hic[10] fama est, quod, expulsa[11] nave mercatorum nitri,[12] cum sparsim[13] per litus epulas pararent nec essent lapides[14] pro attollendis vasis, lapides, glebas nitri vasi subdiderunt.[15] Quibus accensis, permixta arena littoris, translucentis novi liquoris, vitri scilicet,[16] fluxisse rivos,[17] et hanc fuisse originem vitri.

Mox, ut[18] ingeniosa hominum[19] solertia non fuit contenta solo vitro, sed et aliis mixturis hanc artem studuit[20] in melius ampliare, levibus enim et] aridis lignis concoquitur, adjecto cipro ac nitro,[21] continuisque fornacibus, ut æs, liquatur, massæque fiunt. Postea ex massis rursus funditur in officinis, et aliud flatu figuratur, aliud torno teritur, aliud argenti modo celatur. Tingitur etiam multis modis ita ut jacinctos saphirosque virides imitetur,[22] et onichinos, et aliarum gemmarum colores. Neque est alia speculis aptior materia, vel picturæ accommodatior. Maximus tamen in candido vitro, proximaque in cristalli similitudine, unde et ad potandum argenti et auri metalla[23] repulit. Vitrum olim[24] fiebat[25] in Italia, et per

---

[1] *Deinde* P. [2] *Proprietatem habet* supplet P. [3] *Vero* omittit R. [4] *Quælibet* supplet R. [5] *Taliter* R. [6] *Clarius* R. [7] Inter hæc duo verba lacunam habet R. [8] *Belus rivus* R. [9] *Decrescente* R. [10] *Hæc* P. [11] *Quod expulsa* P. ; *pulsa* R. [12] *Mercatorum nitri* omittit P., et loco ejus *ibidem* supplet. [13] *Sparsius* R. [14] *Lapides* omittit R. [15] Ex R. ; *cum ad ignem in navi apponi deberent pro ferculis decoquendis, glebas igitur nitri, loco lapidum utendas, navi subdiderunt;* P. [16] *Vitri scilicet* omittit R. [17] *Asseritur* supplet P. [18] *Est* supplet R. [19] *Hominum* omittit R. [20] Ex P. ; *nam* R. [21] *Et vitro* supplet P. [22] *Immittetur* P. [23] *Argenti metalla et auri* R. [24] *Enim* P. [25] *Et* supplet R.

furnaces.   This mass was called "Admovitrius," and from
this, when re-melted, pure and white glass was made.   Among
the kinds of glass, the stone obsidian [1] is also enumerated.
This is black and occasionally greenish, and sometimes translucent, and of a coarser appearance, and when used for mirrors,
shows a shadow instead of an image.   Many persons make
gems of it.   It is said that this stone is produced both in India
and Italy, and in Spain near the ocean.

VI.   [256] *How that a person was beheaded by order of the Em-*
peror because he had discovered the art of making flexible glass. [2]
—It is related that in the reign of Tiberius Cæsar a certain
artist had discovered a way of making glass flexible and ductile.
When he was admitted into Cæsar's presence, he handed a
phial to him, which Cæsar indignantly threw on the ground,
and it bent like a brazen vessel.   The artist took up the phial
from the pavement, and then taking a hammer out of his bosom
he repaired the phial.   Upon this Cæsar asked the artist
whether any other person was acquainted with that method of
making glass.   When he affirmed with an oath that no other
person knew the secret, Cæsar ordered him to be beheaded,
lest, when this was known, gold and silver should be held dirt
cheap, and the prices of all the metals be reduced.   And,
indeed, if glass vessels did not break, they would be better
than gold or silver.

---

[1] Mr. Phillips observes that obsidian occasionally bears a great resemblance to common glass.   The origin of this substance has been warmly
contested : it is common in the neighbourhood of volcanoes, and has
been considered as vitrified lava, whence it has obtained the familiar
name of *volcanic glass*.   It is found on Hecla, and in almost every part of
Iceland, in the Lipari Islands, in one of which it constitutes the greater
part of the mountain " della Castagna"; near the Peak of Teneriffe ; in
Peru, Mexico, and New Spain.   In Europe, obsidian is made into reflectors
for telescopes ; in Mexico and Peru, it was made into looking-glasses and
knives.   Phill. Min. p. 135, 136.

[2] It is merely necessary to observe with respect to this tale, which is
repeated by every writer on the subject, that it is universally disbelieved.

The

Gallias, et in Hispania. Arena alba mollissima pila molaque terebatur. Dehinc miscebatur tribus partibus nitri pondere vel mensura, ac, liquata, in alias fornaces transfundebatur quæ Massa vocabatur Admovitrius,[1] atque hæc recocta fiebat vitrum purum et candidum. In genere vitri et obsianus lapis adnumeratur. Est autem virens interdum, et niger, aliquando et translucidus crassiore visu, et, in speculis parietum, pro imagine umbras reddente.[2] Gemmas multi ex eo faciunt. Hunc lapidem et in India, et in Italia, et ad Oceanum in Hispania nasci tradunt.

VI. [256] *Quod quidam decapitatus fuit jussu Imperatoris, quia modum faciendi vitrum flexibile invenerat.*[3]—Fertur autem sub Tiberio Cesare quendam artificem excogitasse vitri temperamentum ut flexibile esset et ductile. Qui, dum admissus esset ad Cesarem, porrexit[4] fialam Cesari, quam ille indignatus in pavimento projecit, quæ complicaverat se tanquam vas æneum. Artifex autem sustulit fialam de pavimento, deinde martulum de sinu protulit, et fialam correxit. Hoc facto, Cesar dixit artifici, numquid alius scit hanc condituram vitrorum? Postquam ille jurans negavit alium[5] hoc scire, jussit illum Cesar decollari, ne, dum hoc cognitum fieret, aurum et argentum[6] pro luto haberentur, et omnium metallorum precia abstraherentur. Et revera quod si vasa vitrea non frangerentur, meliora essent quam aurum et argentum.

---

[1] *Admonitem* P. [2] *Reddere* P. [3] Sic P. *De artifice* R. [4] *Prorrexit* P. [5] *Alterum* R. [6] *Et argentum* omittit R.

The problem, however, of making malleable glass was always a favourite subject with the alchemists, and Raymond Lully expressly declares, that " one of the principal effects of the philosopher's stone was to render glass malleable." The Hon. Robert Boyle mentions (Philosophical Works, vol. i. p. 58), on the authority of an expert chemist, a piece of transparent red glass which, after receiving several strokes with a hammer, was found to have stretched under it (although it had begun to crack on the edges), growing more thin on the beaten part, and leaving visible impressions made on it by the edge of the hammer. Mr. Boyle, very prudently, declines expressing his own opinion on this subject.

VII. [257] *How to make white glass, and glass of various colours.*—Glass is made with the ashes both of fern and of "faina"[1]—that is, of the small trees which grow in the woods. The fern is cut before the Feast of St. John the Baptist, and well dried, and is then put into the fire and reduced to ashes. So also the "faina" is reduced to ashes in the fire. Then take two parts of fern, and one-third part of "faina," and mix them together. Then make a furnace of stones, faced with clay mixed with horse-dung. You must make the foundation quite smooth to the height of half a cubit, and leave a hollow in the furnace without any materials—that is, you must put nothing in the middle of the furnace, because the fire must be in the middle of the furnace while it is at work. Upon the foundation of the furnace you must begin to make three small compartments, which are called "archæ," in which there must be small windows. You must make the middle arch large, with two windows in it, one on one side, and one on the other. In the middle arch, just opposite the door of the arch, must be placed two jars, very well baked, which they call "mortariola," in which the ashes, or sand, as it may be called, is melted, and the glass is made. And you must make the other arches, one on the right hand and one on the left of the middle arch, and the one on the right hand smaller than the one on the left. In the arch on the left hand side you must heat the ashes for a day and a night; and you must heat them until they cohere into a mass. In this arch also you must bake your melting pots perfectly, in order that they may be firm and hard, so as to hold and melt the glass without breaking. When the whole of the ashes have been well baked, and for a very long time, put them into your melting pots with an iron spoon, and melt them until they become white. If you wish it [the glass] to become red,

---

[1] Theophilus employs the ashes of beech-wood, "ligna faginea." It seems to me, therefore, not improbable that "faina" may have been an old French term for the seedling beeches which grew wild in the woods, the beechnut being still called in French "faîne." The ashes of the beech-tree are mentioned afterwards, in treating of the purple and flesh-coloured glass.

VII. [257] *Quomodo efficitur vitrum* [*album*[1] *et etiam de diversis coloribus*].—Vitrum efficitur de cineribus, id est,[2] de filicis cinere,[3] et de faina, id est,[4] de parvulis arboribus quæ sunt vel crescunt in sylvis. Accipitur autem filix ante Festum S. Johannis Baptiste, et optime siccatur, deinde ad ignem mittitur et fit cinis. Similiter et faina efficietur cinis per ignem. Accipies itaque duas partes de filice, et terciam partem de faina, et simul misces. Deinde facies furnum de petris argilla linitis mixta de stercore jumentorum. Fundamentum ejus altitudine dimidii cubiti totum planum facies; profundum furni dimittes sine materia, id est,[5] in medio furni nihil facies, quod in medio ejus ignis quando operatur semper faciendus est. Super fundamentum furni incipies facere tres mansiunculas, quæ arche nominantur, in quibus erunt fenestrellæ. Mediam archam magnam facies, in qua duæ fenestræ erunt, una ex parte una, et alia ex parte altera. In istam archam intus ante os archæ duas ollas optime coctas ponunt,[6] quas mortariola vocant, in quibus cinis sive[7] arena, ut dicetur, funditur, et vitrum efficitur. Alias autem archas facies unam a dextris mediæ archæ, et alteram a sinistris. Illam autem quæ est a dextris minorem facies illa quæ a sinistris est.[8] In archa sinistræ partis una die et una nocte cinerem coques. In tantum vero coqui facies, ut simul[9] sit agglutinatus.[10] In hac quoque archa mortariola tua penitus[11] coqui facies, et, ut firma sint et duriora ad vitrum sustinendum et coquendum, ne frangantur. Quando autem cinis totus et diutissime et optime coctus fuerit, tunc mittes eum in mortariolis tuis cum coclea ferrea, et funde eum tamdiu, donec efficiatur album. Si vero vis ut efficiatur rubeum, de cinere non[12] bene cocto, sic facies. Accipe limaturam cupri, et arde eam quousque pulvis sit, et mitte illum in mortariolis, et erit vitrum rubeum, quem Galienum vocamus. Viride vero vitrum ita facies. De eodem

---

[1] Ex P. [2] *Id est* P.; *Et* R. [3] *Cinere* omittit R. [4] *Id est* P.; *Aut* R. [5] *Id est* P. *Et* R. [6] *Ponunt* omittit R. [7] *Seu* P. [8] *Quæ est a sinistris* R. [9] *Similiter* R. [10] *Conglutinatus* P. [11] *Primitus* P. [12] *Tamen.* Cant.

you will do as follows, with ashes not well baked.   Take copper filings, burn them until they are reduced to powder, and
throw them into your melting pots ; and this will make red
glass, which we call " galienum."   Green glass you will make
thus.   Throw, of the same powder of burnt copper into your
melting pots, as much as you think proper, and stir it, and it
will be green.   Yellow glass is thus made.   Take raw ashes,
and put them into the melting pot and melt them, and throw a
little sand in with them, and a little, if I am not mistaken, of
the powder of copper, and stir the whole together ; and it will
make a yellow glass, which we call " cerasin."   Purple and
" membranaceum " are made differently, with the ashes of the
beech-tree, which are baked like white ashes, and put into a
melting pot, and melted and boiled until they burn to a purple
colour.   While the glass is boiling, stir it about frequently, like
the other glass, as we have said before.   When you see it turn
to a purple colour, take what quantity you like of it, and do
whatever you like with it, until you see it turn pale.   From
this pale colour it changes to another colour, which is called
" membrun."

But when you wish to make tablets or plates, take iron tubes
of the length of one cubit, more or less, as you may think fit,
and at the end of each tube a little wooden tube, having a very
small hole, through which you must blow when you wish to
make a vase.   When you begin to work the glass, take one
tube, and look into the melting pot to see whether the glass is
well cleared and melted.   Then dip the tube into the melting
pot and take up a little glass upon it, like dough, and whirl it
round in your hand, and form whatever you please upon the
iron slab which is placed at the mouth of the furnace.   And
you must make a screen of brickwork, to avoid being scorched
by the fire ; and inside this you must put the iron slab, which
is called " marmor," upon which you must shape the glass
which you are working, and you may form whatever kind of
vase you like.   When your vase, or cup, or saucer, or phial, is
made, you must put it into the arch which is on the left hand

pulvere cupri combusti[1] in mortariolo pones quantum tibi
visum fuerit, et movebis, et erit[2] viride.   Croceum quoque
vitrum sic efficitur.   Cinerem crudum accipies, et mittes in
mortariolo, et fundes eum, projicies que modicum sabuli intus
cum eo, et parum, ni fallor, de pulvere cupri, et movebis simul,
et efficietur croceum vitrum, quod nos Cerasin vocamus.   Purpureum et Membranaceum[3] aliter efficiuntur[4] de cinere arboris
fagi, et, sicut cinis albus, ita coquitur, et mittitur in olla, et
tamdiu funditur bulliendo, quousque vertatur in colorem purpureum.   Dum bullit sepe movebis, sicut et aliud vitrum,
ut[5] supra docuimus.   Quando videbis[6] eum verti in purpureum
colorem, illico tolle quantum vis, et fac opus quod volueris
usque dum videris eum mutari [in pallorem.[7]   De colore pal-
lido mutatur] in aliud quod membrun[8] vocatur.

Quando vero vasa vel tabulas facere volueris, habebis virgas
ferreas intus cavatas longitudine unius cubiti, aut plus, vel
minus [ut videbis opportunum[9]] et in summitate virgæ parvu-
lum lignum intus cavum, habens[10] unum foramen parvissimum
per quod sufflabis quando operari volueris aliquod vas ; et
quando de vitro operari incipies, accipies virgam unam, et in
mortariolo, si sit[11] bene purgatus vel fusus[12] fuerit cinis, aspicies.
Tunc mittes virgam in mortariolo, attrahesque modicum vitri
quasi parumper pastæ, et circumduces manu tua in girum, et
formabis quod tibi placuerit super marmorem ferri qui positus
est juxta os furni.   Nam ibi[13] facies obstaculum quoddam[14] ma-
cerie, ne ab igne consumeris, in quo pones tabulam ferri quæ
marmor vocatur, super quem formabis vitrum quando operaberis, et facies qualecunque vas placuerit tibi.[15]   Facto autem
vase vel[16] cipho vel scutella vel fiala, mittes in archa quæ est in
sinistra parte furni ut ibi temperetur donec refrigescat.

---

[1] *Cupri combusti* omittit R.   [2] *Et erit* R. ; *eritque* P.   [3] *Membranum.*
Cant.   [4] *Efficitur vel efficiuntur* P.   [5] *Sicut* R.   [6] *Videris* R.   [7] Ex R.
[8] *Membranum.* Cant.   [9] Ex P.   [10] *Concavum habentem* P.   [11] *Sit* Inserit P.
[12] *Fondatus vel fonditus* P.   [13] *Tibi* P.   [14] *Quadam* R.   [15] *Qualecunque
vas sicut placuerit in oculis tuis* P.   [16] *Id est* P.

side of the furnace, that it may be annealed there until it is cool.

But when you wish to spread out plates of glass—that is, to make them smooth—heat them again in the furnace, and spread them out in the small window, which is called "explanaria," which is near the left hand side of the arch. When they are spread out, put them into a small furnace made on purpose, and let them remain there until quite cold. And there must be put live coals in the furnace, and as they go out, so the glass cools.

VIII. [271] *How glass is made of lead, and how it is coloured.*[1]—Take good and shining lead, and put it into a new jar, and burn it in the fire until it is reduced to powder. Then take it away from the fire to cool. Afterwards take sand and mix with that powder, but so that two parts may be of lead and the third of sand, and put it into an earthen vase. Then do as before directed for making glass, and put that earthen vase into the furnace, and keep stirring it until it is converted into glass. But if you wish to make it appear green, take brass filings, and put as much as you think proper into the lead glass; and then, if you wish to make any vase, do so with the iron tube. Afterwards take out this vase with the glass, and let it cool. You may, if you like, mix some of this leaden glass with a grossinum of sapphire for painting on glass, adding to it one-third part of scoria of iron. And this pigment is to be ground on an iron slab.

IX. [235] *How to cut glass and other stones.*[2]—The Saracens whip the udder of a goat well with sting-nettles, and then rub it with their hands to get the milk down into it. It is then

---

[1] The latter part of this chapter should be compared with No. xlix., "Quomodo pingitur in vitro."

[2] See Mappæ Clavicula, p. 63.

Tabulas autem vitri quando volueris extendere, id est, planas facere, recalefacies in furnum, et extendes[1] in fenestra parva quæ explanaria vocatur, quæ est juxta sinistram partem archæ. Explanata vero repones eam in parvum furnum ad hoc opus factum, et ibi dimittes donec omnino sit frigida. Carbones autem vivi erunt in furno preparati, qui quanto magis extinguitur[2] tanto plus refrigescit[3] vitrum.

VIII. [271] *Quomodo efficitur vitrum de plumbo, et quomodo coloratur.*[4]—Accipe plumbum optimum[5] et nitidum, et pone in ollam novam, et arde in ignem usque quod[6] pulvis sit. Deinde tolle eam ab igne ut refrigeretur. Postea sabulum sume, et misce cum pulvere illo, ita tamen ut duæ partes sint de plumbo, et tercia de sabulo, ponesque in testeo vase. Facies vero sicut supra[7] scriptum est ad vitrum faciendum, et illud vas testeum pones in furnum, et semper movebis, usque dum vitrum efficiatur. Si vero ut videatur[8] virideum facere cupis, accipe limaturam auricalci, et intus cum plumbeo vitro quantum tibi visum fuerit pone. Deindeque[9] si aliquod vas facere[10] volueris cum fistula ferrea facies. Postea[11] vas illud cum vitro tolle et refrigerari sine. [De isto[12] vitro plumbeo poteris, si vis, cum gallino[13] saphireo miscere ad pingendum in vitro, apposita tercia parte de scoria ferri. Et hæc pictura in marmore ferreo est terenda.][14]

IX. [235] *Quomodo inciditur vitrum*[15] [*et alii lapides*].—Cum acri urtica ubera capræ Saraceni acriter urticant,[16] et palmis tundunt,[17] ut in eis lac[18] descendat. Postea[19] lac in vas emulgitur,[20]

---

[1] R. lacunam habet sic— ; . . . . . *tendes.* [2] Sic emendavi. *Quanto extinguitur* R. *Tanto magis extingueritur* P. [3] *Refrigescet* P. [4] Sic P. *Quomodo efficitur de plumbo* R. [5] *Di Vitro,* Cant. [6] *Quod* omittit R. [7] *Superius,* Cant. [8] *Efficitur* P. [9] *Denique* R. [10] *Facere vas* R. [11] *Posthæc* R. [12] *Pisto,* Cant. [13] *Grossino,* Cant. [14] Sic R. ; in P. vero, *de isto vitro plumbeo, illo scilicet qui cæruleus est, quæ de duobus coloribus potest fieri, poteris, si vis, cum pulvere saphireo miscere ad pingendum in vitro.* [15] Sic P. In [ ] omittit R. *Ad vitrum incidendum* C. [16] *Saraceni acriter urticant* sic C. ; *urticantur* R. ; *acriter urticantur* P. [17] *Tenduntur* P. R. [18] *In ea* C. [19] *Ex eis* supplet P. [20] Sic C. ; *mulgetur in vas* R. ; *mulgatur in vas* P.

*

milked into a vase, into which the glass, with the iron with
which it is to be cut, is to be put for one night until it becomes
soft. The iron must be tempered in the milk itself. When
necessary the milk should be warmed to the same degree of
heat which it had when first milked. The glass must be always
kept warm in it, and so it must be cut. Other stones are cut
in the same way. The goat must be fed on ivy.

X. [236] *How precious stones are cut and polished and made
brilliant.*[1]—Sume hircum qui nunquam coierit, et pone in cuppa
per tres dies [quousque totum digerat quod in ventre habet.
Postea hederam da ei edere per iiij. dies]. Posthæc purgabis
dolium, ut urinam ejus accipias. Posthoc occides hircum et
sanguinem ejus urinæ commiscebis ; et sic lapidem impone per
unam noctem, et posthæc vel comprime in figuram, vel sculpes
si vis. To make it beautiful, procure a leaden plate, and
sprinkle upon it white flint, ground fine like pepper, and rub
the stone upon it until you have ground down the roughness of
it. Then tie up some of the said powdered flint in a linen
cloth, with which rub down the angles which you could not do
on the plate. And then, in order to restore it to its former
lustre, make some nut oil, and rub over it. You must also
rub it down with a waxed cloth to make it shine and remove
the greasy appearance.

XI. [254] *How to cut crystal.*[1]—Take the crystal, and wrap
it up in a linen cloth wet with sudore capræ, and bury it, together with the cloth, in cow-dung ; and afterwards cut it with
a knife just as you like, but with care. After you have done
this, put the crystal into cold water, and then polish it with a
leaden plate, and with flour or bran.

---

[1] See Mappæ Clavicula, p. 64.

et in eo per unam noctem, vitrum cum ferro ponitur[1] cum quo
debet incidi [temperabitur in ipso lacte ferrum, aut in lotio
parvæ puellæ rufæ, quod excipitur ante ortum solis[2]]. At vero
lac,[3] cum necesse fuerit, recalefiat cum[4] eadem calitudine, qua
fuit prius[5] mulsum, et in eo semper vitrum calefiat [donec[6]
molle fiat] et sic incidatur. Sic et alii lapides.[7] [Capra vero
hedera pascatur.][8]

X. [236] *Quomodo sculpuntur preciosi lapides, poliunturque,
et splendificantur.*[9]—Sume hircum qui nunquam coierit, et pone
in cuppa[10] per tres dies [quousque totum digerat quod in ventre
habet. Postea hederam da ei edere per iiij. dies].[11] Posthæc
purgabis dolium, ut urinam ejus accipias. Posthoc occides[12]
hircum et sanguinem ejus urinæ commiscebis;[13] et sic lapidem
impone per unam noctem, et posthæc[14] vel comprime in figuram,
vel sculpes si vis. Ut pulcrum facias, fac tibi tabulam plumbeam, et super hanc asperges album silicem contritum, ut piper,
et lapidem desuper fricabis, quoadusque asperitatem lenies.[15]
Postea liga de eodem silice contrito in laneo panno, et inde
fricabis angulos quos prius[16] aptare nequisti[17] in lamina.
Deinde, ut pristinam lucem recipiat, fac tibi oleum de nucibus,
et inde fricabis. Adhuc debes eum linire panno cerato, ut
splendeat et sudore deficiat.[18]

XI. [254] *Quomodo incidatur[19] cristallum.* —Accipe cristallum, et involve in panno lineo intincto in sudore capræ, et cum
ipso panno in fimo bovis involve, et sic cum cultro incide, ut volueris, et tamen caute. Postquam[20] feceris, mitte in aquam frigi-
dam. Dehinc lica cum lamina plumbea, et farina vel furfure.[21]

---

[1] *Ponatur* P. R.   [2] Ex C.; alii omittunt.   [3] *At vero lac* C.; omittit P.;
at vero R.   [4] *Cum* omittunt P. C.   [5] *Primitus* C.   [6] Ex C.   [7] *Aliæ
petræ* C.   [8] Ex C.   [9] Ex P.; *quomodo sculpuntur lapides* R.; *ad cristallum
comprimendum in figuram* C.   [10] *Cupam* P. R.   [11] Ex C.   [12] *Vel incides*
supplent P. R.   [13] *Miscebis* P. R.   [14] *Posthoc* P.   [15] *Lenieris* R.; *Linieris* P.   [16] *Prius* omittunt P. R.   [17] *Nequivisti* C.   [18] *Et sudare desinat* C.
[19] *Incidetur* P.   [20] *Posteaquam* R.   [21] *Cum farina vel sulfure* P.

XII. [266] *How stones are polished.*—Take the stone which is called hæmatite, which must not be too hard, or veined, but very smooth and bright; and go to a grindstone, and make it as smooth as you can.   When it appears sufficiently even, make it still smoother upon a tile, and afterwards, that it may be still smoother, rub it upon a whetstone.   Then polish it upon a leaden plate, and again polish it still better upon the hairy side of a cow's skin, which must be very smooth and clean.   Afterwards polish it again on a very smooth and polished piece of the wood which is called aspen or poplar.   You may also polish the teeth of beasts in this way, and not only teeth, but also whatever gold you have used either on walls, or wood, or even on parchment.

XIII. [276] *Of gilding [tin foil].*—Gilding is composed of quicksilver and tin, in the proportion of three parts of quicksilver to four of tin.   Take a plate of tin, and varnish it very thinly two or three times, and let it dry.   Then take soot[1] and cervisia, and mix them together.   Then strain them and place them upon charcoal.   When they have boiled a little, dip the tin into the dish containing the soot and cervisia, and when you see that it is sufficiently done, take it out of that colour, and put it into a saucerfull of cold water, and it will then appear to you to be good.   Afterwards, when you take it out, it will look like gold.

XIV. [253] *How to gild.*—Take seven parts of quicksilver and one of gold, and mix them together, and then put them into a saucer, or cup, or basin, and wash them with water, and gild whatsoever you like with them.   But if you wish to keep the gold very long, squeeze out the quicksilver through a clean cloth, and the gold will remain, which you may put into a vase, and so you may preserve it.   And when you wish to gild with it, mix it afresh with quicksilver, and wash it.

---

[1] Probably the soot from burnt wood, of which the pigment called " Bistre " was made.

XII. [266] *Quomodo politur lapis* [*et dens animalis.*][1]—Sume lapidem qui dicitur emantes, qui non sit nimis durus, neque venatus,[2] sed admodum planus, et clarissimus, et vade ad molam fabri, et ut volueris planum facies.   Cum tibi visum fuerit satisfactum, inde super tegulam levius planabis ; postea iterum, ut dulcius fiat, cum cote ; deinde super tabulam plumbeam, ut poliatur.   Hinc iterum super corium vaccæ illa parte quæ[3] pilosum fuit, quod planissimum et mundissimum[4] sit volo, super quod[5] iterum melius polies.   Posthoc super lignum quod tremulum vel populus[6] vocatur, optime et multum planatum, polies iterum.[7]   Dentem vero bestiarum poteris hoc modo polire ; non tantum dentem, sed et aurum, quocunque posueris, sive in muro, seu in ligno,[8] vel etiam in perchameno.[9]

XIII. [276] *De deauratura* [*petulæ stagni.*][10]— Deauratura efficitur de vivo argento et stanno[11] ita ut tres partes sint de vivo argento, et quatuor,[12] de stagno.   Sume laminam stagni, et vernicia illam duabus vel tribus vicibus multum tenuiter, et dimitte siccare.   Postea accipe fuliginem et cervisiam, et misce simul.[13] Postea[14] cola.   Deinde pones super carbones.   Cumque aliquantulum bullierit, tunc in patella cum fuligine et cervisia mitte, et cum videris satisfactum, abstrahe de hoc colore,[15] et mitte in scutella plena aqua frigida,[16] et tunc tibi non videbitur bonum. Postea, cum eum tuleris, velut aurum eum[17] videbis.

XIV. [253] *Deauratura quomodo fit.*—De argento vivo vii. partes,[18] et unam de auro accipies, et misces simul.   Deinde in scutella vel in[19] cipho vel in bacino mitte, et de aqua ablue, et deaura quod volueris, [si[20] vero diu multumque servare volueris] per pannum nitidum[21] argentum vivum projicies foras, et remanebit aurum, et in vase pones.   Sicque servare poteris.   Quando vero deaurare volueris, iterum cum argento vivo misces, et ablues.

---

[1] Ex P.   [2] *Veratus* P.   [3] *Quæ* P. ; *vel qua* R.   *Quod.* Cant.   [4] *Mundum* R.   [5] *Qua* R.   [6] *Vel populus* omittit R.   [7] Novum capitulum hic incipit R. [8] *Sive in ligno sive in muro* R.   [9] *Pergameno* P.   [10] Ex P.   [11] *Stagno* R. [12] *Quarta* R.   [13] *Similiter* R.   [14] *Post* P.   [15] *Calore* R.   [16] *Et plena aqua frigida in scutella mitte* R.   [17] *Eum* omittit R.   [18] *Partes* omittit R.   [19] *In* omittit R.   [20] Ex P.   [21] *Accidum* R.

XV. [252] *How brass, or silver, is gilt.*—Take soot and pure salt, and grind them well, and take white of egg, and distemper them with it. Then spread it over the silver, or gold, or copper, or whatever else you wish to gild, laying this mixture on those parts between which you wish to gild it, and put it upon charcoal, and when it is dry, gild those parts upon which the mixture was not laid, and when it is gilt, wash off the mixture, and burnish.

XVI. [249] *How to gild brass.*—Take three parts of atramentum and one part of salt, and grind them with vinegar; then mix quicksilver with them, and grind them all together again. Next take a clean cloth and dip it in atramentum, and rub the brass strongly with it. Then put it into the fire until it is thoroughly red-hot, when it must be removed from the fire and suffered to cool. You may then gild it like gold or copper.

XVII. [237] *How to gild iron.*[1]— Grind brass filings with vinegar in a brass mortar, with salt and alum, to the consistence of honey: some persons use water instead of vinegar. Then the iron, well cleaned, and slightly warmed, must be anointed and rubbed with this, until it is of the colour of brass. It is then washed with water and wiped, and gilt like silver, and the quicksilver driven off in the usual manner by heat; and in order to make it shine it is rubbed with an iron.

XVIII. [238] *Otherwise.*— Globular alum (?)[2] and salt, which is called sal gem and calcanthum, are ground with vinegar

---

[1] See Clavicula, p. 37.

[2] The different readings of these words have cast much obscurity over the passage. The word "glumen," however, does not appear to be susceptible of any other explanation than the reading in the Mappæ Clavicula (p. 39), which has been followed in the text. Additional weight is given to this construction by the word "alumine" being used in a manner somewhat similar in the recipe immediately preceding. The correspondence of the other parts of the recipes will also be observed. Salt, which is mentioned in the first, is substituted for the sal gem (the purest kind of rock salt) of the second, and the brass filings of the first recipe for the calcanthum (sulphate of copper) of the second.

XV. [252] *Quomodo deauratur æs, vel auricalcum, vel argentum.*[1]—Accipe fuliginem et purum sal; teres fortiter, accipiesque glaream ovi et distemperabis. Deinde linies aurum, vel argentum, vel cuprum, vel aliud quod volueris deaurare, et ibi ubi volueris interim deaurare illam distemperaturam superpones,[2] et super carbones mittes. Cum fuerit siccatum, deaurabis ubi non fuerit positum, et quando deauratum fuerit, ablues distemperaturam, et burnies.

XVI. [249] *Quomodo deauratur auricalcum.*[3]—De atramento tres partes, et salis unam partem accipies, et cum [aceto[4] fortiter teres, deinde argentum vivum cum eis misces, et in simul iterum teres]. Postea accipe pannum nitidum, et intinges in atramentum, et auricalcum fortiter fricabis. Deinde mitte in ignem quousque totum rubeum fiat. Postea retrahe[5] ab igne, et sine refrigerari. Tunc poteris deaurare sicut aurum vel cuprum.

XVII. [237] *Quomodo ferrum deauratur.*[6]—Eris [pulvis[7] vel] limatura teritur[8] cum aceto in mortario æreo,[9] et[10] cum sale et alumine, usque ad mellis spissitudinem. Aliqui pro aceto aqua utuntur. Deinde ferrum bene purgatum,[11] et leviter calefactum, hac mixtura inungitur,[12] et fricatur, donec colorem æris[13] accipiat. Posthæc[14] abluitur aqua,[15] et tergitur,[16] et sicut es vel[17] argentum deauratur[18] et calefactum, recedente[19] vivo argento, sicut mos est,[20] ut splendorem accipiat, ferro defricatur.

XVIII. [238] *Aliter.*[21]—Alumen rotundum, et sal, quod gemma vocatur,[22] et calcanthum,[23] ex aceto acerrimo teruntur in æreo

---

[1] *Quomodo deauratur vel aurum vel argentum* R.   [2] *Suppones* R.   [3] *Oricalcum* R.   [4] Ex P., R. habet *eis misces et insimiliter tercium teres.*
[5] *Trahe* P.   [6] Sic P. R.; *inauratio ferri* C. (p. 64). In C. (p. 37) partem alterius capituli facit.   [7] C. (p. 37).   [8] *Teratur* P. R.   [9] *In eneo mortario* C. (p. 37), *in hereo mortario* C. (p. 64).   [10] *Et* omittit C.
[11] Sic C. (p. 64); *Deinde ferrum multum purgatum* P. R.   *Denique bene purgatum ferrum* C. (p. 37).   [12] *Inungatur* P.   [13] *Eis* P., *Heris* C. (p. 64); *eris* C. (p. 37).   [14] *Posthoc* P.; *posthac* R.; *tunc* C. (p. 37).
[15] *Abluta aqua* R., *aqua abluitur* C.   [16] *Teritur* C. (p. 37).   [17] *Aurum et* R.; *es vel* C.; omittit P.   [18] *Deauratum* P.   [19] *Recedendo* R.   [20] *Et* supplet P.   [21] Sic P. R. C. (p. 64). In C. (p. 37) partem facit capituli cxlvj.
[22] Ex C. (p. 37).   *Glumen rotundum et salvandum, quod sal Gemma vocatur* P. R.; *alumen rotundum et salvandum, quod salis gemma vocatur* C. (p. 64).
[23] *Calcantum* C.

in a brass mortar. This is rubbed over the clean iron with a cane or any other light stick, and, when it has the colour of brass, it is washed and gilt. The quicksilver is then driven off, and it is cooled with water, and then rubbed down with a very smooth and bright iron until it is well polished.

XIX. [239] *How ivory is bent and ornamented.*—If you wish to bend and adorn ivory, put it into the aforesaid mixture for three days and three nights.[1] Having done this, hollow out a piece of wood in whatever manner you like, and then put the ivory into the cavity, and turn and bend it just as you like. A plate of copper, 10 inches in breadth, and the same in length, can be gilt with [the weight of] one denarius[2] of gold.

XX. [250] *How to restore gold.*—If you have gilt any vase which, through negligence, has lost the gilding, take atramentum and salt, well ground together, and spread some of it over the vase. Then place it before the fire to dry; and give it another coat, then place it again before the fire. Do this three or four times, and it will recover its former colour, which it had lost.

XXI. [267] *How to varnish gold so that it will not lose its colour.*—If you wish to varnish gold that has been laid upon gypsum, varnish over the gold, not with pure varnish, but with that colour which is made for preparing auripetrum,[3] mixed, however, with oil, and a little varnish, lest it should be too thick. And so, if in any part the colour of the gypsum should appear through [the gold], it may be covered with this colour. But you may varnish figures and other colours with pure varnish or with thick oil.

XXII. [248] *How to solder gold, or silver, or copper, or brass.*—Take three parts of brass, and three parts of tin, and melt

---

[1] See Clavicula, p. 64.

[2] It is obvious that the author is here speaking of the weight of the coin, for the denarius was not a gold coin. Celsus informs us that, from the time of Tiberius to that of Vespasian, seven of them were made from one ounce Troy weight. At a later period eight were made from the ounce Troy. In the lower empire they scarcely weighed half so much in pure silver.

[3] The composition of this colour is described in No. xliv., which is not in the Cambridge MS. From this it would appear that the MS. published by Raspe was really defective.

mortario. Ex [1] his ferrum purgatum, cum ferula,[2] vel alia qualibet levi hastula,[3] defricatur, et, cum æris habuerit colorem,[4] detergitur,[5] et deauratur; deinde,[6] exfumigato vivo argento[7], aqua refrigeratur,[8] et [9] usque ad splendorem, ferro valde plano et limpido, defricatur.

XIX. [239] *Quomodo dirigitur et ornatur ebur.*[10]—Quod si volueris ebur dirigere et ornare,[11] in hac supradicta confectione mittatur tribus diebus et tribus [12] noctibus. Hoc facto, cavabis lignum quali modo volueris; deinde, posito ebore in cavatura,[13] diriges illud, et plicabis ad placitum.[14] Tabula cupri quæ decem pollices habet in latitudine, et totidem in longitudine, denario auri deaurari [15] potest.

XX. [250] *Quomodo recuperatur deauratura.*—Si aliquod vas habueris deauratum, et per negligentiam deauraturam perdiderit, accipe atramentum, et sal cum eo bene tritum, et lini illud vas. Postea pone ad ignem seccare, et iterum linies, et ad ignem pones. Hoc facies tribus vel [16] quatuor vicibus, et recuperabit colorem pristinum.[17]

XXI. [267] *Quomodo vernicietur aurum ne perdat colorem.*— Si aurum super gypsum positum verniciare volueris, non de [18] puro vernicio, sed de illo colore qui efficitur ad auripetram [19] faciendum, mixto tamen [20] cum oleo modico vernicio, ne nimis sit spissum,[21] vernicietur [22] super aurum. Ideo si aliquid [23] gipsei coloris apparuerit,[24] hoc colore operiri poterit. Imagines vero et alios colores de puro vernicio, vel de crasso oleo, poteris verniciare.

XXII. [248] *Quomodo poteris solidare aurum vel argentum vel cuprum* [25] *vel auricalcum.*—Accipe tres partes de auricalco, et

---

[1] *Ex* omittit C. (p. 37). [2] *Ferura* C. (p. 64). [3] *Hattula* R.; *astula* P. [4] *Cum eraminis colorem habuerit* C. (p. 37); *cum heris colorem habuerit* C. (p. 64). [5] *Extergitur* C. (p. 37); *retergitur* C. (p. 64). [6] *Ac deinde* C. [7] *Argento vivo* C. (p. 37). [8] *Refrigeratum* C. (p. 37). [9] *Et* omittit C. [10] Sic P.; omittit R., qui septem prima verba capituli rubricavit. *De ebore* C. (p. 64). [11] *Vel carvare* C. [12] *Tribus* omittit C. [13] *Cavitura* R. P. [14] Quod sequitur omittit C. [15] *Decorari* R. [16] *Et* R. [17] *Pristinum colorem quem perdiderat* R. [18] *Circumde (conde)* R. [19] *Aurum petrum* R. [20] *Unde* R. [21] *Ne sit spissum nimis* P. [22] *Verniceter* R. [23] *Aliqui* R. [24] *Apparuerunt* R. [25] *Vel cuprum* omittit R.

them together in a ladle over the fire, and reduce the mass to powder, and put it away in a box. Then take three parts of paramentum, and burn it in an earthen vase in the fire like atramentum. Then take salt, and dry it well upon coals. Then grind the salt and paramentum together with wine. When you wish to solder brass or copper, put some of this preparation, made with the salt, upon the brass or copper, wherever you wish to solder it. Then immediately put some of the aforesaid powder on it, and heat it in the fire and it will be firmly soldered.

XXIII. *On trying gold and silver.*[1]—All pure gold, of whatever weight, is denser, by one-twentieth part of itself, than any silver, similarly pure. This may be proved as follows: If one pound of pure gold be weighed in the balance, under water, with an equal weight of pure silver, the gold will be found heavier than the silver, or the silver lighter than the gold, by xii denarii, or one-twentieth part of its weight. Wherefore if you have any article made of gold, with which silver appears to have been mixed, and you wish to know how much gold, and how much silver, is contained in it, take silver or gold, and having found the weight of the said article, make a mass of either of the metals, of exactly equal weight, and, putting them into the scales, immerse them in the water. If the mass which you made is of silver, the said article will preponderate. If the mass is of gold, the gold will preponderate, throwing up [the scale containing] the said article. And it will happen, that by as many parts as the gold is heavier, by so many parts the silver is lighter; for whatever there may be in the said article, under water, besides the usual weight, belongs to the gold on

---

[1] This chapter does not form part of the MS. of Le Begue; but it will be found, with some variations, in Mappæ Clavicula, p. 45. From the chapter in the text, it will be seen that the value of the denarius was much diminished, since, at the time the above was written, 20 denarii were equal to an ounce, and 240 to a pound.

tres partes de stagno, et funde [1] simul in conca ad ignem, pul-
veremque facias, et in buttam [2] recondes. Postea accipe paramentum tres partes [3] et quasi atramentum in testeo vase arde in
igne. Accipiesque sal, et super carbones optime siccabis.
Deinde paramentum et sal [4] macerabis simul cum vino. Cum
vero auricalcum vel cuprum solidare volueris, pones super
auricalcum vel cuprum de ista confectione, et de sale, et temperamento facta ubi volueris solidare. Statimque de pulvere
supradicta [5] pones, et ad ignem calefacies, et firmiter solida-
bitur.

XXIII. *De probatione auri et argenti.*[6]—Omne [7] aurum
purum, cujus libet ponderis, omni argento similiter puro, ejusdem [8] tamen ponderis, densius est parte sui vicesima ;[9] quod ita
probari potest. Si purissimi auri libra cum equo [10] puri [11] argenti
simili pondere [12] sub aqua conferatur in statera, xii denariis,[13] id
est [14] vicesima [15] sui parte, aurum gravius argento, vel argentum
levius auro invenietur. Quapropter si inveneris opus aliquod [16]
auro formatum, cui argentum permixtum esse [17] videatur,
scireque [18] volueris quantum auri, quantumque [19] in eo argenti
contineatur, sume argentum sive aurum, et examinato supra-
dicti operis [20] pondere, nec [21] minus pensantem massam de utro-
vis [22] metallo fabricato, atque utraque et opus et [23] massam
stateræ [24] lancibus imponito,[25] aquisque immergito. Si argentea
fuerit [massa quam fecisti, opus preponderabit ; si aurea
fuerit [26]] alleviato [27] opere, aurum inclinabitur. Hoc tamen ita
fiet, ut quot partibus inclinatur aurum, totidem partibus sub-
levatur [28] argentum ; quia [29] quicquid in ipso opere fuerit sub
aquis præter solitum pondus,[30] ad aurum, propter densitatem,

---

[1] *Fonde* P. [2] *Buscam* P. [3] *Tres partes paramentum* P. [4] *Sal et para-*
mentum P. [5] *Suprascripta* P. [6] Sic R. ; *de auri pondere* C. (p. 45).
[7] *Omnem.* Cant. [8] *Eidem.* Cant. [9] *Parte sui xxiiij. et insuper ccxl.* C.
[10] *Eque* C. [11] *Puri.* Omittit Cant. [12] *Ex.* Cant. [13] *xj. denariis* C.
[14] *Et* R. [15] *xxiiij. et ccxl.* C. [16] *Opus aliquod inveneris* C. [17] *Per com-*
mixtionem inesse C. [18] *Que* omittit R. [19] *Quantumve* C. [20] *Examinato*
inspectione C. [21] *Non* C. [22] *Utrius* R. [23] *Utrumque opus scilicet, et* C.
[24] *Stantem* C. [25] *Imposito* R. [26] *Ex* R. [27] *Allevato* C. [28] *Sullevetur* C.
[29] *Quod* R. [30] *Ponderis* C.

account of its greater density; and whatever deficiency there may be is to be attributed to the silver, on account of its greater rarity. And in order that you may perceive it more easily, you must bear in mind that, in weight for gold, and in lightness for silver, x denarii signify a pound, as I have already stated in the former part of this chapter.

XXIV. [268] *How wood is to be prepared before painting on it.*[1]—Whoever wishes to adorn any wood with divers colours, let him hear what I say. First make the wood very flat and smooth by scraping it, and lastly by rubbing it with that herb which is called shave-grass. But if the piece of wood is such that you cannot smooth down its inequalities, or you have reasons for not wishing to do so, and at the same time are not willing to cover it with leather or with cloth, grind dry white-lead upon a stone, but not so finely as if you were going to paint with it. Then melt wax over the fire in a vase, add tiles ground fine. Then mix it with the white-lead which you had ground, stirring it frequently with a small stick, and so let it cool. Then heat an iron, and with it melt the wax into the little fissures, until they are level, and then scrape off the rough parts with a knife. And if you hesitate about mixing white-lead with the wax, know that the more you mix with it, the harder it will be. And when you have made it smooth, as I was saying, mix plenty of white-lead very finely ground, with linseed-oil, and lay an excessively thin coat of it wherever you intend to paint with a brush of ass's hair adapted for that purpose. When this is dry, lay on, as you did before, another and a thicker coat of it, not thicker by having a greater quantity of colour, but by having less oil in it. For you must take very great

---

[1] The mode of preparation described in this chapter differs essentially from those usually followed; inasmuch as several coats of white lead and oil are laid immediately on the wood, without a previous preparation of glue and gesso.

pertinet; quicquid autem levitatis, ad argentum, propter raritatem, conferendum est.[1] Et, ut hoc[2] facilius possit adverti,
considerare debes, tam in gravitate auri, quam in levitate
argenti, x denarios[3] significare libram, sicut in[4] prima lec-
tionis hujus fronte prefixum est.

XXIV. [268] *Quomodo aptetur lignum antequam pingatur.*—
Quicunque aliquod lignum ornare diversis coloribus satagis, audi
quæ dico. Imprimis ipsum lignum multum rade equalem, et
planissimum radendo, et ad ultimum fricando cum illa herba
quæ dicitur asperella. Quod si ligni materies talis fuerit, ut
non possis equare ejus asperitates,[5] vel non velis, propter ali-
quas occasiones, nec tamen[6] cum corio illud[7] velis cooperire,[8]
vel panno;[9] album plumbum teres super petram siccum, sed
non tantum[10] quantum si inde pingere[11] velis. Deinde ceram
in vase supra ignem[12] liquefacies, tegulamque tritam subtiliter;
albumque plumbum, quod ante trivisti,[13] simul commisces, sepius movendo cum parvo ligno, et sic sine refrigerari. Postea
aliquod ferrum fac calidum, et, cum ipso, ceram[14] funde in
ipsas cavernulas donec equales sint, et sic cum cultello desuper
abrade ea quæ sunt scabrosa. Si autem album[15] plumbum
miscere cum cera dubitas, scito quod quantum plus miscueris,
tanto durius erit. Et, sicut dixi, jam equali facto, habundancius plumbum, valde subtilissime tritum cum oleo lini,[16] desuper, per totum ubicunque pingere vis, tenuissime exten-
dendo[17] cum pincello asinino,[18] sic aptato; deinde ad solem exiccari bene permitte. At post,[19] cum siccatus fuerit color,
iterum superpone, sicut prius fecisti, de eodem, et spissiorem
pones; sed non ita spissiorem, ut abundancius[20] colorem super-

---

[1] *Est referendum* R. [2] *Hoc* omittit R. [3] *Denarios* xj. C. [4] *In* omittit C.
[5] *Asperitatem* P. [6] *Id* supplet P. [7] *Illud* omittit P. [8] *Operire* R. [9] Quod
sequitur novum capitulum facit P., cum titulo " *Quomodo ligni caverna-
culas seu fossulas implebis.*" [10] *Tantum* omittit P. [11] *Inpinge* P. [12] *Super
igne* R. [13] *Trivisses* P. [14] *Ipsam* supplet P. [15] *Album* omittit R. [16] *Lini*
omittit R. [17] *Extendo* P. *Exterende* Cant. [18] *Afornio* vel *Aforino* P.
[19] *Post* omittit R. [20] *Abundanciorem* R.

care never to lay on the colour too fat, for if you do this, and
lay on a great deal of it, when it begins to dry, wrinkles will
form on the surface of it.[1]   But now, in order that I may omit
nothing that relates to the subject, I beg you will let me return
to where I was speaking of the bare wood [if you were willing
to cover it with a leather or with a cloth].   If the wood, which
you wish to paint upon, is [not] smooth, cover it with leather
made of horse-skin or with parchment.

XXV. [262] *How a column is prepared for painting.*—If you
wish to paint on a column or slab of stone, first let it dry very
perfectly in the sun or before a fire.   Then take white, and grind
it very finely with oil upon a marble slab.   Afterwards, the column being well smoothed and polished, without any crevices,
lay on it two or three coats of that white, with a broad paint-
brush.   Then rub very stiff white over it with your hand or
with a brush, and let it remain a short time.   When tolerably
dry, press your hand strongly over the white surface, drawing
your hand towards you.   Continue to do this until it is as
smooth as glass.   You will then be able to paint upon it with
all colours mixed with oil.   But if you wish to imitate the
veins of marble on a general tint (brown, black, or any other
colour), you can give the appearance, when the ground so prepared is dry.[2]   Afterwards varnish it in the sun.

XXVI. [280] *If you wish to paint a linen cloth, and to lay
gold upon it, prepare it thus.*—Take parchment, or clippings of
parchment, and put them into a jar with water, which must be
placed over the fire and made to boil as before directed; then
dip a cloth into it, take it out immediately, and stretch it out
on a wet panel, and let it dry.   Then burnish or polish it all
over with a glass muller, and stretch it out, fastening it on to a

---

[1] See Mr. Eastlake's remarks on this subject, in his recent work, Materials for a History, &c., p. 37.

[2] I have adopted Mr. Eastlake's translation of this sentence.   Ibid.
p. 34.

ponas, sed ut oleum minus habeat. Nam et in hoc multum cavendum est ut nunquam crassiorem colorem superponas; quod si feceris et abunde posueris, cum exiccari cœperit, rugæ desuper erunt. Nunc autem ut ea quæ supersunt[1] simul omnia dicam, superius queso me redire permitte, ubi de ligni nuditate locutus sum, [si[2] illud corio vel panno operire volueris]. Quod si lignum, quod pingere volueris, non[3] fuerit equale, corio equino vel perchameno operi illud.

XXV. [262] *Quomodo preparatur columpna ad pingendum.*— Si vis aliquam columnam vel laminam de petra pingere, inprimis optime ad solem vel ad[4] ignem siccare permittes.[5] Deinde[6] album accipies,[7] et cum oleo super marmorem clarissime teres.[8] Postea illam columpnam jam bene sine aliqua fossula planam et politam, de illo albo cum lato pincello superlinies duabus vel[9] tribus vicibus. Postea imprimes cum manu vel brussa de albo spisso, et ita dimittes paululum. Cum vero modicum siccatum fuerit,[10] cum manu tua album[11] planando fortiter retrahes. Hoc tamdiu facies donec planum sit quasi vitrum. Tunc vero poteris desuper[12] de omnibus coloribus[13] cum oleo distemperatis pingere. Si vero marbrire volueris, super unum[14] colorem, vel brunum, vel nigrum, vel alium colorem, cum siccata fuerit[15] marbrire poteris. Postea vernicia[16] ad solem.

XXVI. [280] *Si vis pingere lini pannum, et aurum in ipso ponere, sic præpara.*—Accipe pergamenum vel minutias pergamenorum, et mitte in ollam cum aqua, et pone ad ignem, et fac bullire sicut suprascriptum est, et mitte in ea pannum, statimque extrahe, et desuper tabulam in aquam extende, et ita dimittes siccare, et tunc cum petra vitrea burnies, seu lissabis, per totum; postea extendes ipsum, ligando in lignis cum filo,

---

[1] *Superius* R.   [2] Ex P.; omittit R.   [3] *Volueris, non* P.; *vis* R.   [4] *Ad* omittit P.   [5] *Permittas* P.   [6] *Dein* R.   [7] *Accipe* P.   [8] *Tere* P.   [9] *Vel* omittit R.   [10] *Fuerit album siccatum* P.   [11] *Album* omittit P.   [12] *Desuper poteris* P.   [13] *Et* supplet P.   [14] *Unum* omittit R.   [15] *Fuerunt* R.   [16] *Verniza* P.

wooden frame with the thread. You may then paint upon it with colours distempered with size, or egg, or gum.[1]

XXVII. [281] *How to lay gold on the cloth.*—And if you wish to lay gold on the cloth, apply it with the before-mentioned size, and polish it.

XXVIII. [285] *Of the general practice in grinding all colours.*—You must know, however, that all colours may be ground with clear water, if they are afterwards allowed to dry ; and then with white of egg, or oil, or gum-water, or wine, or cervisia, when they are mixed or tempered.

XXIX. [260] *How oil is prepared for tempering colours.*—Put a moderate quantity of lime into oil and heat it, continually scumming it ; add ceruse to it according to the quantity of oil, and put it in the sun for a month or more, stirring it frequently. And know that the longer it remains in the sun, the better it will be. Then strain and keep it, and distemper the colours with it.

XXX. [263] *How alumen*[2] *is distempered.*—Grind the alumen with gum and water upon marble, and let it dry ; and when you wish to do anything with it, distemper it with white of egg.

XXXI. [284] *Of the manner of preparing white of egg for tempering colours.*—When you are going to prepare white of egg, take a filter, and dip it in water, and wet it well, and afterwards receive the white of egg mixed with water in this filter, which must be folded up so as to be pointed at the bottom and open at the top ; and so, squeezing it, make it pass through seven or eight times, or oftener or less frequently, if necessary, for you must do this until the white of egg becomes like water, and runs through without drawing into threads. Then take it and put it by ; or, if you wish, write with it. Two vases are necessary for preparing it.

---

[1] The sized cloth mentioned in this recipe was probably used for the transparent painting practised by the English and Germans. See Eastlake, Materials for a History, &c., p. 100.

[2] See No. L., where alumen is said to be a white colour.

deinde cum coloribus, cola, vel ovo, vel gummi distemperatis, desuper pingere poteris.

XXVII. [281] *Quomodo aurum ponitur in panno.*—Et si aurum desuper ipso panno ponere cupis, cum distemperatura suprascripta pones et polies.

XXVIII. [285] *De pratica generali in movendo omnes colores.* —Sciendum autem est quod omnes colores cum aqua clara moli possunt, si postea exsiccari permittantur, ut postea glarea, vel oleum, vel aqua gummata, aut acetum, seu vinum, necnon cervesia, quomodo misceantur aut temperentur.

XXIX. [260] *De oleo, quomodo aptatur ad distemperandum colores.*—Calcem in oleo mensurate pone, et illud despumando coque ; cerosium in eo secundum quod de oleo fuerit pone, et ad solem, per mensem, vel eo amplius, frequenter removendo, pone. Scito quod quanto diutius ad solem fuerit, tanto melius erit. Postea cola, et serva, et colores inde distempera.

XXX. [263] *Alumen quomodo debet distemperari.*—Alumen cum gumma et aqua super marmorem tere, et dimitte siccári, et cum aliquod ex eo facere volueris, cum glarea ovi distempera.

XXXI. [284] *De modo parandi glaream ovorum, ad colores ex ea temperandos.*—Glaream paraturus sume staminium, et in aqua intinge illud ; et madidum sit, ut postea glaream aque mixtam, in eodem staminio duplicato, subter summato (*acuminato ?*), desuper autem expanso, excipe, et sic exprimendo, fac transire vel septies vel octies, vel sæpius, vel minus, si necesse fuerit, tamdiu scilicet debes hoc facere, donec glarea quasi aqua fit, et tenuis, sine filo, distillet. Hinc susceptam reconde, vel, si vis, scribe. Ad hanc autem parandam, duo vascula sunt necessaria.

XXXII. [270] *How yolk of egg is prepared.*—Orpiment is ground and prepared with the yolk of egg in the following manner, and the yolk of egg is thus prepared :—Take the yolk in the middle of your hand, and prick it with a thorn or a needle, and, putting your finger upon it, press it out, and receive it in a vase ; and, adding a drop of water to it, mix it with the orpiment.   If you mix oil with it, it will never dry.   Mix it therefore with yolk of egg.

XXXIII. [258] *How Cordovan leather is dyed.*—Take the leather which is called " Cordovan," not dyed with colour, but pure and white, and wash over the side on which the hairs grew with alum.   Then take madder, and heat it over the fire in a brass vessel with wine or with water, so that you can just bear your finger in it.   Then dip the aforesaid leather into the vessel, and take it out ; see if the colour is sufficiently deep ; if it is, well and good ; if not, dip it in again.   Then spread it out on a smooth table, burnish it with a piece of box-wood ; and then take fat, and grease the skin all over, and suffer it to dry.

XXXIV. [277] *How to make use of brasilium.*—Take a brass dish, and scrape as much brasilium into it as you may think necessary ; then fill it up with urine ; add powdered alum to it, and so let it remain for a night.   The next day set it upon the coals, make it boil up once or twice ; remove the dish from the fire, and put a little quick-lime with the brasilium and alum and stir it up, and so let it stand till it settles thick, and the water floats on the top ; then throw away the water, and let the remainder dry in the sun, and keep it as long as you like. You may use this colour both on wood and on walls ; but with greater brilliancy on parchment.

XXXV. [289] *To make a rose-colour with braxilium.*—To make rose-colour, add urine to the braxilium before you put the alum ; and this is the way it is to be done.

XXXVI. [288] *How ceruse is made, and how red minium is made from that.*—If you wish to make red minium, or the white which is called ceruse, take lead plates, and put them into a

XXXII. [270] *Quomodo vitellum ovi paratur.*—Auripigmentum cum vitello ovi molitur et distemperatur sic, et vitellus
hoc modo paratur. Sume vitellum in media manu, et spunge
vel spina vel stila, et digito superposito, exprime, et in vase
recipe, mittens guttam aque ex auripigmento misce. Si autem
oleum miscueris, nunquam siccabitur. Ideo misce cum vitello.

XXXIII. [258] *Quomodo corduanum tingitur.*—Accipe corium, quem corduanum vocant, nondum coloribus tinctum, sed
purum et album, illamque partem, quæ prius pilis tegebatur, de
alumine ablues. Accipiesque Waranciam, et ad ignem in vase
æreo calefacies cum vino, vel cum aqua, et tantum ut digitum
tuum in ea mittere possis, et tunc corium antedictum in vase
merges et trahes, videbisque ; si fuerit rubeum, bene quidem ;
si non, iterum merge, dimittesque siccare ; postea super tabulam planam extendes, et cum baculo buxeo burnies ; deinde
adipem accipies, et pellem per totum inunges, sicque siccare
permittes.

XXXIV. [277] *Quomodo poteris de bresilio operari.*—Accipe
patellam æream, et brasilium intus rade, quantum tibi visum
fuerit. Postea imple eam urina, pulveriza desuper alumen, et
sic una nocte dimittes. In crastino super carbones mitte, unam
aut duas undias bullire facies, et retrahe ab igne patellam, et
pone parumper de viva calce cum brisillio et alumen, et insimul move, et ita dimittas ; dum spissum fuerit, et aqua desuper nataverit, projice foras, et reliquum ad solem permitte
siccum fieri, et serva quantum volueris. De hoc colore in
ligno et in muro operari poteris, mirabilius tamen in pergamenis.

XXXV. [289] *Quomodo rosa color fit de ligno braxillii.*—
Rosam faciendo, urinam pones cum brixillio priusquam pones
alumen, et sic faciendum.

XXXVI. [288] *Quomodo fit cerusa, et de ipsa rubeum minium.*
—Si vis facere rubeum minium, vel etiam album, qui cerusa
dicitur, accipe laminas plumbeas, et mitte in ollam novam, et

new jar, and so fill the jar with very strong vinegar, and cover it up and set it in some warm place, and leave it so for a month. Then open the jar, and put what you find adhering to the slips of lead into another jar, and place it upon the fire, and keep stirring up the colour until it becomes as white as snow. Then remove it from the fire, and take as much as you like of that colour, which is called ceruse. Put the rest back over the fire, and keep stirring it until it becomes red minium. I recommend you to continue stirring it, because, if it is not stirred, it turns back again to white lead. Then take it from the fire and let the jar cool.

XXXVII. [265] *How terre verte is distempered.*—Take mallow, and distemper it with vinegar or with very good wine, and with this juice distemper the terre-verte, and it will be a good colour for walls.

XXXVIII. [273] *How to make a green colour from salt.*—I have often mentioned a green colour, and now I will tell you how I make it. I take a piece of oak, of whatever length and breadth I please, and scoop it out into the shape of a scrinium. I then take copper, and cause it to be hammered out into plates as long as I choose; that is, so that their length may cover the breadth of the hollow wood. Afterwards I take a ladleful of salt, and pressing it strongly down, I put it into the fire for a night, and cover it up with coals; and the next day grind it very carefully upon a dry stone. I then take small twigs, and place them in the aforesaid wood, so that two parts of the hollow wood may be underneath and the third above. Then smearing the copper-plates on both sides with honey, I sprinkle the salt all over the honey, then shake the plates over the ladle to avoid waste, and then place the plates upon the twigs. I next cover up the hollow wood with another piece made for this purpose, and lute it all round with clay well mixed with asses'-dung. But before I cover up the hollow wood, I pour into it hot vinegar or hot urine, so as to fill one-third part of it, and then cover it up, and afterwards do as before directed with this colour.

sic imple illam ollam fortissimo aceto, et cooperi, et mitte in
aliquo calido loco, et sic uno mense dimitte ; et tunc aperies
ollam, et quod inveneris in circuitu laminarum plumbearum
mitte in aliam ollam, et pone super ignem, et semper movebis
ipsum colorem, donec efficiatur albus sicut nix, et tunc tolles
ab igne, et sumes de ipso colore quantum vis, et iste color
vocatur cerusa ; reliquam partem pone super ignem, et semper
movebis donec efficiatur rubeum minium. Propterea moneo ut
moveas, quod si non moveris, semper iterum vertetur in album
plumbum, et sic tolle ab igne, et ipsam ollam dimitte refrigerari.

XXXVII. [265] *Quomodo distemperatur viride terrenum.—*
Accipe malvam, et distempera cum aceto, vel optimo vino, et
de isto jussu terrenum viridem distempera, et erit boni coloris
in muro.

XXXVIII. [273] *Quomodo efficitur viridis color cum sale.—*
Sæpe tractavi de viridi colore, quali modo efficiatur. Nunc vero
quomodo id ipsum facio narrabo. Lignum quercinum sumo
quantæ latitudinis et longitudinis voluero, et illud in modum
scrinii cavo ; deinde cuprum accipio, et facio illud attenuari in
laminas tam longas quantum mihi placet, scilicet ut longitudo
ejus operiat latitudinem concavi ligni. Posthoc accipio scutellam
plenam salis, et, comprimens eum fortiter, mitto in ignem per
noctem, et cooperio carbonibus, et in crastinum super lapidem
molo diligentissime siccum. Postea accipio surculas graciles,
colloco eas in predictum lignum, tamen ita ut duæ partes ligni
cavi sint inferius, et tertia superius, sicque liniens laminas
cupreas utraque parte melle, et desuper mel sal aspergens per
totum, moxque excutio laminas in scutellam, ne pereat, sicque
super surculas illas laminas pono. Tunc lignum concavum
altero ligno adhuc aptato cooperio, et in circuitu totum argilla
bene fimo asini mixto linio. Antequam autem lignum illud
concavum cooperuerim, ponam intus vel acetum calidum, vel
urinam calidam, ita ut tertia pars impleatur, et mox cooperio ;
tunc deinceps facio quod de hoc colore suprascriptum est.

XXXIX. [287] *A manner of making green with copper or brass.*—Fill a basin with white wine vinegar, and put into it strips of copper, and throw into it any other copper that you can procure; let it remain there for the space of one, two, or three months, and you will then find an excellent green colour.

XL. [261] *How orpiment is prepared for use.*—Crush the orpiment in leather, and afterwards grind it with water upon marble, adding to it a little calcined bone, and so let it dry there.   Distemper it afterwards with egg for painting on wood, or on walls; but on paper, distemper it like ceruse.   If it is not good, mix ochre with it, and then it will do.

XLI. [264] *How to lay on gold.*[1]—Take ochre and distemper it with water, and let it dry.   In the mean while make glue with vellum, and afterwards whip some white of egg.   Then mix the glue and the white of egg, and grind the ochre (which will by this time be well dried) strongly upon a marble slab, and, as soon as the ochre is dry, lay it on the parchment with a paint-brush, wherever you wish to lay the gold on the parchment, and then apply the gold, and let it remain so without pressing it with the stone.   When it is dry burnish it well with a tooth.   This is what I learned by experiment, and have frequently proved, and you may safely believe that I have told you the truth.

XLII. [278] *How to gild on parchment.*[2]—Take gypsum and white of Apulia, and carminium,[3] that is to say, cinnabar, namely, one third part of gypsum, and two equal parts of white and of carminium.   Mix them well, and grind them on a marble slab, and add to them only a little thin glue; and with this mordant you may lay on gold wherever you like, and you may keep it a long time.

---

[1] See Sloane MS. No. 1754.   [2] Ibid.

[3] Carminium is here represented to be synonymous with Cinnabar; but at p. 252 it is said to be composed of white and ochre.

XXXIX. [287] *Modus faciendi viridem cupri vel æris.*—Imple pelvim de aceto albo vini, et quicquid cupri poteris habere, projice intus, et sic stare permittes per spatium unius mensis vel duorum vel trium, et postea optimum viridem procreatum invenies.

XL. [261] *Quomodo auripigmentum præparatur ad operandum.*—Auripigmentum confringe in corio, postea tere cum aqua super marmorem, addens ei parum ossis combusti, et ibidem siccare permitte. Postea distempera cum ovo ad ponendum in ligno vel in muro, sed in carta pone sicut cerosium. Si non est bonum, misce ocrum ; postea valet.

XLI. [264] *Quomodo ponitur aurum.*[1]—Accipe ocrum, et distempera cum aqua, sicque dimittes siccare. Interim de pergameno [2] vitulino colam facies. Postea glaream de ovo facies. Tunc colam et glaream insimul misces, et ocrum jam [3] bene siccatum [4] fortiter super marmorem teres, et ubi volueris ponere aurum in pergameno, statim ut molitum fuerit ocrum, super pergamenum cum [5] pincello trahes, sicque aurum desuper illico pones, dimittesque siccare [6] ita sine impressione coti.[7] Postea, cum siccatum fuerit,[8] cum dente fortiter burnies.[9] Ecce ut sæpe experimento didici, multociens probavi, et tua certa fide verum dixi.

XLII. [278] *Quomodo aurum in pergamenis ponitur.*[10]—Accipe gipsum, et album de Pullia[11] et carminium, i. e. cinobrium,[12] tertiam partem de gipso, et de albo, et[13] de carminio[14] duas partes equales, et misce simul, et tere super marmorem, adjungesque eis[15] modicum colle, tenue tamen,[16] et de hac distemperatura poteris aurum ubicunque volueris ponere, et multum[17] diu servare.

---

[1] Sic P.; *De temperamento auri* S. No. 63. [2] *Percameno* passim S. [3] *Jam* omittit S. [4] *Teres* hic inserit et post omittit P. [5] *Percameno illo* S. [6] *Siccare* omittit P. [7] *Et* supplet S. [8] *Cum siccatum fuerit* omittit S. [9] Quæ sequuntur omittit S. [10] Sic P. *Item de distemperatura auri* S. [11] *Apuleya* S. No. 64. [12] *Carominium id est sinobium* S. [13] *Quod* P. [14] *Carominio* S. [15] *Cum iis* S. [16] *Tantum* P. [17] *Multum* omittit S.

XLIII. [279] *How to write with gold.*[1]—Take a glass vase and fill it with urine, and let it rest until it appears clear. Then take the white of an egg well whipped, and divide it into two parts, and mix it with the urine, and stir them both together, and put them into a horn with gold dissolved, that is, ground, and then washed. You may write with this gold as with any other colour.

XLIV. [274] *Of auripetrum.*—Secundum Magistrum R. Take oil made from linseed, and put it into a new jar, and take the bark of "vesprum" very well dried and well ground in a mortar, and let it lie for a night in the oil. The next day boil it as long as you may think proper, but not much, and then pass it through a cloth into another jar, and boil it again a little over the fire with myrrh and aloes. Strain it again, and immediately put *vernix* with it, and heat it upon the coals. But if you have no *vernix*, take *glassa*, and put it with the aloes and myrrh instead of *vernix*, and, as I said before, strain it again. If you have not the bark of *vesprum* take dry *incaustum*, or else the bark of black-thorn dried and ground, and, as I said before, boil it with the myrrh and aloes, and afterwards remove it from the fire, and when it is cold, put it away in a vase to preserve as long as you like. You must collect the bark in March or April, and dry it in May, and keep it as long as you like.

XLV. [275] *How to gild upon tin.*—Take tin and place it on a tablet well whitened for this purpose, and well dried. Hammer the tin out well, and polish it with water and flint, rubbing it both along and across. Then take a polished iron made for this purpose, and polish it again with water. When it is very bright, let it dry, and then take it again and lay it on a table and burnish it with flint. And you may work with this gold on wood or on walls, and wherever you wish to gild.

---

[1] See Sloane MS. No. 1754.

XLIII. [279] *Quomodo scribitur de auro.*[1]—Sume tibi vas vitreum, et urina tua illud imple ; sicque, donec appareat clara, requiescat ; postea accipe glaream ovi optime fractam,[2] et fac duas partes, miscesque cum urina, et movebis utrumque [3] insimul, et pone in cornu cum auro soluto [*i.e.* molito et postea lavato [4]], itaque [5] poteris de tali [6] auro scribere sicut de alio colore.

XLIV. [274] *De auro petro.*—Secundum magistrum R. Accipe oleum de lini semine factum, et pone in ollam novam. Accipies que corticem de vespro optime siccatam, et in mortario bene tritam, et in oleo eam unam noctem jacere permittes. In crastino ad ignem bullies ; quando satis tibi visum fuerit, tamen non multum, protinus per medium pannum in aliam ollam transire facies, deinde iterum ad ignem cum mirra et aloe parumper bullies. Iterum colabis, statimque vernix cum eis pones, et super carbones calefacies. Si autem vernix non habueris, accipies glassam, et pones cum aloe et mirra pro vernix, et, ut dixi, iterum colabis. Si autem corticem de vespro non habueris, accipe incaustum siccum, vel etiam corticem de nigra spina siccatam et tritam, et, sicut supra scripsi, cum mirra et áloe bullies, post hoc retrahes ab igne, et, cum frigidum fuerit, ad servandum in vase, quanto tempore volueris, repone. Cortices autem in Martio vel in Aprili accipies, et in Majo siccabis, et servabis quamdiu volueris.

XLV. [275] *Quomodo ponitur aurum super stagnum.*—Accipe stagnum, et pone super tabulam ad hoc opus optime dealbatam, et bene siccatam, extende, et cum silica et aqua in longitudinem et latitudinem poli ; deinde sume ferrum totum aceratum, ad hoc opus factum, et iterum cum aqua poli. Cum multum et stans fuerit, sic siccare dimittes ; postea accipies iterum, et super tabulam pones, et cum silice burnies eum. Poterisque de hoc auro in ligno vel in muro operari, et ubi volueris ponere.

---

[1] *De* omittit S. No. 65.   [2] *Factam* S.   [3] *Utrumque* omittit S.   [4] Ex P. Omittit S.   [5] *Et* S.   [6] *Tali* omittit S.

XLVI. [246] *How borax¹ is distempered and kept.*—Take bean-ashes, and strain them through a cloth into a jar three or four times, and afterwards boil them [with water] over the fire unt^l the ley is thick like ink, and then take the liquor which is called borax, and grind it in a vase or cup like cummin or pepper, and then mix it with the aforesaid ley. Then make it boil again, and keep stirring it, and then remove it from the fire, and put it into a leaden vase, and you may keep it as long as you like.

XLVII. [247] *Also on the same subject in another manner.*— Also, take the same ley, fresh made, and mix it with a little borax previously well ground in a shell, and then take copper reduced to powder of the weight of 12 denarii, (├∴┤), and grind it well in a shell, like pepper, and mix it with the ley and borax, and boil it over the fire, and afterwards let it cool, and put it into a copper vase, and preserve it as long as any remains.

XLVIII. [248] *How to make nigellum.*—When you wish to make nigellum, take quicksilver, and copper, and lead, in equal quantities by measure, and put them into a shell to fuse together. Then take 6 denarii by weight of sulphur, and mix with the other ingredients, and stir them well. Then remove the mixture from the fire, and let it cool, and put it into a vase; then take atramentum distempered with wine, and draw what you like upon the silver with the atramentum, and immediately lay the powder made of the quicksilver, copper, and lead upon it [and heat it] until it melts, and it will make a beautiful nigellum.

XLIX. [272] *How to paint upon glass.*—I must tell you how to paint upon glass. Take a grossinum of sapphire, and the scales which are beaten off red-hot iron upon the blacksmith's anvil; and you must put one-third part of this with the grossi-

---

¹ I have no doubt that " Bures " should be read " Borax," and I refer to the note on this subject in the Table of Synonymes. It will be observed that the Bures of the text is said to be a liquor; it is unnecessary to remark that this is scarcely consistent with the direction to " grind it like cummin or

XLVI. [246] *Quomodo distemperatur bures et servatur.*—Accipe cinerem fabarum, et cola per pannum in ollam tribus vicibus aut quatuor, postea ad ignem bullire facies donec spissum sit quasi incaustum ; deinde accipias illum liquorem qui vocatur bures, et teres in vase vel cipho quasi caminum vel piper ; tunc misces cum laxiva suprascripta, iterumque bullire facies, semperque movebis. Postea tolle ab igne, et in plumbeo vase pone, et poteris servare quamdiu volueris.

XLVII. [247] *Item de eodem aliter.*—Item accipe eandem laxivam cum nuper fuerit facta, et misces cum ea parum de bures bene in conca prius maceratum ; deinde accipies pulverem de cupro factam pensantem xii^{cim} denarios, et macerabis fortiter in conca velut piper, et cum lexiva bures misces, et ad ignem bullire facies. Postea sine refrigerari et in vase cupreo mitte, et serva quantum duraverit.

XLVIII. [248] *Quali modo nigellum facies.*—Quando volueris nigellum facere, accipe de argento vivo, et de cupro, et plumbo, equali mensura, et mitte in conca, ut simul coquantur. Tunc accipe sulphuris pondus vj denariorum, et cum eis misces, et movebis. Postea retrahe ab igne, et sine refrigerari, in vase pone ; deinde accipe attramentum cum vino distemperatum, et facies quod volueris super argentum de attramento, statimque pulverem de argento vivo et cupro et plumbo superpones, donec fundatur, fietque pulcrum nigellum.

XLIX. [272] *Quomodo pingitur in vitro.*—Dicendum quomodo pingere debes in vitro. Accipe grossinum de saphiro, et palleam, quæ excutitur de calido ferro super incudem fabri, cum grossino tertiam partem pones, et plumbeum vitrum, Judeum

---

pepper." A similar direction is repeated in the following recipe. I consider that in both cases the Borax was prepared as a flux for the nigellum in No. xlviii.

num, and mix it with lead glass, that is, Jewish glass,[1] and grind it well on an iron slab, and so you will be able to paint.

L. [240] *On the various kinds and names of the principal and intermediate colours. And on the advantage of mixing them together; and on the places in which they are found, and are produced. or exist, and on the means of knowing the goodness of them.*—Of colours, some are white, and some are black, and some are intermediate. And the species of white are ceruse, lime, and alumen. The blacks are fuscus and those which are made from twigs. The intermediate colours are red, green, yellow, purple, prasinus, azure, and Incicus [Indigo ?], which are each of them, in themselves, beautiful; but are more so when mixed, because, by their variety, they give beauty to one another. And then, in composition they have a different hue, for as in medicinal preparations the various drugs mixed together modify each other; so colours of different kinds are mixed together, in order that they may partake of the nature of the others as well as of their own, and make as many, and beautiful, and pleasing, varieties as possible.

In this mixture, and in the order in which one is laid over another in painting, great skill is exercised. For after white, black or red should be put as an intermediate, because yellow, in composition, is in the second degree of mediocrity, for a colour too thick or too thin, soon alters.

Reds are produced in many places, but the best are found in Pontus and Spain.[2] "Paratonium"[3] is named from the place where it is dug. In the same manner, also, "Meline earth," a kind of metal, is found in some of the Cyclades, and receives its name from it. Green earth[4] is found in many

---

[1] In an extract published by Mr. Hendrie from a copy of the MS. of Le Begue, "judicatim scilicet" is inserted instead of "Judeum scilicet." So little is known of the history of glass-making, that it is impossible to say whether the glass mentioned in the text resembled in *any* respect the "Jews' glass," which used to be sold at Birmingham.—(See a paper in the 'Philosophical Magazine' for Dec. 1836.) The latter was a ruby-coloured glass, coloured with gold; but as Bulengerus says ('De Pictura,' &c. lib. ii. cap. v.), "Sine plumbo nullum metallum in vitrum transire

scilicet, misces, et super marmorem fortiter teres, sicque pingere potes.

L. [240] *De diversis colorum principalium et intermediorum speciebus et nominibus et de utilitate mixtionis eorum ad invicem, et de locis in quibus inveniuntur, et nascuntur, vel sunt, et de cognicione perfectionis eorum.*—Colorum alii sunt albi, alii nigri, alii sunt medii. Et albi quidem species, cerusa, calx, alumen. Nigri vero, fuscus, et qui ex sarmentis componitur. Medii, rubeus, viridis, croceus, purpureus, prasinus, azur, et incicus; quorum expressio per se cujuslibet pulcra est, sed interdum sic invicem permixti pulcriores fiunt, quia sua varietate graciam alter alteri præstant: Dein compositi aliud monstrant, nam ut in medicinæ confectionibus species sibi permixtæ invicem conferunt, sic colores non ejusdem qualitatis, ut partem ex alterius natura, partem ex sua trahant, et quam plurimas eorum varietates pulcras et delectabiles reddant, simul commiscentur. In qua commixtione, et in eo modo quo in pictura alter alteri post se ponuntur, summa est subtilitas; siquidem post album, niger, aut rubeus medius, convenit; quoniam crocus, in temperacione, mediocritas secunda est, quia color nimium spissus, et nimium tenuis, cito deficit.

Rubi itaque multis locis generantur, sed optimi Ponto, et in Hispania, nascuntur. Paratonium ex ipso loco unde foditur habet nomen. Eadem racione et melinus quidem, metalli species, per insulas Cycladis, inde dicitur. Creta viridis pluribus locis nascitur, sed optima in Creta Cirina, quæ Græce dicitur Theodote quædam, in cujus solo primum est inventa. Arzicon, id est, auripigmentum, in Ponto nascitur. Sandaraca

---

potest," it is not improbable that glass coloured with gold was composed partly of lead; and if, as appears from the text, lead glass was called " Jewish glass," this may sufficiently account for the appellation given to the glass made at Birmingham.

² See Vitruvius, lib. vii. cap. vii.

³ Paratonium and Meline earth, or Melino, are both white minerals.

⁴ The author of the French Commentary on Pliny, published at London in 1725, observes that Isidore mentions green earth, which he calls " Prasinus."

places, but the best in "creta cirina," which in Greek is called
Theodote,[1] in which territory it was first found. "Arzicon,"[2]
that is, orpiment, is found in Pontus. "Sandaraca"[3] is found
in many places, but the best is found in Pontus, and by the
river Ysparis.[4] Azure is mentioned as having been first found
in the Ephesian territory and afterwards in Spain, and with it
are connected the following inventions.[5]

LI. [241] *On trying azure.*—Now azure must be tried in the
following manner: Put it on an iron plate, and hold it over the
fire until it is red-hot. Then take it out and let it cool. If it
does not change colour, it will be good; but if it does change
colour, it is adulterated.

When ice,[6] therefore, is first cut off metals, drops of quicksilver are pressed out, which artificers collect for various purposes, for neither silver nor brass can be gilt without it. When
the drops of quicksilver are run together, so as to fill a measure
of 4 sextarii, they will weigh one hundred pounds. If upon
this liquor you place a stone weighing a hundred pounds,
it will float on it. If you put a scruple into this liquor, it will
sink, whence you may see that the difference does not consist
in the weight of the substance but in the nature of it. Also, if
the goldsmith wish to obtain the gold from the tinder of burnt
frieze, let him wash it, and mix it with quicksilver, and then
press it in a linen or cotton cloth, so that the quicksilver may
be expressed, and the gold remain.

---

[1] Vitruvius says it was called "Theodotion," because the name of the
owner of the estate where it was found was Theodotus.

[2] The word Arzicon appears to be a corruption of "Arsenicon," the
Greek name for Orpiment.

[3] The term "Sandaraca" is applied to red orpiment and also to red
lead; both are occasionally found native.

[4] Hypanis, according to Vitruvius.

[5] A native mineral azure is here described, which appears, from the test
mentioned in the next chapter, to be Lapis Lazuli. The author of this work
appears to have been unacquainted with the azure described by Vitruvius,
which consisted of a blue glass formed of nitre, sand, and copper filings.

[6] This obscure passage appears to be an abridgment of cap. viii. of the
7th book of Vitruvius. The original MS. may have been imperfect, or

pluribus locis generatur, sed optima in Ponto et juxta flumen Ysparim. Azurii autem natura, primum Ephesiorum solo reperta, memoratur deinceps in Hispania, cujus natura has invenciones habet.

LI. [241] *De probatione azurii.*—Verum probacio azurii sic erit observanda. In lamina ferrea mittatur, et super ignem ponatur, tamdiu donec lamina rubescat. Tunc retrahatur ut refrigescat. Si colorem non mutaverit, optimum erit; si autem mutaverit, viciatum erit.

Glades itaque, vel glaciens, cum ex metallis primum exciduntur, argenti vivi guttas exprimunt, quas artifices ad plures usus colligunt. Neque enim argentum, neque æs, sine hiis inaurari possunt. Nam confuse in unum guttæ argenti vivi, ita ut quatuor sextariorum mensuram habeant, centum libræ pondus efficiunt. Supra cujus liquorem centenarium saxi pondus si posueris, sustinebit; scrupulum si posueris, descendit. Unde intelliges non ponderis esse, sed naturæ distinctionem. Itaque si aurifex pannis tostilibus adustis ex friso in rudi vase fictili solidari pulverem voluerit, lava, postea mixtum argento vivo, vel in panno, vel in linthiolo, cumprimis, ut liquor argenti vivi expressus emanet, et aurum extrinsecus remaneat.

---

something may have been omitted by Le Begue, for this paragraph is evidently unconnected with the first part of the chapter. The following extract from Vitruvius (lib. vii., cap. viii.) may render the passage more intelligible :—" Ingrediar nunc Minii rationes explicare.....Foditur enim gleba, quæ Anthrax dicitur antequam tractionibus ad minium perveniat, vena uti ferreo magis subrufo colore, habens circa se rubrum pulverem ; cum id foditur, ex plagis ferramentorum crebras emittit lacrymas argenti vivi, quæ a fossoribus statim colliguntur."

LII. [242] *On the mixture of colours, and what the colours are,*
particularly lakes, which are used for want of other colours.—
It is evident that all colours are corrupted by mixing them ;
although, indeed, in tempering " folium," lime made from hard
stone is used, lest the colour should fade for want of body.
For when "folium" is distempered with a pernicious quantity
of albumen, that is white of egg, it can [not?] be employed
with great beauty and advantage.   The juice of dragon's blood,
and "sandis," that is, madder—is used either pure or with red
chalk ; other juices of a similar kind are also mixed with green
or yellow earth.   " Crisicula¹" [chrysocolla] comes from Ma-
cedon, and is dug in copper mines.   *Indicus* by its name shows
whence it is brought.

LIII. [243] *How atramentum of various kinds is made.²*—
The method of making ink is as follows, for it is necessary, not
only for use in painting, but even for every day writing.   A vase
is put into a hollow chamber ; and a furnace is made so as to
have nostrils, that is, apertures, through which the smoke can
penetrate into the vase.   Some tiles must then be laid in the
furnace, and upon these hot tiles resin must be put, so as to
drive all the smoke and soot into the vase.   Afterwards grind
the soot very fine, and you will make a very bright atramentum, with which you must mix painter's size.   To accelerate
the process, soft charcoal of wood, or of peach-stones, ground
up with glue, is useful.   Charred twigs also will imitate the
appearance of atramentum ; but the blackest twigs must be
used.   If good wine is poured over them, and glue be added,
they will form a colour which will appear to imitate the softness of daylight.

LIV. [245] *How to make a "purpurino"³ colour out of various*
things in various ways.—Stones or flints, that is, stones emitting
fire, seem very necessary for painting, when they are heated in
the fire, and quenched with very strong vinegar, and they will give

---

¹ See Vitruv., lib. vii. c. ix.   ² Ibid. c. x.

³ Ibid. cap. xi. This chapter treats of red or crimson colours, and not
of the " Purpurino " of the Italians.

LII. [242] *De colorum commixtione, et quales ipsi colores sunt, præcipue infectivi, quibus utitur propter aliorum colorum inopiam.*—Colores autem omnes commixtione corrumpi manifestum est. Siquidem in temperamento folii utilitur calx ex duro saxa facta, ne minus pressus pereat. Quippe aqua distemperato folicio, cum perniciosa quantita albuginis, id est, glarea ovi, pulcherrime et utiliter miscetur. Sanguis drachonis aut sandis, id est, garancia; ejus autem purus succus, aut creta rubea, viridi quoque, et croceo, alii suæ qualitatis permiscentur. Crisicula a Macedonia venit, foditur autem ex metallis ærariis. Indicum ab ipsis ostenditur ubi nascitur.

LIII. [243] *Quomodo fit attramentum diversarum specierum.*—Attramenti vero compositio sic erit observanda, quæ non solum ad usum picture necessaria videtur, sed etiam at cothidianas scripturas. Vasculus curva camera servatur : fornacula sic componatur, ut nares, id est, suspiracula, habeantur in vasculo, quibus fumus possit intrare. Tegulæ in eadem fornace intendantur. Super tegulas ardentes resina mittatur, ut omnem fumum et fuliginem per nares in vasculum exprimat. Postea fuliginem diligenter conteres, et attramentum facies nitidum, pictorum autem gluten misceas ipsi. Ad accelerationem etiam operis, carbones molles ligni, et ossium persicorum, cum glutino contriti, valent. Nec minus sarmenta exusta attramenti qualitatem imitabunt, sed sarmenta quæ nigrioris coloris sunt, si in optimo vino perfundantur, postea exusta fuerint, addito glutino, imitari etiam diei suavitatem monstrabunt.

LIV. [245] *Quomodo fit purpurinus color ex diversis diversimode.*—Utique plurimum necessaria in operibus picturæ videntur glebæ vel silices, id est, lapides ignem emittentes, cum in igne cocuntur, tunc, aceto acerrimo perfuso, extinguuntur, et

a purple colour.   Copper burnt becomes ceruse.[1]   The oster [2]
also, the blood of which is used for a purple colour, is found in
many places, but the best are found in the island of Cyprus,
when they grow with the sun [i. e. in the spring].   Having,
therefore, cut them round, pound them, and they will give out
drops of a purple colour, which, being run together, are tempered as a purple pigment.   This pigment is called "oster,"
because it is obtained from the above liquor, which soon solidi-
fies on account of its saltness.

LV. [245] *Of lakes ; and how they are made of various substances in various manners.*[3]—Purple colours are also made by
straining [a decoction of] boiled madder roots. So also other colours are dyed with flowers.   Thus, when painters wish to imitate
sil atticum they put dried violets[4] into a vase of water over the
fire to boil, and, when boiled down, they are strained through
a linen cloth, and rubbed down in a mortar with chalk, and so
a colour like sil atticum is made.   In the same manner, tempering "vaccinium" with milk, a very elegant purple colour is
made ; so the herb which is called "litea"[5] gives out an azure
juice ; and a very deep green colour is also made.   These are
called "infectivi ;" and are used for want of simple colours.
In the same manner, also, mixing formosa or angularia[6] with
glass, they make colours with it.

LVI. [282] *On mixing colours together in painting, and in
illuminating ; and of the ways in which pictures are filled in with
them, and how the lights and shades are laid on.*[7]—Mix azure
with ceruse ; shade it with indigo ; lay on the lights with white-
lead.   Shade pure vermilion with brunum or with dragon's

---

[1] There is probably some mistake here.   See Vitruv., lib. vii. cap. xii.

[2] Ibid. cap. xiii.

[3] Ibid. cap. xiv.

[4] The Viola lutea, or Wall-flower.

[5] Lutea—The Reseda Luteola—Dyer's weed, Weld. See Vitruv., ibid.

[6] The annularia of Vitruvius and Pliny.

[7] This chapter and the next are certainly translations from some Byzantine MS. The term Bisctum, Biseth, occurs frequently. It is a corruption

reddent purpureum colorem. Cuprum adustum fit cerusa. Oster autem, cujus sanguinem qui pro colore purpuræ temperatur, pluribus locis nascitur, sed optimum in insula Cipri, cum solis cursum habentur. Concute itaque, cum circumcisæ fuerint, lacrimas in purpureum colorem emittunt, quibus collectis, purpureus color temperatur. Hoc autem oster est appellatum, quod ex humore licetur, qui cito ex salsugine inhærescit.

LV. [245] *De coloribus infectivis, et quomodo fiunt ex diversis diversimode.*—Fiunt etiam purpurei colores, infecta cocta rubea radice. Similiter ex floribus alii colores inficiuntur. Itaque pictores, cum voluerint silvaticum imitari, viola arida in aqua cum vase ad ignem ponatur, ut ferveat, et decoctam in linteolo exprimunt, et in mortario cum creta terunt, et faciunt silasacetum colorem. Eadem ratione, vaccinium cum lacte temperantes, purpureum faciunt eleganter, uti herba quæ litea appellatur, succum efficit cæruleum, et utuntur viridissimo colore. Hæc infectiva appellantur, quibus utitur propter inopiam colorum simplicium. Simili modo cum in formosam seu angulariam vitro miscentes, inficiunt ex ea colores.

LVI. [282] *De miscendis inter se coloribus pingendo et illuminando, et de modis cum de ipsis implentur opera et matizantur et inciduntur alter ex altero.*—Azurium misces cum cerosio; incides de indico; matizabis de albo plumbo. Vermiculum purum incides de bruno, aut de sanguine draconis; matizabis

---

of Pezzette, the Italian name for those pieces of rag dipped in the juice of certain plants, which were used in painting, and for other purposes. The Turks and inhabitants of the Levant still call them " Bezerere Rubré " (see Pierre Pomet, Histoire Générale des Drogues, Tit. Tornesole). In the west of Europe they were called Bezette or Bezeth. From the term " Vergaut," which occurs in this recipe, and which appears to signify " Vert bleu," " blue green," or " Verde azzurro," I should think the translation was by a Frenchman.

blood ; lay on the lights with orpiment or minium. Also mix vermilion with white-lead, and make the colour which is called rosa ; shade with vermilion ; lay on the lights with white [and] rosa, or with white-lead. Also make a colour with dragon's blood and orpiment ; shade it with brunum ; lay on the lights with orpiment. Shade carminium with brunum ; vary with minium. Shade folium with brunum ; lay on the lights with bisetum folii. Also mix folium with white ; shade it with folium ; lay on the lights with white-lead. Shade ochre with vermilion ; lay on the lights with white [and ?] ochre. Also shade ochre with green ; lay on the lights with white. Shade white with pure minium ; and vary with azure. Shade brunum with black ; lay on the lights with azure or minium. Also mix brunum with white, and it will make a beautiful rose colour ; shade with brunum ; lay on the lights with white or with bisetum folii. Also mix brunum with minium ; shade with black ; and lay on the lights with red minium. Mix orpiment with azure or indigo, or ochre with indigo, or green, and it will be good " vergaut ;" then vary with brunum or black ; lay on the lights with orpiment or with bisetum. Shade green with black ; lay on the lights with bisetum. Mix green with white ; shade with green ; lay on the lights with white. Shade brunum with black ; lay on the lights with vergaut or with minium mixed with brunum. Shade indigo with black ; lay on the lights with azure, or vergaut, or bisetum. Shade orpiment with vermilion ; lay on the lights with white [and ?] orpiment. Carminium is made with white and ochre.

LVII. [283] *On colours incompatible with each other.*—Now, if you wish to know which are the colours that are incompatible with each other, they are these :—Orpiment does not agree with folium, or with green, or with minium. Nor does green agree with folium, namely, in the mixture of the materials of the said pigments, and in the works in which they are employed together.

de auripigmento aut de minio. Item, vermiculum misce cum albo plumbo, et facies colorem qui vocatur rosa ; incide de vermiculo ; matizabis de [alba[1] rosa, aut de] albo plumbo. Item, facies colorem de sanguine draconis et de auripigmento ; incide de bruno ; matizabis de auripigmento. Carminium incide de bruno ; de rubeo minio undabis.[2] Folium incide de bruno ; matiza de biseto folii.[3] Item, misce folium cum albo ; incide de folio ; matiza de albo plumbo.[4] Ocrum incide de vermiculo ; matiza de albo ocro. Item, ocrum incide de viride ; matiza de albo. Album minii purum incide, et undabis simul de azuro. Brunum incide de nigro ; matiza de azurio vel minio. Item, misces brunum cum albo, fietque pulcra rosa ; incide de bruno ; matiza de albo, vel de biseto folii. Item, brunum misces cum minio ; incides de nigro ; matiza de rubeo minio. Misce auripigmentum cum azurio vel indico, aut ocrum cum indico, vel viride, et erit bonum vergaut ; inde de bruno, aut de nigro, undabis ; auripigmento aut de biseth matizabis. Viride incide de nigro, et matizabis de biseto. Misce viride cum albo ; incide de viride ; matiza de albo. Brunum incide de nigro ; matiza de vergaut, aut de minio mixto cum bruno. Indicum incide de nigro ; matiza de azurio, vel de vergaut, aut biseth. Auripigmentum incide de vermiculo ; matiza de albo auripigmento. Carminium fit de albo et ocro.

LVII. [283] *De coloribus sibi contrariis.*—Modo si vis scire qui sunt colores qui sibi invicem alter alteri sunt contrarii, hi sunt. Auripigmentum non concordat cum folio, nec cum viride, nec cum minio. Nec viride concordat cum folio, scilicet in mixturis materiarum ipsorum colorum, et operationibus mixtis eorum, quæ discordantiæ non sunt in qualitatibus colorum, nec

---

[1] Ex P. ; in alteris omittitur.   [2] *Matizabis de rubeo minio.* C.
[3] *De albo plumbo* C.   [4] *Albo folio* P.

And these discordances are not in the mere [optical qualities of
the pigments, nor in their accidents of colour ; for there are no
colours, or qualities of colours, either simple or mixed, which, as
regards the colour only, do not agree with any other sorts of
colours in mixtures, namely, for composing other different mixtures ; and you may thus have at pleasure almost innumerable
varieties of colours. But the said discordances are, and are to
be understood as being, in the other natural conditions, incident
to the substance of the said pigments, they being contrary to each
other in such manner that, if they are mixed together, one substance, by a certain natural incompatibility, either changes the
other or is changed by it ; and so the quality and beauty of
the pigments themselves, as well separate as mixed, and their
own substance, and the work done with them, are spoiled and
destroyed. They therefore do not bear to be mixed together ;
and so, in the art of painting, besides the consideration that
is to be had for the varieties of colour, and these and other
things relating to the said art, we must not forget the proper
and necessary considerations, drawn from a true theoretical and
practical knowledge of and acquaintance with the natural conditions and contrarieties existing in the materials and liquors of
the said colours, and of the contrarieties of the other things incident to that art.

LVIII. [286] *Of the care which must be taken with regard to
the nature of the colours and of the way of mixing them together,
and of the method to be observed in shading and laying on the
lights, on which another chapter has been inserted.*—If you wish to
know well the natures of the colours, and the mixtures of them,
as whether they are transparent or opaque, give attention to what
follows. And note, that you must shade azure with black ; and
lay on the lights with white lead. Also mix azure with white
lead ; and shade [with azure, and lay on the lights] with white
lead. Shade vermilion with brunum ; and lay on the lights with
orpiment. Also mix vermilion with white lead, and make the
colour which is called rosa ; shade it with vermilion ; lay on the
lights with white lead. Shade orpiment with vermilion, and orpi-

ex accidentibus colorativis eorum ; quia nulli colores, nec colorum qualitates, sunt, simplices aut mixtæ, quæ et qui,
quantum ad colores, non conveniant quibuslibet aliis in mixturis, ad componendas, scilicet, alias diversas et quasi innume-
rabiles qualitatum varietates ad placitum habebis : sed dictæ
discordantiæ intelliguntur et sunt, quantum ad ceteras natu-
rales conditiones insistentes in materiis ipsorum colorum invicem taliter contrarias, quod, si simul miscentur, una materia,
ex contrarietate quadam naturali alterius, vel alterat alteram,
et altera alteram, et colorum ipsorum qualitas et pulcritudo,
tam distincta quam mixta, necnon eorum materia, et opus ex
ea factum, vastatur et deletur. Igitur mixtiones ad insimul
invicem non tolerant ; et sic non prætermittendum est, quin in
arte pictoriæ, ultra debitas considerationes quantum ad colorum
varietates, ac eorum et aliarum rerum in ipsa arte concurren-
tium differentias, habeantur etiam debite et necessarie considerationes, ex vera theorecali vel practicali scientia et cognitione conditionum et contrarietatum naturalium, insistentium
materiis et liquoribus ipsorum colorum, et rerum contrarialibus
in ipsa arte intervenientium.

LVIII. [286] *De diligentia quæ haberi debet circa naturas
colorum, et de modis miscendi, eos inter se, et incidendi, et mati-
zandi, cum in operibus distinguuntur, ut etiam aliud capitum de
hoc antepositum est.*—Si vis bene scire naturas colorum et mixtiones eorum, ut hi sunt clari et spissi, diligenter autem intentum
appone. Et nota quod lazurium incides de nigro ; matizabis
autem de albo plumbo. Item, misces lazurium cum albo plumbo
[incides[1] de azur, matizabis] de albo plumbo. Vermiculum
incides de bruno ; matizabis auripigmento. Item, miscebis vermiculum cum albo plumbo, et facies colorem qui vocatur rosa ;
incides de vermiculo ; matizabis de albo plumbo. Auripigmentum incides de vermiculo ; et illi matizatura non est, quia ster-
corat omnes alios colores. Tum si vis facere gladium viridem,

---

ment has no light tint, because it mars all colours. Then, if
you wish to make lily-green, mix orpiment with indigo; shade it
with black; lay on the lights with orpiment. Shade dragon's
blood with black; lay the lights on with white lead. Also mix
dragon's blood with orpiment; shade with dragon's blood; lay
on the lights with orpiment. You must shade green with black,
and lay on the lights with white lead. Also mix green with
white lead; shade with green; lay on the lights with white lead.
Shade granetum with green; lay on the lights with white lead.
Shade indigo with azure; lay on the lights with white lead.
Also mix indigo with white lead; shade with indigo; lay on
the lights with white lead. Shade flesh colour with black; lay
on the lights with white lead. Also mix saffron with white lead;
shade with saffron; lay on the lights with white lead. Shade
folium with black; lay on the lights with white lead. Mix
folium with white lead; shade with folium; lay on the lights
with white lead. If you wish to make a colour like lily green,
mix azure with white lead; shade it with azure; lay on the
lights with white lead; and when it is dry, cover it over with
clear saffron. Orpiment does not agree with green, or with
folium, or with red minium, or with white minium, as we have
already said.

auripigmentum misce cum indico; incides cum nigro; matizabis auripigmento. Sanguinem draconis incides de nigro; matizabis de albo plumbo. Item, misces sanguinem draconis cum
auripigmento; incides de sanguine draconis; matizabis de albo
plumbo. Item, misces sanguinem draconis cum auripigmento;
incides de sanguine draconis; de auripigmento matizabis. Viride incides de nigro; matizabis de albo plumbo. Item, miscebis viride cum albo plumbo; incides de viridi; matizabis de
albo plumbo. Granetum incides de viridi; matizabis de albo
plumbo. Indicum incides de lazurio; matizabis de albo plumbo.
Item, misce indicum cum albo plumbo; incides de indico, matizabis de albo plumbo. Carminum incides de nigro; matizabis de albo plumbo. Item, misces crocum cum albo plumbo;
incides de croco; matizabis de albo plumbo. Folium incides
de nigro; matizabis de albo plumbo. Misces folium cum
albo plumbo; incides de folio; matizabis de albo plumbo.
Si vis facere colorem similem gladio viridi, misce lazurium
cum albo plumbo; incides de lazurio; matizabis de albo plumbo;
et quando fuerit siccus operi de claro croco. Auripigmentum
non concordat cum viridi, nec cum folio, nec cum rubeo minio,
nec cum albo minio, ut antea jam dictum est.

THE FOLLOWING IS

A TREATISE UPON COLOURS
OF VARIOUS KINDS.

AND FIRST

THE INTRODUCTION.

290. In the year of the Circumcision of Christ 1398, on Sunday, the 28th day of July, JOHN ARCHERIUS wrote and noted down, at Paris, the following chapters concerning colours for painting, according to the words and instructions given him by Jacob Cona, a Flemish painter then residing at Paris, who, as he said, had himself tried, and used, during the whole period of his life, the recipes contained in the following pages.

And afterwards in the month of December, in the year of Christ 1411, the said John, more than a year after his return from Lombardy, corrected them in several places, according to various information which he had since received, both from other authentic books relating to such things, and otherwise; and which he copied fairly as follows:—

291. *For laying gold in different ways upon various articles so that it may be burnished, and the cautions to be observed concerning this in painting.*—For laying gold on parchment,[1]

---

[1] *Carta et papiro.* It is difficult to translate these words accurately: there is no doubt that in this sentence *carta* means *parchment*, which would otherwise be omitted in enumerating the substances on which gold was laid. *Papirus* also may be understood to mean *paper*, since cotton and linen paper were both in use at this time. The next time the author mentions the word "carta" he explicitly speaks of that kind called

DE COLORIBUS DIVERSIS MODIS TRACTATUR
IN SEQUENTIBUS.

ET PRIMO

MODUS PROHEMII.

290. Anno circumcisionis Christi 1398 die dominicæ
28 Julii, Johannes Archerius scripsit et notavit in
Parisiis sequentia capitula de coloribus ad pingendum,
per verba et signamenta quæ sibi dixit Jacobus Cona
flamingus pictor commorans tunc Parisiis, qui toto tempore suo ut dixerat temptaverat et usus fuerat ipsemet
de contentis in sequentibus. Et post ea anno Christi
1411 de mense decembris, idem Johannes reversus de
partibus Lombardiæ jam per plusquam unum annum,
correxit ea in pluribus locis secundum plures informationes, quas inde postea per ceteros libros autentiquos
de talibus narrantes et aliter habuerat, et ad nettum
rescripsit ut sequitur.

291. *Ad ponendum aurum burniendum super diversis diverse
mode et de cautelis habendis circa hoc pingendo.*—Ad ponendum
aurum in carta, papiro, tela linea; sindone, et in ligneis tabulis

---

" parchment " (pergamenum), of the clippings of which, he adds, the size
might be made. In the earlier part of this MS. I have translated the word
" carta " always by " parchment," but it appears that it was also applied to
paper at this period, 1382—1411.

The exact date when the Egyptian paper, made of the papirus, fell into
disuse in Europe is not known, but it appears from the testimony of Eusta-

paper, linen cloth, sindone,[1] and on primed wooden panels,
which gold may be burnished, that is polished.   Take the white
gersa, which is otherwise called white chalk, which is found
in abundance at Bologna and at Paris ; and a little Armenian
bole, in quantity about one-fourth of the chalk, or a little *crocus*,
which is commonly called saffron.   This Armenian bole and
this saffron are not added because they cannot be omitted without great inconvenience by any one who wishes to do so, but
merely that the colour may not be white, but yellowish or
reddish ; and not for any other reason than this, namely, that
when it is laid upon the paper, it may differ from the whiteness
of the paper, and thus the things which are made of it are
better seen than they would be if the colour of it was white
like that paper which is called parchment.   Grind all these
things very fine upon a hard stone, well polished, and broad,
with another stone to be held in the hand, polished in the same
manner with clear water from a well or a spring, and let the

---

chius, the learned commentator on Homer, that it was no longer in use in
his time, 1170.

The invention of paper made from cotton is believed to have occurred in
Greece in the tenth century.   The most ancient MS. that Montfaucon saw
on this paper, with the date, was written A.D. 1050.

Theophilus, lib. i. c. xxiii., mentions " *pergamenum græcam quæ fit ex
lana ligni.*"   This is the reading of Raspe, from a MS. of the thirteenth
century, and may certainly be understood to apply to the cotton paper made
in Greece, which was called by the Italians " Carta Bambagina ;" but the
copy of the MS. of Theophilus, which formed part of the MS. of Le Begue,
which is of the fifteenth century, and which is in his hand-writing, instead
of " ligni," has the words " *lini id est papirum.*"   Le Begue then may be
considered to have understood this passage, if indeed he did not interpolate
the words " *id est papirum,*" as applying to paper made of rags or linen.
We may therefore, I think, consider that, where *papirus* is used in the MS.
of Jehan Le Begue, paper made of rags is meant.

I am the more strongly inclined to this opinion, because the author of the
article ' Paper ' in the ' Encyclopædia Britannica,' quoting the work of the
Abbé Andrez, published at Parma in 1782, entitled ' Dell' Origine, Pro-
gressi, e Stato attuale d'Ogni Letteratura,' says that paper made from silk
was anciently fabricated in China, and that the art of making this paper was

---

[1] *Sindone*, a kind of very fine linen, such as cambric or lawn.

dealbatis, quod aurum burniatur, id est, poliri possit. Accipe
gersam albam quæ aliter dicitur creta alba de qua habundanter
reperitur bononiæ et Parisiis,[1] et accipe parum bularmenii circa
quantitatem quartæ partis cretæ, vel parum croci, qui vulgariter
dicitur safran et qui bularmenius et saffranus non ponuntur
quia non possunt absque magno inconvenienti dimitti qui vult,
sed ponuntur solum ut ipse color non sit albus sed sit croceus
vel rubescens et non per alia causa, ad hoc quod dum ponitur in
opere super cartam quæ differenciet ab albedine cartæ et quod
per hoc melius videantur quæ fiunt de ipso quod videri possent
si ipse color esset albus ut est carta quæ dicitur pergamenum.
Et ea omnia tere valde subtiliter super lapidem durum bene
politum et latum et cum alio lapide manuali similiter polito,
viz. cum aqua clara putei vel fontis et fiat tempera seu color
qui in gallico dicitur *assiete*, quæ postea si vis tamen antequam
penitus siccet, dum tamen induratus jam sit, quia postquam
siccus sit potes distemperare cum aqua colata, ex cola facta de

---

carried from China to Persia about the year 652, and to Mecca in 706.
The Arabs substituted cotton, the production of their own country, for silk,
and introduced the paper into Spain. The Spaniards, from the quantity of
linen to be found in the kingdom of Valencia, seem first to have adopted
the idea of using linen rags, and the most ancient paper of this kind is that
of Valencia and Catalonia. From Spain it passed into France, as may be
learned from a letter of Joinville to St. Louis about 1260. It is discovered
to have been in Germany in 1312, and in England in 1320. In consequence
of the paper made from cotton in the Levant, the paper from linen was
introduced much later in Italy. " Carta Bambagina " is frequently mentioned in the MS. of Cennino Cennini, written at Florence in 1437, and it
is still made in the Levant.

The precise period of the introduction of paper made from rags into
France and Italy is not known, but Montfaucon could find no book on this
paper antecedent to the death of St. Louis.

We may then conclude, that during the time of Jehan Le Begue, paper
made from linen rags was used in France and Germany, and that in Italy
paper was made from cotton, while parchment, which had become scarce,
was employed occasionally throughout Europe.

It will be observed that in the following chapters Alcherius writes " per-
gamena *seu* carta."

---

[1] Sic sublin. in MS., sed in atramento recentori.

mixture or colour be made, which in French is called *assiete*,[1] which you may afterwards, if you like, before it is quite dry, but after it has set, distemper with glue water, made with glue from cuttings of the white leather of which gloves are made. Clippings of parchment also are good for this purpose, but the cuttings of the white leather make the glue stronger. Lastly, let the size, or sized water, be warm; I say warm, lest it may be conglutinated, because if the size is as it ought to be, when it is cold it will be congealed like jelly for *galantina* [brawn] not very hard, and this on account of the glue which is made to enter into the water by the decoction of the cuttings of leather or of parchment in that water, which is congealed by cold. And therefore summer weather is very convenient for this, both because it does not allow the colour to congeal or chill, and because it makes the colour dry quickly when it is laid on. And with this warm size, you must, as has been said before, distemper the said powdered colour or tempering for laying on gold, so that it may be soft and liquid like good ink for writing, or as it may seem convenient. Having done this, write, draw, and fill in or paint whatever you wish with it, and rather with a paintbrush than a pen, because if it were done with a pen, and were to become chilled in the pen, it would not flow so well as with a paintbrush; moreover, when using a paintbrush, the colour may be held in the hand, which, by its warmth or heat, will not allow it to congeal; this, however, can also be done well with a pen, but a paintbrush is much more convenient. And, in painting with a pen, as well as with a paintbrush, it is a good thing to keep the colour over a slow fire of charcoal, at such a warmth, that it may not congeal, but may remain liquid. Afterwards let those things dry which you have drawn and painted, and when they are dry burnish them, that is, polish or smooth them gently with a tooth of a horse or a boar, or with a polished hard stone fitted for this purpose, in order that all the roughness may be softened down,

---

[1] Hence our terms " size " and " gold size."

inciseriis corii albi de quo fiunt chirothecæ, et minutiæ pergamenorum etiam sunt bonæ ad hoc, sed meliores sunt dictæ
incisæ corii albi quia faciunt colam firmiorem ; denue cola seu
aqua colata sit tepida, dico tepida ne sit conglutinata quod si
ipsa aqua sit qualis debet esse cum ipsa erit frigida erit con-
gelata in modum gelii galantinæ non multum duri, et hoc
causa colæ in ipsa aqua insertæ ex decoctione dictarum minu-
tiarum corii vel pergameni facta in ipsa aqua, quæ per frigidum
congelatur. Ideo tempus æstatis in hoc multum prodest, tam
quod non permittit colorem congelari neque frigidari quam
quia facit colorem cito siccari cum positus est in opere. Et de
ipsa aqua colata tepida debes ut dictum est distemperare dictum colorem tritum seu temperamentum ad ponendum aurum
taliter quod sit mollis et liquidus quantum est bonum incaustum
ad scribendum, vel ut conveniens videbitur. Et hoc facto
scribe pertrahe et imple seu pinge quæ vis ex eo, et potius
cum pincello quam cum calamo, quod si fieret cum calamo et
infrigidaretur in calamo, non tam bene curreret sicut facit cum
pincello ; ac etiam operando cum pincello potest ipse color ex-
tendi super manum, quæ pro tepiditate sua seu caliditate non
permittit ipsum colorem congelari, quod tamen potest etiam
bene fieri cum calamo sed multo melius pincello convenit. Et
operando tam cum calamo quam cum pincello, bonum est quod
color ipse teneatur cum lento igne carbonum in tali tepiditate,
quod non possit conglutinari, sed stet liquidus ; et postea dimitte siccari ex quæ scripseris pinxeris et protaxeris [protraxeris]
et quando siccati fuerint, burnias, id est polias seu lisses leniter cum dente equi vel apri, vel cum lapide duro polito ad hoc
apto, ut adæquentur omnes scabrositates in ipsis præcipue locis
in quibus ipsam assisam seu colorem posuisti, deinde rettera et
adhuc in ipsis locis repone pinge et pertrahe tanquam prius
cum ipso colore et postea permitte siccari et adhuc polies et
burnias ut prius. Postea vero tertia reponas et repinge ea
ipsa quæ prius de eadem assisia seu colore, sed fac quod ista

particularly in those places in which you have put this size or colour. Then grind some more, and again paint over and draw upon those same places, with this colour, as before, and afterwards let it dry, and then polish and burnish it as before. Afterwards go over and repaint those places which you did before, with the same mordant or colour, but let this third and last coat of colour be tempered with white of egg whipped or beaten, so as to be liquid and without any particles conglutinated or adhering together; because this white of egg makes a size or vehicle sufficiently strong to hold the gold for burnishing and to resist the shaking and violence of the friction and rubbing the burnisher over the gold. Then, before the colour on the places in which you put it, is dry apply the gold quickly, and allow it to dry, and afterwards burnish all these things with the same tooth, stone, or other instrument, you used before as above mentioned, but first pressing lightly and drawing the burnisher over the gold; then rather harder, and afterwards harder still, particularly on parchment, paper, and panels; but on cloth and sindone not pressing so hard, and taking great care lest what has been done should crumple up and be broken, and so those things which you drew and painted, and upon which you laid the gold, will remain clean and polished; and the forms and lines made with this colour will remain brightly gilt.

But it must be observed, that on parchment, paper, and panels it is sufficient for the said colour to be put on once only, tempered with size, and afterwards, for the last coat, with white of egg, provided that it is laid on well the first time when tempered with size. But on cloth or sindone it is more necessary that this colour should be laid on twice, while tempered with size, before it is put on for the last coat tempered with white of egg. And this is because sindone and cloth, owing to their porosity, are too absorbent, flowing, flexible, and unstable, and therefore soak up the colour, so that there does not remain a good and firm substance of colour upon the cloth or sindone, unless, as useful experience tells us, it is laid on several times.

tertia et ultima vice temperatus sit ipse color de clara ovi
spongiata aut verberata, ita quod sit liquida absque aliquibus
partibus conglutinatis et sibi adhærentibus quia ipsa clara ovi
facit ipsam assisiam seu temperam fortem satis ad tenendum
aurum ad burnissionem et ad strepitum et violentiam fricationis
et deductionis ipsius super ipso auro.   Et tunc velociter antequam siccetur color in locis in quibus posueris, pone sursum
aurum et sic permitte siccari, et postea ea omnia burnias cum
eodem dente lapide vel alio instrumento quo prius ut supra,
sed primo leniter premendo et trahendo burnissorem desuper
aurum, postea aliquantulum fortius, et postea adhuc fortius,
præcipue in carta papiro et tabulis, sed in telis et sindone non
tam fortiter et cum majori studio ne plicetur et diripietur quod
factum est, et sic remanebunt quæ pertraxeris de ipso colore
pinxeris et auro ut dictum est posueris purgata polita et ex
ipsa deauratura lucida juxta formas et pertractiones ex dicto
colore factas.

Sed notandum est, quod in carta, papiro, et tabulis, sufficere
quod ponatur dictus color solum una vice, temperatus cum
cola et postea ultima vice cum clara ovi, dum bene ponatur ad
primam vicem cum cola temperatus.   Sed in tela et sindone
magis est necesse poni bis, primo cum cola temperatus ipse
color, antequam ultima vice ponatur temperatus cum claro
ovi etc., et hoc quod sindon et tela, pro raritatibus eorum sunt
nimis labiles, decurrentes, flexibiles, et instabiles ; et ideo
bibunt colorem ipsum nisi pluries, prout expediens experientia
doceat, reponatur ita quod in superficie telæ vel sindonis non
remanet bene valida substantia coloris ; neque etiam dicta
flexibilitas et ductibilitas ipsorum, sindonis et telæ, per aliquem alium modum corrigi potest, et ad stabilitatem quandam,
quam illis ex hoc causa viscositatis et tenacitatis colæ infertur
reduci potest.   Ideo haberi debet etiam advertentia, quod si
tempus sit ventosum, impedit, nisi ponens aurum sit in loco
recluso ; et si aer sit nimis siccum, color non bene capit aurum ;
et si nimis humidum, color non tenere potest aurum ad burnissorem.   Et provideatur etiam quod tela et sindon cum ca-

And this flexibility and instability of the cloth or sindone can be corrected and reduced to firmness in no other way than by the tenacity and viscosity of the glue laid over them for this purpose. And therefore care must be taken as regards the situation, because windy weather is a hindrance, unless the gilder is in a closed place ; and if the air is too dry, the colour does not take the gold well ; and, if too wet, the colour cannot hold the gold under the burnisher. Care must also be taken that the linen or sindone which is chosen for this purpose be well woven and strong, and as close in the texture as possible. The colour itself ought not to be applied too thick or too cold, lest by the curve made in folding them the colour should scale off and fall away along with the gold ; particularly under the stroke of the burnisher, while the gold upon it, as has been already mentioned, is being burnished ; and so your labour should be thrown away. And even supposing that the cloth, sindone, paper, or parchment, on which gold has been laid in the manner hereinbefore described, should be folded into slight creases, as frequently happens spontaneously and by chance, and unless they are folded and rubbed together, cracking the priming by violent and voluntary force, the gold will not fall off or start from the places in which it was laid.

292. *For laying on gold in various ways, and upon various articles, when it is not to be burnished.*—For laying gold on parchment, paper, cloth, and sindone, with size alone, or with a mordant tempered with size, and this by a short and quick method, but so that it ought not, nor can be burnished, particularly on cloth and sindone, which, on account of their flexibility, instability, softness, and porosity, can ill bear the stroke and pressure of the burnisher, nor can they stand it so that the gold will not be spoiled in burnishing ; and also because the size which is to be used for laying on the gold, or for tempering the colour on which the gold is to be laid, is not strong enough to hold the gold against the stroke of the burnisher, as white of egg would be, if it were tempered with white of egg. Take the glue with which bows and spears are glued, and put it to soak in cold

piuntur pro operando sint bene texti et fortes, et minus rari in eorum textura quam possunt. Sed neque etiam debet ipse color esse nimis grossus seu spissus et frigidus, ne ex ductu plicationum contingentium eis, ut necessario convenit, cadat et resiliat color cum auro, et specialiter ad strepitus burnissoris, quando aurum desuper, ut dictum est, burnitur, et quod sic opus perdatur. Et dato quod tela, sindon, papirus, et carta in quibus positum erit aurum modo quo dictum est complicentur aliquantum in rugas sicut a casu per se accidit, dum modo non violento et voluntario rigore confringendo plicentur et fricentur, aurum tamen non cadit nec resilit a locis in quibus positum est.

292. *Ad ponendum aurum diversi mode super diversis, quod non burniatur.*—Ad ponendum aurum in carta, papiro, tela et in sindone cum cola tantum vel cum colore de cola temperato et hoc brevi modo et veloci, quod burniri non debeat, nec possit, præcipue in tela et sindone qui pro eorum flexibilitate ductibilitate mollitie et raritate strepitum et impressionem burnissoris male sustinent nec possint pati quin burniendo aurum deleretur, et etiam quia cola imponenda ad ponendum aurum vel ad temperandum colorem, de quo poni debet, non est fortis ad tenendum aurum ad strepitum burnissoris ut esset clara ovi si de clara ovi distemperetur. Accipe colam de qua colantur arcus et hastæ et pone ad distemperandum in aqua frigida, et quum est bene mollis pone ipsam in vase cum circa totidem de dicta aqua, quotidem debito respecta est colla et non plus, et pone ad ignem

water, and when it is well softened put it into a vase with about
an equal quantity of the said water, that is, as much as the glue
requires, and no more, and put it on the fire so as not to boil,
but only keep hot, until the glue is dissolved in the water, or is
melted, and incorporated with the water. And having done
this, not allowing the glue to cool, but keeping it at a moderate
heat with a slow fire, for fear it should be congealed, so that it
could not be used, write and draw whatever you wish with this
glue, upon a linen or other cloth, or upon sindone, or even on
parchment, or paper, with a soft pen, or a small paintbrush
of hogs' bristles, which brush must be obtuse, that is, must
have short bristles which are stiff or hard, that is to say,
like those which are used to mark the canvass upon bales
of goods with ink ; and write, fill in, or paint, and draw any
letters or other broad designs, whatever they may be, with the
said stiff and blunt paintbrush. But if you are working on fine
cloths or sindone, and on parchment and paper, it is better for
the paintbrush to be made of the hairs of the tails of minever,
blunt or pointed as you see best, according to the nature of the
work you have to do. When you have done this, leave it to
dry, and afterwards with the same glue go again over those things
which were drawn before, particularly on cloth and sindone,
which usually absorb the first coat of size so strongly, that
scarcely any of it remains upon the surface to hold the gold
which is to be laid on them. It is therefore proper to lay it on
twice, if it should seem necessary ; afterwards at the last coat,
before the letters and drawings are dry, apply the gold and
allow them to dry. And know, that if the cloth, sindone, paper,
and parchment, on which the gold is laid in the above mentioned manner, are folded into a crease, and rubbed, as sometimes happens accidentally, and not by violent and voluntary
force, yet the gold laid on in this manner will not fall off, or be
spoiled. This is because the size, with which the gold is laid
on, or with which the mordant is tempered, if a mordant is
used, makes the mordant itself less rigid and more flexible and
yielding, by reason of its soft condition and nature, than the
white of egg, which is firmer and stiffer.

ita quod non bulliat sed solum calefiat, usque ad hoc quod colla fundatur in aqua seu sit liquefacta et incorporata cum aqua. Et hoc facto, non permittendo infrigidari colam, sed tenendo ipsam ad temperatam caliditatem cum lento igne, ne conglutinetur, ita quod de ipsa possit operari, scribe et pertrahe quod vis de ipsa cola super telam lineam vel aliam, vel super sindonem, aut etiam super papirum, aut pergamenum, seu cartam cum calamo non duro vel cum pincello parvo setarum porci, qui pincellus sit obtusus, id est, habeat setas curtas ut sint rigidæ seu duræ, viz., sicut sunt pincelli ad signandum balas mercium super earum cavenatiis [canevatiis?] cum incausto; et scribe, imple, seu pinge et pertrahe, quascumque literas et alias pertractiones grossas, quæque sint, fac cum dicto pincello sic rigido et obtuso. Sed si operaris in telis subtilibus; vel in sindone, et in carta, aut in papiro, melius est quod pincellus sit de pilis caudarum vayrorum, obtusus vel acutus secundum quod videbis magis convenire juxta qualitatem operum faciendorum. Et hoc facto dimittas siccari, postea de eadem cola rescribe et reimple iterum semel, et repertrahe quæ pertracta jam fuerant; specialiter super telam et sindonem quæ solent lambere tam fortiter primam colam, quod de ipsa quasi nil remanet in superficie eorum quo possit aurum desuper ponendum teneri. Ideo advertatur de ponendo vis si necesse videatur, et postea, ad ultimam vicem, antequam siccentur literæ et pertractiones pone aurum desuper et dimitte siccari. Et scias, quod dato quod tela, sindon, papirus, et carta, ubi positum erat aurum modo supradicto, complicentur in rigam et fricentur sicut accidit a casu, et non cum rigore violento et voluntario, tamen aurum illo modo positum, non cadit, seu non vastatur, etiam quia cola qua positum est aurum, vel qua temperatus est color de quo positum est aurum si de colore ponatur, reddit colorem ipsum magis flexibilem, non rigidum, et consentientem contingentibus flexionibus ex sua molli conditione et natura, quam facit clara ovi quæ fortior et rigidior est.

293. *A good rose colour for linen cloth, sindone, parchment, or paper, and primed panels, is made in this way.*— Take *brasilium* rasped or scraped with a knife, or with glass, pounded in a mortar; but it is much better to have it scraped; then let it be put with a little raw alum in powder into a ley, or into urine. Then make it boil for a long time over a charcoal fire, not a wood fire, lest by chance the smoke, which the wood makes, should spoil the colour. Afterwards let it be strained through a linen cloth, retaining in the cloth the substance of the wood brasilium, lest it should be mixed with the colour that is to be made, and then let it be put into a glazed jar with white chalk or gersa [gesso], in powder, or with powdered bracha [biacha—biacca], which is otherwise called white lead, otherwise ceruse, otherwise Spanish white; and let it be allowed to incorporate with the said chalk or ceruse. Next let it be ground altogether upon a hard stone without adding water or urine, on the contrary, keeping it as little liquid, *i.e.*, as thick as it can be ground; and although it should be less liquid than it was at the beginning before it was ground, and yet not sufficiently thickened in the grinding, because the water of the ley or the urine had not been sufficiently poured off or dried; let the colour be put to dry upon a hollow stone of chalk or gersa, or upon a concave brick made of clay, and baked in the furnace, which will immediately absorb the moisture of the ley, so that the colour remains suddenly almost dry, *i.e.*, inspissated. Afterwards let the colour be put away; and when it is necessary to use it, take whatever is wanted of it and temper it with white of egg, or with gum water made of gum arabic, in the way cinnabar is used. But if it is used with white of egg, it shines where it is used, and is more beautiful. And write and draw and paint with this colour whatever is wanted on parchment, and primed panels, as well with the pen as with the paintbrush. And the less ceruse or chalk there is in it the darker will be the colour; and so, on the other hand, the more there is of it the lighter the colour will be.

293. *Color rosæ bonus in tela linea, sindone, papiro, pergameno, seu carta et in tabulis dealbatis fit hoc modo.*—Accipe bri-
silium raspatum seu rasum cum cultello vel cum vitro aut pis-
tum in mortario, sed multo melius tamen est habere rasum ;
deinde cum pauco aluminis crudi pulverizati ponatur in lexivio
vel in urina hominis ebriatoris quæ optima est, et melior est
vetera et diu facta quam nova. Et fac bullire diu ad ignem
carbonum ; non lignorum, ne fumus quem ligna faciunt vastet
colorem. Et postea coletur dictus color ita callidus per telam
lineam, dimittendo in tela substanciam ligni brisilii ne immis-
ceatur colori faciendæ, postea ponatur in vase vitreato cum
creta seu gersa alba pulverizata vel cum bracha pulverizata
quæ aliter dicitur album plumbum aliter cerusa, atque
aliter album Hispaniæ, et dimittatur incorporari cum ipsa
creta vel cerosio. Et postea teratur totum simul super lapidem durum absque addendo aquam nec urinam ymo minus
liquidum, *i. e.*, magis spissum quam teri poterit vel possit ;
deinde si minus liquidus erit quam sic esset a principio antequam tereretur, et quod terendo non satis inspissatus fuerit,
quod aquositas lexivii vel urinæ non erat satis comminuta et
desiccata ponatur ad siccandum super concava lapide cretæ vel
gersæ aut super latere concavo facto de terra et cocto in fornace,
qui subito bibunt humiditatem lexivii taliter quod remanet color
subito quasi siccus, viz., inspissatus. Postea reponatur et quando
oportet operari accipiant de illo quantum necesse sit, et distemperetur cum clara ovi vel cum aqua gummata de gummi arabico
ut distemperatur cinobrium. Sed si distemperatur cum claro
ovi, relucet cum in opere est, et pulcrior est. Et scribantur
ex eo et pertrahantur ac pingantur in carta in papiro et in tabulis dealbatis de ipso colore, quæ velint tam cum calamo quam
cum pincello. Et quanto erit in ipso minus de cerusa aut de
creta, tanto erit color plus obscurus ; et quanto plus, sic converso magis clarus.

294. *A blue colour, that is, azure, which is not ultramarine, nor is it so beautiful, but which is good on linen, sindone, parchment, or paper, and primed panels, that is panels covered with gersa.*—Take fine indigo, which is called by the name of Bagadel, and Spanish white, otherwise called ceruse or blacha, and mix both together, and grind them on a hard stone, with white of egg beaten and mixed with pure water, or with gum water, made with gum Arabic, and in the manner in which sinobrium, that is, sinopis is ground when alone. When it is ground, temper it in a shell or a horn with the clear part of beaten white of egg, not mixed with water, as has been already directed for the rose colour, and write or draw whatever you want with this colour. This is the way in which it must be made if you wish to use it immediately. But if you do not want this colour for immediate use, but wish to keep it, you must not add any egg or gum water to it when you grind it on the stone, but only mix it with pure and clean water; and when it is ground up with water, let it dry up or inspissate upon a brick of baked clay, or a hollow stone of white chalk, which immediately absorbs the moisture in such a manner, that the colour remains thickened and like juice, and afterwards allow it to dry completely in the shade, or in the sun, and put it away and preserve it. And when you wish to use it, take some of it and temper it in a shell or a horn, with white of egg not mixed with water, or even with the said gum water, and make it of a reasonable and moderate softness or liquidity, according to what is required for the work you intend to do with it, and just as you would do with sinopis. And the lighter or less dark you require it, the more blacha or ceruse you must mix with it; and, on the other hand, the darker you wish it, the less you must put of the said ceruse, that is, white-lead, that is to say, while you are grinding the colour upon the stone.

295. *To make letters of a green colour, and to draw and paint all other things on linen, parchment, or paper, primed panels, and sindone.*—Take fine indigo, called Bagadel, and

294. *Color blauetus id est celestis, qui non est de lazurio, nec tam pulcher, et est bonus in tela linea, sindone, papiro, pergameno seu carta et in tabulis dealbatis, id est gersatis.*—Accipe Indicum finum qui cognomine bagadellus vocatur, et de albo hispaniæ aliter cerusium vel blacham, et misce ambo simul et tere super lapidem durum cum claro ovi spongiato et mixto aqua clara, aut cum aqua gummata de gummi arabico, et ad modum quo teritur sinobrium solum, id est sinopis ; et postquam erit tritum, distempera in conchilla vel in cornato cum claro ovi spongia liquidato, non mixtum aqua ut dictum est antea de colore rosæ, et scribe et pertrahe quæ vis cum ipso colore. Et hic est modus quo fieri debet, volendo ipsum de præsenti ponere in opere. Sed si non vis ipsum colorem de præsenti ponere in opere et quod velis ipsum servare, debes isto modo nullum ovum nec aquam gummatum ponere quum ipsum teris super lapidem, ymo solum ponas de aqua munda pura et simplici, et cum tritum sit cum aqua, fac ipsum siccari vel inspissari super laterem terræ coctum aut super laterem coctæ albæ concavum qui subito bibit humiditatem aquæ taliter, quod remanet color subito inspissatus et quasi succus ; et postea desiccari penitus permittas ad umbram aut ad solem et repone et serva. Et cum vis operari accipe de ipso et distempera in conchilla vel in corneto cum claro ovi non mixto aqua, vel etiam mixto vel cum dicta aqua gummata, et fac ipsum de rationabili et moderata mollitie, seu liquidate secundum quod requiritur in faciendo ea quæ vis de ipso facere et sicut de sinopide faceres. Et quanto vis clariorem seu minus obscurum, tanto pone plus de blacha seu cerosio ; et e converso, quanto vis magis obscurum, pone minus de dicto cerosio, id est de albo plumbo, scilicet quando teres ipsum colorem super lapidem.

295. *Ad faciendum literas viridis coloris et ad protrahendum et pingendum omnia alia in tela in papiro in carta seu pergameno in tabulis ligneis dealbatis et in sindone.*—Accipe Indicum

orpiment, and mix and grind them together upon a hard stone
with clear water from a well or a spring, and it will be a green
colour, and the lighter you require it, the more orpiment
you must add ; and the darker you require it, the less orpiment
you must put, and the more indigo.   When you have ground
it very fine, let it dry ; and if it is put upon a stone of white
chalk, that is gersa, or upon a clay brick baked in the furnace,
and concave so that it may hold the colour, the moisture will
directly dry up or be absorbed into the stone, and the colour
itself will remain hard and thick, and you may then allow it to
dry by itself, and when it is dry, put it away and keep it. And
when you wish to use it, take as much as you want of it, and
put it into a horn, or into a shell which is found in fresh water,
or even a sea-shell that is fit for this purpose, and temper it
with white of egg, or with gum water, as is done with sinopis,
and with it write and draw whatever you like, in the same
manner as is done with vermilion or sinopis.   But if, omitting
and not putting the indigo, you mix fine ultramarine with the
said orpiment instead of indigo, you will have a much finer
green.

296. *To prepare parchment, or paper, primed panels,
and linen, so that you may be able to draw upon them in black,
with a pencil or stile of gold, silver, bronze, or brass, as is done
upon panels of boxwood whitened or covered with bone or stag's-
horn burnt and whitened in the fire.*—Take bones of any animal
or bird, or stag's-horn, which is better, and burn it, and make
it white and friable and soft by long and violent boiling, and
afterwards grind it upon a hard stone with pure water.   Then
put it on a brick of baked clay or of white chalk, that the
moisture may enter into it, and that the bone may remain
thickened and almost dry.   Remove it from the stone, and
burn it a second time in a charcoal fire, and make it perfectly
white and fine in a crucible in which silver or gold is usually
melted, and afterwards, that it may be made still more fine
and white, grind it a second time upon a stone with water,
in the same way as you did before ; and then if you wish to use

finum quod bagadellum nominatur, et auripigmentum, et misce
et tere simul super lapidem durum, cum aqua putei vel fontis
clara et erit color viridis.   Et quanto volueris ipsum magis
clarum, pone magis de auripigmento.   Et quanto magis obscurum pone minus de dicto auripigmento et plus de Indico.   Et
cum tritus sit valde subtiliter, pone ad siccandum, et si ponatur super lapidem album cretæ i. e. gersæ aut super laterem
de terra coctum in fornace et concavum ita quod capax sit
coloris, subito aquositas siccabitur seu intrabit in ipso lapide et
color remanebit durus et spissus, et postea permittas per se
siccari et cum siccus sit repone et serva.   Et quando vis de
ipso operari, accipe quantum vis de ipso et pone in cornu vel
in conchilla quæ reperitur in aquis dulcibus vel etiam in mari
apta ad hoc et distempera cum claro ovi, aut cum aqua gummata ut fit sinopis, et de illo scribe pinge et pertrahe quæ vis
ut fit de vermiculo seu sinopide.   Sed si cum dicto auropig-
mento, loco Indici, præmisso Indico et non posito, misceris
finum azurium multo pulcriorem viridem habebis.

296. *Ad aptandum papirum, et pergamenum, seu cartam, tabulas ligneas et telam, modo quo possis super ipsas protrahere
nigro, cum grossio seu stilo auri, argenti, latonis, vel æris, sicut
super tabulas busuli dealbatas seu intinctas cum osse vel cornu
cervi combusto et dealbato in igne.*—Accipe de osse cujusvis animalis vel avis, aut de cornu cervi, quod melius est, et arde
illud et albifica et tritibilem et dulcem facies longa et forti decoctione, postea tere super duro lapide cum aqua clara ; postea
pones super latere terræ coctæ, aut cretæ albæ, ut in ipso
entret humiditas et inspissetur et remaneat ut quasi siccum :
postea eleva a lapide, et iterum in ignem carbonem secundo
decoque et perfectissime albifica et subtilem facies illud in cru-
sibulo in quo solet fondi argentum vel aurum ; postea ut iterum
magis subtilietur et dealbetur, tere illud secundo super lapidem
cum aqua ut prius feceras ; deinde si prompte vis operare, de
ipso distempera quantum velis in conchilla vel in scutella figuli

it immediately, wet up as much of it as you require in a shell
or a glazed earthen jar, with size made from glue or from clippings of white leather or parchment, and which must be of a
moderate consistence and warmth. Having done this as directed, paint or draw with it, with a broad paint-brush, upon
paper which has been polished with a boar's tooth. Also lay
it over parchment, cloth, sindone, and wooden panels, and
permit it to dry. And then, if the first coat is not sufficient for
it (which may be known by drawing on it with a stile of brass,
or bronze, or copper, or still better of silver, and seeing whether
it makes black marks or not), you must give it another coat of
the said bone-dust, keeping it warm in the vase in which it
stands over a slow fire, particularly in winter, lest it should be
congealed by the cold, on account of the glue with which it is
mixed, which hardens with cold; afterwards let it dry, and try
it again by drawing upon it with a stile as before. And so you
must apply this bone or horn as many times as you see necessary, though it is true that the second coat usually suffices,
and frequently the first. And note, that if you wish the paper,
after it is thus painted, to be very smooth and polished and without any inequalities or roughnesses, that it may be better to
draw upon, you must polish and burnish it, holding it under
another paper not painted on, upon which you must rub a boar's
tooth, or a hard and polished stone, or any other instrument fit
for burnishing. And know, that if you wish to make this preparation of various colours, it is necessary, while grinding the
horn or bone upon the said stone, and wetting it in a shell or a
glazed earthen vessel, when you wish to paint the paper, that
you should mix with the horn or bone whatever colours you
wish, separately, which must however be ground very fine upon
the said stone with pure water. Afterwards, if any of the said
horn remain, whether white or coloured, it can be preserved,
because, although what remains becomes dry by keeping, it may
still be of use to lay upon other paper, like any other colours,
by being wetted up with pure water, not sized; because,
although the water of the first wetting dries up, yet the glue of

vitriata, cum aqua colata de cola seu de incisuris corii albi vel
pergameni, et quod sit colata moderato modo et tepida.   His
itaque talimodo factis pinge vel pertrahe de ipso cum pincello
grosso super papyrum quod primo sit lissatum cum dente apri.
Item pinge de eo pergamenum telam sindonem et tabulas ligneas, et permitte siccari ; postea, si prima depinctio facta non
sufficit, quod scitur protrahendo desuper cum stilo æris vel
latonis aut cupri ; et melior esset de argento ; si non bene per-
trahit nigros tractus.   Quod si sic sit debes iterum repingere
de eodem osse, tenendo ipsum tepidum in vase in quo est lento
igni, præcipue si sit in hyeme ne conglutinetur ex frigore pro
cola qua temperatus est, et quæ pro frigore induratur ; postea
dimitte siccari et iterum tempta protrahendo desuper cum stilo
ut prius.   Ita sic ipsum ossem vel cornu totiens ponas quotiens
videbis esse necessarium, dato quod verum est quod si secunda
vice pingatur, solet sufficere et multotiens pro prima.   Et nota
quod si velis ipsum papirum postquam taliter pictus sit esse
valde politum et equale absque fossulis et scabrositatibus ut
melior sit ad protrahendum super, ipsum lisses et burnias tenendo ipsum sub uno alio papiro non picto super quem trahes
imprimendo dentem apri, aut lapidem durum politum, aut
aliud instrumentum ad burniendum aptum.   Et scias quod si
de diversis coloribus ipsas depictiones facere velis, oportet quod
terendo cornu vel osse super dictum lapidem distemperando
illud in conchilla vel scutella figuli vitriata, quando papirum
vel cartam vis pingere, quod in ipso cornu vel osse misceas
separatim quales colores velis, tritos tamen ut subtiliores super
lapidem cum aqua clara.   Postea si de dicto cornu tam albo
quam de coloribus remanent partes illæ residuæ possunt ser-
vari, quia dato quod resedentiæ postea stando siccentur, possunt
tamen sicut est de omnibus aliis coloribus adhuc alias valere ad
ponendum in opere, scilicet distemperata cum aqua clara non
colata ; quia dato quod aqua primæ distemperaturæ sit desiccata, tamen iterum remanet ibidem cola ipsius primæ distem-
perationis, quæ sufficit ; quia in exhalatione et desiccatione
aquositatis primæ distemperaturæ, non frustrata nec exalata

the first wetting still remains there, and in sufficient quantity;
for in the exhalation and evaporation of the moisture of the
first wetting, the strength or substance of the glue is not exhaled or evaporated, but only the water. And if any of the
first quantity of bone or horn, not mixed with any colour or
glue remains in the vase, shell, or saucer, you may put it on a
lump of chalk, or on a brick of baked clay, that the water
which is contained in it may be dried up, and may be exposed
to the air or the sun, that it may dry completely; and afterwards, when you wish to use it, you must temper it with size
as originally directed, as there is not any size or glue mixed
with it. You can also colour it with various colours, mixing
them with it, as before, according to your taste, as above mentioned. And note, that if you have no stag's-horn, the bones
of the stag are good, as also those of any other animal or bird,
as has been already mentioned.

est virtus nec substantia colæ, sed solum aqua. Et si de primo
osse vel cornu non mixto de colore ullo et in quo non est cola
remanebit ulla pars in vase seu scutella vel in conchilla, potes
ipsum ponere super lapidem cretæ, aut super laterem terræ
coctæ, ut siccetur aqua quæ in ipso est et reponere ad aërem
vel ad solem, ut ex toto desiccetur, et postea quum de ipso
eges ad operandum, debes illud distemperare cum aqua colata
ut prius dictum est. Ex hoc quia in ipso non fuerat umquam
cola seu aqua ulla colata. Et potes etiam colare illud de
diversis coloribus, ut prius commiscendo eos in ipso ad libitum
tuum, ut dictum est supra. Et nota, quod si non habes cornu
cervi, pro faciendo quod dictum est, bona sunt ossa sua et
etiam ut supra est declaratum ossa aliorum animalium et
avium.

A TREATISE UPON VARIOUS COLOURS,

AND FIRST THE

INTRODUCTION.

297. In the year of the Circumcision of our Lord Jesus Christ, 1398, on Thursday, the 8th day of August, Johannes Alcherius wrote, and noted down, at Paris, in the house of Anthonio de Compendio, an illuminator of books, and an old man, according to the words told him by the said Anthonius, who, as he said, had tried, during the whole time of his life, all the following recipes, namely, the following chapters concerning colours for illuminating books. And afterwards, in the year 1411, in the month of December, the same Johannes, who had then returned more than one year from Lombardy, namely, from Bologna, where there was a *curia apostolica* newly united, corrected them in many places, according to further information, which he subsequently received by means of several authentic books treating of such subjects, and otherwise; and copied them fairly as follows:—

298. *For laying gold upon various articles, so that it may be burnished, and various cautions concerning it, for illuminating.*—To lay gold on parchment, or paper, and on wooden panels primed with white chalk, which gold may be burnished or polished. Take gersa, or white chalk, and a little ocra de ru, equal to one-third part of the chalk, and pound them both together, and grind as thick as you can, i. e. with little water,

DE DIVERSIS COLORIBUS

IN SEQUENTI TRACTATU,

ET PRIMO MODUS PROHEMII.

297. Anno circumcisionis domini Jesu Christi 1398 die Jovis octavo Augusti, *Johannes Alcerius* scripsit et notavit in Parisiis in domo *Anthonii de Compendio* illuminatoris librorum, antiqui hominis, a verbis quæ ipse Anthonius sibi dixit. Et qui omnia quæ sequuntur tentaverat toto tempore vitæ suæ, ut dixit, de coloribus scilicet ad illuminandum libros, sequentia capitula. Et postea anno 1411 de mense decembris, idem Johannes qui jam per plusquam annum reversus fuerat a partibus Lombardiæ, viz., a Bononia, ubi erat curia apostolica noviter unita, correxit in pluribus partibus ea, secundum plures informationes quas inde postea per plures libros autentiquos de talibus narrantes, et aliter habuerat, et rescripsit ea ad nettum ut sequitur.

298. *Ad ponendum aurum super diversis quod burniatur, et de diversis cautelis utendis super hoc, illuminando.*—Ad ponendum aurum in papiro, in pergameno, seu carta, et in tabulis ligneis, creta alba dealbatis, quod aurum burniatur seu poliatur. Accipe gersam seu cretam albam et modicum ocræ de ru, per tertiam partem quantitatis cretæ et totum simul subtilia, et tere cum aqua clara magis spissum quam poteris,

upon a smooth hard stone, with a muller also made of stone. Afterwards put the colour, which is otherwise called the tempera or size of the gold, in a shell or a glazed earthen saucer, or a glass vase. And when you wish to use it, take as much as you like of it in another smaller shell, and temper it to a reasonable softness or consistence, with whipped white of egg, in order to paint or write with it; and if you have time, allow the mordant to get stale, for several days or weeks, for it will be better putrid than fresh. Afterwards write, paint, and draw whatever you like, and where you like, and let it dry. Then, when you wish to lay on the gold, go into a closed place and choose a proper time, as has been before mentioned. And having chosen a fit time and place, and used the proper precautions, lay the gold on those parts of the parchment or paper on which you put the colour or mordant, and draw over it, first pressing lightly, and afterwards more forcibly, the burnisher, namely, the tooth of a boar or a horse, and polish the said gold until it adheres to the colour, and becomes shining, as was said before. Therefore, when the gold is to be laid on, the mordant which was left from a previous gilding is better than any other, provided that in the interval, by looking at it, stirring it and mixing egg or water with it, it has been kept sufficiently liquid, so that it may not be completely dried up, or have been too much putrified or altered.

299. *To make a rose colour.*—To make a rose colour for painting on parchment, paper, and wooden panels primed with chalk. Take brixillium scraped very fine with a knife or with glass, and tie it in a fine piece of linen, not tight, but loose and easy. And put it, tied up in that manner, into a new glazed earthen jar, to soak in ley, or in urine; and if the urine is stale, so much the better. If you cannot have any such, take very strong ley and put with the said piece of linen containing the brixillium, some of the white chalk of three or four times the weight of the brixillium, more or less, as by looking at it you may think fit, according to the goodness of the brixillium. Afterwards add some

i. e. cum pauca aqua, super lapidem equalem durum cum mol-
leta lapidis similiter.   Postea pone ipsum colorem qui aliter
tempera vel assisia auri dicitur, in conchilla aut in scutella
figuli vitriata, aut in vase vitri.   Et cum operari vis, accipe de
ipso in conchilla alia parviori quantum vis et modera ipsum
cum claro ovi spongiato ad rationabilem mollitiem seu liquida-
tem pro pingendo aut scribendo de ipso, et si habes tempus
cum temperaveris, dimittas inveterari per plures dies vel septi-
manas ipsam temperam, quia melior erit putrida quam recens.
Postea de ipso scribe pinge et pertrahe quæ vis et ubi vis et dimittas siccari. Postea sis in loco recluso cum aurum vis ponere
et elige tempus idoneum ut supradictum est. Et habitis idoneis
loco et tempore et remediis; ponas aurum in locis cartæ aut pa-
pyri quibus ipsum colorem vel assisiam posuisti, et super trahe,
et premendo primo leviter, postea fortius burnissorem, scilicet
dentem apri vel equi et polias tantum dictum aurum quam ad-
hæreat colori et lucidum fiat ut supra jam dictum est. Ideo
cum aurum poni vult, color talis remansus de alia positione
auri alias facta melior est dum ex interpolata visitatione de-
ductione et ovi aut aquæ interpositione conservatus sit in debita
liquiditate, ita quod ad totalem siccitatem vel nimiam putrefactionem et alterationem deductus non sit.

299. *Ad faciendum Rosam.*—Ad faciendum rosam pro operando in carta, et in papiro, et in ligneis tabulis creta dealbatis.
Accipe brixillium rasum subtiliter cum cultello vel cum vitro,
et liga in subtili pecia lini non stricte sed late et fluctuanter.
Et sic ligatum pone in vase figuli vitriato novo ad temperandum in lixivio aut in urina hominis ebriatoris potantis forte
vinum, et si urina sit vetera tanto melius, et si non possis
habere talem, accipe lessivium fortissimum et pone de creta
alba in ipso lessivio, cum dicta petia in qua est brixillium et
per quantitatem de tribus vel quatuor vicibus quantitatis brixillii ad pondus et etiam sicut inspiciendo melius videbis convenire plus et minus secundum bonitatem brixillii. Postea pone

pulverized raw alum, in quantity about one-fourth part of the chalk or thereabouts, more or less, and mix all these things together, always leaving the said brixillium tied up in the said piece of linen, and leave it so for about one hour. Next, place the jar upon a fire, not of wood, but of charcoal, and let it boil, but not too fast, for the space of a quarter of an hour or less, so as just to melt the alum. Then take the said bag of brixillium out of the vase, and press it and screw it out well, in order that the whole of the colour may run out of it into the said vase; and then remove the colour, hot as it is, from the fire, and put it on a hollow lump of chalk or upon a brick of baked clay, in order that the urine or ley may be immediately absorbed into the stone, and the colour itself remain thickened and half dry. Afterwards let it dry completely in the sun, and then remove the colour, which is of a rose colour, from the stone or brick with a knife, and put it by for use. When you wish to use it, take as much as you require and powder it, that is, grind it upon a hard and smooth stone with gum water, which must be made of two-third parts of gum arabic dissolved in so small a quantity of water as barely to cover the colour when the water is added and strained through a linen cloth, and one-third part of clear water mixed with the said gum so dissolved and strained. And with the gum water, thus made, temper your rose colour to a proper consistence, and use it for whatever you please, as well for writing, as for painting and drawing.

300. *To make corrosive green, without substance or body.*— To make a green transparent in its nature, and without body, that is, having no substance, such, for example, as is the colour of saffron, *i. e.* of crocus, which does not cover up other colours so as to conceal them, on account of its thinness, transparency, and rarity, owing to which other colours appear through it, wherefore this colour as well as the said green colour is over-powered, and shows little or not at all, nor can it be much seen over other colours. But this green colour is not mild like saffron, on the contrary it is, by nature, acrid and corrosive, so

de alumine glaro crudo pisto in pulverem, quod sit tantum
quantum est quartum dictæ cretæ vel circa, et autem plus
quam minus, et misceas hæc omnia insimul dimittendo semper
ligatum in dicta pecia dictum brixillium et dimittens sic per
horam unam vel circa. Postea ponas vas ad ignem non lignorum sed carbonum et bulliant non nimis fortiter et per spatium
quartæ partis horæ vel minus, ita quod solum alumen fondatur.
Postea de ipso vase tollatur dicta pecia brixillii et exprimatur
et extorqueatur fortiter ut color de ipsa totaliter exeat in eodem
vase ; postea tollatur ipse color ita callidus ab igne et ponatur
super lapidem cretæ concavæ vel super lapidem de terra &c.,
ad hoc quod urina seu lessivia intret in lapidem subito et
color ipse remaneat ibi inspissatus et semisiccus. Postea facias
ex toto siccari ad solem, deinde eleva ipsum colorem, quæ rosa
est cum cultello a lapide vel latere, et repone servando pro usu.
Et cum de ipsa operari vis, accipe de ipsa quantum vis et
subtilia, id est tere super lapidem durum et planum cum aqua
gummata quæ fit per duas partes gummi arabici fusi in tam
pauca aqua, quod pene cooperiatur ipsa aqua cum in ipsam ponitur aqua, et colati postea per telam lineam, et per tertiam
partem fit aqua clara insimul cum dicto gummi fuso et colato ;
et de ipsa aqua gommata ipso modo factam distempera dictam
rosam ad debitam mollitiem et operaberis de ipsa quæ volueris,
tam scribendo quam pingendo ac protrahendo.

300. *Ad faciendum viride corrosivum absque substantia seu
corpori.*—Ad faciendum viride in substantia clarum et non corpulentum id est substantiam non habentem, ut verbi gratia
clarus atque sine substantia est color safran, i. e. croci qui non
cooperit alios colores pro ejus subtilitate claritate et raritate,
qua alii colores apparent per medium ipsum, et ex hoc ipse
pro raritate sua ut et dictus color viridis remanet obfuscatus, et
nil vel minimum apparet, neque multum apparere potest super
alios colores. Sed ipse color viridis non est dulcis sicut est
dictus color croci, ymo ex sua natura est acer et corrosivus,

that it destroys and corrodes other colours if it is put over
them, or they over it, and this on account of the verdigris
which is in it ; and such is its nature, and it is used upon
parchment and paper.   Take verdigris and a little of the
dried lees of wine, which in Latin is called *tartarus,* and in
French *gravelle*,[1] and pulverize it and grind both the ingredients
together upon a hard and smooth stone with vinegar.   Afterwards draw all those things which you wish, both in parchment
and paper, and the empty spaces which are between the lines
of black ; afterwards fill in with the green colour made in the
above manner, and colour according to your taste, the things
which you have so drawn as aforesaid.   And note, that no
other colour can be laid over this green colour, as has been
already observed, nor can it be laid over others ; nor can it be
used otherwise than by itself and upon white paper and parchment, because this green colour, made as above, is corrosive
and acrid, and, by reason of its acrid nature, it destroys other
colours, as has been already mentioned above.

301. *To make a green colour, which has body and is not corrosive.*—To make a mild green body colour, for painting on
parchment, on paper, on linen, and on primed wooden panels.
Take verdigris and the juice of the herb which is called in
French *flamma*,[2] and strain the juice of the herb through a
linen cloth, and grind up the aforesaid green with it upon
a stone, adding a little gum water to it.   Then put it into a
shell or a glazed earthen saucer, and temper it with the gum
water, and the juice of that herb.   The gum water must be
made of clear gum arabic, and must be strained, lest, when the
gum is poured into the colour, it should contain any straws, earth,
or other impurities.   Afterwards write, draw, and paint whatever you like with this green colour, and note, that the juice
of rue would be better than that of the above written herb for
putting into the above-mentioned composition of the said green

---

[1] Anglicè " Tartar."
[2] Flambe, Glayeul. It. Gladiola ; E. Cornflag ; L. Gladiolus Communis.

taliter quod destruit et rodit alios colores si ponatur super ipsos, vel ipsi super ipsum, et hoc pro viride æris qui in ipso ponitur et est talis conditionis et ponitur in carta et in papiro. Accipe viride æris et modicum de fæce vini sicca, quæ dicitur in latino tartarus et in gallico *gravella*, et subtilia et tere super lapidem durum et planum insimul quæ dicta sunt cum aceto. Postea omnia quæ in carta et in papiro protrahere vis, protrahe, ac vacuum, viz. per lineas de colore scilicet nigro, postea de ipso colore viridi sic facto ut dictum est colora ad libitum ea quæ ut dictum est protraxeris. Et nota quod super ipsum colorem viridem ut dictum est, nullus alter color debet poni neque ipse super alios nisi solum super cartam albam vel papirum, et non super colorem aliquem album artificiatum seu pictum, quia ipse color viridis illo modo factus est fortis seu acer et pro sua acritudine destruit alios colores ut supra jam dictum est.

301. *Ad faciendum colorem viridem cum corpore et non corrosivum.*—Ad faciendum colorem viridem dulcem et corpulentum, pro operando in pergameno, in papiro, in telis, et in tabulis ligneis dealbatis. Accipe viridem æris seu arani et succum herbæ quæ dicitur in gallico flamma et ipsum succum herbæ cola per telam lineam et cum ipso tere super lapidem viridem suprascriptum addendo aliquantulum de aqua gommata, postea ipsum pone in conchella, vel in scutella figuli vitriata, et distempera cum dicta aqua gummata et cum dicto succo ipsius herbæ, et dicta aqua gummata debet fieri de gummi arabico lucido, et collata, ne cum infusum sit gummi in ipsa, adsint in ipsa ullæ palleæ, terra vel aliæ turpitudines. Et postea de ipso colore viridi scribe protrahe et pinge quæ vis. Et nota quod succus rutæ esset melior quam suprascriptæ herbæ ad ponendum in dicta compositioni dicti viridis coloris. Et alii sunt

colour.   There are some persons who put the juice of certain other herbs.

The aforesaid colour is such that you may paint upon it with other colours, and lay gold upon it, &c., in the same manner as upon sinopis or ultramarine, or upon rosa, and other similar things, because there is no vinegar in it, and the acrid nature of the verdigris is corrected by the juice of the said herb.

302. *Introduction to the following chapter, concerning the manner of making writing ink.*

Also in the aforesaid year, 1398, on Saturday the xijth day of October, the aforesaid Johannes Alcherius wrote at Paris, and in this place, after the preceding, added this chapter concerning the way to make good atramentum, or incaustum, which chapter had been long previously, even before the year 1382, given to him in writing at Milan, by the since deceased Master Alberto Porzello, who was most perfect in all kinds of writing and forms of letters, and who, while he lived, kept a school at Milan, and taught boys and young men to write ; and who, as he said, had frequently tried and made ink in the manner described in this chapter, and had found it very good, as he told the said Johannes. And the said Johannes, himself, afterwards tried this method at Milan, and also found it very good. And afterwards in the said year, 1382, in the month of March, when the said Johannes Alcherius went from Milan to Paris, he carried with him a copy of the said recipe, which is as follows. But afterwards, in the year of Our Lord Jesus Christ, 1411, in the month of December, having then been returned to Paris more than one year from Lombardy—viz., from Bologna, from the newly-formed Apostolical *curia*, he corrected in some places the following recipes, and copied them fairly as follows :—

303. *To make ink for writing.*—Observe that choice and tried writing ink must be made in this way.   Take iij ounces of galls, the goodness of which may be known by their being wrinkled.   Take an equal quantity of gum arabic, the goodness of which may be known by its being bright and easily broken, and the smallest is the best.   *Item.* Take $3\frac{1}{2}$ oz. of Roman vitriol [sulphate of copper ?], the goodness of which may be known by its being of a blue colour, and solid, and coarse after the manner of coarse salt.   Afterwards take four pounds,

qui ponunt succos quarundam aliarum herbarum. Et color suprascriptus est talis quod potest super ipso pinge cum aliis coloribus, et super ipso poni aurum etc. sicuti posset fieri super sinopide vel super lazurio, vel super rosa et aliis similibus, quia ibi non est acetum, et acritudo viridis æris mitigata est ex dicto succo herbæ.

302. *Prohemium super capitulo sequenti de modo ad facien-dum incaustum pro scribendo.*

Item anno prædicto 1398, die sabati xii. Octobris, antedictus Johannes Alcherius scripsit in Parisiis, et hic post precedentem addidit hoc capitulum de modo faciendi bonum atramentum seu incaustum ad scribendum, quod capitulum jam diu usque ante annum 1382 sibi dederat in scriptis in Mediolano nunc quondam magister *Albertus Porzellus* perfectissimus in omnibus modis scribendi et formis lite-rarum, qui tunc dum vixit tenuit scolas in Mediolano et docebat pueros et juvenes ad scribendum. Et qui temptaverat ipsemet multotiens et fecerat attramentum in modum in ipso capitulo con-tentum, et invenerat valde bonum ut dixit dicto Johanni. Et postea dictus Johannes ipsum modum temptavit Mediolano et invenit similiter valde bonum. Et postea dicto anno 1382 de mense Martii, quum dictus Johannes Alcherius ivit a Mediolano Parisiis, portavit secum copiam dicti capituli quæ talis est ut sequitur. Sed postea anno ejusdem domini nostri Jesu Christi 1411 de mense decembris dum jam per plusquam annum de partibus Lombardiæ viz., a Bo-nonia veniens, ab apostolica Curia noviter unita, rediisset Parisiis, in aliquibus partibus ea quæ dicta sunt sequentia, et rescripsit ad nettum ut sequitur.

303. *Ad faciendum incaustum seu atramentum pro scri-bendo.*— Nota quod atramentum electum et probatum hoc modo debet fieri. Accipe unciæ tres gallæ, cujus bonitas ap-paret si minuta in crispa est. Totidem accipe de gummi ara-bico, cujus bonitas apparet si lucidum et de facili frangatur, et minutum magis valet. Item accipe oncias tres et dimidiam vitrioli Romani, cujus bonitas apparet si est cœlesti coloris et solidum et grossum, quasi in modum salis grossi. Postea accipe quatuor libras de onciis duodecim per libram aquæ claræ, quæ si

of twelve ounces to the pound, of clear water, which if it is rain water, or water from a cistern in which rain water is kept, is better than well, spring, or river water; and put into a new metal or glazed earthen jar, which has never been used for any thing else, in order that it may be pure and clean from all filth; and into this water, put the galls roughly pounded so that each grain of gall may be broken into four or five pieces, and then let the galls boil in the water without gum or vitriol, until the water is reduced to one-half. Then let it be strained through a cloth or piece of linen, and be put back without the substance of the galls in the vase over the fire, and let it remain there until it begins to boil, and then put into it the gum ground and pulverized, and let it boil gently for a short time, namely, until the gum is dissolved. Having done this, pour into it directly two pounds of the best pure and white wine, and stir it a little, and immediately add the vitriol well pulverized, stir it again a little, and then immediately remove the vase from the fire, and mix the whole together in order that the vitriol may be well incorporated with the galls, and the gum, and the water. Having done all these things in order, put the vase with the ink in the open air, and let it stand for one night, in order that the air may make it brilliant and more black. And therefore if it be done in fine weather, it will be better and finer. Afterwards strain it through a cloth, and put it by, and keep it for use.

303a.[1] *Another Recipe to make Ink.*

> Another recipe for making one quart of good atramentum, or incaustum, which, however, does not belong to the present treatise; but was added in this place on account of its connexion with the matter of the preceding chapter, by me, Jehan Le Begue, licentiate in law, who wrote with my own hand, although not accustomed to it, the present work, or the chapters in this volume contained, in the Year of Our Lord MCCCCXXXJ, and in the year of my age lxiij, as I found the same recipe elsewhere, written as follows:—

Take a quarter of a pound of gall-nuts of the weight of iiij.

---

[1] The succeeding chapters, to the end of the volume, were added by Le Begue.

est pluvialis vel de cisterna reservante aquas pluviales melior est
quam putei nec fontis nec fluvii et pone eam in vase metallino
vel figuli vitriato novo, quod non sit alteri usui deputatum, ut
sit purum et mundum ab omni sorde, et in ipsa aqua mitte
gallam grosso modo tritam, ita quod de quolibet grano gallæ
fiant quatuor vel quinque particulæ, et sic bulliat galla in aqua
absque gummi et vitriolo, donec aqua reddatur ad medium
comminuta.   Postea coletur per pannum seu telam et absque
substantia gallæ reponatur in vase ad ignem et sic tantum stet
quod incipiat bullire, et tunc gummi tritum et pulverizatum
mittatur in ipsa et bulliat aliquantulum, scilicet leniter usque :
quo gummi liquefactum sit.   His factis, immediate apponas
duas libras optimi vini puri et albi et aliquantulum misce, et
immediate mitte vitriolum bene pulverizatum et misceas parum, et statim eleva vas ab igne, et misceas simul totum, ita
quod bene incorporetur vitriolum cum galla, et gummi, et
aqua.   Omnibus his peractis ex ordine pone vas cum ipso
attramento ad aerem serenum, et stet per unam noctem, ut serenum reddat ipsum lucidum et magis nigrum.   Et ideo si fiat
sereno tempore, magis valet et pulcrius est.   Et postea coletur
per telam, et reponetur, et usui servetur.

303a. *Autre Recepte pour faire encre.*

Alia recepta pro faciendo unam quartam attramenti seu incausti boni,
quæ tamen non est de præsenti compilatione, sed hic, propter con-
nexitatem materiæ capituli precedentis, fuit addita per me *Johannem
Le Bégue licentiatum in legibus* qui præsens opus seu capitula in hac
volumine aggregata, propria manu, licet non assuetus, scripsi Anno
Domini MCCCCXXXI ætatis vero meæ lxiij, prout eandem receptam
alibi scriptam reperi sub hac forma.

Prenes ung quarteron de noiz de galle de iiij deniers parisis

Parisian deniers, and let them be beaten to powder. Put it
[the powder] into a quart and a half of water, and let it boil
for an hour and a half or more on a good charcoal fire until the
water is reduced to a quart; and when it has thus boiled put
into it a quarter of a pound of gum of the weight of iiij. Parisian
deniers and a cup full of vinegar; and then make it boil another
hour, and when it has boiled, take it off and put into it a quarter
of a pound of copperas in powder of the weight of iij. Parisian
deniers, and let it cool, and then put it into an inkstand. And
if it is too pale add to it a little more copperas, and you will
have good ink.

304. *To make a rose colour from Brazil wood.*—Take a mixture of equal quantities of water from a cistern, and wine, and
boil in it shavings of the said brexillium; and, having extracted
and pressed out the colour, and strained the red liquid through
a linen cloth, and removed the substance of the wood, add to
the water a little roche alum in powder; and when it is dissolved, put in some white gypsum, which has been ground
upon a stone with pure water and dried, or some bracha prepared and ground in the same way as the gypsum is directed to
be done, in sufficient quantity, and mix and incorporate them all
well together, and keep for use. This water can also be used without putting in gypsum or bracha, but only for shading, and not
as a body colour, for it has no body or substance; and when
the bracha or gypsum is added, then it can be used as a body
colour as well as for shading, because the gypsum or bracha,
which have body, give their body to the colour.

305. *Tracing paper*, through which all things are visible that
are drawn and figured on other parchment or on paper or on
panels when laid under it, and therefore all drawings which are
put under it, or all drawings or pictures over which it is put,
can be drawn correctly and perfectly on this tracing paper. It
is made in this way. Grease thinly with mutton suet a smooth
and polished stone of the breadth and length you wish your
tracing paper to be. Then, with a broad brush, spread clear
and transparent melted glue over the stone, and let it dry.

et faites batre en pouldre, puis la metez en quatre et demie
diaue et la faites boulir une heure et demie ou plus a beau feu
de charbon et jusques atant que leaue soit revenue a la quarte ;
et puis quant elle aura ainsi bouli, y mettez un quarteron de
gomme de iiij deniers et plain gobelet de vin aigre ; et puis le
faites boulir une autre heure et puis quant elle aura boulu, la
descendez et y metez un quarteron coperose en pouldre de iij
deniers parisis, et le laissiez refroidier puis metez en un cellier.
Et se elle est trop clere blanche si y metez encore un pou de
coperose et vous aurez bon encre.

304. *Ad faciendum colorem ligni Brexillii rosaceum.*—Accipiantur aqua cisternæ et vinum album per medietatem, et in
ipsis coquatur rasura dicti brexilii et extracto colore postea expressa et colata dicta aqua rosacia per telam et ablata substantia ligni suprascripti ponatur in ipsa aqua parum aluminis rosiæ
triti quo fuso ponatur in ipsa aqua de gipso albo bene trito super lapidem cum aqua clara et desiccato aut de bracha eodem
modo ordinata et trita quo dictum est de gipso ad quantitatem
quæ sufficiat et incorporentur et misceantur et operetur de hoc,
et etiam potest operari de ipsa aqua antequam ponatur gipsum
nec bracha, sed solum umbrando, et non ad corpus, quia corpus
seu substantiam non habet, et quando apposita est bracha vel
gipsus, tunc potest operari ad corpus et etiam umbrando quia
gipsus seu bracha qui corpus habent incorporant colorem ipsum.

305. *Carta lustra,* per quam transparent quæ sub ipsam sunt
posita protracta et figurata in aliis cartis vel in papiris aut in
tabulis et possunt igitur in ipsa carta lustra penitus et recte ab-
strahi qualia sunt quæ sub ipsam ponuntur protracta vel protractiones et picturæ super quas ipsa extenditur.   Fit hoc modo.
Perungas subtiliter sepo arietino lapidem æqualem et politam
latitudinis et longitudinis tantæ quantæ vis facere cartam.
Postea cum pincello lato lineas ex colla liquefacta clara et lucida
lapidem ipsum et dimitte siccari.   Postea eleva ab uno angulo

Afterwards lift up from one of the corners of the stone a little
of this skin of dried glue, which will be as thin as paper, but
transparent; and see whether it is thick enough, that is, whether it is not too thin; if so, do not pull it off, but leave it there
and give it another coat of the same glue, and let it dry; and
then again, as before, try whether it is thick enough.   And
repeat this until it is sufficiently thick.   Afterwards take it
quite off the stone, because the above-mentioned greasing with
mutton fat will enable you to take off the said coat of glue easily,
for it will not allow it to fasten or stick to the stone; and so you
will have tracing paper for the purposes aforesaid.[1]

306. *How the colours are tempered.*—All colours are distempered with the gum of the pine or of the sapin,[2] except minium
and ceruse, which are tempered with white of egg.   All kinds
of green must be tempered with glue except Spanish green,
which must be tempered with vinegar.

307. *To clean and renovate minium that is too old and dirty.*—
Put it into water mixed with one-fourth part of wine in a horn,
and stir it up well; then let it settle well and pour off and remove the water, and pulverize the colour and distemper it with
whipped white of egg, and do as you please with it.

308. *To make a colour which makes all other colours, except
orpiment, sinople, and saffron, bright, brilliant, and lustrous, and
which is called " Clare."*—Put gum arabic to soak in clean water
in a clean vessel, until it is dissolved, and with this distemper
your colours, or stir them with it and leave them moist for a day
or two; and if you wish the clare to be made quickly, place it
over hot ashes.

309. *To make a very good lake.*—Take an ounce of lake,[3] and

---

[1] Compare this with Cennino Cennini, chap. xxv.

[2] The article being repeated, it would seem that the author intended two
kinds of pine resin.   The latter was the Pinus Picea of Linnæus, the
Silver Fir of the English, the Abete of the Italians—whence they procured
the Olio di Abezzo, which was used in making varnishes.   See Nemnich,
art. ' Pinus;' and see Matthioli, pp. 118, 120.

[3] The lac lake.

lapidis aliquantulum linituram illam collæ siccatæ quæ erit subtilis ut carta sed erit lustra, et vide si non sit satis grossa seu
spissa, viz., quod sit nimis subtilis, et non eleves sed permittes,
et adhuc linias desuper de eadem cola et permitte siccari, et ut
prius tempta si satis grossa sit.   Et totiens hoc reiteres quod
fiat sufficienter grossa.   Postea ex toto eleva a lapide quia suprascripta perunctio lapidis ex adipe arietino facta dabit facili-
tatem elevandi ipsam cartam quam non permisèrit lapidi glu-
tinari nec adhærere et sic habebis cartam lustram ad ea quæ
dicta sunt facienda.

306. Toutes couleurs sont destrempées de gomme de pin ou
de sapin, fors mine et ceruse qui se destrampent de glaire dœufs.
Tout vert droit estre destrempe de glux, se ce nest vert des-
pagne qui doit estre destrempez de vin aigre.

307. *Se mine est trop vielle et trop orde pour la renouveler et
abellir.* —Mettez le en yaue avecques la quarte partie de vin,
en un cornet et la mouvez tres bien, puiz la laissiez bien rasseoir, puis purez et ostez leaue et le brisiez et destrempez de
glaire dœf et en faites vostre volente.

308. *Pour faire une couleur qui fait toutes autres couleurs
reluisans clers et replendissans qui est nommee clare ; hormis
orpiment sinople et safran.*—Mettez tremper gomme arabice
en eaue nette en un vaisseau net tant que elle soit fondue et
soit expresse par raison, et de ce destrempez vos couleurs ou
vous les mouvez avecques, et les laissiez moitier par ung jour
ou deux.   Et se vous voulez qu'il soit tost fait si le mettez
dessus les cendres chaudes.

309. *Pour faire très bonne laque.*—Prenez une once de laque

rasp finely a little Brazil wood, put it into a clean vessel, then add to the Brazil wood some clean and clear beaten white of egg, and a little alum water. Grind the lake with that water and dry it in the sun, and when you wish to use it, distemper it with this water, especially on parchment; and the more you grind it up with this Brazil wood water, the better it will be.

310. *To write or paint with gold.*—Put quicksilver with powdered gold into stag's leather, and press it; the quicksilver will pass through the leather, and the gold will remain; then put the gold with the quicksilver over the fire, but take care that the crucible does not burn. And you must add to it a little well-pulverized salt, until the mercury evaporates, which you may catch in a vessel anointed with grease, and suspended above it. Then wash the powdered gold with water in a basin as you would wash minium; and when it is dry, stir into it a glue made with parchment or vellum, which you must put into a vessel over hot water, and it will presently be dissolved. When this is the case, grind it well, and fill with it your pen or pencil, and write or paint with this distempered gold.

311. *To illuminate a book or other thing with minium.*[1]—Do not use minium alone, for the letters would be too light coloured, and would not look well, but put minium with vermilion; and if the vermilion is very red and new, put two parts of that to one of minium. And if it is old and brown, put equal quantities of each, or two-thirds of minium, for the older the vermilion the darker and browner it is. When it is ground up with clear water and dried in heaps, if you wish to use it and to have it appear brilliant, distemper it with varnish and white of egg beaten to a froth, and add a little clean water; with this you may write large letters [initial] and small on parchment. If the colour is

---

[1] This is nearly a repetition of No. 177.

et rayez un pou de bresil soubtillement et mettez le en un vaissel nett, puiz mettez dedens le bresil glaire dœf batu clers et net et puiz un pou deaue en quoi il ait un pou dalun mis avecques, et puis de celle eaue moules le laque, puiz le laissiez secher au soleil et quant vous en voulez ouvrer vous le destremprerez de ceste yeaue especialment en parchemin. Et quant plus de foys le ferez broyer et mouldre a cette yaue de bresil, et resuer, tant mieulx vauldra.

310. *Pour escrire ou paindre dor.*—Mettez argent vif avecques or molu en pouldre en cuir de cerfs, et le espraignez si passera largent vif par le cuir et lor demourra ou cuir, puis mettez lor avecques largent vif sur le feu maiz gardez bien que le crosel narde. Et mettez avecques un pou de sel bien moulu et crible tant que le vif argent se parte par fumee, lequel vous pouez recevoir en une escuelle ointe de graisse pendue au hault au dessus puis lavez la pouldre dor en un bacin en yaue, comme vous feriez mine. Puis mettez la pouldre dor quant elle est seche en glus faite de parchemin orculin [ou velin] lequel mis en vaissel sur eaue chaude est **tantost** resolu et quant tout sera resolu moelez bien et mettez en vostre plume ou pincel et escrisiez ou paindez dicellui or trempe.

311. *Pour enluminer de mine, soit livre ou autre chose.*—Ne mettez pas mine par soi, car la lettre en seroit trop clere et mal parant, mais mettez mine avecques vermillon, et se le vermillon est bien rouge et novel si en mettez deux parties et le tiers de mine. Et sil est viel et obscur ou brun mettez de mine la moitié ou les deux pars, car plus est vermillon viel et plus est noir et obscur, et quant il sera mouluz ensamble a leaue clere et sec par monseaux se vous voulez eu ouvrer et quil soit luisant trempez le de vernix et de glaire dœufs rompue a lespurge, et y mettez pou deaue clere et de ce escrisiez en parchemin grosse lettre et menue et quant il est sech, sil nest bien luisant, et que

not brilliant when dry, and the weather is moist, dry it by the
fire, and thus it will shine; but if the weather is dry and hot,
it will be better to dry it in the sun.

312. *To write with brass, gold, and silver.*—File some brass
of a good colour very finely, then grind it on the porphyry,
which is a very hard stone ; put it into a clean vessel and let it
settle ; then pour off the water and prepare your tempera of
gum arabic. Distemper it with this, and use it on your pencil,
and when it is dry you must rub and burnish it well with the
stone which is called *ametiste* [hæmatite]. You will act in
the same manner for writing with gold and silver.

313. *Orpiment [atramentum] is thus made.*[1]—Take oil and
ink, and juice of the blackthorn, and its middle bark well
ground in a mortar ; put the whole together in a pot, and let
it stand for a night. Then boil it gently and strain it ; boil it
gently again with myrrh and aloes, and again strain it. Then
add to it a little verjuice or glace,[2] and put the whole to boil
gently over the coals without flame; then take it off and
keep it.

314. *To make a blue colour like azure.*—Take the juice of
the corn-flower,[3] and make on wood or parchment a ground of
white-lead ; lay the juice on the said ground, three, four, or
five, or more times, if necessary, and thus you will have an
azure colour.

315. *To paint walls.*—Put a little lime with ochre, that it
may be lighter coloured, or mix it with simple red or prasin,[4]
or with a colour which is called posce,[5] which is made with
ochre, green, and membrayne ;[6] or you may take of a colour

---

[1] See *ante*, No. 189.

[2] Glace, probably Alumen Glacie, or glarum, as in No. 41.

[3] The blue-bottle, the Corn Centaury, the corn-flower. Ciano delle
biade, Ciano ceruleo, Blaveolo, Fiore di Zaccaria, Centaurea cyanus.

[4] *Prasinus.* See Theophilus, lib. i. c. ii., and see *ante*, pp. 236 and
244. This colour was sometimes called " Prasminem ;" and by the Italians
" Verde Porro."

[5] *Posce.* See Theophilus, lib. i. c. iii.

[6] See Theoph., lib. i. c. i. See also *ante*, pp. 144 and 180, where this

le temps soit moite, sechez le au feu, si resplendira ; et se le
temps et sech et chaut elle seroit mieulx sechee au soleil.

312. *Pour escrire de laton et pareillement dor et dargent.*—
Limez tres subtilement laton de tres pure couleur et puis le
molez soutiliment sur le porphire qui est pierre tres seure,
puis le mettez et un net vaisel et le laissiez asseoir, puis ostez
leaue et ayez vostre detrempe de gomme arabiche, et len destrempez puis en ouvrez de vostre pincel, et quant ce sera fait
et sech, si le frotez et burnissez tres bien, d'une pierre qui est
nommee ametiste et ainsi povez vous escrire dor et dargent.

313. *Orpiment se fait ainsi.*—Prenez oille et encre et jus
despine noire et son escorce moienne bien broyee en un mortier et mettez tout ensemble, en un pot, et li laissiez une nuit
reposer, puis le metez un poi boulir, puis le colez, puis le
metez boulir un pou avec mirre et aloes et derechief le coulez.
Puis metez avee un po de verjus ou de glace, et remetez tout
ensemble sur les charbons sans flamme un petit bolir, puis le
ostez et le gardez.

314. *A faire couleur blauet comme d'azur.*—Prenez jus de
bleues net et faites en bois ou en parchemin un camp de blanc
de plomb, puis mettez le jus dessus le dit champ, trois ou
quatre ou cinq lis ou plus si mestier est ; si avez couleur
dazur.

315. *Pour peindre murs.*—Mettez un po de chaux avec ocre
pour avoir plus grant clarte, ou vous la mellez avec rouge
simple ou avec prasin ou avec une couleur qui est nommee posce
qui est faite de ocre vert et de membrayne ou vous pouvez

---

colour is described by S. Audemar under the name of " Olchus seu Membrana."

The method of mural painting described in the text was probably that
which was generally practised by the painters of the middle ages ; and
there is reason to suppose that the old paintings recently discovered on
the walls of churches in so many parts of England were painted in this
manner.

which is made of sinople, ochre, lime, and posc, &c. And walls should be painted rather moist than otherwise, because the colours unite together better, and are firmer. And all the colours for walls should be mixed with quicklime.

316. *Black* is made with charcoal ground with water or wine, and distempered with oil or garlic; but the best is made with atramentum, unless it is charcoal which is made of scales of iron boiled and heated with oil. Or take the bark of alder and grind it with iron filings in water, and put it with atramentum, and distemper it.

317. *The flesh colour of images is thus made.*—Take terre verte, white, and lake, mix them together, and fill what you please with them. Then make a shade [tint] of green and ochre so that it may be like green, and mix with it a little lake, and mark out the shadows with it; then make the rose colour with white and synople, and lay it wherever you may think proper. Then make the flesh colour of ochre and white, with a little synople, and fill up the solid parts, but that which is laid on the rose colour should be very thin. Then take some of that colour and lay it on the eyebrows, and under the feet, on the mouth, chin, neck, and ears. Then draw as it were veins, and then with pure lake mark the eye-lashes, nostrils, eyes, and limbs. Then shade again lightly with lake mixed with a little oil; then whiten the lights with pure white, and then draw the eyelids, eyes, and other members.

318. *To gild with gold leaf.*—Grind well some gypsum with pure clean water, dry it; then grind it with synople like rose, and with fish-glue dissolved in very good white wine, and with the pencil spread it where you please, covering well with it the part to be gilded. Then dry it, and make it smooth with the knife, apply the gold, fix it with the hæmatite and polish it,

prandre dune couleur qui soit faite de synople et docre et de
chaux et de posc etc. ; et doivent estre murs paint plus moiste
que aultre chose pour ce que les couleurs se tiennent mieulx
ensembles et soient plus fermes. Et doivent toutes couleurs
pour murs estre melles avecques chaux vive.

316. *Noir* est fait de charbon broye avec eaue ou vin et
destrempez doile ou deil, mais le bon est fait darrement,[1] etc.
Se ce nest carbon qui est fait de paille de fer boulu et cuie
avec oille. Ou vous prenez escorce dalne et le broiez en eue
avec molure de ferre en yaue, et mettez avec arcement et
destrempez.

317. *Charnure dymages se fait ainsi.*—Prenez vert terrin
blanc et laque, et mellez ensemble et emplissiez la ou vous
vouldrez, puis faictes ombre de vert et ocre en telle maniere
que ce soit comme vert et mellez avecques un po de laque, et
signez vos lits, et puis ombre et puis rose de blanc et de
synople, et roses la ou vous plaira, puis faites charnure docre
et de blanc et dun po de cinople et mettez dedans les signe-
mens espes et cil qui sera sur la rose sera tres sutil, puis
prenez de celle couleurs et mettez sur les surcils et dessoubs
les piez et sur la bouche et au menton et a la goile et aux
oreilles. Et en faut si comme se fust vains, puis designez de
pur lac les cilles et narines et les yeulx et tous les membres.
Et metez de rechief dedens umbre legierement et de lac loig-
nez un petit, puis le blanchissez de blanc pur, puis designez
les cilles et les yeulz et les autres membres.

318. *Pour mettre or de feuilles battues.*—Molez gipse tres
bien avec yaue pure et nette, puis le sechiez, puis le molez
avec cinope si comme rose, et avec cole de poisson qui soit
fondue avec tres bon vin blanc et le mettez au pincel la ou
vous vouldrez et soit bien couvert et le sechiez puis le raez dun
coustel plainement et mettez lor dessus et le fermez de ame-

---

[1] That this word is really " atramentum," is proved by a similar passage
in S. Audemar—see *ante*, No. 172. See also ' Materials for a History of
Painting in Oil,' by Mr. Eastlake, p. 132, n. ; and Halliwell's ' Dictionary
of Archaic and Provincial Words.'

and if it does not succeed well, take the above-mentioned glue, spread it over the drawing, and over that the gold leaf.

319. *If you wish to prepare oil for distempering all kinds of colours.*—Take quicklime, and equal quantities of ceruse and oil; expose these to the sun without moving it for a month or more, as the longer it remains the better it will be. Then strain it and preserve the oil well. With the oil, thus kept and prepared, you may distemper all colours either separately or mixed.

320. *To write with gold and silver.*—Take leaf gold, grind it with salt on the marble, leave it for a long time in water, stir it and let it settle. Then pour off the water to remove the salt, and the gold will remain at the bottom. Distemper it with gum for writing, and the letters you make will be dark; but when they are dry, polish them with a tooth and they will be of a beautiful yellow shining gold colour. If you choose you may write with silver in the same manner.

321. *To make silver letters without silver.*—Grind alum with salt; then wash it in order to remove the salt; then distemper it with gum and write with it. When it is dry, if you polish it with the tooth, it will lose its darkness, and will take the colour of silver.

322. *A recipe for grinding gold.*—Take some very fine and pure gold filings, grind them in a mortar such as is used by the apothecaries, which is made of three parts copper and one part of tin or lead; such are their mortars. But previous to this, your gold filings should be well washed in a basin or in a shell with a pencil. Then grind all your gold in the above-mentioned mortar, so that when finished it shall be left clear. And in like manner you may grind copper, silver, brass, pewter, and all other metals; but take care that the gold does not burn, as it would then be necessary to regrind it. When the operation is finished, remove the water and impurities, let the gold settle, then place it over the coals with water, and warm, and stir it.

tiste, et le lissez. Et se il ne vient bien prenez de la cole dessus dicte et metez au dessein, et tantost la feuille de lor dessus.

319. *Si vous voulez appareiller oïle pour destremper toutes manieres de couleurs.*—Prenes chaux vive avec autant de ceruse comme est de loile, puiz metez au soleil et ne le movez jusques a ung moyt ou plus tar quant plus y sera, et mieulx vaudra, puis le colez et gardez tres bien loile, et de celle oille gardee et ainsi preparee, povez destremper toutes couleurs ensemble et chacun par soy.

320. *Pour escrire dor et dargent.*—Pren feuille dor et la broye sur le marbre avec sel, puis le fay estre longuement en eaue, et le leve et laisse rasseoir puis prenez leaue pour oster le sel, si demourra lor au fons. Si le destrempe a gomme et en escri, si auras lettre noire et quant elle sera seche, si la poli dun dent, si sera belle et gaune et luisant en bonne couleur dor, et ainsi puez tu escrire de argent se tu veulz.

321. *Pour faire lettre dargent sans argent.*—Broyez alun avec sel, puis le leve pour oster le sel puis le destrempe a gomme et escri et quant il est sec, si le poli du dent, si perdra sa novete et ara couleur d'argent.

322. *Pour or mouler recipe.*—R. tres fin or lime bien menu et le broyez en un mortier suzille tel que les appoticaires ont, cilz de cuivre les trois pars et la quarte partie de staing ou de plomb, tels sont leurs mortiers ; mais avant ce doit estre votre limeure d'or bien lavee en un bachin ou en une conche de limeterie a un pincel et en ce mortier dessus dit, molez tant or que have qui y sera mise soit au departir clere. Et en telle maniere pourrez molez cuivre argent loton estaing et tout autre metail, mais gardez que lor ne se haerde car il le fauldroit remouldre de rechief. Et quant ce sera fait, ostez liaue et les ordures et laissiez lautre rasseoir, puis le metez sur les charbons avec eaue et le chauffez et mouvez.

323. *To grind gold, and how it should be softened.*—Take well-filed gold, grind it well on a porphyry slab with two parts of sal gem [rock salt], a little yellow sulphur in a glass vessel, changing it frequently from one vessel to another until it is well washed and purified. Then put it into a horn, and when you wish to use it, distemper it with gum arabic, which must be put into a glass vessel with water and exposed to the rays of the sun, until it is dissolved. When it is dissolved put it into a saucer with as much silver as water, and let it be tepid when you write with it, which you must do the same day before the fire. When dry, let it be burnished with a tooth.

324. *To make what appear to be gold and silver letters, without the use of either gold or silver.*—Make very thin plates of fine brass for gold letters, of fine tin for silver letters, and each separately; and let the plates be as thin as gold leaf, and let them be well ground and bruised with water and dried in the sun, and then strained through a cloth; afterwards regrind the coarser portion which remains in the cloth in a mill or mortar of iron or copper, such as is used by the apothecaries. Then fill the letters or portraits with minium, if you mean to gild, but if you intend to lay on silver put no minium; and when the minium is dry, fill those letters or portraits, by means of an ass'-hair pencil, with a glue made in the following manner.

Boil some clean and white pieces of the leather of cows, oxen, calves, or sheep, early in the morning, until two-thirds have evaporated. Then pour off that water, add some fresh water, and boil again for an hour. Then pour off one-third of the water and let the rest boil for two hours more, when you must take out the leather and keep it in a clean vessel; and if it is then thick and sticks to the fingers, it is good; if it does not do so, you must boil it again. Then take some of this glue and put it into a vessel over the coals, and while hot or tepid, lay it on those portraits or letters with the pencil. Afterwards dust on to it the said brass powder or tin powder, and leave it for a day to dry, then polish it with a tooth. Again, an-

323. *Pour escrire dor et comment il se doit mollir.*—Recevez or bien lime, et le moulez tres bien sur une porfire avec ij pars de salgemme et un poy de souffre jaune et moulez tout ce tres bien ensamble avec lor puis en vaissel de voire, et le mettez souvent de vaissel en autre tant qu'il soit fort bien lavez et bien purifiez, puis le mettez en un cornet.   Et quant vous en vouldrez ouvrer si le destrempez de gomme arabic et lequel mettez avec yaue en ung vaissel de voire au soleil afin quil fonde.   Et quant il sera fondu, mettez avec argent autant comme et de leaue en une paelle et faites que elle soit tiede quant vous vouldrez escrire et escresiez ce jour devant le feu. Et quant elle sera seche si le burnissez dun dent.

324. *Pour faire lettre qui semble dor et dargent, qui na ne or ne argent.*—Face plattes moult tenues de fin loton pour lettre dor, et de fin estaing pour lettre dargent, et chacun a part, et soient les plates tenues comme feuille dor a dorer, et soit molu tres bien et crible avec yaue et laissie seichr au soleil et coule par ung drapel et remoler le plus gros qui demorra en le drapel et moule tous dits en ung moulin ou mortier de cuivre ou de fer tel quil sont chieux les appothicaires, puis emplissiez les lettres ou pourtraictures de mine, en cas que veuillez faire dor ; et se dargent, ne y mettez point de mine, puis quant le mine est mis et est sech, mettez a un pincel de poil dasne en icelles lettres ou pourtraictures cole ou glus facte en tele maniere.

Faites boulir pieces de cuir de vaiche ou de bœuf ou de veau ou de mouton purs et blans, du matin jusques a tierce, pus ostez leaue et metez de lautre et faittes boulir une heure puis ostez le tiers de leaue et laissiez boulir lautre encore ii heures puis ostez les cuirs et gardez leaue en un vaissel pur et net, et se lautre tour elle est expresse et que elle se tienne aux doiz elle est bonne.   Et se non faictes boulir de rechief puis prenez une partie de ceste cole et la mettez en un vaissel sur les charbons et la mettez chaude ou tiede a tout le pincel sur icelles lettres ou pourtraictures.   Et tantost mettez dessus de la dicte pouldre de loton ou de celle de estaing et laissiez

other way, without using brass powder: boil parchment with
the said glue, then take out the parchment, and put much
saffron with the glue, and let them cool together. In the
morning give your parchment a coat of glue on a very smooth
table, lay your tin powder on it, and then leave it exposed
to the sun for four or five hours, that it may dry; after this
you must polish it with a boar's-tooth, when it will be of the
colour of gold. Or thus, scrape your parchment with a knife
where you wish to draw, and make the glue with the saffron
boil a little. Then put a little of this into an iron spoon, warm
it over the coals, and while tepid, lay it where you please, by
means of the pencil, having your powdered tin in the other
hand, which you must then apply all over it, and burnish it
with a tooth. Also, if you wish to make gold letters, put
saffron with your tin and glue; but if you wish them to be
of the colour of silver, use no saffron; after this you may
put on other colours. And you must know that sometimes
the letters become pale; this arises either from its not being
sufficiently polished, or from the too small quantity of saffron.

325. *If you wish to make a water proper for distempering
all colours.*—Take a pound of lime and 12 pounds of ashes;[1]
then take boiling water and put the whole together, making
them boil well; after which let the mixture settle and strain
it through a cloth; then take four pounds of that water, heat
it well, take about two ounces of white wax, and put this to boil
with the water; then take about $1\frac{1}{2}$ oz. of fish-glue, put it in
water, and leave until it is well softened, and as it were melted,
when you must manipulate it until it becomes like paste, and
throw it into the water with wax, and make all boil together;
then add to it about an ounce and a half of mastic, and boil
it with the other ingredients. Take some of this water on a
knife-blade, or piece of iron, to ascertain whether it is done: if
it is like glue, it is all right. Strain this water while hot or

---

[1] I have no doubt that the word originally written was *cendres*, and not
Flandres.

secher par un jour, puis polissiez dun dent. Item autrement
sans pouldre de laton boulez parchemin avec la dicte cole et
ostez le parchemin et metez foison safran avecques la cole et
laissiez refroidier ensamble, et au matin faictes ou liniez le
parchemin de vostre cole sur une table bien pleine, et mettez
vostre pouldre destaing dessus, et puis le laissiez au soleil
secher par quatre ou cinq heures, puis le polissiez dun dent de
porc et sera couleur dor. Ou ainsi ; raez vostre parchemin
dun coustel la ou vous vouldrez pourtraire et faictes la cole
avec le safran un tant et boulir et en mettez un poy en une
cuiller de fer et faictes a tiedir sur les charbons, et en prenez
tout tiede et en mettez au pinceau la ou vous voulez et tenez
la pouldre de vostre estaing en lautre main et le appliquez
tantost dessus et laissiez secher et burnissez a un dent. Item
se vous voulez faire lettre dor mettez safran avecques vostre
estaing et vostre cole. Et se vous voulez dargent, si ny mettez
point de safran. Et apres pourrez vous mettre les autres couleurs, et est a savoir que la lettre aucune fois palist, et cest
quant elle nest mie bien polie ou quant on ni met pas le safran
a point.

325. *Se vous voulez faire yaue conosite a destremper toutes*
couleurs.—Prenez une livre de chaux et douze de Flandres
puis prenez eaue boulant et metez tout ensemble et les faictes
assez boulir puis le laissiez bien reposer, puis le coulez bien
parmy un drapel et de celle yaue prenez livres quatre et la
faictes bien ardoir, puis prenez cire blanche environ ii. onces et
la mettez boulir avec lyaue puis prenez cole de poisson environ
j once et $\frac{1}{2}$, et la mettez en eaue et li laissiez tant quelle soit
bien emollie et si comme fondue puis la maniez tant que elle
soit comme paste puis la mettez en lyaue avec la cire et la
faites ensemble boulir, et mettez mastic dedens environ once et
demie et faictes boulir ensemble, puiz prenez de ceste eaue et
mettez sur un coustel ou sur fer pour savoir sil est bien cuit
et sil est comme glue il est bien. Puis adonc coulez celle

tepid through a linen cloth, let it settle, and cover it well. With this water you may distemper all kinds of colours.

326. *To make skins and all other things of a red colour, or any other colour.*—First put the skins in alum-water which has been boiled with some bran, and then skim it well and let it settle, and when the heat of the water is so reduced that it is just tepid, so as not to burn the skins, throw them in. After this you must dry them ; then boil some brazil wood in the above-mentioned water, and when it is well boiled sew your skins into the form of bags, and fill them with the said water while tepid and not boiling, as in that case the skins would burn : they will thus be well coloured. And in this manner you may stain anything with any colour.

327. *To gild copper or brass without gold.*—Take clean and pure brass or copper, and scrape it well with a knife, and burnish it with a boar's tooth ; then grind some ox-gall or other suitable thing ; then take your pen or pencil, soak it in the gall, rub it on the above-mentioned brass or copper, and let it dry. Do this three times and you will have a colour similar to gold.

328. *To make fine letters of gold.*—Grind gold and mercury together, put them into a crucible over the fire until the mercury is evaporated ; then stir the gold well until it is reduced to powder, when you must grind it up with saffron boiled in water, and expose it to the sun in a phial with gum-water. When you use it, take it from the sun and write with it.

329. *If you wish to make three kinds of vestures on parchment, one purple or red, another violet, and another white.*—Mix together a green made from the juice of any herb with a little ochre, and with this fill the vesture of the pourtrayed image. As to the second mix a little cinople with orpiment, and with this fill the dress of the other image. For the third mix orpiment with the juice of a tree called in Latin sambucus, and in

yaue chaude ou tiede parmi ung drap linge, et laissiez reposer
et la covrez bien et de celle eaue povez destremper toutes
manieres de couleurs.

326. *Pour taindre peaux et toutes autres choses en couleur
rouge, et en toutes autres couleurs.*—Mettez les peaulx premiere-
ment en eaue alumee, qui soit boulie et du son dedens et puis
laissiez bien escumer et reposer, et quant leaue ne sera que
tiede tellement que en mettant les peaulx dedens elles nardent,
mettez lors dedens celle eaue les dictes peaulx puis les mettez
sechier, puis faictes boulir bresil dedens leaue dessus dicte et
quant elle sera tres bien cuite cousez vos peaulx en maniere
de sacz et mettez leaue dessus dicte dedens, tiede comme dit
est et non boillant afin que les peaulx nardent, et ainsi seront
elles tres bien coulorees. Et par ceste maniere povez taindre
toutes choses et de toutes couleurs.

327. *A dorer cuivre ou arain sans or.*—Prenez arain ou
cuivre pur et net, et le reez bien dun coustel, puiz le burnissiez
dun dent de porc puis moulez fiel de torel ou autre chose con-
venable, puiz prenez vostre penne ou vostre pincel et le moil-
liez au dit fiel et en frotez sur le cuivre ou arain dessus dit, et
laissiez secher, et se faictes pour trois fois, si aurez couleur
semblable dor.

328. *A faire lettre dor fin.*—Molez or et vif argent ensamble
et mettez en un crosol sur le feu tant que le vif argent soit
evapore, puis le movez tres bien tant que ce soit pourre, puis
molez safran avecques et les cuisez en yaue, puis le metez en
yaue de gomme au soleil en un fiale, et quant vous vouldrez
escrire prenez la fiale au soleil et du dit or escrisiez.

329. *Se vous voulez faire trois manieres de vestemens en
parchemin, lun pourpre ou rouge, lautre violet, et lautre blau.*
—Mellez ensemble vert avec jus daucune herbe et y adjoustez
un po docre et emplissiez le vestement de limage pourtraicte.
Et en aprez pour le second, mellez un po de cinople avec orpiment et emplissiez le vestement de lautre ymage. Tierce-
ment mellez orpiment avec jus des feuilles dun arbres qui es

French seur,[1] and fill the third dress with this. But these are not good on walls.

330. *To make a colour which is called venede or veneda.*[2]— Take black, and mix white lead with it, if it is to be used on parchment, but if it is to be used on walls employ lime instead of the said white lead.

331. *To make a green colour for writing.*—Mix good vinegar with sour honey, and put it in a [copper] vessel under very hot dung. In 12 days it will be of a beautiful green.

332. *To make a blood-like colour which is called lake.*—In the month of March cut some ivy, which in Latin is called edera, and which climbs on the trees and forests, and put the juice which exudes into a glass vessel every three days; then boil it in urine and use it in drawing with the pencil.

333. *The following is for tempering iron and steel.*—When the he-goat is in heat take his blood and temper your iron or steel in this; it then becomes very hard. The he-goat is an animal whose Latin name is hyrcus.

334. *To make the colour of red roses.*—Put some Brazil wood raspings into an earthen vessel glazed with lead, adding urine and powdered alum; let it stand for a night, and in the morning place it over the coals without flame and boil it well for a little; then take it off the fire, add a little powdered quick lime, and mix it well with the other ingredients; then pour off the clear part, and dry that which is thick so that you may use it when necessary.

335. *If you wish to redden tables or other things.*—Take linseed, or hemp-seed, or nut-oil and mix it with minium or cinople on a stone without water; then with a pencil illuminate what you wish to redden with this.

336. *To write with gold.*—Grind gold with clear and pure wine, then pour off the wine and distemper it with gum or ox-gall. When you desire to paint or write with it, you must stir

---

[1] The elder.   [2] See Theophilus, lib. i. c. vi.

nomme en Latin *sambucus*, et en Francais *seur*, et emplissiez
le tiers vestement, mais en murs ils ne sont pas bons.

330. *A faire une couleur qui se nomme venede ou veneda.*—
Prenez couleur noir et y mellez un pou de blanc de plomb
avec pour mettre en parchemin, mais se vous voulez le mettre
en mur, mettez en lieu du dit blanc plomb de la chaux.

331. *A faire couleur verde pour escrire.*—Mellez bon vin
aigre avec miel aigre, et le mettez en un vaissel en fiens bien
chaut et li laissiez douze jours et sera bon vert.

332. *Pour faire couleur sanguine qui est appelee laque.*—
Trenchiez du mois de mars yerre, qui est une herbe en Latin
appelee *edera*, et rampe sur les arbres et forets, et recevez en
un vaissel de voirre le jus qui en ystra de iij jours en trois
jours, et le cuisiez en orine et puis en ouvrez au pinceau vos
portraictures.

333. *Trempeure de fer et dacier forte se fait ainsi.*—Quant
le bouc est en amour, se on prent son sang, et on y trempe dedens fer ou acier. Il est moult dur, et le bouc est beste que
on nomme en Latin *yrchus*.

334. *A faire couleur de roses vermeilles.*—Raez bresil en un
vaissel de terre plomme et y metez de lorine et aussi pouldre
dalun, et le laissiez une nuit reposer, et a landemain le mettez
sur les charbons sans flambe, et le faites tres bien boulir une
onde ou deux, puis lostez du feu et mettez avec un pou de
chaux vive en pouldre, et mellez tres bien ensamble, et ostez
le cler, et mettez lespez secher pour garder et pour en ouvrez
quant est besoing.

335. *Si vous voulez rougir tables ou autres choses.*—Prenez
oile de lin ou de chanvre ou de noiz, et mellez avec mine ou
cinope sur une pierre sans yaue. Puis en luminez a un pincel
ce que vous voulez rougir.

336. *Pour escrire dor.*—Molez or avec vin cler et pur, puis
lostez du vin et le destrempez de gomme ou de fiel de torel,
et quant vous vouldrez paindre ou escrire, si le mouvez et en

it and use it with a pen or pencil, and when dry polish with a boar's tooth.

337. *Several modes of distempering saffron.* — Saffron is sometimes distempered with water, sometimes with egg, sometimes with wine ; but the best way is to put the saffron into a clean vessel with a great quantity of water until it is soaked, and then to boil it over the coals. You may then write or paint with it whatever you please, and you must know that saffron is redder when distempered with wine.

338. *To make green.* — Boil the leaves of the Morelle [solanum nigrum] with ochre and grind them on a stone. If you were to put saffron instead of ochre, or saffron and ochre, the colour would be very good.

339. *To paint and write with gold on cloth, parchment, tables, and everything else.*—Fill a glass vessel with urine and let it settle until it is clear, then take two parts of white of egg and mix it with your fresh urine and put it with some dissolved or ground gold into the horn ; and with this gold you may write as with any other colour, and paint on cloths and all other things.

340. *To make the colours of flowers.*—At the rising of the sun go into the fields and collect divers corn flowers and other herbs ; bruise and grind each kind of flower separately with well-baked gypsum, then dry them and keep each colour separately so as to be ready when wanted for use ; and if you wish for a green colour mix quick lime with the flowers and you will have a good colour.

341. *To make a good liquid varnish for painters.*—Take glasse aromatique, which is dark or dull outside, and inside when broken is clear and shining like glass ; put some of it in a new jar, which must stand on the mouth of another jar, which must be well luted to it. The upper jar must be well covered so as to be smoke-proof, and its bottom must be pierced. Then light a fire beneath it, and leave it until the glasse is melted, when you must take two parts of linseed, or

ouvrez a la penne ou au pincel et quand il est sec polissiez le
dun dent de sangler.

337. *A destremper safran en plusieurs manieres.*—Safran est
aucunefoiz destrempez dyaue aucunefois dœuf aucunefois de
vin, mais la meilleur maniere et de mettre le safran en yaue
en un vaissel bien net jusques a tant quil soit confis et fault
quil ny ait une grant quantite deaue, puis le mettez sur les
charbons boulir un po ensamble et puis en ecrisiez ou paindez
ce que vous vouldrez ; et est a savoir quant le safran est destrempe de vin, il est plus rouge.

338. *Pour faire vert.*—Cuisez feuille de morelle avec ocre
puis le broyez sur la pierre.   Et cui y mettroit safran en lieu
de locre, et autour avec locre, bon seroit.

339. *A paindre et escrire dor sur telles, parchemins, ou tables,
et toutes autres choses.*—Emplissiez de votre orine un vaissel de
voirre et si le laissiez reposer tant que elle soit bien claire,
puis prenez glaire doefs tres bonne deux parties et les meslez
avec vostre orine novelle ensemble, et le mettez avec or solut
ou broye, dedens le cornet et de cest or povez escrire comme
dautre couleur, et paindre sur draps et toute autres choses.

340. *A faire couleurs de fleurs.*—Alez au matin soleil levant
aux champs et assemblez diverses fleurs de bles et dautres
herbes, et criblez bien et molez chacun par soy avec gips bien
cuit, et mettez le sechier et gardez chascun par lui et en ouvrez
quant est besoing.   Et quant vous vouldrez avoir couleur
verde, meslez chaux vive avecques les dictes fleurs, et avez
bonne couleur.

341. *A faire bonne vernix liquide pour paintres.*—Prenez
glasse aromatique qui est obscur par dehors et par dedens
quant on le brise il est clair et luisant a maniere de voirre et en
mettez une partie en un pot neuf qui soit assis sur la bouche
dun autre pot et soient bien lute ensamble, et le pot denhault
bien couvert que fumee nen ysse et soit percie au fons et faites
feu dessoubz, tant que vous santez que la glasse sera fondue.
Puis prenez oile de lin, ou de chanvre, ou de noix deux parties,

hemp-seed, or nut-oil, and heat this oil slowly over a fire, not making it too hot. You must then pour it on to the said glasse, make the fire hotter, and let it boil for an hour, taking care that the flame does not touch it. Then take it off the fire and put it into a clean vessel, and when you wish to varnish any dry painting take some of this liquid and spread it over the painting with your fingers, for if you were to do it with a pencil it would be too thick and would not dry. You will thus have good varnish.

342. *To make a yellow colour.*—Cook some vernide well in a clear ley, add to it a little verdigris, and distemper it with black, and the more verdigris you add the redder it will be ; for instance, 2 oz. of verdigris and 5 of vercande, put the thread in while it is hot or boiling and it will give you satisfaction.

343. *The nature and condition of minium, sandaraca,*[1] *and ceruse, and the way to distemper them.*—They are all of the same kind and nature, but when exposed to heat they change their name, strength, and colour ; for that which is the most heated is the reddest, and that which is the least heated is the whitest or palest, and they should be distempered with water for mason's work, with egg for parchment, and with oil for wood.

344. *To make a colour which is called posc for the undraped parts of images.*—Mix a little cynobre with simple flesh colour and a little minium and you will have the said posc[2] colour, with which you will redden teeth (gums), nostrils, mouths, hands, the under part of necks, the wrinkles of foreheads, the temples, and the articulations and other members in all the undraped parts of painted and round figures.

345. *To make two colours, one called lumine*[3] *and the other cedre or excedre, for the undraped parts of figures.*—Mix flesh

---

[1] The colour here called sandarace appears from the description to have been massicot.

[2] See *ante*, p. 300, No. 315.

[3] See Theophilus, lib. i. c. v. ix. and xiii.

et le chauffez au feu petit a petit et ne li laissiez pas trop chauffer, puis le getez par dessus avec la dicte glasse, et faites bon feu et le faites bien boulir par lespace dune heure, et gardez tres-bien que la flamme ne la touche. Puis lostez du feu et mettez en vaissel cler et net, et quant aucune euvre de painture sera faite et seche et la voulez vernicier si prenez de ceste liqueur et la tandez dessus la painture a voz doiz ; car se vous le fasiez du pincel il seroit trop espez et ne pourroit secher, et ainsi avez bonne vernix.

342. *A faire couleur jaune.*—Cuisiez bien vernide en lexive clere et nette et y mettez un po de vert de gris et le destrempez de seurs et quant plus y mettez du vert de gris et plus sera rouge s. ij oz. de vert de gris et v de vercande, puis mettez dedans le fil tiede ou boulant, et sera a vostre plaisir.

343. *La nature et condition de mine, sandarace, et ceruse, et la maniere de la destremper, et que ils sont dune maniere et dune nature, mais par feu ilz muent, noms, force, et couleurs.*—Car celui qui est plus cuit et plus rouge et le moin cuit est le plus blanc ou plus pale, et doivent estre destrempez deaue en maconnage et de œufs en parchemin, et de oille en sustages.

344. *A faire une couleur qui est appelee posc pour faire le nus de ymages.*—Mettez avec simple membrane un poi de cynobre et un poi de mine, et vous avez la dicte couleur posc, de laquelle vous rougirez dens, naselles, bouche, mains, col par dessoubs, et les fronces du front, et les tremples, et les articles et les autres membres en tous nus dimages pourtraictes et rondes.

345. *Pour faire deux couleurs, lune appelee lumine et lautre cedre ou excedre, pour le nud des ymages.*—Mellez avec cynobre

colour, well-ground ceruse, and verblee [vertbleu] with cynobre, and you will have a colour which is called *lumine*, with which you will illuminate the eyebrows, the upper part of the nose, and the nostrils with very fine lines. The other colour is made by mixing red with a little black, which produces a colour called cedre or excedre, with which you will make the touches round the pupils of the eyes.

346. *To make a glue for flesh.*—Take the root of the plant which is called "stipatum," put it into a cauldron or kettle with pieces of flesh boiled in water ; when cold, the water will coagulate, and is called "gelantina." And pure water in which the said roots are boiled is useful for distempering colours on account of the glutinous properties which it takes from the root ; and even if that root alone was left in water for a day and night without being boiled it will be of equal value.

347. *Water for tempering colours.*—Water in which linseed-oil has been steeped for a day and night receives a glutinous quality from that seed, which makes it proper for distempering colours.

348. *To prevent anything made of burnished iron or steel from rusting.*—Take saltpetre, otherwise called afronitre,[1] or sal nitre, of the size of a nut, and half a goblet of olive oil, distemper and boil the whole together, then strain through a linen cloth and keep it clean, and anoint with it the said things, or armour, or other works by means of a linen or woollen cloth, which must be moistened with the oil without laying it on too thickly ; for it is better to lay it on thinly and then at any time after two or three months the articles may be again rubbed down with the oiled rag.

349. *To make fine azure.*—You must take the Indian or Persian azure stone which comes from beyond the sea, and which is kept by the apothecaries, who use it in some of their medicines. That which has white veins is better than that which has gold veins, and if you heat it over the fire on a hot

---

[1] Froth of nitre. The saline excrescence which forms on walls.

membrane ceruse bien molue et verblee si avez couleur qui
est appellee lumine, de laquelle vous enluminerez les sourcils,
le nez au long, et sur les pertuis des narines, faisant les trais
soubtilz ; et lautre est se vous mellez avec rouge un po de noir
vous avez couleur qui est nommee cedre ou excedre, de quoi
vous ferez les trais environ les pupilles.

346. *Ad gellantinam carnium faciendam.*—Herba quædam
stipatum vocata est, ejus radix in cacabo vel lebete posita cum
carnium frustris in aqua coquentibus ea coagulat cum ad fri-
gidatem reducuntur quæ sic gelantana vocantur, et aqua pura
in qua bulirentur ipsæ radices dictæ herbæ utilis esset ad temperandum colores, pro ejus glutiniositate ab ibsa radice sumpta.
Ac etiam si solum radix ipsa in aqua staret per diem et noctem
saltim, absque quam bulita æque valeret.

347. Aqua in qua semen lini diu per diem et noctem saltim
steterit, recipit ab ipso semine glutinositatem quæ ipsam facit
aptam ad distemperandum colores.

348. *Pour garder denreullir aucune chose de fer ou dacier
burnies.*—Prenez salpetre, autrement appellee assafetide [afro-
nitre ?] ou salnitre, le gros dune noiz et la moitie dun gobelet
duille dolive, et deffaites tout ensemble, et le faites boulir, et
puis le coulez par un drapel de lin et le gardez nettement et
en oindez les dictes choses armoures ou autres besoignes a un
drapel de lin ou de laine qui seroit meilleur moillie en icellui
ille sans le mettre trop gros, car il est mieulz a le mettre
delie, et puis aucune fois de deux ou troiz moiz les torcher et
remettre.

349. *Pour faire fin azur.*—Vous devez prendre la pierre de
lazur qui est Inde ou Pers, et vient des parties doultremer, et
se treuve sur les appothicaires qui en font aucunes medicines ;
et celle qui a vaines blanches vault mieulx que celle que les a
dor, et se vous le mettez ou feu recuire, ou sur une platine de

plate of iron and when cool find it of the same colour as before, it is good. If you buy the said stone in powder, you must prove it in this manner, and then pound and grind it well on a flat piece of porphyry or other hard stone; then make a cement of turpentine and to a quarter of a pound of the said powder by weight add 4½ ounces of turpentine, and mix and incorporate together the powder and turpentine in a well-glazed earthen vessel, the turpentine being tepid before the powder is put into it. You must leave them in this state for the space of sixteen hours or thereabouts; then heat some water until it is tepid, throw it into the pot until the said mixture is covered with it, and stir the whole well together quickly and for a long time with a stick; then take the water, which will be rendered opaque by the blue colour, let it clear, and throw it into another new well-glazed earthen vessel, and let it settle, when the blue will fall to the bottom; then pour some more water on the mixture and stir it harder than before, and throw the water, which will thus be full of the blue colour, into another clean glazed vessel, and let it settle, when the blue will fall to the bottom. Then pour in tepid water for the third time, and stir the said mixture of turpentine and blue; pour off the water into another pot and let it settle, then pour the water off all three vessels, dry the blue and keep it. The first will be worth its weight in gold, the second its weight in silver, and the third is good for making grounds. For this reason each sort should be kept apart.

350. *When a horse has bad and troubled eyes.*—Take three or four leaves of *waide* [woad?] and the white of an egg, with salt of the size of a bean; put all these things in an egg-shell; sweep the hearthstone clean; put it on it, and let it dry until it can be easily powdered, then apply to the eye of the horse.

351. *To cure quartan fevers.* — Take an herb which is called " tettes de souris," of the size of a gall-nut, distemper it with white wine, and make the sick person drink it on the day he expects to be seized with this fever: he will be immediately cured.

fer chaude chaufer et puis le laissiez refroidier et il revient ou
est de telle couleur que devant il est bon. Et pareillement
eprouverez au feu la poudre de la dicte pierre se vous lachetez
broye puis le devez bien broyer et mouldre bien sutil sur une
pierre platte de porfire ou autre bien dure. Puis faites siment
de termentina et pour un quarteron de la dicte pouldre a pois
fault iiij onces et demie de termentine, et doit on en une paelle
de terre bien plommee encorporer et mesler la dicte pouldre et
pierre ou azur, avec la termantine qui soit un pou tiede, avant
que la pouldre y soit mise et laissier ainsi par lespace de seize
heures ou environ ; et puis chauffez de leaue que elle soit tiede
et en boutez en la paelle grant foison tant que celle mixtion
soit couverte et remues ce bien et fort et hastivement et
longuement a un bastonnet. Et liaue qui lors sera bien
trouble de lazur, purez et boutez en une autre paiellete de
terre neufve bien plommee et la mettez rasseoir et vostre azur
se traira au fons. Puis mettez encor sur la dicte mixtion de
leaue tiede et remuez plus fort que devant, et puis leaue qui
ainsi sera trouble de lazur et la boutez en une autre paelle
nette plommee et le laissiez aussi rasseoir et lazur descendre
au fons. Puis remettez la tierce fois de leaue tiede, et remuez la dicte mixtion de trementine et dazur, et purez leaue
en une autre paelle et laissiez rasseoir, et de toutes trois getez
leaue et sechez et gardez lazur. Le premier vault son poiz
dor, le second son poiz dargent, et le tiers est bon pour faire
assiete. Et pour ce chacune sorte soit tenue apart.

350. *Quant un cheval a mauvais yeux et troubles.*—Prenez
troiz ou quatre feuilles de waide et le blanc dun œufs et du
sel le gros dune feve et mettez toutes ces choses en lescaille de
lœf et netoiez lastre du feu et le metez dessus, et le laissiez
tant secher que on en puisse faire pouldre et en mettez en leul
du cheval.

351. *Pour garir de fievres quartainnes.*—Prenez dune herbe
que lon appelle tettes de souris, le gros dune noiz galle, et le
destrempez de vin blanc, et en faites boire le malade le jour
que les fievres le doivent pranre, et tantot garira.

352. *To make cleret, which in Lombardy is called stellerie.*—
Take an ounce of chanelle [canelle ?], half an ounce of ginger,
6 cloves, 8 grains of paradise grains, a little nutmeg, all these
things well pulverized, half a pint of virgin honey, and a little
wine. Distemper all these things together and strain them
through a bag, the bottom of which is pointed into the vessel
which contained the wine ; and if it is not clear the first
time of straining, replace it in the bag over the other, which
meanwhile has been dripping, and on straining it will become
clear.

THANK GOD.

This Book is composed by Master Jehan Le Begue,
a Licentiate in the Law, Notary-General of the Masters
of the King's Mint, at Paris, Anno Domini 1431, when
he was 63 years of age.

----

352. *Pour faire cleret qui en Lombardie est appelle stellerie.*
—Prenez une once de chanelle et demie de gingembre et six
clox de girofle et viij grains de grainnes de paradis, et un po de
noiz muscade, tout broye en pouldre, et demie pinte de larme
de miel et un pot de vin, et les trempez tous ensamble, et puiz
les coulez par le sachet agu dessoubs en le pot ou estoit le vin ;
et se le premier qui descend nest bien cler, remetez le au dit
sachet sus lautre qui tondis coule et il revenra cler.

DEO GRATIAS.

Compositus est liber iste a magistro Johanne le
Begue, Licentiato in Legibus, Greffario Generalium
Magistrorum Monetæ Regis Parisiis, anno Domini
1431, ætatis vero suæ 63.